Readings in
African Politics

Reviews of
Readings in African Popular Culture
Edited by Karin Barber

'...likely to become the main source book for African culture studies during the next decade ... the enormous value of Readings in African Popular Culture in bringing together such a heterogeneous selection of nuanced, well-researched, thought-provoking articles from the emerging field of African Cultural Studies.' – David Kerr in *African Theatre in Development*

'... extraordinarily rich collection full of informative detail and excellent interpretative analysis. There is not a single piece that fails to fascinate ... The bibliographical information brought together is worth the price of the volume alone.' – Martin Banham, Emeritus Professor of Drama and Theatre Studies in the University of Leeds, in *Leeds African Studies Bulletin*

'... a critical testament of African popular culture. I strongly recommend it to readers and libraries.' – Tanure Ojaide in *African Studies Review*

'... (one of) a rich diet of delicious scholarship on contemporary African culture...' – Graham Furniss, Reader in Hausa Cultural Studies and former Director of the Centre of African Studies, School of Oriental and African Studies, in *African Affairs*

'... an impressive collection of inspiring and thought-provoking essays' – Francis B. Nyamnjoh in *Media Development*

Readings in African Popular Fiction
Edited by Stephanie Newell

'... forces a reconsideration of the idea of "African literature".' – Eileen Julien, Indiana University

'... the unique primary materials and the arrangement of the resources will make this volume valuable to many scholars and library collections.' – Elizabeth Blakesley Lindsay in *H-Net*

'This is a rich and intelligently conceived anthology ... the examples presented here also challenge the usual paradigms now taken for granted in postcolonial studies, and demonstrate that "subaltern voices" so often assumed to be silent or suppressed can be heard loud and clear if one cares to locate oneself outside Western academies and networks. ...' – Lyn Innes, Professor of Postcolonial Literatures, University of Kent at Canterbury

Forthcoming
Readings in Gender in Africa
Edited by Andrea Cornwall

General Editors

Karin Barber is Professor of African Cultural Anthropology at the Centre of West African Studies at the University of Birmingham. She has published widely in the field of Yoruba, oral literature and popular culture. Her most recent book *The Generation of Plays: African Popular Life in Theatre* (Indiana University Press 2000) won the Herskovits Award. She also edited the first and widely acclaimed book in this series *Readings in African Popular Culture*.

Tom Young is Senior Lecturer in Politics at the School of Oriental and African Studies. His areas of interest are Mozambique; Africa as an object of Western intervention; the theoretical foundations and practices of human rights and democracy agendas as part of a globalisation process. He is the author of (with Margaret Hall) *Confronting Leviathan: Mozambique since Independence* (Hurst and Co. 1997).

Readings in ...

This series makes available to students a representative selection of the best and most exciting work in fields where standard textbooks have hitherto been lacking. Such fields may be located anywhere across the full range of Africanist humanities and social sciences, but the emphasis will be on newly emerging fields or fields that cross older disciplinary or subject boundaries. It is in these areas that the task of accessing materials is most difficult for students, because relevant works may be scattered across a wide range of periodicals in different disciplines. The aim is to bring together central, key works – classics that helped to define the field – with other significant pieces that cut across established or conventional positions from different angles. Within reasonable limits all the sub-regions of Africa will be covered in each volume.

Each Reader will include materials from journals and books, condensed or edited where appropriate. Work published or produced in Africa which, because of the widening economic divide, may otherwise be unavailable in Europe and the US, will be included wherever possible. Readers may also include new work invited and hitherto unpublished where there are significant gaps in the field or where the editors know of exciting developments that have not yet been represented in the literature.

The significance of the readings and the overall nature of the field they contribute to, will be discussed in an introductory essay in each volume. In some cases these introductory essays may be significant contributions to the development of the field in their own right; in all cases, they will provide a 'reading map' to help students explore the materials presented.

The material included will obviously vary in complexity and difficulty, but the overall level will be appropriate for second- and third-year undergraduate courses and for postgraduate courses.

Edited by TOM YOUNG

Readings in
African Politics

The International
African Institute
in association with

INDIANA UNIVERSITY PRESS
BLOOMINGTON & INDIANAPOLIS

JAMES CURREY
OXFORD

First published in the United Kingdom by
The International African Institute
School of Oriental & African Studies
Thornhaugh Street
London WC1H 0XG

in association with
James Currey Ltd
73 Botley Rd
Oxford
OX2 0BS

and in North America by
Indiana University Press
601 North Morton Street
Bloomington
Indiana 47404-3797
Tel: 1 800 842 6796
http://iupress.indiana.edu

British Library Cataloguing in Publication Data
Readings in African politics
  1. Africa - Politics and government
  I. Young, Tom II. International African Institute III. African
  politics
  320.9'6

ISBN 0-85255-257-2 (James Currey paper)

Library of Congress Cataloging-in-Publication Data
available on request

ISBN 0-253-21646-X (Indiana paper)
ISBN 0-253-34359-3 (Indiana casebound)

Typeset in 9.5/9.5 pt Bembo by Long House, Cumbria
Printed and bound in Britain by Woolnough, Irthlingborough

Contents

Notes on Contributors

Jon Abbink is senior researcher at the African Studies Centre Leiden, where he heads the research group on Culture, Politics and Inequality in Africa,. He is also Professor of African ethnic studies at the Vrije Universiteit in Amsterdam. His research interests include political change in Africa, the comparative study of ethnic relations in (especially Northeast) Africa, the anthropology and history of Ethiopia, and the relation of culture and violence. He has recently published *Meanings of Violence: A Cross-Cultural Perspective* (edited with G. Aijmer, 2000), *Rethinking Resistance: Revolt and Violence in Africa History* (edited with K. van Walraven & M. de Bruijn, 2003), and numerous papers in scholarly journals.

Jocelyn Alexander is lecturer in Commonwealth Studies at the University of Oxford. Her research focuses on the social and political history of southern Africa. She is the author of numerous articles on the history and politics of the region, and co-author of *Violence and Memory: One Hundred Years in the 'Dark Forests' of Matabeleland* (2000). She is currently completing a book manuscript entitled *The Unsettled Land: Land and Politics in Zimbabwe, 1945–2002*.

Adam Ashforth is Visiting Associate Professor of Social Science at the Institute for Advanced Study. He is the author of *The Politics of Official Discourse in Twentieth-Century South Africa* (Oxford: Clarendon Press), and *Madumo, A Man Bewitched* (Chicago: The University of Chicago Press) as well as numerous articles on state formation, violence, witchcraft, and AIDS. His book on witchcraft, violence, and democracy based upon field work in Soweto during the 1990s will be published in 2004.

Robert H. Bates is Eaton Professor of the Science of Government and Faculty Associate of the Center for International Development at Harvard University. He is currently focusing on conflict in Africa and his most recently published book is *Prosperity and Violence* (2001).

Jean-François Bayart was Director of the Centre d'Etudes et de Rechereches Internationales in Paris from 1994 to 2000 and Director of Critique Internationale from 1998 to 2003. A specialist in comparative politics, he has conducted research on the historical sociology of the state, with particular reference to sub-Saharan Africa, but also to Turkey and Iran. He co-founded the journal *Politique Africaine*, which he edited from 1980 to 1982. Since 1990, he has been permanent advisor to the Centre d'analyse et de prévision of the French Ministry of Foreign Affairs. He lectures at the Institut d'Études Politiques de Paris and contributes regularly to the French media.

Rémy Bazenguissa-Ganga is Maître de Conférence de Sociologie at the University of Lille 1. He has written several articles on the Congolese political system and political violence in Africa. He is the author with Janet MacGaffey of *Congo-Paris. Transnational Traders on the Margins of the Law* (2000).

Patrick Chabal is Professor of Lusophone African Studies at the University of London. He has taught and done research in a number of (West, Southern and Eastern) African countries as well as in the USA, France, Italy, Sweden, Portugal and the UK. He is the author of a large number of books and articles on political change, leadership, identity, culture and literature in Africa.

Jean-Pascal Daloz is a CNRS Senior Researcher and is based at the Bordeaux Institute of Political Science. He is also Executive Secretary of the Research Committees on Political Elites (IPSA) and on Comparative Sociology (ISA). He specializes in the comparative study of elites, with an emphasis on the symbolic aspects of political representation.

Mamadou Diouf teaches history at the University of Michigan. His publications include *Liberalisations politiques ou transitions democratiques* (1998). His current research is on popular urban culture in Senegal.

Toyin Falola is Frances Higginbothom Nalle Centennial Professor in History at the University of Texas at Austin. He has written many books most recently *The Culture and Customs of Nigeria* (2001) and *Nationalism and African Intellectuals* (2001).

Richard Fanthorpe is a research fellow at the School of African Studies at the University of Sussex. He is currently engaged on a two-year research project funded by DfID on the local government and chieftaincy issues in post war Sierra Leone.

Robert Fatton, Jr. is Professor and Chair of the Woodrow Wilson Department of Politics, University of Virginia. Within the field of Comparative Government he is the author of *The Making of a Liberal Democracy: Senegal's Passive Revolution, 1975–1985* (1987); and *Predatory Rule: State and Civil Society in Africa* (1992).

Mitzi Goheen is Associate Professor of Anthropology at Amherst College. She is the author of *Men own the Fields, Women own the Crops: Gender and Power in the Cameroon Grassfields* (1996). She is currently working on the relationships between regionalism, ethnicity and nationalism and the various ways both national and local leaders use and manipulate media, especially but not exclusively television broadcasting in Cameroon.

Sten Hagberg is Assistant Professor at the Department of Cultural Anthropology and Ethnology, Uppsala University, Sweden. His current research concerns how ethnicity is articulated in discourses of history, religion and development in Burkina Faso. His recent publications include *Poverty in Burkina Faso: Representations and Realities* (2001); the co-edited book *Bonds and Boundaries in Northern Ghana and Southern Burkina Faso* (2000); and several articles published in journals and edited books.

Margaret Hall has worked for the Foreign and Commonwealth Office as an area specialist and researcher since 1975, concentrating on Southern Africa (especially Mozambique, Zimbabwe & Malawi) and the western Indian Ocean islands (Mauritius and Seychelles in particular). Besides the politics of this area, she has a general interest in the history and international relations of lusophone Africa.

John Hamer is Adjunct Professor of Anthropology at the University of the South, Sewanee, Tennesee. He has published a book *Human Development: participation and change among the Sidama of Ethiopia* (1987), and numerous articles on the Sidama.

Bessie House-Midamba (now known as Bessie House-Soremekun) is Professor in the Department of Political Science at Kent State University. She is the author of *Class Development and Gender Equality in Kenya 1963–1990* and co-editor of *African Market Women and Economic Power: The Role of Women in African Economic Development*.

Goran Hyden is Distinguished Professor in the Department of Political Science at the University of Florida. He is the author of several books and articles on various aspects of politics and development in Africa, especially Kenya, Tanzania and Uganda. Among his recent publications are *African Perspectives on Governance*, co-edited with Dele Olowu and H.W.O. Okoth Ogendo (2000), and *Media and Democracy in Africa*, co-edited with Michael Leslie and Folu Ogundimu (2002). He has served as consultant to a number of international organisations involved in the development field.

Robert Jackson is the author/editor of nine books including *Quasi-States: Sovereignty, International Relations and the Third World* and *Personal Rule in Black Africa* (co-author). He teaches at Boston University. He has been a Visiting Fellow at Jesus College, Oxford University, The London School of Economics, and the Hoover Institution, Stanford University.

Mikael Karlström is Assistant Collegiate Professor of Social Sciences in the Collegiate Division of the University of Chicago. He has published on political culture, democratisation and civil society in Uganda.

Ronald Kassimir is a Program Director at the Social Science Research Council, responsible for its Africa Program and the International Dissertation Field Research Fellowship Program. He holds a PhD in Political Science from the University of Chicago and has conducted extensive field research in Uganda. Among other publications, he is co-editor of *Intervention and Transnationalism in Africa: Global-Local Networks of Power* (2001).

Mahmood Mamdani is currently the Herbert Lehman Professor of Government and Director of the Institute of African Studies at Columbia University in New York City. He has served as A.C. Jordan Professor of African Studies and as the Director for the Center for African Studies at the University of Cape Town (South Africa), and has taught at the University of Dar es Salaam and Makerere University. He is the founding Director of the Centre for Basic Research in Kampala, Uganda, and was the President (1999–2002) of the Council for the Development of Social Research in Africa.

Roy May is Director of the African Studies Centre at Coventry University. He has published widely on Chad, the Franco-African relationship, the role of NGOs and militarism and peacekeeping in Africa.

Sally Falk Moore is Professor of Anthropology (Emerita) at Harvard University. She received her BA from Barnard College, a PhD in Anthropology at Columbia university and an LLB from Columbia Law School. A specialist in legal and political anthropology she has done fieldwork in East Africa, and consulting in West Africa. She came to Harvard in 1981, where she taught in the Faculty of Arts and Sciences and in Harvard Law School. From 1985 to 1989 she was Dean of the Graduate School at Harvard, and was Master of Cunster House. Her books include *Law as Process* (1978, 2nd ed 2000) *Social Facts and Fabrications 'Customary' Law on Kilimanjaro 1880–1980* (1986) and *Anthropology and Africa* (1994).

Aili Mari Tripp is Associate Dean of International Studies, Director of the Women's Studies Research Center, and Associate Professor of Political Science and Women's Studies at the University of Wisconsin-Madison. She is author of *Women and Politics in Uganda* (2000) and *Changing the Rules: The Politics of Liberalization and the Urban Informal Economy in Tanzania* (1997). She has also published numerous articles and book chapters on women and politics in Africa; women's responses to economic reform; and the political impact of transformations of associational life in Africa.

Wim van Binsbergen is Professor of the Foundations of Intercultural Philosophy, Erasmus University Rotterdam, and Senior Researcher at the African Studies Centre, Leiden. His research interests are African religion including Islam and Christianity; intercultural philosophy especially the epistemology of African Studies; African and Ancient history; Afrocentricity and the Black Athena debate; ethnicity and globalisation. His recent books include *Black Athena Ten Years After* (1997), *Modernity on a shoestring* (with Fardon and van Dijk, 1999), *Trajectoires de libération en Afrique contemporaine* (with Konings and Hesseling, 2000) and *Intercultural Encounters* (2003).

Tom Young is Senior Lecturer in Politics at the School of Oriental and African Studies, University of London. His areas of interest are Mozambique; Africa as an object of Western intervention; the theoretical foundations and practices of human rights and democracy agendas as part of a globalisation process. He is the author of (with Margaret Hall) *Confronting Leviathan: Mozambique since Independence*, (1997).

Aristide Zolberg is Walter A. Eberstadt Professor of Political Science at the Graduate Faculty of New School University in New York City and Director of its International Center for Migration, Ethnicity, and Citizenship. He has published extensively in the fields of comparative politics and historical sociology. He is currently completing *A Nation by Design? Immigration Policy in the Fashioning of America* (forthcoming, 2004).

Preface

This book aspires to provide students and, hopefully, that anonymous hero, the general reader with, if not a completely comprehensive set of readings, at least sufficient material to follow the main contours of theoretical discussion about African politics and a great deal of empirical material to reflect on, drawn from a wide variety of African countries. Two leanings should be noted. First, there is a bias (both in the selection and the structuring) towards the contemporary debates although the international dimensions of African politics (to be the subject matter of a companion volume to this) have been largely excluded. Second, political scientists might grumble at the inclusion of so much 'anthropological' material and the (relative) omission of some central political themes, say military regimes or corruption. I will only note as to the second that I am not a trained anthropologist but incline to the view that a close reading of 'anthropological' writings is important for politics students, whose discipline, in its Western version at least, is irrevocably marked by a concern with the state.

These readings are prefaced by an introductory essay whose purposes and biases should also be noted. I have not attempted a systematic commentary on the texts which, aside from being rather dull, would suggest that they cannot speak for themselves, when all of them do so, invariably more eloquently and persuasively than I. Nonetheless some guidance seems useful even in the event that one does not share the guide's viewpoint. My essay is therefore a sketch of one way of looking at how the debate on African politics has changed and what has shaped it. This account might be regarded in certain circles as rather eccentric but since semi-'official' and mainstream views are widely available there seems no reason to apologise for that.

I need only add that this volume was put together in the shadow of a sustained assault on intellectual and collegial life in British universities which has deeply impoverished the lives of many of those who work in them. In such circumstances unpaid and uncontracted aid from colleagues has become less a debt to be acknowledged than a marvel to be wondered at. Richard Jeffries and Roger Charlton provided good advice about what should go in although not all that advice could be followed. Tim Kelsall was thoughtfully tough about some of my arguments and made me rethink and rewrite. Without Elizabeth Dunstan's unstinting help the book might never have seen the light of day. Finally I am most grateful to Barbara, for finding time within the rhythms of family life to read many drafts of the introductory essay, thus greatly helping to secure whatever clarity it may have.

Sources & Acknowledgements

The publishers and editor are grateful to the following authors and publishers for permission to republish articles:

Aristide Zolberg, *Creating Political Order: The Party States of West Africa*, University of Chicago Press, 1966 [Ch. 5]

Robert H. Bates, *Markets and States in Tropical Africa*, Berkeley, University of California Press, 1981 [chs 6 & 7]

Goran Hyden, *No Shortcuts to Progress: African Development Management in Perspective*, London, Heinemann, 1983 [pp. 36–45]

Robert H. Jackson and C.G. Rosberg, 'Personal Rule: Theory and Practice in Africa', *Comparing Politics*, No. 4, July 1984, pp. 421–42 [pp. 430–40 from 'some characteristic practices' to the end of the text]

Robert Fatton Jr, 'Bringing the Ruling Class Back In: Class, State and Hegemony in Africa', *Comparative Politics*, 20/3 1988, pp. 253–64 [complete]

Jean-François Bayart, L'Etat pp. 213–28 in C. Coulon & Denis-Constant Martin (eds), *Les Afriques Politiques*, Paris, Editions La Découverte, 1991 [complete minus bibliography]

Mahmood Mamdani, *Citizen and Subject: Contemporary Africa and the Legacy of Late Colonialism*, London, James Currey; Princeton, NJ, Princeton University Press, 1996 [ch. 8]

Patrick Chabal and Jean-Pascal Daloz, *Africa Works: Disorder as Political Instrument*, London, IAI; Oxford, James Currey; Bloomington & Indianapolis, Indiana University Press, 1999 [pp. 155–63]

Roy May, 'Internal Dimensions of Warfare with Chad', *Cambridge Anthropology*, vol. 3, no. 2, 1988/89, pp. 17–27

Margaret Hall & Tom Young, *Confronting Leviathan: Mozambique Since Independence*, London, Christopher Hurst & Co., 1997 [ch. 7]

Toyin Falola, *Violence in Nigeria: The Crisis of Religious Politics and Secular Ideologies*, Rochester, University of Rochester Press, 1998 [pp. 194-221]

Jon Abbink, 'Ritual and Political Forms of Violent Practice among the Suri of Southern Ethiopia', *Cahiers d'Etudes Africaines*, 150-52, XXXVIII-2-4, 1998, pp. 271–95 [complete]

Rémy Bazenguissa-Ganga, 'The Spread of Political Violence in Congo-Brazzaville', *African Affairs*, vol. 98, no. 390, Jan 1999, pp. 37–54 [complete]

Mitzi Goheen, 'Chiefs, Sub-Chiefs and Local Control: Negotiations over Land, Struggles over Meaning', *Africa*, 62/3, 1992, pp. 889–411 [complete]

John Hamer, 'Commensality, Process and the Moral Order: An Example from Southern Ethiopia', *Africa*, 64/1, 1994, pp. 126–44 [complete]

Richard Fanthorpe, 'Locating the Politics of a Sierra Leonean Chiefdom', *Africa*, 68/4, 1998, pp. 558–83 [complete]

Sten Hagberg, *Between Peace and Justice: Dispute Settlement between Karaboro Agriculturalists and Fulbe Agro-Pastoralists in Burkina Faso*, Uppsala, Uppsala University, 1998 [ch.10]

Mamadou Diouf, 'Urban Youth and Senegalese Politics: Dakar 1988–1994', *Public Culture*, 8, 2, 1966, pp. 225–50 [complete]

Ronald Kassimir, 'The Social Power of Religious Organisation and Civil Society: The Catholic Church in Uganda' in N. Kasfir (ed.), *Civil Society and Democracy in Africa*, London, Frank Cass, 1998 [complete]

Aili Mari Tripp, *Changing the Rules: The Politics of Liberalisation and the Urban Informal Economy in Tanzania*, Berkeley & Los Angeles, University of California Press, 1997 [ch.6]

Bessie House-Midamba, 'Gender, Democratization and Associational Life in Kenya', *Africa Today*, 43, 3, 1996, pp. 289–306 [complete]

Jocelyn Alexander, 'The Local State in Post-War Mozambique: Political Practice and Ideas about Authority', *Africa*, 67/1, 1997, pp. 1–25 [complete]

Sally Falk Moore, 'Post-Socialist Micro-Politics: Kilimanjaro, 1993', *Africa*, 66/4, 1996, pp. 587–605 [complete]

Wim van Binsbergen, 'Aspects of Democracy and Democratisation in Zambia and Botswana: Exploring African Political Culture at the Grassroots', *Journal of Contemporary African Studies*, 13, 1, 1995, pp. 3–33

Mikael Karlström, 'Imagining Democracy: Political Culture and Democratisation in Buganda', *Africa*, 66/4, 1996, pp. 485–504

Adam Ashforth, 'Witchcraft, Violence and Democracy in the New South Africa', *Cahiers d'Etudes africaines*, 150–152, XXXVIII-2-4, 1998, pp. 505–32

TOM YOUNG
Introduction

'The French have taught us we are like women; if someone comes from the town to tell us what to do, all we can do is say Yes; that's the way it was under the French and that's the way it still is'.[1]

'When the President of Malawi said, 'I don't care what the world calls me, a dictator or what, my job is to develop this country', he spoke in a European voice'.[2]

Political science has, perhaps more than other branches of social science, long prided itself on its hard-headedness, its lack of squeamishness in the face of brute realities, its assertion, even celebration, of power and domination as the bedrock phenomena, however decorously draped on occasion in more gentle or dignified garb. In part this stems from some of its most memorable intellectual forbears. The prose of a Machiavelli or a Hobbes still exudes a striking violence and ruthlessness. In part because of course in politics, perhaps more than other fields of human action, the distance between words and deeds can seem so wide as to make the deepest scepticism about political words the only plausible position to take. In the study of African politics, particularly in recent years, a general tendency towards a relative disinterest in political language is also very apparent; or rather a tendency to celebrate the everyday language of politics while evincing considerable hostility to that of states and rulers. This is perhaps because much of this academic (and policy) discourse is rather populist, comfortable with denunciations of African elites (provided that term is kept appropriately vague), and complicit in a sense with a populism in Africa itself which ascribes all the continent's ills to the machinations of 'Big Men'. What is then often called political rhetoric becomes little more than the self-interested mendacity of predatory elites.

The political kingdom

It was not always so. At least in their words the first generation of African leaders saw it as their task 'to combat prejudices, routine, inferiority complexes and the fatalistic spirit'; to place themselves in step with 'evolutionary laws'; to emancipate the 'spiritually and mentally bewitched'; to 'goad [their societies] into the acceptance of the stimuli necessary to rapid economic development'; to 'create a new mentality and way of seeing things'.[3] Re-reading these and many other such statements from the vantage point of the twenty-first century is sobering indeed but it seems fairly uncontroversial to suggest that these (and many other) texts articulated aspirations to extremely ambitious programmes of social transformation, in which modernity is exemplified by science, progress, discipline, themselves all embodied in the form of the modern state. There are often (rather vague) acknowledgements of the need to adjust this to local realities, an acknowledgement which often shades into some realism about the obstacles confronting a modernising project in Africa, and even, occasionally, some ambivalence about the relationship between Africa and modernity. But, despite this cautious note, what

stands out is an almost magical wishing into being of modernity, a tendency which, to be fair, was by no means restricted to African elites but extended to their (then) friends in the West. After all, Professor Bates 'observed' (in 1976) 'a score of cities of 100,000 or more persons' in Zambia, when in fact four years later there were only seven.[4] Nor should this be taken as an isolated oddity. Africanist scholarship was formally constituted as a legitimate endeavour within the academic division of labour during a period in which modernisation was the ruling idea. The newly independent African countries were to be transformed into modern, dynamic societies in which the combined forces of economic growth, urbanisation, education and the mass media would sustain new forms of associational life and create informed, participant citizens with both of these providing the essential props, at least eventually, of a liberal democratic political order.

So the huge emphasis placed by Nkrumah (and others) on 'the political kingdom' did not then seem the self-interested absurdity it has since become fashionable to mock. Virtually all the main approaches to the question of the 'new states', in both economics and political science, shared the concern with the strong state as the vehicle of modernisation. Within these approaches there were of course differences and debates about the relative importance of order and participation or of economic growth and transformation but almost none doubted that the state must play a central role in these processes of change. Even approaches outside the mainstream, for example the various forms of dependency theory, did not dissent from an emphasis on the central role for the state as an agent of growth or development.[5] And if the state was the vehicle then nationalism was the fuel of modernisation. African nationalism, unlike other nationalisms, was not (or at least not then), 'the starkest political shame of the twentieth century'.[6] Rather it was 'the bearer of positive goods'.[7]

The centrality of modernisation, the state and nationalism ensured that history and political science became prominent, indeed predominant, in the new African Studies, anthropology having become increasingly suspect as the handmaiden of colonialism or worse, as the purveyor of a patronising account of Africans, implying they were incapable of modernity. The new disciplines by contrast were heavily complicit in the modernising project, uncovering glorious historical pasts for modern African nation-states, praising African nationalism and its continuities with the pre-colonial 'struggles for freedom', and vaunting the new political organisations that would lead African countries to the New Era. In sum (it is perhaps excessively obvious to say) these efforts were as much to do with ideological and political agendas in the West as they were to do with the discovery of 'new facts' or the exercise of social 'science'.

Anthropology's revenge?

This particular bundle of concepts and understandings now seems a world away. The modernising project in all its variants has signally failed in Africa to effect the transformations promised or anticipated. More than this the whole framework of categories clustered round modernisation, indeed the very idea of a transition from 'tradition' to 'modernity', appeared confounded by what was happening in independent Africa. Perhaps most poignantly 'tribalism' or 'ethnicity', far from dissolving in the face of progress, appeared to acquire increased virulence; indeed as African nationalism evaporated, to become the main currency of the new state politics, often in urban locations once thought to be the very engine rooms of modernity. It no longer seemed plausible to regard ethnicity as a cultural hangover or even a temporary compass in a rapidly modernising environment, but rather it appeared to be a veritable product of modernisation itself, driven by increasingly bitter struggles for power and resources within the structures of the new states. The results of empirical enquiry were supported by theoretical interrogation and critique. This suggested that 'tradition' came to be a sort of residual category that meant little more than the not-modern; the effect of that being that no real differences in traditions could be registered and the only change that this terminology could recognise was transition towards the Western experience; and finally that tradition and modernity represented mutually exclusive and functionally interdependent clusters of attributes so that urbanisation was naturally bundled with capitalism, democracy, secularisation and so on, an assumption that precluded various forms of mixture of the traditional and the modern. Beyond these descriptive and analytical points the categories of tradition and modernity came under fire on normative grounds. This was part of a much larger shift of Western sensibilities, particularly but by no means exclusively exemplified in academic discourse, which considers the attribution to 'others' (or, more portentously, the 'Other') of such notions as 'tradition' as not only empirically and conceptually empty, but both morally offensive and complicit in, if not directly constitutive of, oppressive forms of social and political relations.

The combined weight of these criticisms has generated a dilemma very clearly posed in an Africanist context by Feierman - 'If we define the people of a given society as different from us, then we have defined them as other, distant from us, not subject to the same historical forces or living in the same moral universe. This is unacceptable. But if we say that we are indeed coeval, living in the same era, subject to the same historical forces, struggling with the same issues, then we lose the picture of cultural variation which is the heart of anthropology'.[8] The perceived solution to this difficulty has prompted, across the social sciences and humanities, a pervasive assertion of 'agency' on behalf of social actors and loud calls for (anti) essentialism. 'Agency' connotes a repudiation of 'victimhood' and a robust assertion of the social and cognitive capabilities of ordinary individuals. Anti-essentialism questions both the idea that identities are naturally given and that people can have integral and unproblematic identities. By extension such arguments 'challenge accounts of collective identities as based on some "essence" or set of core features shared by all members of the collectivity and no others'.[9] So in the field of African studies more generally such arguments have provided some of the intellectual resources to proclaim a new world of 'creolisation' and 'glocalisation'.[10] The old myth of a Merrie Africa of cultural authenticity gives way to a post-modern Africa of endlessly ecstatic bricolage and multiple modernities.[11] Not the least of the benefits of such a view (at least for its proponents) is that the 'historicity' of African societies is restored and by (very strong) implication the standing of Africans as full members of (one) human family is re-asserted.

All of these shifts finally have had their impact on understandings of African politics. They have contributed to furious polemics against old paradigms, now to be dismissed as 'mere ideological preconceptions' which have 'abysmally failed the test of plausi-bility'.[12] 'Dependency is a fairy tale' and development is a 'disastrous notion'.[13] Both are characterised by dogma and hypocrisy.[14] Modernisation theory can see only a failed state to be explained by

'tradition', its explanatory framework allowing only a vacuous teleology or a facile exoticism. Dependency theory is no better, seeing African realities only as externally determined by global class forces. But beyond such polemics several positions are posed. Firstly, an explicit assertion that African politics should be understood by means of universal concepts, not that is treated, as Stephen Ellis puts it, in terms of 'otherness'.[15] Secondly, it is argued that political analysis is now informed by a great deal more knowledge and particularly historical knowledge. The frequent and passionate assertions of 'historicity' register a claim to Africa being a part of history, that is having a capacity to be understood in its own dimension and not as a function of something else (say Western imperialism). This requires the 'de-exoticisation' of tradition, essentially a critique of ethnicity as tradition and its re-under-standing as a strategy simultaneously asserting the capacity for action amongst subordinate as well as ruling groups. As a result it becomes possible to emphasise the continuities in African political life. Thirdly, and most importantly, it has led to the view that the modern African state is precisely that, a modern African state; it has, in the words that are frequently used, been grafted onto African societies.[16] It is to its foundations and the associated political strategies that we should attend rather than such irrelevancies as the form of state or the ideological statements of leaders and so on.

The return of modernisation

There is no doubt that this onslaught has had effects, bringing about dramatic changes in words and usages. No-one now dare talk of imparting 'civilisation' or 'making men modern'. In academic and policy circles alike slogans abound calling for 'African solutions' or 'African imprints' or even 'African alternatives'. These shifts are not mere changes of tone or rhetoric, yet another threadbare mask to cover the ever sinister play of Western interests. But their importance need not obscure the fact that, concurrent with them, the modernisation framework (and its dependency cousin) far from disappearing, has rather shifted its ground. The key to this remains the state. It was the state, the political kingdom, that was to open the door to progress and it is the state that is now seen to have failed. Although there are considerable differences in theoretical provenance and language a cluster of themes has emerged to constitute the new mainstream understanding. African states lack legitimacy because there is no real political representation or participation. To the extent that states are linked to the wider society it is through forms of clientelist politics. Clientelism breeds corruption and arbitrariness and the scope for all these is greatly increased by a large degree of state intervention in the economy. The form of politics that results is a ruthless struggle for power and resources by individuals and cliques and leads to the state's development policy being made against the interests of society as a whole. Over time African societies, or elements of them, have resisted these tendencies causing both politics and states to fail. And so debate has shifted to firstly, how to make the state work better and secondly, how to achieve by other means things that should have been achieved by the state. Simplifying somewhat, both of these are seen to point in the direction of the market and civil society because the former removes opportunities for rent-seeking and corruption and because accountability comes from the existence of independent power bases in society. Thus both together will constrain the possibilities of the abuse of office by state officials and both will make possible the emergence of a properly constituted public authority properly committed to the public interest.[17]

Not surprisingly then on this shifted terrain the (new look) modernisation school suggest either that things really are changing this time (or at least have the potential to do so) as vibrant civil societies and democratisation bring corrupt and tyrannical regimes to heel. Voluntary associations or non-governmental organisations have come to be seen as the key to strengthening African civil society. It is true that within this context much more attention is paid to 'the indigenous' (and this is a particular fancy of Western NGOs) but this is to the degree that the indigenous suits or is conducive to the processes of modernisation. This emphasis on the indigenous also suits a kind of policy discourse as it suggests that while it is appropriate for 'the international community' to intervene in the affairs of African states this is in order to assist the (good) domestic forces agitating for change against the (bad) old elites and preserves at least a (very threadbare) notion of sovereignty. Of course just as there was an early wave of scepticism about modernisation from within modernisation theory we may well be in a wave of liberal scepticism about the degree to which a post-Cold War world offers the opportunities to finally restructure the non-Western world.[18]

If modernisation theory has been reworked rather than buried it is not unlikely that some form of dependency theory continues to survive; and so it proves. This (new look) dependency school no longer places the same emphasis on structural economic variables (terms of trade, capital flows and the like) but rather on political strategies. But against the mainstream positions it suggests that, what it often calls a neo-liberal agenda does not promise a genuine modernisation because it is constructed to sanction only the enhancement of technocratic control over African societies within a globalising capitalist order. Despite a fig-leaf of commitment to democracy and empowerment, the policies of structural adjustment have done great damage to those groups in African societies in the forefront of struggles for democracy, groups who are, in addition, often most vociferously opposed to structural adjustment and related policies.[19] It follows that what is really needed in Africa is a *genuine* civil society and *real* democratisation involving popular participation as the means to a rekindling of the nation-state building strategy.

This reconfiguration of modernisation theory also involved a shift in some time-honoured assumptions about democracy. The effective operation of this form of political order was long thought to involve certain structural pre-requisites, including a certain level of economic prosperity, a large middle-class, fairly high levels of education for the mass population and so on. Now the presumed causalities are reversed so that the lack of democracy (or at least an accountable state) becomes the root cause of the lack of development. While acknowledging this shift it is important to note that, in both its 'mainstream' and 'radical' variants, it is not a politicisation of modernisation theory (the political was always central) but rather a shift, from an emphasis on a modernising state to one on a modernising civil society; and that, while it may have important implications for policy and certain kinds of empirical research, in no sense does it part company with the dominant analytical and normative assumptions prevalent in Western liberal social and political theory.

Far from sounding the death knell of modernisation theory 'new historical knowledge' can comfortably find its place within the new formula. Thus, as the debate about ethnicity shows, the old orthodoxies about 'tribalism' gave way to (very) confident assertions that new historical knowledge confirmed ethnic identity to be a purely modern phenomenon rooted in colonial experience. But this view has in turn been outflanked by new arguments that ethnicity can be found in pre-colonial history (often accompanied by that rather threatening undertone which says: who dares suggest that Africans were not capable of inventing ethnic identities or whatever for themselves).[20] But this is not surprising. It has already been noted that the writing of African history in modern times suggests that historians have produced new knowledge in response to current ideological and political agendas: when resistance to colonialism was to be lauded 'continuities of resistance' proliferated all over the continent; when states were fashionable (they were once) the African past suddenly teemed with states; indeed in that brief moment when everyone had to have a 'mode of production' Africa acquired one too. These gyrations suggest, to say the least, that the notion of an unproblematic discovery of 'new knowledge' is something of a conceit. Historians may now be engaged in telling different stories, 'recognising and respecting the identities and traditions of various communities, yet emphasising their interactions and their commonality' or reporting the 'triumph of indigenous economic rationality'.[21] Whatever the historical plausibility of these stories, their ideological agendas are, to put it mildly, not difficult to discern. As Lee notes, 'scholars of Africa seem to have an urgent need to demonstrate that Africa was and is truly part of World history'.[22] In this, of course, they find themselves at one with the much reviled modernisation theorists whose most intellectually acute representatives emphatically asserted that, 'the categories we employ are the same as the ones we employ in our studies of our own societies, and they postulate the fundamental affinities of all human beings'.[23]

These considerations suggest that both the sheer resilience and the analytical ambiguities of 'modernisation theory' are much more deeply rooted within Western (liberal) social and political theory than is generally acknowledged. Within that theory the problem of the state is that it must be both weak and strong. Weak because, on the one hand, the state is purely an enabler, little more than a neutral mechanism providing the security to allow free, equal individuals to pursue their life projects, unhindered by others. In this understanding a strong state is a potential threat to free persons. These threats are two fold. Firstly the state may attempt to impose some particular social order, which will invariably embody some set of values, that constrains peoples' freedom (think here of Western denunciations of 'fundamentalism') and secondly, that the offices of the state may be abused by their incumbents (and the stronger the state the greater the possible abuses). The way to counter these threats is to institutionalise some form of accountability and historically, as a general tendency, this has taken the form firstly, of a universal legal code to which state officials are also subject, and secondly a complex of institutions now generally referred to as liberal democracy and comprising universal suffrage, political parties, rights of political participation and so on.

But this is only half the story. The other half is a series of arguments that require that the state be strong. This strong state must to a certain extent be disengaged from social interests and certainly not be overwhelmed by them. It must be capable of imposing and maintaining a certain kind of social order, essentially a liberal capitalist order. Far from being merely accountable to social interests it must be capable of ensuring that only the right kind of interests are in play; indeed in terms of the European experience it is not implausible to suggest that the state itself is committed to the constitution of social classes as a new form of social order.[24] In this half of the story it is quite impossible for the the liberal state to be neutral and indifferent to values; rather it must actively interfere in what people believe and how they live, even to the extent of inculcating certain kinds of values and dispositions. Such elaborate processes of transformation of both 'structures' and 'values' require not a minimalist state, but a state constituted in the form of an immense bureaucratic apparatus with all the capacity for fine-grained social surveillance and social control which that makes possible.

A liberal project

These endless ambiguities about the state, accountable but not captured, autonomous but not oppressive, neutral but interventionist, are not resolved at the purely theoretical level. Rather they can only be made sense of as a project, a project the nature of which is sharply illuminated by the debate about Africa because liberal capitalism is not yet hegemonic there and the processes by which such hegemony is constructed cannot be so easily obscured as in the West. There is increasingly an international dimension to all this. The Cold War, it is generally agreed, gave African countries some room for manoeuvre as between the two superpowers and their junior allies and, it should be added, legitimated some elements of global pluralism in the social systems of sovereign states thereby making intervention in their internal affairs somewhat problematic (though of course, and especially in francophone Africa, it did sometimes occur). The dramatic shift in the correlation of forces since the end of the Cold War has allowed not only Western states but the 'intergovernmental' agencies they control (which is essentially all of them) to contemplate and, arguably, begin the imposition of their own agendas on the rest of the world.

The World Bank provides an excellent example of all these developments, both domestic and international.[25] Looking back over some twenty years in which its actions in Africa have become more and more obtrusive, it is clear that there has been a twin track attempt both to weaken states (in certain sorts of ways) and to strengthen them (in other sorts of ways). This approach must be seen as a project though of course shaped by many contingencies, the international political situation and the policy shifts of Western states and elites, being only the most obvious. Yet through all these exigencies, the trajectory of the Bank and latterly other international institutions, illustrates how this project has expanded and diversified from a narrow focus on economic growth to a concern with structures of governance, to programmes of social reconstruction which in their scale and aspirations (if not yet the political will and the resources committed to them) are paralleled only by nineteenth-century colonialism and the post-war occupations of Germany and Japan. Despite the dismissal of these efforts in certain quarters little evidence is offered that they are going to recede. They are complemented indeed by a growing amount of private sector involvement in this new civilising mission that goes far beyond 'development' in any of the conventional senses and, (let us use the robust language of the colonial era) whose 'ultimate object is moral improvement'.[26]

For some of course it may be sufficient to repeat the charges of naiveté against the World Bank, to locate its undertakings in the tradition of the crasser forms of modernisation theory and leave it at

that. For those not content with such a manoeuvre a question remains as to whether the notions of tradition and modernity are quite as bankrupt as they are now usually said to be. In approaching that issue it is sensible to acknowledge that there is little doubt that these terms have come to carry an insupportable weight subsuming transitions as varied as custom to law, communal to private property, barter to exchange, seasonal to clock time, craft to automated production and so on; and that the idea that all these continua straightforwardly join in two contrasting bundles is the 'error of seeing everything modern as belonging to one Enlightenment package'.[27]

But at their most intellectually serious the various conceptual schemes devised by European social theory were intended to distinguish forms of social order characterised by the presumption of the universality and equality of individual interests conjoined with a universal morality, all under the aegis of a universal reason; and forms of social order that were not. Modern societies would take the form of a differentiation of spheres of activity - the economic, the political, the familial, and so on to which different values and orientations, could be deemed appropriate. The values appropriate to one sphere could be positively dysfunctional in another. Various accounts provided more or less elaborate pictures of this form of social order, especially the problems of ensuring its coherence, but undergirding them all was a distinction between 'private' and 'public'. The public sphere, comprising both the state proper and the market in its formal constitution and operation, embodied rationality and impersonality. As we have seen it is the failure of African societies, and especially states, to respect (and police) this boundary that forms the core of the contemporary mainstream explanation of African state and wider social failure.

But these boundaries (notably between public and private) are not firm and there there has been and is always a tension between them. The dilemma of the weak/strong state, discussed earlier, perfectly exemplifies this. What exactly is private and what exactly public has varied historically and can only be made sense of as part of the attempt to construct a liberal capitalist order. Liberal authors often comfortably suggest that, 'we know directly of communities without markets, bound by unspoken obligations in which altruism and reciprocity appear to govern and in which cohesion is maintained without coercion. These are our families'.[28] There is an important sense in which this is right not least in acknowledging that such relationships certainly have existed, and perhaps still do, inside the heartlands of liberal capitalism and require no 'othering' or 'exoticising' of strange peoples. But such assertions are deeply misleading if they imply that private and public comfortably co-exist. It is true that over long historical periods the (nuclear) family in various forms has been tolerated as an institution which more or less looks after itself and remains an appropriate place for the practical business of child-rearing and early moral socialisation. But this tolerance has been and is always under siege by more hostile stances towards the family, either insinuating it is nothing more than an ersatz contract or denouncing it as an 'oppression', in whichever case insisting it is not what it says it is. It is these understandings that inform past and current efforts to subject the family to the logic of contract and 'rights' both within the boundaries of states, and increasingly, across them.[29] The reactions to communities larger than families is virtually identical in liberal discourse, social science and state practice - either they do not really exist, or perhaps more generously, culture is really 'epiphenomenal'; or if they do, they may be of the 'wrong' kind. The 'enthusiasm for writing out of human history every instance of authentic and autonomous "Others"' is not, *pace* Professor Lee, an aberration of a few scholars, but a deep-seated constant of Western discourse and practice.[30]

Such considerations may enable us to identify the rational kernel of modernisation theory. What marks non-modernised communities and cultures is extensive interaction on all dimensions of social life within the boundaries of those communities, the relative impermeability of the boundaries, at least where that would threaten the integrity of the group and the self-sufficiency of the culture's own moral and normative standards, that is to say that the main source of moral and normative standards is from within the culture. None of this precludes 'borrowings' provided that these do not overwhelm the boundaries of the culture. What modernisation precisely means is the disembedding of people from their cultures and communities and it can therefore be understood as 'the increase of individualism and individuality'.[31] But it is also about re-embedding individuals in new forms of social groups which, even if they are not wholly reduced to the impersonality of the state and the market, come to substantially depend on those forms of social order. Effecting these transformations is complex and difficult and the outcomes in the West within the framework of each nation-state are enormously varied.

A liberal project in Africa

To say the least, effecting such transformations was, and is, likely to be no easier in Africa – as Cahen puts it, counterposing Third Republic France with contemporary Mozambique, 'things do not go anywhere near as smoothly in the capitalist periphery, where the authoritarian modernising state is not a source of upward mobility. Its policies are in these conditions a stick with no corresponding carrot. Its political identity is experienced as alien by its peoples, who thus develop defensive, centrifugal, anti-state identities in response'.[32] It certainly could be argued that African elites have not been as adept as they might have been. In retrospect both the sheer fragility of African 'nationalism' in the absence of the colonial master, and the prodigious difficulty, in the face of bewildering diversity, of providing it with any cultural content, have become clear. Even its development content has been excessively aspirational, often quite unrealistic, not infrequently downright fanciful, and more often than not seemingly innocent of the processes and instruments of social change in the West (and indeed in the East) the effects of which it sought to emulate.[33] Of these the most important, yet again, was the state. The mesmeric effect of the modern state on African elites had never been in doubt (the political kingdom) but an understanding of the real sinews of the Western state which lie, not so much in a rather threadbare rhetoric of 'mobilisation', but in endlessly painstaking processes of individuation, homogenisation, surveillance and discipline, this perhaps eluded them. Nkrumah spoke for many when he demanded social change 'like jet propulsion' but the harsh judgment must be that African elites understood as little of the former as they did of the latter.[34]

Thus there is little disagreement that the states constructed by African elites are weak, poorly focused, and their writ rarely runs through the 'political kingdom'. The Central African Republic is doubtless an extreme case in which 'the state stops at PK 12' (i.e. twelve kilometres from the capital).[35] But generally speaking Herbst is probably right to assert that, 'no large African country can be said to have consolidated control over its entire territory'.[36] There can surely be little doubt either that, to a considerable degree, 'national'

and 'local' politics remain poles apart. Political scientists may ritually protest that they are 'not attempting to *resuscitate* the tradition versus modern dichotomy', but the substitution of a focus on the 'cultural logic of African politics' but not in a narrowly culturalist way, suggests that the dreaded dichotomy is not so easily escaped.[37] Redefined along the lines suggested here it is hardly surprising that political science constantly uncovers distinct 'logics', suggesting that for example, 'State law and local normative orders constitute different logics' or that 'In law, official functioning and budget it [the state] is totally Western. In practice it is otherwise traversed by logics in drastic contradiction with the original model'.[38]

But the other side of this is that many African peoples and communities retain a coherence and a capacity for action that people elsewhere in the world (though notably in the West) have long lost. Thus the Senegalese Family Code which is (needless to say) in line with 'international standards' but not (of course) African ones, hardly regulates Senegalese families, despite being the product of years of work and passed in the teeth of opposition from the marabouts, usually regarded as an essential pillar of the Senegalese state. This is doubtless in part because of the lack of capacity of the Senegalese state to enforce it and indeed many other laws. But it is also because the laws do not fit local communities and cultures who have alternative traditions and therefore other options.[39]

Similarly in many African countries, land laws, which are often not merely in line with 'international standards' but taken over lock, stock and barrel from the colonial powers remain unenforced, land registers are not maintained and indeed local officials do not know what the laws are. None of this suggests particularly efficient or competent states or at the least it suggests proliferations of competing jurisdictions and accompanying 'brokering' of access to such jurisdictions.[40] But even today 'most land tenure systems are "communal" in character' and 'groups often restrict alienation of land to outsiders, and thus seek to maintain the identity, coherence and livelihood security of the group and its members'.[41] Generalising this it might be argued that (many) Africans have not yet been disembedded from land both as a means of security but also of prestige and social and cultural value. They are practical Marxists and they know that to lose one's means of production is to become dependent on (unknown) others; better than Marx they know that to lose one's material means of production is to lose one's cultural means of production. The music of the spheres is the siren song of cultural destruction.

From this vantage point the endless denunciation of tradition, the denial of culture and community as anything more than endless flux, and the proclamation of an abstract 'agency', may lose some of their persuasiveness. For some, of course, such denials and proclamations signify the passing of illusions and 'replacing romanticism with complexity'.[42] They are an essential step on the road to a better and more secure knowledge. But in a globalising world the advantages of this latest vocabulary, just like its predecessors, are not lost on modernisers of all kinds, tirelessly alert to the possibilities of reworking fragments of existing cultures. Of course the Western world is not short of those happy to contemplate a continuous 'assault' on other people's beliefs.[43] But this does not preclude more subtle approaches. As a joint statement of the WHO, UNICEF and UNFPA puts it, in the context of campaigns to eradicate female circumcision in Africa '...culture is not static; it is in constant flux, adapting and reforming. People will change their behaviour when they understand the hazards and indignity of harmful practices without giving up meaningful aspects of their culture'.[44] But, as

Hopgood points out, this cultural material is precisely to be reworked to ends set by other agencies, and these reconfigurations always remain subject to 'reason' whether exemplified as in the nineteenth century by standards of 'civilisation' or in the twentieth by charters of 'human rights', in either case policed by agencies outside the cultures on which they are to be imposed.

It may be of course that, with romanticism replaced by complexity, the Utopia offered by Professor Appiah is the best we can hope for – a world in which we all drink Coca-Cola but it 'means' different things to different people.[45] In any event, or at least so I have tried to suggest here, the study of contemporary Africa and its politics both offers us a glimpse of a world beyond Coca-Cola and poses hard questions about ourselves.

Notes

[1] Anonymous Maka peasant quoted in Wim van Binsbergen and Peter Geschiere (eds), *Old Modes of Production and Capitalist Encroachment: Anthropological Explorations in Africa*, KPI, 1985, p. 131.

[2] Michael Oakeshott, *On Human Conduct*, Oxford, Clarendon Press, 1991, p. 297.

[3] Respectively Leopold Senghor, *On African Socialism*, London, Pall Mall Press, 1964, pp. 158-9; Botswana Democratic Party, 1965 Election Manifesto clause 8; Sekou Toure, *Africa on the Move*, London, Panaf Books, 1977, p. 311; K. Nkrumah, *Africa must Unite*, London, Panaf Books, 1963, p. 105; Samora Machel, 'The Peoples's Republic of Mozambique: The Struggle Continues', *Review of African Political Economy*, no.4, 1975, p. 20.

[4] R. H. Bates, *Rural Responses to Industrialisation: A Study of Village Zambia*, New Haven, Yale University Press, 1976, p. 1. For a full treatment of the numbers see D. Potts, 'Shall we go home? Increasing Urban Poverty in African Cities and Migration Processes', *The Geographical Journal*, vol.161, part 3, 1995, pp. 245–64. Professor Bates later became an expert on urban bias. There is some interesting discussion of Zambian urbanisation in James Ferguson, *Expectations of Modernity: Myth and Meanings of Urban Life on the Zambian Copperbelt,* Berkeley, University of California Press, 1999.

[5] For dependency theory within African studies see Peter J. Schraeder, *African Politics and Society*, Boston, Bedford/St. Martins, 2000, ch.3.

[6] J. Dunn, *Western Political Theory in the Face of the Future*, Cambridge, Cambridge University Press, 1979, p. 55.

[7] Emerson quoted in Crawford Young, 'Nationalism, Ethnicity and Class in Africa: A Retrospective', *Cahiers d'Etudes Africaines* XXVI-3, 1986, pp. 421–95 at, p. 425.

[8] Steven Feierman, *Peasant Intellectuals: Anthropology and History in Tanzania*, Madison, University of Wisconsin Press, 1990, p. 38.

[9] Craig Calhoun, *Critical Social Theory*, Oxford, Blackwell, 1995, p. 198.

[10] Ulf Hannerz, 'The World in Creolisation', *Africa*, 57, 1987, pp. 546-59.

[11] A good recent example with copious references to appropriate literature is Charles Piot, *Remotely Global Village Modernity in West Africa*, Chicago, University of Chicago Press, 1999.

[12] Patrick Chabal, *Power in Africa An Essay in Political Interpretation*, Basingstoke, Macmillan, 1992, p. 197 &, p. 9.

[13] Jean-François Bayart, *The State in Africa*, Harlow, Longmans, 1993, p. 33 and in James Manor (ed.), *Rethinking Third World Politics*, Harlow, Longmans, 1991, p. 52.

[14] Bayart, *The State in Africa*, p. 5.

[15] Stephen Ellis, 'Democracy in Africa: Achievements and Prospects' in D. Rimmer (ed.), *Action in Africa*, London, James Currey, 1993, p. 134.

[16] Bayart, *The State in Africa*, p. 265.

[17] I have condensed this summary of the mainstream literature on African politics from a broader account in Tim Kelsall, *Subjectivity, Collective Action and the Governance Agenda in Tanzania*, SOAS PhD 1999, to which I am much indebted.

[18] See for example Roland Paris, 'Peacebuilding and the Limits of Liberal Internationalism', *International Security*, 22(2), 1997, pp. 54-89, where an explicit parallel is drawn between modernisation theory and contemporary 'peacebuilding'.

[19] See Adebayo Olukoshi, *The Elusive Prince of Denmark*, Uppsala, Nordiska Afrikainstitutet, 1998, for this position and extensive references to the appropriate literature.

[20] For useful surveys of the ethnicity debate see Bill Bravman, *Making Ethnic Ways: Communities and their Transformations in Taita, Kenya, 1800–1950*, Oxford, James Currey, 1998 and R. Atkinson, 'The (Re)Construction of Ethnicity in Africa: Extending the Chronology, Conceptualisation and Discourse', in Paris Yeros (ed.), *Ethnicity and Nationalism in Africa: Constructivist Reflections and Contemporary Politics*, Basingstoke, Macmillan, 1999, pp. 15–44. This outflanking phenomenon is a common feature of Western discourse about Africa and reflects almost unmentionable anxieties about 'rationality'. See for example the squabbles reported in John L. and Jean Comaroff, *Of Revelation and Revolution* vol.2, Chicago, University of Chicago Press, 1997.

[21] Patrick Manning, *Slavery and African Life: Occidental, Oriental and African Slave Trades*, Cambridge, Cambridge University Press, 1990, p. 196, and Gareth Austin, 'Mode of Production or Mode of Cultivation: Explaining the failure of European cocoa planters in competition with African farmers in colonial Ghana', in W.Clarence-Smith (ed.), *Cocoa Pioneer Fronts since 1800,* Basingstoke, Macmillan, 1996, pp. 154-75, p. 158.

[22] R. B. Lee and M. Guenther, 'Problems in Kalahari historical ethnography and the tolerance of error', *History in Africa*, 20, 1993, pp. 185–235, p. 186. For copious documentation of this point see Anne. B Stahl, 'Perceiving variabilty in space and time: the evolutionary mapping of African societies' in Susan Keech McIntosh (ed.), *Beyond Chiefdoms: Pathways to Complexity in Africa*, Cambridge, Cambridge University Press, 1999. See also D.M. Anderson and R. Rathbone (eds), *Africa's Urban Past*, Oxford, James Currey, 2000.

[23] E. Shils, 'On the Comparative Study of the New States' in C. Geertz (ed.), *Old Societies and New States: The Quest for Modernity in Asia and Africa*, New York, Free Press, 1963, p. 8.

[24] See G. Burchell et al. (eds), *The Foucault Effect*, Chicago, University of Chicago Press, 1991, esp. ch.1.

[25] For my understanding of the World Bank I am greatly indebted to D. G. Williams, *The Emergence and Implementation of the World Bank's 'Good Governance' Agenda*, SOAS PhD, 1997.

[26] Sir Charles Grant (speaking in 1832) quoted in Uday Mehta, *Liberalism and Empire: Essays on Nineteenth Century British Liberal Thought*, Chicago, University of Chicago Press, 1999.

[27] Charles Taylor, 'Two Theories of Modernity', *Public Culture* 11(1), 1999, pp. 153-74, p. 160.

[28] William James Booth, *Households. On the Moral Architecture of the Economy*, Ithaca, Cornell University Press,1993, p. 292.

[29] The promoters of such agendas are often helpfully frank about shifts in the notion of public/private. Cf. Geraldine van Bueren, *The International Law on the Rights of the Child*, Dordrecht, Martinus Nijhoff Publishers, 1995, ch.3.

[30] Richard Lee, 'The Primitive as Problematic', *Anthropology Today*, 9(6), 1993, pp. 1–3, p. 2.

[31] Peter Wagner, *A Sociology of Modernity*, Routledge, 1994, p. 6.

[32] M. Cahen, 'Nationalism and Ethnicities: Lessons from Mozambique' at www.dundee.ac.uk.cphrc/sections/articles/cahen1.htm, p. 15.

[33] The Mozambican government put forward a plan in 1980 to industrialise the country in 10 years. For the details see M. Hall and T. Young, *Confronting Leviathan,* Hurst and Co., 1997. It should be added that, whatever else it was, the plan was not the self-interested mendacity of a venal elite. See also John Saul, *Millenial Africa*, Trenton, NJ., Africa World Press, Inc., 2001, ch.4.

[34] K. Nkrumah, *Autobiography*, Nelson, 1957, p. x.

[35] A popular saying quoted in T. Bierschenk & Jean-Pierre Olivier de Sardan, 'Local Powers and a Distant State in rural Central African Republic', *Journal of Modern African Studies*, 35(3), 1997, pp. 441–68, p. 441.

36 J. Herbst, *States and Power in Africa: Comparative Lessons in Authority and Control*, Princeton, Princeton University Press, 2000, p. 254.

37 Bruce J. Berman, 'Ethnicity, Patronage and the African State: The Politics of Uncivil Nationalism', *African Affairs*, 97, 1998, pp. 305–41, p. 340 and p. 308 my emphasis. Cf. the rather different tone in Bruce J. Berman, 'African Capitalism and the Paradigm of Modernity: Culture, Technology and the State', in B. Berman and C. Leys (eds), *African Capitalists in African Development*, Boulder, Co., Lynne Rienner, 1994.

38 Cf. Sten Hagberg, *Between Peace and Justice: Dispute Settlement between Karaboro Agriculturalists and Fulbe Agro-pastoralists in Burkina Faso*, Uppsala, Uppsala University, 1998, p. 231. Olivier de Sardan, 'A Moral Economy of Corruption in Africa', *Journal of Modern African Studies* 37(1), March 1999, pp. 25–52, p. 47. There seems to be a similar use of 'logic' (insofar as I can follow the argument) in A. Mbembe, 'Provisional Notes on the Postcolony', *Africa*, 62(1), 1992, pp. 3–37.

39 For the details see L. Villalon, *Islamic Society and State Power in Senegal*, Cambridge, Cambridge University Press, 1995, chs. 3 and 6.

40 For an example see Christian Lund, 'A Question of Honour: Property Disputes and Brokerage in Burkina Faso', *Africa* 69(4), 1999, pp. 575–94.

41 Camilla Toulmin and Julian Quan (eds), *Evolving Land Rights, Policy and Tenure in Africa*, International Institute for Environment and Development, 2000, p. 152.

42 Thus, H. Englund, 'Waiting for the Portuguese: Nostalgia, Exploitation and the Meaning of Land in the Malawi–Mozambique Borderland', *Journal of Contemporary African Studies*, 14(2), 1996, pp. 157–72 at p. 157. Bear in mind that just about the most awful thing you can say to an academic is that they or their views are 'not complex'.

43 Claude E. Welch Jr., *Protecting Human Rights in Africa, Strategies and Roles of Non-Governmental Organisations*, Philadelphia, University of Pennsylvania Press, 1995, p. 95.

44 As quoted in Stephen Hopgood, 'Constructing the Unencumbered Self: The Eradication of Premodernity in Global Civil Society', unpublished paper, p. 35 See also the same author's, 'Reading the Small Print in Global Civil Society: The Inexorable Hegemony of the Liberal Self', *Millenium*, 29 (1), 2000, pp. 1–25.

45 K. A. Appiah, 'Cosmopolitan Patriots', in L. Wohlgemuth et al. (eds), *Common Security and Civil Society in Africa*, Uppsala, Nordiska Afrikainstitutet, 1999, p. 201.

1 Appraising the Modern African State

ARISTIDE ZOLBERG
The Party-State in Perspective

Reference
Creating Political Order: The Party States of West Africa
University of Chicago Press, 1966, ch. 5

Although in the preceding chapters the emphasis has been on the common characteristics of the regimes of the five countries studied, we have remained very close to empirical reality and operated at a relatively low level of generalization in order to sketch a somewhat detailed and fairly realistic composite portrait of the West African party state. Given the misconceptions that prevail in much of the literature on this subject, our main purpose has been frankly revisionist. Nevertheless, in order to round out the analysis and suggest the beginnings of an alternative approach to the study of African politics, we shall now attempt to view the West African party-state at a somewhat higher level of generalization. This chapter will therefore adopt the vantage point of the society in which the party-state operates, raise some questions concerning the relationship of the party-state to the political system of that society, and conclude by introducing the perspective of time.

The perspective of the political system

The level of generalization at which we now attempt to view the politics of the five West African countries under scrutiny approximates that of the political system as conceptualized by David Easton, which is 'the most inclusive system of behavior in a society for the authoritative allocation of values.'[1] Therefore, instead of merely analyzing the structure of the party-state, as we have done so far, we shall attempt to provide at least a sketchy answer to the following questions about West African countries: 'How are values authoritatively allocated for the society?' and 'What role does the party-state play in this allocative activity?' The usefulness of the systemic perspective becomes clear because of immediate difficulties we encounter in answering. Usually, political scientists who speak of political systems have in mind at least implicitly the context of an identifiable concrete society, be it contemporary Great Britain or a small tribe of highland Burma or northern Togo. It is more difficult, however, after a moment of reflection, to take as a given the existence of a 'society' which encompasses all the individuals living within the territorial confines of any of the five countries under consideration here.

A century ago or less, there existed on the African continent, within the area encompassed today by any of the five countries (or by all of them and their neighbours as a group), a large number of societies varying in size, in social structure, and in culture, each with a corresponding political system. They also varied from relatively undifferentiated ones in which political and kinship structures were almost indistinguishable to highly differentiated

ones usually referred to as 'states'. They did not exist in isolation but constantly interacted so as to warrant the designation of the area as an international political system, or, if we wish to relate the area to the world at large, as a regional subsystem of the international system.[2] The relationships between the individual political actors within the subsystem and those between the subsystem as a whole, or some of its parts, and the international system, varied greatly over time. About a century ago, however, certain international actors (principally France and Great Britain) extended the boundaries of their own political community to include some of the societies of the African continent.

The definition of new political units such as 'Senegal', 'French West Africa', or 'Gold Coast', did not, of course, result automatically in the creation of a new society within these legally defined territorial boundaries. There is no doubt that initially at least the various societies caught within the net cast over a particular geographical area retained their identity. The changes that occurred, however, particularly affected their individual political systems, as well as the interactions between them that constituted the regional international subsystem. What form these changes took constitutes the major theme in the political history of the colonial period. It ranged from the limiting case of almost complete preservation of an African political system and the establishment of a federal type of relationship between it and the European system (as in a pure type of indirect rule), to the complete destruction of the African political system and an extension of the European political system over the corresponding society (as in a pure type of direct rule). In practice, however, neither of these limiting cases was ever met.

During the past three or four decades, the impact of cultural, social, economic, and political change has been heightened. A growing number of Africans who were members of particular societies began to interact across the boundaries of these societies. At the same time the colonial power developed its central bureaucracy, territorial political organizations began to appear. Thus it could be said that a new territorial society was in the making and that corresponding to this incipient society there arose an incipient political system. Nevertheless, although Africans have taken control of the central bureaucracy, it is reasonable to assume that the pre-existing African societies and their corresponding political system have not totally disappeared. Hence, any consideration of the authoritative allocation of values in countries such as these must come to grips with the persisting duality of political processes.

This duality of societies and of political systems coexisting within the territorial boundaries of new states can be grasped intuitively, but it is difficult to express it with conceptual precision. Although it may be useful for some purposes to adopt a conceptual approach which views each country as being composed of numerous interacting societies, and hence to consider the territorial political process as merely the sum of the interactions within and between the political systems it contains, this approach takes us very far afield and necessitates the abandonment of most of the available conceptual apparatus of comparative politics. Before adopting it, other alternatives should be considered. It is also possible to assume that to each new country there corresponds a single, albeit imperfectly integrated, society, and also, by definition, a single political system dealing with the authoritative allocation of values for that society. Unless this is qualified, however, it leads to a loss of the intuitive grasp we have acquired of the duality of the political process.

While adopting this approach, the duality could be retained and even made operational by classifying individuals living in these countries into two or more appropriate political categories. Karl Deutsch, for example, has distinguished, on the basis of degree of political participation and exposure to political communications, two sets in any population, the 'mobilized' and the 'non-mobilized'.[3] Following a similar procedure, Daniel Lerner has distinguished between 'moderns', 'transitionals', and 'traditionals'.[4] But this sort of approach raises a serious conceptual difficulty, in addition to the practical problems stemming from the difficulty of distinguishing between participants and non-participants in countries where the government is intent on demonstrating unanimity. Although it is a heuristic device to help us understand the process of national political integration, it can tell us mostly whether or not and at what rate this process is occurring. It tells us very little about the vital problem before us, namely, *what the political system of an unintegrated country is like* and tends to gloss over the fact that even the individuals who are not 'mobilized' participate in politics *of some sort*.

We can avoid the problem of struggling with the notion of multisocietal states and still retain the sense of political duality by stressing the 'allocation of values' aspect of Easton's definition of the political system. It is possible to suggest that the *values* that are authoritatively allocated in West African countries can be classified into two categories, one set to be called 'modern' and the other – avoiding the word 'traditional', which will be reserved for another purpose – to be called simply 'residual'. Furthermore, it is also possible to distinguish analytically between political structures that deal with authoritative allocation of the first set and others that deal with the second. We can then speak of a political system with two sectors, the one modern, the other residual. Since this is an analytical distinction, it can be stated also that any member of the political system occupies more or less important roles in both sectors. Although some individuals are more active in the one than in the other, these roles are not mutually exclusive. It is not only analytically possible, but empirically probable that we shall find individuals who occupy important roles in both sectors at the same time, while it is not possible to speak of someone who is *both* politically mobilized and non-mobilized without substantially modifying Deutsch's approach.[5]

The applicability of the distinction of two political sectors to the West African countries with which we are concerned and the consequences for the understanding of their politics can be illustrated as follows. If we wish to examine, for example, the activities of the party-state in the economic sphere, with which it is greatly concerned and where it is well known that it desires to play a determining role in value-allocation (through state entrepreneurship, regulation of economic activity, taxation, redistribution of income, etc.), we can take as one rough index the proportion that the total annual budget represents of the estimated GNP. The figure we obtain is in the range of 15 to 25 per cent, with the Ivory Coast and Ghana in the lower range and the remaining countries in the upper.[6] The significance of these figures is highlighted by Deutsch's finding that the budget of richer, non-Communist countries in the mid-1950s averaged about 30 per cent of the GNP. This somewhat surprising result can be understood once we take into account the fact that although the party-state plays an important role in the relatively modern economic sector (monetary transactions, import-export, industry), this sector itself is only a part of the total economic system. Much of what goes into the computation of GNP is in a residual sector, including subsistence agriculture and husbandry, locally marketed products, and even traditional imports and exports such as cattle, fish, kola nuts, and salt, which follow century-old trade routes. Most of the economic activity in this sector, which varies in importance from country to country, is, practically speaking, outside the domain of the party-state's allocative authority, even when it claims the legal right to make decisions that affect it'.[7] Yet there can be no doubt that in this residual sector rules and regulations exist, together with authoritative agencies to settle disputes, change rules, enforce obligations, etc.[8]

The distinction applies even more strikingly, albeit in a less tangible manner, to the entire sphere of norms and regulations relating to personal status. The inclusion of this apparently private sphere in the political system is so well established in modern societies that it is thought of as non-political. But such activities as the registration of births and deaths, the enforcement of rules concerning marriage and divorce, the definition of personal rights, the inheritance of property, the regulation of work, are clearly important areas of policy-making, as the consideration of the political history of any of these items or the recurrent debate over some of them (segregation, birth control) quickly reminds us. It is therefore highly significant to note that the activities of the West African party-state in this entire sphere are extremely limited. The regime is concerned with extending its authority in this direction by making laws that will affect these activities, but of course, there is a vast difference between the staking of a claim to do so and the genuine operation of allocative authority. Yet, perhaps even more than in the sphere of residual economic activity, we know that rules exist, that they are enforced, that they undergo change, that conflicts occur, and that they are settled, hence that the political system allocates values authoritatively in this sphere.

The party-state thus deals primarily with the authoritative allocation of one set of values; in a sense, its activities do not fill the entire political system of the society in which it operates. We can adopt as a working hypothesis that there is a residual political space which is filled by other structures. The fact that political activity in this sector is not immediately visible to us does not mean that it is unimportant or irrelevant, but rather, as we have indicated earlier, that the conceptual apparatus of political scientists and other observers leads them to gather information of a certain type only. What we do not see, however, is at least as important for our understanding as what we do see. How then are these residual values allocated? In countries where traditional political structures have been assigned a legitimate role – such as in Nigeria or in Uganda, for example – the answer is relatively obvious. Although it is more difficult to imagine what occurs in countries such as Mali or Guinea, where traditional rulers have been deprived of all legal authority, we know that only a limited amount of allocative activity is carried out by the party-state. The most likely answer is therefore that traditional structures still perform extremely important political functions. It is noteworthy in this respect that a similar hypothesis was advanced nearly forty years ago by Raymond Buell, who remarked, when discussing the role of chiefs in French Africa, that although these chiefs had a lesser official role in the judiciary than they were given in British Africa, their actual authority may have been greater because it was unchecked by the colonial authorities.[9]

The verification of the working hypothesis proposed here requires research that has not yet been carried out. Meanwhile, however, the view of the political system it suggests reveals the paradox of the party-state. An examination of West African politics which is concerned only with the modern sector easily leads to a characterization of the political process as one in which a single political organization has achieved a monopoly of authority. The alternative approach recognizes the importance of this feature but stresses that it is an incomplete characterization since much of the political activity that is carried on in the society remains outside the modern sector. It enables us to understand how it is possible to suggest that the party-state is authoritarian within its domain, but that at the same time this domain is very limited, and that on the whole the regime has little authority. Thus, while it is perhaps appropriate to speak of the 'one-party state', at the level of the political system there are other authorities than the rulers of the party-state, and hence it is misleading to speak of a 'one-party system'.

The nature of authority in the party-state

If we now re-examine the political patterns discussed in previous chapters the general trends appear to be as follows. First, the party-state is attempting to expand the domain of its authority to encompass a broader sector of the political system. It is doing so by extending its party and governmental apparatus to reach farther down into the society and farther out to distant regions, or as they put it in Mali, by weaving a dense spider's web. It is also extending its domain by making rules in spheres of human activity hitherto outside the sphere of modern politics. How successful the party-state has been in achieving these goals is difficult to estimate. We know, however, that realities seldom correspond to the intent of the rulers. The announcement by an African government that an institution such as chieftaincy has been abolished, that a new one such as a network of village party committees has been established, that older norms have given way to new ones, must not be taken as an indication that the old no longer exists or that the new is operational above a minimal level. On the whole, such announcements are indicative of a change of norms at one level of the political system, but not necessarily in the norms and structures that prevail throughout much as even in a very modern polity such as the United States, Supreme Court decisions declaring segregated schools unconstitutional, however significant, cannot be used as evidence even ten years later that segregated schools are no longer a characteristic feature of the American society. In Africa, much more than in the United States, such announcements can seldom be adequately checked against realities and must therefore be evaluated on the basis of experiential rules of thumb founded on tough-minded skepticism. Nevertheless, it is true that the efforts of the party-state in this direction have borne some fruit.

The second major trend suggests a steady drive to achieve greater centralization of authority in the hands of a very small number of men who occupy top offices in the party and the government, and even more in the hands of a single man at the apex of both institutions. Since the opposition was eliminated, the major source of political tension has stemmed from the contest between the paramount leader and important lieutenants, as well as between the center and regional officials in the apparatus. How successful the top leadership has been in this respect is also difficult to evaluate. Whether he acts primarily through the party or through the government, the top leader has been able on the whole to consolidate his position by making sure that subordinate leaders who have a power base in specific regions are effectively restricted to these regions, while his own personal authority is beginning to

rest on a territorial base; he has also acquired a great deal of leverage by creating multiple chains of command which coexist in a state of tension. Nevertheless, negative evidence such as the top leaders' recurrent admonitions concerning lack of discipline, the persistence of regionalism, and the pursuit of selfish interests, suggests that in spite of all efforts, the party-state retains a great measure of decentralization, with relatively autonomous subordinate authorities.

At the present level of generalization, the spectacle of the expansion of the domain of the state's authority into new fields, of the struggle between the centre and the regions, and of the tension between a supreme leader and his lieutenants, is by no means visible only in the West African party-state, or in the strikingly similar case of Tanzania. A very similar drama is taking place in African countries where federal arrangements and numerous parties prevail, as in Uganda or Nigeria; in states dominated by a party which has never acquired a 'mass' character, as in Niger; and even in spectacular fashion, with recurrent failures and continuing suspense, in the Congo. It is a continuation everywhere of the process which began with the establishment of a central administration by the European conquerors over newly defined political units during the colonial era. It also resembles the process which Lloyd Fallers believes led to the transformation of Buganda society into the Buganda kingdom in Uganda. Pointing out that African political systems were most commonly composed of segments and that the unilineal descent group was the basic building block of society, he states that 'it provided a foundation for local corporateness and autonomy which stood in the way of greater centralization and royal despotism. Highly centralized states like Buganda could develop only by suppressing this autonomy ....'[10]

Fallers goes on to suggest that

> One is reminded ... of Max Weber's discussion of feudalism and 'patrimonialism' in medieval European history – the struggle between the centralizing efforts of kings, expressed in their attempts to build up bodies of patrimonial retainers responsible to themselves alone and the decentralizing tendency of subordinate authorities to become locally rooted hereditary lords.[11]

A similar feeling of *déjà vu* is evoked when one contemplates the behavior of the top leaders in the West African party-states. In a revision of his book on Ghana, Apter characterizes Kwame Nkrumah in 1962–63 as a 'Presidential monarch'.[12] Nowhere, perhaps, is the historical parallel with Europe as striking as in Mali, where Modibo Keita has appointed a set of regional governors directly responsible to him in his capacity as President, and also a set of roving party commissioners directly responsible to him as Secretary-General of the *Union Soudanaise*. In addition, he spends about one-quarter of every year touring the regions with a suite consisting of party officials, elected representatives, and important bureaucrats. He holds court at daybreak in towns and villages, learning about local conditions, teaching the population concepts of national citizenship, and making sure that the authority of his office is clearly understood to be tangible and paramount. He encourages the population to bring to his attention a variety of complaints, including grievances stemming from abuses committed by administrators or party officials, and settles village or town disputes that have been held in abeyance for years. In spite of the use of modern Marxist phraseology, the mood is akin to that of premodern Europe. But where does this analogy lead us? Is it merely an entertaining historical parallel, or does it contain a serious clue to the understanding of the West African party-state?

Beyond drawing attention to similarities in the behaviour of rulers, the parallel suggests possible fundamental similarities in the very nature of the systems of authority which characterize these otherwise very different polities. It invites an inquiry into the legitimacy on which the authority of the rulers of the West African party-state rests.

In Weber's now classical formulation, no regime can rely on coercion alone: 'In general, it should be kept clearly in mind that the basis of every system of authority, and correspondingly of every kind of willingness to obey, is a *belief*, a belief by virtue of which persons exercising authority are lent prestige.'[13] It is the examination of the variety of such beliefs that led Weber to the construction of three major types of 'imperative coordination' or of 'domination', based upon three corresponding bases of legitimacy: the legal-rational, the charismatic, and the traditional.[14] Before attempting to consider the West African party-state in this light, however, we must remember Weber's own admonition that 'The composition of this belief is seldom altogether simple.'[15] Even legal authority – the system which prevails in the United States, for example – contains traditional elements (as with the Constitution and the Presidency, hallowed by time and tradition) but also a charismatic element 'at least in the negative sense that persistent and striking lack of success may be sufficient to ruin any government, to undermine its prestige, and to prepare the way for charismatic revolution.'[16]

If these beliefs can co-exist, how can they form the basis for distinguishing between classes of polities? it might be useful to consider them as traits distributed according to varying patterns among the members of any political system, possibly even cumulatively, rather than as mutually exclusive sets in which the dominance of one type of belief necessarily implies the absence of others. Systems can then be characterized as clusterings of legitimacy variables and it would be possible to understand how the salience of these types of beliefs can vary over time within the same system, denoting important changes at the level of the regime.[17] With this in mind we can approach the question of the legitimacy of the 'modern' set of authorities in the party-state.

Apter's fundamental insight concerning the charismatic nature of the authority of the leader of the nationalist movement in Ghana is useful as an initial proposition and can be extended to include leaders elsewhere. Some qualifications are needed, however. First the term 'charismatic', which has rapidly entered into popular usage to refer to some general quality of flamboyance recognizable even by non-members of a particular system, has led to serious confusion exemplified by debates as to whether this or that African leader is 'charismatic'. It is obviously difficult for an American visitor meeting a man of small stature, wearing a conservatively cut Continental suit, drinking lemonade brought in by a frock-coated usher into his air-conditioned office, to feel mesmerized by President Houphouet-Boigny, but there is absolutely no doubt that this man is believed by many of his countrymen to be among the elect, specially designated to rule over them, and that it is on the basis of this belief that many of them have obeyed him for nearly twenty years. Thus, it is the relationship rather than objective qualities that counts. Second, 'charisma' must be extended from a reference to a single leader's relationship with his followers to include the whole set of such relationships which provided the basis of legitimacy for the early nationalist movements. Typically, roles were not clearly defined, collegiality was important, gifts and hospitality were all-important forms of support, and at the height of the movement's activity many leaders had no other regular occupation, often because they had become ineligible for employment in schools or in the colonial bureaucracy because of their political activities. 'CPP' and 'RDA' became names to conjure with rather than mere party labels, as illustrated by the fact that the success of the RDA in Mali was partly due, according to one qualified observer, to the favorable outcome of the arithmetic sum of the numerical values of the Arabic equivalents of the three letters which compose the party's initials.[18] The Mahdist tradition in Islam, as well as the messianic tradition in Christianity, contributed to the reinforcement of these beliefs. Third, however important this type of belief may have been, it coexisted from the very beginning with other types. For many individuals who had begun to internalize European norms, the legitimacy of these new men was based on democratic values. Furthermore, in most cases leaders and movements also stressed their relationship to pre-European states and movements and claimed to embody hallowed traditions.

During the period of militancy or 'positive action', which occurred early in the Ivory Coast and Ghana, but much later in Guinea and Mali, the charismatic aspects of legitimacy were most salient because they were especially compatible with the future-oriented outlook of nationalist movements. Within a short time, however, these movements became ruling organizations concerned to a considerable extent with institution-building and self-maintenance. During this later period, the charismatic basis of legitimacy is no longer sufficient. In Weber's terminology, charismatic authority must be 'routinized' if the system of domination is to last. For Weber, the major motive for routinization is

> naturally the striving for security. This means legitimization, on the one hand, of positions of authority and social prestige, on the other hand, of the economic advantages enjoyed by the followers and sympathizers of the leader. Another important motive, however, lies in the objective necessity of adaptation of the patterns of order and of the organization of the administrative staff to the normal, everyday needs and conditions of carrying on administration.[19]

Furthermore, 'it is not possible for the costs of permanent, routine administration to be met by "booty", contributions, gifts and hospitality, as is typical of the pure type of military and prophetic charisma.'[20] One is reminded here of the great stress placed by African leaders on the regular payment of party dues and appropriate taxes after self-government was attained. Another motive for routinization stems from the negative aspects of charisma referred to earlier: it is very risky for a system of authority to have to rely in the long run solely on its continued ability to distribute psychic and material benefits to its followers.

Routinization, according to Weber, leads to the transformation of a charismatic type into one of the other two, legal or traditional. Among others, he specified the conditions under which it was likely to lead to the emergence of a particular subtype of the traditional type, the patrimonial system. The crucial process involved is the *appropriation of offices*, which, he believed, tends to occur

> in all states resulting from conquest which have become rationalized to form permanent structures; *also of parties and other movements which have originally had a purely charismatic character*. With the process of routinization the charismatic group tends to develop into one of the forms of everyday authority, particularly the patrimonial form in its decentralized variant or the

bureaucratic. Its original peculiarities are apt to be retained in the charismatic standards of honour attendant on the social status acquired by heredity or *the holding of offices*. This applies to all who participate in the process of appropriation, the chief himself and the members of his staff.[21]

As for the patrimonial system itself, Weber characterized it as follows:

The object of obedience is the personal authority of the individual which he enjoys by virtue of his traditional status. The organized group exercising authority is, in the simplest case, primarily based on relations of personal loyalty, cultivated through a common process of education. The person exercising authority is not a 'superior,' but a personal 'chief'. His administrative staff does not consist primarily of officials, but of personal retainers. Those subject to authority are not 'members' of an association, but are either his traditional 'comrades' or his 'subjects.' What determines the relations of the administrative staff to the chief is not the impersonal obligations of office, but personal loyalty to the chief.[22]

Although the presence of a bureaucracy would at first thought appear to be incompatible with the patrimonial system, Weber remarked that it would be possible for a patrimonial ruler 'in the interest of his own power and financial provision' to develop 'a rational system of administration with technically specialized officials' if the following conditions were met: technical training had to be available; there must be an incentive to have such a policy; and finally, it required 'the participation of urban communes as a financial support.'[23]

We might add that to the extent that these conditions were met, the system would not be resting on traditional legitimacy alone but would be clearly a particular clustering of traditional and bureaucratic traits. When the process of routinization occurs in the second half of the twentieth century, it can naturally be expected to include additional 'rational-legal' aspects such as written constitutions and formal electoral procedures. Furthermore, the charismatic aspects themselves need not entirely disappear and a serious attempt may be made to maintain them in order to retain enthusiasm and instill a willingness to sacrifice present satisfactions in order to reap rewards in the future.[24] Hence, we should expect to witness a shift in the mixture of beliefs rather than the total replacement of one particular set by another.

With these qualifications in mind, it can be seen that the West African party-state approximates Weber's patrimonial type in many important respects. The relationships between the individual at the top and his subordinates, as well as between the ruling group and their followers, are indeed based on personal loyalty. The conditions under which the patrimonial system can coexist with a bureaucracy are precisely met by the accidental inheritance of both the bureaucracy itself and of the taxation system that makes its survival possible. But the most telling factor is evidence concerning the appropriation of offices. It is indeed striking that the occurrence of this process has been noted by a variety of observers of the African scene, beginning with Frantz Fanon, who in 1961 bitterly charged that the leaders of one-party states had become 'chairmen of the board of a society of impatient profiteers'.[25] The ruler and his personal entourage, together with a corps of ranking officials and underlings, 'satraps' (top-ranking territorial agents) and their blood relations and clients, have begun to constitute a genuine

'bureaucratic gentry,' a class based not on their relation to property but on their relation to the state apparatus.[26] Since the holding of political office in many poor countries, where there are relatively few opportunities for economic entrepreneurship, is the major source of economic and social status as well, continued political control is necessary, much as Michels suggested that it was necessary for the leaders of labor unions and European socialist parties.[27]

This tendency is reinforced by the pursuit of economic policies which, in the name of socialism or development, have as their major consequence a redistribution of national income to the benefit of the bureaucratic managers of the economy.[28] This also is compatible with Weber's model. In analyzing the relations of traditional authority to the economic order, he indicated that 'running through patriarchalism and patrimonialism generally, there is an inherent tendency to substantive regulation of economic activity.' Competitive capitalism is usually neither fostered nor tolerated, but 'it is possible for patrimonialism to be organized on a monopolistic basis of meeting its needs, partly by profit-making enterprise, partly by fees, partly by taxes.'[29] The contemporary African version of this pattern takes the form of a preference for state enterprises, or at least state participation in enterprises; and a preference for large-scale foreign investors operating under something like a licensing system over small-scale autonomous indigenous investors who are much more difficult to control. In this manner, as Weber pointed out, 'The immediate effect of charisma in economic as in other connexions is usually strongly revolutionary; indeed often destructive, because it means new modes of orientation. But in case the process of routinization leads in the direction of traditionalism, its ultimate effect may be exactly the reverse.'[30] This is clearly what a critic of Guinea had in mind when he concluded a recent study with the suggestion that after an initial revolutionary orientation, the country had now become a bastion of 'neo-colonialism.'[31]

The resemblance noted earlier between tendencies visible in the West African party-state and historical examples drawn from Europe or elsewhere is thus far more than a fortuitous parallel but indicates that patterns of authority may be genuinely similar. Since the patrimonial system is one of Weber's 'traditional' types, however, at first sight this view raises a serious problem: how can one speak of regimes that are still so to speak in their first generation as being based on traditional authority? The problem is much less serious if we do not require as evidence the disappearance of all other forms of legitimacy, but accept as a significant indicator the coming to light of certain attitudes that stress tradition and if we furthermore broaden the latter concept to include not only pre-European Africa, but other references that imply legitimacy based on the notion 'this is how things have always been' as well.

Evidence of this sort is not difficult to find. As was already mentioned earlier, Apter, who initially anticipated routinization of charisma into a legal-rational direction in Ghana, has revised his judgment and now strongly suggests on the basis of new evidence the emergence of a kind of 'neo-traditionalism.' He stated, in the revised edition of his book, 'It seems to me that Ghana politics makes little sense unless one appreciates that what has occurred is a new relationship between traditional and secular politics in the form of the mobilization system. At the top of this system is a Presidential monarch – a kind of chief.'[32] Furthermore, 'Substantive integration, such as it is, has been achieved by the ritualization of charisma into a peculiar mixture of socialism and neo-traditionalism. It is a uniquely Ghanaian blend and the new, non-charismatic role at the top is the Presidential monarch, increasingly backed by force.'[33] Suggesting that this is a self-conscious effort on the part of the regime, he examined ideological change and concludes:

> One view is that of society as a continuation of the clan and the chief. The position of Nkrumah is that of a chief. The entire society is composed of clans. The local party figures are related to the clans, and thus the web of association between community and chieftaincy is maintained on a national level. The concept of chieftaincy is the essence of the African personality. The leader is duty bound to serve the state because the state is the ensemble of clans, and the leader himself derives from the clans. Hence the principle of legitimacy is a traditional one.[34]

The last sentence exaggerates the situation; in Ghana as elsewhere, several principles of legitimacy coexist, and legal-rational aspects, expressed through both representative institutions and the bureaucracy, are very important as well. Nevertheless, the recent emergence of tradition as a salient principle is very significant. It indicates a shift from legitimacy based on a future-orientation to legitimacy based on past-orientation. Similar observations can be made about the other countries under consideration. Almost everywhere an attempt has been made to relate the present regime to pre-European African states, most obviously in the case of Mali which views itself as having been 'reborn' in 1960. Advocates of African socialism everywhere have stressed that their proposed economic policies are anchored on African traditions.[35]

But 'tradition' in today's Africa, does not merely refer to pre-European times. Many political institutions created during the colonial period have become, in the eyes of living men, part of the natural order of things: district commissioners, provincial commissioners, commandants and governors are offices hallowed by time; the African occupants of these offices derive their authority partly from the fact that they are legitimate successors to the original charismatic founders.

Finally, 'tradition' now includes the dominant party's glorious past. Almost every major speech delivered at a party congress or on some other solemn occasion is devoted to a considerable extent not to a discussion of the present but to the recitation of a litany of milestones in the party's history. Even as this chapter was being written, the Ivory Coast government announced the publication of a 'history of the party,' which turned out to be none other than the reprinting of a three-volume report gathered in 1950 by a committee of the French National Assembly on the origins of the RDA and the troubled times of 1949–1950.[36] In Mali, Modibo Keita's claim to rule is based not only on the fact that he was properly elected, that he bears the name Keita, but also on the fact that he alone is the legitimate successor of the party founder, Mamadou Konaté. In the midst of rapidly changing circumstances, in a society where history remains primarily a matter of verbal record, events that occurred fifteen to twenty years ago can easily become part of a hallowed tradition on which the regime attempts to base its contemporary legitimacy.

The real test of the nature of authority in West Africa, however, can only be provided by a systematic examination of the beliefs of followers. This alone can reveal whether and on what basis they are willing to obey. That this sort of investigation has not yet been carried out illustrates how much we do not yet know and points to some of the tasks that await new waves of political scientists.

The perspective of time

Much of the discussion about the West African party-state concerns not its present but its future. Many projections, however, rest on an erroneous view of its present characteristics, and it is hoped that the present work will provide a useful corrective. But what of the method of projection itself? On the whole, observers concerned with long-term trends tend to peer into the contemporary party-state and then debate whether they can detect embryonic democracies or embryonic totalitarian systems. This suggests that in borrowing the concept of 'development' or 'growth' from biology, political science has tended to include the notion that 'the adult is "implicit" in the egg in the sense that one day it will be possible, after determining certain parameters, to read off the constitutional properties of the adult animal from a detailed knowledge of the chemical structure of the egg it arose from.'[37]

Is it really useful to view, say, the England of Magna Carta as an embryo of contemporary Great Britain, or the United States of 1789 as an infant who grew into the present giant? To pursue the analogy, it might be useful instead to conceive of political systems as they exist at any given time as fairly mature organisms. Long-term changes then appear to be more akin to the biological notion of evolution, *a change from one system to another*, like the evolution of earthworm-making instructions into instructions for making frogs. Although this concept cannot serve as a theoretical guide for the study of political change and development, it can clarify our thinking about change itself. As in biology, 'there is no useful sense in which the structure of the mammal is implicit in the structure of a protozoon' – although one can always trace the links in the evolutionary chain *ex post facto*[38] – so we cannot hope to find out, by deciphering the structural code of contemporary political systems, the instructions which will rule one which is to appear in the future.

Instead, we might choose a medium-term view – say, two decades at the most – and then focus on important environmental parameters such as the international system, demography, the economic system, social stratification, about which we can obtain a fair amount of reliable information for this time period, project them into the future, and try to imagine, with the help of evidence drawn from analogous clusterings of variables elsewhere in the political universe (including its extension to include the historical past) what states of the political system would be most compatible with these parametric values, distinguishing with Easton between the levels of 'political community', 'regime,' and 'authorities.'[39] This approximation might then be modified to take into account the heritage of political culture that is now being created, as well as the more general feedback of the system to its environment, which is but another way of saying that any attempt to understand the evolution of the universe must now take into account the phenomenon of man.[40] To do this systematically is another challenging undertaking for the political science community. Although this task lies beyond the scope of this book, it is nevertheless tempting to make a few suggestions.

A major question concerns, for example, the effects of the international environment on the West African political systems. The situation in this respect is fundamentally different from what it was during the period of state-formation in Europe or from what it is at the present time in other underdeveloped regions such as Asia. The West African party-states are not surrounded by powerful neighbors that can absorb or dismember them. They are surrounded mostly by other countries like themselves which also have a limited capability for bringing about fundamental change, although they can contribute to the instability of incumbent authorities by sponsoring opposition groups, etc. Furthermore, as authorities in one country are threatened, the process is likely to have a generalized effect on its neighbors by escalating the cycle of insecurity-repression-subversion-coups. Although the West African party-states could theoretically bring about fundamental changes in their political community through voluntary mergers, such as federations, this is unlikely to happen because the maintenance of the regime and the authorities is closely tied up with the manage-ability afforded by territorial political control.

The most powerful contemporary political actors may have an interest in influencing particular authorities and even in replacing them with others more amenable to certain policies, and be capable of bringing that change about if necessary; but on the whole they are not likely to divert their resources in attempts to bring about fundamental changes at the level of the political community or even at the level of the regime. Indeed, the present international political system is most likely to guarantee the survival of the political communities of West Africa, not only by not interfering with them, but by providing tangible reinforcements of their identity through devices such as international organizations in which they have an assigned place, and even by intervening if necessary to maintain their integrity. In short, in the medium term the international political system is likely to effect few changes at the level of the political community or of the regime, but it may contribute to the instability of the authorities.

Turning now to the other social systems within the society, we find that there already exist some important economic differences among the countries in the group. Estimated per capita income in 1961 ranged from about $200 for Ghana, with Senegal and the Ivory Coast not far behind, to about $60 for Guinea and Mali. The absolute size of GNP, which gives us an idea of the total pool of resources available, varied even more, ranging from a high of about $1,375 million for Ghana to a low of about $185 million for Guinea. Other economic indicators confirm this ranking. It is likely that the relatively richer countries in the group will make more progress in economic development than the poorer ones (1) because their present level of achievement already reflects the availability of certain resources; (2) because the relative magnitude of the economy provides at least some opportunities for internal savings and investment by either private entrepreneurs or government; and (3) because external resources (from foreign governments as well as private capitalists) are more likely to flow there than to countries that have no prospects at all for development.

In the poorer countries, unless there are radical changes in the demographic situation, the economic welfare of the bulk of the population will tend to remain at its present level. Since on the whole there has been less exposure to modernity, the population is less likely to undergo what is usually called 'the revolution of rising expectations.' Nevertheless, since even in poorer countries current policies favor the growth of education, it is likely that there will be a larger group of individuals with higher aspirations, who will be particularly concerned with access to the sole source of social mobility, the bureaucracy. In the immediate future the annual budget, which averages around $50 million in Mali and Guinea, together with some external aid, will enable the party-state to support its bureaucrats, in governmental administrations and by providing a few additional opportunities in state enterprises. But the saturation point is likely to be reached very quickly without an equivalent increase in over-all governmental capability. Hence the

economy and the social stratification system are likely to remain compatible with the present regime, a patrimonial system *cum* bureaucracy. Intergenerational tensions, crises of succession, and other difficulties, however, are likely to create instability at the level of the authorities.

In the richer countries the situation is likely to be very different. Without going into details, it is possible to suggest that as some economic development takes place, the society will continue to undergo tangible transformation. These countries are already characterized by the fact that a substantial proportion of the population is involved in growing cash crops for export, such as coffee and cocoa. In the Ivory Coast, this continues to be encouraged; but even in Ghana, in spite of much talk of funda-mental change, 'socialism' has not yet affected the agricultural sector of the economy in serious fashion. In these countries there is thus already, and it is likely that there will continue to be, an economic as well as a bureaucratic bourgeoisie, with some overlap between the two. With further changes in social communications, the already substantial stratum of 'transitionals' will increase at a rapid rate. Although these systems appear to have a greater capability for the distribution of tangible satisfactions to members, an inflationary process of demand-formation is likely to develop. For these same reasons the struggle between central authorities and their sub-ordinates is likely to be more acute. On the whole, all these factors suggest that the stresses at the level of the authorities *and of the regime* are likely to surpass their capacity to adjust.

What will happen to the party-state under these circumstances? In the first place, it is important to note one characteristic of these systems that is seldom discussed, the factor of *size*. As Servoise has suggested, most of these countries can be thought of as 'micro-states.'[41] Ghana has about seven million inhabitants, and the others are in the three to four million range, but not all of the inhabitants are actually involved in the modern political sector in a substantial way. The total resources secured and redistributed by the party-state, as indicated in annual budgets, bring home even more dram-atically the smallness of total political operations even in the richer countries of the group: this ranges from a maximum of about $250 million in Ghana to about $120 to $150 million in Ivory Coast and Senegal. A major consequence of size is that until major trans-formations in the society occur, politics will remain manageable with the use of existing methods. In addition, even with anticipated serious stresses at the level of the regime, it is difficult to find alternative sources of authority in the society. Many may have the desire not only to upset the incumbent authorities but to remake the regime in their own image, but few have the capability to pursue the latter goal. Military groups exist and can create disturbances – as they have already done in Togo and Dahomey, for example – but they have only a capacity to bring down governments and to apply pressure on authorities, not to effectively remake the polity.[42]

If grave stresses prevail at the level of the authorities and the regime, the political systems of the richer countries in the group are likely to be characterized by periods of substantial disorder which permeate the entire regime, rather than merely causing changes in a particular set of rulers. After a time, however, the new regime is likely to resemble its predecessor because of the absence of alternative possibilities. The painful conclusion is thus that we might expect a sort of institutionalized instability, just as in Latin America over many decades the 'coup' became an institution. We shall often see dramatic change, but will probably conclude that *plus ça change, plus c'est la même chose.*

Notes

1 David Easton, *A Framework for Political Analysis* (Englewood Cliffs, N.J.: Prentice-Hall, 1965), p. 56.
2 For a conceptualization of the international system, see Morton A. Kaplan, *System and Process in International Politics* (New York: John Wiley & Sons, 1957).
3 Karl A. Deutsch, 'Social Mobilization and Political Development,' *American Political Science Review*, LV, No. 3 (September, 1961), 492–514.
4 Daniel Lerner, *The Passing of Traditional Society* (Glencoe, Ill: The Free Press, 1958), *passim*.
5 Deutsch, does, of course, distinguish between mobilization in various sectors (political, economic, etc.), but within a given sector, an individual can only be inside or outside the set.
6 'The economic indicators used in this entire chapter are very sketchy, and they are used for illustrative purposes only; GNP and per capita income are from AID, as reprinted in *Africa Report*, VIII, No. 3 (August, 1963); budgets for French-speaking countries are taken from figures published in *Europe-France-Outremer*, No. 397 (May, 1963).
7 Malien officials, for example, estimated that the country's traditional exports were much greater than its 'modern' exports and produced a net surplus in trade, but the government cannot 'reach' this income in any way.
8 For traditional economic activity, see, for example, Paul Bohannan and George Dalton (eds.), *Markets in Africa* (Garden City, N.Y.: Doubleday and Co., 1965).
9 'Raymond Buell, *The Native Problem in Africa* (New York: Macmillan, 1927), 1, 1000.
10 Lloyd Fallers, *The King's Men* (London: Oxford University Press, 1964), p. 99. Reprinted by permission of the East African Institute of Social Research.
11 Ibid. Professor Jan Vansina has suggested broadening this universe to include pre-European Morocco and Ethiopia during certain phases of its history.
12 David Apter, *The Gold Coast in Transition* (Princeton: Princeton University Press), pp. 331, 337.
13 Max Weber, *The Theory of Social and Economic Organization* (New York: The Free Press, 1957), p. 382.
14 For a general background to the problem under discussion, see ibid., part III, 'The Types of Authority and Imperative Coordination,' especially pp. 324–86; also Reinhard Bendix, *Max Weber: An Intellectual Portrait* (London: Heinemann, 1960), pp. 289–368.
15 Weber, *The Theory ...*, p. 382.
16 Ibid.
17 I am particularly grateful to Professor David Easton for his suggestions concerning this section.
18 Vincent Monteil, *L'Islam Noir* (Paris: Editions du Seuil, 1964), p. 332.
19 Weber, *The Theory ...*, p. 370.
20 Ibid., p. 371.
21 Ibid., pp. 369–70 (italics mine).
22 Ibid., p. 341.
23 Ibid., pp. 357–58.
24 For a discussion and extension of Weber's use of 'Charisma,' see Edward Shils, 'Charisma, Order and Status,' *American Sociological Review*, XXX, No. 2 (April, 65), 199–213.
25 Frantz Fanon, *Les damnés de la terre* (Paris: François Maspero, 1961), especially pp. 124 ff.
26 This concept of social stratification is based on Karl A. Wittvogel, *Oriental Despotism* (New Haven: Yale University Press, 1957), pp. 301–68.
27 Robert Michels, *Political Parties* (Glencoe, Ill.: The Free Press 1958), especially Chapter IV, 'The Need for the Differentiation of the Working Class,' pp. 304–11.
28 Harry Johnson, 'A Theoretical Model of Economic Nationalism in New and Developing States,' *Political Science Quarterly*, LXXX, No. 2 (June, 1965), 169–85.
29 Weber, *The Theory ...*, pp. 357–8.
30 Ibid.
31 That is the theme of the bitter attack by B. Ameillon in *La Guinée, bilan d'une indépendance* (Paris: François Maspero, 1964).
32 Apter, *Ghana in Transition*, p. 331.
33 Ibid., p. 337.
34 Ibid., p. 365.
35 See, for example, the author's analysis of this theme at the 1962 Dakar Conference on African Socialism, in William H. Friedland and Carl G. Rosberg, Jr. (eds.), *African Socialism* (Stanford, Calif.: Stanford University Press, 1964), pp. 122–23.
36 *Fraternité*, August 13, 1965. For the character of this report and its history, see the author's *One-Party Government in the Ivory Coast* (Princeton: Princeton University Press, 1964), p. 111, n. 13.
37 P. B. Medawar, 'Onwards from Spencer,' *Encounter*, XXI, No. 3 (September, 1963). pp. 37–38.
38 Ibid.
39 Easton, pp. 85–86, 116–17.
40 Pierre Teilhard de Chardin, *The Phenomenon of Man* (New York: Harper and Brothers, 1959).
41 R. Servoise, 'Whither Black Africa?' in B. de Jouvenel (ed.), *Futuribles* (Geneva: Droz, 1963), pp. 262ff.
42 For the limitations of the military in countries of this type, see Morris Janowitz, *The Military in the Political Development of New Nations* (Chicago: University of Chicago Press, 1964). Although Ghana must now be added to the list, the proposition itself appears to remain valid.

ROBERT H. BATES
Rental Havens & Protective Shelters

Reference
Markets & States in Tropical Africa
University of California Press, 1981, chs 6 & 7

Organizing support among the urban beneficiaries

The new nations of Africa were born in a moment of hope. It is difficult to recapture the emotional tone of that moment. But the depth of it, the fullness of it, and the promise it offered left its mark on all who were in any way touched by events of that era. It was called a new dawn, a rebirth, a reawakening.

For many, the dreams of that period have given way to disillusion. Social scientists studying the United States long ago learned to listen to the 'little man from Missouri.' The sullen cynicism of the common man of Africa today offers no less insight into the reality behind the public-spirited rhetoric of the policy process. Public institutions no longer embody a collective vision, but instead reinforce a pattern of private advantage that may often be socially harmful – that is the message of disillusion in Africa today.

In re-evaluating the promise of the nationalist period, many have charged its spokesmen with cynical manipulations of popular hopes and with self-interested proposals of programs of questionable merit. There is much to this interpretation, but it captures only part of the truth. For during the nationalist period, there were in fact striking instances of public spiritedness. People made major sacrifices for the sake of national independence. Careers were abandoned, educations sacrificed, and lives lost as persons turned from normal pursuits and entered the political arena. And many did so for high-minded reasons: to get rid of foreign rule, to end racial oppression, and to escape colonial bondage. Above all, they did so in order to seize control of the state. They sought to secure for the people of Africa the power to create and implement public policies and thereby secure greater prosperity.

The words of Kwame Nkrumah – 'seek ye first the political kingdom and all else shall be added unto it' – best represent the vision of that era. And in keeping with Nkrumah's injunction, public servants sought to use the power of the state to manipulate major markets and thereby induce a flow of resources that would generate rapid development.

The forms of economic manipulation chosen were compatible with prevailing economic doctrines. Many of those who formulated and implemented the development programs of the new African states had studied the theories of the leading development economists. That industry is the engine of growth; that savings come from the profits of industry and not from the profits of farmers; that resources should be levied from the countryside and channeled into industrial development; that the rural sector should be squeezed for development and can be made to give up resources without major declines in production – these were and remain today important tenets in development doctrine (see Lewis; Ranis and Fei; Jorgenson; and readings in Stiglitz and Uzawa).

It would therefore be a mistake to see the policies chosen by governments in Africa as representing commitments made without regard for the public interest. But what is notable is that the mix of policies chosen to secure economic development has permitted the entrenchment of enormously powerful private interests, and that this fact has become an important source of the durability of policy commitments.

Public policy and private advantage

The dynamics are simple but powerful. The government enters certain markets. For development purposes, it lowers prices in those markets. With lower prices, demand increases; private sources of supply furnish smaller quantities; and scarcities therefore occur under circumstances of excess demand. The result is that the commodity in question – be it foreign exchange, capital for investments, or whatever – achieves new value. Insofar as a public institution controls the market for that commodity, it then has control over this new value.

The administrators of such an institution can consume that value themselves, which is financial corruption. Or they can apportion it to others whose influence they wish to secure, which is political corruption. In either case, the bureaucracy that is mandated to control the operation of a market for public purposes finds itself in control of financial and political resources – resources that render the program economically useful to those in control of it and a means for generating a political following. Market intervention leads to the formation of vested interests in policy programs.

The process is outlined in Figure 1. P_0 represents a price at which the market is in equilibrium; at P_0 the quantity demanded (Q_{D_0}) equals the quantity supplied (Q_{S_0}). Assume that the government, desiring some policy objective, intervenes in the market and lowers the price to P_1. At this lower price, consumers demand more of the good, so the quantity demanded increases ($Q_{D_1} > Q_{D_0}$) But at the lower price producers will supply less of it, so the quantity supplied declines ($Q_{S_1} < Q_{S_0}$). At P_1 the quantity demanded therefore exceeds the quantity supplied ($Q_{D_1} > Q_{S_1}$) and the market cannot allocate the good; too little is available for the level of demand at the new price. Rather, the good will have to be given to some and withheld from others who want it at that price. It will have to be rationed.

Being subject to excess demand, the good increases in value. At the quantity supplied (Q_{S_1}) it is scarce by comparison with the demand for it. As seen in Figure 1, some consumers would be willing to pay $P\star$ for the good. $P\star$ lies above P_1, the officially mandated price; it also lies above the market clearing price, P_0. The difference between $P\star$ and P_0 can be regarded as a premium created by the scarcities induced by government intervention. We will call this premium an *administratively generated rent*: a value in excess of the market value which has been created by an administratively generated fixity in the supply of a commodity (see Krueger; Posner).

The value of this rent can, of course, be appropriated in the form of bribes; or those in charge of the market can confer it upon others by giving them rations of the commodity at the administratively lowered price. In the latter case, the bureaucracy creates grateful clients – people who owe their special fortunes to public officials who choose them, from among competing claimants, for privileged access to these resources. Government intervention, excess demand,

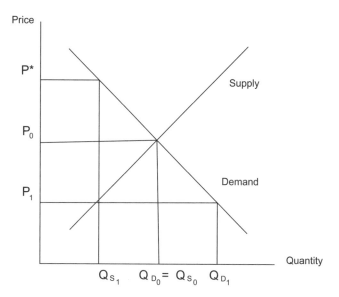

Figure 1 Excess demand in a market.

and the conferral of privileges are thus all part of the political process by which public programs create vested interests in policies of social and economic reform.

The Urban Sector These dynamics characterize the operation of programs designed to promote the development of urban-based industry by extracting capital from export agriculture. This is best illustrated by the material from Western Nigeria. There, as we have seen, the marketing board lowered the prices offered peasant producers for export crops and thereby accumulated surplus revenues. A portion of the proceeds thus generated by the board was transferred to development agencies, which provided capital for loans at subsidized terms to potential investors in the urban industrial sector.

As our analysis would suggest, this policy in Nigeria was in fact self-contradictory, and its contradictions became a source of political opportunity. One of the results of making capital available at lower prices was to create a 'shortage' of capital; artificially lowering the price of capital led to excess demand for it (Schatz 1977, pp. 66ff). And it was precisely at the time of the capital shortage that characteristic loans were made – loans whose bene-ficiaries were members of the agencies themselves, or politically influential persons whose support the agency heads wished to secure (Schatz 1970, pp. 41ff).

Further evidence (much of which is cited by Schatz) is contained in the volumes of the Coker Commission of Inquiry into the affairs of statutory corporations in Western Nigeria. There we find that the persons in charge of the development agencies used their powers to secure the transfer of funds into banks and corporations in which they themselves held directorships. In effect, they consumed the administratively created rent themselves. As directors of the banks they gave themselves large, unsecured, interest-free loans. In the words of the Commission, one witness 'told us of how between the years 1958–1959 he received a total amount of over £1 million

from the National Bank without signing any papers for the amounts' (Nigeria 1962, vol. 2, p. 7). And as directors of the corporations these persons secured both fees and profits.

The ability to ration capital not only led to personal gain, but was also employed to build political coalitions. In evidence of this, one of the major Nigerian corporations that secured subsidized loans, the National Investment and Properties Company, published the newspaper chain owned by the Action Group, the party that held power in the Western Region. The Commission of Inquiry noted that the company and the party were virtually identical (Nigeria 1962, vol. 1, p. 55). Furthermore, major corporations owned by politically influential persons, including the 'father' of the Action Group, received major loans during the period of supposed capital scarcity.

In their efforts to promote the growth of urban-based industries, governments in Africa not only intervene in the markets for capital; they also artificially increase the value of the domestic currency, thereby cheapening the costs of capital equipment which is scarce domestically and must be imported from abroad. The result of the maintenance of an overvalued currency is, once again, the creation of an excess demand for foreign goods and the elaboration of means for rationing access to them. Financial corruption and the apportionment of privileged access are once again correlative results; and both create private incentives for persons to support the continuation of this policy measure.

Perhaps the best known examples come from Ghana. Following the 'big push' of the post-independence industrialization programs, Ghana began to run large deficits in foreign trade; its massive international reserves which had been accumulated from cocoa exports began to erode, and 'by November 1961 the government felt it had only one instrument left to deal with the situation: stringent import licensing' (Leith, p. 23). The evidence strongly suggests that those in charge of the regulation of foreign exchange rapidly converted the scarcities in this market into personal wealth. The first minister in charge of the program, Mr. A. K. Djin, owned a trading firm which, by privileged access to import licenses, grew from a minor corporation into one of the major import houses in Ghana. His successor, Mr. Kwesi Armah, also secured major personal benefits. As noted in a government report: 'He introduced the system whereby all applications for import licenses had to be addressed to him personally under registered cover and he alone was responsible for processing the said applications.... Import licenses were issued on the basis of a commission corruptly demanded and payable by importers on the face value of the import licenses issued. The commission was fixed at 10 percent, but was in special cases reduced to 7.5 or 5 percent' (Ghana 1966, p. 26).

As suggested in this quotation, the value of access to quantities of foreign exchange was not consumed solely by those who administered it: it was also apportioned to others. Kwesi Armah, for example, gave the right to negotiate with petitioners for licenses to selected Members of Parliament; they then became his protégés, with grateful clients of their own (Republic of Ghana, 1967, pp. 4–5). And after the overthrow of the Busia government, the military government found that the Minister of Trade 'had varied the normal procedures for allocating licenses to favor specific individuals and companies who were [backing] the ruling party' (Killick, p. 281).

Thus far we have indicated how government intervention, by depressing prices in markets, creates opportunities for conferring privileged access to commodities that have been rendered scarce in comparison to the demand for them. Privileged access is used by the elites in charge of the programs for direct personal gain or to create a political following. The political attractions are obvious. And they help to explain why, when given a choice between market and nonmarket means for achieving the same end, African governments often choose interventionist measures.

Leith, for example, notes that the foreign exchange crisis in Ghana in the 1960s could have been resolved either by devaluation or by import licensing. Ghanaians were demanding more foreign exchange than was being supplied by exports; their currency was overvalued and there was thus an excess demand for foreign imports. As Leith points out, the government could have devalued; by raising the price of foreign currency, it could lower the quantity demanded. Alternatively, the government could employ a system of rationing. Leith then states: 'The immediate ... difference between the two [approaches] was nil. Curiously, though, a given volume of foreign-exchange use at a lower *cedi* price to the initial recipients seemed preferable to the same volume at a higher *cedi* price' (Leith p. 156).

In our analysis, an appreciation of the *noneconomic* difference between the two approaches dissipates any puzzlement over the preference for administrative controls. Those who received the lower-priced foreign exchange were given special favors, and those who apportioned it amassed a political following. To have allocated foreign exchange through the market would have given no comparable chance for the exercise of discretion, and thus no comparable opportunity for creating a political clientele.

Urban industry, public policy, and political power
In earlier chapters we have seen how governments create highly sheltered markets for urban-based industries. Protected by government policies, these markets confer benefits upon those who produce within them. The benefits take the form of noncompetitive prices, which generate *noncompetitive* rents: they are increases in the earnings of firms created by the ability of prices in the protected industry to rise above the level that would be sustained if the industry were subject to competition. Like the administratively generated rents, these rents too are consumed by the elite or distributed to the politically faithful.

It will be remembered, for example, that in order to secure Firestone's investments in a tire factory, the government of Kenya gave Firestone a virtual monopoly over the tire market for ten years, sheltering it from both domestic competition and from foreign imports. This agreement virtually guaranteed Firestone monopoly profits. It also generated advantages to public officials and their political allies. As part of its agreement, the company shared with the government the right to name its distributors; the government could then pick those persons who could share in the monopoly profits. The company also brought prominent Africans, including one former Cabinet Minister and 'one of the chief negotiators' on the Kenyan side of the deal, into managerial positions in the sheltered firm (Langdon, p. 173).

As a World Bank report states, the system of protection in Kenya 'created absolute protection for many manufacturers of consumer goods. On the basis of the mission's interviews *it would not be an exaggeration to suggest that several firms have a license to print money*, being subject to no competition at home or abroad' (IBRD 1975, p. 298, emphasis added). These profits are shared with the administrators of the public policies that helped create them. Cohen and Swainson document the tendency of the political elites in the

Ivory Coast and Kenya, respectively, to hold directorates in private firms and state industries; Shivji does the same for permanent secretaries in Tanzania (p. 89). Moreover, the policy-generated rents are also apportioned among political allies. Arthur Lewis, for example, in reviewing the state industries of Ghana, wrote that they have 'suffered greatly from outside interference, in the shape of members of Parliament and other influential persons expecting staff appointments to be made irrespective of merit, redundant staff to be kept on the payroll, disciplinary measures to be relaxed in favor of constituents' (quoted in Killick, p. 245). When attacked for using the state industries to provide sinecures for political allies, N. A. Welbeck, a minister and sometime Secretary General of the ruling party in Ghana, simply replied: 'But that is proper; and the honorable Member too would do it if he were there' (quoted in Killick, p. 245). That subsequent regimes have behaved in the same way only underscores the sagacity of Welbeck's reply.

Inflated payrolls are a characteristic of many state industries in Africa, as elsewhere. In part, this is another indication of the artificially inflated prosperity of the urban industries. But it is also indicative of the political uses of these policy-induced rents. Protective measures inflate the profits of firms. These revenues can be shared with political clients. And recruitment to jobs in state industries becomes a basis for allocating these profits so as to form political organizations.

In his study of the membership of the boards of Ghanaian state enterprises, Henry Bretton, for example, noted that they 'had been staffed not with the most competent but with the ... friends and associates of the President,' that 'thousands of employees ... were at the President's mercy and disposal,' and that 'the efficiency-oriented staff members in the Secretariat who attempted to halt the drift to institutionalized incompetence and corruption were fighting a losing-battle' (quoted in LeVine, pp 74–5). Less dramatically, perhaps, but in accordance with the same logic, is the conduct of Daniel Arap Moi, President of Kenya. In an effort to consolidate his power after succeeding Jomo Kenyatta, Moi made a series of high-level appointments to state corporations. These appointments were overtly political and were made in the wake of the Ndegwa Commission's condemnation of the inefficiency of these bodies, and its call for their reform (*Weekly Review*, May 16, 1980, and May 23, 1980). That Moi would choose to do this emphasizes the overriding importance of political considerations and suggests the ways in which economic inefficiency can be used for political purposes.

A more egregious example is provided by the rule of President Mobutu in Zaire. An important basis of Mobutu's power is his capacity to make appointments to state-regulated industries. Efforts at economic reform repeatedly founder on his determination to manipulate these industries in order to generate privileges for himself and his followers, and to reward those whose support he needs to remain in power. And in Liberia, when Master Sergeant Doe began his 'revolution' the heads of government firms were prominent among those listed as exploitative members of the old order (*Los Angeles Times*, April 26, 1980). A key signal of the limited nature of Doe's rebellion in the eyes of many was that the lives of these persons were spared. The revolution did not, as it had promised, break up the pattern of privilege characteristic of the 'old Liberia' – a structure of advantage and power based in large part on the consumption and distribution of rents in state-dominated markets.

By intervening in markets for capital and foreign exchange, and by influencing the structure of markets for manufactured items, the governments of Africa have sought to use government power to promote urban industrial development. Industrial development is equated with the public good. These policies create economic environments which generate rents. The rents are both economically valuable and politically useful, and from them are forged bonds of self-interest that tie African governments to their miniscule industrial base. Thus policy choices, made to serve a new vision of the public good, have created a network of self-interest which has proved more enduring than the faith which that vision initially inspired.

The origins of political marginalism: evoking compliance from the countryside

In Africa, as elsewhere, governments use force to quash peasant resistance to measures intended to create a new political and economic order. By frustrating those who would seek fundamental changes, governments remove proposals for comprehensive reforms from the political agenda and forbid organized efforts to alter the collective fate of the disadvantaged. Instead they allow only efforts to seek marginal adjustments to the status quo or petitions for individual exceptions to it. The capacity to coerce is thus used to defend and perpetuate basic policy commitments and the political and economic order they create.

Among the primary objects of government coercion in Africa are opposition parties. In this book we are concerned with parties that mobilize rural populations against the agricultural policies of governments in power. African governments use their control of the courts and the legal system to harass such parties, to ban them, and to arrest and imprison their leaders.

We have already noted the effort of the Government of Ghana to counter the appeals of the National Liberation Movement (NLM) which was organized in the cocoa belt to oppose the government's cocoa pricing policy. Accounts of political life in rural Ghana during the struggle with the NLM are filled with accounts of roadblocks, beatings, assassinations, and clashes between armed groups of party militants (Dunn and Robertson; Owusu). What was decisive in the end, however, was the government's control over the police and the courts. The opposition party was banned, its activities proclaimed illegal, and its organizers arrested for 'reasons of state.'

A similar tale emanates from Kenya, where in the 1960s a dissident faction of the ruling party, the Kenyan African National Union (KANU), opposed the government's program for establishing private rights in land. This faction correctly claimed that the program tended to confer disproportionate benefits on the wealthy, who could afford to buy land, while failing to safeguard the assets of the poor, and in particular the former freedom fighters. Because demands for land had furnished much of the impetus for the struggle for independence in Kenya, this critique was politically telling. To forestall damage to their political standing among the militant rank and file of the governing party, members of the dominant faction therefore altered the party's constitution. The changes they made enabled them to remove from party office the principal spokesman for the dissidents. The dissident faction thereupon split from the KANU and joined an opposition party, the Kenya People's Union (KPU). By controlling the police and the courts, KANU was able to frustrate the growth of this opposition party. In the local government elections of 1968, for example, the judiciary found technical faults in all but six of the nomination papers of KPU candidates; none of the papers filed by candidates for KANU were found defective (Leys, p. 216; Buijtenhuijs). Then, after clashes between KPU and KANU supporters, including one in which the President's bodyguard fired into a crowd of KPU loyalists, the KPU was banned and its leaders detained. Suppression of the KPU put an end to attempts to change the government's agricultural policies by organizing a political movement capable of removing incumbent elites from office.

The fate of the NLM in Ghana and the KPU in Kenya is paralleled by the fate of opposition parties in a host of other African nations. Because the majority of the African people live in rural areas, it is inevitable that their fate becomes central in the appeals of any political opposition. With the use of the state's instruments of coercion to emasculate the political opposition, governments in power thus eliminate one of the basic elements of political life which, by the sheer weight of self-interested political calculation, would champion the interests of the rural majority.

Instruments of coercion are also used against political entrepreneurs who seek to build their careers on protests against agricultural policies. An example would be J. M. Kariuki of Kenya. A former freedom fighter, Kariuki attained prominence in post-independence Kenya as a private secretary to President Kenyatta, a member of parliament, and a member of the government as well. Increasingly, however, Kariuki dissented from the government's position. The principal source of his disaffection was the tendency of members of the political elite to use government programs to acquire large agricultural holdings. Foremost among these new landholders, of course, were the President and his family. As described by one political observer, Kariuki 'was not only pointing to the vast lands that every peasant believes, correctly, the Royal Family has acquired. He was inviting his audience to remember that Mau Mau had sprung from the land issue. Finally, he even said it plain: "Unless something is done now, the land question will be answered by bloodshed"' (*Sunday Times*, London, August 10, 1975, p. 3).

The question did indeed lead to bloodshed, but the blood was Kariuki's own. In February of 1975, President Kenyatta's fields in Rongai were burned. His cattle were hamstrung. Leaflets were circulated describing the wealth of his family. Kariuki was suspected in having a role in organizing these activities. On March 1, he was abducted, taken into the hills outside Nairobi, and murdered. A subsequent Parliamentary investigating commission implicated persons close to the President: his bodyguard, his brother-in-law, his Minister of State, and his closest friend. For their efforts to uncover the truth about the murder of Kariuki, members of the commission were themselves jailed by the government of Kenya.

Rural demobilization

Besides using their power to forbid collective efforts at altering the social standing of the peasantry, governments in Africa also use their control of markets to fragment the rural opposition. They accomplish this by making it in the private interest of individuals to cooperate in programs that are harmful to the interests of producers as a whole.

As we have seen, under many governments, all producers in the countryside are subject to a depressed price for their products; this is particularly the case for export crops. Through the pricing policies of government agencies, the public sector accumulates revenues. What is critical is that the governments return a portion of these revenues in the form of divisible benefits, which they confer upon supporters and withhold from political dissidents. The apportionment of these divisible benefits becomes a basis for attracting allies and building political organizations.

In part, this tactic underlies one of the most paradoxical features of agricultural programs in Africa: the coexistence of taxes (through the imposition of low prices on products) and subsidies (through the reduction of prices of factors of production). Deference to pricing policy is obtained by the manipulation of subsidy programs. The use of subsidy programs to build political support in the countryside for governments in power, and particularly for their agricultural programs, is a prominent feature of agrarian politics in Africa.

In Ghana, for example, in 1954 the Convention People's Party (CPP) government of Kwame Nkrumah passed the notorious Cocoa Duty and Development Funds (Amendment) Bill; it thereby froze the producer price for cocoa for four years, anticipating increased government revenues from the trading profits in this commodity. An immediate result was the formation, in the cocoa-growing regions, of a powerful opposition party, the National Liberation Movement (NLM), which opposed the new ordinance. The NLM threatened to unseat the CPP throughout the cocoa-growing regions, and so the CPP fought back. One of the resources at its command was the allocation of subsidized inputs. The government loan program, for example, became a weapon in the struggle to build a pro-government organization in the cocoa-growing region and to counter growing resistence to the government's pricing policy.

The 'farmers wing' of the governing party was the United Ghana Farmers' Council (UGFC); keeping this in mind, the following comments in a government report are instructive] 'The declared policy of CPC [the Cocoa Purchasing Company] not to grant loans to any farmer who is not a member of the UGFC is to be found at page 80 of the CPC Minutes Book (Exhibit 157), where it is laid down that before a farmer is considered for a loan, the officer dealing with the application must satisfy himself that the applicant is a bona fide cocoa farmer and that he is a member of the UGFC' (Ghana 1967a, p. 1). The report also noted that 'the distribution of gammalin [an insecticide], cutlasses, etc., gave the United Ghana Farmers' Cooperative Council officials an opportunity to accord preferential treatment to their favorites and party members' (ibid., p. 18). Through the manipulation of these subsidized inputs, the government was able to erode support for the NLM and its opposition to the freeze in cocoa prices.

The use of government agricultural programs to organize rural support is also revealed in materials from Senegal. The government of Senegal secures much of its revenues from the marketing of groundnuts; and at least one quarter of the country's groundnuts are grown in areas controlled by an Islamic sect commonly known as the Mourides. The leaders of the Mourides are known as Marabouts. With the postwar expansion of the franchise in French West Africa to include residents of the countryside, the Marabouts gained in power. As Donal Cruise O'Brien (1971) states:

> The result of postwar rural enfranchisement was that the *marabouts* became political agents for the major parties, whose feeble organizations were inadequate to reach the mass of ordinary peasants, and which were often unable to capture their interest in political programs which had little obvious relevance to the immediate problems of rural life. The easy way to win rural votes was through notables who could guarantee the votes of their followers, and of all the notables the most important

were the *marabouts*. [P. 262]

The problem of securing the backing of the Mourides became more urgent with the advent of self-government in Senegal, for the government relied heavily on the profits of the groundnut trade to provide revenues for its expanded development programs. Maintaining a producer price for groundnuts well below the price realized from sales in the French market, the government of Senegal curried favor with the Marabouts by giving them privileged access to publicly subsidized inputs: fertilizers, mechanical equipment, land carved out from forest reserves, and above all massive amounts of government credit. The government, in short, has used its control over the allocation of subsidized farm inputs to build a political organization. Donal Cruise O'Brien, citing Brochier, refers to the end result as the creation of a 'technically oriented feudality' As he states:

> J. Brochier correctly points out that the projects involving technical co-operation with the marabouts have always reinforced the hierarchical structure of the brotherhood. The Government, by providing land, credit and various forms of technical assistance for the Mouride leaders, has in general contributed to the marabouts means of domination, and has more particularly helped to bring about a concentration of resources in the hands of a few notables with significant political influence. [Cruise O'Brien 1971, pp. 227–28]

By conferring privileged access to subsidized inputs upon the Marabouts, the government thus enhanced their power over the rural masses; and by so doing, it helped to build its own political machine in the countryside of Senegal.

The cases just cited are to some extent exceptional. Nonetheless, the tendency to use control over farm implements to build organized rural support for governments in power is a pervasive one. In Zambia, the cooperative movement formed an important basis for the rural political organization of the United National Independence Party (UNIP), the governing party. It was through the movement that smallscale farmers could gain access to loans, seeds, fertilizers, and mechanical implements. And the UNIP's domination of the movement enabled it to apportion these benefits to the political faithful. Rationing access to farm inputs became a means of consolidating political power in the countryside (Bates 1976).

Moreover, the government credit agency in Zambia was heavily staffed by persons transferred over from UNIP. One former UNIP Regional Secretary whom I knew moved from the party to the credit organization. He regarded his work with the agency as a continuation of his career as a political organizer. And though he was professional enough not to want to 'waste the government's money' by lavishing funds on political figures who were poor economic risks, he nonetheless regarded the money he could distribute as a useful tool for convincing the people of the beneficence and power of the governing party. The political use of loan funds has also been recorded in Nigeria (Northern Nigeria 1967, vol. 3, p. 6). And the capacity of the government of Tanzania to mobilize its population into Ujamaa villages has been attributed partly to its ability to link access to subsidized farm inputs to village membership (Raikes; McHenry).[1]

Through the use of violence, the governments of Africa have forestalled the mobilization of the rural majority against policies that harm their interests. And by granting or withholding farm inputs, they gain the backing of individual farmers for programs which, taken as a whole, do basic violence to the interests of agricultural producers. The agricultural programs of African governments thus become basic units of rural political organization.

But this organization is narrowly based – its members are the better-off few, and most of the peasantry remain outside it – and therefore vulnerable. During the nationalist period in central Africa, for example, those mobilizing the rural masses against the colonial regimes attacked the elite farmers who benefited from access to inputs whose costs were subsidized by the colonial governments. In many locations, the progress of the rural insurrection was measured in terms of the rate of defection of these elite farmers from government agricultural programs. (Interviews in Zambia, 1971–1972; see also Baylies; Dixon-Fyle). The progressive farmers, employing new technologies disseminated by their governments, are thus a frail base on which to build a rural constituency.

These organizations are also vulnerable because they are expensive. When governments are poor, when other programs win out in the competition for scarce resources, and when international organizations fail to contribute significantly to the costs of agricultural development, then governments must lower the level of the subsidies they provide farmers. At this point, the elite farmers lack the incentive to act as persons whose interests lie apart from those of the larger rural population. They may then offer leadership in organizing the collective opposition to the policies of the governments in power. The rural strategies of African governments are thus vulnerable to the vagaries of their fiscal base and the means by which they attempt to ensnare the larger farmers.

Public services and public projects:
constructing a system of spoils

In their efforts to organize political support in the countryside, African governments also manipulate the structure and performance of their public services. Governments everywhere supply roads, clinics, schools, water supplies, and the like. In Africa, and in other developing nations, 'development' projects are also standard fare. And whether it be in Mayor Daley's Chicago or Awolowo's Western Region of Nigeria, the supply of such services can be, and is, tailored to the quest for political support.

Studies of the behavior of members of parliament in Africa uniformly stress the emphasis they give to securing schemes and projects for their districts (Cliffe for Tanzania; Barkan for Kenya; Dunn for Ghana; Bates for Zambia). Moreover, studies of the attitudes of African electorates indicate that citizens seek, and expect to get, material improvements from those with access to public power (Barkan, Bates, and others). Holders of public office fully realize that in order to remain in power, they must manipulate the bureaucracy of the state to secure such benefits. The result is a general tendency to try to orchestrate public programs to secure political advantage.[2] And, of greater relevance to this work, the tendency is particularly strong with respect to agricultural programs.

Several features of the agricultural programs of the states of Africa can be attributed to the quest for political support. One of these is the preference for production schemes as opposed to pricing policies in the attempt to secure greater food supplies. Another is the structure of these production programs – their number, their location, and their staffing.

Positive pricing policies are politically unattractive to African governments seeking greater food production. Their political costs are high in terms of loss of support in the urban areas; and their political benefits are low in terms of their ability to secure support

from the countryside – or at least they are low by comparison with those which can be secured from the allocation of production projects. Were the governments of Africa to confer a price rise on all rural producers, the political benefits would he low; for both supporters and dissidents would secure the benefits of such a measure, with the result that it would generate no incentives to support the government in power. The conferral of benefits in the form of public works projects, such as state farms, on the other hand, has the political advantage of allowing the benefits to be selectively apportioned. The schemes can be given to supporters and withheld from opponents. Project-based policies, as opposed to pricing-based policies, are thus relatively attractive from the point of view of organizing a rural constituency in support of the government in power.

Governments can choose where to locate such schemes. They can also choose with whom to staff them. Both decisions offer opportunities for organizing political support.

The importance of political motivations is suggested in features of the state farm programs in Western Nigeria and Ghana. In both cases (reported by Wells and Dadson, respectively), the programs 'overexpanded': state farms were provided for every electoral district! By most accounts, this decision crippled the programs from an economic point of view; having so many farms meant that too few resources were provided for each, with the result that most operated inefficiently. But, from a political point of view, structuring the programs so as to provide a state farm in each constituency made available to government backers in each district public resources with which to organize support of the government in power. Moreover, within each district, the state farms were often poorly located, again from the point of view of maximizing production. A principal reason for this, apparently, was a desire to put them in areas where they would provide a 'public works' benefit to the supporters of the government in power. As Wells states, in a bemused comment on Nigerian farming schemes: 'allocations were used in an attempt to solve essentially political problems, often at the cost of considerable economic efficiency' (p. 353).

Once their locations were established, the farms had to be staffed. In Ghana, three of the four agencies that staffed the state farms were units not of the public administration but rather of the governing party! In hiring laborers and staff, the managers of the farms were required to give priority to party activists (Dadson, pp. 26ff). As Dadson states: 'A foremost objective … as with other public projects, was to extend the control [of the party in power] over the rural population, or to buy the political support of the rural population. Therefore, to begin with, only [party] members were recruited into socialist units' (p. 261).

Lowered prices, such as those for export crops, alienate all rural producers. But the normal outputs of public administration can be selectively offered as compensation and so used to build a coalition supportive of the government in power. We have already noted the passage in 1954 of the bill which froze the cocoa price in Ghana, thereby inspiring the formation of a powerful opposition party, the National Liberation Movement. John Dunn and A. F. Robertson, in their fascinating study of Brong Ahafo, one of the cocoa-growing districts in Ghana, document the government's manipulation of public services there in an effort to cripple opposition to its pricing policy. They note, for example, that 'communities in Ahafo which had supported the [government] throughout, like Acherensua … and Kukuom duly received their rewards in the form of major items of government development expenditure, like the secondary school provided by the Ghana Educational Trust' (Dunn and Robertson, p. 327).

Not only the allocation of services but also the structure of public administration in Ghana was manipulated to secure political backing. The government dismissed holders of public office, such as chiefs and headmen, who were supporters of the opposition; it replaced them with those willing to stake their futures on backing the government in power. Also, the local administration was removed from the greater Ashanti Region and given a regional standing in its own right. The result was a virtual regionwide promotion in the status and emoluments of public officeholders, as they moved from district to regional status, or, in the case of the chiefs, from mere chiefly to paramount rank. The cocoa farmers remained primarily concerned with the price of cocoa, and so long as it remained low, they remained disaffected. Nonetheless, through the manipulation of public services, political control was reasserted over the region. As Dunn and Robertson note, the opposition's 'hegemony' was 'overturned from outside' (p. 341).

Among the public services, it is the agricultural agencies that are of foremost interest to many persons in the countryside, and in building political organizations the governments of Africa manipulate the patronage potential of these agencies. For example, in analyzing the rural base of the governing party of Senegal, Schumacher notes that the party's 'strength in the countryside was undoubtedly buttressed by the promotion of party supporters and protégés into key posts in economic and administrative structures directly in touch with the rural population. In addition to cooperative officials, these included produce inspectors [and] secretaries of storage facilities' (p. 16). Schumacher uses this fact to explain the party's rural strength in the face of adverse government pricing policies. Additionally, the cooperatives, which in many countries serve as the local agencies for many government programs, are the bases for governing parties as well. This is true in Kenya, Tanzania, Zambia, and Senegal. In Senegal, efforts to divest the governing party of political control over the cooperative societies led to massive political opposition by rural party leaders and to the downfall of the 'technocrats' who advocated this measure (see Schumacher; Donal Cruise O'Brien 1975). The agricultural bureaucracy and its ancillary organizations thus form a fund for political patronage.

By making the attainment of particular benefits – whether a project for a community or a job or promotion for an individual – the substance of rural politics, the governments of Africa have augmented their control over their rural populations. Through the promise of benefits they can secure cooperation; through their conferral, they can reward compliance; and through their withdrawal, they can punish those who protest.

In interviewing a rich cocoa farmer in Ghana in 1978, I asked him why he did not try to organize political support among his colleagues for a rise in product prices. He went to his strongbox and produced a packet of documents: licenses for his vehicles, import permits for spare parts, titles to his real property and improvements, and the articles of incorporation that exempted him from a major portion of his income taxes. 'If I tried to organize resistance to the government's policies on farm prices,' he said while exhibiting these documents, 'I would be called an enemy of the state and I would lose all these.' He was a cocoa farmer and we were discussing cocoa prices. The price of Ghanaian cocoa is indeed one of the most politically sensitive topics in African agrarian politics. But in systems where producers operate in markets which are increasingly controlled by public agencies, his point was generally valid.

Through coercion, governments in Africa block the efforts of those who would organize in attempts to achieve structural changes; only the advocacy of minor adjustments is allowed. Moreover, through the conferral of divisible benefits, they make it in the interests of individual rural dwellers to seek limited objectives. Political energies, rather than focusing on the collective standing of the peasantry, focus instead on the securing of particular improvements – subsidized inputs, the location and staffing of production schemes, the allocation of jobs, and the issuance of licenses and permits. Rather than appeals for collective changes, appeals instead focus on incremental benefits. The politics of the pork barrel supplant the politics of class action. Debates over the fundamental configuration of policies remain off the political agenda of the African countryside, and individual rural dwellers come, as a matter of personal self-interest, to abide by public policies that are harmful to agrarian interests as a whole.

Notes

[1] It is notable that in the rural portion of their program in Afghanistan, the Soviet-backed government in Kabul offered the peasants 'new farming tools, fertilizers, and liberal loans in an apparent effort to blunt rebel recruitment' (*Los Angeles Times*, February 29, 1980).
[2] Illustrative of the general tendency is Michael Cohen's analysis of the behavior of the Parti Democratique du Côte d'Ivoire (PDCI), the ruling party in the Ivory Coast. As he states: 'The failure to express sufficient militancy for the PDCI and the government leads to neglect.... On the other hand, support for the government or one of its key figures is rewarded with the granting of public resources. Thus when [the] Minister of Construction and Town-Planning ... had to choose one hundred villages to receive ... improvements, he received a list of localities from [the] president of the National Assembly and PDCI secretary-general. The list had been drawn up by députés from all over the country in an effort to reward loyal populations and encourage support from opposition groups' (p. 90).

Selected bibliography

Barkan, Joel D. 1975. 'Bringing Home the Pork: Legislator Behavior, Rural Development and Political Change in East Africa.' Occasional Paper No. 9 Iowa City: Comparative Legislative Research Centre, University of Iowa.
Bates, Robert H. 1976. *Rural Responses to Industrialization: A Study of Village Zambia.* New Haven and London: Yale University Press.
Baylies, Carolyn, 1979. 'The Emergence of Indigenous Capitalist Agriculture: The Case of Southern Province, Zambia.' *Rural Africana*, Nos. 4–5, 65–82.
Buijtenhuijs, Robert. 1973. *Mau Mau: Twenty Years After.* The Hague: Mouton and Company.
Cliffe, Lionel, ed. 1967. *One Party Democracy: The 1967 Tanzania General Elections.* Nairobi: East African Publishing House.
Cohen, Michael A. 1974. *Urban Policy and Political Conflict in Africa.* Chicago and London: University of Chicago Press.
Cruise O'Brien, Donal B. 1971. *The Mourides of Senegal: The Political and Economic Organization of an Islamic Brotherhood.* Oxford: Clarendon Press.
——. 1975. *Saints and Politicians: Essays in the Organization of a Senegalese Peasant Society.* African Studies Series No. 15. London and New York: Cambridge University Press.
Dadson, John Alfred. 1970. 'Socialized Agriculture in Ghana, 1962–1965.' Ph.D. Dissertation, Department of Economics, Harvard University.
Dixon-Fyle, M. 1974. 'The Genesis and Development of African Protest on the Tonga Plateau, 1900–53.' Seminar Paper No. 13. Department of

History, University of Zambia. Mimeographed.

Dunn, John, and A. F. Robertson. 1973. *Dependence and Opportunity: Political Change in Ahafo.* Cambridge: Cambridge University Press.

Ghana. 1967. *Government Statement on the Report of the Committee Appointed to Enquire into the Local Purchasing of Cocoa* (White Paper No. 3). Accra: Government Printer.

——. 1966. Office of the President. *Report of the Commission of Enquiry into Trade Malpractices in Ghana.*

IBRD (International Bank for Reconstruction and Development). 1975. *Kenya: Into the Second Decade.*

Jorgenson, Dale W. 1969. 'The Role of Agriculture in Economic Development: Classical vs. Neoclassical Models of Growth.' In *Subsistence Agriculture and Economic Development*, edited by Clifton R. Wharton. Chicago: Aldine Publishing Company.

Killick, Tony. 1978. *Development Economics in Action.* New York: St Martin's Press.

Krueger, Anne O. 1974. 'The Political Economy of the Rent-Seeking Society.' *American Economic Review* 64, No. 3: 291–303.

Langdon, Steven. 1978. 'The Multinational Corporation in the Kenya Political Economy.' In *Readings on the Multinational Corporation in Kenya* edited by Raphael Kaplinsky, pp. 134–200. Nairobi: Oxford University Press.

Leith, J. Clark. 1974. *Foreign Trade Regimes and Economic Development: Ghana.* A Special Conference Series on Foreign Trade Regimes and Economic Development, Volume II. New York: National Bureau of Economic Research, Columbia University Press.

LeVine, Victor T. 1975. *Political Corruption: The Ghana Case.* Stanford, Calif.: Hoover Institution Press.

Lewis, W. Arthur. 1963. 'Economic Development with Unlimited Supplies of Labour.' In *The Economics of Underdevelopment*, edited by A. N. Agarwala and S. P. Singh. New York: Oxford University Press.

Leys, Colin. 1975. *Underdevelopment in Kenya.* London: Heinemann and James Currey.

McHenry, Dean E., Jr. 1979. *Tanzania's Ujamaa Villages.* Berkeley, Calif.: Institute of International Studies.

Nigeria. 1962. *Report of the Coker Commission of Enquiry into the Affairs of Certain Statutory Corporations in Western Nigeria.*

Northern Nigeria. 1967. *A White Paper on the Northern Nigeria Military Government's Policy for Comprehensive Review of Past Operation and Methods of the Northern Nigeria Marketing Board.* Kaduna: Government Printer.

Posner, Richard A. 1975. 'The Social Costs of Monopoly and Regulation.' *Journal of Political Economy* 83, No. 4: 807–827.

Raikes, Philip. 1978. 'Rural Differentiation and Class Formation in Tanzania.' *Journal of Peasant Studies* 5, No. 3: 285–325.

Ranis, G. and J. C. H. Frei. 1961. 'A Theory of Economic Development.' *American Economic Review* 51: 533–565.

Schatz, Sayre P. 1970. *Economics, Politics and Administration in Government Lending: The Regional Loans Boards of Nigeria.* Ibadan: Oxford University Press, for the Nigerian Institute of Social and Economic Research.

——. 1977. *Nigerian Capitalism.* Berkeley and Los Angeles: University of California Press.

Schumacher, Edward J. 1975. *Politics, Bureaucracy, and Rural Development in Senegal.* Berkeley and Los Angeles: University of California Press.

Stiglitz, Joseph E., and Hirofumi Uzawa, eds. 1969. *Readings in the Modern Theory of Economic Growth.* Cambridge, Mass. and London: The Massachusetts Institute of Technology Press.

Wells, Jerome C. 1974. *Agricultural Policy and Economic Growth in Nigeria, 1962–68.* Ibadan: Oxford University Press, for the Nigerian Institute of Social and Economic Research.

GORAN HYDEN
Conditions of Governance

Reference
No Shortcuts to Progress:
African Development Management in Perspective
Heinemann, 1983, pp. 36–45.

African leaders govern under conditions very different from other societies. Because they are placed between, on the one hand, a multitude of small producers whose structural dependence on other social classes for productive and socially reproductive purposes is virtually nil and, on the other, owners and agencies of foreign resources, they really operate in a social vacuum, or as we tried to describe it in the first chapter, in the context of a state that is suspended in mid-air above society. In this respect, it is difficult to call the Africans holding state power a 'ruling class'. They are not the carriers of a hegemonic 'bourgeois' culture and prefer to act as patrons of their respective home communities. Because the bourgeois culture is associated with colonial and neo-colonial practices, most African politicians have hesitated to embrace it. Thus, although they may have occupied positions of influence and control in society they have not exercised these opportunities to establish themselves as members of a bourgeois class in the sense of developing an economic system over which they have increasing control. Some political economists have argued that such an entrenchment has not been possible because of the dominance of foreign capital in Africa.[10] The agents of such capital really constitute the ruling class in Africa, according to this argument. This point, however, seems quite far-fetched. The influence of foreign capital is exercised in relation to estates and plantations run by multinational corporations, but beyond these micro-level operations it is hard to see that foreign owners of capital in a general sense constitute a ruling class in Africa. They do not control the behaviour of Africa's multitude of smallholder peasants and can no more than government leaders lay claim to having them in their hands through the manipulation of economic systems variables. To be sure, in some countries there is evidence that government leaders prefer a 'comprador' relationship to foreign capital owners. This, however, as indicated in the previous chapter, is not a historical inevitability although it may be right to assume that such a relationship could develop in situations where the emerging African bourgeoisie fails to enhance organizational efficiency and labour productivity. Where the economic policies are such as to facilitate the development of a class of local entrepreneurs such a 'comprador' relationship seems in the long run much less likely.

The main reason why in many African countries there is no ruling class in the sense we know it from other societies is that the political strategies after independence have not supported the rise of a class of people who, by cutting their ties with the economy of affection, can establish themselves as guardians of a public morality that protects the integrity of economic institutions serving the nation-state as a whole. African governments have proved unable to break the hold of the economy of affection on society. Political interventions like leadership codes, while noble and well-intended, have made only marginal contributions to improvements in public morality. In recent years when economic scarcities have arisen, the leadership codes have been put on particularly serious tests. Experience suggests that either they are unenforceable or, where capacity exists to oblige people to follow them, those affected have frequently become demoralized.

Violations of leadership codes have normally been attributed to 'evil capitalist' behaviour but it is clear that the issue is much more complex than that. Many of these breaches are the result of normal affective behaviour. Nobody has better captured this behavioural phenomenon than Donal Cruise O'Brien in his study of 'clan' politics in Senegal. As he makes clear the clan in local Franco-Senegalese parlance has nothing or very little in common with the normal usage of the term among social scientists. The modern clan is not defined by kinship, real or imagined, although kinship relations may exist and may help to reinforce political solidarity within a given clan group: there is no requirement for a common revered ancestor, real or imagined; no clanic name; no shared taboo; no role of exogamy. Instead, as he argues:

> The clan is a political faction, operating within the institutions of the state and the governing party: it exists above all to promote the interests of its members through political competition, and its first unifying principle is the prospect of the material rewards of political success. Political office and the spoils of office are the very definition of success: loot is the clanic totem[11]

This phenomenon exists in varying degrees throughout Africa. In the Swahili-speaking parts of the continent, it is referred to as *kula* (literally 'to eat'), that is, the ability to take advantage of public resources for purposes other than those officially prescribed. The present author was able to observe it in an earlier study of cooperatives in Kenya where affective ties, operating under the guise of political factions, steered resources away from these organizations.[12] Particularly notable was the incident of a society chairman being accused of theft and corruption by a co-operative auditor in front of a general meeting, yet returned at that same meeting by an overwhelming majority by virtue of the strength of his clan. It is not at all uncommon in Africa that a person who can demonstrate generosity at public expense is not only forgiven by his people but also seen as having acted correctly.

The unauthorized use of public funds for purposes of building political constituencies has featured prominently in virtually all inquiries conducted by African governments. Reports by state auditors give further indications of this phenomenon through references to unreturned cash imprests, unauthorized travelling and uses of public vehicles, just to mention a few of the more common accusations.[13] Featuring in these public inquiries are also frequent reports of appointments of excessive numbers of employees, often from among the same ethnic groups as those controlling employment. While it would be wrong to attribute all these incidents to political factionalism, they are indicative of the weak adherence to the kind of public morality that is a prerequisite to acceptable performance in modern large-scale organizations. The report of the commission appointed to make an inquiry into the affairs of the Nigerian Railways in 1967 is chosen here as representative of the findings and sentiments expressed in most such documents:

> We consider, however, that many of the ills of the Corporation would have dropped out if the commercial attitude had been present even in the diluted form envisaged by the Act. It seems that the Corporation had taken refuge under the cloak of public utility in its gross acts of financial indiscipline and mismanagement. Even if the Corporation was not expected to undertake full-scale commercial exploitation of the railway nothing debarred the Board and Management from keeping up the efficiency of the system. The large pool of redundant workers could have been reduced; inefficient workers could have been trained or removed; skills and dexterity could have been improved; materials could have been bought at reasonable prices, stocked in adequate quantities, cared for and issued as necessary, and used responsibly. Wastages and frauds could have been avoided.[14]

These examples illustrate the various ways by which public resources are being diverted for other uses and confirm the difficulty managers have, often as a result of pressures from clan politics, to conform with prescribed organizational rules. In fact, as Moris points out in his interesting analysis of the transferability of a western management tradition to East Africa, some of the distinctive features which to outsiders epitomize bureaucratic inefficiency, in their local context arise out of well-intended efforts to incorporate proximate rationality within administrative decision-making. For indigenous officials, their organization's flexibility and sensitivity to individual human needs is a source of pride, Moris notes.[15] What he suggests is that rationality in the public context in Africa must be seen to operate at two different levels. To fully understand this point it may be helpful to draw yet another historical comparison with western society and its development, here borrowing from a perceptive analysis by the Nigerian political scientist, Peter Ekeh.[16]

In his view, the public realm – that is, the sphere of state action – and the private realm in western societies share a common moral foundation. That is to say, what is considered morally right or wrong in the latter is also considered morally right and wrong in the public realm. His argument is that for centuries, Christian beliefs have provided a common foundation for both private and public ethic. There may be exceptions to this pattern, as manifested for example in Banfield's study of 'amoral familism' in southern Italy,[17] but by and large these are in the contemporary context marginally important.[18]

In post-independence Africa, by contrast, there is no monolithic public realm morally bound to the private realm. Instead, Ekeh maintains, there are two public realms with different links to the private realm. At one level is the public realm in which primordial groupings, ties and sentiments influence and determine the public behaviour of individuals. This realm is moral and operates on the same moral imperatives as the private realm. At another level there is a public realm which is historically associated with colonial rule and which is based on the civic structures created in those days: the civil service, the judiciary, the police, the military, and so on. Its chief characteristic is that it has no moral links with the private realm. In Ekeh's view, this civic public realm is amoral and lacks the generalized moral imperatives operative in the private realm and in the primordial public realm. The latter is a reservoir of moral obligations, which one works to preserve. The civic public realm, by contrast, is a place from which one seeks to gain, if possible in order to benefit the primordial public realm.

What Ekeh refers to in western societies is the process of rationalization, which began long ago in ancient Greece, but which was not really complete until the maturation of capitalism in the twentieth century. The congruence between the private and public realms is evidence to some people of successful modernization, to others of effective capitalist penetration. Whichever way looked at, the individual has succumbed to the moral imperatives of a public collectivity and its chosen instruments of social action. He is engulfed by the *nature artificielle*, a captive of the system or, perhaps more appropriately, a cog in a wheel.

Because there is as yet no ruling class that has established its hegemony over African societies and succeeded in capturing other social classes for its purposes, the situation is different. The primordial public realm, or the economy of affection as we prefer to call it here, manages to survive and exercise its influence over public policy.

In order to understand its resilience, it is important to accept that it is not only the absence of a ruling class that perpetuates the public influence of affective criteria on social action. Following the point made in Chapter I about the important role the economy of affection plays as a support mechanism for otherwise virtually autonomous economic units, there is a strong tendency in Africa to look for insurance against hardship and calamity among people who by virtue of wealth or access to resources may be able to offer it. This phenomenon, which in the anthropology literature is often referred to as 'primitive social insurance',[19] is still invoked in most African societies. Public expectations are very much in that direction. They encourage not only an inclination to assume the obligation of public figures or institutions to provide such insurance but also the institutionalization of a patronage type of politics. Thus clan politics or factionalism is funnelled from below, giving rise to tensions between the centre and the regions and the supreme leader and his lieutenants. It provides the foundation for local corporateness and autonomy which may pose a threat to central rule. As Fallers notes in his study of this phenomenon in the transformation of Buganda into a highly centralized kingdom:

> One is reminded … of Max Weber's discussion of feudalism and 'patrimonialism' in medieval European history – the struggle between the centralizing efforts of kings, expressed in their attempts to build up bodies of patrimonial retainers responsible to themselves alone and the decentralizing tendency of subordinate authorities to become locally rooted hereditary chiefs.[20]

While the patrimonial tendencies were inherent in many African kingdoms prior to European colonization, few countries can really claim a genuine feudal tradition. A notable exception is imperial Ethiopia where the Emperor tried to keep his country together under a centralized form of rule through allocation of fiefs to the Orthodox Church and to individual officials ready to serve as retainers of the Emperor in the regions.[21] Although a similar system of retainership was used in pre-colonial times to establish the Moroccan kingdom,[22] there are no other significant examples of a feudal system of land tenure replacing the communal ownership of land. This is another reason why central authority and a hegemonic class are still developing on fragile grounds. Those saddled with the responsibility to govern are neither landlords nor capitalist barons controlling the economy through ownership of important means of production. On the contrary, they are spokesmen and representatives of political clans or groupings derived from the economy of affection, over which they have no direct control without ability to dispense favours and benefits to members. This makes the whole polity naturally tense and normally requiring public resources to contain.

Approaches to governance

Having tried to show that the economy of affection permeates politics in African society. it is time to look at how African leaders have tried to cope with the challenges posed to effective government by the prevalence of affective criteria. The almost unanimous choice of one-party systems denotes a natural, if not inevitable, response to the uncertainty that characterizes a society under the influence of the peasant mode of production. In the absence of any advanced structural dependencies, there are few institutions in which officials and peasants share a common interest. The scope for the protection and development of public institutions through adherence to formal rules is very limited. Instead, networks developed under the economy of affection tend to become politicized and used to pursue political objectives. That is why politics, as Jackson and Rosberg note in their book, tends to be much more personalized and less restrained in Africa. In this kind of situation, where the principal social cleavage is between factions based in local communities, be they ethnic, religious or defined by any other affective criteria, the institutionalization of factional rivalry into a two- or multi-party system carries the risk of a crack in the very fundament of society. The examples of multi-party systems surviving without intensifying ethnic rivalry are few. Senegal has a system where parties have been assigned a certain space along a given ideological spectrum accommodating views from right to left. Nigeria is another special case because of its size and federalism and the experience of the civil war in the 1960s which has enabled the Nigerians to approach the question of constitutional and political arrangements with greater maturity and sophistication. It can be argued that it needed a civil war – that is, the loss of control of the political situation – in order to generate this new outlook. Most African leaders, however, would like to pre-empt a threat to national unity and they prefer to adhere to a one-party system, in which leaders of various clans are co-opted. In pursuing this strategy of cooptation, African leaders have used either of two approaches.

The first has been to develop a loose alliance of clan leaders who through participation in the ruling party and government have been given opportunity to secure benefits for their respective constituencies. While it would be wrong to imply that such considerations have been singularly dominant, they have constituted a legitimate, albeit unformulated, aspect of governance. Serving as political patrons, these leaders have been able to command the diversion of public resources to their clans or constituencies in spite of the cost of these activities to the economy. The supreme leader normally accepts this use of public resources as a necessary means of buying the support of the various clan leaders but he must also be careful not to give away too much. None of the other leaders must be allowed to grow too powerful or autonomous, as that may threaten the ability of the supreme head to govern effectively. Thus, normally the president of an African country can apply the brakes on the use of public resources for support of individual clan leaders. Usually such measures are taken behind closed doors and never become publicly known, although when they also lead to demotion or transfer from a given position of prominence, one can normally deduce that the person has been 'cut to size' by the supreme leader. The president may in rare cases publicly rebuke a clan leader, particularly if the latter poses a serious threat to his power. Another way by which the president of an African country can counteract the influence of a clan leader is by appointing persons with no connection to his clan as senior party or government officials in the area where thst clan is powerful. These officials may be unofficially awarded because of their loyalty to the president and rise to prominence without being clan leaders.

The most outstanding feature of this approach to governance is the ability of individual politicians to command resources for their respective constituencies even though official policies make no mention of such allocations. Furthermore, unofficial channels are often used to settle disputes. As Cruise O'Brien notes with respect to Senegal, access to patronage helps to explain the otherwise surprisingly docile attitude of peasants in the face of bureaucratic exploitation.[23] There are many ways around the system and where patronage politics prevails it is an expected means of resolving conflict or meeting demand. The success of the patronage approach presupposes ability on the part of the supreme leader to placate the various clan leaders. Particularly in cases where these men have access to external resources independently of the former, the danger of secession or civil war is imminent, as the case of Chad demonstrates.[24]

The second approach is characterized by the deliberate creation of a vanguard group of leaders who by virtue of some agreed-upon criteria can control access to the political arena. This approach has been particularly common in states using a socialist approach to development but has been applied also by military juntas. The essence of this approach has been to try to place a 'lid on the system', that is, discourage the demands for patronage handled by clan leaders and elevate the allocation of resources needed for governance or political management purposes to the level of official policy-making. The reigning ideology has normally been used to legitimize the handling of these issues in an official context. Tanzania is a case in point where access to party leadership has been carefully controlled through various screening and selection mechanisms and where, as a result, the level of unofficial patronage has been low but where instead some of the same purposes have been served through official party channels. This approach has enabled the leadership to free itself from some of the most immediate pressures of affective criteria and it has been possible within the national leadership to agree upon a measure of official redistribution of resources and services to benefit the poorer and more backward regions of the country.[25] Yet, political clans have not been totally eliminated in Tanzania and pressures for more use of unofficial channels have continued to exist. As a way of combating these pressures the political leadership has made party work more remunerative. Thus, for instance, party salaries are generally higher than those in government and elected politicians are eligible for retirement benefits after only one period of five years in Parliament. Although Chama cha Mapinduzi (CCM) collects dues and subjects income-earners to monthly deductions in order to finance party activities, its expenditures are also met from regular government revenue. Thus, some of the public resources that under the 'patronage' approach are used to sustain the loyalty of political clans are here channelled into the official party machinery and used for the same political management purposes. While the latter approach appears less illegitimate, it is often at least as costly. Officials handling the allocation of resources in the name of the ruling party are normally persons working outside their respective home areas. As a result, they are not always sensitive to local needs. While they do have a stake in demonstrating to superiors their ability to accomplish results in the name of the party, they often do so over the heads of the local population. The overall effect may be not only bad projects, as we will discuss in Chapter 4, but also strained relations between officials and the local people. Because the party has 'hijacked' rights associated by most people with the prerogatives of the economy of affection, there is a tendency for people to feel alienated.

It would be wrong to conclude, however, that these vanguard parties are watertight entities who can preclude affective considerations altogether. The social realities of African society are such that attempting it would be tantamount to committing political suicide. To that extent, vanguard parties or military juntas tend to be influenced by the prevailing affective forces in society. The clans do exist, albeit in a more subdued form and the problems of effective co-optation manifest themselves even in this approach. The PAIGC in Guinea-Bissau and the MPLA in Angola are cases in point. Although they were both liberation fronts and their leaders comrades-in-arms, post-independence politics has taken its toll in the form of factional struggles based not only on ideological but also affective criteria.

There is a certain similarity between the vanguard approach and that of the colonial powers in that both have tried to govern in isolation of the prevailing social forces in African society. Although the rationale for doing so obviously has differed, both have shared the view that in the interest of effective government the doors to society must remain closed and tightly controlled. While the British found it easy to be consistent on this point, it is clear that African leaders, operating in the name of a vanguard party, have found it much more difficult to cut their ties with prevailing cultural and social values.

Personal rule and authoritarianism

This similarity is not just coincidental as it does reflect the point made in the previous chapter that the predicament of the post-independence rulers is the same as that of their colonial predecessors. Because capitalism was not able to complete its historical mission of transforming pre-capitalist formations, changing social behaviour, and freeing labour for use in efforts to enhance productivity on land and in factories, the same challenge is still there. The fact that the state is still not structurally rooted in the prevailing systems of peasant production in Africa invites authoritarianism and often arbitrariness in political decisions. As Francis Sutton noted already over twenty years ago: 'Authoritarianism in the new African states … is – perhaps paradoxically – a feature of government in which there is a basic continuity from colonial to African control.'[26] By and large, the comparison still stands.

Certainly Jackson and Rosberg provide plenty of evidence to support the thesis. Whether the African leader appears in the figure of 'prince', 'autocrat', 'prophet' or 'tyrant', his style of governance assumes unquestionable authority and consequently a good measure of authoritarianism.[27] This does not mean that these styles are the same in all respects. For instance, it would be an insult to compare Nyerere ('prophet') with Amin ('tyrant'), since the latter clearly violated even the most basic norms of civil rule while Nyerere, in an enlightened fashion, has tried to use authoritarian interventions only when absolutely necessary.

Because personal rule and authoritarianism characterize governance throughout Africa it is easy to become cynical about the prospects for democracy and the safeguarding of civil and political rights in these countries. Given that the general conditions on the continent certainly are so different from those that support democracy in other parts of the world, credit must go to at least some regimes in Africa which in spite of the alien character of political democracy as it is known in western countries have tried to implant some of its principles in their society.

While these measures may not have been enough to guarantee civil and political rights, their violation has often been the result not of lack of political will but of circumstances ruling out their effective implementation. With an intrinsically unstable base of governance, African leaders, often against their will, have been forced to sacrifice democratic principles of rule.

The dilemma facing African leaders is that because the state is not structurally tied to society they are not in a position to exercise systemic power. They lack the more subtle institutional means that are at the disposal of a government in societies where the state is firmly rooted in the productive system of the country and where, therefore, it can be used to shape the system at large. Seen in this perspective, the image of the African leader as being extremely powerful is mistaken. While it may be true that if one enters the political kingdom in Africa a lot of other private benefits will follow, there is reason today to be more sceptical about the capacity of politics to accelerate development. There are definite structural impediments to such a possibility in the contemporary situation in most African countries and as long as these are not adequately dealt with and leaders prefer to politicize latent affective relations the scope for exercise of systemic power is going to be very limited. Personal rule and authoritarianism are likely to continue. An editorial comment in one of the newspapers at the occasion of Kenya's move to legalize its one-party system in 1982 is not unrepresentative of political beliefs in the nature of rule in African countries:

> Authoritarianism is a necessary ingredient of political power, for it is impossible to conceive of a sovereign without authority to enforce obedience or moral and legal supremacy or to influence the conduct of public affairs... The function of the top, in addition to using power like the Leviathan to preserve the state, is also to act like a referee between many competing centres for power.[28]

The conclusion one can draw from an analysis of the political situation in Africa is that while authoritarianism is a prevalent feature of rule that by many is regarded as legitimate, or at least as a necessary evil, these countries (with the possible exception of South Africa) are not totalitarian. The preconditions for such a system simply do not exist where society and state are structurally so separate as they are in Africa. The marginal presence of a culture penneated by science and technology – a *nature artificielle* – limits for the foreseeable future any attempt to establish such a system of rule.

Notes

* Please note that original footnote numbering has been retained.

[10] See, for instance, the debate about the 'post-colonial' state, notably the contributions by Colin Leys, 'The "over-developed" post-colonial state: a re-evaluation', *Review of African Political Economy*, No. 5 (January–April 1976), pp. 39–48; and Michaela von Freyhold, 'The post-colonial state and its Tanzanian version', *ibid.*, No. 8 (January–April 1977), pp. 75–89.

[11] Donal B. Cruise O'Brien, *Saints and Politicians: Essays in the Organization of a Senegalese Peasant Society* (London, Cambridge University Press, 1975), p. 149.

[12] Goran Hyden, *Efficiency versus Distribution in East African Cooperatives* (Nairobi, East African Literature Bureau, 1973).

[13] The present author has a set of Reports by the Auditor-Generals of Ghana, Kenya and Tanzania. In spite of constant warnings in these reports and ventilation in Public Accounts Committees of the Parliaments, no improvement is registered. In fact, over the years financial discipline has declined.

[14] Federal Republic of Nigeria, *Report of the Nigerian Railway Corporation Tribunal of Inquiry Appointed under the Tribunal of Inquiry Decree 1966 to Inquire into the Affairs of the Nigerian Railway Corporation* (Lagos, Federal Ministry of Information, 1967), p. 260.

[15] Jon Moris, 'The transferability of the western management tradition into the public service sectors: an East African perspective', *Management Education in Africa: Prospectus and Appraisals* (Arusha, East African Management Institute, 1977), p. 82.

[16] Peter Ekeh, 'Colonialism and the two publics in Africa: a theoretical statement', *Comparative Studies in Society and History*, vol. 17, no. 1 (1975), pp. 91–112.

[17] Edward C. Banfield, *The Moral Basis of a Backward Society* (New York, The Free Press, 1958).

[18] One should not of course underestimate recent 'revolts against the heavy taxes imposed in many European countries'. A Reuters dispatch, dated 22 March 1982, tells of moonlighting and other 'underground economy' measures threatening to undermine Denmark's cradle-to-grave welfare state, disrupt public finances and hinder recovery in the official economy. The author claims that this phenomenon has grown in recent years as a result of falling incomes and a record unemployment level. This certainly confirms the importance of economic growth in developing and sustaining loyalty to the public realm.

[19] See, for example, Raymond Firth (ed.), *Themes in Economic Anthropology* (London, Tavistock Publications, 1967), and Marshall Sahlins, *Stone Age Economics* (New York and Chicago, Aldine Atherton, 1972). For the application of the subject of the soft state to Africa, see S. Egite Oyovbaire, 'Politics and development planning' in Martin Dent and Dennis Austin (eds), *Operation of the Nigerian Political System under the Second Republic* (Manchester, Manchester University Press, 1981).

[20] Lloyd Fallers, *The King's Men* (London. Oxford University Press, 1964), p. 99.

[21] See, for example, Richard Pankhurst. *State and Land in Ethiopian History* (Addis Ababa, Haile Selassie I University, 1966).

[22] In pre-colonial Moroccan history distinction was made between *Bled el-Makhzan* (centralized authority) and *Bled es-Siba* (tribal domain), the latter having gradually been incorporated under the control of the central monarchical authority through co-optation of local chiefs.

[23] Cruise O'Brien, *op. cit.* p. 151.

[24] For a useful overview of the events leading to the war between the forces of President Goukouni and his former Foreign Minister, Hissen Habre, in 1982, see Virginia Thompson and Richard Adloff, *Conflict in Chad* (Berkeley, Institute of International Studies. University of California, 1981).

[25] This is the subject of a volume by Professor Paul Maro, Department of Geography, University of Dar es Salaam. due to be published by the Dar es Salaam University Press.

[26] Francis X. Sutton, 'Authority and authoritarianism in the new Africa' in Robert O. Tilman and Taylor Cole (eds), *The Nigerian Political Scene* (Durham, NC, Duke University Press, 1962), p. 262.

[27] This classification of the leaders is borrowed from Jackson and Rosberg, *Personal Rule in Black Africa* (Berkeley and Los Angeles: University of California Press, 1982).

[28] *The Standard* (Nairobi), 28 May 1982.

ROBERT H. JACKSON
& CARL G. ROSBERG
Personal Rule

Reference
Comparative Politics, no. 4, July 1984, pp. 430–40.

Some characteristic practices of personal regimes in Sub-Saharan Africa

Largely by utilizing indigenous political-cultural materials readily at hand as well as by accommodating the necessity of pragmatism, many African politicians have improvised a makeshift polity that is not modelled on any design and lacks effective institutions but is characterized by a number of distinctive practices.[32]

By 'practices,' we mean activities in which political actors are commonly engaged. As such, they are recognized and frequently used ways of pursuing one's power or security goals. It is important and useful to distinguish political 'practices' from social 'processes': while the former are the activities of political actors, the latter are the operations of a more impersonal social system. It is also necessary to distinguish between 'practices' and 'institutions': like all practices, those of personal rule are entirely pragmatic and carry no legitimacy or value that is independent of their effective uses, unlike formal political institutions and procedures which are valued not only for what they enable but also for their own sake.

Among the most important practices in personal regimes are conspiracy, factional politics and clientelism, corruption, purges and rehabilitations, and succession maneuvers. We do not regard these as the necessary 'functions' of personal political systems, but we do regard them as the kinds of political behavior one might expect in countries in which formal institutions are ineffective. Not all of these practices contribute to political order, stability, and civility; in fact, some of them, such as conspiracy, are harmful to the provision of such political goods. However, taken together, they appear to accurately characterize the kind of politics to which politicians in the great majority of sub-Saharan countries have resorted over the past two decades.

These practices have been widely noted – and often deplored – in the study of contemporary African politics. Indeed, they have been the subjects of considerable commentary, and an already sizable literature deals with some of them, such as coups and corruption. However (as we have noted), as yet there has been little inclination to view them as integral elements of a distinctive type of political system, personal rule. Instead, they have usually been viewed from the rationalist perspective as shortcomings in the endeavor to establish modern social politics and policy government in Black Africa. As indicated, we are inclined to regard such practices as the very essence of political and governmental conduct in most countries south of the Sahara. While it is evident that most contemporary African states have not acquired the rationalist characteristics of social politics and policy government, they nevertheless have become something more than can adequately be described in terms merely of the absence of such characteristics. The

political system of personal rule and its distinctive practices are the reality of what they have become.

Before we begin to examine the distinctive political practices of personal rule in Black Africa, it may be appropriate to remind ourselves of the obvious fact that all political systems, and not only systems of personal rule, consist of persons and systems of personal relationships. Political institutions that are effective – that is, those which are not simply unrealized, abstract rules – always give rise to informal relationships and practices that enable them to work: 'To each of the legal organs of the state corresponds, more or less exactly, a social system, which consists in effect of persons brought together by legal relationships, existing together in social relationships.'[33] Thus the House of Commons is not only a primary political institution of Great Britain but also the 'best club in London.'[34] In contrast, in contemporary African regimes of personal rule we find informal social systems that have evolved not out of sympathy and loyalty to the formal political institutions but out of indifference or antagonism to them. The personal system has displaced rather than augmented the legal system of rule; where a concern for legality has been displayed, it has always been dependent on the interests of powerful individuals rather than the other way about. (Why this has happened is a question we address briefly in the conclusion.)

Political conspiracy

Individuals or groups usually resort to conspiratorial politics either when they are deprived of a fair opportunity to compete openly for government positions or when they believe they cannot win by open competition. In contemporary Black African countries both conditions have frequently been present, and coups and plots have emerged as characteristic political practices. By 1983 there had been at least fifty successful coups since the end of colonial rule in twenty-three countries, and many others that were unsuccessful. By definition a coup is an unlawful action, an action in violation of constitutional rules. Similarly, to engage in political plotting is to undertake actions such as scheming and spying aimed at displacing a ruler or leader – or protecting him. There have been widespread reports of plotting in Black Africa, including bogus as well as genuine plots, by rulers as well as by their opponents. Plotting is generally associated with conspiracies against rulers and regimes, but it has been alleged that at least one African despot – Toure of Guinea – has governed 'by plot.'[35] While it is impossible to know with certainty how widespread such practices have been owing to their secretive nature, there is little doubt that many African politicians have engaged in them.

The relationship of weak political institutions and the prevalence of coups has been given considerable attention by political scientists.[36] The absence of effective institutional restraints is undoubtedly a critical consideration which disposes ambitious individuals or groups with access to power to contemplate and engage in unlawful bids for political control. In contemporary Black Africa, as elsewhere in the Third World, members of the military, or factions within it, have found themselves in a position to contemplate political intervention. During the initial post-independence years, African soldiers were less disposed to intervene, probably owing more to their inexperience and peripheral position in the state than to the strength of political institutions. But with the passing of time and the increasing contravention of constitutional rules by civilian rulers, the self-restraint of soldiers has declined, and their political ambitions have increased. By the second half of the 1960s they had become less hesitant to assert their power. In place of constitutional-democratic government, there appeared contrary expectations and practices in which the checks on powerholders became merely the power of others or personal loyalty to one's supporters. Politically ambitious African soldiers who were lacking in loyalty to the ruler and his regime and who in addition possessed more than sufficient power to take command of the government became disposed to intervene in politics. Once some successful coups had been perpetrated, others were contemplated and attempted. It is perhaps understandable that in such circumstances it was not long before the coup was established as a recognized political practice which was most frequently – but not exclusively – engaged in by soldiers. Today military rulers are as common in sub-Saharan Africa as civilian ones. Indeed they have been for some time. However, the distinction between military and civilian rule – which has received much attention in African political studies – is probably less important than the fact that *both* soldiers and civilians are attempting to rule without the benefit of effective institutions and that *both* have been victims of coups.

Factional politics and clientelism

The politics of faction has been evident in African political life throughout the independence era, especially as political pluralism declined, and political monopoly increased in the years immediately following independence.[37] By 'factional politics' we mean jockeying and maneuvering to influence a ruler and to increase one's political advantage or security in a regime, an inherently nonviolent political activity (unlike conspiratorial politics, which may involve violence). By its nature, factionalism tends to be an internal competition for power and position within a group rather than an open contest among groups. Under political monopoly, factionalism is ordinarily the prevalent form of nonviolent politics because open, legitimate political competition based on parties is forbidden. When a factional struggle is transformed into a public, nonviolent contest which is governed by rules of some kind, factions in effect have become parties. To our knowledge this has never happened in contemporary African politics, undoubtedly owing to the fact that open political competition has seldom been permitted. Moreover, a factional struggle may deteriorate into violent conflict and civil warfare; this has happened in Chad, Burundi, post-Amin Uganda, and Ethiopia following the overthrow of Emperor Haile Selassie in 1974.

It is to factional politics (and clientelism) that Senghor is referring in employing the term 'politician politics.' Ordinarily, the objects – the prizes and spoils – of factional politics are government positions and the patronage they control.[38] The less autocratic and the more diplomatic and tolerant a personal ruler is, the more likely factional politics is a common practice in his regime. Outstanding examples of politics based on faction (and also clientelism) are Senghor's sagacious rule in Senegal (1960–80), Kenyatta's courtly but stern governance in Kenya (1963–78), William Tolbert's paternalist style in Liberia (1971–80), Numeiri's adroit and resolute rule in Sudan (1969–present), and Kaunda's somewhat self-indulgent and utopian pursuit of socialism in Zambia (1964–present). By comparison, in a few highly autocratic regimes there has tended to be less factional politics because the ruler is sufficiently strong and confident to attempt to dominate the state without sharing power with other leaders if he so desires. Such is definitely the case in Banda's Malawi and Ahidjo's Cameroon; these two rulers have displayed a type of personal regime reminiscent of European absolutism, where the country is virtually the ruler's estate and the government is his personal apparatus to deploy and direct as he wishes without consulting anyone. Thus while factional politics is practiced widely in sub-Saharan Africa, it is by no means practiced everywhere or to the same extent.

Closely related to factionalism in idea and expression is the practice of clientelism. The image of clientelism is one of extensive chains of patron–client ties extending usually from the center of a personal regime, that is, from the ruler to his lieutenants, clients, and other followers, and through them to their followers, and so on. The substance and conditions of such ties can be conceived of as the intermingling of two factors: the resources of patronage (which can be used to satisfy wants and needs and can be allocated by patrons to clients) and personal loyalty (which is an affective relationship that helps to sustain dyadic relations during times of resource scarcity).[39] Clientelism is primarily personal: unlike institutions, individual patron–client linkages are contingent upon the persons in a relationship and ordinarily cannot outlast them. A change of ruler or leader – as a result of a successful coup or assassination plot, for instance – can alter greatly both an existing clientelist pattern and the political fortunes of those entangled in it. When Tom Mboya and Josiah Kariuki, each a 'big man' in Kenyan politics, were assassinated (Mboya in 1969 and Kariuki in 1975), the political fortunes not only of personal clients and followers but also of clans and large segments of ethnic communities were adversely affected. Clientelist relations are the outcome of a stratagem of pursuing power and position by securing the support of others in exchange for patronage (or vice versa) in societies in which democratic political organizations and interest groups are weak or nonexistent.

Political corruption

Unlike clientelism, corruption is an unlawful practice; it is the disregard of the rules and requirements of one's office for the sake of a personal advantage, such as a bribe. While corruption occurs whenever officials accept bribes, corrupt governments can develop only where such practices are widespread and are sustained by social attitudes: it is more difficult and offensive to be corrupt in Sweden than in Italy. Where corruption is widely practiced, it is evidence of the weakness of public institutions and the strength of private appetites and desires as determinants of political and administrative behavior.[40]

Corruption is a widely noted practice in contemporary African states.[41] In addition to the weakness of civil and political institutions, the incidence of corrupt behavior in personal regimes depends greatly on the conduct of those leaders who are in the best position to be corrupt. If a ruler and other prominent leaders strenuously oppose corruption, are able to police it, and refuse to engage in corrupt practices themselves, then it may not be as prevalent. This is clearly the case in Banda's Malawi, where such practices have been kept in check. But if the ruler or other prominent leaders indulge in such practices themselves, then the demonstration effect upon the rest of the country can be profound because such practices can reinforce existing social expectations in which family, friends, associates, clients, clansmen, and tribesmen have a higher claim on a public official's conduct than do government rules and regulations.

In some African countries corruption has been virtually 'a way of life,' for example in Ghana, Sierra Leone, Liberia, Amin's Uganda, Bokassa's Central African Empire, Nigeria, and Zaire. In these countries the expectation of corruption is probably more difficult for officials to ignore than the institutional regulations which prohibit such practices. Nigeria's pervasive corruption has been viewed as part and parcel of 'the present accepted value system of Nigerian society.'[42] Nonetheless, it is probably Zaire which enjoys the dubious status of being the most thoroughly corrupt country in sub-Saharan Africa. Corruption is so extensive that observers have virtually had to invent new phrases to describe it; it is termed a 'structural fact,' and Zaire is referred to as 'an extortionist culture' in which bribery is common and has been described as 'economic mugging.'[43] Probably the most corrupt individual of all is the ruler, Mobutu, who is reputed to be one of the world's richest men and to have amassed an enormous fortune (in the millions of dollars) by personally appropriating or misusing the funds of the Bank of Zaire, the state trading companies, and other government agencies.[44] What Mobutu debases on a vast scale, lesser leaders debase on a diminishing scale from the upper levels of government to the lower ones, where soldiers and minor officials act virtually as if they possess 'a license to steal.'[45] Zaire is an extreme case of a country where government is personally appropriated by the governors.

Political purges and rehabilitation
Like factionalism, purges and rehabilitations are entangled with political monopoly. A purge is an action which expels from an organization members who are accused of disloyalty, disobedience, or excessive independence. If there is but one political organization in a country to which all politicians must belong, the threat or use of expulsion may be a method of controlling them, while offers of rehabilitation may reduce their temptation to conspire against the regime from outside the ruling group. In most African countries the political monopoly is a monopoly not only of power but also of wealth and status; there is no comparable source of privilege outside of politics. Therefore, to be deprived of membership in the ruling monopoly of an African country or to be restored to membership is to have one's life and fortune dramatically altered. For politicians everywhere the political wilderness is a lonely place; for African politicians it is also a misfortune.

With the decline of political pluralism and the rise of political monopoly in sub-Saharan Africa in the past two decades, there has been a corresponding increase in purges and rehabilitations as rulers have endeavored to maintain control of their regimes. Such practices were in evidence in Nkrumah's Ghana soon after his Convention People's Party (CPP) acquired its political monopoly in 1960.[46] In autocratic Malawi these practices have been a jealously guarded prerogative of the ruler, Dr. Banda. Since 1964 he has not hesitated to exercise his prerogative, and during this period there has been a consistent emphasis on the requirement of absolute obedience and devotion of all politicians to the ruler.[47] In a few countries, leading politicians have been purged for a lack of expressed ideological fervor, as in Guinea, where Toure has periodically removed notables from his regime on these grounds, and in Congo-Brazzaville, where a 'purge commission' with the authority to remove cadres who failed to meet contrived standards of 'socialist' behavior was established in 1975.[48]

Succession maneuvers
The ultimate prize in most regimes is the attainment of rulership. In multiparty democracies the allocation of the prize is determined by rules: the president or prime minister has won his party's nomination and a general election contested with other parties, or he has succeeded to office in accordance with constitutional provisions. In contrast, in personal regimes the struggle of rulers to maintain their position or to pass it on to a designated successor, and the efforts of other leaders to become the ruler or to prevent their rivals from attaining rulership, is a direct struggle of power and skill unmediated by political institutions. Therefore, uncertainty always surrounds the question: 'Who shall rule and for how long?' For elites the prospect of succession is likely to be a catastrophic destabilizing political issue because the regime is tied to the ruler. When he loses his ability to rule or passes from the scene, his regime can be jeopardized; a change of ruler might augur a change of regime. 'Succession' is the replacement of a ruler who has died, become incapacitated, or resigned; it differs from a change of ruler by election, a termination of office, or a reconstitution of a country after an interlude of unconstitutional rule. In personal regimes succession is an important problem precisely because the rules governing succession – like all constitutional rules in personal regimes – lack legitimacy and therefore the predictable capacity to shape political behavior.

Succession uncertainties have affected politics in some African personal regimes, although perhaps not to the extent that the theory of personal rule would lead us to expect. Furthermore, there have been several, albeit qualified, constitutional successions. The uncertainty of who would succeed Kenyatta and whether the succession would be peaceful or violent affected Kenyan politics for a decade prior to his death in 1978. As it happened, the succession of Vice-President Moi to the presidency was orderly and appeared to comply with constitutional procedures, an indication that Kenyan politics is becoming institutionalized at least in this respect. The succession of Vice-President Tolbert to the Liberian presidency following the death of President William Tubman in 1971 also complied with constitutional provisions. In 1983 there appeared to be a possibility of a constitutional succession in Tanzania, where Nyerere has declared his wish to leave the presidency by 1985, when elections are scheduled. However, if he is still alive and in good health the personal legitimacy of Nyerere himself, rather than the constitutional rules, may be the deciding factor in an orderly succession. Such was the case in Senegal, where Senghor took the step – extremely unusual in African politics – of voluntarily resigning his office on December 31, 1980, and passing it on to his prime minister and protégé, Abdou Diouf. The succession had the quality of being orchestrated by Senghor insofar as he had arranged a revision of the constitution in 1976 to make the prime minister, who is appointed by the president, the automatic successor to the presidency.[49] Senghor's example may have been followed by Ahmadou Ahidjo, the autocratic ruler of the Cameroons for more than two decades, who resigned from the presidency in November 1982 and was succeeded by his own nominee, prime minister Paul Biya.[50] Therefore, the Senegalese and Cameroonian successions more nearly correspond to the model of the 'dauphin,' in which the ruler manipulates constitutional procedures to arrange for a successor of his own choosing, than to the model of a fully institutional succession. The dauphin model was also apparent in Gabon, where ailing President Leon M'Ba created a vice-presidency in 1966, designated its incumbent the rightful successor, and appointed a loyal and capable lieutenant, Bongo, to the post. (Bongo became president in 1967).

Conditions of personal rule

In conclusion, let us explore two questions. First, what conditions appear to be the most important in encouraging and sustaining the practices of personal governance in sub-Saharan Africa? All political systems are provisional; they are all built on sand, not on the rock of Gibraltar. Personal rule is no exception. It is dependent on the inclination and ability of people, particularly politicians, to understand and utilize its practices. Second, since personal rule is the converse of institutional government and since political institutions in the great majority of sub-Saharan countries are present formally as abstract rules but not substantively as effective restraints on political behavior, it is important to ask what conditions discourage the realization of concrete political institutions in these countries and what the prospects are of changing them.

Neither of these questions is easy to answer, and we have the space to offer only some suggestions as to the direction in which we believe answers might be found. It is somewhat easier to conjecture an answer to the first question because the practices of personal rule are essentially pragmatic and can be understood in terms of a rational politician who must operate in a country in which state institutions are merely forms and duties other than those of his office compete with self-interest as a claim to his conduct. In other words, the practices of personal rule are the sort in which a rational politician would engage if he found himself in a world in which the official rules and regulations of the state were not well understood or appreciated and were poorly enforced, and if he knew that others were aware of this and were not likely to conform to the rules in their own conduct. In such circumstances political and administrative conduct would be shaped by a combination of expediency and whatever obligations were owed to family, friends, allies, clansmen, tribesmen, and any other moral community to which an actor belonged. Most African politicians and administrators find themselves in more or less such circumstances.

At the center of any answer to the second question there must be an explanation as to why personal, arbitrary rule has not been widely condemned as political misconduct in sub-Saharan Africa. Why has personal rule not become sufficiently established as misconduct to effectively discourage the kinds of practices that we have reviewed in this essay and to encourage the realization of institutional rules and regulations? These questions are difficult to formulate, let alone answer, but if an answer is to be found, it will probably be connected with the widely acknowledged arbitrariness of most African states and its political and sociological roots.

In political terms, almost every sub-Saharan African state was the successor of a geographically identical, preexisting colonial entity. From the perspective of the European colonial powers a colony was not arbitrary. It was an extension of the sovereignty of the metropole, and its officials were subject to imperial policy and colonial regulations; far from being arbitrary rulers, colonial officials were considered responsible servants. However, from the perspective of subject Africans, colonial government was essentially arbitrary. It was imposed from outside and worked in accordance with alien and unfamiliar rules and regulations, in disregard, often in ignorance, of indigenous institutions. The British in effect acknowledged that colonial rule was arbitrary in their practice of indirect rule, but even indirect rule could not cancel the fundamental political reality that colonialism was essentially the imposition of government by an external, superior power.

The African states were arbitrary entities in sociological terms as well. It is well known that the size and shape of almost every sub-Saharan country was the result of boundaries arbitrarily drawn by colonialists who rarely acknowledged, or were not even aware of, the preexisting boundaries of traditional African societies. (Even if they had been aware of such boundaries, the traditional political systems were usually too small to be viable as separate colonial entities.) Consequently, there were no territory-wide traditional institutions that could be resurrected at independence and used to identify legitimate conduct and condemn misconduct by a state's new rulers. (It must be acknowledged that even if such institutions had existed, most of the new leaders, who were usually intellectuals, would very likely have been as hostile to them as they were to the traditional institutions that existed at the sub-national level. However, in some cases such institutions might have been sufficiently strong to command the reluctant compliance of the new rulers.)

Sociologically, most African countries are multi-ethnic societies with populations that are sharply divided along racial, cultural, linguistic, religious, and similar lines of cleavage. Most are composed of several and some of many different traditional societies, each with distinctive institutions to which members of other traditional societies are not only detached but also disinclined, if not actually opposed. Multi-ethnic societies are not confined to sub-Saharan Africa, but they appear to be a characteristic of most new states. Roth suggests that

> one of the major reasons for the predominance of personal rulership over legal-rational legislation and administration in the new states seems to lie in a social, cultural, and political homogeneity of such magnitude that a more or less viable complementary and countervailing pluralism of the Western type, with its strong but not exclusive components of universality, does not appear feasible.[51]

Roth sees the divided plural society as an impediment to the realization of modern, rational-legal institutions. But it is no less an impediment to the realization of traditional institutions or any other kind of general political institutions. All institutions that are realized in conduct must rest upon some kind of general understanding and acknowledgment by most of the people who live under them.

The attempts by the colonial authorities – very belated in the case of Belgium and Spain, and scarcely undertaken in the case of Portugal – to introduce modern political institutions as an essential stage of decolonization were not successful owing to the political and sociological impediments we have noted. British parliamentarianism and French republicanism were as alien to most Africans as colonial bureaucracy. Indeed, they were probably more difficult to understand since they are inherently less pragmatic and rational and more exotic and ritualistic in their rules and offices. It is easy for the forms and rites of (for example) parliamentary government to be mistaken for its substance, which is what happened not infrequently in some African countries before the forms too were discarded or fundamentally altered to suit the interests of those in power.

Imported European political institutions had no greater inherent capacity to overcome the centrifugal effects of sub-Saharan Africa's multi-ethnic societies than did any other institutions. The British were sensitive to this sociological problem, as indicated by their preference both for bicameral legislatures (with upper chambers to give representation to traditional rulers) and for federalism. Nonetheless, the checkered history of federalism in Nigeria, where politicians have striven to make it work, suggests that federalism, like any other national political institution, requires a commitment of the parts for the whole, of the whole for the parts, and of each part for each other part. In no sub-Saharan country to date has federalism proved to be a workable and durable institutional arrangement, although the Nigerians must be given full marks for persevering in efforts to make it a reality and not merely a formality in their political life. In short, the borrowing of institutional forms from abroad – even the most widely admired models – in no way guarantees their substantiation in political conduct.

In regard to changing the conditions that presently encourage personal rule and obstruct the realization of institutional government in sub-Saharan Africa, there seems to be very little prospect, if any, of altering the political and sociological conditions mentioned above, at least in the short and medium terms. Such fundamental change is a long-term historical process. But if institutional development is to occur in the foreseeable future, it will very likely begin at the top and not at the bottom of African political systems. It is not inconceivable – and there is some evidence to support the contention – that rulers and other leading politicians might begin to value the limited security of official tenure more highly than the uncertain possession of personal power and, beyond this, the greater stability and order attainable only under institutional government. Periodic attempts to reconstitutionalize some states which had been ruled by soldiers, as in Ghana (1969 and 1979), Nigeria (1979), and Upper Volta (1978), are evidence. However, wholesale attempts at constitutional engineering hold out less promise of success owing precisely to their very ambitious character: they literally ask leaders and their followers to transform their political attitudes and behavior overnight. Institutionalization in politics is a transformation involving piecemeal social engineering and time.[52]

A less improbable course of political institutionalization in sub-Saharan Africa is the incremental steps taken by some rulers and their associates to find acceptable and workable procedures to organize political competition and to prevent violence and other political evils. Constitutional rules of succession tend to be accepted for preventive reasons: leaders who face the prospect of a succession may fear the threat of uncertainty, dislocation, violence, bloodshed, and other hazards more than they desire the prize of becoming the successor or his associate. This 'negative' political rationality, which we usually associate with the political theory of Hobbes, is also evident in electoral institutionalization in sub-Saharan Africa.[53] For example, in Senegal under the prudent and judicious rule of Senghor the one-party system was liberalized in the late 1970s to allow other parties to compete openly with Senghor's party, but only under labels approved by the regime with Senghor's party preempting the most popular 'democratic socialist' label. This experiment in 'guided' democratization apparently reflected Senghor's conviction that a de facto one-party system – such as had existed from 1963 to 1976 in Senegal, with its numerous and various ethnic and ideological tendencies – invited conspiratorial politics and threatened national stability.[54] But the success of Senegalese liberalization to date probably must be attributed to Senghor and to his successor, President Abdou Diouf, who in 1981 accepted the challenge of governing a multi-party democracy.

Senegal is a fascinating experiment in moving from a party monopoly to a multi-party state and would reward study by political scientists who are interested in political institutionalization. But to date it is unique and has not inspired imitation by other African rulers. A more typical path of electoral development in sub-Saharan Africa is the encouragement of institutionalized competition within a ruling party. Kenya and Tanzania are good examples of this tendency. Kenya is probably the most unrestricted of Africa's one-party democracies, where elections regularly result in a high level of participation and a large turnover of elected politicians. In the November 1979 general election, more than 740 candidates competed for 158 elected parliamentary seats in the national assembly; seventy-two incumbent MPs, including seven ministers and fifteen assistant ministers, were defeated.[55] Similar results have occurred in previous Kenyan elections and also in Tanzanian elections, although the latter are more strictly controlled and do not exhibit the freewheeling character of Kenyan one-party democracy. Neither of these countries has suffered a successful military coup, which reinforces our impression that they have established the beginnings of a democratic tradition during their two decades of independence. The Kenyan experiment is the more impressive of the two, since that country has also experienced a presidential succession following the death of the founding father, Jomo Kenyatta, in 1978. Nyerere has been at the helm since Tanzania's independence in 1961 and lends his personal authority to that country's political procedures. The real test for the Tanzanian experiment will occur after Nyerere exits from the political stage that he has dominated for so long. These experiments in expanded political choice have more recently encouraged others in Zambia, Ivory Coast, Sierra Leone, Malawi, and Gabon. This may indicate that one-party democracy is better suited than multi-party democracy to the personal and communal idioms of African politics.

These African political experiments suggest the following conclusions, one practical and the other theoretical. First, democracy can be promoted by inventive political practitioners as well as by favorable socio-economic processes, and the former do not necessarily have to wait upon the latter. Statesmen are to political development what entrepreneurs are to economic development. Indeed, they may be more important insofar as political development is less dependent on material resources and consists essentially in appropriate inclinations and conduct. Political development may be within the reach of countries such as those in sub-Saharan Africa, which are as yet too poor in resources to achieve much in the way of substantial economic development. Second, politics can therefore be understood theoretically as a (constructive and destructive) human activity as well as an impersonal process, and can be studied profitably in terms of choice, will, action, opposition, obligation, compulsion, persuasion, possession, and other elements of individual and intersocial volition, that is, in terms of neo-classical political theory.

Notes

* Please note that original footnote numbering has been retained.

[32] For an interesting analysis of the necessity of pragmatism or prudence in politics, see R. L. Nichols and D. M. White, 'Politics Proper: On Action and Prudence,' *Ethics*, 89 (July 1979), 372–84.

[33] W. J. M. Mackenzie, *Politics and Social Science* (Harmondsworth: Penguin Books, 1967), p. 347.

[34] Ibid.

[35] See Ladipo Adamolekun in *Afriscope*, 5 (March 1975) 45.

[36] See especially Samuel P. Huntington, *Political Order in Changing Societies* (New Haven: Yale University Press, 1968), ch. 2; Claude E. Welch, Jr., 'Soldier and State in Africa,' *Journal of Modern African Studies*, 5 (November 1967), 305–22; and Samuel Decalo, *Coups and Army Rule in Africa: Studies in Military Style* (New Haven: Yale University Press, 1976).

[37] See, for example, Donal B. Cruise O'Brien, *Saints and Politicians: Essays in the Organization of a Senegalese Peasant Society* (London: Cambridge University Press, 1975); Jonathan S. Barker, 'Political Factionalism in Senegal,' *Canadian Journal of African Studies*, 7 (1973), 287–303; J. M.

Lee, 'Clan Loyalties and Socialist Doctrine in the People's Republic of Congo,' *The World Today*, 27 (January 1971) 40–46; Dennis L. Dresang, 'Ethnic Politics, Representative Bureaucracy and Development Administration: The Zambian Case,' *American Political Science Review*, 68 (December 1974), 1605–17; and Richard Stren, 'Factional Politics and Control in Mombasa, 1960–1969,' *Canadian Journal of African Studies*, 4 (Winter 1970), 33–56.

38 O'Brien p. 149.

39 See Carl H. Lande, 'The Dyadic Basis of Clientelism,' in Schmidt et al., eds., pp. xiii–xxxvii.

40 Huntington, pp. 59–71.

41 For two explanations of the attractions of corruption as a practice, see Opoku Acheampong, 'Corruption: A Basis for Security?,' *West Africa* (January 5, 1976); and 'The Battle of Corruption,' *ibid*. (February 8, 1982). For an excellent case study from which many generalizations can be drawn, see Victor T. LeVine, *Political Corruption: The Ghana Case* (Stanford: Hoover Institution, 1975).

42 Colin Legum, ed. *Africa Contemporary Record: Annual Survey and Documents, 1971–72* (New York: Africana Publishing Co., 1972), p. B653.

43 Ghislain C. Kabwit, 'Zaire: The Roots of the Continuing Crisis,' *Journal of Modern African Studies*, 17 (1979), 397.

44 See Crawford Young, 'Zaire: The Unending Crisis,' *Foreign Affairs*, 57 (Fall 1978), 173; and 'Political and Economic Situation in Zaire – Fall 1981,' Hearing before the Subcommittee on Africa of the Committee on Foreign Affairs, House of Representatives, September 15, 1981 (Washington, D.C.: U.S. Government Printing Offce, 1982), esp. pp. 4–6.

45 Kabwit, 'Zaire: The Roots of the Continuing Crisis,' p. 399.

46 See David E. Apter, *Ghana in Transition*, 2nd ed. (Princeton: Princeton University Press, 1972), p. 348.

47 See Legum, ed., *Africa Contemporary Record, 1973-74*, pp. B210–11; and ibid., 1974.

48 See ibid., 1975-76, p. B471.

49 See the account in ibid., 1980–81, pp. B592–93.

50 *Africa Research Bulletin: Political, Social, and Cultural Series*, 19 (December 15, 1982), 6647C–6650B.

51 Guenther Roth, 'Personal Rulership, Patrimonialism, Empire-Building in New States,' *World Politics*, 20 (January 1968), 203.

52 Huntington, pp. 13-14; and Karl Popper, *The Open Society and Its Enemies*, vol. I (Princeton: Princeton University Press, 1967).

53 Thomas Hobbes, *Leviathan*, ed. by Michael Oakeshott (New York: Collier Books, 1962), chs. 13 and 17.

54 See a seminal article by William J. Foltz, 'Social Structure and Political Behavior of Senegalese Elites,' in Schmidt et al., eds, pp. 242–49.

55 *African Research Bulletin: Political, Social, and Cultural Series*, 16 (December 15, 1979), 5466.

ROBERT FATTON Jr
Bringing the Ruling Class Back In

Reference
Comparative Politics, 20/3, 1988, pp. 253–64.

The vital role which the state plays in postcolonial and late industrializing nations has generated a vast literature on the nature, scope, and function of state activities. The state is increasingly portrayed as a bureaucratic apparatus of domination endowed with an autonomy of its own as well as with its own material interests and political agenda. In this literature the state is no longer an agent of social classes; it no longer reflects their relative power; the state is now above society and struggling against society itself.[1] A certain conceptualization goes as far as to contend that the state is capable of opposing antagonistically and frontally the fundamental interests of the ruling class.[2] Thus, for this conceptualization the state is not just relatively autonomous from ruling classes, it challenges their domination, threatens their supremacy, and transcends their structural power. This article contends that such a conceptualization is seriously flawed.

While it is true that in exceptional situations the state may achieve a relative autonomy from the ruling class, it constitutes and is bound to constitute in a class society the ultimate organizer and defender of the long-term interests of the ruling class.[3] The existence of a ruling class implies necessarily the existence of a state whose role is to preserve and reproduce the social, political, and economic structures of the ruling class's dominance. This is not to say that the state can effectively fulfill this role. It may be constrained by the ruling class itself and/or transnational agents, and/or it may be challenged by the subordinate classes. Indeed, in Africa ruling classes have demonstrated an inordinate capacity to 'mess up' and to undermine their very rule. This is not surprising however. African ruling classes are in the process of 'becoming.' They lack hegemony, and they are likely to be fragmented and hesitant about their interests and aspirations. Their ability to engage in coherent and sustained collective action is thus limited, uncertain, and contradictory. In this perspective, the extent to which the state can protect successfully the position of the ruling class, that is, the extent to which the state is an effective state, is directly dependent on the degree of hegemony which the ruling class itself has achieved.[4] Thus, to make sense of the state is to decipher the relations of class power, the processes of class formation, and the hegemonic propensity of the ruling class. Before 'bringing the state back in,' it is crucial to proceed to 'bringing classes back in.'

The aim of this paper is to do precisely that in the political context of Africa. Special attention is paid to the hegemonic projects of the ruling class. It will be argued that ruling classes exist throughout Africa but that they have yet to become hegemonic. Their domination and their rule express more the threat and use of direct violence than their moral, material, and intellectual leadership. Politics is not consensual but Hobbesian, and the rule of the ruling class is not democratic but dictatorial. Thus, the absence of hegemonic ruling classes explains African despotism. It is suggested also that this absence of hegemony limits the relative autonomy of the African state. African ruling classes are ruling classes because they control the state and use it as a political and material apparatus to further their narrow corporate interests. In other words, the state in Africa is the prime instrument with which a class can hope to become a ruling class. To be absent from the state is to be condemned to a subordinate and inferior status. In Africa, class power is state power; the two are fused and inseparable.[5]

Hegemony and ruling class in Africa

The nonhegemonic character of African ruling classes has compelled them to take direct charge of the state itself, to staff it, and consequently to obliterate the political space required for the effective exercise of statecraft. Paradoxically, because state power and class power are one, the state has lacked the relative autonomy necessary to effect those reforms and concessions necessary for the preservation of the rule of the ruling class. With their eyes fixed on immediate and selfish interests and their hands in direct control of the levers of the state apparatus, African ruling classes have been unable to take the long view and organize in an appropriately flexible way the conditions of their own continued dominance. Because those staffing the main agencies of the state form the ruling class, and are part of the ruling class by virtue of this very fact, their relative independence in deciding how to serve the long-term interest of their own class is seriously inhibited.

The nonhegemonic status of African ruling classes deprives the state of the relative autonomy that makes reform possible, despotism unnecessary, and liberal democracy viable. The state is almost exclusively an authoritarian structure of dominance; expressing the narrow corporate interests of the ruling class, it has failed to become integral. The integral state is the state of a hegemonic ruling class and as such is capable of 'expansion.'[6] It is capable of integrating and coopting into its own institutions potential allies and even antagonistic elements. The integral state is thus relatively autonomous since it can extract certain sacrifices from the ruling class and make certain concessions to popular classes. The integral state, however, is not above society; it is integral precisely because the ruling class has achieved hegemony. In other words, the integral state can emerge only when the ruling class has consolidated its rule to a point where its material, intellectual, and moral leadership is unquestioned or at least consensually accepted by the subordinate classes. Thus, hegemony makes possible the integral state.

In African conditions, where hegemony is nonexistent or embryonic, the state is not likely to take seriously into account the interests of those classes over which the ruling class seeks to impose its domination and authority. Not surprisingly, the rule of most African ruling classes is authoritarian, brutal, and violent. Compliance is the result of coercion and not consensus, and popular resistance is seldom frontal and revolutionary. Resistance takes the form of withdrawal from the public realm rather than confrontational assaults against the state. 'Exit' is the preferred means of voicing discontent since it does not necessarily provoke the immediate exercise of state repression.[7] Exit demonstrates also that African ruling classes are nonhegemonic: they are unable to penetrate certain popular political and economic spaces which exist independent of state authority.

The study of the state presupposes, therefore, the analysis of classes, and in particular the degree of hegemony which the ruling class has attained. It is hegemony, or the lack of it, which determines the nature of the state and the scope of its autonomy. Instead of approaching politics from a 'state-centered model,' this paper seeks to reaffirm the primacy of class in the shaping of society and in the authoritative allocation of values. To do otherwise is to assume that the state can stand undisturbed above society and impose in an antagonistic manner its own policies and its own preferences on a recalcitrant ruling class. It is to assume that the ruling class can exist without ruling; it is to assume that the ruling class does not exist at all.

In reality, the state is neither a balloon floating freely in midair, nor an omnipotent autonomous organism. It is grounded in class processes and practices; it is ligatured to the exercise of class domination. This is particularly so in Africa where an intense and accelerated process of class formation is taking place. While still fragile and weak, African ruling classes are clearly discernible. Their conspicuous life styles and life chances distinguish them from the vast majority living in poverty. Irving Leonard Markovitz defines them as an 'organizational bourgeoisie:' 'a combined ruling group consisting of the top political leaders and bureaucrats, the traditional rulers and their descendants, the leading members of the liberal professions, the rising business bourgeoisie, and the top members of the military and police forces.'[8] Markovitz then argues that the members of the organizational bourgeoisie are 'located at pivotal points of control in those overarching systems of political, social and economic power ... the nation-state and capitalism.'[9] They have integrated the private and public spheres into their own corporate domain for the advancement of their productive and political power.

This power is inextricably tied to their control of the state. Class power in Africa is fundamentally dependent on state power. Capturing the state is the best and perhaps exclusive means for acquiring and generating the material wealth necessary for becoming a ruling class. The absence of a hegemonic African bourgeoisie, grounded in a solid and independent economic base and successfully engaged in the private accumulation of capital, has transformed politics into material struggle. State power provides the fundamental opportunity to build class power in a context of great and increasing scarcity. Not surprisingly, once an incipient ruling class takes over the state, it monopolizes it for its exclusive material and political gain and uses it for the violent exclusion of potential rival groups. In this sense the power holders inside the state constitute the dominant fraction of the African ruling class, but they are a dominant fraction in formation, *in statu nascendi*, and accordingly they rule without having achieved hegemony. As Frederick Cooper has remarked, '[African ruling classes may] be better defined by their "project" than by their current situation.... But it is not a project that has been altogether successful....'[10]

The fragility of the ruling classes' project is directly related to the peripheral nature of African societies.[11] The dependent and backward character of African capitalism has contributed to the material and hegemonic fragility of most African bourgeoisies and thus to authoritarian political forms of governance. Such authoritarian forms, however, mask the ruling classes' relative incapacity to transform their power into effective political, economic, and cultural policies. The African state has yet to develop the means and resources with which to penetrate all the sectors of society. Authoritarianism coexists therefore with a definite lack of authority. This paradox of African politics can be partly explained by the articulation of different modes of production.

In this perspective Goran Hyden has introduced the concept of an 'uncaptured peasantry' capable of resisting and neutralizing state policies.[12] The uncaptured peasantry operates its own 'peasant mode of production' as a separate material and institutional structure. Such a structure constitutes the 'economy of affection' which represents an alternative 'space' to the dominant state system. In other words, this alternative space allows the peasantry to 'exit' from the demands and policies formulated by central political authorities. Thus, in Hyden's perspective, the state is incapable of sustaining and reproducing existing social relations and specifically of controlling the labor force in the interest of any program of economic growth. Suspended in midair, without roots in a strong, indigenous bourgeoisie and without the power to enforce the systemic and authoritative allocation of values, the state is 'soft' and impotent. As a result, the vast majority of the population, the peasantry, has the option of rejecting its integration in the state system; it remains 'uncaptured.' And precisely because it can choose to remain uncaptured, it promotes the continued survival of the economy of affection as an alternative mode of production to the macro-economic program of the state. In Hyden's view, then, the peasant mode of production challenges and erodes the implantation of modern industrial structures and sustains traditional economic methods and ideologies. In this respect, the softness of the state represents a serious constraint on the overall development of African societies. No social class is powerful enough to impose its hegemony and construct an effective and productive economic system.

For Hyden, therefore, African politics is a politics without ruling classes and a politics marked by the absence of institutionalized power.[13] This, however, does not preclude the existence of authoritarianism, dictatorial rule, and tyranny. Paradoxically, as Hyden himself acknowledges, the soft state creates the perfect terrain for these arbitrary and violent forms of governance.

The question this inevitably implies is, why and how can the state unleash its arbitrary violence particularly against the lower and working strata of the population if its stands in midair uncontrolled by any ruling class? Hence the important issue is not whether the state is soft, but whether it is soft for or harsh against particular groups and classes. In short, who benefits best from the softness of the state? It is true that in most African countries social discipline is weak and power lacks institutionalization, but this general systemic weakness favors in disproportionate ways the interests of the privileged ruling circles. In fact, the soft state is neither neutral nor in midair. It unleashes its power, often violently, to defend the interests of the dominant faction of the ruling class. It depoliticizes the subaltern groups by eliminating their independent organs of representation and by reducing their participation in decision making. The emergence of the one-party state throughout Africa is the means to these ends. In addition, the one-party state is the vehicle through which material resources are acquired and distributed, since the state in Africa is the fundamental agent of capital accumulation and extraction. In these circumstances, it is not surprising that the struggle for control of the state, in conditions of monolithic political structures and generalized material scarcity, becomes Hobbesian, violent, and deadly.

Such a situation of political insecurity has transformed the one-party state into a system breeding disorder rather than order. This in turn has generated a process of escalating repression as those ruling the state have sought to maintain and preserve their absolute monopoly of power. Political instability in Africa is therefore rooted more in the extreme politicization of the state as an organ to be monopolized for absolute power and accelerated economic advancement than in the softness of the state as Hyden would have it. To characterize the state as being soft is to miss the class relationships and class struggles that provide the social context which molds and shapes the state itself. Thus, if the state in Africa is relatively weak in terms of its capacity to impose its authority on all sectors of society, it is nonetheless powerful enough to unleash its violence against particular groups and classes. The relative impotence of the state to enforce its own rules is biased impotence. It is an impotence that consistently favors and enhances the power, interests, and status of the well-off and privileged classes.

This is not to say that the organization, modalities, and efficiency of the state embody the most rational and paradigmatic representation of ruling class interests. Far from it, the African state is still incapable of taking charge, as it were, of the ruling class's political interests and hence of establishing its autonomy. This is why ruling class power in Africa is expressed in terms of state power. The nonhegemonic character of African ruling classes impels them to seize state power as the means of constructing their class power. The fusion of state power and class power precludes the development of the political space required for the crystallization of compromises between dominant and dominated classes. Liberal democratic practices are thus impossible. To survive and avoid catastrophe, dominated classes are forced to seek refuge in their 'exit' from political society. They move into those spaces of civil society that have yet to be fully captured by the ruling classes. This is not to imply that such spaces exist independent of the ruling class, but rather that they are tolerated by the ruling class because they paradoxically represent sources of ruling class power.

In this instance it is significant to note the benign opposition of the state towards the illegal acquisition and reproduction of wealth through the rapidly expanding black markets of Africa. The phenomenon of the black market economy known as the *magendo* in East Africa indicates that the softness of the state is more a symptom of ruling class interests than institutional weakness and fragility. The *magendo* persists because it serves the material and political purposes of the ruling class. It constitutes a source of wealth and a means of ascending to membership in the ruling class. Accordingly, the *magendo* depends inevitably on the power holders for its continued survival and expansion in spite of its autonomy from the formal structures of state power. The state will not close down the *magendo* operations because they are too profitable for both state agents and *magendo* entrepreneurs. As Nelson Kasfir has remarked in his study of Uganda:

> … neither the Amin nor the interim post-liberation govern-ments acted to plug [*magendo*] loopholes, presumably because civil servants from top to bottom were highly conscious of their vested interest in permitting the state to maintain them. As *magendo* operators moved into legitimate economic sectors, their involvement with state officials would necessarily have had to grow more extensive. The operation of *magendo* in Uganda was significantly dependent on and continued to be related to the state.[14]

In contrast to this symbiotic relationship between state and *magendo*, the state-peasant relationship, in spite of the peasant's capacity to exit, has been characterized by domination and subordination. Indeed, the fact that peasants enjoy certain means of exit from governmental policies should not conceal the negative and pervasive impact of the state on their livelihood and mode of production. The peasants' exit is a choice of last resort, reflecting their desire to avoid the adverse effects of official policies. It is not an indication of the peasants' victorious independence from state interference. The peasants withdraw from the public realm precisely because of the harshness of state decisions. Thus, the exit of the peasantry is more a symptom of the hard-centered nature of the state than of its softness. As Robert Bates has argued:

> The fact is that the peasants avoid the state by taking refuge in alternatives that are clearly second best. They move out of the production of the crops that are most profitable and into economic activities that have become more profitable only because they are less heavily taxed. In thus changing the way they employ their resources, they incur economic losses.[15]

In this sense, while the state may be soft in so far as it is incapable of both enforcing the totality of its authority on all sectors of society and penetrating effectively all the realms of social activity, it is not uniformly soft in its impact on the different social classes. The concept of the soft state is therefore misleading because it masks the authoritarian character of most African states and the uneven and biased impact of state intervention. In this instance it is preferable to allude to Gramsci's notion of the integral state, a state which crystallizes the 'organic relations between ... political society and "civil society".'[16]

Because the African state has yet to become integral, the ruling classes have failed to obtain the 'spontaneous' consent of the masses to the general direction they wish to impose on society. In these circumstances social discipline and order are imposed by direct domination on those who do not consent either actively or passively to the rule of the governing classes. Thus, while the state cannot effectively expand the domain of its authority to obtain the obedience of all its subjects, it has the capacity to crush fundamental political challenges. Thus, the state may lack the power to eliminate all existing means of exit, but it possesses sufficient coercive might to repress serious contending and opposing 'voices.'[17] In fact, the means of exit represent a safety valve for the continued survival of most African political systems. Exit embodies the safest and most profitable expression of discontent as the popular articulation of voices is much too costly and dangerous in the African context of authoritarian, one-party states.

In Africa most ruling classes have restricted so stringently the level of voice that the masses have found in exit the only means of expressing their opposition without risking the brutal suffering of state repression. Hence it is the incapacity of the ruling classes to tolerate and institutionalize a relatively high level of voice which has paradoxically contributed to the development and persistence of exit. Such an incapacity indicates the ruling classes' failure to control, shape, and guide political participation; it is symptomatic of their nonhegemonic status. African ruling classes have been unable to impose their "intellectual and moral leadership;" they have been besieged by a continuous and persistent "crisis of authority." They lack the necessary legitimacy to establish an integral state which can command obedience without the pervasive use of force.[18]

This absence of legitimacy has stemmed in great part from the ruling classes' peripheral and weak position in the world of production. The stagnating, declining, and dependent nature of most African economies has imposed obdurate limitations on the hegemonic capacities of these ruling classes. The conquest of state power has yet to generate the hegemonic mechanisms of class power. Paradoxically this has resulted in both the emergence and decay of authoritarian regimes. The African ruling classes' incapacity to transform effectively their state power into class power has created the terrain for violent and often mutually destructive confrontations between contending fractions vying for domination. In this instance the state may move toward autonomization to prevent the catastrophic explosion of internecine class struggles resulting from the absence of a hegemonic class power.

Such internecine class struggles are conducive to the emergence of Caesarism whereby 'a great personality is entrusted with the task of arbitration over a historico-political situation characterized by an equilibrium of forces heading towards catastrophe.'[19] In this perspective, the role of personalities, the nature of leadership, and the talents of specific individuals have a significant impact on the making of African politics. Historical figures do emerge and do make choices.[20] They have opportunities that they can seize, and they can open doors to new alternatives. At each juncture there is some room for choice. Caesarism can therefore reinvigorate the rule of the ruling class by paradoxically distancing the ruling class itself from the direct and unmediated exercise of state power. An autonomous political space is thus created in which a Caesar can maneuver his statecraft and individual *virtù*. But statecraft and *virtù*, choice and leadership are all decisively molded and limited by the processes of class formation, the fluidity of the class structure, and the power of class interests. As Marx remarked long ago, 'Men make their own history, but they do not make it just as they please; they do not make it under circumstances chosen by themselves, but under circumstances directly found, given and transmitted from the past.'[21]

This is why, as Callaghy has convincingly argued in his study of Mobutu's Zaire, Bonaparte rules in Africa without Bonapartism.

> Absolutism ... fits the conditions of Mobutu's Zaire more closely than Bonapartism primarily because socioeconomic and class development are much less advanced and patrimonial forms of politics, leadership, and administration are more important than in Bonapartism. Above all, the class situation is simply more fluid, more in flux, under absolutism ... than it is under ... Bonapartism.... Political, territorial, and above all administrative unity and centralization are still being struggled for, are still problematic, under absolutism while they are assured and assumed characteristics under Bonapartism.[22]

What exists in Africa are thus absolutist forms of governance in which presidential monarchs maintain their patrimonial power through the illegal appropriation of massive state revenues. Corruption is therefore the rampant and pervasive cement binding the monarch to his loyal followers in a predatory ruling class.

Class, patrons, and clients

Corruption in turn leads to the creation of patron–client networks. These networks reflect great inequalities of exchange and thoroughly lopsided structures of power. Patron–client relationships form bonds of coercive dependence rather than ties of genuine reciprocity. Coercive dependence, however, does not entail nor necessarily call forth the consciousness of suffering exploitation or a sense of moral outrage. Patron–client relationships have routinized and legitimized coercive dependence by projecting it as a form of benevolent paternalism; they have established the moral authority of obedience and stifled the sense of injustice. They have frozen the emergence of class conflict and enshrined as natural the existing hierarchy of domination and subordination.[23]

This is so because patron–client relationships prevent the political organization of subordinate classes as classes by maintaining and accentuating their isolation, individualization, and ethnic attachments. On the other hand, they unify the dominant classes by linking them into a framework of cooperation closely associated to the state. In this sense, patron–client relationships integrate the patrons into, and exclude the clients from, the centers of national power.

The individualized and ethnically determined bonds of patron-client relationships should not mask, however, the more pervasive and profound reality of class domination. As Crawford Young has pointed out:

> [The] intensity of ethnic conflict exists despite the fact that inequality is much more clearly linked to social class – where it is indeed axiomatic. Ethnic inequality, on the other hand, is largely in the eye of the beholder. A belief that ethnic inequality exists can gain currency when substantial numbers of elite members of a given group become highly visible. In reality, the great majority of members of all groups are poor, and the social advantage of a given ethnic community is usually quite relative.[24]

In addition to blurring class differentiations, patron–client relationships are also processes of resource extraction and capital accumulation. Their economic structures and paternalistic ethos strengthen and enhance the material and political power of the patrons. Thus, patron–client relationships are means of political control and financial aggrandizement.[25] Indeed, the relatively peaceful extraction of the economic surplus from the masses for the benefit of a privileged and small state bureaucracy rests on the maintenance of the personalistic and individualized bonds of dependence that clientelism entails and nurtures. Clientelism also generates certain factional divisions within the ruling class as different sections of this class struggle over the spoils of political power in their effort to build popular followings. These divisions, however, are contained within a common framework of understanding and interests, and they do not stem from principled political options and commitments. As Richard Sandbrook put it, 'Factionalism is a form of conflict over access to wealth, power, and status, frequently with only minor ideological and policy implications in which members of the conflict units are recruited on the basis of mercenary ties.'[26]

In addition, factionalism is inherently unstable as clients are always prepared to shift their allegiances to the highest bidder and to the patron best suited to defend their collective and individual interests. Accordingly, clients are continuously calculating which patrons are most effective in representing their demands and in articulating their grievances. Similarly, patrons are permanently struggling for the influence and means necessary to maintain and expand their following. Patron–client relationships are therefore based more on self-interest than on the principles of the collective good. In these circumstances, the competition for power breeds nepotism and corruption at the highest political levels. A widespread cynicism undermines developmental goals and makes a mockery of the leadership's demands for hard work and sacrifices. The result is the unethical and factional quest for acquiring and monopolizing the vital administrative resources of the state.[27] Indeed, the state itself becomes the superpatron of society, or, to put it more precisely, its top bureaucratic managers are the ultimate and decisive builders of clienteles.

As builders of clienteles, the managers of the state can develop political bases and control the regional and sectoral allocation of resources. Such control confers on them the capacity to penetrate at least indirectly the peripheral areas of society. The penetration, however, can hardly be rationalized since it is mediated by local notables who depend on patronage itself to maintain their status and wield effective authority. Not surprisingly, the consolidation of state power is constrained by the serious limitations of peripheral clientelism and by the necessity of strengthening this very periphery to counterbalance urban unrest and disaffection.[28]

As a result, the conflicts between the modernizers of the center and the traditionalists of the periphery tend to lose their intensity since they are completely subordinated to the imperatives of political stability and order. Moreover, the traditionalists are not necessarily threatened by the implantation of a new mode of governance; in fact they have always manipulated such implantation by inserting it into their own modified structure of dominance. Accordingly, the traditionalists are not inherently opposed to change; what they seek is to direct and control it in the interest of consolidating and expanding their own privileged position. They form therefore a conservative class, a class that knows that its economic and political power depends on modernizing tradition. To this extent, central and peripheral ruling classes are in symbiosis even if their objectives and policies differ in some instances.

Finally, patron–client relationships are also a manifestation of the patterns of dependence and misdevelopment characterizing the world capitalist economy. African ruling classes bent on preserving their status – in an environment of growing scarcity – are forced to rely on external capitalist forces to obtain more resources with which to finance their patronage. They are inevitably drawn into linkages of dependence on imperialist centers. As Kasfir explains:

> Without a source of external resources – or a locally controlled bonanza – patrimonial organization must squeeze subordinate classes in order to continue. Consequently, where the opportunity occurs, patrimonial states are likely to become more dependent on transnational corporations and international lending agencies. Demands for patronage, then, allow additional points of entry by external capitalist forces into African economies.[29]

Thus, the linkages of dependence and relative subservience to external forces from which African ruling classes derive part of their power are reproduced locally to preserve the highly unequal access to wealth and prestige. In turn, the domination of external forces in African societies is mediated through a structure of superordination and subordination embodied in patron–client relationships. In other words, the bonds between external and internal forces constitute a complex whole reflecting both the reality of the center's exploitation of Africa and the coincidence of interests between African ruling classes and their imperial patrons.

Such coincidence of interests is rooted in what may be called the cross-national instrumental friendship of ruling patrons. In this friendship each patron promotes the interests of the other even if some patrons are clearly more equal than others. The crucial question for the friendship is not whether it is thoroughly reciprocal, but whether it maintains the structures of the status quo at the national and international levels. It is true, however, that, the more 'peripheralized' a ruling class, the more difficult it is for it to establish its hegemony, and the more difficult it is for the state to achieve what I shall term a degree of transnational autonomy. By transnational autonomy I mean the capacity of both class and state power to be exercised without the interference of major international actors. In this sense, colonialism would be a situation *par excellence* in which transnational autonomy would be obliterated. Transnational autonomy is thus a function of a ruling class's dependence on external constellations of power: the greater such dependence, the more restrained and inhibited transnational autonomy is, and the more problematic it is for the ruling class to establish and consolidate any type of hegemony.

In spite of their great dependence on capitalist centers of dominance, African ruling classes have demonstrated a remarkable capacity to maintain a tolerable level of transnational autonomy. While they are junior partners to imperial bourgeoisies, African ruling classes have their own project and their own independent aspirations, to which they can give rein by manipulating existing conjunctures of dependence. As Young has remarked in his essay on Zaire:

> The very bonds of economic dependency have been used with virtuosity. The regime adroitly trades on the premise that its creditors cannot afford either to see it fall, or to see Mobutu fall. Bankruptcy would be as inconvenient for the banks as for Zaire; at each negotiating brink, a temporizing formula is found, the debt rolled over one more time, while all await the millennium of higher copper prices.[30]

The bilateral tension characterizing the relationship between African ruling classes and their external mentors creates the space in which the former can exercise their statecraft to expand the limits of their transnational autonomy. African politics and its associated processes of class formation and state building are therefore primarily determined by endogenous forces even if they are severely constrained by external constellations of power. While these endogenous forces are volatile, fluid, and in flux, they have solidified to the point where class differentiation and class conflicts are clearly identifiable. As Jan Vansina has put it, 'the closure of classes is becoming accentuated.'[31]

This closure of classes so pronounced in the life styles and life chances separating the affluent minority from the poor majority finds its full expression in the monopolization of state offices. Class power being state power, the premium on access to such offices is extremely high, and it is becoming increasingly denied to new aspirants. Accordingly, power holders have to rely on naked force to maintain their position of wealth, status, and prestige. In this sense, the state is not suspended in midair. The ruling classes use it to enforce the closure of classes.

Conclusions

In this article I have argued that the African state has a very limited organic autonomy because the ruling class is a ruling class in so far as it is capable of occupying directly the main offices of the state. The ruling class expresses its class power through its unmediated control of state power. This fusion of state and class power reflects the nonhegemonic character of the ruling class. Accordingly, coercion rather than persuasion, domination rather than leadership, and corruption rather than legitimacy constitute the stuff of African politics.

Finally, this article posits the need for a study of the state as an organ of domination ligatured to the hegemonic project of incipient ruling classes. The state, however autonomous it may be, cannot transcend the parameters of class power. In Africa it is the vehicle to attain such power, and the means to protect, maintain, and reproduce it.

Notes

I wish to acknowledge a summer grant from the University of Virginia, without which this research would have been impossible.

1 Thomas Callaghy. *The State–Society Struggle: Zaire in Comparative Perspective* (New York: Columbia University Press, 1984).
2 Fred Block, 'The Ruling Class Does Not Rule: Notes on the Marxist Theory of the State,' *Socialist Revolution*, 7 (1977), 6–28; Peter B. Evans, Dietrich Rueschemeyer, and Theda Skocpol, eds., *Bringing the State Back In* (Cambridge: Cambridge University Press, 1985); Eric A. Nordlinger, *On the Autonomy of the Democratic State* (Cambridge. Mass.: Harvard University Press, 1981). Nordlinger asserts (p. 203): 'the democratic state is frequently autonomous in translating its own preferences into authoritative actions, and markedly autonomous in doing so even when they diverge from those held by the politically weightiest groups in civil society.' Theda Skocpol, *States and Social Revolution* (Cambridge: Cambridge University Press, 1979); and 'Political Responses to Capitalist Crisis: Neo-Marxist Theories of the State and the Case of the New Deal,' *Politics and Society*, 10 (1981), 155–201. In this article Skocpol contends (pp. 199–200) that 'no existing neo-Marxist approach affords sufficient weight to state and party organizations as independent determinants of political conflicts and outcomes … so far, no self-declared neo-Marxist theory of the capitalist state has arrived at the point of taking state structures and party organizations seriously enough.'
3 Ralph Miliband, *Marxism and Politics* (New York: Oxford University Press, 1977): and *Class Power and State Power* (London: Verso Editions, 1983), pp. 3–78; Nicos Poulantzas, *Political Power and Social Classes* (London: Verso Editions, 1978): and *State, Power, Socialism* (London: Verso Editions, 1980). For a detailed analytical survey of studies on the state, see Martin Carnoy, *The State and Political Theory* (Princeton: Princeton University Press. 1984).
4 In this article, the term hegemony is used in its Gramscian connotation. As defined by Gramsci it is characterized by 'the "spontaneous" consent given by the great masses of the population to the general direction imposed on social life by the dominant fundamental group; this consent is "historically" caused by the prestige (and consequent confidence) which the dominant group enjoys because of its position and function in the world of production.' Antonio Gramsci, *Selections from the Prison Notebooks* (London: Lawrence and Wishan, 1971), p. 12. The question of hegemony, however, is not merely material stuff; it is also a politics of moral and intellectual leadership. To assert its hegemony, the ruling class must be able to defend its own corporate interests by universalizing them, by ensuring that these interests can 'become the interests of the … subordinate groups' (*ibid.*, p. 181). To this extent hegemony implies consent rather than domination, integration rather than exclusion and cooptation rather than suppression.
5 Miliband, *Class Power and State Power*, pp. 40-41.
6 A ruling class is hegemonic when it has established both its material dominance and its intellectual and moral leadership over society and when it succeeds in persuading subaltern classes that positions of subordination and superordination are just, proper, and legitimate. This requires that the ruling class be prepared to make certain concessions, which, while not fundamental, contribute to the political cooptation of popular sectors and the progressive expansion of the productive process. In this instance, as Gramsci points out, the ruling class 'really causes the entire society to move forward, not merely satisfying its own existential requirements, but continuously augmenting its cadres for the conquest of ever new spheres of economic and productive activity' (*Selections from the Prison Notebooks*, p. 60). This is the moment of 'historic unity' when

the ruling class has established its material, ethical, and political leadership over society and when the relationships of superordination and subordination are accepted by all as organic and not contradictory and as legitimate and not exploitative. When such a situation crystallizes, the ruling class has achieved what might be called paradigmatic hegemony.

[7] The notion of exit is developed in Albert Hirschman, *Essays in Trespassing: Economics to Politics and Beyond* (Cambridge: Cambridge University Press, 1981).

[8] Irving Leonard Markovitz, 'Continuities in the Study of Power and Class in Africa,' in Irving Leonard Markovitz. ed., *Studies in Power and Class in Africa* (New York: Oxford University Press, l987), p. 8.

[9] Ibid.

[10] Frederick Cooper, 'Africa and the World Economy.' *The African Studies Review*, 24 (1981), 20–21.

[11] Claude Ake, *A Political Economy of Africa* (New York: Longman, 1981); Walter Rodney, *How Europe Underdeveloped Africa* (Washington. D.C.: Howard University Press, 1972).

[12] Goran Hyden, *No Shortcuts to Progress* (Berkeley: University of California Press, 1983), pp. 8–29.

[13] Hyden contends: 'As the productive and reproductive needs of the peasants can be met without the support of other social classes, relations between those who rule and those who till the land are not firmly rooted in the production system as such. Instead, appropriations by those in control of the state are made in the form of taxation and as such they are simple deductions from an already produced stock of values. These are tributary rather than productive relations and they do imply a much more limited degree of social control. In this respect, African countries are societies without a state. The latter sits suspended in "midair" over society and is not an integral mechanism of the day-to-day productive activities of society....' (Ibid., pp. 7–8.)

[14] Nelson Kasfir, 'State. Magendo, and Class Formation in Uganda' in Nelson Kasfir, ed., *State and Class in Africa* (London: Frank Cass, 1984), p. 95.

[15] Robert H. Bates, *Markets and States in Tropical Africa: The Political Basis of Agricultural Policies* (Berkeley: University of California Press, 1981), p. 87.

[16] Gramsci, *Selections from the Prison Notebooks*, p. 52.

[17] Hirschman, *Essays in Trespassing*, p. 224.

[18] This is not to say that all African ruling classes are incapable of establishing their hegemony. The establishment of a liberal democracy in Senegal is indicative of the hegemonic potential of these ruling classes, but it simultaneously demonstrates the difficulties of the successful implementation of any hegemonic project. See Robert Fatton Jr., *The Making of a Liberal Democracy: Senegal's Passive Revolution, 1975–1985* (Boulder: Lynne Rienner Publishers, 1987).

[19] Gramsci, *Selections from the Prison Notebooks*, p. 219.

[20] Robert Jackson and Carl G. Rosberg, *Personal Rule in Black Africa* (Berkeley: University of California Press, 1982).

[21] Karl Marx and Friedrich Engels, *The Marx-Engels Reader*, 2nd ed. (New York: W. W. Norton & Company.

[22] Thomas M. Callaghy, 'Absolutism, Bonapartism, and the Formation of Ruling Classes: Zaire in Comparative Perspective,' in Markovitz, ed., *Studies in Power and Class in Africa*, pp. 98–99.

[23] Robert Fatton Jr., 'Clientelism and Patronage in Senegal,' *The African Studies Review*, 29 (forthcoming).

[24] Crawford Young, 'Patterns of Social Conflict: State, Class, and Ethnicity.' *Daedalus*, 3 (1982), 93.

[25] René Lemarchand. 'Political Clientelism and Ethnicity in Tropical Africa,' in Steffen W. Schmidt, James C Scott, Carl Land and Laura Guasti, eds., *Friends, Followers and Factions* (Berkeley: University of California Press).

[26] Richard Sandbrook, 'Patrons, Clients and Factions: New Dimensions of Conflict Analysis in Africa,' *Canadian Journal of Political Science*, 5 (1972), 115.

[27] Colin Leys, 'What Is the Problem about Corruption?.' *Journal of Modern African Studies*, 3 (1965) 228.

[28] Clement Cottingham. 'Political Consolidation and Centre-Local Relations in Senegal,' *Canadian Journal of African Studies*, 4 (1970), 103-104. See also Christian Coulon, 'Elections, factions et idéologics au Sénégal,' in Centre d'Etude d'Afrique Noire. ed., *Aux urnes l'Afrique! Elections et pouvoirs en Afrique noire* (Paris: Editions A. Pedone, 1978), p. 80.

[29] Nelson Kasfir, 'Relating Class to State in Africa.' in Kasfir, ed., *State and Class in Africa*, p. 15.

[30] Crawford Young, 'Zaire: The Unending Crisis,' *Foreign Affairs*, 57 (1978), 117.

[31] Jan Vansina, 'Mwasi's Trials,' *Daedalus*, 3 (1982), 59.

JEAN-FRANÇOIS BAYART
The State

Reference
Translated by A.M. Berrett from 'L'Etat', in C. Coulon &
Denis-Constant Martin (eds) *Les Afriques Politiques,*
Editions La Découverte, 1991

The roots of the relative specificity of African societies on which so much stress is laid in much writing about Africa undoubtedly lie in history; it may well arise from the predominance in the distant past of a model of social organization which, while it was not totally unfamiliar with the principle of the State, limited its centralization and surplus-extracting capacities, compared to the situation that prevailed in Europe and Asia at the same period. The price of this singular historical trajectory was undoubtedly to make the subcontinent, or at least parts of it, dependent from a very early date on civilizations that were materially more powerful: those of Mediterranean Antiquity, then later the Arab-Muslim world, and later western Europe as it gradually asserted its supremacy from the fifteenth century onwards. In this respect, the dynamic of the contemporary state in Africa is indeed 'fatherless', as Bertrand Badié and Guy Hermet characterize it:[1] it has no great State tradition like that provided by States in the West, central Asia or the Far East, nor does it have a heritage of a multidisciplinary culture of writing and monotheism. All this suggests the extent to which hybridization between indigenous repertories of politics and repertories imported from outside – a phenomenon that is necessarily part and parcel of the construction of the State in the 'Third World' – is occurring in Africa in unique conditions.

But it would be wrong to conclude from this that the State is 'no more than an imported artifact',[2] tacked on to social and cultural realities to which it is totally alien. Nor can it be deduced from it that all the ills of the subcontinent derive from this original distortion, originating in the colonial rape. This manner of presenting the problem stresses the arbitrary character of the borders drawn by Europeans at the Congress of Berlin. However, apart from the fact that, in a few cases, the political formations that exist today coincide more or less with those of earlier times (Lesotho, Swaziland, Rwanda, Burundi, Ethiopia), it still remains the case that these so-called 'artificial' borders were endorsed, rather sensibly, by the Africans when the Organization of African Unity was established in 1963.

The fact is that the State introduced by the colonial powers was immediately appropriated by the peoples subject to it in two ways. On the one hand, it was adopted by indigenous social actors to the best of what they thought to be their interests. But, on the other, it was interpreted by them in the light of their own cultural representations. From both these viewpoints, the contemporary State in Black Africa has a historicity of its own. Many features of political life in Africa south of the Sahara attest not to its lack of adaptation, as is too facilely said, but, on the contrary, to its rootedness in local societies.

The primacy of factional struggles

This is notably the case with the major political phenomenon which transcends differences of institutional organization or ideological orientation: factional struggles, sometimes described as 'struggles of influence' (as in Cameroon) or 'clan struggles' (as in Senegal).

What African political regimes have in common is that they are dominated by the intensity of the competition that divides their political actors. It may be argued that competition between political entrepreneurs accounts for much of the institutional instability in the subcontinent. Be that as it may, it is a fact that instability varies from country to country. Several countries have rather enjoyed remarkable stability, excessive stability even, if we think of the longevity of certain presidents of the republic in Côte d'Ivoire, Zambia, Togo, Gabon or Zaire or seen controlled constitutional transitions, in Senegal, Cameroon, Kenya, Tanzania or Sierra Leone. Whatever the case, power is always the fruit of a confrontation between rival factions, concealed though this is from the observer by the apparently monolithic character of the single party or the army. The ways in which these factional struggles are fought are many: ministerial reshuffles, coups d'état, political trials or assassinations, meetings of 'elites' in the provinces, campaigns of rumours peddled in the 'chantiers', 'maquis' and other 'circuits' by 'deuxièmes bureaux',[3] fetish gatherings and ritual crimes, marriages, business associations. That is, there is a political life in Africa in the fullest sense of the term, although a reading of the official or semi-official press, subject to censorship and police intimidation in most countries, offers a very inadequate picture of it.

But it has not been sufficiently stressed, outside Africa, how much competition among political entrepreneurs can be effectively mediated by established institutions. Even within single-party regimes, the electors contribute to it: either they are competitive and involve several candidates who all belong to the Party (as in the Tanzanian and Kenyan systems, which have tended to spread to other countries, notably French-speaking ones since the late 1970s) or the fight goes on at a higher level, in the Party apparatus, and is over nomination by ruling bodies of single candidates (according to a system that has long prevailed in Cameroon and Côte d'Ivoire).

Conversely, it is not only political institutions that are involved in intense struggles for influence. Similar intense struggles are to be found too in other structures or other social forces, such as bureaucracies, local authorities, chiefdoms, trade unions, employers' organizations and even Christian Churches, Islamic brotherhoods, so-called 'independent' religious movements or sects.

What is at stake in these conflicts, whether it be a matter of great or of no importance, reflects the institutions or social forces within which they are fought. At the national level, they naturally focus on the holding or sharing of supreme power. In other words, factional struggle is not something occurring at the periphery of political systems. It does not contradict the centralizing presidentialist principle which has generally won out under cover of the single party or military rule. It is rather what made this development happen. The ground was often laid before independence by rivalries within the nationalist movement, and the construction of the post-colonial order has consisted in the assertion of a presidential network over rival factions. In a few extreme cases – Sekou Touré's Guinea or Macias Nguema's Equatorial Guinea – the holder of political power has secured his absolute predominance by eliminating his rivals, politically or physically, and seizing control of the country's wealth. But most of the time, political competition has remained relatively open, despite appearances, and the autonomy of the presidential faction has been only relative.

The integration of African political systems

In this context, the fundamental focus around which political life is conceived is that of the succession to the head of state, although of course there can be no question of raising it officially. The whole art of governing then consists in regulating the play of factions in such a way as to divide and rule and assemble supports without being taken over by them. Herein lies the explanation for the paradoxical and hesitant character of the action of many presidents, so disappointing in regard to economic management or grand ideals, but ultimately consistent in terms of what in Senegal Senghor described as 'politique politicienne' [politicking]. Herein too lies the explanation for the interlocking of political processes and other social dynamics, Factional conflicts within State institutions or dominant parties are interlinked with struggles for influence in the hidden reaches of society. Thus the everyday events of local life – the appointment of so-called traditional chiefs, local elections, civil service appointments – are rarely without national ramifications. In the same way, economic nationalization measures adopted in most countries in the late 1960s or during the 1970s were often a means for power-holders to check or control the resources of factional networks which might compete with them; but, in turn, the austerity programmes implemented at the behest of the IMF and the World Bank in the 1980s and the consequent privatizations enabled presidents such as Abdou Diouf in Senegal or Félix Houphouët-Boigny in Côte d'Ivoire, to transfer public enterprises to their family and friends and to deprive the 'barons' threatening to harm them of some of their sinecures.

Seen in this way, African political systems are much more integrated than is generally accepted. First, the ethnic or regionalist connotation of the factions engaged in 'politicking' must not be exaggerated. The reality is that the major political entrepreneurs, those involved in winning or sharing supreme power, endeavour to mobilize support wherever it may be found, as failure to do so condemns them to marginality. The regions or ethnic groups, so named as matters of linguistic convenience, are historically, socio-economically and, often, culturally, diverse; as a consequence of that diversity, and through the interplay of individual ambitions, they are divided among several leaders, like the Kikuyu or the Luo in Kenya, for example. Thus the ethnic or regionalist label of some ruling cliques always takes second place to their quality as a political machine: Marshal Mobutu's faction in Zaire, is indeed mainly made up of Ngbandi from the province of Equateur, the people of the 'promised land' as the Kinois (the people of Kinshasa) say to highlight the privileged relationship they have with power and its fruits; but not all the Ngbandi native to Equateur are part of it, or benefit from it, while political entrepreneurs from other regions have been coopted into the presidential circle. What is more, this domination by a regional or ethnic faction does not rule out the contradictions within it, including in the form of plots and coups d'état, as witness Burundi (within the Bururi Tutsi group) or the Central African Republic (within the 'Yakoma clan'). In this sense, ethnicity is not the opposite of the State. It is rather a product of it, and a mode of conflictual participation in it, a means of demanding a share in it, both economically and politically. The categorical imperative of national unity, which has served to legitimize post-colonial authoritarian regimes, has never been as threatened as their ideologists have asserted.

Next, the dichotomy between rulers and ruled is less sharp than the institutional appearances suggest. It is striking to note how well informed the 'small men', the 'en-bas du bas', as they say in Côte d'Ivoire, are about everything the 'big men', the 'en-haut du haut', are doing, if only through the bush telegraph ('Radio trottoir'). This political communication is one sign among many of how African societies are networked. There are horizontal networks which promote alliances between the elites of different regions and which link the towns to the rural areas through a vast number of demographic, material or symbolic exchanges. But there are also, at the same time, vertical networks in the framework of which transactions between political entrepreneurs and their clients are conducted. The classic distinction between State and society must thus be qualified when it comes to Africa, even though the former, allegedly modernizing, has claimed to define itself against the latter, allegedly traditional, in direct continuation of the colonial bureaucratic and ideological heritage. In reality, public institutions, such as the civil service or the army, are shot through by the conflictual interests of society. Factional struggles which interfere with their functioning are simply the expression of this osmosis.

This stress on the interplay of factions implies a rejection of three readings of the postcolonial State which have confused political science for thirty years: one that views it in terms of ethnic conflicts, since these are simply a shadow play and involve political machines that cannot be reduced to intangible primordial identities; one that sees it in terms of regimes, since these are impossible to define according to strict institutional criteria and are subject to the deleterious effect of struggles for influence; and one that sees it in terms of fully fledged social classes, since political entrepreneurs and their networks never absolutely coincide with the categories of production or exchange relations and tend to straddle them, thus giving factional conflicts more weight than class conflicts.

The postcolonial State lives as a rhizome, as a set of underground roots of which the parts above ground, the political institutions, are less important than the happenstance roots, their multiple correspondences with the various social formations and in particular in the provinces, the hierarchies of the historical terroirs [home areas, with their roots in the precolonial past]. It rests on force, which it freely uses, but it also rests on permanent negotiations and compromises among all these forces; in other words, it is closely dependent on the individual performances of its actors.

State, social inequality and political systems

Does this mean that this State can be seen as simply the product of the strategies of political entrepreneurs, crowned, to an extent that varies from country to country, by the preeminence of the President? Some writers have seen fit to assert as much and have preferred to speak of 'personal rule' rather than 'State'. In doing so they have taken the appearance of personality cults, celebrated by the regime ideologues, for the reality, and have not gone beyond paraphrasing journalistic commentaries on the enlightened Prince (Senghor, Houphouët-Boigny, Ahidjo) or the evil despot (Idi Amin Dada, Bokassa). But there are at least three key objections to this way of seeing things.

First, it plays down the role of power in the formation of a global system of social inequality. Redistribution from above of sinecures and other benefits obtained through the holding of a position of authority in the State apparatus must be treated carefully. It is not unheard of for a 'big man', influenced by the cultural code of munificence, to make a point of honour of doing so. It is more common for it to be imposed upon him by meetings of collective savings societies in his home area and by the continuous stream of favour-seekers, masters of either the language of kinship and flattery, or, more disturbingly, that of witchcraft accusations. But such redistribution does not always happen: far from it. The personal relationship on which it supposedly rests is by definition highly unequal and hierarchical.

In this context, too systematically or too loosely described as 'clientelist', factional struggles are not simply concerned with the distribution of status and power. They are also about the distribution of wealth, or more precisely, the distribution of the possibilities of realizing a genuine primitive accumulation, in the strict sense of the concept, through confiscation of the means of production and exchange. To describe this conception of politics, Nigerians speak of 'sharing the national cake', and Cameroonians of the 'politics of the belly'. It is surely not warranted to go from there and see in power the sole vehicle of the system of social inequality, given that power almost never, even in situations of extreme patrimonialism, such as in Mobutu's Zaire, Houphouët-Boigny's Côte d'Ivoire or Sékou Touré's Guinea, succeeds in totally monopolizing the channels of accumulation and has to come to some sort of terms with autonomous economic networks such as the Swahili, Indian or Arab merchants in east Africa, the Nande traders in Zaire and the Bamileke ones in Cameroon, the great Muslim trading families in the Sahel or the 'nana Benz'[4] along the Gulf of Guinea. Nevertheless, the position of power is by definition a position of accumulation: either directly, or indirectly through the administrative permits, commercial licences and tax levies which it alone can grant.

It is this strong relationship between the exercise of power, factional rivalry and access to the State apparatus, even if it is merely in terms of a wage, on the one hand, and the formation of a system of social inequality, on the other, that British historians have conceptualized in the term 'straddling' and that Cameroonians refer to in a spicy saying: 'goats nibble where they are tethered'. Its most fateful manifestation is perhaps the private appropriation of land by 'big men', in a historical situation where land ownership was unknown (with the possible exception of Ethiopia) before the formation of big European plantations in settler colonies, most notably South Africa, Southern Rhodesia, Kenya and Angola. Thus, in Kenya, the postcolonial 'land reform' transferred to the new holders of State power many farms that the British settlers had carved out for themselves at the expense of the land users. Similarly, in Côte d'Ivoire, the 'agrarian bourgeoisie', in which some writers thought they could detect the ruling class, is not made up of planters who achieved social mobility through agriculture but of the political and bureaucratic personnel who took power in 1960 on the coat-tails of Mr. Houphouët-Boigny. More generally, the surplus produced by the various ways in which rent is extracted from African economies – particularly the export of major agricultural crops, oil, minerals or diamonds, and management of development aid or foreign investment – is seized by the holders of political authority. In the twists and turns of the convoluted struggles for influence carried on in the shadow of the State a ruling class is indeed being forged; its formation is as yet too incomplete for it to be possible to characterize it definitively, but its capacity to reproduce itself must not be under-estimated. In many respects, the presidents are the proxies of this ruling class in formation, rather than *dei ex machina*.

The historical trajectories of the State

Second, the action of power-holders and in particular of the first among them, takes place in a political arena on which it is dependent. Even the founding presidents of the postcolonial state – Julius K. Nyerere in Tanzania, Jomo Kenyatta in Kenya, Ahmadou Ahidjo in Cameroon, Félix Houphouët-Boigny in Côte d'Ivoire or Kwame Nkrumah in Ghana, for example – were confronted with relations of force, with cultural, economic or social obstacles that constrained their projects and which factional rivalries introduced into political bodies. Nothing can be more erroneous than to see in decolonization ' a sort of *tabula rasa*', as Frantz Fanon did. The postcolonial State inherited a particular colonial and precolonial history. And itself soon produced history too. Contemporary political actors are to a greater or lesser degree the prisoners of these historical trajectories, which vary from country to country. First, they relate in a particular way to a number of defining events which constitute the historical memory of their society: for example, the manner in which the slave trade, colonial occupation and decolonization was effected, or the succession of postcolonial events (revolutions, disturbances, rural uprisings, coups d'etat, etc.). Then they are ensnared in an established institutional fabric which itself bears the imprint of the different colonial heritages, from the French Jacobin tradition to the British conception of government, by way of Salazar's corporatism, each one equipped with its own logic, whatever freedoms may be taken with constitutional texts.

In thirty years of independence, a not insignificant number of regimes have achieved a degree of institutionalization (Senegal, Côte d'Ivoire, Mali, Togo, Cameroon, Gabon, Congo, Zaire, Zambia, Kenya, Malawi, in particular); such institutionalization limits the freedom of action of political entrepreneurs. Finally, and in a more diffuse way, these entrepreneurs act in a legitimate problematic of politics, it too engendered by history and made up of various repertoires, some indigenous, some imported, some implicit, others explicit, and the baroque combination of these repertoires gives political mediation its particular character.

For, ultimately, what is striking is the extreme diversity of these political arenas, ranging as they do from the shores of the Indian Ocean and the banks of the Limpopo to the the Sahara and the shores of the Atlantic Ocean: in Congo-Brazzaville, a regime which claims to be Marxist-Leninist but rests on a territorial organization of a French Jacobin type maintains a subtle equilibrium with the indigenous lineage hierarchies and leaves space for the occult practices of witchcraft; in Kenya, a presidential power which seeks to escape from factional struggles long contained in the competitive framework of the single party by increasing resort to coercion in the name of a philosophy imbued with a Christian religiosity; in Senegal, there is 'politicking' in a multi-party framework which represents a reasonably happy compromise, as yet still fragile, between the electoral experience of the four communes of the French Third Republic and the *zawiyya* spirit of the Islamic brotherhoods; and in Côte d'Ivoire, a munificent presidential regime which long channelled factional struggles through a style of government that was extremely familial, paternalistic and sinecure-based, and later sought to head off the rising power of a new generation of graduate cadres through universal suffrage.

In such circumstances, to speak of personal rule or personal power is to flatten out the many different historical paths of politics in Africa south of the Sahara, and replace them with a dubious culturalist hypothesis that posits the existence of a specifically African conception of authority, something to which claim is laid notably by the doctrine of 'authenticity' so dear to Mobutu Sese Seko in Zaire or Gnassingbé Eyadema in Togo, and according to which 'there cannot be two male crocodiles in a single pond'.[5] It also amounts to dismissing as of no consequence the actual debates that go on inside political institutions, including those with a monolithic facade such as armies and the leading bodies of single parties.

Third and last, the fable of the enlightened Prince and the evil despot overshadows the popular forms of political action that helped create the postcolonial State. Continuing on from the colonial period, the exercise of power resorts massively to coercion and expects from the population docile adhesion in the form of routine participation in elections, 'spontaneous' demonstrations of support, neo-traditional oaths of allegiance, obedience to the various instructions issued by government and acceptance of the various levies that the agents of public authority are in the habit of demanding. All insubordination is treated automatically as an act of subversion and put down as such, if need be by force. In addition, those dismissively regarded as the 'small men' or 'children' of society are subjected to continuous political surveillance, as a preventive measure, through police raids and the widespread practice of informing. That suggests the scope of domination in a postcolonial Africa which regularly supplies Amnesty International with some of its most terrible pages. But it would be wrong to reduce the political arena to this one aspect. In addition to their direct resistance or protest, in the form of urban riots, strikes or rural rebellions, the 'small men' participate in the State in a more or less routine or conflictual way through its institutions, electoral procedures and clientage networks, but with their own objectives.

There too political mediation is intensely rich, as is revealed in analyses of elections in Kenya, Tanzania, Cameroon, Nigeria, Côte d'Ivoire or Senegal, for example. Yet the weight of 'those of no importance' on the postcolonial State mainly makes itself felt by what does not happen, as if by default, and – apart from the ambiguous case of Congo-Leopoldville in 1964–1965 and the quite special case of the Republic of South Africa – has not led to the crystallization of enduring social or revolutionary movements, once the aim of anticolonial liberation has been achieved. The 'exit option', so highly valued in old Africa, is often preferred to the 'voice option'. First, there is flight through humour and derision, or banditry, currently the most banal form of subversion of the State, both in the towns and in the countryside. Flight too into the religious and the occult: Christian, Islamic or 'Independent' cult practices are growing enormously and are helping to reorder the political arena. And finally there is flight in the literal meaning of the word, in the shape of migration, refugee flows and the brain drain. Thus the space of domination in contemporary Africa is not set once and for all. Its definition is one of the issues at stake in the social struggle between 'big men' and 'small men'. The former deal with it by resorting to coercion and promoting their conception of the State, according to a variety of legitimate problematics of politics; the latter, by endorsing these latter but also by relativizing their effectiveness.

State scenarios

Once we begin to ask about the invention of the State in Black Africa (and not about its varying nature, whose shifts and changes attempts are made to classify into a typology), once we grasp this State as a historical phenomenon that varies from one national situation to another, we then need, on the one hand, to assess the paths travelled since independence, and, on the other, to envisage likely developments in the closing years of the century.

Regarding social inequality, the State in Africa south of the Sahara has been the matrix of three broad scenarios.

In a first series of cases, it has been the vector of a conservative modernization to the benefit of a dominant class which succeeded in 'changing everything so that everything stays the same' (in the famous words of Tancredi in *The Leopard*). The best example of this strategy is in Nigeria. The *sarakuna* aristocracy which dominated the north successfully manipulated indirect rule to its own advantage during British colonization, overcoming its historical divisions, co-opting commoner elites alongside it and taking the lead in social change without renouncing its adhesion to Islam and its other cultural values; in doing so it not only withstood the twin threat coming from the popular, even revolutionary pressure of the *talakawa* (commoner) masses and competition from the Christian elites in the south, better trained in Western ways, but also parlayed its regional hegemony into preeminence at the federal level over the whole country through the successive civilian and military regimes that have followed one another after independence in 1960 (apart from the brief and bloody interlude of the Ironsi government in 1966, which sought precisely to subject it in the framework of a unitary State).

In a second series of situations, the dominant classes or groups have been overthrown by new elites that arose during the colonial period. Thus, in Rwanda, the Tutsi aristocracy was swept aside by the Hutu counter-elite, belatedly educated by Catholic missions, in the revolts of 1959, while in Sierra Leone, Zanzibar or Liberia, political power or influence was taken from non-native elites under the combined pressure of population imbalance and universal suffrage in the first case, and through a coup d'état in the other two.

But midway between these two extreme scenarios, it was often a middle way that won out – for example in Senegal, Côte d'Ivoire, Cameroon, Gabon, Kenya or Tanzania – in the shape of a fusion and reciprocal assimilation of various old and new elites, and through political alliances at the level of political power, economic deals in the business world and marriage exchanges in the private sphere. In many respects, this intermediate path has the hallmarks of the 'passive revolution' which the Italian Marxist theoretician Antonio Gramsci saw at work in his country, from unification by Cavour to fascism under Mussolini: the same compromise between 'old' and 'new' dominant groups; the same capacity of the State to coopt into its service radical political groups and above all popular counter-elites, such as peasant and worker cadres; the same geographically unbalanced construction of the political space, built on the preeminence of a single region; the same alternation of resort to the most brutal use of force and ideological legitimation through the intermediary of an exaggerated nationalism, the monopoly of modernity and leadership cults. If this comparison is well founded, it would confirm that postcolonial authoritarianism south of the Sahara is less the product of some cultural archetype of 'African power' than of one of those paths to democracy and dictatorship explored in the historical sociology of the State in Europe, Asia or Latin America.[6]

Regime crises

Whatever the case, the regimes that are the vectors of these three scenarios are today in crisis. On the one hand, they are now suffering from a major legitimacy deficit; the great ideological myths that they claimed allegiance to – the single party in the service of development and national integration; an 'African' conception of the leader; socialism – are now discredited and have been replaced by a strong resurgence of the demand for liberal democracy. On the other hand, and above all, these regimes that rest on exploitation of economic resources and permanent aid from abroad are seeing both dry up and are faced with a recession which the structural adjustment programmes of the International Monetary Fund and the World Bank have failed to overcome. But it is unlikely that Africa will be able to escape from this crisis through democracy. The authoritarian powers have not said their last word. They can grant a multiparty system at the drop of a hat and put it in the service of their interests, while continuing to rely for the most part on their security agencies and repressive laws. In addition, successful structural adjustment economic policies would require an intensification of the exploitation of labour power, and authoritarian regimes would be better able to assure that. Finally, the determination by both the existing authorities and the social categories contesting them to have done with the 'politics of the belly' which has brought about the collapse of the postcolonial State may not be all that it seems: the mass movements of 1990 were aimed perhaps less at the extractive, even predatory conception of the State than at its redistribution mechanisms, and they were perhaps not so far removed from the established play of factions – notably the classic issue of the presidential succession – as was said at the time.

In short, the apparent liberalization of authoritarian regimes which began in the early 1980s in a number of French-speaking countries, such as Côte d'Ivoire or Cameroon, or even as early as the mid-1970s in Senegal, does not necessarily rule out a continuation of authoritarian situations, in the light of a distinction that experts on authoritarianism have highlighted in Latin America, and especially Brazil.

There is thus a very real risk that the armed scenario of factional struggles which has already become established as the mode of political production in a number of African countries (Chad, Uganda, Angola, Mozambique, Somalia, Sudan and, more recently, Liberia) will become the rule, under the cumulative impact of the economic crisis and the digging-in of authoritarian regimes under serious threat: in the countries mentioned, movements organized into proto-presidential systems around more or less charismatic warlords, of which Jonas Savimbi, the leader of UNITA in Angola is the archetype, are turning to rebellion and making part of the country an area of dissidence, before going on to try and seize central power, usually with the support of outside powers. To date, two leaders have been able to achieve this, succeeding where revolutionary movements in the 1960s had failed: Hissène Habré in Chad and Yoweri Museveni in Uganda. These sub-continental precedents, along with other comparable situations in Latin America or Asia, tend to suggest that what is at issue is not so much a calling into question of the State but of another way of regulating and appropriating it. It is moreover revealing that such movements reject all partition of the national territory, despite their often marked regional connotation, and accept the State framework inherited from colonization. Deep down, the strength of this scenario lies in its compatibility with several of the key contemporary dynamics of sub-Saharan societies. It can live with the unbridled exploitation of economic resources (mining or oil-producing enclaves, extraction and secret marketing of diamonds,

poaching, smuggling, storing of industrial waste etc.); it rests on a historical memory, the memory of the slave trade, the trading posts and the caravans; it retains 'affinities', in the Weberian sense of the term, with the repertory of the invisible and with the reordering of the political arena through the intermediary of various religious cults; better than delinquency, it ensures a legitimate social mobilization and access to wealth to uneducated young people subject in peace-time to the tutelage and exploitation of adults. In any event, it should be noted that the primacy of the war leader, in movements of this sort, should not be a matter for surprise either; like what is happening in institutionalized single-party regimes, it is never more than relative and precarious, as witness the competition between Hissène Habré and Goukouni Oueddei in Chad or between Charles Taylor and Prince Johnson in Liberia, and it belongs in a global social or historical context, the complexity of which is illustrated by the civil wars in Sudan and Mozambique, for example.

Ethnonationalism or universalism?

Are we seeing the institutionalization or militarization of the play of factions? The restoration of the great productive balances or the accentuation of extraction and predation? There will be no single continent-wide response to these dilemmas, and that response will be partly influenced by international factors because of the emergence of regional powers (Nigeria, South Africa), the relative disengagement of some external actors (Western Europe, USSR) and the arrival or return of other external actors (Arab countries, Asian commercial networks). But in one way or another these alternatives come down to a choice between two conceptions of political modernity, which is to be found in different forms throughout the countries south of the Sahara, although it is in southern Africa that the debate can be best grasped. On the one hand, there is a particularistic, ethnonationalist conception of politics, through the ideological and mythical reconstruction of an allegedly primordial traditional identity: this option, of which the highest expression was the apartheid system, has been shared by many political forces in the region within Pretoria's orbit; further north, it also inspired the single-party presidential systems that lay claim to a highly problematic 'African authenticity', in Zaire and Togo in particular. The authoritarian, even totalitarian implications of this version of modernity are obvious.

On the other hand, there is a universalist conception of the City, defined in liberal, Christian or Marxist-Leninist terms, or even (why not?), Islamist terms, which would give a broader freedom of action to strategies of democratization, but this potential has been almost entirely systematically stifled by the nationalist emphasis on 'African-ness'. In many respects, this dilemma is symbolized by the two-track negotiation embarked on by Frederik De Klerk in South Africa with, on the one hand, Gatsha Buthulezi, strong-arm leader of Zulu ethnonationalism, and, on the other, Nelson Mandela, vice-president of the African National Congress. And, in many respects, the outcome of this two-track negotiation in South Africa will help to crystallize the type of modernity which the rest of the subcontinent will adopt in turn in the coming decades. Nevertheless, the very fact that this debate is occurring is a reminder that Black Africa has not let itself be caught in the political trap of what the Congolese novelist Sony Labou Tansi called ironically, the better to denounce it, its 'tropicality'.

Notes

[1] Bertrand Badié, Guy Hermet, *Politique comparée*, Paris, Presses universitaires de France, 1990, pp. 231 et seq.

[2] Bertrand Badié, Pierre Birnbaum, *Sociologie de l'État*, Paris, Grasset, 1979, pp. 178 et seq., p. 181 [American tr. Arthur Goldhammer, *The Sociology of the State*, Chicago, University of Chicago Press, 1983, pp. 99 et seq.].

[3] 'Chantiers', 'maquis' and 'circuits' are common names used to describe drinking places in French-speaking Africa, especially Côte d'Ivoire and Cameroon. 'Deuxièmes bureaux' refers to mistresses and favourites of 'big men', that is those who are commonly described in the rural areas as the 'elites'.

[4] 'Nana Benz': an expression used to describe wealthy businessmen, usually specialized in the cloth and dried fish trades, alluding to the famous Mercedes Benz saloon cars, distinct signs of social success.

[5] This thesis, which is often taken up by the French media, gives short shrift to anthropological studies that show how African societies often rested on a dual social and political hierarchy (for example, on a more or less institutionalized balance between a conquering warrior minority and a conquered religious hierarchy).

[6] See in particular Barrington Moore Jr., *Les origines sociales de la dictature et de la démocratie*, Paris, Maspero, 1969 [original American ed. *The Social Origins of Dictatorship and Democracy*, Boston, Beacon Press, 1966].

MAHMOOD MAMDANI
Linking the Urban & the Rural

Reference

Citizen & Subject: Contemporary Africa & the Legacy of Late Colonialism
James Currey; Princeton University Press, 1991, ch. 8

As the dawn of independence broke on a horizon of internal conflict, reconsideration of the African colonial experience began. Could it be that the African problem was not colonialism but an incomplete penetration of traditional society by a weak colonial state or deference to it by prudent but shortsighted colonizers? Could it be that Europe's mission in Africa was left half finished? If the rule of law took centuries to root in the land of its original habitation, is it surprising that the two sides of the European mission – market and civil society, the law of value and the rule of law – were neither fully nor successfully transplanted in less than a century of colonialism? And that this fragile transplant succumbed to caprice and terror on the morrow of independence?

With the end of the cold war, this point of view has crystallized into a tendency with a name, Afro-pessimism, and a claim highly skeptical of the continent's ability to rejuvenate itself from within. Whether seen as a problem of incomplete conquest or as one of unwise deference to traditional authorities, both sides of the Afro-pessimist point of view lead to the same conclusion: a case for the recolonization of Africa, for finishing a task left unfinished. Part of the argument of this book is that Afro-pessimism is unable to come to grips with the nature of the colonial experience in Africa precisely because it ignores *the mode* of colonial penetration into Africa.

Yet another set of questions coheres around a perspective that is not evolutionist but particularistic, whose impetus is not toward highlighting African 'backwardness' but underlining its difference. That difference is said to be the tendency to fragmentation and particularism, hitherto held in check and obscured by a shared dilemma, colonial racism. Was not racism the general aspect of the African experience – its colonial and external aspect – and tribalism its particular, indigenous and internal, aspect? Generally emancipated from racism with the end of colonialism, did not Africa once again come to be in the grip of a specifically African particularism: tribalism, ethnic conflict, and primordial combat? Another part of the argument in this book is that it is too naive to think of racism and tribalism as simple opposites, for alien (racial) domination was actually grounded in and mitigated through ethnically organized local power. In the colonial period, ethnic identity and separation were politically enforced. Although forged through colonial experience, this form of the state survived alien domination. Reformed after independence, purged of its racial underpinnings, it emerged as a specifically African form of the state.

The form of the state

Colonial genesis

I have argued that to grasp the specificity of colonial domination in Africa, one needs to place it within the context of Europe's larger colonizing experience. The trajectory of the wider experience, particularly as it tried to come to grips with the fact of resistance, explains its midstream shift in perspective: from the zeal of a civilizing mission to a calculated preoccupation with holding power, from rejuvenating to conserving society, from being the torchbearers of individual freedom to being custodians protecting the customary integrity of dominated tribes. This shift took place in older colonies, mainly India and Indochina, but its lessons were fully implemented in Africa, Europe's last colonial possession. Central to that lesson was an expanded notion of the customary.

Britain was the first to marshal authoritarian possibilities in indigenous culture. It was the first to realize that key to an alien power's achieving a hegemonic domination was a cultural project: one of harnessing the moral, historical, and community impetus behind local custom to a larger colonial project. There were three distinctive features about the customary as colonial power came to define it. First, the customary was considered synonymous with the tribal; each tribe was defined as a cultural group with its own customary law. Second, the world of the customary came to be all-encompassing; more so than in any other colonial experience, it came to include a customary access to land. Third, custom was defined and enforced by customary Native Authorities in the local state – backed up by the armed might of the central state.

To appreciate the significance of this, we need to recall only one fact. Although the use of force was outlawed in every British colony in the aftermath of the First World War (and in French colonies after the Second), this applied to the central state and usually to European officials supervising Native Authorities in the local state, but not to the Native Authorities. For this, there was one reason. So long as the use of force could be passed off as customary it was considered legitimate, and – to complete the tautology – force decreed by a customary authority was naturally regarded as customary. No wonder that when force was needed to implement development measures on reluctant peasants, its use was restricted to Native Authorities as much as possible. In the language of power, custom came to be the name of force. It was the halo around the regime of decentralized despotism.

The customary was never singular, but plural. As far as possible, every tribe was governed by its customary law. Europe did not bring to Africa a tropical version of the late-nineteenth-century European nation-state. Instead it created a multicultural and multiethnic state.[1] The colonial state was a two-tiered structure: peasants were governed by a constellation of ethnically defined Native Authorities in the local state, and these authorities were in turn supervised by white officials deployed from a racial pinnacle at the center.

Another peculiarity of this form of the state was that the relation between force and market was not antithetical. It was not simply that force framed market institutions. It was more that force and market came to be two alternative ways of regulating the process of production and exchange. To the extent that the scope of the customary included land and labor, that of the market was limited. To flush either labor or its products out of the realm of the customary required the use of force. Clearly, there was and is no particular and fixed balance between force and market. Its degree remains variable: the customary was never a Chinese wall keeping the tide of market relations at bay; nor was it of nominal significance. The customary was porous. Within its parameters, market relations were enmeshed with extra-economic coercion. Free peasants were differentiated, and those better off were shielded from the regime of force.

Postcolonial reform and variations

Characteristic of Afro-pessimism, whether in its left-wing or right-wing version, is a 'roots of the crisis' literature that reduces the past to a one-dimensional reality. The result is a reconstruction of the past as if the only thing that happened was laying the foundations of a present crisis. The result is not an analysis that appropriates the past as a contradictory mix, but one that tends to debunk it.

The core agenda that African states faced at independence was threefold: deracializing civil society, detribalizing the Native Authority, and developing the economy in the context of unequal international relations. In a state form marked by bifurcated power, deracialization and detribalization were two aspects that would form the starting point of an overall process of democratization. By themselves, even if joined together, they could not be tantamount to democratization. Together, this amalgam of internal and external imperatives signified the limits and possibilities of the moment of state independence.

Of this threefold agenda, the task undertaken with the greatest success was deracialization. Whether formulated as a program of 'indigenization' by mainstream nationalist regimes – conservative or moderate – from Nigeria to Zaire to Idi Amin's Uganda, or as one of nationalization by radical ones, from Ghana to Guinea to Tanzania, the tendency everywhere was to erode racially accumulated privilege in erstwhile colonies. Whether they sought to Africanize or to nationalize, the historical legitimacy of post-independence nationalist governments lay mainly in the program of deracialization they followed. The difference between them, however, was an effect of the strategy of distribution each one employed. Whether the tendency was privatization or statism, both strategies opened opportunities for nepotism and corruption, for clientelism.

In contrast to deracialization, the task undertaken with the least success was democratization. Key to democratization was the Native Authority in the local state: its detribalization would have to be the starting point in reorganizing the bifurcated power forged under colonialism. The failure to democratize explains why deracialization was not sustainable and why development ultimately failed. Without a reform in the local state, the peasantry locked up under the hold of a multiplicity of ethnically defined Native Authorities could not be brought into the mainstream of the historical process. In the absence of democratization, development became a top-down agenda enforced on the peasantry. Without thoroughgoing democratization, there could be no development of a home market. This latter failure opened wide what was a crevice at independence. With every downturn in the international economy, the crevice turned into an opportunity for an externally defined structural adjustment that combined a narrowly defined program of privatization with a broadly defined program of globalization. The result was both an internal privatization that recalled the racial imbalance that was civil society in the colonial period and an externally managed capital inflow that towed alongside a phalanx of expatriates – according to UN estimates, more now than in the colonial period!

But if the limits of the postindependence period were reflected in a deracialization without democratization, I will argue that the Achilles' heel of the contemporary 'second independence movement' lies in its political failure to grasp the specificity of the mode of rule that needs to be democratized. Theoretically, this is reflected in an infatuation with the notion of civil society, a preoccupation that conceals the actual form of power through which rural populations are ruled. Without a reform of the local state, as I will soon show, democratization will remain not only superficial but also explosive.

Mainstream nationalism The mainstream nationalists who inherited the central state at independence understood colonial oppression as first and foremost an exclusion from civil society, and more generally as alien rule. They aimed to redress these wrongs through deracialization internally and anti-imperialism externally. The new state power sought to indigenize civil society institutions and to restructure relations between the independent state and the international economy and polity.

In the absence of the detribalization of rural power, however, deracialization could not be joined to democratization. In an urban-centered reform, the rural contaminated the urban. The tribal logic of Native Authorities easily overwhelmed the democratic logic of civil society. An electoral reform that does not affect the appointment of the Native Authority and its chiefs – which leaves rural areas out of consideration as so many protectorates – is precisely about the reemergence of a decentralized despotism! In such a context, electoral politics turned out to be about more than just who represents citizens in civil society, because victors in that contest would also have a right to rule over subjects through Native Authorities, for the winner would appoint chiefs, the Native Authority, everywhere. More than the rule of law, the issue in a civil society-centered contest comes to be who will be master of all tribes. As a Kenyan political scientist once remarked to me, the ethnicity of the president is the surest clue to the ethnic tinge of the government of the day. This is why civil society politics where the rural is governed through customary authority is necessarily patrimonial: urban politicians harness rural constituencies through patron–client relations. Where despotism is presumed, clientelism is the only noncoercive way of linking the rural and the urban.

Confined to civil society, democratization is both superficial and explosive: superficial because it is interpreted in a narrowly formal way that does not address the specificity of customary power – democratization equals free and fair multiparty elections – and explosive because, with the local state intact as the locus of a decentralized despotism, the stakes in any multiparty election are high. The winner would not only represent citizens in civil society, but also dominate over subjects through the appointment of chiefs in the Native Authority. The winner in such an election is simultaneously the representative power in civil society and the despotic power over Native Authorities.

Tribalism is more one-sidedly corrosive in an urban context than in the rural one. Stripped of the rural context, where it is also a civil war, tribalism in urban areas has no democratic impetus. It becomes interethnic only. This practice is not confined to propertied strata. We have seen that migrants who became involved in the interethnic politics of civil society did so partly to protect customary rural rights. In the absence of the democratization of Native Authorities and the custom they enforced, the more civil society was deracialized, the more it came to be tribalized. Urban tribalism appeared as a postindependence problem in states that reproduced customary forms of power precisely because deracialization was a postindependence achievement of these states.

Radical nationalism The accent of mainstream nationalism was on deracializing civil society, but it is the radical regimes that sought to detribalize Native Authority. The institutional basis of that effort was the single party, the inheritor of militant anticolonial nationalism, which symbolized a successful linkup between urban militants and rural insurrectionary movements against Native Authorities. Militant urban nationalism was the social and ideological glue that cemented otherwise heterogeneous peasant-based struggles. From that experience arose the single party as yet another noncoercive link between the rural and the urban.

The single party was simultaneously a way to contain social and political fragmentation reinforced by ethnically organized Native Authorities and a solution imposed from above in lieu of democratization from below, for the militants of the single party came to distrust democracy, by which they understood a civil society-centered electoral reform. A democratic link between the urban and the rural was in their eyes synonymous with a civil society-based clientelism. Seen as the outcome of an urban multiparty project, clientelism appeared as the other side of a deepening fragmentation along ethnic lines.

Whereas multiparty regimes tended toward a superficial and explosive democratization of civil society, their single-party counterparts tended to depoliticize civil society. The more they succeeded, the more the single party came to be bureaucratized. As the center of gravity in the party-state shifted from the party to the state, the method of work came to rely more on coercion than on persuasion. Whether heralding development or waging revolution, the single party came to enforce it from above on a reluctant peasantry. Although depoliticization contained interethnic tensions within civil society – and as a consequence within the whole polity – the result of a forced developmental march was to exacerbate tensions between the rural and the urban. The single party turned from a mobilizing organ into a coercive apparatus; in the words of Fanon, militants of yesterday turned into informers of today. True, there was a significant break with the formal institutions of indirect rule, but there was no such break with the form of its power. An

institution such as chiefship may be abolished, only to be replaced by another with similar powers. The ideological text may change from the customary to the revolutionary – and so may political practice – but, in spite of real differences, there remains a continuity in administrative power and technique: radical experiences have not only reproduced, but also reinforced fused power, administrative justice and extra-economic coercion, all in the name of development.

The reform of decentralized despotism turned out to be a centralized despotism. So we come to the seesaw of African politics that characterizes its present impasse. On one hand, decentralized despotism exacerbates ethnic divisions, and so the solution appears as a centralization. On the other hand, centralized despotism exacerbates the urban-rural division, and the solution appears as a decentralization. But as variants both continue to revolve around a shared axis – despotism.

The lesson of oppositional reform

The two tensions the specific form of the African state generated, the interethnic and the urban-rural, have also been faced by oppositional movements. In chapter 6 we surveyed some rural movements, and in chapter 7 the urban movement in post-1973 South Africa.

These movements bring out the two dimensions of the ethnic question, the internal and the external. Because the context in which rural movements organize is more often than not multiethnic, they face a common question: is a resistance against a tribal Native Authority possible which does not at the same time exacerbate interethnic tensions within the resulting movement?

I have argued that a peasant movement in the parameters of a Native Authority is at the same time an ethnic civil war. Yet this should not be understood as a claim that every such movement is committed to rooting out the institution of chiefship. Of the South African movements we surveyed, only the Mpondo sought to implement a democratic program whose target was the institution of chiefship. The rest fell short of it, some more than others. But all of them, without exception, sought to redefine the notion of the customary, to limit the powers of chiefship within traditional constraints. If 'customary' is the name that power gives to the untraditional force with which it arms Native Authorities, it is also the language of peasant movements that seek to reform the same Native Authority in the name of a custom anchored in notions more historical and popular. When I speak of tribalism as civil war, my notion of civil war is a continuum along which muted tensions coexist long before they break out into open confrontation.

Notwithstanding the colonial claim that traditional Africa was a tribal checkerboard, with each tribe in its own place, we have seen that tribal culture was highly textured and elastic, with the stranger often present on rural ground. For no reason other than to expand their following, the tendency of chiefs was to encourage strangers to settle in their domain. With a state-enforced and tribally circumscribed notion of custom, two related changes occurred. First, the tendency was to homogenize and flatten cultural diversity within the tribe in favor of an official tribal version. Second, the imposition of a tribal law as customary, to be defined and dispensed by a tribal authority, necessarily turned the simple fact of ethnic heterogeneity into a source of tension.

If the rural movements I surveyed were all to some degree marked by ethnic civil war, only the experience of the NRA in

Uganda brought out clearly the intertribal tensions that surface in peasant movements. As it sought to weld together a common oppositional movement in a context where settled and migrant populations rubbed shoulders, the NRA defined rights as an attribute not of citizenship but of labor. To say that rights belonged to all those resident in a locality, regardless of geographical or ethnic origin, was to say that all those who labor have a justifiable claim to rights. Once labor was understood as the life-sustaining activity of laboring humanity, and not as wage labor, the accent shifted from citizens' rights to human rights.

To view rights as an attribute of labor is also to transcend the opposition between customary law and civil law, for the opposition notwithstanding, customary law and civil law share a common premise. Both see rights as an attribute of individuals belonging to a common land-based community. The difference lies in the definition of the community. From the point of view of customary law, that community is defined in ethnic terms, as the tribe; from that of civil law, the community is a nation, whether defined ethnically or territorially. Both subject and citizen derive their rights, customary or civil, through membership in a *patri*: a tribe for the subject, a nation for the citizen.

Although the NRA was able to bring a creative insight into resolving the interethnic tension in its rural base, the Luwero Triangle, it found great difficulty in addressing the urban-rural tension from a position of power in the city. It saw urban civil society demands for a representational multiparty democracy – a demand reinforced by many Western donors – as a threat, both to its hold on power and to the unity of power holding the country together. It was faced with the old dilemma that had plagued single-party regimes. Would not a multiparty contest in the city be about not just who would represent citizens in the city, but also who would be the master of tribes in the countryside? Would not such a contest both exacerbate clientelism in civil society and extend it to the countryside, thereby also activating and reorganizing demo-cratic politics around interethnic tensions?

If the failure of the NRA – at the time of this writing, in late 1994 – was in making a transition from the rural to the urban, from democratizing Native Authority to democratizing civil society, that of the urban movements in post-1973 South Africa was the opposite. The independent unions successfully fought attempts by the apartheid state to drive a wedge between migrant and resident labor in the townships but remained prisoners of a civil society-centered perspective. Although they disagreed on many issues of principle, the workerists and populists inside the independent unions agreed on one thing: the community meant the township. If the IFP – and in retrospect, also the ANC – succeeded in bridging the rural and the urban in the context of a multiparty contest, it did so at the cost of exacerbating interethnic tensions in civil society. Whereas the IFP was an urban extension of a Native Authority-based organization that it sought to conserve, the ANC was unable to arrive at a program to democratize Native Authority; instead, it turned to embracing those in the Native Authority who were willing to join it in an electoral alliance.

The Ugandan case shows that the democratization of the rural and the local cannot be stabilized unless extended to embrace the urban and the central, and the South African case illustrates the other side of the same proposition: without a democratization of rural customary power, urban civil power must inevitably degenerate. So long as rural power is organized as a fused authority that denies rights in the name of enforcing custom, civil society will remain an urban phenomenon. Surrounded by tribally organized customary powers, urban civil society is subject to a dual pressure: deracialization from within and retribalization from without. We can see this reflected in the dilemma the ANC faced in the 1994 elections.

Without a presence in either the reserve or the hostel – and without a program for democratizing customary rule in either – the ANC could reach the rural only from above, through Native Authorities. Confined to waging a democratic struggle in the urban and reduced to reaching rural communities through its customary authorities, the ANC found itself trapped in a Catch-22 situation. Its only option of linking the urban to the rural was through a tribal logic: either an intertribal alliance or an intertribal conflict, or more likely both, an alliance with those who are friendly (such as the chiefs of the Congress of Traditional Leaders of South Africa, CONTRALESA) and a conflict with those who are not (such as Inkatha). In either case, the structure of customary power would remain intact. This is the context in which the 1994 election assumed a significance both civic and ethnic.

Critical to the shape these elections came to assume were migrant workers, the social force that more than any other straddled the rural and the urban. Without a democratic reach to either hostels or reserves, the ANC remained alienated from hostel workers, the very reason Inkatha raced to embrace those Zulu as the custodian of their customary rights in KwaZulu, a custom it promised to defend with arms if necessary. The more successfully Inkatha executed this project, the more the tribal logic of customary authorities came to contaminate urban civil society. As the hostel-township-shanty triangle was engulfed by violence in the early 1990s, this fact registered on popular consciousness with the impact of an explosion. Unable to isolate Inkatha from its social base, the ANC explored a tactical alternative to a fast-expanding conflict. To defuse an intertribal collision, it settled for an intertribal alliance from above. The promise of that alliance was a federated civic power. Its price was unreformed customary power in the reserves. The compromised federal solution of South Africa closely resembled the one arrived at in Nigeria after the civil war.

A methodological point

There is also a methodological significance to the argument advanced in this book. It is that issues of democracy and governance cannot be directly deduced from the analysis of a mode of production; nor can they be read off as prescriptions from a general theory of democracy. In grappling with the question of democracy and governance, I have both shifted perspective from the mode of livelihood to the mode of rule and argued that there is a historical specificity to the mode of rule on the African continent. This shift underlines a critique – more in the nature of a sublating than a simple negation – of two kinds of contemporary discourses, that of political economy and that of civil society.

The critique of the standpoint of political economy is clearest in my analysis of the South African experience. In South African studies, the finest fruit of the political economy perspective was the cheap labor power thesis: it argued that apartheid was functional to capitalism, critical to ensuring a regular supply of cheap labor power. I have shifted attention from the cheapness of labor power to its semicoercive and controlled nature, in the context of a broader shift, from a focus on the labor question to one on the native question. My locus of analysis has been less the mode of accumulation than the mode of domination.

More than a response to the question of securing cheap labor power in a semi-industrial setting, I have argued that apartheid needs to be understood as the outcome of an unending quest for order in a setting both semi-industrial and colonial. Without denying the importance of the semi-industrial context, I have illuminated the significance of the colonial context in understanding apartheid as a form of the state. Rather than debunk or discard the perspective of political economy, my purpose has been to build on its insights while questioning its holistic claims.

Whereas in South Africa political economists generated a rich debate on the role of the state in reproducing a regime of semicoercive labor, the same cannot be said of the political analysis offered by their counterparts to the north of the Limpopo. Their claim was that the problem of Africa is one of 'backwardness,' of precapitalist relations of production, of insufficient proletarianization; in sum a lack of 'development.'[2] The key to democracy, then, is development. Ironically, this crude reductionism still finds defenders on both the Left and the Right, from militants advocating a single-party solution to champions of an IMF-style structural adjustment.

No less convincing, however, is the multiparty discourse of the so-called prodemocracy movements in equatorial Africa. Unlike their single-party counterparts, theirs is an explicitly political discourse. But it has turned a concrete historical experience – of civil society in the West – into the basis of a general and prescriptive theory. It has thereby turned democracy into a turnkey institutional import. Arguing that the problem of Africa is the absence or weakness of civil society institutions, it speaks the language of exclusion and marginalization, unable to unravel the form of power through which large numbers of Africans – in many cases the majority – are ruled.

Both perspectives presume rural areas to be residual, signifying a lack and an absence. That absence may be defined as economic or as political; the rural may be seen as lacking in urban modes of livelihood or in institutions of civil society. Whether it is activists in the trade unions and civics of South Africa or their more liberal counterparts in prodemocracy movements to the north, both have failed to arrive at a political program that addresses the mode of power containing rural populations on the continent. In contrast, my emphasis has been more on the mode of incorporation than that of marginalization. It is an emphasis less on the regime of rights from which the colonized were excluded on grounds of race than on the regime of custom into which they were incorporated and through which they were ruled.

In an analysis concerned not just with the colonial legacy, but also with postcolonial attempts to reform it, the shift has not simply been from the labor question to the native question; it has also involved placing the native question in the context of a broader problematic, the subject question. In practice, this latter shift took place with independence, with the birth of a decolonized and deracialized state. With it, the duality native–non-native gave way to another, subject-citizen. Inasmuch as reform in postcolonial Africa crystallized along two distinct paths, known as the conservative and the radical, one can speak of two subject prototypes. In the conservative states, which reproduced Native Authorities as the locus of a decentralized despotism, the prototype subject was stamped with an ethnic identity. In the radical states, which detribalized Native Authorities but where reform degenerated into a centralized despotism – most dramatically illustrated when the central state branded poor and unemployed urban residents as vagrants and forcibly repatriated them to their 'home areas' in the countryside – the prototype subject was simply a poor inhabitant in the rural areas, a peasant.

My point, then, is not only that the mode of rule is not deducible from the mode of livelihood. It is also that the specificity of the political in the African experience lies not as much in the structural defects of a historically organized civil society as in the crystallization of a different form of power. This is why the point of democratization cannot be just a simple reform of civil society. It also has to be a dismantling of the mode of rule organized on the basis of fused power, administrative justice, and extraeconomic coercion, all legitimized as the customary.

The antidote to a mode of rule that accentuates difference, ethnic in this case, cannot be to deny difference but to historicize it. Faced with a power that fragments an oppressed majority into so many self-enclosed culturally defined minorities, the burden of resistance must be both to recognize and to transcend the points of difference. If there is a lesson in the experience of oppositional movements – whether rural, such as the Ruwenzururu, the NRA, and the Sungusungu or the urban, such as the independent trade unions in post-1973 South Africa – it is that to create a democratic solidarity requires joining the emphasis on autonomy with the one on alliance, that on participatory self-rule with one on representational politics. In the specific circumstances of contemporary Africa, to create a democratic majority is to transcend two divisions that power spontaneously imposes on resistance: the rural-urban and the interethnic.

The way ahead

The point of this book is that any effective opposition in practice, and any theoretical analysis that would lead to one, must link the rural and the urban in ways that have not yet been done. This is why Uganda and South Africa are the paradigm cases today. Uganda, though the home of the most serious attempt yet to democratize Native Authority, has been unable to address the democratic demands of civil society movements. In South Africa, though the home of the strongest and the most imaginative civil society-based resistance on the continent, reform has floundered on the walls of customary power. As paradigm cases, both allow one to see in one place phenomena that appear as fragmentary elsewhere.

What social forces can link the urban and the rural? The only successful attempt yet to bridge the two has been the militant nationalist movement that followed the Second World War. The political impetus of this movement came from the disenfranchised native strata of the towns. Whether the 'verandah boys' of Nkrumah's CPP, migrant workers in many powerful trade union movements, or the 'boatmen' of Cabral's African Party for the Independence of Guinea and the Cape Verde Islands (PAIGC) a decade later, they shared a common social position: they lay beyond the reach of customary law and yet had few entitlements to civil rights. Though in civil society, they were not of civil society.

Faced with a growing and militant nationalism, colonialism embarked on its most ambitious reform program yet. Part of that postwar reform was a stabilization of migrant labor. Colonial governments raised 'bachelor' wages to 'family' ones, technically upgraded and differentiated the work process, and extended official recognition to trade unions. A similar process unfolded in South Africa in the wake of the post-Soweto Wiehahn and Riekert

Commissions, but the reforms were of limited significance. In South Africa the end of influx control brought a wave of migrants from rural areas to urban ones – mainly into hostels and shantytowns. To the north of the Limpopo, the 'informal sector' burgeoned as a combination of economic crises and structural adjustment led to a shrinking domestic industry alongside deregulated markets. Today it is migrant labor – and those in the informal sector – that forms a class that is in civil society but is not of it.

The social role of migrants varies, depending on the political choices available to them. As the South African case demonstrates, that role can be progressive or nonprogressive. The point about the prodemocracy movement of today is precisely that it lacks a program for linking the urban and the rural on the basis of democratizing rural power, as the ANC in South Africa. In the absence of such a democratization, the customary will remain a rallying cry lining up urban-based migrants behind customary authorities in their ethnic homes and behind city-based champions of the customary – so as to defend customary rights, however residual these may be. In the linkage between the urban and the rural, the rural is the key. So long as the rural is not reformed, the perversion of civil society is inevitable. This is why the limits of the current South African reform are so serious.

The most serious attempt yet to reform the rural was, as I have already noted, that of Museveni in Uganda, following earlier and more partial attempts, Qaddafi in Libya, Sankara in Bourkina Faso, and the early Rawlings in Ghana. They all highlight one lesson: decentralized democracy confined to the local state is both partial and unstable. It harbors contradictory possibilities: the point of reform of rural power can just as easily be to link up with representative demands from urban civil society as it can be to check these. If the objective is an overall democratization, it requires a balance between decentralization and centralization, participation and representation, autonomy and alliance. But if it is to checkmate civil society, a one-sided glorification of decentralization, autonomy and participation will suffice because, in the final analysis, it is bound to exacerbate the breach between the urban and the rural. Yet it is precisely such a tendency that is a growing orientation in left-oriented intellectual thought, on the one hand opposing and upholding participation against representation, on the other championing autonomy against alliance. If the experience of oppositional movements and the record of regime strategies reviewed in this book are anything to go by, this tendency needs to be seen as a negative development.

Colonial legal theory justified the subordination of subjects to a fused power as the continuation of a customary law and gave it the name of indirect rule; in contrast, it termed as direct rule the racially defined exclusion of colonized persons from citizen rights guaranteed by civil law in a differentiated form of power that framed civil society. Postindependence governments seeking to overcome this duality took one of two alternatives: either preserving the customary in the name of defending tradition against alien encroachment or abolishing it in the name of overcoming backwardness and embracing a triumphant modernism. But if indirect rule characteristic of Native Authorities was anchored in participatory forms, however distorted, and direct rule over civil society in representational forms, however exclusive, then was not the point to transcend both through a creative synthesis?

The reform of indirect rule systems in postindependence Africa built on the practice of participation without representation. In the second phase of radical African governments – from Qaddafi and Sankara to early Rawlings and Museveni – this reform became the basis of dismantling authority in the local state without democratizing power in the central state. Each of the peasant movements considered in chapter 6 tended toward participatory reforms, but none was able to stabilize these on the basis of participation alone. Participatory forms ('empowerment',) that stress the autonomy of a bounded group – only to undermine any possibility of an alliance-building majority-based representation – can justify and uphold the most undemocratic forms of central power. One only needs to look at the experience of self-initiated squatter settlements in South Africa: many began with an emphasis on participation and ended up with a warlord.

At the other extreme, there is the phenomenon of representation without participation. This is characteristic of a multiparty electoral reform whose target is the central state while leaving intact the decentralized despotism crystallized in the local state. Without an accent on participatory forms (and, as we will soon see, autonomy), the tendency is for representation to turn into its opposite: instead of a representation of popular strata in the state, the representative turns into an agent of the state power to popular sectors.

If democratic politics calls for joining participation at the local level with direct representation at higher levels, a similar perspective also needs to be forged when it comes to the relationship between autonomy and alliance. If the rationale for autonomy is the legitimacy and particularity of the local, then the fragmentation produced by a one-sidedly localized perspective underlines the need for alliance as a way to transcend it. And if participation and representation, autonomy and alliance, cannot be viewed in a one-sided opposition, neither can the customary and the civil. In spite of the practice of Native Authorities to justify their writ as custom, the customary was never a single, noncontradictory whole. Not only the Native Authority but also many peasant movements spoke the language of the customary. For every notion of the customary defined and enforced by the state, one could find a counternotion with a subaltern currency. A democratic appreciation of the customary must reject embracing an uncompromising modernism or traditionalism. As a start, it needs to disentangle authoritarian from emancipatory possibilities in both.

The point is neither to set aside dualisms that mark social theory nor to exchange one set for another more adequate to describing the contemporary situation. Rather it is to problematize both sides of every dualism by historicizing it, thereby underlining the institutional and political condition for its reproduction and for its transformation. Although theory cannot by itself transform reality, without a theoretical illumination reality must appear a closed riddle.

The fall of Soviet-type regimes in the late eighties was followed by an uncompromising critique of single-party regimes. In the African context, these have been followed by equally single-minded and prescriptive reforms embracing multiparty elections on the one hand and decentralization on the other. With every fresh round of lessons, however, we seem to lose historical depth. Once again, the impact of multiparty elections – in the absence of a reform of rural power – turns out to be not just shallow and short-lived, but also explosive. Too many presume that despotic power on this continent was always or even mainly a centralized affair, in the process forgetting the decentralized despotism that was the colonial state, and that is one variant of the African state today. In the absence of alliance-building mechanisms, all decentralized systems of rule fragment the ruled and stabilize their rulers. No doubt this is the great attraction of the current wave of decentralization – and the historical amnesia accompanying it – to Africa's current rulers.

But for the opposition that must take stock of social fragmentation as its historical starting point, it makes more sense to appropriate critically the experience of militant nationalism of yesteryears than just to debunk it. The strength of that experience lay in its ability to link the urban and the rural – politically. Its Achilles' heel was the failure to ground the link in an ongoing process of democratic reform, one with a focus on reforming the bifurcated state inherited from colonialism. Once in power, militant nationalists pursued reform in both civil society and Native Authority, deracializing the former and detribalizing the latter. But they reformed each sphere separately, and they did so from above. As reform from above substituted administration for politics, a bifurcated reform strategy recreated the bifurcated state. That failure corrupted a hitherto political link between the rural and the urban into a coercive one, cutting the ground from under their own feet. So the attempt to reform decentralized despotism degenerated into a centralized despotism, the other and more unstable variant of the African state.

The second round of reformers, those of the 1980s and 1990s, learned one lesson from their predecessors but also reproduced a limitation. They began the reform process from below, by dismantling Native Authorities and reorganizing village communities on the basis of self-administration. Detribalization was thereby joined to democratization, but in the local sphere only. Their dilemma is how to reform the center and thereby how to join the rural and the urban through a single – overarching but differentiated – reform process.

The record of state reform has been mixed. The tendency of African governments has been to play reform in one sphere against repression in the other. The result, inevitably, is a truncated reform. Of the two tensions aggravated by the form of the African state, the interethnic and the rural-urban, the latter is key. Hitherto, there have been two ways of linking the rural and the urban: the administrative and the political. The administrative link has turned out to be coercive. The political link has taken the form of a noncoercive clientelism. To bridge the rural and the urban through a politics both noncoercive and democratic, it is necessary to transcend the dualism of power around which the bifurcated state is organized. To do so requires that the nature of power in both spheres, the rural and the urban, be transformed, simultaneously. Only then will the distinction rural-urban – and interethnic – be more fluid than rigid, more an outcome of social processes than a state-enforced artefact.

Notes

[1] Notwithstanding Basil Davidson's claim to the contrary in *The Black Man's Burden: Africa and the Curse of the Nation-State* (James Currey).

[2] Expressed in non-radical terminology, the problem is 'the politics of the belly' to cite the title of Jean-François Bayart's latest book. It is a politics that he explains as 'the rush for spoils in which all actors – rich and poor – participate in the world of networks.' My point about clientelism is that it is more an effect of the form of power than an explanation of it.

PATRICK CHABAL & JEAN-PASCAL DALOZ
The Instrumentalization of Disorder

Reference
Africa Works: Disorder as Political Instrument
The International African Institute, James Currey, & Indiana University Press, 1999, pp. 155–63

The heart of our paradigm is the notion that in contemporary Africa politics turns on the instrumentalization of disorder. The three parts into which the book is divided represent the three areas on which we think it is essential to provide a fresh analysis. This is not to say, as should be obvious to the reader, that we neglect other political considerations or that we deem them of little interest. It is only that we concentrate our efforts on those aspects of socio-economic life which we believe have the most profound political resonance on the continent.

Our interpretation could appear controversial. Indeed, taken literally our view might even seem perverse. How can it seriously be suggested that the political arrangements which govern the lives of such a large number of contemporary nations amount to no more than the exploitation of disorder? Is not modern politics generally to be understood as the construction of political order? Is it not immoderate to imply that Africans should not just resist political order but positively prosper on disorder?

While we recognize these concerns, what we mean is that the disorder of which we speak is in fact a different 'order', the outcome of different rationalities and causalities. It appears as disorder only because most paradigms are based on a notion of a form of social, economic and, therefore, political development which reflects the experience of Western societies. The view that societies could modernize without becoming Westernized is one which most political analysis does not readily entertain. We can still make sense of countries, like those in Asia, that achieve economic success on different cultural bases because at least they are modern in ways which we do understand. But the experience of Africa, where there has been little or no appreciable economic or technological achievement, simply defies our usual notions of order.

Our approach is an attempt to explain how apparent disorder can in fact have its own logic – even if at first that logic seems hardly to contribute to the future prosperity of the continent. Once it is accepted that there are in Africa well-recognized norms of political practice which do not conform to those we find elsewhere, it becomes imperative to predicate our analysis on an interpretative framework which makes sense of those norms. This is what we have sought to accomplish both in the presentation of concepts that can be profitably used and in the development of a political analysis reaching beyond the surface of social, economic and political processes which appear either paradoxical or incomprehensible.

Let us now bring together the various strands of our analysis and present those notions which are most crucial to our paradigm. The point here is not to offer an exhaustive list of all aspects of African life which we consider politically significant but to illustrate the analytical irmport of our paradigm through a discussion of a judicious selection of key issues in the politics of contemporary Africa. We thus want in the remainder of this chapter successively to touch on: (1) the notion of the individual, (2) the salience of reciprocity, (3) the importance of vertical links, (4) the concept of success, and (5) the imperative of the short-term view and micro-perspective.

(1) We have already discussed at length the notion of the individual. Here we explain how this aspect of social life is relevant to our paradigm. The kernel of our analysis of the concept of identity in sub-Saharan Africa is that individual rationality is essentially based on communal logic. What we mean is twofold. First, individuals act on the whole with a preponderant respect for the psychological, social and religious foundations of the local community from which they are issued. Second, and more generally, relations of power are predicated on the shared belief that the political is communal.

The reverse is usually the case in the West, where the socio-political order is built on the notion that individuals are primarily discrete and very largely self-defined citizens of the nation. This is, of course, a question of emphasis. In the West, individuals are not entirely dissociated from the communal context of social life. Nor are individuals in Africa mere prisoners of their own community, bound by the imperatives of communal logic. On balance, however, there is a fundamental distinction on this question between the two forms of political 'rationality'.

The implications of this communal notion of the individual in Black Africa are both complex and profound. At the very least, it means that we cannot consider the place and role of the individual within the political system as we would do in the West. This may appear a relatively minor point but in some very crucial way it invalidates most existing interpretations of politics in contemporary Africa. Indeed, if we cannot simply assume what individual behaviour may mean politically, as most paradigms do, we have in effect to reconstruct one of the foundation concepts of modern political analysis. We need to conceive of individuals as the nodal points of larger communal networks rather than as single, free and intentional agents.

We can illustrate the importance of this point by reference to one of the latest, and perhaps one of the most sophisticated, studies of political change in present-day Africa.[15] Apposite as the authors' views are on the political-institutional approach best suited to understanding present 'democratic' political transitions on the continent and judicious as their conclusions may be, nowhere in this large volume is there any recognition of the pitfalls of conceptualizing individuals as 'citizens'. The notion of citizen is very precisely one which we would take to be Western (or Euro-centric) in that it implies a degree of individual differentiation within society which is almost nowhere to be found in Africa. Moreover, Bratton's and Van de Walle's analysis simply takes for granted that a process of democratization along the present lines will, *ipso facto*, bring about the consolidation of the reality of citizenship, regardless of existing socio-economic conditions.

We would in fact suggest that the reverse is a more likely outcome: democracy might well be Africanized in that the impact of multi-party elections will be seen in a communal rather than an individual framework. In our view, multi-party elections are unlikely to bring about significant change in the nature of individual differentiation in the present context of social, economic and political disorder. We would thus be wary of any suggestion

that such transitions might usher in a fundamental mutation in the contemporary political order. The experience of South Africa where, uniquely on the continent, Western and African notions of identity both have deep historical roots, will be an interesting test case of the extent to which Western-style democracy evolves in Africa.

(2) Our conception of the individual leads immediately to a consideration of the importance of the notion of reciprocity, the full significance of which is of great import to the workings of politics in Africa. Our emphasis on this aspect of socio-economic life is due to the observation that political action is in large degree driven by what we might call the imperative of exchange. We do not mean here simply the commerce of reciprocal favours – important as that undoubtedly is in everyday life – which is to be found everywhere in the world, albeit under different guises. We mean instead a more profound notion of what is expected of relations between individuals and the communities which are most relevant to their lives.

What we would say is that, in Africa, the logic of any action (whether political or not) lies in what it induces by way of expectations of reciprocity between the parties involved. Because of the conception of the individual on the continent, relations between people must also be seen as taking into account the communal of which they are a part. This can only be done when there is a clear recognition of the nature of the exchange involved. Relations, as it were, must be propitiated by reciprocity because they are not seen as distinct from the context within which they take place. Thus, political acts are played out on the market place of the various patrimonial networks concerned.

Whereas Western political theory starts from the premise that an individual political act such as voting can be meaningful regardless of the social context within which it is cast, our paradigm makes clear how this context cannot be disregarded in the case of Africa. Any political action is couched in an environment of reciprocity which dictates its symbolic and instrumental value. To return to present political transitions, the process of voting in a multi-party election must be understood as part of (very largely informal) relations of political exchange which impinge directly, if sometimes obscurely, on the electoral result.

For example, it is clear that in many African countries (like Côte d'Ivoire, Mozambique. Senegal or Guinea Bissau) ruling parties were returned to power in part simply because they were perceived to be more able to deliver on expected patrimonial promises than their competitors. Conversely, in other settings (like Zambia, Benin or São Tomé e Príncipe) they were swept from power in part when it was clear that they could no longer deliver. Whatever other considerations may induce voters to prefer one presidential candidate to another, the fact remains that such political support as may be given is expected to bring with it suitable reciprocity: hence, for example, the disillusionment with Frederick Chiluba's austerity measures in Zambia.

(3) That this is the case is, not fortuitously, connected with the third factor we wish to stress: the overriding importance of vertical links within the political system. We know, of course, that such links are the defining features of patrimonial systems. We know too that even Western legal-bureaucratic organizations are not immune to this kind of influence. Our point, however, is rather different. What is significant in Africa is the extent to which vertical and/or personalized, relations actually drive the very logic of the political system. It is not just that politics are swayed by personal

considerations or that the personal is manipulated for political reasons. It is also, and perhaps more importantly, that the overall aim of politics is to affect the nature of such personal relations.

What this means is that the ultimate ambition of those who have power is most often to establish their standing as Big Men. Such standing is, by its very nature, subjective and can only be achieved within a context of personalized relations where clients, or dependants, will ensure its recognition. It is not, therefore, sufficient to be acknowledged as the supreme political ruler. It is also necessary to be recognized as the *primus inter pares* among all Big Men, within what Hyden called an economy of affection.[16] The aim of the political elites is not just to gather power. It is much more fundamentally to use that power, and the resources which it can generate, to purchase, as it were, the 'affection' of their people.

Politics is thus about the search for a position of esteem which derives in large part from such subjective factors as status, respect and 'affection'. That is why, for example, the question of corruption in Africa cannot be understood simply within the context of the abuse of power. A well-managed moral economy of corruption does involve the abuse of formal power for personal gains. But, ultimately, personal gains are aimed at achieving a position of legitimate respectability recognized by all. While petty corruption is usually despised by the population at large, because it is merely self-serving and usually arbitrary, there is often a recognition that the elites' much more significant abuse of power serves larger and more legitimate 'moral' purposes.

Our argument here is not to downplay the extent to which personalized relations undermine the very viability of legal and bureaucratic institutionalization - which it most assuredly does. It is, rather, to explain how such personalized relations fit within the more general moral economy of esteem described above. This is not to say that such a moral economy is not itself widely abused by those, like Idi Amin or General Abacha, who sought to remain in power at all costs. Dictators are dictators anywhere in the world and Africa has had more than its fair share of tyrants. It is simply to remind ourselves that we need to be more discriminating in our analytical interpretation of personalized political relations in Africa. Here, as elsewhere, we could do worse than to start with the notion of accountability.[17] People in Africa can tell whether personalized relations are legitimate or not.

A paradoxical consequence of the factors outlined above, particularly in view of the present condition of Africa, is our conviction that a useful paradigm of politics in Africa needs to accommodate the concept of equilibrium. Our argument is that, because there is such a high degree of instability and uncertainty in contemporary Africa, the search for order has led to a strong demand for a state of equilibrium in society. That demand has fuelled a desire to find in existing beliefs and societal values the framework within which some stability could be achieved. In other words, the taming of disorder has heightened what we described in Part II as the 're-traditionalization' of society.

The problem, however, is that development requires the productive use of disequilibrium, meaning here the channelling of the resources generated by inequality into productive investment. There is currently in Africa neither the (technical, social, professional and legal) infrastructure nor, more importantly, the political will to drive development in this way. Consequently, the search for equilibrium takes the form of what we have conceptualized as, the political instrumentalization of disorder. The rapid gains reaped by exchange, much of which is now of a 'criminal' nature, are, more likely quickly to deliver the resources needed by the neo-patrimonial System than the long and arduous journey which Western-style economic development entails.

(4) Crucial to the comprehension of current politics on the continent is a notion of what achievement or success means. Development demands, as we know, the kind of productive investment which is most compatible with what Weber identified as the Protestant work ethic. The success of capitalist development is measured in growth, which in turn implies deferred reward. The opposite is the case in Africa. The measure of achievement has long been, and seemingly continues to be, found in the immediate display of material gain – that is, consumption rather than production. At a most fundamental level, then, the logic of the notion of success is antithetical to the economic 'mentality' under-pinning development.

There is debate as to why this should be the measure of achieve-ment in Africa.[18] What is cause and what is effect? Do such norms of success only apply because the continent is poor? Would they change if development were initiated successfully or are they themselves one of the main impediments to development? Whatever the most plausible answers to these questions, there is no doubt that at present such norms do apply and that they do have a deleterious effect on Africa's potential for economic development. And, from our observations, there are no indications of a change towards a different set of attitudes.

Ostentation remains, and is likely to remain, one of the chief political virtues in Africa. Or to put it another way, it continues to be more important for political elites to display the right kind of ostentation (including redistributing resources to clients) than to demonstrate the potential achievement of the Protestant work ethic.

From a Western perspective such attitudes exhibit the limits of political ambition in Africa. Few politicians meaningfully engage the population in a discussion of the changes required to achieve a higher rate of growth and more sustained development in the country. Fewer still show by what they do rather than what they say - that they are even remotely concerned about such issues. There may be talk of development - there have even been in the past development plans - but the reality of the exercise of power does not give much evidence of a commitment to the sort of structural and infrastructural reforms which would make development possible. Oil revenues, for instance, are usually dissipated on conspicuous consumption (such as the construction of a new capital city in Nigeria) and other patrimonial expenses.

Far from becoming less prevalent, the present norm of success seems in practice to be pushing politicians into an ever more frantic search for the means of patrimonial ostentation. The apparently stunning speed with which political liberalization and democratiza-tion were embraced (between 1990 and 1994) by the political elites in Africa can, without undue cynicism, be seen in part at least as an attempt to instrumentalize Western political conditionalities for the purpose of making possible the continued, or even increased, delivery of foreign aid which their regimes so desperately required.[19] This concept of achievement entails two further characteristics of politics which we think important: the dominance of the short-term view and the imperative of the micro- (as opposed to macro-) perspective.

(5) These two attributes of modern politics in Africa are easily understood, as they are entirely consistent with the socio-economic norms currently found on the continent. Indeed, the criteria of

success identified above make it inevitable that the outlook of the political elites should be both short-term and concerned with the micro- rather than macro-picture of society. The political system (as we have outlined it in Part I) functions in the here and now, not for the sake of a hypothetical tomorrow. It can only work if it meets its obligations continuously. In other words, its legitimacy rests with its immediate achievements, not with its long-term ambitions. It does not allow for delayed reward or achievement – much less for long-term investment.

Similarly, the logic of neo-patrimonialism is focused on the proximate: the local and the communal. Its legitimacy depends on the ability to deliver to those who are linked with the political elites through the micro-networks of patronage and clientelism. There is no scope within such a perspective for deferring to a larger but less immediate macro-rationality, most significantly to the greater good of the country as a whole. Clients will not readily accept sacrifices for more ambitious national goals in a context where it is assumed that patrons only work for their clients. So that the claim by one Big Man that he must reduce expenditures on his clients because resources are needed for national development would not normally be credible or acceptable.

By stressing what we take to be two powerful political imperatives, we do not thereby mean to imply that other factors are not at work. Because political elites operate on a number of different registers both modern and 'traditional' – the analysis of politics in Africa needs to take into account the ways in which those registers impinge on political outcomes. It is obvious that politicians will try to maximize the effect of their action in terms which are not limited to the short-term and micro-perspective. They quite naturally want to be seen to succeed in the modern developmentalist ambitions which are at the centre of their political ideology. They will, accordingly, rationalize what they do by means of a discourse which will omit to highlight the considerations we have stressed.

Some, like Nyerere or Museveni, may well have a relatively modest personal need for the status of Big Man and may genuinely aim to transcend the short-term view in favour of longer-term developmental goals. A few, like Nelson Mandela, may in fact embody the highest virtues of the Protestant work ethic.[20] The fact remains, however, that the ability of such exceptional leaders to move the political system beyond its present rationality is limited, not primarily because of a lack of ambition but much more fundamentally because of the nature of existing forms of political legitimacy. In the end, there is an interlocking neo-patrimonial logic between the deep ambitions of the political elites and the well-grounded expectations of their clients.

❖❖❖

Our (admittedly far from cheering) conclusion is that there prevails in Africa a system of politics inimical to development as it is usually understood in the West. The dynamics of the political instrumentalization of disorder are such as to limit the scope for reform in at least two ways. The first is that, where disorder has become a resource, there is no incentive to work for a more institutionalized ordering of society. The second is that in the absence of any other viable way of obtaining the means needed to sustain neo-patrimonialism, there is inevitably a tendency to link politics to realms of increased disorder, be it war or crime. There is therefore an inbuilt bias in favour of greater disorder and against the formation of the Western-style legal, administrative and institutional foundations required for development.

Consequently, the prospects for political institutionalization are, in our view, limited. Nor is it likely that the recent democratic experiments in Africa will lead to the establishment of the constitutional, legal and bureaucratic political order which is required for fundamental reform. Such change would have to be driven by popular will. Only when ordinary African men and women have cause to reject the logic of personalized politics, seriously to question the legitimacy of the present political instrumentalization of disorder and to struggle for new forms of political accountability, will meaningful change occur. Tempting as it is to think that political liberalization, the so-called democratization of Africa, will facilitate such change, there is in the foreseeable future little likelihood that it will. We simply cannot know how Africa will evolve politically.

Our paradigm offers a method for understanding the present condition of Africa which is neither normative nor teleological. Its analytical import is to make it possible to explain how it is that Africa 'works' in the absence of proper political institutionalization or sustained economic development. We do not present solutions to the problems of Africa, merely a diagnosis of its predicament. That is why it is worth stating again that our argument cannot be used as evidence to support the view either that Africans are 'inherently' different from us or that they are 'inherently' incapable of changing the condition of the countries in which they live. Nor can it remotely be construed as condoning what is happening on the continent today. As Africanists we can only deplore the consequences of the present economic, social and political crisis. As political analysts we can do no more than offer what we believe to be a well-considered appraisal of that crisis.

Notes

⋆ Please note that original footnote numbering has been retained.

[15] M. Bratton and N. van de Walle, *Democratic Experiments in Africa: Regime Transitions in Comparative Perspective*, Cambridge, Cambridge University Press, 1997.

[16] G. Hyden, *Beyond Ujamaa in Tanzania*, Heinemann, 1980.

[17] Patrick Chabal, *Power in Africa. An Essay in Political Interpretation*, London and Basingstoke, Macmillan, 1992, ch. 3.

[18] We have reviewed the debate on these issues in chapter 9.

[19] As we have shown in chapter 8.

[20] The paradigm we present is, in our view, not necessarily applicable to South Africa, which we believe to be structurally different from the rest of Black Africa because of its distinct historical experience.

2 Dimensions of Conflict

ROY MAY

Internal Dimensions of Warfare in Chad

Reference
Cambridge Anthropology, Vol 3, No 2, 1988–9, pp. 17–27

Some of the most vivid images of the recent history of Chad have been those of the external interventions and involvements by other states and of internal dislocation. The major external actors have been France, the United States and Libya though there have also been important inputs from other African states, particularly some of the more conservative Francophone states, and the OAU. In particular the major military operations of the 1980s have highlighted the role of France, which 'whilst characterised by weakness, vacillation and either choosing the wrong option or at best being forced to make constant adjustments to its policies … to (remain) Chad's predominant military patron'[1] has led her to intervene with five specific military interventions in 1968, 1969–72, 1978–86 and *Operation Manta* in 1983–84 and *Operation Eperviev* 1985. United States support has been of less value quantitively, but it is clear that without the CIA-funded support of Habré in 1981–82 that, 'Habré could not possibly have returned to power'.[2] Meanwhile Gadaffi's international and continental aspirations have highlighted her role, although Libyan influence and support has in its opportunistic and fickle manner ranged across most factions within Chad and has resulted in both the high point of Libyan troops and armour installing Goukouni in Ndjamena in December 1980 to the low point of her disastrous military defeats at the hands of the Chadian armed forces in 1987 when the Libyan military, 'showed deep-seated flaws in command, tactics, weapons mix and motivation'.[3]

However, it is the contention of this paper that these important actions and the attention they have received should not distract us from the crucial dynamics and processes within Chad and from asserting that these internal dynamics are the crucial bedrock upon which external interventions have been built. Whilst agreeing with Lemarchand[4] that, 'the vectors of factional strife are both domestic and foreign, internal fragmentation and external involvement are crucially important dimensions for grasping the roots of factionalism', it is asserted that, without that combination of regional, ethnic, religious, cultural and historical factors *peculiar* to Chad, external intervention would have been unlikely. Further the recently attempted coup of 1st April 1989[5] reinforces this by being quite clearly the result of *internal* tensions and processes within the ruling coalition and reflecting difficulties resulting from a switch from the historical reliance of President Habré upon his Forces of the Army of the North (FAN) to the wider groupings brought in by the 'ralliement' and now reflected in both government appointments and membership of Union of Independence and Revolution

(UNIR), the quasi party created by Habré in 1984. Some of these tensions had been noted as early as 1987[6] and were apparent at the time of the UNIR congress in Ndjamena in October 1988[7] with discussions around the issue of UNIR as either a movement (*animation politique*) or a political party with implications of more representative structures.

Many variables can be used to explain the slow breakdown of the Chadian state from the 1960s to the early 1980s when not only did it not meet Jackson and Rosberg's[8] criteria of empirical statehood, but probably not also their concept of juridical statehood. The transformation that has occurred has seen the state rise from the dead and reconstitute itself, 'with American and French assistance as a viable political and military, if not yet economic entity under Hissene Habré'.[9] The key question revolves around the role of Habré for this has been crucial both in military and political terms where Foltz[10] argues that he is 'intelligent and tough' but 'no remote autocrat or one man band' and a 'thorough-going pragmatist who has kept his eye on the central goal of seizing and ruling Chad'. The test will be whether the pragmatist will be able to handle the tensions caused by the recent partial rapprochement with Libya with its implication both for Chad's relationship with France (who have already talked of troop reductions) and the United States *and* the problems inherent in the process of 'ralliement' with the careful balancing required to maintain stability. To assess the possibilities of such careful balancing requires an explanation of these factors that have led to political fragmentation and the emergence of factions.

Regional and ethnic factors

Regionally Chad can be divided into three, the Northern desert belt containing the prefectures of Borkou, Ennedi and Tibest (BET), the middle belt of more populated Sahelian region and the southern, Sudanic belt being both the most populated and the most economically viable. As will be shown ethnic and political groupings are not coterminous with these regions. There are both divisions and overlap. French colonial perceptions however, tended to view Chad in a more sympathetic light, seeing the southern five prefectures of Mayo-Kebbi, Logone Oriental, Logone Occidental, Tandjil and Moyen-Chari (about 10% of the country) as *La Tchad utile* and the rest as *La Tchad inutile*. These perceptions were reinforced by policy which, acting upon indigenous institutions, led to the considerably differential impact of economic, educational and social change, with the south gaining disproportionately.

The population of Chad was estimated to be 5.2m in 1985, though the last partial sample survey was taken in 1963–64, and is divided into a large number of ethnic groups, between 150 to 192 depending upon the classification used. This population is widely spread and Lemarchand shows both the major grouping and the schismatic elements within these. Using the simplistic definition of the North (excluding the five southern prefectures) it is possible to identify three major groupings, the Toubou (also known as the Gorane), the Arabs and the Sahelian populations. The majority of the Toubou may be found in the BET with the majority living in Ennedi although small numbers may also be found in Kanem and Ouaddai; the major division within the Toubou is between the Teda living mainly in the north west and the Daza living mainly in the south east of the region, although again in both cases these classes are split into smaller groups that nomadise specific areas.[12] The ethnic origins of the Toubou are still unknown, 'their skin is black but their features are caucasian' and 'whilst converted to

Islam, they remain animists under a Muslim veneer'[13]. It is significant for an understanding of Chadian politics that the two major figures of recent political history Hissene Habré and Goukouni Oueddei are both Toubou, Habré from the Daza and Goukouni being from the Teda.

Also in the north are the Arabs estimated at over half a million and within these 'countless subdivisions based on origin (Jahauna and Hassauna) lifestyle (Abbela and Baggara) factions (Missirye and Rattanine) and class'.[14] These subdivisions have led to inter-Arab strife for example in 1947, when the Missirye turned against the Rattanine resulting in 180 deaths and a later inter-Frolinat conflict in 1972.[15] An important group amongst the Arabs, the Ouled Suleyman, are differentiated from other Arabs by their strong links with Libya which in some ways they regard as their homeland. The Ouled Suleyman have proved to be a strong basis for factional support and of resistance to all Chadian governments; evidently they have also been open to Libyan influence. In the cases of both Toubou and Arab societies Lemarchand[16] observes that power in the segmentary societies is so widely diffused that it leads to extraordinary fluidity of alliances and oppositions, and the 'principle of freedom (is) raised almost to the level of anarchy' with important consequences for the stability of governments.

Spread across the Sahelian belt are a large number of loose and arbitrary groupings which include the Maba, Moubi, Haddad, Hadjeray, Zaghawa, Kanembou and Massalit. A complicating factor here is the existence of strong sultanates particularly those of Kanem, Bagurmi and Ouaddai. These originally pagan sultanates had become Islamic and had been utilised by the French in the process of indirect rule with some important consequences for the nature of their authority. Amongst the Sahelian peoples the Hadjeray is a name given to a loose grouping of 14 to 18 peoples who speak a variety of languages and have a wide variety of social structures, but who are 'united by a common habitat, the rough hill country of the Guera'[17] (Jadjeray is Arabic for hill people), and common religious traditions resistant to both Islam and Christianity. It was amongst another Sahelian group, the Moubi, that a chieftaincy dispute is said to have sparked off a set of events that led to the eruption of the Mangalme riots in 1965 and really started the rebellions.

In the south the major group are the Sara although it is clear that there are a number of linguistically related sub-groups within this collectivity and that Sara ethnicity is a recent construction.[18] Within this Sara consciousness sub-loyalties persist and while their shared consciousness of the threat posed to their political hegemony was the most powerful force of intra-Sara cohesion during the early days of the civil war 'the events of the 1970's under Toubalbya and the 1980's showed their susceptibility to ethnic demobilisation and cultural fragmentation'.[19] There are also significant non-Sara populations in Mayo Kebbi such as the Massa, Toubouri, Kera and Moundang who were resistant in various degrees to Sara hegemony.

Political decay and the Tombalbye era

In this section we argue that a crucial determinant of the rise of opposition groupings, based on the elements mentioned in the preceding section, was misrule of the first Chadian President Francois Tombalbye between independence in 1960 and the coup of 1975.

Despite opposition from colonially backed parties, regionally based parties and political groupings around individual leaders, the Parti Progressiviste Tchadien (PPT) became the ruling party at independence with Tombalbye (a Sara) as the leader. The PPT was largely a Sara supported party but there were some northern and Muslim elements. In the early years of independence there was a rapid movement towards consolidation of power by the PPT and by 1963 the one party state was established with the banning of all other parties mainly northern and Muslim. This movement was reinforced by purges within the PPT, for example in 1965 when three ministers and three deputies were arrested in connection with a supposed plot to put the Sultans and tribal chiefs into power. Tombalbye's rule became increasingly onerous. Tax excesses and administrative brutality led to the outbreak of serious riots in Batha prefecture in 1965 which spread to most of the Sahelian region by 1966. These riots, which might be termed a populist revolt, became more channelled into political action with the emergence of two guerilla movements; the Front for the Liberation of Chad (FLT) operating largely in Biltine, and the Front for National Liberation (FROLINAT) in Batha, Guera and Ouaddai. FROLINAT became the more significant body. In the BET the departure of the French military and the assumption of administration by a Chadian government rapidly led to tensions between the southern administrators and military and the local population. A series of arbitrary actions followed an incident at a dance in Bardai in which a Chadian soldier was killed. The local sous-prefect imposed harsh sanctions including the mistreatment of a whole village and the imposition of fines for such things as the wearing of turbans, the growing of beards and public meetings. Further disturbance in the north led to a revolt by Toubou members of the nomad guard and finally, intervention by French troops in August 1968. Meanwhile FROLINAT had become so successful that they controlled a large part of the centre and east of the country and it required a French expeditionary force to operate from 1969–72 in order to prevent them from taking Ndjamena. Two crucial points to emphasize here are that firstly there were two separate bases of revolt which later became labelled under the FROLINAT title and secondly, that in both cases it was internal dynamics that led to growth of these bodies not external stimuli.

During the period of French involvement (1969–72) Tombalbye had to make some adjustments suggested by the Mission d'Reform Administratice (MRA) which included reforming the administration, and recognizing that the complaints of the centre and east had some substance by the release of some prisoners and attempts at dialogue with FROLINAT. The result of these actions were short lived however, and the early 1970s saw a number of attempts by Tombalbye to strengthen his grip upon the country. Amongst these was the institutional renovation of the party in 1973 by replacing the PPT 'a cadre of permanent discard' by the Movement National pour la Revolution Culturelle (MNRCS). More serious were the attempts at cultural renovation and the trend to authenticity (introducing African names for people and places) following the example of Tombalbye's mentor President Mobuto. (A similar relationship appears to exist between Habré and Mobuto.) These cultural trends also included the introduction of an ideology of 'Tchaditude' and the spread of Yondo rites. These 'rites de passage' were male initiation ceremonies amongst the Sara and included painful and humiliating ordeals. Tombalbye's decision that these should be performed for all Sara males between 16 and 50 and to all public servants, members of the government and the higher ranks of the armed forces was the key to splits amongst the Sara. The Yondo rites were borrowed from the Sar subgroup and their imposition upon other subgroups led to the crystalisation of intra-Sara antagonisms along class and regional lines which eventually led to the coup that over-threw the President in 1975 and to his replacement by another Sara, General Malloum.

The demise of the state

By the middle of the 1970s a number of factors had conspired to break down the initial and limited cohesion of FROLINAT: the defeat by the French troops in 1969–72, the involvement of Libya particularly since their acquisition of the Aouzon strip in 1973 that caused tactical disagreements between factions and also the dispute between Goukouni and Habré over the capture and ransom of the French archaeologist Madame Claustré that reinforced traditional intra-Toubou rivalries. However, Lemarchand argues that, 'the extraordinary rapid disintegration of FROLINAT after 1975 can only be understood by reference to the centrifugal forces at work in the social structure of northern societies'.[20] A number of groups had emerged with regional bases of support, the most prominent of these were the Forces Armées Populaire (FAP) led by Goukouni, largely Toubou with bases in the Tibesti; Forces Armées du Nord (FAN) based in Biltine prefecture; Conseil Démocratique de la Révolution (CDR) Arab-supported mainly in Guera prefecture; Forces Armées Occidentales (FAO) mainly Kanenbou with a base just north of Lake Chad; the 1st Vulcan army operating in the south of the BET; Movement Populaire pour la Libération du Tchad (MPLT) in the Lake Chad area. Other groups included the Forces Populaire de la Libération (FPL), FROLINAT Originel, and FROLINAT Fondamental. As has been argued elsewhere[21] these leaders exhibited many characteristics of 'warlord' politics: personal authority, a regional base of support, military success reflected in political claims and the development of political ability. Chad also exhibited similar characteristics to those of China in the 1930s: a fluidity of groups, the lack of an unifying ideology or policy, the collapse of central state authority and some external intervention. The two crucial and related processes involved here were the 'de-institutionalisation and organisational decay at the level of central government' and a 'concomitant and progressive growth of regionalism ultimately emerging as a regionalisation of the whole political process'.[22]

In the south the major group was the rump of the old Chad army, the Forces Armées Tchadien (FAT) led by Kamouge, with other minor groups led by Djogo and Kemto.

The military government of General Malloum from 1975–78 transformed itself into the Council of Defence and Security (CDS) in 1978 with Habré brought in as Prime Minister. This fell apart with the first battle of Ndjamena in February 1979 when FAN effectively took control of the city with important support from Guarra Lassou and some elements of the Moundang from Mayo-Kebbi prefecture. After the defeat of Malloum there were pogroms against Muslims in the southern towns of Sarh and Moundou. Also, a number of political organisations in the south came together under the umbrella organisation of the Comité Permanent du Moudou led by Kamougue and operated as a personal fiefdom. There was some distrust of Kamougue, and his acceptance of Libyan help did nothing to allay this though his defeat of Habré's FAN expeditionary force in its attempt to capture Pala and Bongor in Mayo Kebbi did a great deal to strengthen his position.

During a protracted set of conferences in 1979 the 'onze tendances' (eleven factions) come together in a Transitional Government of National Unity (GUNT) that included Goukouni as President, Kamougue as Vice President and Habré as Minister of Defence. But this rapidly broke down, unsurprisingly given the 'Chadians' centrifugal regional and ethnic tendencies, intensified by their leaders, political ambitions, competitive foreign sponsorship, and pervasive suspicion of any centralised authority'.[23] The internal wars, shifts of alliances and external support led to Habré becoming President by 1982 and the GUNT faction split into two major groupings, those supporting the GUNT led by Goukouni. In this period, immediately after Habré's accession to power, the defeat of Kamougue and the heavy handed actions of FAN troops led to a number of splits in Sara ranks with the emergence of a number of groups known as commandos or 'codes', principally the 'codos rouge' of Lt. Col. Kotiga in the south of Moyen Chari, 'codo espoir' around Moundou, 'codo logtan' in the south of Tandjil and the less significant 'codo vert'. The splits in the south after 1982 are important as they demonstrate the strength of conflicts but also point to the need for Habré to reconcile these groups if he was to establish effective control of the state.

Finally,[24] the combination of this situation with external interventions meant that effectively between 1983 and 1987, the country north of the fifteenth parallel (sixteenth after February 1984) was under the control of GUNT, and Chad was effectively partitioned. Further it can be argued that from the period 1975–82 and 1983–87 there certainly has not been a Chadian state in the empirical sense and that the demise of this state has stimulated the emergence of yet more groupings competing for power. Paradoxically it is possible to argue that despite this, 'a sense of Chadian identity has taken root' and this 'reflects a growing realisation amongst northern and southern leadership groups that their respective societies are simply too fragmented as shown by the fact that at no stage has secession been viewed as a viable alternative'.[25] One may argue that this very fact has reinforced the vigour of struggles to control the state and given greater impetus to the emergence of regionally based factions.

The Habré solution

Habré's success in achieving power in 1982 lay in the military wing of FAN which had been remarkable for its political cohesion and its fighting prowess, 'it (had) kept together a core force of combatants drawn from the Gorane, Zaghawa, Bideyat, Hadjeray, Arab, Moundang and Kim with a sprinkling of individuals from most other subgroups in the north and the middle of the country'.[26] The expansion of the armed forces, the proliferation of intelligence networks, the use of the Sécurité Présidentielle (SP), and the favoured treatment of the SP, have all caused difficulties but none so great as the political needs of reconciliation. The creation of UNIR in June 1984 was a brave and risky step by Habré as it signalled he was searching for a coalition of interests beyond those which had brought him to power. The creation and use of UNIR was to be an institutional manifestation (in addition to government appointments) of the process of 'ralliement'. The difficulties inherent in this process can now be seen clearly in two ways.

Firstly one of the key groups of the alliance that brought Habré to success, the Hadjeray, have been in dispute with the government. An Hadjeray leader, Idris Miskine, was Habré's no. 2 until his death from malaria in 1984. Rumours that his death was not accidental were reinforced by difficulties in November and December 1986 when, after incidents between Hadjeray and Gorane soldiers, a senior Hadjeray officer was tortured on the orders of the Gorane commander. Problems escalated with incidents and arrests in Ndjamena, the death of an arrested Hadjeray journalist and more disturbances in Guera. An underground organisation, the Mouvement pour le Salut National du Tchad (MOSANUT) led by a junior Hadjeray officer was created.

Secondly the process of ralliement had continued as most rebel leaders joined Habré, with the exception by late 1988 of two important figures, Goukouni and the leader of the CDR Achiek Ibn Oumar.[27] Protracted and difficult negotiations concluded with the return of Achiek and the CDR in December. This was followed by Achiek's rapid promotion to Foreign Minister which appeared to stimulate the recent coup attempt. It seems FAN could accept Kamougue, Djogo, Kotiga (other rallied leaders) etc., but accepting Achiek was going too far! The significance of the attempted coup lies in two areas: firstly, the *seniority* of those involved (Hahamat Itno was Minister of the Interior and Idris Deby an ex-forces commander, Hassan Djamous was the Commander-in-Chief of the armed forces and architect of the brilliant victories of 1987), *and* secondly, in their ethnic origins. All three are Zaghawa from Biltine prefecture. It remains to be seen whether processes that have resulted from the internal needs of reconciliation, and those tentative moves to re-establish relationships with Libya, can be easily and happily resolved.

Conclusion

It would be foolish to argue that external powers have not had an important role in the decline, fall and re-emergence of Chad but it needs to be reiterated that, 'the determining influence of competing external actors in maintaining Chad in a state of constant disequilibrium was perhaps exaggerated in earlier accounts'.[28] What has been suggested in this paper is that the particular nature and character of Chad's ethnic groups have proved especially vulnerable to pressure. These pressures can be identified as unequal regional economic and social development, the inequitable and disastrous rule of Tombalbye, the subsequent decline of the State and the emergence of 'warlords'. If we accept the 'warlord' analysis, the important questions are whether Habré's rise is part of an incipient state building process, whether he can move from a successful politics of extraction to a more effective politics of control and whether it is possible to turn warlord commanders into a conventional military bureaucracy and synthesise them further into a civilian administration. Habré's recent resurrection of the 'Chadian State'[29] at least raises the possibility that he may be that state's Chiang, though it seems improbable that he is Chad's Mao!

Notes

1 Roy May and Roger Charlton, 'Chad: France's Fortuitous Success'. *Review of Association for the Study of Modern and Contemporary France*, No. 37, April 1987, p. 3.
2 W. Foltz, 'Chad's Third Republic: Strengths, Problems and Prospects'. *CSIS Africa Notes*, 27th October, 1987, p. 4.
3 Ibid, p. 5.
4 R. Lemarchand, 'Chad, The Misadventures of the North–South Dialectic', 29th March, 1986, p. 28.
5 West Africa, 24–30th April 1989. Le Monde, 17th April 1989.
6 W.Foltz, *op. cit.*, p.6.
7 Interviews, Ndjamena, October 1988.
8 R Jackson and C. Rosberg, 'Why Africa's weak states persist'. *World Politics*, Vol. 35, No. 1, 1982.
9 Roger Charlton and Roy May, 'Chadian Politics: A Warlord Perspective', paper to African Studies Association of the USA, Conference, Denver, Colorado, November 1987.
10 W. Foltz, *op. cit.*, p. 3.
11 V. Thompson and R Adloff, *Conflict in Chad*, Hurst, London 1981, p. 3. R Lemarchand, *op. cit.*, and R. Lemarchand, 'Chad. The Roots of Chaos.' *Current History*, December 1981.
12 S. Decalo, 'Regionalism, Political Decay and Civil Strife in Chad.' *JMAS*, 18th January, 1980, p. 277.
13 Thompson and Adloff, *op. cit.*, p. 5.
14 R Lernarchand, *Roots*, p. 30.
15 R Lemarchand, *Misadventures*, p. 417.
16 R Lemarchand, *Roots*, p. 35.
17 W. Foltz, *op. cit.*, pp. 7-8.
18 R Lemarchand, 'The Politics of Sara Ethnicity.' *Cahiers d'études Africains*. 20th April, 1980.
19 R Lemarchand, *Roots*, p. 416.
20 R Lemarchand, p. 415.
21 Roger Charlton and Roy May, *op. cit.*, p.13.
22 Ibid, p. 11.
23 V. Thompson and R Adloff, *op. cit.*, p. 97.
24 Roy May and Roger Charlton, *op. cit.*
25 R Lemarchand, *Misadventures*, p. 31.
26 W, Foltz, *op. cit.*, p. 6.
27 There was a period of disputed leadership in the CDR with Libyan support for Rakmis Mahni.
28 Roger Charlton and Roy May, *op. cit.,* p. 2.
29 Ibid., p. 13.

MARGARET HALL
& TOM YOUNG
Mozambique at War
with Itself

Reference
Confronting Leviathan: Mozambique Since Independence
London: Christopher Hurst & Co., 1997, ch. 7

We didn't realise how influential the traditional authorities were, even without formal power.... We are obviously going to have to harmonize traditional beliefs with our political project. Otherwise, we are going against things that the vast majority of our people believe – we will be like foreigners in our own country. I think we are gathering the courage to say so aloud. We will have to restore some of the traditional structures that at the beginning of our independence we simply smashed, thinking that we were doing a good and important thing.[1]

Traditional spirit mediums and diviners, sometimes Ndau but more often local specialists, also play a pivotal role in regulating daily life on Renamo bases. No major decisions … are ever undertaken without a prior consultation with the spirits.[…] Diviners and spirit mediums are also kept busy magically protecting Renamo bases, making them invisible to Frelimo soldiers, 'vaccinating' Renamo combatants to make them bulletproof, identifying witches amongst the civilian population and captives contemplating flight. All residents on Renamo bases are obliged to participate on a regular basis in such religious ceremonies – ceremonies in which the ancestral spirits ideologically legitimate Renamo's war against Frelimo.[2]

As we have shown, Frelimo understood its war of liberation as part of a process of building a nation out of diverse groups kept separated and divided by colonialism. Although the anti-colonial revolts of the nineteenth and early twentieth centuries (and even the earlier pre-colonial wars) marked the beginnings of drawing together some of the ethnic and regional threads, even if in temporary and geographically limited alliances against the enemy, Portuguese colonialism finally triumphed because Mozambicans had failed to unite. Frelimo's armed struggle had overcome these divisions, thereby providing a base for the construction of the new nation. As the political process became more radicalised, a second theme of social progress was added to national freedom. 'Liberation' came also to mean, negatively, the defeat of 'feudalism' as incarnated by Nkavandame and the social strata he represented; positively, it meant the prospect of both development and social emancipation. For a considerable period these political beliefs shaped Frelimo's understanding of Renamo's war: as little more than an attack on Frelimo's nation-building and development project. This was an attack, moreover, largely if not wholly directed by hostile external forces, utilising Mozambican collaborators, either former stooges of the colonial regime or Frelimo's own traitors and defectors. This combination of elements in turn accounted for Renamo's tactics, especially the extreme violence visited on civilians along with the deliberate destruction of development projects and the economic infrastructure.

This account of Renamo as a violent apolitical movement whose only rationale must be that it operated on behalf of some malevolent outside interests was assiduously cultivated by the Mozambican government and its academic and journalistic publicists with considerable skill and success.[3] Nor was it wholly false. Renamo's persistent assaults on the transport infrastructure serving Mozambique's neighbour states was the most unambiguously South African-inspired aspect of Renamo's war. It directly damaged the Mozambican economy as well as further internationalising the conflict by drawing in other actors in defence of their own interests. The destruction of the development infrastructure and the national transportation network was also, in part at least, clearly inspired by South African destabilisation strategies.[4] South African support for Renamo, while often exaggerated, remained important. The organisation was not afforded substantial rear-base or sanctuary facilities inside South Africa, and although re-supply continued by devious routes after the Nkomati Accord (the need for restraint and subterfuge having become paramount), the South African military pursued a 'minimalist' strategy of ensuring Renamo's survival by providing intelligence and arms when it seemed in danger of defeat.[5] Thus re-supply was not lavish, and had to be supplemented by what Renamo managed to obtain by capture from the Mozambican army.

Waging war

The niggardliness of suppliers and the absence of a secure rear sanctuary meant that the war remained one fought at a low level of military technology, and that Renamo had to adapt to living off the land – in practice off the peasantry. The main weapon on both sides was the AK47 assault rifle. Renamo also habitually employed knives and machetes, especially in the north and centre of the country, but it also had an ill-assorted array of weaponry as well as a few SAM-7s, which the group was unable to operate.[6]

But the low level of military technology favoured mobility and guerrilla tactics over conventional forces; and although areas of established Renamo operation certainly existed, bases within them usually remained mobile, although perhaps less so in Zambézia than elsewhere. Even the largest and most important bases, including Dhlakama's headquarters (normally situated in or near the Gorongosa), shifted periodically in response to the threat or reality of government or Zimbabwean assaults. Renamo had the ability to concentrate forces for offensives, but was not equipped for anything beyond hit-and-run tactics and sabotage on a sustained basis. Thus persistent destruction of the development infrastructure and anything representative of the Frelimo state continued to guide its day-to-day operations.

These particular features of its military situation (including, as we have suggested, Renamo's need to extend its theatre of operations extremely widely, and extremely fast, throughout Mozambique), in part account for the widespread intentional use of extreme violence against civilian populations.[7] The 'Gersony Report' found that by far the most important reason for the massive increase in Mozambican refugee numbers in neighbouring countries was the violence perpetrated by Renamo. The author of this report assessed that Renamo had been directly responsible for at least 100,000 civilian deaths, as well as for systematic and coordinated violence against civilians in all parts of the country. He observed:

The level of violence reported to be conducted by Renamo against the civilian population of rural Mozambique is extraordinarily high. That the accounts are so strikingly similar by refugees who have fled from northern, central and southern Mozambique suggests that the violence is systematic and coordinated and not a series of spontaneous, isolated incidents by undisciplined combatants.[8]

Among the implications of Gersony's findings were that Renamo found it necessary to extract food and labour from the peasantry on the spot, while trying to prevent the escape of manpower from areas under its control, and that it used the toughest of methods to do so. Gersony identified three notional areas of Renamo operation: in ascending order of oppression, these were 'tax', 'control' and 'destruction' zones. The last category is self-explanatory. 'Control' areas near Renamo bases experienced extreme degrees of forced labour, especially involving porterage duties, and other abuses. The inhabitants of the more sparsely populated 'tax' areas escaped more lightly.

While it may be that Gersony's three-zone typology creates the impression of something closer to the Khmer Rouge system of slave camps in Cambodia in the 1970s and 1980s than to the more haphazard and far less fanatically ordered African reality, its broad outline remains plausible.[9] Despite the conventional wisdom about guerrilla movements, extreme brutality appears to have played a part in Renamo's rapid spread throughout Mozambique after 1980 (even if it later proved counter-productive in the attempt to achieve international support and recognition).[10] This violence had two purposes. The first and more significant was the attack on the Frelimo state. Government and party officials were the priority targets here. In rural areas their physical elimination served to isolate communities and remove them from the authority of the central power, and it thus complemented the destruction of the economic infrastructure and the severing of communications. Essentially, it worked to disarticulate the state. Secondly, violence was exemplary, intended 'to instil a paralysing and incapacitating fear into the wider population … by conjuring a vision of inhumanity and maniacal devotion to the infliction of suffering, that sets them outside of the realm of social beings and hence beyond social control and even resistance'.[11]

K.B. Wilson imputed to Renamo a 'cult of violence' distinguished from other violent activity naturally associated with warfare by ritualistic elements which the perpetrators believed imbued the activity with value or power. He distinguished between Renamo's numerous massacres, especially in the south, where large numbers were despatched in order to destroy local morale, and killings with ritualistic or symbolic elements. The numbers involved in what he termed 'ritualised violence' designed to terrify and impress need not be great, as his own researches in Zambézia suggested, but the spectacle of gruesome public killings was designed to have psychological impact over a wide area. Within rural communities isolated and reordered to support a semi-permanent Renamo presence, exemplary killings served to cow the population and maintain control. The effect of this violence may have been to induce passivity and a sense of fear, anxiety and helplessness.[12]

The argument that the violence directed against civilians was indeed purposeful and instrumental was supported by an apparent lessening of such activity in areas where the local Frelimo influence and presence had been eliminated and Renamo was relatively well established. Such situations did prevail in central and northern Mozambique in some localities and certainly where some base of popular support existed, grounded in ethnic or regional factors. In the Gorongosa region there was reasonably good and cooperative coexistence with the civilian population and little apparent fear.[13] The Renamo presence in Zambézia seemed at this time to have been less brutal and better organised than its first arrival in the area had been.[14] But in southern Mozambique, where Frelimo had a strong base, and where by virtue of the numbers involved the elimination of its supporters could not be achieved by simply picking off a handful of local party officials, there was a significantly high incidence of atrocities.[15] This probably also explains why it was above all in the south where Renamo resorted to the widespread use of child-soldiers.

Induction into Renamo's own ranks was also draconian, perhaps reflecting its Rhodesian and South Africa training during the organisation's formative period. Forced recruitment was widespread, certainly from the early 1980s onwards.[16] A variety of control mechanisms deterred escape; principal among these was the fear of execution, while the practice of transferring captives away from their home area was also significant. Recruits were kept in separate training bases attached to, but not integrated with, operational bases, and underwent two or three months' military instruction. In certain cases the harshness of the treatment meted out to new recruits was in itself a disincentive to volunteer. Renamo's recruitment process in Nampula province centred on incarcerating all recruits, whether volunteer or captives, in a cage or chicken coop, called a *jaula*, for long periods during which they were subjected to various forms of deprivation and trauma in order to break them psychologically before formal military training began.[17]

Alongside harsh internal discipline and forced recruitment, however, some foreign captives held at Renamo bases observed high morale, and although many recruits were press-ganged, others appeared to have joined voluntarily out of boredom or because of hunger and poverty.[18] Even when recruits were originally press-ganged, the excitement they experienced – compared to the dull, impoverished life in the countryside – was enough to induce some to stay willingly.[19] While most recruitment in Gaza province, where Renamo had no natural base, was forced (including the recruitment of children), there was also some voluntary enlistment on the part of marginalised youths. Despite the harshness and danger of life in Renamo ranks, it held the attractions of excitement and access to luxury items and women, as well as providing a means for settling old scores with neighbours and local authorities in their home areas.[20]

Violence seems to have been a crucial rite of passage for forced recruits. John Burlison, held prisoner by Renamo for several months in 1982, reported seeing hundreds of recruits kept under armed guard until they committed their first attacks, after which they were warned that if they fled and were captured by government troops, they would be executed as terrorists.[21] There are reports of Renamo recruits who were compelled to kill fellow villagers or even relatives, to bind them to the movement through guilt and fear of retribution, and plentiful evidence exists of the gradual induction of children into the art of slaughter (by killing first animals and then people). The more extreme acts of exemplary violence, especially those involving young guerrillas, were clearly used as part of a battle-hardening technique.[22] Renamo's young peasant abductees in Inhambane province were initially ill-treated, humiliated and beaten, and then exposed to short periods of kindness and understanding, as an inducement to wholehearted involvement in training and then participation in Renamo's military activities. Those who could not stand this treatment sought to run away, sooner or later, despite the dangers if they were caught. (Among a group of forty-eight former Renamo recruits the average period spent as an active guerrilla before escape was found to be a surprisingly short twelve months.)[23] In practice, reliance on such methods as these was dictated by the size of Renamo's field of operations, and the narrowness of its support base. In the absence of any rewards in the leadership's gift – other than the guerrillas' access to a gun, loot and a relatively well-organised system of first aid – violence was probably the most effective and cheapest means of obtaining obedience both within the ranks and outside them.[24]

None of this, of course, precluded the existence of semi-formal military structures. Indeed until the late 1980s Renamo arguably remained an almost purely military organisation; there were few attempts at building political structures in Renamo-held areas, or at political teaching within the military itself, save for rare instances of political commissars (in Tete and Manica) who had gone through a course of Frelimo political education.[25] The reality was that Renamo retained all the features of an army. In 1985 Renamo's then secretary-general, Evo Fernandes, described a fairly conventional military structure:

> We have the President, Afonso Dhlakama, who is also commander in chief. Then we have generals. The generals have military commanders under them. The regional commanders have sector commanders. The sector commanders have zone commanders under them. Then there are battalions and platoons and so on.[26]

A somewhat later version was more elaborate: Renamo's military council was said to consist of fifteen generals: three chiefs of staff, ten provincial commanders, and Afonso Dhlakama's personal staff. The chiefs of staff were in command in three operational areas: north (from the Rovoma to the Zambezi rivers); centre (the Zambezi to the Sabié rivers); and the south (from the Sabié river to the South African border). The ten generals, each in command of all the forces deployed in any one province, were all technically subordinate to the chiefs of staff in their respective operational areas. Below this level the organisation became less clear.[27] Renamo statutes merely stipulated the existence of a military council comprising regional commanders and military service directors, which assisted the commander-in-chief in military issues. A slightly different version of the military hierarchy published in mid-1986 spoke of twelve generals (one for each province and two from Dhlakama's general staff), plus the operational commanders.[28]

This army had an effective system of command and control under strict military discipline based upon a formal rank structure.[29] A German hostage held at a Renamo base for a month in 1986 noted that the officers sat according to rank in the officers' hut at the centre of the village. They adhered to a rigid military etiquette, asking permission of their superiors before every stage in the proceedings: entering the hut, washing, drinking water, serving, smoking and leaving the table. Rank was colour-coded. The 'general' in command of the 200-strong Angonia company (part of the Matenje regiment) wore a dark red necklace as an insignia of rank. The platoon leaders beneath him, each in charge of forty to fifty men, wore blue cravats on duty and signalled their authority by the use of whistles. Group leaders commanding twelve to fifteen men wore pink cravats and, like their platoon leaders, used whistles for issuing orders. Leaders of specialist units (radio operators, mine-layers or grenade-throwers) had yellow cravats.[30]

Renamo also possessed an efficient radio communications system (superior to that of the Mozambican army), donated by the South Africans, which played an important part in its mobility and effectiveness as a guerrilla force. This gave it the ability to mass large numbers of small units for attacks and to disperse them rapidly for strategic retreats.[31] This military hierarchy and centralised co-ordination coexisted with regional variations in tactics. Child guerrillas were active with Renamo units in the south but not in the north. In some parts of the country, small Renamo gangs engaged in hit-and-run tactics, while in Zambézia in particular they operated at battalion strength, taking towns and holding the areas around them for substantial periods, although evacuating the town itself. Their communications network allowed for this regional variation within an overall coherence of military strategy and purpose. It made possible a change in tactics in most areas, moving towards smaller and more mobile bases. This followed the loss of Casa Banana in the latter part of 1986, a decrease in logistical aid reaching Renamo from South Africa, and the loss of Malawi sanctuaries.[32] The radio net linked Renamo's shifting headquarters in central Mozambique to subordinate bases throughout the country (though smaller outposts might still need to rely on runners or motorcycle messengers).

A final characteristic of its military organisation which gave Renamo organisational coherence was the domination of its military leadership by Shona-speakers from central Mozambique, especially the Ndau subgroup to which Dhlakama himself belongs.[33] This appears to have been not a matter of policy but an accident of the organisation's own history and early operations out of Rhodesia and into Manica and Sofala provinces, although it may also have been an effect of the leadership struggle following the death of André Matsangaíssa in 1978.[34] At the middle levels the picture is mixed, with significant regional variation. In Zambézia almost all the officers were local. In general, however, a large majority of the military commanders were Shona-speaking 'veterans', although the rank and file include men from all ethnic groups.[35] This held good for most parts of Mozambique. In Nampula in the late 1980s, those of sergeant-major level and below in Renamo were said to be local Macua who had been captured, while those of officer rank above them were all Ndau from central Mozambique.[36] Doubtless this reflected both Renamo's recent rapid spread throughout Mozambique and its practice of compulsory local recruitment. In one area of Gaza province, for instance, the composition of Renamo bands reportedly changed over the years – by the end of the 1980s many of the troops were local but the commanders were still all Ndau-speakers from further north.[37] Yet some battalions were known to be all-Ndau, such as the crack Grupa Limpa, which was used to spearhead offensives and attracted a reputation for toughness and effectiveness.[38]

Even at the topmost level of the command pyramid there were non-Ndau who had risen through ability; for example Raul Domingos, a Sena from Zambézia who was southern commander before promotion to Foreign Affairs Secretary, and then Secretary for Organisation. There appears to have been no ethnic bar to such internal promotion. There is, however, a sense in which the Ndau set their stamp on Renamo's military, with others required to adapt or acculturate to their pattern. Accusations were made of Shona linguistic hegemony. Constantino Reis claimed that his problems at Gorongosa headquarters arose 'because I didn't speak Ndau, only Shangaan. And when I spoke Portuguese, they said I was showing contempt for the national languages.'[39] Conversely, Minter observes from his interviews that while the majority of Renamo commanders were Shona-speakers, the language used in any particular Renamo unit depended on the ratio of different ethnic groups represented in its ranks.[40] However, Ndau does seem to have developed as Renamo's military lingua franca and the language of its radio communications. Renamo even made reference to 'initiation schools' at which both military skills and the Ndau language were taught to specialist grades, such as radio operators, and those destined for promotion into the officer corps. That such linguistic training was overlaid with supernatural associations – initiates acquiring power from learning the 'language of the spirits' – did little to make the Renamo military less opaque to outsiders.[41] In Gaza province, not only were the Ndau dominant at both officer and rank-and-file level in the Renamo military, but Renamo was widely perceived to be a Ndau political project.[42]

The war of the spirits

Despite occasional references to health, education and economic officials, Renamo appears to have lacked a comprehensive system of direct administration for civilian areas. However, it did make efforts where possible to provide some basic services – establishing schools, for example, as well as destroying them, notably in Manica, Sofala and Zambézia provinces. Evidence for these and for the medical treatment of civilians by Renamo male nurses and first-aid orderlies appears to have come especially from the Gorongosa region.[43] Apart from a vestigial provision of education and health care, Renamo generally relied on a system of indirect administration. A significant Renamo-eye view of the guerrilla–civilian relationship was provided by Secretary-General Fernandes in 1985:

> Administration doesn't have anything to do with the military. We are based on the traditional system: the administrative system depends on the area the chieftain has. There are the lower chieftains, but we also have what we call *mujeebas*. [...] What happens then if a military unit needs new bases? We ask the chieftains where we can settle a base in their area. Then they say such and such a place is better because there is water there, and a nice, thick forest. The *mujeeba* is our representative at the village level. He knows everybody in his village. Nobody can come without being known. Then nobody also can betray us because he surveys the area. He has a weapon – not an automatic weapon but a Mauser or something ... these chieftains, if they don't live too far away from military units, are in mobile connection with us because they are involved in some military activities. For instance, if we need to haul captured ammunition from a cache, we call people to come and carry it. And we have specific bases only for receiving food from the people. They come to give it to us every time, and nobody forces them.[44]

This form of indirect rule allowed for alliances to be struck with local representatives of traditional power, and provided the basis for elements of a cultural revival. It was well adapted to the mobility of guerrilla war, so that once forced to shift base, a Renamo company or platoon could remake its previous relationship with a new civilian population. It was also simple and effective, ensuring local provision of food and labour by the simple expedient of using and resuscitating the very traditional mechanisms which Frelimo had been trying, often ineffectually, to suppress. *Mujibas* (usually young civilian collaborators of the guerrillas, who provided auxiliary services) were appointed to police the system and formed an effective spy and surveillance network.[45] They existed as part of a usually strict social and spatial division between Renamo military structures and the civilian population. Normally this was expressed in the layout of the base. In the case of the highly mobile Renamo camps in Gaza, which depended on a semi-military life of pillage and for sustenance on bovine meat, it was defined rather by means of a rigid physical and hierarchical allotment of separate areas for combatants, and civilian living and sleeping quarters.[46]

At the Renamo base at Mariri in Nampula the civilian-military relationship was rigidly compartmentalised.[47] The only civilians to be found inside its confines were actually imprisoned there (wives and child-servants of soldiers), or else were temporary captives (male recruits taken locally and held pending intensive military training and transfer to another base elsewhere, often hundreds of kilometres away). Any contact between soldiers at the base and the civilian world outside (including the chiefs) was effected at the control-post on its periphery. Within its confines all important military infrastructures (such as the armoury) were situated at the core, near the huts of the officers and within what – figuratively speaking – seems to have been a series of concentric circles of increasing authority and power whose secrets were guarded against outsiders (*mujibas*, for example, were completely excluded from the base). Near the centre, too, was the radio transmission point, which permitted officers to communicate with the national headquarters in Gorongosa, 1,000 km. away, as well as with each other when out on operation in the bush.

Right up till the 1990s Renamo was widely described as crudely anti-Communist and anti-Frelimo, with no political programme as such. It has already been suggested that the 'ideology' Renamo presented to the outside world was very much for international consumption. However, the remarkable tenacity and expansion of the organisation have to be explained, and the difficulties involved in doing this are compounded by analytical assumptions that all Western observers tend to make that politics presupposes programmes, ideological beliefs, calculations of political support from different kinds of groups and so on – so that, in the absence of these, what does exist must be 'social banditry' or 'destabilisation' inspired by 'traditional animist superstition [which] has replaced political mobilisation'.[48] Yet Renamo's widely reported practice of consulting the local land chief before setting up a new base, in order to obtain the support of the legitimate owners of the land (that chief's ancestral spirits), can surely be seen as a political statement of sorts, albeit one couched in symbolic language that is obscure to outsiders.

The elaboration of a symbolic language drawing on religious idioms seems largely to have occupied the space left void by the dearth of Renamo policies as such. Elsewhere in Africa, peasant concerns have often been channelled into a religious idiom. Traditional forms of belief particularly lend themselves to protest in this form, because of the usually strong association between the spiritual realm and the land. It was therefore natural that Renamo's peasant-soldiers should articulate grievances related to forced villagisation in this mode. This accompanied the destruction of communal villages and the slaughter of Frelimo officials running them, while the evacuation of their inhabitants to their former more dispersed settlements, under the restored authority of chiefs, brought the civilian population into Renamo's system of indirect rule. But this seems also to have gone hand in hand with enormous religious eclecticism and an exaggerated respect paid to the outward symbols of religious observance. The local church or mosque was often the only building left undamaged in a Renamo attack on a settlement.[49] Captives of Renamo and other observers have remarked on their habit of carrying bibles, and their approving and enthusiastic attitude to religion – any religion, it sometimes appears. At one large base, 'religion was much in evidence: pictures of Jesus, bibles in huts, an Islamic mosque, and churches for Ethiopian Copts, Seventh Day Adventists and Catholics.'[50] The most intimate connection, however, seems to have been with traditional systems of belief, although Renamo bases also hosted religious healers from African Christian churches, especially Zionists, who like their non-Christian colleagues practise spirit possession and exorcism and had been subject to state repression for this reason.[51] It seems clear that some local chiefs as well as traditional healers and magicians provided support for Renamo, at least in some parts of the county.[52] Disgruntled traditional healers, who retained their status and importance for the peasantry, proved an ideologically compatible instrument for Renamo in fostering its insurgency.[53] In the Shona-speaking areas of central Mozambique where Renamo originally operated and recruited, spirit mediums are of social and potentially also political importance, as they are in neighbouring Zimbabwe. Some have certainly been associated with Renamo bases in Manica and Sofala – at Casa Banana, for example, and at other bases in the Gorongosa area. Renamo's first military commander, André Matsangaissa, died in late 1979 in an attempt to retake Gorongosa town, having been assured of victory by a spirit medium.[54] Ranger suggests there were residual elements of organisational methods based by Renamo's early Rhodesian tutors on those used by ZANLA:

> Interpreting the most recent evidence on Mozambique somewhat freely one can construct the following picture. The MNR was begun by the Rhodesians as an ironic tribute to ZANLA; it was taught by its Rhodesian mentors to operate like ZANLA; to sing *chimurenga* songs; to make use of spirit mediums. It was sent in first of all to Shona-speaking areas in Mozambique and was provided with gifts to win over the people, whom it was taught to seek to persuade rather than to terrorise. Of course, since then the MNR has lost its Rhodesian and gained South African backers; it has spread far beyond the Shona zones of Mozambique; and it has notoriously had recourse to appalling terror. Nevertheless, there remain traces of that parody ZANLA origin.[55]

Renamo of necessity drew on religious idioms outside of Shona culture, and sought to adapt itself to local practices. Indeed, the proportion of Shona-speakers in the Mozambican population is so small, and Renamo's geographical spread was so wide, that it could hardly do otherwise. Yet Renamo is known to have carried with it elements from the belief systems of central Mozambique, which it introduced into new areas of military expansion. The protective presence of 'lion' spirits to accompany and guard Renamo soldiers has, for example, been claimed by Renamo members themselves in some fairly remote and unlikely places.[56] In parts of Zambézia and northern Tete, Renamo tried to extend the role of 'lion spirit' mediums of Shona conception into non-Shona areas through a systematic hierarchy of mediums attached to its bases. One such medium (a Ndau brought in from central Mozambique) at the important Maqueringa base of northern Zambézia during the 1985–90 period, on the one hand, received regular instructions and medicaments from the provincial base of Alfa Zema; on the other, he interacted with local religious powers by displaying an essentially Zambezian pattern of possession and holding rituals in a local

graveyard.[57] In Tete, Renamo detachments operating in the valley of the Zambezi typically practised traditional local cults, while Renamo political commissars in southern Tete and in Manica existed alongside much more numerous 'witch doctors and sorcerers who have their strong psychological influence on the rank-and-file'.[58]

There were also military advantages in the reputations that Renamo fighters, and especially the Ndau, had for supernatural powers. Renamo recruits in Tete adopted Ndau as their language of communication, linking in with a popular belief in such powers, and particularly that the Ndau had special powers of vengeance after death.[59] The language implicitly derived symbolic power from this belief, so that in drawing on this existing resource Renamo may have been able to reinforce what Wilson would term the 'cultic' aspects of violence. Ndau has elsewhere been called 'the language of the spirits' by Renamo officials, and in southern Mozambique it is a language employed in exorcisms.[60] Finally, beneath the externally-oriented claims that Frelimo had betrayed and abandoned the political heritage of Eduardo Mondlane by adopting un-Christian and un-African 'Communist' ways, it was common on Renamo bases for the claim to be made that a 'war of the spirits' was being waged by Renamo to return Mozambique to its ancestral and traditional ways.

Explaining the conflict

These general features of the conflict in Mozambique made possible a wide variety of local dynamics in different parts of the country which still elude comprehensive analysis. In Érati district of Nampula province, Frelimo policies, particularly villagisation, proved alienating and divisive to the point where a number of local (Macua) chiefs organised wholesale support for Renamo among sections of peasant society when it entered the area in the mid-1980s. Local Macua patterns of land tenure gave the advantage to the lineage which controlled the land on which the communal village was built, creating serious contradictions between different traditional political and kinship groupings which Renamo was able to exploit. As well as 'loser' lineages, alienated rural youths initially joined in the war, made possible by the incursion of Renamo arms and military organisation, with 'joy'.[61] Beyond the impact of communal villages Frelimo's suppression of key Macua cultural and religious practices, along with the marginalisation of traditional authorities, had elicited considerable antagonism. Under Renamo's system of indirect rule, traditional chiefs were able to return their followers to something resembling their traditional way of life. Yet only some populations in Érati rallied to Renamo, the pattern of pro- and anti-government allegiances following pre-existing lines of conflict between historically opposed rival ethnic groupings. In the no-man's land between the Macuane (who supported Renamo) and the Érati (who clung to the protection of the government forces) people did their best to survive by placating both sides. And where Renamo had established itself, it did not develop into anything resembling a political movement but, on the contrary, remained a military machine largely reliant on capturing men from Government-held areas for the recruitment of its soldiers. Economically, it remained predatory towards the peasantry. Chiefs played a key role, helping to recruit a corps of local police responsible for collecting a tax in food to sustain the Renamo base, and also *mujiba* auxiliaries.

Arguably Nampula represented a 'worst case', where forced resettlement into communal villages after 1980, but most especially after 1984, created widespread popular disaffection which Renamo was able to turn to its advantage. Moreover, the province had other peculiarities, notably that traditional authorities enjoyed an unusual degree of respect and popular prestige, since the colonial pattern of forced peasant cash cropping which had prevailed in Nampula and elsewhere in the north permitted the survival of pre-colonial political institutions to a much larger extent than in the more developed economies of the centre and south. These authorities had been instrumental in providing Renamo with recruits, intelligence and logistical support, while their political and kinship networks provided Renamo with an important avenue of penetration into new areas of the province.[62] This meant that although in the conventional sense Renamo had no extensive social base for waging guerrilla war, it was able to count on the widespread neutrality of the peasantry, who in no real sense supported Frelimo.[63]

Yet such adaptive strategies had their limitations, especially in relation to the south of the country. Frelimo's villagisation policy was not a comparable factor in Gaza, with its dependence on migration for wage labour, since it never posed the serious threat to subsistence that it did for the largely cash-cropping peasantry of the north; nor was the involvement of traditional authorities with Renamo (which were in any case very weak in this part of Mozambique) of significance. In the densely populated southern third of the province, where the flood plain of the Limpopo favours agriculture, villagisation had been accepted, if not welcomed. (Most communal villages in Gaza were created in the south of the province, and in the wake of floods which devastated the Limpopo valley in early 1977.) However, Renamo succeeded in establishing its major bases in the dry hinterland of the province, from where it mounted incursions against existing communal villages in the river valley areas. Vlllagisation might have been perceived as an economic threat to the extensive cultivators and cattle-herders of the dry northern hinterland, yet few communal villages were established here, and the more obvious explanation for Renamo penetration relates to the area's remoteness from large centres of population. Nonetheless Renamo had little local support in Gaza as a whole, where it was viewed as very much a Ndau political project. Virtually all Renamo commanders and most of the trained combatants were Ndau speakers from central Mozambique. Local recruits (the vast majority of them were initially captives) were integrated into logistical and procurement units, engaging in combat only if attacked. They were expected to learn Ndau, which served as the official language of the base. Widespread use was made of children, inducted into military training at about eight or nine years of age.[64] The Ndau military commanders actively propagated a 'neotraditionalist culture of insurgency'. Base commanders drew upon the symbolism used in religious ceremonies and healing practices in southern Mozambique. They frequently dressed in the symbolic garb of the spirit world; wearing, for example, two sashes crossed over their chests: the black sash symbolic of the *munguni* spirit used for divining purposes by southern Mozambican religious specialists, and the white sash symbolic of the *mandau* spirit used for exorcisms. This duality refers back to the nineteenth-century Nguni migration from Zululand and the subjugation of the Ndau, who were incorporated into the regiments of the Nguni Gaza empire. Today most traditional healers in southern Mozambique utilise both Nguni and Ndau spirits when treating patients. Indeed, the two spirits coexist in the person of the Nyamasoro, who simultaneously exercises the functions of diviner and healer, and they aid him or her in those functions.[65] But this practice is peculiar to southern

Mozambique, and does not extend north into the Shona-speaking areas of the centre from which the Ndau commanders came. It therefore represents a Renamo adaptation of its symbolic message to the culture of the south, albeit one with limited persuasive power there. Thus while Renamo's religion-based propaganda had found resonance among the rural population of Gaza, it was not translated into popular support, for essentially cultural and ethnic reasons. Fear and mistrust were displayed in Gaza towards the Ndau,

> ....who are renowned for their custom of taking a particular medication when alive that enables their spirit to return from the dead to persecute and bring misfortune upon those people who wronged them...and the Ndau are believed to have the power to transform themselves into such a spirit after death.[…] It is significant that virtually all Ndau Renamo combatants are said to have taken this medication as a way of obtaining revenge on those who might kill them or wrong them in some way.[66]

But ethnic reasons were perhaps paramount. Many Frelimo leaders come from Gaza, a province where the party has always had real support, so that forced to choose 'between the ideologically appealing – but foreign – traditionalism of the Ndau, and the ethnically familiar but sometimes socially disruptive policies of Frelimo, the people of southern Mozambique have tended to come down on the side of Frelimo'.[67]

Clearly, there was no simple correlation between the level of villagisation in a province and the intensity of Renamo activity; Cabo Delgado amply demonstrates this, as the province least affected by the insurgency but where villagisation was most vigorously pursued. No doubt the strong tradition of support for Frelimo in some areas, as well as its remoteness from the main theatres of conflict and lack of enticing strategic targets, were all relevant. Nonetheless, peasant discontent with the communal villages had been manifest even here and in Mueda district, the historical cradle of Frelimo's struggle for Mozambican independence. The Makonde peasants of Ngapa near the Tanzanian border withdrew from communal villages to set up autonomous villages of their own, but they did not turn towards Renamo.[68] Conversely, Zambézia province, with very few communal villages, was profoundly involved in Renamo's war. Indeed, sporadic anti-government guerrilla and bandit activities occurred after independence even before Renamo made its presence felt in August 1982. Other factors at work have undoubtedly included the military effort Renamo was willing to make because of the position and natural fertility of this area (and probably also because of its ease of access from Malawi), as well as the way these considerations interacted with the region's special traditions and idiosyncratic social and cultural fabric. Probably also significant was the absorption of Africa Livre by Renamo in 1982, giving it some structure, support-base and local political legitimacy in western Zambézia. Moreover, Zambézia is a deeply socially divided society, in which the old *patronato* system has proved resilient enough to absorb Frelimo officials, mainly those of *assimilado* background. Nor did the province ever really support Frelimo, either before or after independence, as Samora Machel himself recognised.[69] Ordinary people often welcomed the looting of captured commercial centres in late 1986 even where there was little distribution of goods, while many *comerciantes* were also looted by their own employees and dependants under cover of Renamo banditry.[70]

It was in Zambézia that the Renamo administration attained its most organised form. In 1986–7 Renamo established a food production system in many areas, based on taxation and labour on special fields, as organised by former chiefs, for example in the district around Milange.[71] Even after the area was retaken by the Mozambican army in mid-1988, Renamo still retained important bases in the south of the district, and in areas under its control cultivation continued, some health care was provided (there was even a maternity unit at Renamo's 'district hospital') and attempts were made at elementary political mobilisation.[72] However, all the Zambézian towns taken by Renamo had their populations evacuated. At Gilé, controlled by Renamo from October 1986 until July 1988, surrounding villages were put under the authority of the chiefs, who had the task of organising food, recruits and porterage.[73] Morrumbala in southern Zambézia was deserted for the whole nineteen months of Renamo occupation, the entire population of the town having been marched off into the bush. All subsequent dealings with them were effected through the medium of *régulos* and *mujibas*. Food produced at Morrumbala was distributed to Renamo bases in Manica and Sofala to the south.[74] The 'war of the spirits' also took a different form here; one that was more akin to a cult of magical protection and competitive spiritual prowess associated with attainments by specific military leaders in accordance with Zambézia's more 'individualistic' traditions.[75] As elsewhere in the country, Renamo cultivated local spirit mediums and healers, whose increase in numbers and influence also reflected the social strains and *anomie* induced by the war.[76]

The history of the war at Derre in Morrumbala district illustrates how Renamo became a Zambézian phenomenon. In the initial stages of the war (1982–4) most ordinary people had an indifferent or mildly positive attitude towards Renamo. Although conditions deteriorated during the following two years, it began to use the Zambezi valley and local auxiliaries, who behaved less unpredictably and harshly than expected. By now Renamo-supporting chiefdoms also existed where conditions had stabilised. Derre fell to Renamo in 1986 for a second time, and during an initial period after the capture the population went into hiding in camouflaged pits called *camblinha* (a traditional resort in threatening and dangerous conditions). But a *modus vivendi* was eventually attained. Until the army counter-offensive in the area in late 1990, Renamo operated an administrative regime which was neither particularly intrusive nor violent, and which provided very basic health and educational services and allowed for some market activity. The key to this relatively benign state of affairs (in relation to other parts of the country) was probably the ease with which an agricultural surplus could be produced locally to support the Renamo soldiers, and the existence of a social base which allowed for voluntary local recruitment. After 1986 new troops, mostly of Zambézian origin, were moved in, and more were recruited locally. They created a more civil-based administration which tried to mobilise the support of the people. The level of food tax collected by the chiefs for Renamo was not onerous, and tribute labour on Renamo-managed fields engaged only one adult household member per household for two days a week.[77]

Fragmentation and disorganisation

Clearly, widely varying local circumstances in Mozambique, and Renamo's tactics in dealing with them, suggest that Frelimo's understanding of the conflict was limited and that it became rooted in structures and practices that proved much more resistant to eradication than Frelimo's leaders had ever imagined. Material factors were not unimportant, and had indeed previously constrained the colonial regime. The country's size and shape alone make effective control difficult, and these difficulties are compounded by the lack of north-south communications (the important arteries bisect the country laterally), and by the existence of several natural regional centres, while all power is concentrated in the capital, 1,900 km from Mozambique's northernmost border but only 102 km from South Africa. Colonial rule failed to integrate the country economically or indeed administratively until late in the day, so that a marked legacy of the colonial past has been Mozambique's fragmented economic development. Historically, the country comprised corridors of communication linking Central and Southern Africa to the coast, so that there is no major rail line which both begins and ends inside Mozambique.[78] This economic legacy dovetailed with considerable regional and ethnic diversity, which Frelimo did not manage to overcome.

With independence in 1975, coming after a long guerrilla war but actually precipitated by the collapse of the metropolitan power in Lisbon, Frelimo had still to establish a presence over large areas of this elongated country, but the conflict in neighbouring Rhodesia meant that in much of central Mozambique it had little opportunity to do so. Indeed, in as much as Renamo can be said to have developed a regional base during the war, it was located in Manica and Sofala, where the insurgency began and where Renamo was able to count on some support, if only tacit, from the peasantry. During the early 1980s Renamo was able to attract some voluntary recruits from the area by claiming that Frelimo was southern-dominated.[79] In particular Gorongosa in northern Sofala was long the main area of its shifting headquarters, regarded as a centre of support for Renamo, as well as being an area where the connection between it and the Shona spirit cult was particularly strong and close.[80] Some commentators in Mozambique have even claimed to discern underlying elements of the past in the conflict: the 'people of Monomotapa' versus the Gaza empire established by Soshangane.

In addition to the difficulties of integration associated with geographical and cultural diversity, Mozambique under Frelimo displayed all the structural weaknesses of the African state to an extreme degree, with an acute lack of qualified cadres, weak infrastructure and hence poor administrative control. These factors interacted with, and reinforced, the regional and ethnic fragmentation. They also severely affected the military capacities of the state; Renamo faced an army which was 'under-trained, underequipped, underpaid, and underfed'.[81] Military logistics suffered *inter alia* from Renamo assaults on the transportation system, so that more than one garrison is known to have been driven to forage for its food. Morale was widely recognised to be poor, and during the war there were plenty of rumours of troops illicitly collaborating with, or even spying for, Renamo. Logistical problems aside, the army was encumbered by a post-independence overemphasis on conventional weapons that was inappropriate to countering a rural guerrilla insurgency.[82]

Contingent factors also had their effects. In the early 1980s an unusually severe drought affected much of central and southern Mozambique, and there were many deaths in Tete as a result of famine. In Gaza and Inhambane provinces, where Renamo activities were most intense, people had lost much of their remaining foodstocks and cattle to Renamo forces and were running out of roots and berries in the bush.[83] Their suffering was greatly exacerbated by Renamo tactics, which in Inhambane not only targeted relief vehicles for attack, but also focused on starving peasants seeking to make their way to government feeding stations. An estimated 25% of the normally marketed grain overall was lost due to Renamo action, compounding rural hardship just as the distribution and commercialisation networks were disappearing throughout rural Mozambique. In circular fashion, this provided further fertile ground for Renamo expansion. In so expanding, Renamo was destroying the development infrastructure linked to the communal villages which Frelimo had created (health posts and schools).[84]

These structural and contingent factors did much to shape the war into a confusing patchwork of shifting local engagements. Yet to make sense of Renamo it is essential to bear in mind three elements: the nature of the indigenous African societies; the policies pursued by the Frelimo government in the first phase of its rule; and the South African involvement. Many of Frelimo's policies antagonised sections of the population. Its more or less open door policy for the ANC antagonised Pretoria. The South Africans were able to capitalise on these discontents to shape a force whose main *raison d'être* was the destruction of economic targets and of the skeletal framework of political and administrative control that Frelimo had been able to set up in the rural areas. It is not clear whether Renamo ever had any meaningful political goals as such. It was able to exploit a deteriorating social and economic situation and maintain in the field a fairly large body of armed men effectively living off the countryside. It acquired a momentum of its own by exploiting the prevailing social crisis and economic collapse in the rural areas. Geffray's comment perhaps summarises as well as anything a very complex series of truths: 'The responsibility for the development of the war can be divided as a follows: only the South African intervention can account for the beginning of the war – that country has a major responsibility for the conflict – while the political choices made by Frelimo in building its power in the countryside can explain the fact that this war was grounded in the social fabric of rural Mozambique.'[85]

Notes

1. Luis Honwana, one-time Minister of Culture, quoted in Finnegan, *A Complicated War*, p. 125.
2. Otto Roesch, 'Renamo and the Peasantry in Southern Mozambique: A view from Gaza Province', *Canadian Journal of African Studies*, 26 March (1992), pp. 472–3.
3. For some discussions of this aspect see T. Young, 'From MNR to Renamo: Making Sense of an African Counter-Revolutionary Movement' in P. Rich (ed.), *The Dynamics of Change in Southern Africa*.
4. See especially P. Johnson and D. Martin, *Apartheid Terrorism: The destabilization report*, for the Commonwealth Committee of Foreign Ministers on Southern Africa, London, 1989.
5. Unorthodox methods and ivory smuggling were resorted to. See A. Vines, 'Change and the Military in Mozambique', paper given at a US Defense Intelligence College Conference on Change and the Military in Africa, Alconbury, England, 6–7 May 1993. On DMI/Renamo involvement in poaching and the illegal ivory trade, see 'Under Fire: Elephants in the Front Line', Environmental Investigation Agency, London, 1992. See also the claims of Colonel Jan Breytenbach, *Observer*, 18 April, 1993.
6. Moorcraft, *African Nemesis*, p. 280.
7. Renamo has periodically argued that atrocities attributed to it were part of a propaganda campaign organised by President Chissano. But such atrocities had been reported from a much earlier date (see *The Herald*, 15 June 1982), and in the press of countries not notably hostile (e.g. *Malawi News*, 27 May–2 June 1989).
8. Robert Gersony, *Summary of Mozambican Refugee Accounts of Principally Conflict-related Experience in Mozambique*, Washington, DC: Department of State, Bureau for Refugee Programs, 1988, p. 25. The findings were based on 196 individual interviews with refugees in twenty-five locations, in five countries. The author, Robert Gersony, was an experienced academic who had previously conducted refugee surveys for the State Department.
9. Finnegan, *A Complicated War*, p. 80; although certain deficiencies of methodology have been highlighted e.g. Gersony's acceptance that interviewees spoke entirely freely when they attributed 94% of all murders to Renamo and only 3% to Frelimo. Gersony may have been naive in this because, e.g., in Zimbabwe refugee opinion was monitored by the authorities for evidence of pro-Renamo sympathies which might identify Renamo infiltrators, and to this extent refugees there may well have learned to be self-censoring in their comments.
10. We remain sceptical about the degree to which, as Clarence-Smith puts it, 'it seems axiomatic that a guerrilla force has to be "like a fish in the water"' (correspondence in the *Southern African Review of Books*, June/July 1989, p. 22). Dhlakama himself has occasionally invoked this metaphor: see *Die Welt*, 6 January 1989.
11. K. B. Wilson, 'Cults of Violence and Counter-Violence in Mozambique', *Journal of Southern African Studies*, 18, 3 (September 1992), pp. 527–82.
12. An impressionistic report on both sides of the line, published in *Der Spiegel*, 47/87, tends to suggest this in Renamo-held Mozambique. See also Cole P. Dodge and Magne Raundalen, *Reaching Children in War: Sudan, Uganda and Mozambique*, Bergen, 1991.
13. Nicholas della Casa, held by Renamo for eighteen months, mainly in Gorongosa, and released at the end of 1988, likened the local civilian attitude to Renamo to that of Dorset villagers towards NATO troops in their area – some grumbling, but no real complaints. *Sunday Telegraph*, 18 December 1988.
14. Guardian, 6 October 1982.
15. Lina Magaia's harrowing collection of tales of atrocities is set in southern Mozambique although her Introduction is at pains to point out that atrocities had occurred throughout the country. Lina Magaia, *Dumba Nengue: Run for Your life*, Trenton, NJ, 1988.
16. W. Minter, 'The Mozambican National Resistance (RENAMO) as described by ex-participants', Washington, DC, 1989, puts it at over 90%.
17. Roesch, correspondence in the *Southern African Review of Books*, December 1989/ January 1990.
18. H Moorcraft, 'Mozambique's long civil war' *International Defense Review*, October 1987, pp. 1313–16.
19. Hanlon, *Revolution*, p. 229.
20. Otto Roesch, 'Renamo and the Peasantry', p. 478.
21. Cited by Allen Isaacman in his preface to Magaia, *Dumba Nengue*, p. 12.
22. Finnegan, *A Complicated War*, pp. 25–6.
23. Anders Nilsson, 'From Pseudo-Terrorists to Pseudo-Guerrillas: the MNR in Mozambique', *Review of African Political Economy*, 58 (1993), pp. 35–42.
24. The point about economy is made in the Introduction to D. Riches (ed.), *The Anthropology of Violence*, Oxford, 1986.
25. Georgi Derlugyan, 'Mozambique: a tight knot of problems', *International Affairs* 3, (March 1990), pp. 103–11.
26. Interview in *Defense and Diplomacy*, 3 September 1985.
27. André Thomashausen, 'The Mozambican National Resistance Movement'.
28. *Africa Confidential*, 9 (June 1986).
29. Minter, 'The Mozambican National Resistance' and Paul Moorcraft, 'Mozambique's long civil war'.
30. N. Baron, 'The Struggle Continues: Diary of a Kidnapping in Mozambique by Robert Rosskamp: An Analysis' in A. Vines and K. B. Wilson (eds), *War in Mozambique: Local Perspectives* (forthcoming).
31. Finnegan, *A Complicated War*, p. 58; Alex Vines, *Renamo: From Terrorism to Democracy in Mozambique?*, London, rev. edn, 1996, p. 82–3.
32. Vines, *Renamo*, p. 86; Zambézia was the exception.

33 Mozambique's 1980 census results for home language by province suggests Shona-speakers form only about 8–9% of the total population, the great majority being in Manica and Sofala provinces. The Ndau are the largest Shona-speaking group inside Mozambique and, like the Manyika, straddle the border with Zimbabwe, where they form an estimated 6% of the much larger Shona population of that country.

34 Roesch, 'Renamo and the Peasantry in Southern Mozambique'. See also Vines, *Renamo*, pp. 83–5.

35 Minter, 'The Mozambican National Resistance', p. 12.

36 Information given in interview.

37 Finnegan, *A Complicated War*, p. 210.

38 Vines, *Renamo*, p. 85. Cf. Jovito Nunes, 'Peasants and Survival: The social consequences of displacement – Mocuba, Zambézia', draft paper, April 1992.

39 Interview, *AIM Bulletin* supplement, January 1985.

40 He also observes that only interviewees from central Mozambique differentiate between Shona dialects, the tendency elsewhere being to lump all Shona speakers together as 'Ndau'. See also Vines, *Renamo*, pp. 83–5.

41 See Alex Vines, 'Diary', *Southern African Review of Books*, 4, 4 and 5, issue 20/21, (July/October 1991).

42 Roesch, 'Renamo and the Peasantry', p. 469.

43 Minter, 'The Mozambican National Resistance', p. 8. Constantino Reis, for example, helped to build a primary school in Gorongosa in 1983 and taught there for several months.

44 In *Defense and Diplomacy*, 3 September 1985.

45 *Mujibas* were a feature of ZANLA's campaign in Zimbabwe, and appear to have been copied by Renamo from them. The word itself was first coined by ZANLA.

46 Roesch, 'Renamo and the Peasantry', p. 471.

47 Christian Geffray, *La Cause des Armes au Mozambique*, Paris, 1990.

48 Paul Fauvet and Alves Gomes, 'The Mozambican National Resistance'.

49 *Tempo* 947, 4 December 1988, p. 29.

50 J. Wheeler, 'From Rovoma to Maputo: Mozambique's guerrilla war', *Reason*, December 1985. An ostentatious display of bibles may well have impressed certain missionary sects who assisted Renamo. See, for example, *Southscan*, 4, 34 (15 September 1989), pp. 262–3.

51 Roesch, 'Renamo and the Peasantry', pp. 473–4.

52 Minter, 'The Mozambican National Resistance', p. 8.

53 Roesch, 'Renamo and the Peasantry', p. 475.

54 *Tempo* 780, 22 September 1985.

55 T.O. Ranger, 'The meaning of violence in Zimbabwe', paper delivered at a conference in Cambridge on violence and decolonisation in Africa, April 1991.

56 See the *Southern African Review of Books*, July/October 1991, where in the 'Diary' Alex Vines relates the claim by two Renamo representatives in Lisbon that Lion and Snake spirits protected them from the interference of Portuguese police.

57 K. B. Wilson, 'Cults of Violence and Counter-Violence in Mozambique'.

58 Derlugyan, 'Mozambique: A tight knot of problems'.

59 Magaia, interview, *Race and Class*, 30 April 1989.

60 See Alex Vines, 'Diary'.

61 C. Geffray, *La Cause des Armes*. See also C. Geffray and M. Pedersen, 'Nampula en guerre', *Politique Africaine*, 29 (1988), pp. 18–40.

62 *SARoB*, December 1989/January 1990.

63 For a critical review of Geffray, emphasising the contribution made by destabilisation to the crucial discontents of the countryside, see Bridget O'Laughlin, 'Interpretations Matter: Evaluating the War in Mozambique', *Southern Africa Report*, January 1992, pp. 23–33.

64 Roesch, 'Renamo and the Peasantry', p. 469.

65 We are grateful to Alcinda Honwana for this explanation.

66 Roesch, 'Renamo and the Peasantry', pp. 476–7.

67 Ibid., p. 472.

68 Rudebeck, 'Conditions of People's Development in Postcolonial Africa', unpubl. paper, 1988/9.

69 K. B. Wilson, personal communication. See also the comments in Vail and White, *Capitalism and Colonialism in Mozambique*, ch. 9.

70 K. B. Wilson, 'War, Displacement, Social Change and the Re-Creation of Community: an exploratory study in Zambézia, Mozambique', preliminary report of a field study in Milange district, March–April 1991. Refugee Studies Programme May 1991.

71 *Notícias*, 13 July 1988.

72 K. B. Wilson,'War, Displacement, Social Change'.

73 *Mozambique File*, January 1989.

74 Information from Oxfam fieldworker.

75 K. B. Wilson, 'Cults of Violence and Counter-Violence'.

76 See Jovito Nunes, 'Peasants and Survival'.

77 K. B. Wilson, 'The Socio-Economic Impact of War and Flight in Posto Derre, Morrumbala District, Zambezia', January 1992 (described in the Archivo Historico de Mozambique as forthcoming).

78 M. Newitt, 'Towards a history of modern Mozambique', *Rhodesian History*, 7, 5, pp. 33–47.

79 Joseph Hanlon, *Mozambique: The revolution under fire*, p. 229.

80 *Tempo* 780, 22 September 1985, pp. 10–12.

81 Finnegan, *A Complicated War*, p. 56.

82 See Herb Howe, 'Mozambique at a Standstill' in *Defence: Africa and the Middle East*, 11, 2 (March 1985), pp. 14–15. See also *Indian Ocean Newsletter*, 5 November 1983, pp. 7–10, on the state of the armed forces, and ION, 25 September 1993.

83 Conspicuous Destruction (*Africa Watch* report, 1992).

84 See Glenda Morgan, 'Violence in Mozambique: Towards an Understanding of Renamo', *Journal of Modern African Studies*, 28, April (1990), pp. 603–19.

85 C. Geffray, *La Cause des Armes*, pp. 3–4.

TOYIN FALOLA
Violence & Conflict in the 1990s

Reference
Violence in Nigeria:
The Crisis of Religious Politics & Secular Ideologies
University of Rochester Press, 1998, pp. 194–221

Confronting the state: Yakubu Yahaya and the Katsina riot, 1991

During the last week of March 1991 and continuing into April, the city of Katsina, the capital of Katsina state, laid in wait for an imminent largescale outbreak of religious violence. It came on 19 April, but unlike previous incidents, the Katsina riot lasted just one day. At the center of the violence was Malam Yakubu Yahaya, a preacher who challenged the state's government to a fight. Like the Maitatsine, the Katsina event was a case of violence involving a well-known leader with radical views. Unlike the case of the Maitatsine riots, the government and its security forces were fully prepared for battle in Katsina.

Yakubu Yahaya was the leader of a large Muslim group in Katsina.[3] Innocent-looking but tough, Yahaya was able to popularize the beliefs of Nigerian Shiites through his intransigence and his challenge to the governor of the state. Yahaya was a preacher of modest means. He lived modestly in a small mud house in the town. His living room had only a mat, a standing fan, and a large poster of Ayatollah Khomeini, which he described as his most valuable possession.[4] He spoke only limited English, but he was a highly educated person in the Islamic tradition and in formal Arabic studies. He learned the Qur'an and the Arabic language under his father, after which he went to the Arabic Islamic College in Kaduna for four years. Thereafter, he traveled to Maradi in the Niger Republic to preach. A few years later, he went to Bayero University in Kano to obtain a diploma in Arabic Studies, which qualified him to teach Arabic and Islamic education at the Katsina Teachers College. In the 1980s, he began to show his strength as a fearless anti-government preacher. He was once arrested by security agents for his volatile teachings. He resigned his teaching appointment in 1983 to take to full-time preaching. With a base at Katsina from which he drew his students and followers, he traveled frequently to Kano, Katsina, Maiduguri, Potiskum, Makurdi, and other places to spread the Shiite gospel.[5] At this time a young man in his thirties, Yahaya was able to attract younger followers and to develop both their zeal and commitment to the religion.

Although his hero was Khomeini, he rejected attempts to divide Muslims through Shiite, as he regarded sects as potentially too divisive:

> I can say that there is nothing like Shi'ite in Nigeria.... I know that the Jews always try to divide Muslims into groups. Whenever a movement is raised to work for Islam, they try to give it a name in order to make people avoid it ... to divide Muslims into groups, to disunite us.[6]

One of his followers, Mohammed Amin, a graduate of Kaduna Polytechnic, said that the sect's relations with Khomeini did not make them Shiites, and that Khomeini was just a person whom Allah used to fulfill a promise that whenever Islam experienced a drawback, someone would emerge to raise it up. Like Khomeini, Yahaya believed that he was sent by God to end injustice, oppression, and exploitation in Nigeria.

Labels aside, Yahaya and his followers believed strongly that the Nigerian government must be changed, if necessary by force, as had happened in Iran, Lebanon, and Bahrain. Yahaya did not see himself as the Mahdi, or even as the leader of a new Islamic state. He acknowledged the leadership of another person, Malam Ibrahim al-Zakzaky of Zaria, a prominent preacher and a notable critic of the government. Al-Zakzaky is a veteran protester. As a student at Ahmadu Bello University in Zaria in the 1970s, he was at the forefront of the Muslim Students Society, rising to the position of deputy chairman and organizing a series of pro-Islamic lectures and campaigns. Following unrest on campus, he was expelled on 14 December 1979. He turned his full energies to the propagation of Islam, calling for the overthrow of the Constitution and an Islamic revolution.[7] In widely circulated cassettes, al-Zakzaky had criticized emirs, governors, presidents, politicians, and soldiers.[8] He was opposed to secular authority. One influential cassette that documents al-Zakzaky's beliefs identifies him clearly as a Shiite:[9] he says Muslims must say the *shahada* confession of faith ('There is no god but Allah and Muhammad is His messenger'), adding the line 'and Ali is the friend of God,' a Shiite trademark. Shiites believe that Caliph Ali was the true successor of the Prophet Muhammad, a position with which the rival Sunni disagree. Al-Zakzaky goes on in the cassette to affirm that the Mahdi would soon appear to save Islam, resonating with the Shiite belief that the twelfth and last Imam will redeem the world. He says Nigeria must become like Iran, 'the only country in the world today where Satan has no place to hide.' The Nigerian governments, al-Zakzaky continues, 'are under kaffir, thieves, and satans.' He rejects the Nigerian Constitution:

> Does the Nigerian constitution recognize the law of Allah? Does it recognise the Quran as the supreme law? A section of this constitution you are referring to says that its laws are supreme whatever law that is not consistent with its provisions, are null and void. Now we know for sure that the laws of that constitution run contrary to the provisions of the Quran. So according to Nigeria's constitution the Quran is null and void. And it will be a contradiction, for anybody who accepts the laws of the Quran accepts Allah as the Lord and accepts Muhammed (SAW) as the messenger of Allah too, at the same time, accept the constitution of Nigeria.... We want Islam and no power on earth can stop it.[10]

For his combative style and provocative preachings, al-Zakzaky had a series of confrontations with the law, and by 1989, he had spent a total of eight years in jail. His releases from prison were always met by welcoming crowds of thousands of his followers, who included among them university students and lecturers.

On 25 March 1991, Yahaya marched at least two thousand of his followers to the Katsina office of the *Daily Times*, chanting 'La ilahah il'Allah' (there is no God but Allah), 'Down with *Daily Times*,' and 'Down with the Federal Government.' His mission was simple: to take possession of every remaining copy of the December 1990 edition of *Fun Times*, a humor magazine published by the *Times*. The offending edition contained an opinion poll that asked whether or not respondents would marry prostitutes who repented and became 'born again Christians.' In addition, there was an article on prostitution that investigated the origins of prostitution and argued that many women had abandoned the profession to lead decent lives. The author supported certain claims with references to the Bible and the Qur'an. Mary Magdalene, according to this writer, used to be a prostitute before she became a strong follower of Christ, and the Prophet Muhammad had made love to a woman of easy virtue whom he later married.

How this issue of *Fun Times* reached the hands of al-Zakzaky or Yahaya and their sect has been obscured by time, but they were extremely angered by it. Both the *Daily Times* and *Fun Times* were owned by the federal government, and the attack on Prophet Muhammad was believed to have been endorsed by either the government or some of its high-ranking officials.[11] On 25 March Yahaya and his followers burned all remaining copies of the offending magazine. It was an otherwise peaceful protest, in which no one was hurt and no property was damaged.[12] The police did not disturb the protest march, nor did they come to the aid of the Daily Times office. By then Yahaya had already become popular, according to police records.[13] He was not known to have caused much trouble, although his record at that time said that 'he is capable of doing this because of his preachings and because many of his followers are young and idealistic.[14] This capability had been demonstrated two years earlier. In 1989, a Yahaya disciple was arrested and charged in court. On the day of the hearing, over a thousand 'angry-looking and desperate young men' converged on the court, chased out the magistrate and freed the accused disciple.[15] A similar incident in the small town of Kankia was also attributed to Yahaya, although police reports were divided on the attribution.[16]

Whether or not the incident of 25 March would have died down, Colonel John Madaki, the Christian governor of Katsina, saw it as the beginning of a long protest. He had no evidence, only a suspicion.[17] The leading officials of Katsina state regarded Yahaya as a Shiite, the leader of 'a bunch of fanatical Muslims' whose goal was to overthrow the government at any cost.[18] The governor's action turned what had begun as a small protest into a major crisis that would cause him sleepless nights and two trips to see the president in Lagos. The governor went public with an angry speech:

The leader of the Shi'ites should be aware that I, Madaki, am not afraid of him. I swear to Almighty God in heaven, if he causes trouble again … we will go to his house, take him to the Polo Ground and kill him publicly.[19]

This threat provoked anger from Yahaya. He dared the governor to carry out his threat. asserting that he would protest in the city whenever he wanted and whenever he disagreed with government policy. He was not afraid of death, and he told the governor that 'a true Muslim should not fear death … fear has no meaning in Islam.'[20] He feared neither Madaki nor Babangida, but only the anger of Allah. Yahaya went even further than had the governor, whom he accused of foolishness, asserting that he was not bound by secular law:

I am a Muslim. I have the injunctions of Prophet Mohammed. I have the Holy Qur'an and I am schooled in Islamic Science which my 'ulama taught me. I am under these rules. I am following it and I am not working for anybody. I do not recognise any authority on me but the Holy Qur'an. I do not recognize the Federal Government. I do not recognize the State government and their laws. Whatever my religion permitted me

to do, I will do it without waiting for any permission or without considering whether somebody likes it or not. I will never seek anybody's permission at all.… Do not be surprised we are using our own model of justice. The Federal Government does not recognise the injunction of my Holy Prophet, neither the State government. So this is clean justice. They do their own and I will do my own. Everybody should stand on his own. They are Kaffirs.[21]

He expected a change soon:

There would be an islamic revolution in this country and I am certain that Governor Madaki has started laying its foundation.… The solution is to flush out this corrupt system and establish an Islamic state.… There is no compromise. The solution is not in talking on the table but to shed out all the idol worshippers and their leaders and all these evils. So our aim and target is to do so here, Insha Allah.[22]

One of his disciples added that

this imperialist system has to be changed to an Islamic system. What Islam recognises is that the people who are to lead must be those with Islamic background. Our aim is that the present leadership of the country should go and give way to Sharia which will be governed by the highly placed Islamic scholars.[23]

An Islamic government, they felt, was possible in Nigeria.

Yahaya and his followers accused the governor, a Christian, of working with CAN to spread Christianity in the state and to promote secular policies.[24] He and the entire federal government were also accused of allowing people and the media to abuse the Prophet Muhammad and the Muslims. Yahaya did not see his procession and newspaper-burning of March 25 as constituting any threat to peace. He believed that he was only carrying out a legitimate religious duty. His justification was this:

Sometime in December, the *Fun Times* magazine had abused prophets Mohammed and Jesus. So we were angered by this and we could not tolerate this one because prophet Mohammed has been abused so many times in this country. Awolowo abused him sometimes ago saying that he was more successful and popular than Mohammed and Jesus. One Kaffir in Jos once said that we should not go to Hajj but go to Jos. Many of this. There was somebody who called himself Dauda and said prophet Mohammed sent him from Saudi Arabia in order to perform adultery with women. This is intolerable. We cannot tolerate these abuses. We went in procession and got the Fun Times and Daily Times burnt. Madaki, this so-called Governor, a foolish man, said that he would execute me for arranging the procession. I realise that the Federal Government and the State government are supporting these unbelievers in order to insult our Prophet and our religion. We will not fold our arms or shut our mouths. If everybody shuts his mouth, I will not shut mine.[25]

Unknown to most people at that time was that the person with whom they had to deal with was not just Yahaya but also Malam Ibrahim al-Zakzaky of Zaria. It was al-Zakzaky who instructed Yahaya to make a bonfire of the Fun Times and to defy the governor.[26] Yahaya himself publicly admitted that al-Zakzaky was his leader and that he was under his directive: 'I am doing whatever I am doing under the leadership of my master, Malam Ibrahim

Zakzaky…. Nothing is done here without his consent. Wherever you see the burning of Fun Times, he is the only one behind it…. I am proud to be his student. He is my leader and I am under his directive.'[27] Al-Zakzaky defended Yahaya's action:

Those who actually made the demonstration were the muslims who cared to defend the honour of the messenger of Allah and who also cared to go against the utterances of Governor Madaki and of course, Malam Yakubu Yahaya who featured prominently served as a spokesman.[29]

Al-Zakzaky also mobilized followers in support of their cause by instructing them to head for Katsina. Within a few days, the town was flooded with hundreds of his followers. Asked why those people responded so quickly, Mohammed Ameen, a member of the group and also a lecturer at Kaduna Polytechnic, responded with great confidence:

If the leader of Islamic movement in Nigeria, Malam Zakzaky, gives an order now for the Muslims of this state to go and bring Governor Madaki to this house, I assure you that in no time he will be brought here.[29]

Katsina became tense as members of the public feared an imminent clash between the preacher and the governor. Yahaya's followers became more committed to their beliefs and leaders. There were problems for them and the government. The government had to deal with thousands of youths and angry Muslims who had flooded the city. All other government business had to be suspended to face an imminent security crisis.[30] The governor was now being blamed for having initiated a crisis, for saying that he would kill an enemy and for choosing a strategy of 'confrontation with fanatics.'[31] Newspaper editorials and civil rights movements joined in the attack on the governor for his arrogance and abuse of office. The *New Nigerian* attacked Madaki for granting himself judicial powers, asking, 'where does Colonel Madaki think he is ruling: Katsina State or Soweto in South Africa?'[32] The governor revised his previous statement, saying that Yahaya would not be executed, but that he would face due process of law if he committed any offense.[33] He was allowed to protest if he wished, provided he did not kill or injure anyone or damage property. In addition, he distanced himself from CAN without denying his Christian identity:

I am not an agent of anybody. You will never get anybody as broad-minded as myself. I don't know of the existence of CAN. I am not working under anybody's umbrella. All I am working for is peace in Katsina. CAN did not appoint me as Governor of Katsina.[34]

The governor said that he only wanted peace, that Yahaya was free to criticize him, that he was not afraid of him, and that he would do everything in his power to protect lives and property in the state. Yahaya had not been arrested for the invasion of the *Daily Times* office. Rather than seek compensation for damages, the newspaper carried apologies to assuage feelings.[35] But such pacification failed to impress Yahaya and his master; what Yahaya wanted was for the governor to appear before al-Zakzaky to revoke his death sentence personally, and to apologize for having embarrassed the sect.[36] Yahaya and Al-Zakzaky, having mobilized their followers for action, felt they must either seek the means to disperse them or find avenues to explore their restlessness. Like the Maitatsine, they acquired small weapons – swords, bows and arrows, knives,

catapults, stones, and clubs. Many of them wore uniforms to distinguish them from other Muslims in the town. The uniform was a white gown fronted with bold Islamic inscriptions in Arabic. They wore red armbands, headbands, and carried flags symbolizing rebellion, independence, and the call to action.

Yahaya and Al-Zakzaky felt that they could not disperse their followers without losing credibility, and so they prepared them for action. They strengthened their faith with radical preachings. They prepared them for death, offering it as 'a reward, something to look forward to.'[37] This psychology proved to be a source of strength, and there was no evidence to support a security report claiming that the group had modern weapons.[38] They were bold: 'we feel that we are more powerful than all the superpowers not to talk of their surrogates, the agents of the Jews.'[39] Like their leader, they feared only the wrath of God, and not the guns of the police. Those who might die were assured that their brothers would carry the mission to a successful end.

Their first aim was to prevent the arrest of Yahaya. Next, they would protest government policies as they had always done. Were they to be attacked by the police, they would fight back. They would not antagonize the public. Consequently, they sought ways to present themselves as peace-loving and law abiding. They printed leaflets denying that they were a violent group and saying they would never attack any private person. Referring to the incident of 25 March, they explained their justification for burning the *Fun Times* and reminded readers that they passed through the city's business center without disturbing anyone. Yahaya told a group of reporters that he was not a terrorist but a devout Muslim looking for peace for himself and his fellow-citizens.[40] All Muslims were invited to join them in fighting a government of *kaffirs*, but not in terrorizing innocent people.

By the third week of April, the war of nerves between Madaki and Yahaya had given way to an overt preparation for confrontation. On 16 April, al-Zakzaky traveled to Katsina accompanied by almost two thousand followers. His entry into Katsina was cheered by thousands of people who chanted war songs and called for the head of Madaki.[41] Al-Zakzaky was in town for a day or two, not to incite violence, but to instruct Yahaya to preach and to stage an unauthorized demonstration,[42] no doubt an act of defiance. He instructed Yahaya to attend the forthcoming Friday midday prayer of 19 April, where he was to preach his popular message of defiance of anti-Islamic laws and the call for a return to the true path.

The government responded by increasing police presence. Armored personnel carriers and many truckloads of anti-riot police began to patrol the town. Undercover agents kept a round-the-clock watch on Yahaya. The presence of heavily armed police further added to the tension, but did not scare off Yahaya and his people. The central mosque was heavily guarded, public vehicles near the building were withdrawn, and the staff of the Ministry of Information, Culture, and Home Affairs, which was located close to the mosque, deserted their offices.

On 19 April Yahaya entered the crowded mosque as a hero, with his followers chanting war songs. He preached against the government and its agents, as heavily armed police watched closely. The sermon whipped Yahaya's audience into a frenzy, and some began to shout at the police, daring them to come in and execute Yahaya. The Muslims charged the police, who fired back with heavy tear gas. The battle began as Yahaya's followers dispersed into the town. Fortunately, the protesters intended only to attack the government, not the citizenry, unlike participants in the Maitatsine or Kafanchan riots; damage was limited as a result. Three policemen were killed, and twenty-nine civilians and eight policemen were injured. Public property was damaged; the state subtreasury, the library board, and a section of the state's Ministry of Information were destroyed. Five cars were also destroyed. Yahaya and his followers withstood the tear gas, but they were not as militarily prepared as they had boasted. Their shouts of 'Allahu akbar' (God is great) were met with heavy police fire.

Because the riot had been foreseen, the police were able to contain it that same day. Many people were arrested, but Yahaya escaped. On 22 April, Yahaya and a hundred of his followers surrendered to the police. A few hours later, the state government set up a five-man tribunal, headed by Justice Rabiu Mohammed Danlami, to try Yahaya and others under the Civil Disturbance (Special Tribunal) Decree of 1987. Yahaya became the first leader of a religious riot to be tried and jailed. Al-Zakzaky was untouched, however, and the sect remain intact and continued to act as aggressively as ever.

Shiites in other parts of the country were upset, although they were unable to mobilize another violent protest. They nevertheless protested in other ways. In Yola, the capital of Gongola state, for instance, they marched through the streets singing the praises of Yahaya. In Sokoto, they circulated leaflets criticizing 'pagan Nigeria' and its officials. The governors of both Sokoto and Gongola states, sensing the threat of violence, quickly mobilized police forces and issued warning threats to the Shiites. In Katsina itself, fearing that the remnants of Yahaya's movement might regroup, the police stepped up patrols of the town.[43]

The Nigerian government saw Yahaya as a madman, an erroneous perception that influenced the investigation of the Justice Danlami Tribunal. The media castigated him, criticizing the government for not using security forces to hunt him down before he could cause havoc. While Yahaya's commitment to his religion is not in doubt, which fact is evidenced by the fact that he is called a fanatic, much of what he and his followers stood for is important. They sought full rejection of the British political heritage and the way in which the military authorities defined the state and projected authority. They challenged the jurisdiction of the state over them, claiming the state was illegitimate and that public functionaries were ungodly and corrupt. They called into question the need for loyalty to the state, preferring instead loyalty to Islam and religious leaders. Madaki's threat provided them with the opportunity to test this loyalty and to reject the secular authorities. The members of the sect held Yahaya and al-Zakzaky in much greater regard than they did Madaki. Members of the sect had no confidence in a government presided over by Madaki, a kaffir, whose policies were *shirk* (anathema). Again, Yahaya reaffirmed the well-known Islamic view that government ought not to be separated from religion. For those who blamed the security forces, there was little these forces could have done in a situation where the coercive apparatus of the state was not respected or feared. As soon as the members of Yahaya's sect lost their fear of death, the police and the army lost the ability to prevent the crisis. The Katsina incident demonstrates the limited power of the government to challenge a religious group and to require people to give their allegiance to a secular authority rather than a religious one. Madaki's Pyrrhic victory at the protest failed to see an end to the Yahaya sect.

Each year there has been at least one violent incident involving Shiites, mostly occurring in Kaduna, Kano, and Zaria. The movement's ability to mobilize in large numbers, sometimes of over ten thousand, on a moment's notice makes their actions difficult for the police to anticipate. Al-Zakzaky retains his respect and leadership, and he is under permanent police surveillance. As recently as September 1996, the police and the Shiites clashed in Kaduna in an outbreak that led to the deaths of two police officers and five civilians and hundreds of injuries.[44] This incident was provoked by the arrest of al-Zakzaky, who was alleged to have been importing illegal arms and to have been publishing illegal subversive material.

A particularly vehement protest took place on 20 September. Panic immediately struck the city. The police promised security to the public and issued threats to the Shiites. 'If they are violent,' warned the state police commissioner, 'we will be violent. It is an eye for an eye.'[45] The police arrested many of the protestors and charged about forty of them for disturbing the peace, unlawful assembly, and the murder of police officers. Mohammed Ciroma, a prominent leader unmoved by the police force's actions, spoke for the Shiites:

> We are just trying to continue with our programme as usual, teaching Islamic philosophy and working to deliver Nigeria from this corrupt system of government.[46]

Confronting the state and Christianity: the Bauchi violence of 1991

The riots in Bauchi state from 20 to 24 April 1991 turned out to be even more disastrous than their counterparts in the 1980s. They occurred soon after the Katsina incident, as if Yahaya had planned them as revenge, but they were not engineered by Shiites. Indeed, the Bauchi riots, unlike those of Katsina, had no leader, and were not instigated by any particular sect. The immediate riots began with a confrontation drawn along both ethnic and religious lines. As was the case with the Kafanchan riot, it began with a small grievance but quickly snowballed with hostilities that had been building up for years between different ethnic and religious communities.

The crisis was triggered by a minor incident on Saturday 20 April at an abattoir in the town of Tafawa Balewa, 50 kilometers from the state capital at Bauchi. As was the case in Kafanchan, the details of that day's events have been obscured because no one wants to take the blame, but there are two main versions of the story. According to the first, a Muslim man bought beef from a Christian butcher. A Muslim who was standing by rebuked his fellow Muslim for buying beef from a cow slaughtered by an infidel, and suggested he return the meat for a refund. The butcher refused to refund his money, and a scuffle began. The second version says that a Muslim told the man who bought the beef that the Christian butcher had sold pork to him. The man who had bought the beef was so deeply offended at this deception and the violation of his religion, that without stopping to check whether it was pork or beef he had been given, he attacked the butcher and began a fight.

How did a fight between two people escalate to engulf a whole town? No one knows the details, but like the Kafanchan episode, people were drawn to the scene. Citing an eyewitness, a newspaper reporter wrote that one of the two men initially involved in the quarrel grabbed a knife and slashed the other man's arm. Other butchers, alleged to be predominantly Christian, came to the rescue of their colleague, but they were all overpowered by a crowd of Muslims. A free-for-all melee ensued in which many were either injured or lost their lives.[47]

The crisis moved to the town, where Christians and Muslims attacked one another with all the weapons they could get their hands on. Many lost their lives and homes were looted, vandalized, and set on fire. The police were mere onlookers, making only feeble attempts to quell the riot. From Tafawa Balewa town the violence spread to other parts of the state and became a religious war.

The two versions of the riot's origin read like the well-known mythical creation of a precolonial Nigerian city-state or of a warrior-hero who ascended to heaven on his last day on earth. But if the origin stories are not confirmable because they are too temporally distant, the events in Tafawa Balewa are all too near. These two stories were repeated to me by more than twenty informants in 1992 and 1993, and I was taken to the abattoir and shown the very spot where it all started. The story of the fight in the abattoir was real, not a metaphor, even if the details are lost. The fight spread, and it did in fact begin the widespread violence.

The question, then, is not whether or not this event occurred in Tafawa Balewa, but why such a small event was capable of leading to such a largescale crisis. The answer can be found in some of what I have said before, relating to economic decline in the country, religious divides and manipulation, and attempts by minorities to assert themselves. By the time the riot reached Bauchi City, it had moved beyond the original incident to encompass a general attack on southerners who were perceived to be dominating the economy of Katsina state to the detriment of the indigenes.

In Tafawa Balewa, where the crisis erupted, there was a Christian and ethnic minority, the Seyawa, who had for years complained of the domination of the Hausa-Fulani and the attempts by Muslims to make it difficult for them to practice their religion.[48] They constructed their history and themselves as people who struggle to receive education, but who could hardly use their diplomas to get good jobs and promotions. They regarded themselves as hardworking but poor.[49] However, the majority Hausa-Fulani population did not seem to see things the same way. 'We oppress no one, we prevent no one from practicing their religion' was a common response to the Seyawa construction.[50] In the 1980s and 1990s, the minorities defined politics as seeking 'freedom from Hausa-Fulani oppression.' In some sense, Christianity has made it possible for them to construct a powerful identity of difference from their Hausa and Fulani Muslim neighbors. To this was added a strong desire for Western education. Many were successful in life, and an elite entrepreneur class had emerged among them by the 1980s.

The minorities wanted political freedom. This turned out to be more complicated than they thought. Their number was not enough to win an election, so their only option was to forge political alliances. Even this was not all that easy. In the 1980s, the appointment of two Christian military governors, although not their own men, was interpreted as favorable to them. According to the Muslim political elite, these governors did far too much for the Christians' cause. Political tension continued into the 1990s.

The majority of the politicians in Bauchi belonged to the conservative National Republican Convention (NRC). In the December 1990 local government elections, the NRC won most of the offices, except in Tafawa Balewa, where the Social Democratic Party (SDP) took power. This victory was interpreted in religious terms: minority Christians voted for the SDP to affirm their difference. A goodly number of the Muslim political elite did interpret this not as a victory for democracy, but as an expression of

anti-NRC sentiment and resentment of the majority population.[51] Muslims felt the leaders of the minorities deserved to be taught a lesson by being subjugated and brought into the fold of the NRC. The consequent violence was one way to teach the Christians a lesson.[52]

On 20 April the riots spread to the neighboring town of Dass, where groups of Muslims fought, injured, and killed Christians, outsiders, and even locals. Many people fled the town in panic. In both places, the violence was contained not by the police or local authorities, but because the rioters' goals had already been accomplished. The number of people under attack was small, and once they fled, only their property was left to loot and vandalize. The way the Dass riots ended evidences the long-standing hostility among different groups.

The greatest calamity occurred in Bauchi City, the most heterogeneous part of the entire state. It is difficult to reconstruct how the violence spread here and why the government found it difficult to nip it in the bud, when it was aware that there were already troubles in Tafawa Balewa and Dass. There are two explanations for these questions. The first and most recent explanation holds that reports of the incidents in Tafawa Balewa and Dass spread to Bauchi City, where some Muslim groups thought that they should avenge the death of their 'brothers and sisters' and that the time was ripe to attack all their 'enemies.'[53] The other explanation was popular at the time of the crisis. On Sunday morning, three policemen escorted the vehicle that brought the corpses of riot victims in Tafawa Balewa and Dass to Bauchi to deposit them in the specialist hospital in Bauchi. The vehicle broke down within the city limits before they could reach the hospital. As the victims were being transferred to another vehicle, a crowd who had gathered heard about what had happened. Word spread that mutilated bodies and injured people from other towns were in the hospital, and that all the corpses were Muslims. Very quickly, a mob of Muslims gathered at the hospital,[54] mobilized fully for revenge.

The riots in Bauchi City involved thousands of people who scattered throughout the city wreaking havoc. The Ninth National Sports Festival was happening in the city at the same time, and media attention had already been focused on the city. Within twenty-four hours, about five hundred houses were set on fire. No firemen were available, and the houses burned to their foundations. At the Bayangeri quarter, where most of the hotels were situated, fifteen hotels were set on fire. Bayangeri was in the modern part of the city, with good houses, roads, and amenities. Houses and cars were set of fire. The Deeper Life Bible Church in the neighborhood was set on fire, and rioters watched closely to ensure that it burned to the ground, including every last pew and book. A pharmacy was looted to the last pin, and both of the owner's cars were burned. So close was the pharmacy to police headquarters that the inaction of the police especially infuriated victims. The rioters were too many and too angry, as someone who survived the attack put it.[55]

Having satisfied themselves in the Bayangeri area, the rioters moved next to Hospital Road, where most of the churches in Bauchi City were located. The decision to invade this part of the city could not have been arbitrary, as it was far from the city center. All twenty churches on Hospital Road were burned. They included St. John's Catholic Church, the Basara Baptist Church, Cocin Church, Christ Apostolic Church, and St. Paul's Anglican Church. These were the cream-of-the-crop churches, with the largest congregations and best buildings in the city. The area had long been designated as a Christian zone, to separate them from the large Muslim population and thereby minimize tension. As it turned out, this only made the rioters' destruction easier.

The church was not the only symbol of bitterness. The rioters descended on all the mission houses and destroyed their property, cars, and buses, burning it all. The offices, cars, and other property of the Christian Pilgrims Board were similarly destroyed. Only one church was spared, the ECWA church. An elder of the church attributed this to 'the commitment of the people to God.'[56] But the church's survival was probably attributable more to its location near the army barracks, where rioters decided that an attack could provoke military intervention. When a handful of rioters did come back a few days later, the army simply gunned them down.

Riots occurred in different locations of the city. A truckload of beer and its driver were set on fire. The streets were littered with broken bottles, stones, sticks, and damaged vehicles. Chanting anti-Christian and anti-ethnic slogans, rioters moved with weapons and gasoline against their targets. In many cases, they knew what they were looking for and what to avoid. At Tudun Wada street, home to many non-natives, certain places and people, notably the Seyawa group, were selected for destruction. Even private medical clinics were not spared, if their owners were regarded as enemies.

Casualties were high. Hundreds of homes, hotels, churches, and public buildings were burned or destroyed. While official sources initially put the death toll at eighty, mortuary figures had it at five hundred. Thousands more were injured and hundreds hospitalized. Corpses littered the streets of Bauchi City, and the threat of disease from the decomposing bodies forced health authorities to collect these corpses and bury them in mass graves outside the city. People now callous to death stood by as the corpses were piled into trucks.[57]

Most of the victims were killed brutally – many were burned, macheted, or stoned to death; many more were decapitated.[58] A Christian medical doctor able to escape Tafawa Balewa, thinking that the rioters wanted only his death, was shocked to discover on return that his house had been vandalized, his young boy burned to death, and his mother's head smashed against the wall. He described this as 'a most horrendous act of madness.'[59] A twenty-five-year-old spare parts dealer narrated how his brother, Johnson, was killed on 23 April in their store:

There was smoke everywhere. I ran to the shop. I saw Johnson. He was still inside the shop. He was trying to get out. But they did not allow him to do that. One of them with a long dagger was wielding it before him. Other people used long sticks to push him back into the fire…. The whole shop was burning and falling down on him.[60]

Activities in Bauchi City ground to a halt. The sports festival was suspended, greatly to the embarrassment of the state government. The army was called in to protect participants, who had threatened to abandon the game and head home. Offices and markets were deserted. The roads were deserted, as many people chose to stay at home. Those who were unsure whether or not they would be attacked escaped to other places, notably the nearby city of Jos. The outsiders, who made up the majority of the victims, either ran away or sought refuge in police or army barracks. The hundreds that went to the barracks still suffered; neither food nor sleeping quarters were to be found there. When the governor inspected the city after the riot, he was moved to tears by the enormity of the destruction.[61]

As in previous riots, the police lost control. For three days the rioters were completely unhindered, as the police and everyone else became exclusively concerned with protecting the lives of themselves and their families. The police failed to act promptly, even when one of their own was lynched early on in the crisis. As more Muslims flooded into the city from nearby villages to join in the general destruction, they met with no police resistance. As in most other cases, as soon as the rioters had finished their havoc, the police would come by to inspect, but they were powerless to stop a riot.

On 21 April, a curfew was imposed from 7 p.m. to 6 a.m., but the violence continued. Later that same day, the federal government mobilized the army, instructing them to restore law and order with the maximum force necessary. While the presence of the army brought calm, another round of violence broke out the next day. Hundreds of people were arrested in an attempt to weaken and disorganize the mobs. Muslim leaders claimed that most of those arrested were innocent, and hundreds marched to the emir's house to demand their release. The emir went to the state house to hold talks with the governor, and the mob followed him. Seeing the mob, the commanding officer thought that they were about to attack the government compound, the police, and the army. He ordered that the mob be dispersed, and many were killed and injured in the process. Interpreting their instructions perhaps too literally, the army shot anyone even suspected of attempting to burn down a building.[62] The state itself became a dispenser of brutal violence. Hundreds more people were arrested, many later to be falsely accused of participating in the riots.

More Muslims became very angry and looked for insecure places vulnerable to attack. Sporadic riots occurred on 23 April in Bauchi City. On that day and the next, hundreds gathered in the emir's palace to complain that the police and army were pro-Christian, and that Muslims should not be arrested. Violence spread to the locality of Ningi, which was not heavily policed, and where the divisional police officer, a Christian, was killed after one of his eyes had been plucked out. Five other officers were killed, and the station was burned down. Houses of non-natives were attacked as well, and manhunts were conducted throughout the state to weed out additional outsiders.[63] No figures are available on the number of dead at Ningi.

The violence sent shock waves across the country. Christians were frightened by rumors that a jihad had begun in earnest to engulf the entire country. Archbishop Okogie bitterly proclaimed, 'Nobody is a third rate citizen in this country; it is either we wipe ourselves out for good, or God saves who ever survives because it is going to be a religious war.'[64] CAN questioned the ability of the government to protect Christians. Because many athletes from throughout Nigeria were in Bauchi at the time, national panic was heightened. In a country with undeveloped communication systems, it was impossible for most of the athletes to reach their relatives and friends. Travel to Bauchi City was impossible. The only information coming out of the city was in the form of rumors spread by people fleeing, many of which falsely reported that athletes had been killed. The Bauchi riots were, therefore, not localized in their impact, especially in terms of the deep fear they implanted in the minds of millions of people all over the country. In some southern states, certain groups were already preparing for a retaliatory attack on Muslims. Most governors had to spend days appealing to religious leaders to calm their followers and to pray for peace.[65] The federal minister of information instructed all media under his control to downplay the crisis, leaving the public to fall on private sources of information. Although this is a familiar damage-control strategy, it usually backfires by making the government appear deceitful and supportive of Islam. Police forces across the northern states were put on permanent alert, and major roads leading to all state capitals were monitored.

As in previous cases, a federal commission of inquiry was set up to determine the causes, remote and immediate, of the crisis. Known as the Babalakin Commission,[66] it was given four weeks to assess the damage, determine appropriate levels of victim assistance, determine the causes of the violence, and identify those who were responsible.[67] The Christian community and the media found the Babalakin Commission to be nothing but a joke, a way for the government to seem concerned without actually doing anything. Many people wondered what the government had done with the reports of previous similar commissions. Babalakin's task was nothing new, and no original proposals came out of it.

The wounds inflicted by the violence on intergroup relations in Bauchi have yet to heal fully. Thousands of residents had fled the city, leaving behind their property and their means of livelihood, and not everybody was able to recover from the loss. When the crisis was over, the governor and his leading officers and traditional rulers appealed to southerners not to leave the state. As many sectors of the economy, especially the informal sector and retail trade, were dominated by strangers, Bauchi City suffered greatly from this withdrawal. In addition to launching a propaganda campaign insisting that peace had returned to the region, the state government promised to compensate the victims. The state hoped that the promise of compensation would lure residents back home in order to submit and defend their claims. In an unusual move, the state government sent delegations to the southeastern states of Imo and Anambra to appeal to Bauchi residents to return and resume their activities.[68] Those non-natives who have returned have found it difficult to reestablish trust with their hosts.[69] And as some indigenes complained in 1993, the 'southern traders, ruthless profiteers, will never learn.' Both a lack of trust on the part of non-natives and the perception of southerners as profiteers indicate that tension continues to characterize intergroup relations in Bauchi City and other parts of the state.[70] Riots could recur at any time.

Confronting Christianity: violence in Kano, October 1991

In October, before the dust had settled from the Katsina and Bauchi riots, a massive three-day attack was launched in Kano by Muslims solely against Christians. It was a clear demonstration of the unity among many Muslims to achieve a desired objective and to show Christians in no uncertain terms that the ancient city of Kano was Islamic. A Christian minority also attempted to assert itself, but while willful, it did not have the means to accomplish its goal.

There is no confusion as to the immediate cause of this violence. The Christian Association of Nigeria had invited a German preacher, the evangelist Reinhard Bonnke, to preach in Kano. Many Muslims originally objected not to the preacher's visit or to what he might say, but to the venue – the popular, enormous, and public Race Course – and to the aggressive publicity given the event. Some few months before, an Islamic organization had invited a preacher to use the same place, but it was not granted permission by the government. Thus, when it became known that CAN was to be allowed to use the Race Course for its event, Muslims were enraged.[71]

The state government, not wishing to foment unrest, but recognizing that CAN had a constitutional right to hold a crusade, decided that CAN would have to change the location of its meeting. CAN had meanwhile circulated notices and posters inviting people to the Race Course. Perhaps the crisis would have been averted if the government had offered to publicize the change of venue. But CAN's already printed materials had already antagonized the Muslims, the more militant among whom felt the infidel was challenging them.[72] As if to defy the Muslims and demonstrate their own strength, the Christians embarked upon a renewed publicity campaign for the crusade, using public-address systems and posters to announce to the people of Kano that Jesus Christ would be coming to the city to save souls.

In spite of appeals from the emir of Kano, the governor, and others, and despite assurances that CAN would not hold its crusade at the Race Course, tension in the city remained high. Muslims now demanded that the crusade be cancelled entirely. In retrospect, officials have admitted that such a cancellation, or at least a rescheduling of the crusade, would probably have stayed the violence,[73] but to take this option would have risked offending the Christians and putting Muslim politicians in a position to make additional demands. Muslim leaders said that Christians had polluted the city by raising the name of Jesus over that of Prophet Muhammad, that the minority Christian element was acting outside its place.[74]

Widespread riots broke out on Monday 14 October. Official sources reported twelve deaths and large numbers of injuries. Thirty-four houses, one church, and one mosque were burned. Forty-two shops, four hotels, fifteen cars, eight trucks, and nine motorcycles were also set ablaze. Many public buildings were damaged.[75]

The governor imposed a dusk-to-dawn curfew that very day, but the curfew order was ignored; early the next day, the governor went on the air with an appeal to the Muslims to calm down and exercise restraint. This appeal was also ignored. Later in the evening, he made another broadcast, this time threatening to call in the army. The consequences of this action, he warned, would be grave.[76] But his threats fell on still-deaf ears, and fighting continued in Sabongari (the non-natives' neighborhood) between indigenes and non-natives. Christians and southerners abandoned their homes, fleeing to the air force base and police barracks. Additional police forces were drafted from neighboring states, but the situation could still not be controlled. One senior police officer pleaded with the non-natives: 'Even if the police failed, God would not fail you. We are here to restore peace.'[77] Babangida once again had to rush home from abroad, abandoning the Commonwealth Summit of Heads of Government in Harare, Zimbabwe. It took days of reinforcement from anti-riot police squads to restore order.

The crisis was unprecedented in Kano state. Religious crisis was hardly a stranger to the state, but the sole targeting of Christians for destruction on such a massive scale was something new. State and federal government officials began damage-control initiatives in earnest, seeking to placate non-natives without offending indigenous Muslims. A probe was instituted, promises of compensations were offered, and the business of government went on as usual.

The Kano crisis did recur three years later, when a Christian was beheaded in 1995 by a Muslim mob who accused the man and his wife of desecrating the Qur'an. The violence escalated further over a fracas between a Muslim and an Igbo trader. Widespread riots occurred. As in previous cases, much damage was done before peace could be restored.

The Kano incidents reveal the deep tension between minority Christians and the majority Muslims and the competition between indigenes and southerners. The government laid the blame for the Kano violence at the feet of misguided individuals. This is far from the truth – while every outbreak of violence certainly provides opportunities for looting, it is preposterous to make that sort of activity a motive for religious riots. While young people, thugs, and looters inevitably join in the violence, they are hardly ever instigators.

Most such cases of violence are preceded by a long period of discontent with the government from Islamic leaders, who usually point to societal decadence, rising poverty, unemployment, and materialism. Modern Kano was perceived as degenerate and in desperate need of change. The city is always ripe for revolution. Compounding this problem were unaccounted for declines in economic fortunes and a lack of opportunities for young people. While the government was blamed for these, some also say that southerners compounded the problems by taking a 'big share of our market.'[78] Manipulative Kano politicians find it easier to tell poor people that the outsiders are their enemies. As a result, whenever frustration reaches the breaking point, the outsiders come under attack.

Religion and ethnic nationalism: violence in Zangon-Kataf, 1992

On Thursday, 14 May 1992, one year after the riots in Katsina and Bauchi, another incident broke out in Zangon-Kataf, a small town in southern Zaria in Kaduna state. Muslim Hausa and Kataf Christians engaged in a conflict so bitter and so destructive that the 1987 Zaria crisis paled in comparison. Everything of value was completely destroyed in Zangon-Kataf in the spring of 1992 before the violence spread to the capital city of Kaduna.

The violence of May 1992 was the culmination of an age-old conflict between two groups divided by both ethnicity and religion, the Muslim Hausa and the Christian Kataf. For both groups, the violence was an expression of nationalism, a defense against what each group viewed as an assault on its collective identity by the other. Five days before the crisis, the Zangon-Kataf branch of the Nigerian Aid Group of the Jama'atu Izalatul Bidi'a Ikamatus Sunna, representing the Hausa, wrote to Ibrahim Dasuki, sultan of Sokoto, to alert him that a war was imminent in the town:

As you all know, we moslems in northern Nigeria are patient, peace loving as directed by God. But if we are pressed to the wall, it is possible that the Jihad in Nigeria will begin in Zangon-Kataf. And the moslem if he is killed in such a venture as the Jihad will go to heaven because it is God's war: Consequently God has directed all moslems to ensure that moslems put their heads together and achieve this goal as directed in the Holy Qur'an.[79]

The Kataf, for many years, had been preparing for trouble.[80] By the 1990s, they had already become irritated at what they perceived as the 'ruthless machinations of the Hausa to liquidate them.'[81] Hausa and Kataf alike were prepared for a confrontation.

The atmosphere in Zangon-Kataf had always been charged. Intercommunal conflicts had broken out sporadically for years. The Kataf believed that the Hausa minority marginalized them at all times, abusing their power to take land, dominate resources, and exploit the Kataf, quashing their political and economic ambitions. The emir of Zaria, overlord of the chief of Zangon-Kataf, was accused of treating the Kataf as slaves and supporting the Hausa in

the 'perpetual subjugation of the owners of the land.' The Kataf blamed the crisis on the emir for denying them the right to appoint their own chief, a right their neighbors were given.[82] The emir, the Kataf alleged, usually resolved chieftaincy and land disputes in favor of the Hausa.

The Hausa saw the Kataf as uncivilized, constantly complaining 'pagans.'[83] They believed that the facts of history and conquest gave them both control of the land, saying the Hausa could not be called outsiders, since their ancestors had been living there for hundreds of years. The Hausa viewed the Kataf as hostile, accusing them of bow-and-arrow attacks on innocent Hausa farmers. The chairman of the local government, a Kataf Christian, was accused in 1992 of helping his people to attack the Hausa, the emir, and Islam.

An understanding of these accusations and counteraccusations must reach much further back than the 1990s. The Kataf regarded the Islamic emirate, established in the nineteenth century, as an enemy, along with the pro-emirate colonial and post-independence governments. They themselves feel marginalized by the Hausa. The Hausa and Kataf had intermingled for centuries, beginning in precolonial times, when Zangon-Kataf lay along a regional trade route. It became a thriving colony for Hausa long-distance traders, and over time became a permanent Hausa settlement. The Hausa acquired land, originally as gifts from the Kataf. A population of Hausa traders and cultivators emerged, headed by the *sarkin Hausawa*.

Kataf nationalism developed over the course of the nineteenth century as a result of attempts by Fulani jihadists to extend their control over non-Hausa and non-Fulani people in southern Zaria and many other parts of central Nigeria. The Kataf, like many other groups in central Nigeria, resisted the jihad. When the British conquered northern Nigeria and imposed a system of indirect rule, the power of the emir of Zaria was further strengthened over such people as the Kataf and others in the Zaria province. The Kataf said that the British had forcefully subjugated them and handed them to the emir and the Hausa-Fulani.[84] For those in southern Zaria, who were associated with the Plateau province, problems were fewer because they were able to retain their chiefdoms and enjoy some degree of autonomy. This was not so for the Kataf, who were lumped together with the rest of Zaria province and subjected to the overlordship of the emir, who appointed village heads to govern them.

Missionary activities spread rapidly during the colonial period. The Kataf, having rejected Islam, took to Christianity en masse. Two religions thus became well-established in the areas: Islam among the Hausa, and Christianity among the Kataf. Religion combined with ethnicity to polarize the town. After World War II, an assertive Kataf elite began to question the subjugation of their own chief to the Muslim emir when the Hausa chief was more powerful and had direct access to the emir.

Some reforms were made during the Gowon regime in the late sixties and early seventies, and certain groups in central Nigeria were allowed to appoint their own people as village and district heads, so long as the appointments were ratified by the emir. In the Kataf view, the emir approved only the appointment of puppets. Although a village or district head could be Kataf and a Christian, Kataf nationalists thought that they were 'mere slaves and puppets' to the emir.[85] A village or district head had to obey the emir and carry out his instructions, or risk removal of his title and his income. Resistance to the emir was tantamount to resistance against the Hausa and all Islam. The Kataf accused the emir of using his state-government connections to maintain control over the Kataf. The Hausa in Zangon-Kataf reported not to the Kataf district head, but directly to the emir. All decisions on the town, the Kataf believed, went in favor of the Hausa,[86] and the particularly contentious decisions were those of land rights. The Kataf believed that although they were entitled to all the land in Zangon-Kataf, they had been dispossessed of a large part of their territories by an emir who turned it over to the Hausa. In 1922, a two-kilometer stretch of land was acquired by the district head on behalf of the emir with no compensation to the landowners. For years, land acquisition became a means of support for the district head: all adult Kataf were required to contribute to its cultivation, but all proceeds went directly to the district head personally. In 1966, following administrative reforms, the emir decided to turn this land over to the Hausa community. The Kataf resisted the transfer without success.

For the Hausa and the emir, Kataf nationalism was misplaced and engineered by foreign missionaries bent on destroying northern culture. After 1966, as minority officers began to predominate in the army – General Gowon himself was from southern Zaria, and others included Yohanna Madaki, a colonel and former governor of Gongola State, and Zamani Lekwot, a one-time General Officer Commanding, an ambassador, and a very senior officer – the Hausa began to accuse both the Kataf military officers and the educated elite of being delusional miscreants. As far as the Hausa in Zangon-Kataf were concerned, the Kataf would only be satisfied with the voluntary or forced removal of the Hausa from the town.[87] The Kataf were described variously as anti-Islam, anti-Hausa, anti-northern, and anti-emir. 'What, then, do they stand for?' asked an Hausa imam. His answer, 'destruction of innocent Hausa traders, farmers, families, and religion,'[88] was an expression of a common belief among the Hausa.

In the 1990s, fresh struggles emerged over control of the new local government and market and over questions about allegiance to the emir of Zaria. The Kataf felt that they, and not the emir, should appoint the head of their local government. Kataf nationalists said there would be no peace until the power of the emirate was completely removed from their town and the Kataf were given charge over their own community. Yohanna Madaki explained that Kataf dignity was the cause of all the feuds:

> The people are resisting the emirate incursion into their dignity and culture. The resistance is not anti-government, but a protest of cultural invasion by the emirate. Can you imagine Christians and even those who are village heads are being forced to attend islamic functions in Zaria. If any village head fails to do so, he would be penalised. Another puppet village head will be appointed. The solution is giving the people their independence to manage their affairs. If that is not done, Kaduna will continue to be boiling point.[89]

The Kataf complained that the Hausa traders treated them as slaves in the market that was built on land transferred to them in 1966.[90] Every issue in Zangon-Kataf became identity-based. When the new local government, headed by a Kataf, decided to relocate the main market to a neutral territory in 1991, the Hausa opposed the relocation and appealed to the emir, claiming that the relocation was meant to rob them of their economic power. The Kataf said that by moving the market to a neutral place would they be able to sell burukutu, a local alcoholic beverage, and pork, both of which the Hausa kept out of the old market because of Islamic precepts. The Kataf found no sympathetic ear for their appeals. When the

local government authorized the relocation on 6 February 1992, a bloody confrontation broke out, foreshadowing the May riots. About sixty people were killed in February, property worth two million naira was damaged, farms were destroyed, and many residential houses were burned. After the police had managed to stop the violence, the state government set up the usual judicial commission of inquiry to resolve the communal tension.

The Kataf were suspicious of this commission from the onset. The seven-man commission included four Muslims, and even though the chairman was Christian, they felt it was unfairly biased. The commission met in Kaduna, which the Kataf said prevented their elders from testifying, since they were too frail or too poor to make the journey.[91] They also believed that the emir was determined to conduct a separate one-man investigation of his own, which would no doubt decide in favor of the Hausa.

The crisis of 14 May broke out at a time of especially deep mistrust among these two communities. A pro-Kataf source said that a number of disgruntled Hausa farmers and school children had invaded Kataf farms, where they uprooted yam seedlings and cassava plants. A Kataf party seeking to find out what had happened was met only with insults. The Kataf retaliated by destroying Hausa farms. The Hausa fought back with brutal force, killing the majority of the Kataf.[92] But a Hausa source told the story in reverse, saying that the Kataf were the first to destroy their farms, and that the Kataf youth launched a surprise attack on them while they were worshipping in the mosque.[93] It is clear only that there was a small altercation, brought about by deliberate provocation. Both groups mobilized, fetching bows, arrows, axes, guns, machetes, daggers, and shields.

By noon on 15 May, the clashes had consumed eighty-five lives and incapacitated the local police, and the violence continued unabated for another day. By 16 May, the town had been completely destroyed and hundreds of its residents killed. For three days, the police and the government had done nothing, allowing the people to destroy themselves. By the time three truckloads of mobile police arrived on the afternoon of 16 May, the war had burned itself out. Over four hundred corpses littered the streets, and most of the houses were burned to the ground.[94] Many of the dead had been killed by massive dagger and machete wounds; some were shot through with poisoned arrows and bows. In a few cases, people had been shot with guns, and others had been burned in their cars or homes. All the major churches and mosques were destroyed.

Many were injured, many had fled, and many more were to die later in hospitals or at home from their injuries. Bodies filled the Kafanchan General Hospital and the St. Louis Hospital in Zonkwa, while those who could afford it went to private clinics in Zaria and Kaduna. As the dead and injured were moved, news of the crisis began to spread, spurring many in surrounding areas to seek vengeance. Since the Hausa are in the majority outside of Zangon-Kataf, the Hausa version of the story found a much larger audience. In Kaduna and Zaria, preachers called for a jihad.[95] Corpses of some Hausa victims of the Zangon-Kataf crisis were publicly displayed, rousing tensions further. As in previous cases, the popular response was immediate, as crowds flooded the cities.

By 17 May, news of the Zangon-Kataf crisis had spread far and wide. The state government failed to take adequate damage-control measures, believing that the crisis would be restricted to Zangon-Kataf. But the Hausa in Kaduna, believing that the Kataf had killed their people, launched a massive attack on Kaduna residents of southern Zarian origins. They attacked all the neighborhoods where these people were concentrated: Tundun Wada, Rigasa, Kabala West, Angwar Sanusi, Angwar Sanu, Angwar Rimi, Kakuri, Naraji, Angwar Television, Sabon Tasha, Anwar Dansa, Badarwa, Badiko, Kawo, and Nasarawa.[96]

A pogrom similar to the attack on the Igbo in 1966 resulted. Because the people of southern Zaria were mostly Christians, they made an easy target when they went to church on Sunday 17 May. Many had gone to worship with no expectations of an ambush. The ECWA Church on Aminu Road was a particular venue of disaster. Many worshippers were killed there, including the church's minister, the Rev. Tachio Duniyio. Following the killing, both the vicarage and the church were set ablaze.[97] The Heken Church in Bardawa suffered a similar fate: the Rev. John Wesley and five others were killed. The Baptist Church at Angwar also lost its minister. Other churches were abandoned, but the Hausa had set up roadblocks to entrap fleeing worshippers. Many abandoned their cars and ran to private homes to beg for sanctuary.[98] Among the congregations that suffered the most were the Evangelical Church of West Africa, the African Bethel Church, and the Rehma Church. As they had done in the 1987 crisis, the police merely stood by and observed the rioters.

Far too late, Governor Mohammed Dabo Lere went on the air at 7 p.m. on 17 May to inform the public of the riots in Zangon-Kataf and to assure them that the situation was under control. He appealed for peace and imposed a statewide dusk-to-dawn curfew.[99] But the curfew did not stop the rioters, who spent the night and early morning rallying Muslims to action over loudspeakers.[100] With no police enforcement of the curfew, the rioters were able to move around and to destroy the city. The violence continued on Monday, as the police were more interested in protecting their own buildings than in quelling the rioters. The few arrests that were made only inflamed the Muslim rioters. In the afternoon, an attempt was made to attack the Sanusi police station to free those who had been detained and to assault the hundreds of Christians who had taken refuge there. But for the timely arrival of the army, the attack on the station would have been disastrous. The army dispersed the rioters and took refugees to a military barracks.[101]

The police, panicking and defending themselves, killed indiscriminately. One police sergeant reported that he and his colleagues were besieged by a crowd of hundreds chanting Islamic slogans. The police opened fire to disperse the crowd, killing forty before they themselves ran for protection.[102] The police lost six men of their own, including two inspectors. One was viciously beaten.

But the Kaduna battle was not one-sided. The Christians and southerners fought back in self-defense. The Yoruba and Igbo held solidarity meetings, strategized, and took up arms. They attacked and destroyed mosques, even damaging the national headquarters of JNI.

Southerners and Christians fled the city and thousands sought refuge at police stations and army barracks. When the time came to count the dead and injured, it was discovered that it was not just people of southern Zaria who had been attacked, but also southerners and central Nigerians in general – Yoruba, Igbo, Tiv, and Nupe, among others, were victims of the attacks.

Attacks on the southerners can be explained in two ways. First, many Muslims thought that the southerners and Christians sympathized more with the Kataf than with the Hausa. Second, some informants said that it owed to the problem of identification [sic]. Rioters asked people to identify their religion and ethnicity by reciting verses of the Qur'an or by speaking Hausa with an identifiable accent. Those who failed the test were identified as foreigners and attacked.[103] Over a thousand people lost their lives in this way. As in the Bauchi case, the way in which the killings were conducted reflected the extreme levels of anger and hatred. One pastor and his family were roasted alive in Tundun Wada as cheering crowds looked on.[104]

In Zaria, the Zangon-Kataf crisis provided al-Zakzaky with the chance to avenge his 1991 defeat in Katsina. His men attacked the Zaria prison, where they released their members who were either being detained or serving prison terms. They killed two prison officials and wounded many others. Christians were also attacked; about a hundred who had sought refuge in the prison were killed. When the emir left his palace to appeal for calm, his car was damaged by rioters warning him to stay out of the fight.[105] Bulus Katung, the CAN secretary in Zaria, and three others lost their lives.[106]

In some other small villages and towns in southern Zaria such as Zonkwa and Kagoro, the Hausa and indigenous populations attacked one another. In many other parts of the north like Kano and Abuja, non-natives stayed indoors to avoid any possible attack, while Muslims organized solidarity rallies in various locations.[107]

By Monday evening, when it was decided that the situation warranted army intervention, it was already too late. The situation had become so bad that every major hospital morgue in Kafanchan and Kaduna was filled. Corpses were displayed openly so that people could identify their relatives. In the last week of May, the Kaduna North Local Government Council organized a mass burial for 195 decaying corpses who had not been identified.[108] A number of people remain unaccounted for to this day. Hundreds of motorcycles and cars were destroyed. About twelve churches were burned and five mosques reduced to rubble. It took many weeks for life to return to normal in Kaduna and Zaria. All the schools, and commercial and government offices were unable to open. Non-natives locked their shops, motorists vacated the streets, families were dislocated, and refugees spent weeks in temporary shelters. Many non-natives, having survived the violence of 1987 and 1992, had to reconsider the need to remain in Kaduna and Zaria.

At the end of the violence came a resumption of the verbal warfare between ethnic and religious organizations. As was to be expected, CAN launched a severe campaign against Muslims and the Kaduna state government.[109] CAN blamed both the state and federal governments for failing to use the police and the army effectively. While recognizing that ethnicity was a factor in the conflict, CAN warned all Christians to be on the alert, to seek the means to protect themselves, and not to rely on the government for protection.[110]

The Kataf elite, too, attacked the state and federal governments. Yohanna Madaki granted a series of interviews in which he attacked the emir of Zaria with vehemence, criticizing the government for ignoring people like him who could solve the problem and listening instead to the enemies of the Kataf people and to those who represented entrenched Hausa interests. The crisis as he saw it was both ethnic and religious in nature, which is why minorities and churches were targeted. Rather than arrest the Kataf, the government should engage in dialogue with the Kataf elite and community leaders to seek a lasting solution.[111]

Post-crisis events followed a familiar pattern. Chiefs and leaders appealed for calm, the army and police patrolled cities and towns for a few weeks and then withdrew, markets and offices reopened, people reassessed the situation and planned what they would do the next time to defend themselves. On the part of the government, promises were made about protecting lives and property, promoting religious freedom, compensating victims, and setting up a tribunal to investigate the violence. All these things happened as usual, but there were some new features to the aftermath of the Zangon-Kataf crisis.

In the first place, many people, especially Christians, believed that the violence had escalated as far as it had because the state government was carelessly slow in calling in reinforcements. The Kataf elite blamed the government and the police for failing to prevent the large-scale killings of their people. Madaki railed against the facts that the government had done nothing for three days, had imposed a curfew that it did not enforce, and had failed to coordinate the activities of the police and the army.[112]

Second, while there were investigations aimed at arresting those who had instigated the riots, it was a largely one-sided show. The Hausa elite demanded the punishment of Kataf leaders. Senior Kataf in the army were accused of sponsoring the violence and killing Hausa themselves. Yohanna Madaki and Zamani Lekwot were arrested. By the first week of June, nearly three hundred people had been arrested, including such prominent Kataf leaders as Babon Ayok, the Zangon-Kataf local council head, and Bala Danke, the district head.

Third, the state government dissolved the Zangon-Kataf local government council and appointed Malam Haruna Zock as sole local administrator. Under a military regime, such a dissolution would have been par for the course. But Dabo Lere and the officers of the Zangon-Kataf local government were all elected politicians. The Kataf saw the government's action as yet another deliberate attempt to undermine their own authority over their affairs.

The arrest of Kataf leaders and the determination of top Hausa politicians and military officers to teach the Kataf a lesson has meant that the crisis will not go away for quite a long time. The powerful judicial commission of inquiry set up to investigate the matter quickly became embroiled in political quagmire. The effort to blame Zamani Lekwot for the crisis, and a death sentenced imposed on him by the tribunal, which was later commuted to a short prison term by Babangida, created too many diversions from the actual causes of the 1992 violence. All of the ingredients of crisis continue to fester in Zangon-Kataf and the rest of Kaduna state. By December 1995, Lekwot had received a state pardon and sixty-one Kataf were released from jail, but the Hausa who abandoned Zangon-Kataf had refused to return and the local economy has still not recovered from the destruction.[113]

Notes

* Please note that original footnote numbering has been retained.
3 In addition to my field staff, I must acknowledge the additional support of Murih Muibi, a Katsina-based Islamic teacher and public letter writer, for locating informants and for introducing me to many public officials and the police in Katsina state.
4 'A Mullah's Mission,' African Concord, 22 April 1991, 32.
5 Anonymous, conversations with the author, Katsina, 1993.
6 See the interview with Yahaya in the African Concord, 22 April, 32.
7 Al-Zakzaky, Fadakarwa Ga Musulmin Nigeria (Calling on All Nigerian Muslims) (Zaria: self-published, 1980).
8 These cassettes include 'The Time Shall Come,' 'Ungodly People,' and 'Praying for Forgiveness.' Studio and production dates are not indicated, but none was before 1985, given the references to some political events and names of people. (My translations).
9 The cassette referred to is 'Praying for Forgiveness.'
10 El-Zakzaky, 'I Do Not Respect the Constitution,' Weekend Concord, 20 April 1991.
11 Anonymous, conversation with the author, Katsina.
12 'A Mullah's Mission,' African Concord, 22 April 1991, 31.
13 I was allowed to read but not photocopy police and security reports on Yahaya in Katsina.
14 Ibid.
15 Ibid.
16 Ibid.
17 Anonymous senior public officials, conversations with the author, Katsina, 1993.
18 Ibid.
19 Y. Mohammed, et. al., 'Now the War: Shiite Muslim Leader defies Order and Riot Engulfs Katsina,' Cited in Newswatch, 29 April 1991. See also 'A Mullah's mission,' African Concord, 22 April 1991, 32.
20 'A Mullah's Mission, African Concord, 22 April 1991, 32.
21 Interview with Yahaya by O. Ojudu, 'I Am Not Afraid of Death,' African Concord, 22 April 1991, 37. This view was re-affirmed to me in 1993 by the members of the group.
22 Ibid.
23 'A Mullah's Mission,' African Concord, 22 April 1991, 34.
24 Anonymous members of Yahaya's group, conversation with the author, 1993.
25 Interview with Yahaya by O. Ojudu, 'I Am Not Afraid of Death,', African Concord, 22 April 1991, 36.
26 Anonymous members of Yahaya's group, conversation with the author, 1993.
27 Interview with Yahaya, 'A Mullah's Mission,' African Concord, 22 April 1991, 34.
28 El-Zakzaky, 'I Do Not Respect the Constitution,' Weekend Concord, 20 April 1991.
29 'A Mullah's Mission' African Concord, 22 April 1991, 34.
30 Anonymous public officials, conversation with the author, Katsina, 1993.
31 Isaac Koghe, conversation with the author, Katsina, 1993.
32 Editorial, New Nigerian, 9 April 1991, 1.
33 National Concord, 12 April 1991, 1.
34 Interview with Madaki, 'A Mullah's Mission,' African Concord, 22 April 1991, 33.
35 'Apology' Daily Times, 4 April 1991, 7.
36 Anonymous members of the group, conversation with the author; Yakubu Yahaya's file.
37 Anonymous members of the group, conversation with the author. They still hold to this belief.
38 Yakubu Yahaya's File.
39 'A Mullah's Mission', African Concord, 22 April 1991, 35.
40 Ibid.
41 Anonymous, conversations with the author, Katsina, 1993; 'A Mullah's Mission,' Newswatch, 29 April 1991, 16.
42 Anonymous members of the group, conversation with the author, 1993.
43 Newswatch, 17 May 1991, 17.
44 New Nigerian, 21 Sept. 1996, 1.
45 Ibid.
46 Daily Times, 23 Sept. 1996.
47 'Death and Destruction,' Newswatch, 6 May 1991, 13.
48 Tafawa Balewa, conversation with the author, 1993.
49 Ibid.
50 Ibid.
51 Ibid. (Four NRC politicians joined this particular interview.)
52 'Death and Destruction,' Newswatch, 6 May 1991, 15.
53 Anonymous, conversations with the author, Bauchi, 1993.
54 'Death and Destruction,' Newswatch, 6 May 1991, 14.
55 Anonymous, conversations with the author, Bauchi, 1993.
56 Jacob Gbor, conversation with the author, Bauchi, 1993.
57 'Death and Destruction,' Newswatch, 6 May 1991, 12.
58 See, e.g., 'The Bauchi Massacre,' African Concord, 6 May 1991, 26–33.

59 'Death and Destruction,' *Newswatch*, 6 May 1991, 13; Anonymous, conversation with the author, 1993.
60 'Death and Destruction,' *Newswatch*, 6 May 1991, 14.
61 'The Bauchi Massacre,' *African Concord*, 6 May 1991, 30.
62 'Death and Destruction,' *Newswatch*, 6 May 1991, 15.
63 Anonymous, conversation with the author, 1993.
64 'The Bauchi Massacre,' *African Concord*, 6 May 1991, 32.
65 Ibid.
66 Justice B. O. Babalakin was a Supreme court judge. There were four other members drawn from different parts of the country.
67 'The Bauchi Massacre,' *New Nigerian*, 22 May 1991.
68 *The Guardian*, 15 April 1991.
69 Anonymous, conversation with the author, Bauchi, 1993.
70 Anonymous, conversation with the author, 1993.
71 Anonymous, conversation with the author, Kano, 1993.
72 Anonymous, conversation with the author, Kano, 1993.
73 Anonymous, conversation with the author, Kano, 1993.
74 Anonymous, conversation with the author, 1993.
75 *New Nigerian*, 15 Oct. 1991; *Daily Times*, 25 Oct. 1991, 18.
76 *The Guardian*, 16 Oct. 1991, 1.
77 *The Guardian*, 16 Oct. 1991, 2.
78 El-hajj Mohammad Ahmed, conversation with the author, Kano,1992.
79 Written in Hausa, copies were sent to the Emir of Zaria, the state police commissioner, the director of the State Security Services, JNI, Fitiyanu Islam, the Ansar Ud Deen Society, Islam Forum, Kano, Council of 'Ulama, the Zangon-Kataf local government chairman, and the district head of Zangon-Kataf.
80 Anonymous Kataf indegenes, conversation with the author, 1993. I must acknowledge the support of Dr. Hassan Kukah, a Kataf and the general secretary of the Catholic Secretariat in Lagos, whose name I used to penetrate this community.
81 Ibid.
82 'Mayhem in Zangon-Kataf,' *African Concord*, 25 May 1991, 27.
83 Anonymous, conversation with the author. My assistant and I were able to reach the Hausa community and interview over a hundred of them through the assistance of a school teacher, Yusuf Haruna of Zaria. Yusuf joked that he was risking his life for the pagan Falola for the cause of scholarship. Without Yusuf, it would almost have been impossible for me to penetrate this group; my own identity generates distrust among them. He also assisted with translation of field materials.
84 Interview with Madaki, *African Concord*, 1 June 1992, 29.
85 Ibid.
86 Kataf Youth Association to the Governor of Kaduna State, March 1992.
87 Anonymous, conversation with the author, Hausa community, 1993.
88 Mallam Ibrahim, conversation with the author, Kaduna, 1993.
89 'Heart of the Matter,' *African Concord*, 1 June 1992, 30. (Interview with Col. Yohanna Madaki (rtd.) by Timothy Bonnet.)
90 Anonymous Kataf informants, conversation with the author,1993.
91 'Concerned Kataf Elites' to the Governor of Kaduna state, March 1992.
92 Anonymous Kataf informants, conversation with the author,1993.
93 'Violence Unlimited,' *Newswatch*, 1 June 1992, 12; Anonymous, conversation with the author.
94 'Massacre in Kaduna,' *African Concord*, 1 June 1992, 24.
95 Anonymous, conversation with the author, Kaduna, 1987.
96 *African Concord*, 1 June 1992.
97 Anonymous, conversation with the author, Kaduna,1993; 'Massacre in Kaduna,' *African Concord*, 1 June 1992, 25.
98 Anonymous, conversation with the author, Kaduna, 1993.
99 *New Nigerian*, 17 May 1992, 1.
100 Anonymous, conversation with the author, Kaduna, 1993.
101 'Massacre in Kaduna,' *African Concord*, 1 June 1992, 25.
102 'Violence Unlimited,' *Newswatch*, 1 June 1992, 10.
103 Anonymous, conversation with the author, Kaduna, 1993.
104 Ibid.
105 'Violence Unlimited,' *Newswatch*, 1 June 1992, 15.
106 Anonymous, conversation with the author, Zaria, 1993; 'Massacre in Kaduna,' *African Concord*, 1 June 1992, 26.
107 'Violence Unlimited,' *Newswatch*, 1 June 1992, 15.
108 'Violence Unlimited,' *Newswatch*, 1 June 1992, 10.
109 'CAN Criticizes Government,' *National Concord*, 11 June 1992, 13.
110 Christian Association of Nigeria, press release, 22 May 1992.
111 'Heart of the Matter,' 29–31 for the *African Concord*; 'Mayhem in Kaduna,' *Citizen*, 25 May 1992, 10-19; 'The Immediate Aftermath of Zangon-Kataf,' *Citizen*, 1 June 1992, 6; M. Haruna, 'Zango and Our Conscience,' *Citizen*, 1 June 1992, 9; 'As the Dust Settles,' *Citizen*, 1 June 1992, 9; 'Most Callous and Outrageous Scene,' (interview with Malam Muhammed Mahdi Shehu, the medical director of Ni'ima Hospital, Kaduna) *Citizen*, 1 June 1992, 14; 'A savage carnage,' *African Guardian*, 1 June 1992, 20–23; 'Three Views on the Mayhem,' *African Guardian*, 1 June 1992, 24–28.
112 'Heart of the Matter,' *African Concord*, 1 June 1992, 31.
113 *The Guardian*, 14 Dec. 1995, 1.

JON ABBINK
Ritual & Political Forms of Violent Practice

Reference
Cahiers d'Études Africaines, 150–152, XXXVIII-2-4, 1998, pp. 271–95

Violence as a problem

As a theoretical field, the anthropology of violence has been expanding rapidly[1] in recent years. There has been an upsurge in both case studies and comparative study of conflict and violence. African examples have received prominent attention in this respect, although the continent is not an exception in being more or less violent than other areas. The renewed attention to violence from many academic disciplines study has led to calls for unified 'theories of violence'. While it is not likely that new grand theories will be forthcoming, it is appropriate to put the analysis of violence as interaction more central in social and cultural analysis. Although violence as a subject has not been neglected in general social theory and history or in anthropology, social studies which systematically address violent interaction as a basic dimension in the (re)production of human sociality are still relatively scarce.[2]

For this there are ideological reasons, contained in the long tradition of Western thought on the social order, where violence is – despite its ubiquity – usually seen as a problematic aberration, a non-rational, uncontrolled mode of action signifying a regression to a wild state of 'nature'. There may also be scientific reasons: problems of the definition of 'violence', the reluctance in the comparative study of culture to ground the analysis of violence in the dialectic of basic human predispositions ('biology') on the one hand and the realm of social life and culture on the other, and the relative infrequency of violence in research settings (and its inaccessibility and danger when it occurs).

Various theoretical moments have characterised anthropological studies on violence so far. It has been emphasised, especially in American cultural anthropology, that aggression and warfare are culturally mediated phenomena, and not just the reflection of an innate human urge which just has to come out everywhere. Cultural materialist approaches have stressed the environmental-ecological logic of conflict (cf. Bennett Ross 1980). There has, however, recently been a renewed interest in evolutionary approaches which stress the 'competition for reproductive success' of persons within a population (e.g., Chagnon 1988a, 1988b, 1992; Betzig, Borgerhoff Mulder & Turke 1988), and which counters such earlier culturalist points of view.

In the anthropological study of 'tribal warfare' as developed, e.g., in Papua New Guinea-studies since World War II, ecological-materialist theories have been important. They are revived in modern approaches which emphasise 'resource competition' as the framework of conflict and violence (cf. Ferguson 1984; Markakis 1994). It is often difficult to measure and analyse this theoretical notion. The entities said to 'compete' (individuals or groups) are always assumed to do so largely outside the sociocultural framework within which this definition of reality is constructed and reproduced. 'Competition for scarce resources' can indeed be a concern perceived as such in many societies in conditions of social hierarchy, scarcity, population density and power struggle. But this idea of competition is not sufficient for a theoretical explanation of violence.

Violent action, like other social behaviour, can be more fully understood in a theoretical perspective which sees humans as social animals (i.e. with psycho-biological predispositions) with a capacity for symbol manipulation and social construction of 'meaning'. This capacity is not to be seen as a simple reflection of social conditions, but as a dimension which enters into the very definition of reality itself by both subjects and observers. Such a perspective, based on Weberian ideas about power and legitimacy, should be able to deal also with the ambiguity of the manifold social actions in every society which can be labelled as violent. Few if any societies are consistently 'pacifist' in rejecting all violence: in some conditions it is seen and experienced by many as necessary, inevitable, justified, or even psychologically rewarding.

In this article, we examine the construction and expression of violence among the Suri (or Surma) of southern Ethiopia, a pre-literate, non-industrial society which does not share our (Hobbesian) model of man (Turton 1994a: 21) While in overall terms this group cannot be called more violent than, for instance, people in Western industrial society, it is a setting within which the workings of some 'elementary rules of violent behaviour' might be observed. The case may tell us about this cultural, symbolic dimension of violence in a small-scale non-stratified society, and may enable us to qualify the often-heard statement that violent behaviour is meaningless and irrational – on the contrary, it is nearly always 'meaningful' (cf. Blok 1991). In some respects, violence can be an 'organising principle' in society, not only in moments of crisis but also to structure a part of human experience and values. Whether the Suri or related groups can be said to have a 'culture of violence' is a debatable point. This concept has questionable analytical value, and carries the danger of essentialising a group tradition which is in reality fluid and adaptive. It is, however, a term in the local discourse used by their peasant neighbours, victimised by their raids.

David Riches (1991: 295) has described violence as: '… contestably rendering physical hurt.' This refers to social interaction whereby intentional harm is done, and where the views of perpetrator and victim (and witnesses) are the issue of dispute, these parties being conscious of the problematic aspects and of different views on the (il)legitimacy of the harm done. The definition also points to the fact that violence, even in its most crude and aimless forms, always has an aspect of 'communication' – be it as a statement of social protest, of intimidation, or of self-assertion – and thus of certain cultural values. Violence is also 'rupture', immediate and challenging action, demanding a response. It may in all cases be tied to questions of social honour, of the integrity of the person or of the group.

This communicative, or perhaps performative, definition of violence was perhaps meant as a step toward a theoretical framework and for a more adequate ethnography of violence, which assume its universality but also see the culturally quite varying degrees of defining or contesting some social behaviour as 'violent'. But the definition excludes several forms of action which we would call violence from an outsider's point of view, e.g. when rendering hurt or intimidating persons, or for that matter, animals, is not in a particular culture seen as contestable (yet). For instance, Bloch's description (1992) of the sacrificial rite as being violent (the shedding of blood through killing, with the purpose of 'appropriating' some other being's life force) will not count as such in many cultures.

Here we intend to follow a wider or 'weaker' definition, along Bloch's lines. It is too restricted to only speak of violence when bloodshed among humans and destruction of the social order are involved. The challenge is to look for the cultural roots and antecedents of violent response in order to trace how aggressive, destructive and murderous violence of people could at all emerge. The local people and the representatives of the state in the area which will be described here say that the Suri violence (their disregard for life and property, their raiding, their ambushing and killing others) 'is simply in their culture'. Do such statements make any sense? To answer it, a loose definition of violence is needed: violence is the human use of symbols and acts of intimidation and/or damaging (potentially lethal) physical force against living beings to gain or maintain dominance.

Chai-Suri society: the ecological, political and social setting

The Suri are a Nilo-Saharan (Surmic)-speaking group of agro-pastoralists, somewhat comparable to other East African peoples many of which have been well-studied in anthropology (Nuer, Dinka, Maasai, Turkana, Karimojong). Their history is still shrouded in mystery, although they have clear linguistic and cultural connections to other (Para)Nilotic groups in the region. At present they cultivate a strong group identity, an aversion toward a settled agricultural way of life, a 'warrior ethos' (on which more below), and a cultural focus on cattle. For the most part of their recorded[3] history of some 200 years, the Suri were independent cattle-herders in the Ethio-Sudanese borderland. The Suri-region came under the Ethiopian state in the early 20th century, but, being remote from the central highlands, it was never well connected or integrated into it. The Suri have two sub-groups – Tirma and Chai – , and the rest of this essay will speak about the Chai, some 16,000 people. They live in the area southwest of the small town of Maji, about 60 miles north of Lake Turkana (see Fig. 1).

Environmental and economic factors
The Chai land is a lowland zone south of the Maji highlands of Southwestern Ethiopia, near the border with Sudan. The land is fertile due to the volcanic soil, but rainfall is unreliable, especially in the plains where the Chai keep their cattle-herds. The rain is insufficient for permanent, intensive agriculture, and does not guarantee the successful shifting cultivation of staple crops (maize and sorghum). Apart from cattle-herding and cultivation the Suri are engaged in hunting. At the end of the dry season (March–April), there is a problem of water and pasture, with staple-food supplies running very low. They have both agricultural and agropastoral groups as neighbours.

The most prized possession of the Suri are their cattle-herds. Cattle do not provide more than about a third of the food supply (milk, blood, occasionally meat) but are a store of wealth which can be traded for grain in times of need. In a cultural sense, the possession of cattle is intimately tied up with Chai social personality, adulthood and individual dignity, both for men and women (who also have rights of possession). Young men are expected to be committed to herding the cattle and defending it against raiding

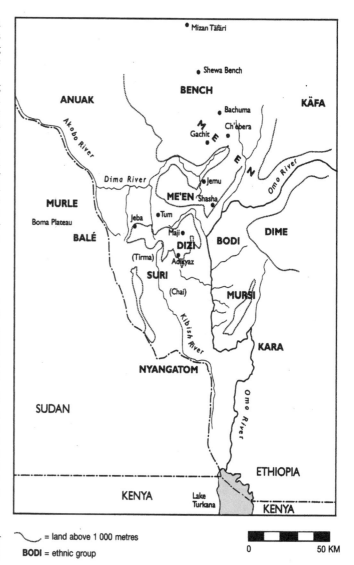

= land above 1 000 metres

BODI = ethnic group

Figure 1 The Maji area, Southwestern Käfa, Ethiopia

outsiders. On this basic level – i.e. that of their mode of subsistence and of 'competition for resources' – the readiness to confront and use violence (repulsing and/or killing the raider-enemies) is an essential 'requirement' of the present Suri way of life, and is not seen in any sense as problematic or contested.

Internal relations
The Chai have no 'chiefs', but only a ritual leader or figurehead (called *komoru*). All *komorus* come from the same ancient clan. He is chosen by consensus, and installed by elders in a special ceremony. He has no executive or commanding authority when in function. His main role is to be a focal point of normative unity of all Chai. The British anthropologist D. Turton, in his work on the related

Mursi (cf. Turton 1975: 180), has called the priest-like figure of the *komoru* a 'conductor of absolute power' (connected to the sky-god Tumu). The *komoru*, through his blessings is expected to emphasise values of restraint, to be nonviolent, and to reconcile the various domestic units, clan groups and local communities if need be.

The Chai also know an age-grade system (for males), with four ritually separated grades, of which the third one (called *rórà*) provides the 'reigning' one and has its own name (like an age-set name). This grade provides the main decision-makers and authority figures. Women derive age-grade status from their husbands, and are not separately initiated.[4]

Chai live in compact villages, with members from various clans. A clan identity is only important for the choice of marriage-partners (exogamy). Several villages form a territorial unit (called *b'uran*), which originated as a co-operative herding unit of its members. Domestic units led by married women are the foci of daily social life. There is little stratification in terms of possessions and wealth. Social relations outside village or *b'uran*-membership are formed on the basis of ritual bond-friendship (established through cattle-exchange), with other Suri as well as with non-Suri.

Inter-ethnic relations

Chai society, both internally and in its relations to other ethno-cultural groups, is marked by frequent violence. The latter comprises, among other things, inter-ethnic conflicts in the form of ambushes, robberies and killings. These seem to have gained in intensity in the last decade (see Abbink 1993b, 1994). There are indications that external factors, such as the nature of state – local society relations, changes in the regional power balance, as well as the influx of technologically advanced automatic rifles have played a decisive role here. These factors, to which we return below, have partly disturbed the 'ritual control' of violence within Chai society itself.

Chai violence has indeed always moved between the two poles of *ritual containment and political strategy*. The former element was related to keeping equilibrium in their own society, the latter to safeguarding access to pasture, water holes, fields, and natural resources vis-à-vis other pastoralist groups (Nyangatom, Toposa and Mursi), and agricultural neighbours (Dizi, highlanders). In recent years there have been additional political-ecological factors at play, and these have brought them in conflict with the Anuak and the agricultural Dizi people as well (see Abbink 1993a). Especially the relations with the latter, now their most immediate neighbours, deserve to be considered.

Historically, the Chai were located near Mt. Naita (also called Shulugui), a border mountain between Sudan and Ethiopia. According to their oral traditions they were formed or just 'arrived' in this area about two-hundred years ago. However, in the past decade, the Chai gradually have filtered into areas formerly used by the Dizi people for cattle-herding, hunting and apiculture. The Dizi were an hierarchical chiefdom society with elaborate rank distinctions, since the early 20th century heavily exploited and decimated by the northern Ethiopian settlers. Relations between Dizi and Chai are important for two reasons: a) both Dizi and Suri traditions maintain that their leading families have a common descent and cannot intermarry; b) they had instituted a kind of ritual alliance in matters of rain-control. While the Chai leaders were ascribed rain-making powers in the lowlands, the final authority on this was ascribed to the Dizi chiefs in the adjacent mountains (see Haberland 1993: 253). Under this 'rain-pact' itself, the Chai – in times of drought, food shortage, cattle disease or other problems –

were permitted to enter the areas claimed by the Dizi. This important cultural agreement was a kind of temporary sealing of a balance between these groups, codifying the exploitation of different but partly overlapping and complementary ecological niches: there was – and still is – economic exchange between them (cattle, pottery, iron products, grain, garden crops). There was also frequent inter-marriage, although mostly in the form of Chai men taking Dizi wives, in itself a sign of Chai dominance.[5]

Suri culture and the ethos of assertiveness

It was noted above that on the level of the Chai mode of subsistence and the readiness to confront raider enemies, violence is emphatically present. What is more, it is not seen in any sense as problematic or contested.

But the Suri attitude towards violence is more than just essential self-defence. An imagery of tension or violent moments is woven into many aspects of Chai life, into ideals of manhood or social personality, and in general in a ritually expressed concern with what we might call 'expansive reproduction': the growth of herds and of family and offspring. For outsiders, this attitude is reflected in many cultural metaphors which permeate Chai (Suri) culture,[6] and even in the self-name 'Chai', taken to mean 'We revenge, we pay (them) back'. For the Chai themselves, this imagery or symbolism of 'violence' does not count as problematic either.

We immediately note two things: first that this 'violent imagery' is mainly an aspect of the construction of the male gender. Females, while sharing the values underlying it, are not socialised to perform it except in a verbal manner. Second, we see that this imagery or symbolism is *not seen as problematic* or as referring to 'violence' by the Chai themselves. This is done only by external observers.

The various realms of social discourse which serve to construct shared cultural scenarios for the Chai – and which are even shared in outline by their pastoralist Nyangatom neighbours, very similar to them in way of life – might also be said to have psychological aims: first, to force new members of society to overcome the *fear* of violence, of armed attack, of wounding and killing. Interestingly, Chai say that young boys have to learn to suppress a 'natural inhibition' against the spilling of blood and against violently inflicting harm. A second aim may be to inculcate the idea of the immanence of violence, i.e. death, or the flowing of blood, in various stages and crucial moments of the life-cycle. When these two aims are achieved, violence is both domesticated, 'embodied', and made instrumentally useful.[7]

This violent imagery is expressed in at least the following three cultural metaphors/schemas, which tell us about the *indigenous* Chai conceptions about human motivations and relations. These are important if we want to advance anthropological theorising about violence and warfare and their relation to culture (cf. Turton 1994b: 25).

- The *sacrificial* metaphor. – The equation of the killing and offering of a consecrated (domestic) stock animal with beneficial effects for humans. This is done at certain ceremonial occasions, for instance: marriage, burial, age-group initiation, a rain-ceremony, installation of a *komoru*, and also at a major public debate, or sometimes in case of serious illness.[8] The core ideas behind putting a consecrated animal to death are perhaps: *substitution* and *vicarious victimisation*, because the violence is performed for the benefit of the human sacrificers. Maurice

Bloch (1992) has called it 'rebounding violence', whereby the 'vitality' of a live being once killed ritually is deflected towards humans (utilised for human purposes). The effectiveness of the sacrifice is predicated upon the close (social) bond between humans and domestic (livestock) animals. The cattle also provide the bride wealth, and thus the medium for marriage and, ultimately, fertility. The flowing of blood thus is seen as essential, yielding beneficial results. The idea of sacrifice was also relevant in the context of inter-group relations (see below).

- The *purification* metaphor. – The idea of purification is pervasive in Chai culture. People involved in homicide or in handling corpses at burials but also in adultery are to be temporarily isolated and cleansed. They can only be made 'normal' members of society again by cleansing themselves with the freshly spilt blood of a stock animal. To purify, in this respect, means to kill and to use the life-force of the animal which was killed, and which stood as the 'killer'. Humans only then are able to re-enter social life. At the same time, to purify with the fresh blood is to redraw a boundary between individuals who were earlier socially separated by their violence.

- The *achievement* metaphor. – A Chai's personal history or social career is important. His/her personality and deeds may live on beyond the lifespan, and in this consciousness, people try to make a name for themselves: as 'warriors', ceremonial duellers, public speakers, important family heads, or ritual experts. Achievements are often laid down in personal favourite-cattle songs (*roga kiyogá bio*) or battle songs (*kírogeñyò*), which every adult male has. They are composed especially by men in the junior age-grade (*tègay*). Most men keep working on such songs during their whole life, changing and adding text. Such songs can speak of deeds done in raids and war, in other dealings with neighbouring and/or enemy peoples, and of actions carried out during the defence of cattle herds and of their own favourite animals. Violent moments or episodes are an inevitable and desired element of such achievements.

Another moment of achievement is, of course, gaining adult-hood. This social adulthood is not 'just there' when people come of age, but must be achieved by having shown valour and personal strength (demonstrated in ceremonial duelling, see below), by capable herding, and by initiation (by elders) into the senior age-grade. For this, they must have demonstrated their 'worthiness'. This is a function both of time passing and of appropriate behaviour of the junior grade (see Abbink 1994). Hence, adulthood cannot just be taken – it is only reluctantly accorded to the newcomers by the outgoing grade of elders. The ritual of the initiation has violent aspects: elders (men and women) insult the new candidates, give them exacting and humiliating tasks to do, deprive them of food, and lash them with whips until their backs bleed.

These domains reveal underlying values and violent motifs active in the constitution of the Chai social person. They are especially articulated vis-à-vis outsiders. In their turn, these motifs and values inform *cultural scenarios* in Chai society. D. Linger (1992) has used the concept of 'cultural scenario' to indicate the expected behavioural 'performances' of values in action. For him, the *briga*, the violent street-encounter in Brazilian urban society, follows a known, shared 'scenario', a scripted course of meaningful action in which the participants know what to expect. It is marked by emotional commitment and shared assumptions and values. Even though the actions are violent and can end in death, they are set in a model, which has psychological and cultural components inhibiting direct aggression but communicating its message. The important point is that *briga* violence, although ambivalent because of its two poles of fascination and restraint, is not aimless, chaotic violence which suddenly erupts. A similar point can be made for Chai violence, which also follows cultural scenarios.

The exercise of violence

In this section, the practice of violence, i.e. the production and enactment of some frequent 'violent' behavioural patterns ('scenarios') in Chai society, is reviewed. Two kinds could be distinguished: the ritually enacted 'domesticated violence', and the external violence, i.e., relating to non-Chai. In the first instance, violence is transformative, i.e. fulfills an essential role for individual Chai in becoming full or accepted members of society; in the second instance, it is constitutive of their own group, a necessary inversion of peaceful social relations in certain conditions requiring distance between them and others.

Ritual enactment of 'domesticated violence'
One finds the following forms expressed within the Chai group:

- Duelling (*thagine*)[9]. – A major event of domesticated violence is male ceremonial duelling. This is done with big poles made of tough wood, of ca. 2.10 to 2.40 metres length. The main contestants are young men of the *tègay* age-grade (unmarried) coming from different territorial settlements and/or clans. They hold several matches and return-matches over a period of a few months every year, supervised by referees (*oddá*). The *thagine*-duel is strictly contained by rules of procedure, and the killing of an opponent, on purpose or accidental, is prohibited. If it occurs, homicide compensation should be negotiated. Social relations are perceived to be disturbed between the family groups of victim and killer as long as a deal is not made.

Three aspects of these duels stand out. First, the *thagine* ostensibly is a forum for male competition and acquisition of culturally approved status among peers and also vis-à-vis girls. They allow young, ambitious men, eager to start life as independent household-heads, to show their strength and virility. This latter aspect is explicitly recognised by nubile Suri girls: the duelling provides a place of male–female contacts, whereby girls among themselves make a first choice as to whom their partners might be, although there is no 100% correlation of being the winner and being the most popular person. Second, it can be interpreted, in psychological terms, as a training ground for youths to explore the fascination and energy of violence in a controlled manner. Thirdly, the duels are forums where competing village communities within Suri society meet (people from the same village can never compete). On these occasions, where thousands of people gather, one might say that these communities (called *b'uran*) are in fact constituted.

- The procedure of homicide compensation (*lígin*).—When an internal homicide has occurred, the lineages of victim and perpetrator are in a state of conflict, whereby in principle revenge can be taken at any moment. People avoid normal social contacts. After some months, negotiations are started, by neutral members from another lineage or clan group. These must lead to the fixing of a compensation sum and to the agreement to hand over a young girl to the victim's group. The killer and the closest male agnate of the victim must also be purified with the blood of a sheep. Without this ordered procedure to restore the peace, feuding would ensue.

- 'Blessing of the raiders' (*dirám*). – This is an essential ritual supervised and carried out by the *komoru*. Before going on a raid for cattle, participants (who virtually all are of the *tègay* age-grade) have to be blessed and ritually protected from death and defeat. This is done in the compound of the *komoru*, and should proceed according to a strict and faultless procedure. The raiders are smeared with a protective black clay and jump across thorn-bush branches, which symbolically stand for the enemy. They also threateningly face the *komoru* as if to attack him – an act to challenge his blessing and divert the power which he has (via the connection with the sky-god).[10] The speeches by elders and the blessings of the *komoru* are full of violent imagery, cursing the enemies, calling upon the raiders to be fearless and dauntless in their attacks. They are expected to make effective use of violence and to come back with glory (they announce their 'successful' mission upon return in their village with a special boasting song). In the knowledge that the opponents do exactly the same, there is here again no controversy on the use of violence.

- The ritual killing of livestock (*nitha*). – This is a very common event, violent although not directed at humans. It is done when people have killed some one (on purpose or by accident), at an initiation ceremony, a divinatory intestine-reading, a marriage, or a burial. The ideas of substitution and of cleansing through blood and death come back here. The manner in which the cattle or sheep are killed has its own meaning, but is seen as cruel by outsiders: it varies from cutting the throat, or slowly bludgeoning an animal to death (cattle), to slitting open the stomach before it is dead (sheep).

- Body culture. – One could see certain Chai *body treatments* as violent, though they are again not 'contested' (except by government agents, who discourage it): the piercing of lips and ear-lobes with sticks and inserting big wooden and clay discs; the making of scarifications with a razor blade on the arms, back and abdomen of women; the kicking out of lower incisors with a stone, and the 'honorific' *rídò*-scarifications (carved in the skin by an age-mate) for people who have killed. In all these cases, blood flows and pain is inflicted, but only in order to enhance *culturally styled personal purposes*: respectively aesthetics, age status, and personal achievement and prestige in the eyes of peers. It is not seen as a contested infliction of harm. This is all part of the self-conscious cultural body-aesthetics which Chai emphasise vis-à-vis other groups, and which is, for instance, completely lacking among the Dizi people.

External violence: ritual and political
We have seen that the Chai had social relations of exchange, ritual friendship bonds (*laale*), and of joint exploitation of pasture and water resources with their Mursi, Nyangatom, Dizi and other neighbours. These groups had close social ties with them, which were fully taken for granted. But, with the exception of the Mursi, such groups remained outside the Suri 'moral community'. As the complementary side of these social bonds, the Chai always knew various forms of violent behaviour and conflict in their dealings with them:

- the stealing of crops and individual cattle without violent assault. These matters, if the culprits could be found, were resolved through talks and compensation on an individual or family level;

- ambushes, to kill an individual or traveller from another ethnic group either to rob grain, clothes, tools, a gun, or cattle, or just to kill to prove personal 'courage' (by a *tègay*, a junior age-grade member);

- the raiding of enemy cattle camps or compounds, with violent deaths of both defenders and attackers. These were short hit-and-run raids, with a brief and intense attack under a barrage of rifle-fire and a quick retreat;

- occasionally: destructive one or two-day battles to destroy enemy settlements or wipe out its people. This was battle-warfare (*kaman*), and was the most serious form of violent interaction between two ethnic groups. Chai have had such fights with all their neighbours, except the Mursi. The primary purpose in such large-scale attacks was to steal cattle, but also women and children were captured, who were then incorporated in Chai society. While the violence used was intense and often deadly (hacking with knives and spears, shooting at close range) forms like rape or torture of the enemies were, however, unknown.

As one can see, the context of this external violence may be partly 'resource competition' and partly political strategy: the (re)drawing of group or territorial boundaries between political units. They do not fight because they are 'separate groups', but the reverse: in order to become different. This also holds for the Chai in their dealings with neighbouring groups (compare the same argument on the Mursi by Turton 1994a).

Relations with the agro-pastoralist Nyangatom were based on an implicit and recognised balance between two similar groups. They had a comparable acephalous organisation and age-group system, a similar subsistence base, etc. Violence was a 'normal' social activity, not problematized as such. It also had a code of conduct: even in serious things like cattle-raiding, for instance, there was the rule of the preliminary marking (in the neck) of a few cattle from a targeted herd before the actual raid would take place. Conflict between the Chai and Nyangatom was, in sum, a way to express or assert a boundary with the 'significant other'. The killing of a Nyangatom allowed a Suri man to make the prestigious *rídò* scarification on his arm.

With the agricultural Dizi people, who dominate the highlands northeast of the Suri and have a very different economy, culture and political ideology, relations were not based on perceived similarity. The Chai always had a disdain for the Dizi and their sedentary, agricultural way of life. But their obvious group differences – despite the myth of common descent of their chiefly families – were codified in an explicit 'contract' of rain control, based on the metaphor of sacrifice. In times of drought, the Chai would pay homage to the Dizi chief of the highlands, bringing a black ox and a black goat for sacrifice by the Dizi chief. The political tension (between two basically *unequal* groups) was 'appeased' in this agreement, thus keeping inter-group violence at bay through the metaphor of ritual sacrifice (substitutive violence). There were incidents between individuals of the two ethnic groups, but no major violent conflicts or battles. Neither did Suri apply the *rídò*-markings.

The above elements shape the Suri practice of violence and define their *habitus* (in Bourdieu's sense defined as human dispositions acquired in society due to a process of internalisation of external 'objective' social conditions). The habitus is also incorporated into action, feeling and thinking of individuals in a specific society, often in a quite literal sense, since the emphasis is on the bodily basis of these dispositions. This is also evident among the Suri. A habitus is, however, not static.

'Deranged' violence? Transformations of the violent habitus

Since a decade, the face of violence among the Chai and their neighbours has changed significantly. Although the traditional situation of 'normal' relations between the ethnic groups in the area was not always harmonious and should not be glorified, it is apparent that the past years have shown a serious crisis in inter-ethnic relations. This kind of situation is becoming general in many parts of Africa due to internal and external factors, often in the context of globalisation, bringing together various spheres of interaction and articulating conflicts of interests. Traditional rituals and customary law usually cannot achieve what they were designed for in bygone days. Local societies are structurally unable to maintain their integrity and moral fibre due to accelerated drought and famine problems, population pressure, faulty state policies, tourism (see Abbink 1998a), modern formal education and criminal activities.

As a result of recent political and other changes in the Maji area, both the internal, thus far ritually contained Suri violence as well as the violence towards other groups tend to break the bounds of custom and to turn into the uninhibited use of force (this was also the opinion of most Chai elders, though expressed differently). While it makes available new options for local people, the new violence tends to endanger the co-existence of groups as well as the peace in Chai-society itself. Relevant factors have been population movements in the Ethio-Sudan border area due to the Sudanese civil war, increased local conflicts about pasture and water holes, periodic drought and famine, epizootics, a temporary retreat of central state authority from the local scene, and generational conflict among the Suri, all this coupled with the rapid spread of automatic weapons among all groups, which changed the extent and intensity of violent encounters (see below). These factors have contributed to more inter-group conflicts, a decline in market contacts and a virtual halting of shared use of the environment and of long-term mutual social contacts (including intermarriage and ritual friendship bonds). A three-year record kept by the author of violent incidents between the Chai-Suri and Dizi (leaving out the conflicts which either group has had with another neighbouring population), shows at least sixty incidents with a fatal outcome, the number of people being killed ranging from one to several dozens per case. (With other ethnic groups like the Anuak and the Nyangatom the Suri also have violent conflicts, but due to geographical separation between them, the number of confrontations and of casualties has been less than with Dizi and highland villagers.)

One of the problems to explain is why violence 'got out of hand' and led to a break-down of social relations between the Chai and other groups. Is it because their cultural models and their *habitus* were, in a sense, 'violent'? In the course of the conflicts with the Dizi, one can see a *qualitative* difference in the view on, and exercise of, violence, especially among the members of the *tègay* age-grade (see Abbink 1994): violent action – attacking and killing – became an aim in itself, a medium of self-glorification and of personal status which, while based on assumptions and ideals within Chai society, has gone well beyond them.[11]

To understand why this happened, we recall two general factors. First, the Chai subsistence base. They are transhumant herders and shifting cultivators, not sedentary farmers: they have never invested in long-term agricultural adaptation but in mobile cattle-herding. For them, boundaries between 'territories' and 'resources' are not to be strictly observed, it is against the nature of their open economy and flexible 'membership policy'. If such a closure occurs, due to conquest and exclusion policies (e.g., of Nyangatom, due in its turn to population growth and also Kenyan military pressure) or to developments of 'sedentarization' and administrative boundary-making, violent conflict cannot but increase. This is what has happened in the past decade. There is less and less room for Chai to follow traditional strategies of conflict resolution: avoidance, migration, or division and territorial spread of groups.

Second, the process of state expansion in the Maji area. Since the turn of the century, when it was nominally incorporated into Ethiopia, Maji has always been a 'frontier area', incompletely administered and on the margins of the state monopoly on violence. Recent efforts to reestablish the state after the change of regime in 1991 have 'problematized' all expressions of Suri violence. The state is by nature presenting itself as the normative, overarching authority which should have the exclusive use of legitimate force as well as combat 'harmful customs'. Local violence of Chai or of any other group is proscribed, regardless of its context (this was already the case under the previous state communist regime of Mengistu). The state representatives have also, at various points, tried to prohibit many Chai activities or customs: not only cattleraiding, ambushing, etc., but also things like animal sacrifice (the killing of cattle for divination or funerals), the customs of ear- and lip-plates, removal of lower incisors, and body scarification (these were called 'harmful customs' in the 1987 constitution of the previous regime, a concept which returns in the policy documents of the post-1991 government). Recently, in 1994 and after, it was also tried to ban the ceremonial duelling contests.

It is obvious that this so-called 'civilisational offensive' represents an assault on the socio-cultural fabric of Chai society. As the Chai are held responsible for most of the violence in the Maji area, state officials think that by reforming the what they see as overall 'violent character' of Chai culture they can halt violent conflicts. It is, however, likely that if this state campaign to 'reform' Chai culture – by banning the customs just mentioned – would be successful (it is not), the violence against non-Chai would notably increase when these domesticated forms of violent expression would cease to exist. In addition, while the state discourages or forbids even Chai self-defence and redressive action against enemy raiders, at the same time it cannot guarantee defending the Chai and their territory against such raiders (e.g., from the south or from Sudan), nor protect them from drought and subsistence crises, factors which necessitate at least some violent action. More immediately important factors stimulating the overall use of violence have been:

1. the wide availability of automatic rifles and ammunition from both Sudanese and Ethiopian sources;

2. continued ecological pressures: drought, cattle disease, more scarcity of bush land for cultivation and pasture for livestock. There was a major famine in 1984-85 and again one in 1994, and one in early 1997. This contributed to theft, ambushes and raiding;

3. the conflict in southern Sudan, which became the source of

population movements in the region, pushing the Toposa to the western borders of the Suri territory, thus making their pastures and their old ritual sites, chiefs' burial places and settlements unsafe, and posing a threat to their physical and also cultural existence.

The effect of such changes in the socio-political and physical environment on the Chai, and on their use of violence in their relations with other groups, has been dramatic, although it is not a one-way causal chain – the developments in their own society have combined with such external factors to reinforce crisis and violent conflict.

It could be seen most clearly in the crisis in the age-grade system, which is the core of their political organisation and internal order (cf. Abbink 1994, and 1998b). In the age-grade system, the elder or reigning age-set of *rórà* is to be accorded respect and obedience from the younger one. They occasionally expect to be honoured and, in a metaphorical sense, 'fed' in recognition of that fact, e.g., by being offered sacrificial cattle.[12] Their blessing of the land and the cattle and their authority on the basis of age is seen as a necessary element in the social order. But it was resented by the reigning age-set called Neebi (= 'Buffaloes') that the *tègay* were always taking violent initiatives on their own, not sanctioned by public decisions at meetings. The *tègay*, mostly younger herders who lived in the cattle camps (in an area six hours' walk from the villages), could assert themselves because of the power of their rifles and on their growing economic leverage (as herders and as gold traders: see Abbink 1993a). Also in other domains the respect of the younger generation toward the elders and parents was diminishing, even within families: personal property and heads of cattle were often taken away by youngsters, without the consent of the parents.

The growing violence perpetrated by Chai youths initially convinced Chai elders (who control the date and the proceedings) that the new age-set initiation, which was already due in the early 1980s, should be delayed. With this, they expressed that the Chai first should formulate an answer to their problems, such as being exiled from their country, recovering from the drought and famine period in the mid-1980s, running into trouble with the Dizi and the Anuak (which endangered normal social relations and trade), and not respecting the elder generation. The *tègay* were blamed for all this, and the elders did not have a clear answer to the problems. The increased violence had brought out internal contradictions in the age-grade system and the authority structure and norms it was supposed to uphold. In fact the metaphor of age organisation as a cultural model of ordering social life was fundamentally disputed.

The availability of automatic weapons, now acquired by virtually all men, led also to changes in the concept of violent action and to new violent practices. Above, we have discussed some core elements of the cultural basis of 'violent imagery' and action among the Chai. In the new situation, their values of male achievement and reputation, raiding and hunting exploits and ceremonial duelling provided a fertile basis for the expansion of violent performance by means of the new weapons, for instance:

- compared to the spears, knives and old three or five-shot rifles of less than a generation ago, the possibilities of the AK-47s (Kalashnikovs), FALs and M-16s seem to have a fascination and momentum of their own. Their availability not only leads to mimetic exercise of violent acts by the *tègay* vainly seeking

recognition still structurally denied to them (see above: the delayed age-set ceremony), but also giving the possessors the idea of 'social self-sufficiency': they explicitly de-emphasised the value or even the need of normal social relationships as formerly maintained with the neighbouring groups;

- the weapons also have been put to new use. For example, there have been some unprecedented instances of Chai killing their own cattle, to prevent them from being captured and taken away by enemy raiders (this has also been observed among the Tirma, and among other newly armed pastoral groups in Uganda and Kenya, the Pokot, Turkana, Karimojong, etc.). There has been the gunning down of Dizi elders and women, and the killing of unarmed Dizi girls in ambushes, things not done in the recent past. Through this violence, exercised largely with impunity, the Chai and Tirma became more and more saturated with the feeling of power, and challenged not only the Dizi peasants but also the state army. This built up until October 1993, when a big Ethiopian army attack reputedly caused several hundred of Chai and Tirma (men, women and children) to die. Only after this obvious defeat the elders decided to hold the age-set ceremony, initiating and conferring adulthood on the 'delayed generation' (see Abbink 1998b). Since then Chai Suri violence has decreased. The Tirma subgroup, which has not yet performed the initiation ritual, shows at present a higher level of violence than the Chai.

Two other internal changes in Chai society are the following:

- in the past six or seven years, the institution of *thagine*, the ceremonial duelling, has undergone a metamorphosis. First of all, the frequency of the contests has much increased. They are held almost every two to three weeks over a period of three to four months after the main harvest of sorghum (September–November, and after that as well, e.g. in January and in the time of the first rains in April–May. Secondly, the influence of the elders (including the *komoru*) and the referees over the contesting parties has diminished: nowadays, the young men and their friends continue as they like, and after one party has 'lost' one contest, they grab their Kalashnikovs and start shooting (usually, but not always in the air) to show their irritation. This has led to several accidental killings. One can hear the Suri elders say that the meaning of duelling is being eroded. We see here another cultural scenario in flux, whereby accepted meanings of violence are transformed;

- there has been an increase in feuding: when a homicide is perpetrated, Suri seem to lose the patience to sit out the traditional compensation talks. The kin group of the victim, if strong enough, demands immediate damages, or else call for retribution. Such feuding conflicts also affected the family of the *komoru*. Among the Tirma-Suri, for instance, there has been a long line of killings between two lineages since one of their two *komorus* was accidentally shot dead: by a Tirma. This in itself is unprecedented.

The above forms of violent behaviour are now also contested within Chai society: elders, the *komoru*, and women especially talk against wanton violence against Dizi and other travellers, against unprovoked killing and robbery of former Dizi bond friends, and against the shooting at duelling grounds.

The changes in the exercise of violence both within and without Chai society points to major shifts of meaning. In fact, we see a movement from ritually contained violence to political and instrumental violence, the aims and meaning of which are less clear to everybody There is a phase of deep uncertainty and sometimes fear, of a transition of meanings. There is an awareness that many of the *tègay* generation have abused the cultural norm of status acquisition on account of killing an adversary: this happened only in battle with recognised, long-standing enemies (i.e., not with Dizi and other highlanders except after manifest injustices). The *tègay* do it repeatedly, 'without a reason', and break the rule of restraint in violent behaviour.

Concluding remarks

Chai-Suri culture is marked by ideals of male personhood and peer status which accord value to assertive behaviour which may translate into violent behaviour when material interests and competitive economic and social relations with other groups are involved. Suri culture can, however, only be called a 'culture of violence' – reproducing violent behaviour as a template, an ideal or a habitus – in its relation to, or opposition to, those outside their 'moral community'.

Chai-Suri expressions of violence have shown important modifications in recent years. While ecological and material conditions play a role in explaining this, an anthropological, cross-cultural understanding of the new dialectics of violent action needs to take into account how violent processes actually unfold on the basis of symbolic-cultural representations and how they establish meaning, either instrumental or expressive.

Violence breaks the bounds of culture, of the social system. The ritualisation of violence is diminishing, more unstructured and unpredictable forms emerge. We see here a society pushing against its own structural and cultural limits. In relations with neighbouring groups (especially Dizi and Nyangatom), this Chai violence can still be seen as a 'language', a communicative act, but mainly one of intimidation. Violence in this sense 'bridges' the communication failures which have emerged, but it grounds group relations in suspicion and fear—in the absence of shared frameworks of control (the breakdown of the rain agreement with the Dizi and of the fighting code with the Nyangatom are cases in point).

A more neo-functionalist explanation of violent behaviour, as in recent evolutionary approaches, seems of limited value, because it tends to assume what has to be demonstrated in each empirical case (cf. Knauft's criticism, 1987, 1991). For instance, the interpretation of Chai violence seems to preclude an easy association between successful raiding or violent behaviour on the one hand and 'reproductive success' on the other. Comparing census-material and involvement or prestige in raiding of dozens of Chai men did not give any direct, meaningful correlation. The most important killers were not more popular with women and did not have more wives and children. Neither did they have larger herds. Certain rules make accumulation of this sort difficult: the captured cattle is being divided among all participants of a raid in a time-consuming and laborious procedure. Other facts which refute such a connection include the position of the *komoru*: he usually has a large number of wives and children and the biggest herd of cattle, but he is noted for his reconciliatory and mediatory role, and his role-model de-emphasises aggressive behaviour and aimless violence. We also saw already that in the *thagine* ceremonial duelling the victors are not the universally popular guys outshining the losers: all participants regardless of their place on the list of honour are esteemed.

What the examination of the Chai case makes clear is that in certain conditions 'violence' is deemed an essential, inherent part of social life, and need not be 'contested' in the sense of categorically rejected by victim and perpetrator. This was true for the Chai and the Nyangatom – both the same focus on cattle herding, both with a stratum of 'warrior-herders', and with the underlying idea that 'violent self-assertion', in ritual as well as in group defence, was, in their view, inevitable. When people were killed it was said to have been 'bad luck' for them, caused by, for instance, failing ritual protection, but it was not contested in itself. With the Dizi case it was different, but we have seen how their perception of illegitimate, excessive Chai violence in recent years was partly generated by the breach of a previous 'historical contract', and by changing regional and state-local society relationships, where different forms of incorporation into overarching political structures and value systems (as expressed in the fight over the monopoly on the means and exercise of violence) of both groups led to regional discrepancies and conflicts.

Traditional Chai violence is a concomitant of their evolved survival strategies as lowland cattleherders in a precarious natural and human environment. Their commitment to the herds, to feeding, defending, and expanding them, has led to a close socio-cultural bond between humans and cattle, symbolically elaborated in their culture and values of social personhood and achievement. Violence is, however, not simply a 'selectively advantageous trait' of Chai behaviour. Their values and ideals certainly reflect a complex violent imagery, but at the same time a pervasive sociality within and beyond their society, suggesting that, on this elementary level also, both are inextricably linked. This again shows the ambiguity of violence as a category of social action: it constitutes and it undermines sociality, the latter especially when released from its cultural formulations.

When the Chai mode of existence is undermined, either by long-term disturbances in ecological conditions or in the inter-group and state relations putting them at a disadvantage, a recourse to more hard violence will be likely. Traditional understandings between local groups then further lose importance, the regional equilibrium is disturbed, and an overarching accepted state structure is not present. Also, the availability of modern weapons and plenty of ammunition has had a seductive effect on Chai young men, prompting them to use violence *beyond* any instrumental necessity. As we saw, this has led to serious internal contradictions within Chai society, and to decisive changes in traditional Chai meanings of violence.

In most of the situations which we presented, violence in Chai society can be seen as a means to symbolically construct a group identity, or 'we-consciousness' – it is not there automatically. This consciousness is based upon ideas of clan descent or affiliation, language, and a cultural aesthetics expressed in decorative customs, but forged into an enduring group identity – or at least into one valid for some purposes – within the network of competitive and exchange relations with other groups in the region. As such, violence is inevitable, a fact of life, and not in any sense problematic or destructive or an irrational regression to evil human nature. When we talk about the violent 'images' in Chai discourse, the usefulness of Riches' definition (1991) is limited: from a Chai point of view, much of their violence is not 'contestably rendering physical hurt', but only uncontested, legitimate self-defence, retaliatory or pre-emptive damaging of enemies, or beneficial sacrifice of animals, with which no one in that context would argue.

Finally, this question of violence being contestable in local Chai terms would only arise on two accounts: a) when according to the normative authority figures such as elders and the *komoru* the people, especially the younger generation, defy the rules and obligations and act on their own account, thus changing or undermining the social order; b) when new forms of aggressively violent and wanton cruel behaviour would appear, such as rape, torture, hired killing, or nihilistic destruction, well-known from our Western societies. The possibility that such forms can emerge may not be precluded (as we know from cases elsewhere in Africa). Subjectively perceived economic exploitation, unbalanced state interference or disturbance, rigidified ethnic boundaries, unsolvable problems of resource competition combined with factors like the easy new technology and power of killing (hand grenades, automatic rifles) may prepare the ground for it. Also more intangible factors connected to the process of globalisation, such as the penetration of a new language of visual images or of a fantasised reality evoked by, e.g., imported 'video-culture', might enhance this process, invalidating – or at least transforming – codes of restraint and social order.[13] It is known that this has happened in extraordinary situations of disturbance such as in Papua New Guinea, Mozambique, Liberia or Sierra Leone. At present, there is one frontier town just north of the Suri country where such videos are now becoming readily available, also for visiting Suri. Such factors might create a new discourse of violence, which would also mark the inclusion of the Suri into the globalised domain of displaced signs and commoditised symbols, and would have an impact on traditional understandings of violent performance. The Suri have, however, not yet reached this 'advanced' stage of development, and whether the process would mean the emergence of 'more' or 'less' violent behaviour cannot be predicted. What seems likely though is that more state authority in the area will transform cultural notions and patterns of violence but not necessarily cause their disappearance.

Notes

* Acknowledgements. Fieldwork among the Chai Suri in southern Ethiopia was done in 1991–1994 with generous support from the Royal Netherlands Academy of Science (KNAW) the African Studies Centre, Leiden, and the Netherlands Organisation for Scientific Research in the Tropics (WOTRO, WR 52–610), which I gratefully acknowledge. I also thank the Institute of Ethiopian Studies (Addis Ababa University) for institutional support, local officials and inhabitants of the Maji and Adikiaz area, and Mr. John Haspels, representative of the EEMCY and LWF in Tulgit, Maji zone. I am most indebted to the Chai people of the Makara settlement. I benefitted a lot from the critical comments on a first draft of this paper from participants in the Seminar on the 'Ambiguity of Violence' at the Institute for Advanced Studies in Social Anthropology, Göteborg University (July 1995).
1 Cf. Balandier (1986), Bloch (1992), Krohn-Hansen (1995), Moore (1994), Riches (1986, 1991).
2 See, however, Knauft (1991).
3 In oral tradition.
4 More on the authority structure among the Chai, in Abbink (1997).
5 In the course of time, the Dizi – who also kept cattle in the lowlands – came to adopt several customs related to the 'cattle-culture' of the Chai, but they never developed a comparable assertive ethos, emphasizing e.g., personal violent performance, militant defence of the cattle herds, or a specific decorative 'body culture'.
6 Culture we define here as the more or less durable, shared and transmitted patterns of behaviour in which collective ideals and norms of a group are expressed and which form an element of identity formation.
7 See part 4.
8 As in most pastoral societies, cattle meat is never eaten outside a ritual context.

9 In this and other sections I draw partly on material first presented in Abbink (1993a and 1994).
10 In the film *The Mursi* (1974, Granada TV, Disappearing World series, UK), the similar ritual among the Mursi, 'spearing the priest', is shown.
11 In fact to such an extent that it endangered the cohesion of Chai society itself. (See Abbink 1998b).
12 Cf. Tornay (1989) on the Nyangatom.
13 Its emergence and adoption in Africa should be investigated in detail. The negative effects of violent and sadistic videos after their displacement to, and appropriation in, other socio-cultural settings are underestimated.

Bibliography

Abbink, J. 1993a. 'Famine, Gold and Guns: the Suri of Southern Ethiopia, 1985–91', *Disasters*, xvii (3): 218–226.
——. 1993b. 'Ethnic Conflict in the "Tribal" Zone: the Dizi and Suri in Southern Ethiopia', *Journal of Modern African Studies*, xxxi (4): 675–83.
——. 1994. 'Changing Patterns of "Ethnic" Violence: Peasant–Pastoralist Confrontation in Southern Ethiopia and its Implications for a Theory of Violence', *Sociologus*, xl (1): 66–78.
——. 1997. 'Authority and Chieftaincy in Surma Society (Ethiopia)', *Africa* (Roma), lii (3): 317–342.
——. 1998a. 'The Production of "Primitiveness" and Identity: Surma-Tourist Interactions', in R. Fardon *et al.*, eds, Proceedings of the EIDOS Conference on 'Globalisation, Development and the Making of Consumers', March 1316, 1997, The Hague (forthcoming).
——. 1998b. 'Violence and Political Discourse among the Chai Suri', in G. J. Dimmendaal, ed., *Surmic Languages and Cultures* (Koln: Koppe Verlag) (forthcoming).
Balandier, G. 1986. 'An Anthropology of Violence and War', *International Social Science Journal*, cx: 499–511.
Bennett Ross, J. 1980. 'Ecology and the Problem of Tribe: a Critique of the Hobbesian Model of Preindustrial Warfare', in E. B. Ross, ed., *Beyond the Myths of Culture: Essays in Cultural Materialism* (New York: Academic Press): 33-60.
Betzig, L., Borgerhoff Mulder, M. and Turke, P., (eds) 1988. *Human Reproductive Behavior. A Darwinian Perspective* (Cambridge: Cambridge University Press).
Bloch, M. 1992. *Prey into Hunter: the Politics of Religious Experience* (Cambridge: Cambridge University Press).
Blok, A. 1991. 'Zinvol en zinloos geweld', *Amsterdams Sociologisch Tijdschrift*, xviii (3): 189–207.
Chagnon, N. A. 1988a. 'Life Histories, Blood Revenge and Warfare in a Tribal Population', *Science*, 239: 985–92.
——. 1988b. 'Male Yanomamö Manipulations of Kinship Classifications of Female Kin for Reproductive Advantage', in L. Betzig, M. Borgerhoff mulder and P. Turke (eds), *Human Reproductive Behaviour. A Darwinian Perspective* (Cambridge: Cambridge University Press): 23–48.
——. 1992. *Yanomamo. The Last Days of Eden* (New York: Harcourt Brace Jovanovich).
Ferguson, R. B. (ed.) 1984. *Warfare, Culture and Environment* (Orlando: Academic Press).
Haberland, E. 1993. *Hierarchie und Kaste. Zur Geschichte und politischen Struktur der Dizi in Sudwest Äthiopien* (Stuttgart: F. Steiner Verlag).
Knauft, B. M. 1987. 'Reconsidering Violence in Simple Human Societies: Homicide Among the Gebusi of New Guinea', *Current Anthropology*, xxviii (4): 457–500; xxix (5): 629–33.
——. 1991. 'Violence and Sociality in Human Evolution', *Current Anthropology*, xxxii (4): 391–428.
Krohn-Hansen, C. 1995. 'The Anthropology of Violent Interaction', *Journal of Anthropological Research*, l: 367–81.
Linger, D. T. 1992. *Violent Encounters. Meanings of Violence in a Brazilian City* (Stanford: Stanford University Press).
Markakis, J. 1994. 'Ethnic Conflict and the State in the Horn of Africa', in K. Fukut and J. Markakis (eds), *Ethnicity and Conflict in the Horn of Africa*

(London: James Currey; Athens, Ohio University Press): 217–37.

Moore, H. L. 1994 'The Problem of Explaining Violence in the Social Sciences', in P. Harvey and P. Gow (eds), *Sex and Violence. Issues in Representation and Experience* (London, New York: Routledge): 138–55.

Riches, D. 1991. 'Aggression,War, Violence: Space/Time and Paradigm', *Man* (N.S.), xxvi (2): 281–98.

——. (ed.) 1986. *The Anthropology of Violence* (Oxford: Blackwell).

Tornay, S. 1989. *Un système générationnel. Les Nyangatom de l'Éthiopie du Sud-Ouest et les peuples apparentés* (Paris, Universite de Paris-X-Labetno), thèse d'État, 2 vols.

Turton, D. 1975. 'The Relationship Between Oratory and the Exercise of Influence Among the Mursi', in M. Bloch (ed.), *Political Language and Oratory in Traditional Societies* (London: Academic Press): 163–83.

——. 1994a. 'Mursi Political Identity and Warfare: the Survival of an Idea', in K. Fukui and J. Markakis, eds, *Ethnicity and Conflict in the Horn of Africa* (London: James Currey): 15-32.

——. 1994b. '"We Must Teach Them to be Peaceful": Mursi Views on Being Human and Being Mursi', *Nomadic Peoples*, xxx: 19–33.

RÉMY BAZENGUISSA-GANGA
The Spread of Political Violence in Congo-Brazzaville

Reference
African Affairs, vol. 98, no. 390, Jan 1999, pp. 389–411

The recent history of the Republic of Congo, the former French colony often known as Congo-Brazzaville to distinguish it from its neighbour, the Democratic Republic of Congo (former Zaire), is a notable example of how the promise of democratization can turn tragically violent. In 1964, four years after independence, Congo became a one-party state under a Marxist–Leninist ruling party. Four years of growing tension between the government and the army led to a coup in 1968 and the formation of a new ruling party, also Marxist-Leninist. A period of great instability, which included the assassination of President Marien Ngouabi in 1977, ended with the rise to power in 1979 of an army colonel, Denis Sassou-Nguesso. Sassou-Nguesso restored good relations with the former colonial power, France, and presided over a period of rapid growth of Congo's oil industry, dominated by the French state oil company Elf. Whereas minerals had provided less than 5 per cent of total exports in 1969, by 1984 they accounted for 90 per cent of export earnings, and mining contributed 43 per cent of Gross Domestic Product.

Congo became one of many French-speaking countries to revert to a multi-party system in the early 1990s. A national conference in 1991–2 led to the resignation of President Sassou-Nguesso and the promulgation of a multi-party constitution, under which a former prime minister, Pascal Lissouba, was elected president. Many of the main players in the period of democratization remained politically active throughout the 1990s and, as rival parties began recruiting armed wings or private militias, political rivalries led to widespread bloodshed in the second half of 1993. A ceasefire was agreed between President Lissouba's party, known as the Mouvance Présidentielle, and the opposition, in January 1994. Official figures for hostilities in 1993–4 record 2,000 people killed, between 100,000 and 300,000 displaced, and 13,000 houses destroyed. As new elections approached in 1997, political rivalries once again led to fighting between rival party militias, this time leading to very heavy fighting and pitched battles in Brazzaville which ended only with the military victory of former President Sassou-Nguesso in October 1997.

The present article examines the role of the various party militias which took part in the second battle of Brazzaville, the fighting which wracked the city from 5 June to 15 October 1997. Those who participated in the hostilities of 1993–4 were mostly young men born and brought up in Brazzaville itself, while those who took up arms in 1997 were mainly people originating in the secondary towns of Congo's provinces. This strongly suggests a need to study the spread of political violence in Congo and to identify the logic which has underpinned the spread of violence. A study of the militiamen, their *modus operandi* and their objectives, thus tells us something not only about the nature of the fighting in 1997, but also about the spread of political violence from the capital to the provinces which took place in the mid-1990s.

The article is organized in five sections, followed by a short conclusion. The first section consists of a brief history of the war of 1997 in Brazzaville. Part two looks in more detail at the various militias which took part. In sections three and four I will consider the forms in which violence occurred, such as the widespread use of roadblocks and the practice of looting. The fifth and final part offers an explanation for the decision by so many young people to engage in political violence.

A chronology

The immediate cause of the fighting of the mid-1990s can be attributed to the tenure of office of Pascal Lissouba, elected head of state in democratic elections in 1992. His hold on power was strongly contested throughout his presidency by powerful opposition parties with support among many army officers. He was frequently accused of showing great ethnic favouritism to people from his own part of the country, the south.[1] His economic policy of liberalization, decentralization and cuts in the public budget brought growing unpopularity in a country where substantial oil revenues had been used to administer a highly centralized policy of public spending on education and other services. Lissouba's unpopularity, and the size and determination of the opposition parties led by such redoubtable figures as the former president, Denis Sassou-Nguesso, and the mayor of Brazzaville, Bernard Kolelas, were apparent in the heavy fighting which took place in 1993–4. Well before Lissouba was due to submit himself for re-election in July 1997, there was a general mood throughout the country that some sort of political renewal was in the air. As he criss-crossed the country on the campaign trail, President Lissouba was often the target of criticism even in areas which had voted for him previously. In contrast, the former president of the republic (1979–92), Denis Sassou-Nguesso, clearly appeared to be the candidate with the greatest popular support. He had left Congo in the middle of 1995 for an extended stay in France and returned to Brazzaville in January 1997 to a triumphal welcome by a crowd of well-wishers and onlookers.

Sassou-Nguesso's participation in the presidential elections led to a marked increase in the intensity of the campaign. In May 1997, in mid-campaign, he toured the regions of Kouilou, Plateaux, and Cuvette-Ouest. In Owando, a middle-sized town in the Cuvette region, a number of violent incidents were provoked by the Cobras, a popular name for the private militia which Sassou-Nguesso was using as his bodyguard. In response, supporters of President Lissouba tried to halt the election campaign. Owando and the surrounding area were the fief of the Rassemblement pour le Développement et la Démocratie (RDD), a party led by Jacques Yhombi Opangault, who also doubled as Lissouba's campaign chief. A few days before Sassou-Nguesso's visit to the town, a leader of the Cobras had shot and killed a soldier from the Owando army garrison who he claimed was plotting to assassinate his leader, Sassou-Nguesso. The following week witnessed a series of clashes between the Cobras and government security forces in the town of Owando. Other fights were also reported, later the same month, between soldiers sent to reinforce the security presence in the area and Sassou-Nguesso's Cobra bodyguards. Some twenty people lost their lives and 4,000 people who had originally come from other areas fled from Owando.

In an attempt to prevent further violence, on 31 May 1997 leading politicians signed a treaty binding them to refrain from the use of violence. However, on 5 June further fighting broke out between two factions, this time in Brazzaville itself: one group was composed of the Cobra militia and soldiers who supported Sassou-Nguesso, and the other camp included soldiers loyal to President Lissouba, making common cause with his own party militias, known respectively as the Cocoye, the Zulus and the Mambas.[2] The two opposing sides gave different accounts of the origins of the clashes. According to the government, a battalion of government security forces, sent to Sassou-Nguesso's residence to arrest those responsible for the killings in Owando, was attacked by the Cobra militia. Sassou-Nguesso's supporters, however, claimed that the deployment of armed forces by the government of President Lissouba was an attempt to murder their own leader.

The fighting which erupted in early June 1997, and which was to last for several months, was markedly different in the various districts of Brazzaville, as some areas were subject to systematic artillery bombardment, while others, which had declared themselves to be neutral, were spared. The districts which suffered the heaviest bombardments were those known to be bases of political support for one or other of the two rival political leaders, principally the four districts called Poto-Poto, Ouenzé, Moungali and Talangaï, which were controlled by the Cobras, and Mfilou, occupied by the President's own militia. Supporters of a third party, the Mouvement Congolais pour la Démocratie et le Développement Integral (MCDDI) led by Bernard Kolelas, the mayor of Brazzaville, were the districts which managed to remain neutral. The urban districts of Bacongo and Makelékélé suffered only minor damage. Nevertheless, these areas too were hit by about twenty shells in July and August, causing several deaths. Some further casualties were sustained as a result of misdirected artillery or small-arms fire. Only after 9 September 1997, when Bernard Kolelas was appointed prime minister in President Lissouba's government, did the bombardment of these formerly neutral areas increase, although it never became really intensive. The Bacongo and Makelekele districts, which remained relatively peaceful throughout, received an influx of displaced and homeless people who, without any family or friends in these areas, were obliged to gather in makeshift camps in the schools and churches. The religious authorities did their best to provide relief, and occasionally the government was able to offer food aid.

Displaced people living in school buildings generally received no help at all.

Officially, the fighting in the second half of 1997 resulted in the deaths of between 10,000 and 15,000 people. Lissouba received the support of most opposition leaders including Bernard Kolelas who had his own militia, known as the Ninjas, but in spite of this, by 10 October 1997 the battle was clearly turning in favour of Sassou-Nguesso who was receiving the support of troops sent by the government of Angola. The armed conflict can be said to have ended on 15 October 1997 with the loss by the government forces of Pointe-Noire, centre of the oil industry and the economic capital of the country.

The militias

The first militias – the Ninjas, the Cobras, the Ministerial Guard ('Reserve ministerielle') and the Zulus – made their appearance in the street battles which occurred between August 1993 and February 1994.[3] The Zulus and the Ministerial Guard supported the Presidential coalition ('Mouvance présidentielle'), a group dominated by Lissouba's own party, the Union Pan-Africaine pour la Démocratie Sociale (UPADS). The Cobras were supporters of Sassou-Nguesso and his party, the Parti Congolais du Travail (PCT). The Ninjas supported Bernard Kolelas, leader of the MCDDI. The continued deployment of these forces after the end of the fighting in 1994 was one reason for a marked increase in crime, including robbery, burglary and rape, in the districts which they controlled. Between 1995 and 1997, the disarmament and demobilization of an estimated 10,000 militiamen was one of the main subjects of political debate. A peace treaty signed in December 1995, marking the official end of the combats of 1993–4, made provision for the incorporation into the gendarmerie and the police of former militia fighters aged between 18 and 24. Each party which had a militia was allocated a quota, with the Presidential coalition receiving 2,000 places, and the opposition 1,000.

At this point of the narrative, it is helpful to consider the structure of the various political militias and armed groups in the contest which then emerged.[4] Their structure was determined by three elements: first, all were originally organized in the secondary towns of the provinces; second, all received at least a minimum of formal training from Congolese or foreign army officers; third, all recruited largely young people from the provinces. The former Ministerial Guard, for example, henceforth known as the Cocoye, received their basic military training at Loudima in the province of Bouenza, from Israeli, South African and Congolese instructors. This organization was headed by the Minister of Public Security and the head of the Presidential security service. It is difficult to evaluate the precise number of Cocoye militiamen. In 1996, the figure of 4,000 people under arms was being widely circulated. During the later battles, each fighter in principle received a wage of 10,000 CFA francs per day. The Cocoye had good access to the army's arsenals and appeared more powerful than the Cobras, but they lacked a really effective organization and sustained logistical supply. This was in part because the leaders of the Cocoye were embezzling some of the funds earmarked for the war effort, and, with many soldiers deserting, few professional officers took part in Cocoye actions during the actual fighting.

The Cobras, on the other hand, received their basic military training at Oyo, Sassou-Nguesso's home town, from officers who had been retired from the Congolese armed forces. (It was rumoured that they also had Chadian, Libyan, Moroccan and Rwandan instructors.) In effect, following the National Conference of 1991–2, the government had implemented a policy of reorganizing the armed forces which aimed to create a more suitable ethnic balance. This process led to the retirement in 1995 of 77 officers, most of them sympathizers with the former government of Denis Sassou-Nguesso. No longer in receipt of a salary, many of these officers were living in Oyo. The most influential among them recruited young men from their home village or the surrounding area, and considerable numbers of young men from the centre and north of the country enlisted in the Cobras in this way. This system of recruitment created a problem in that each Cobra recruit recognized the authority only of his immediate patron rather than of a wider hierarchy. Each fighter, at least during the later engagements, received a per diem payment of 7,000 CFA francs. The Cobras were armed with weapons which Sassou-Nguesso had stocked at Oyo during his own presidency or with arms taken from military arsenals which they had captured during fighting in Brazzaville. Moreover, a considerable number of serving officers and soldiers opted to join Sassou-Nguesso, who retained a residual loyalty in the armed forces even after he had lost the presidency, enabling the Cobras to deploy all over the country. Jean-Marie Tassoua, nicknamed 'General Giap', was the Cobras' military commander, reckoned to have some 2–3,000 troops under him.

In contrast to the Cocoye and the Cobras, the Ninjas, who remained neutral for a long period, did not receive any military training outside Brazzaville itself. After the truce of 1994, most members of the Ninjas had become demoralized as they had not received any payment or other reward for their services. Some, in mid-1997, did not agree with the political leaders of the MCDDI who were urging them to fight alongside the UPADS, their former enemy. Some of the Ninjas' most influential recruiters refused to join this alliance and one of them, Claude-Ernest Ndalla, joined Sassou-Nguesso shortly after the resumption of hostilities in 1997. Others of the Ninja officers who had been the most effective in the battles of 1993–4, such as Willy Matsanga, also led their men over to the Cobras. MCDDI leaders found themselves obliged to organize training courses at the Makala military base in Brazzaville, where some 500 recruits were housed under the authority of the Minister of the Interior. The Ninjas, however, lacked arms and equipment.

Other than the militias, another form of armed group emerged both in Brazzaville and in the provinces in the form of self-defence groups. These were composed of young people who volunteered to defend a particular political group or its leader. Politicians distributed arms to these associations on a huge scale. In Brazzaville, self-defence units undertook the protection of their neighbourhoods. In smaller towns and in the rural areas, their aim was to hold their home territory against all comers and to prevent opponents from occupying it. Members of self-defence groups were paid 1,000 CFA francs per day by various militias to secure their allegiance, and were also promised recruitment into the army at a future stage. The Presidential Coalition used networks of this sort to create the Mambas, the last of the militias to make its appearance. The Mambas included both people from Brazzaville itself and others, the majority, from the regions of Niari, Bouenza and Lékoumou. These militiamen, based in Brazzaville under the orders of some army colonels, underwent one week's military training before being pitched into battle. No figures are available on the number of Mambas.

A few general remarks may be made about the militias as they existed in 1997. In total, they composed between 7,500 and 10,000 young people under arms. There was a marked difference between those with previous combat experience and those without. It should also be noted that the majority were originally from provincial towns or had at least been trained in secondary towns. However, there are certainly points of comparison between this second generation of fighters and those of the previous generation in regard to age (between 15 and 35) and educational qualifications, since most were school drop-outs.

The question of educational level is extremely important because Congo, for a period of almost thirty years, had undergone a system of political administration in which every student was also a political actor. Primary school pupils were regarded as young pioneers of the revolution, and by the time they reached secondary school they had often been incorporated into the youth organizations of the ruling party. Almost all young people in Congo went through an experience of this type. The vast majority of school graduates aspired to a post in the public service, and secondary education was a path to guaranteed individual success. With the massive politicization of the country, political engagement also became an avenue towards success in education. In effect, there was a vast system of co-optation known locally as casologie from the French word cas, meaning 'cases'. Every political actor with any degree of influence would contrive to get certain 'cases', in other words his clients, relatives and dependants, placed on the list of those who had succeeded in gaining an educational diploma or in passing an examination. However, after 1985 Congo was subject to massive budget cuts and economic restrictions through the combined effect of its huge public debt and a fall in oil prices. Under pressure from the International Monetary Fund, the government was obliged to reduce the number of employees in the civil service, to retrench people on short-term contracts and to privatize various state enterprises. This had at least two notable effects on education, namely an increase in the number of school drop-outs and in the number of unemployed school or college graduates. To some extent this was the result of personal failures by individual students, but it was also due to an increase in the rigour of selection as a consequence of the implementation of a structural adjustment programme which included limits on the number of places in higher education. Graduate unemployment was the result of a termination of the practice of giving automatic employment in the public service to holders of secondary school and university diplomas. The growth in the numbers of people who had completed secondary education thus became translated into rising numbers of unemployed people with experience of political mobilization. The growing frustration experienced by such people could only increase the general atmosphere of social tension.

Roadblocks

Militiamen habitually set up roadblocks, called bouchons, in isolated spots, while in densely populated urban areas similar controls were manned by a mixture of militiamen and local residents. Here, militiamen would check the identities of passers-by with a view to preventing enemy sympathizers from entering their zone. The process of identification was of life and death importance, quite literally.

The test of identity most widely used was based on inspection of a national identity document. Since the government had issued an identity card to almost the entire population, the state was in effect the determinant of the categories according to which individual identities were confirmed or regarded as suspect. It is at first sight paradoxical that an official document could play such a crucial role in a country where the forgery of documents of all types is common practice, but since the national identity document was universally regarded as the only foolproof basis for identifying a person, anyone attempting to forge such a document was liable to severe punishment.[5]

Tests of identity varied from one area to another, depending on which militia was in control. Presidential Coalition forces, in their areas, tended to attach particular importance to ethnicity. The Cobras, on the other hand, were primarily concerned to 'casser du mouvancier', as they called it, that is to identify and punish anyone at all whom they regarded as a member of the political elite which had profited from the presidential system, regardless of ethnic affiliation. The Cocoye and Zulus, at their roadblocks, were especially intent on identifying Mbochi, a name collectively attributed to many of the various ethnic groups from the north of the country, the fief of their arch-enemy Denis Sassou-Nguesso. This was a delicate business, because certain supporters of President Lissouba were themselves from the north.[6] In order to determine who was an Mbochi, while taking account of these distinctions, the militias generally applied three different tests according to family name, place of birth and fluency in the mother tongue. Information on the first two of these categories appears plainly stated on a national identity document. Cocoye and Zulu militiamen would relate family names to the area of the country, north or south, with which these names were most likely to be connected. In fact, most Congolese believe that any family name beginning with a consonant is probably of southern origin and any name beginning with a vowel is from the north. In reality, needless to say, this rule-of-thumb is of very doubtful accuracy, but was used by inquirers to establish who was a northerner and who was a southerner. This first indication could then be complemented by the place of birth giving a clue as to who, among the northerners, was regarded as an Mbochi. A further test was linguistic. The militias would ask a person they were checking to speak a few words of the language of whichever ethnic group he or she claimed to belong to. A close check would pay particular attention to accent, to various mannerisms and to the proverbs or other particularities of the group in question.

It is apparent that the ethnic identities established in this manner at roadblocks did not correspond to those of precolonial times. For example, since independence in 1960, every citizen of Congo has borne the name of his or her father. Although most southern population groups are matrilineal, the Cocoye and Zulus made no allowance for matrilineal descent. Hence, the use of the patronym as a mark of identity illustrates that the actors were determining identities by the use of criteria other than the traditional ones. In general, all the indicators of identity used at Cocoye and Zulu roadblocks made use of some external sign and took no account of the subjective views of the person under scrutiny. What counted was the opinion of the interrogators who manned the roadblock.

The Cobras, as we have seen, considered that their task was to 'casser du mouvancier', to identify and punish members of the elite which had sustained President Lissouba. At their roadblocks they also paid close attention to the family names printed on identity documents to check whether the name corresponded to one of those on lists of suspects which had been circulated by their political leaders.[7] Identification of people whose names did not

figure on the list was a matter of considerable improvization. This is revealed in the following two testimonies:

> At the corner of the street, a man was walking by with a walkie-talkie in his hand. He was stopped by a group of armed men. On being asked who he was, he replied with an air of great seriousness that he was from the same group as them. A discussion followed in which it emerged that they suspected him of being a spy. In no time at all a decision was taken: he was to be executed. The man explained, begged, pleaded to be allowed to call witnesses, all in vain. A young Cobra pointed his gun at the man while his comrades egged him on … Shots rang out, and the man fell to the ground.[8]

A second example is of a young soldier in civilian clothes, well known in the neighbourhood:

> At a check point, the Cobras who were searching him found a revolver on him. He was arrested on the spot. He argued that the militiamen knew who he was and should be able to understand that, as a soldier, he needed a gun for his personal security. He was taken to a piece of wasteground. A few moments later, the Cobra who had executed him returned brandishing the jeans which his victim had been wearing as proof that he had accomplished his mission, shouting out 'I've sent him on his way'.[9]

There is a clear connection between the methods used to identify people and the tactics used by the Cobras in particular. When, during a ceasefire between 13 and 15 June 1997, there was large-scale looting of houses in the areas controlled by the various militias, the militiamen changed their method. The Cocoye and Mambas abandoned the use of ethnic criteria in favour of looting the houses of elite members of their own group. The Cobras, on the other hand, tended to adopt an ethnic approach for the first time. Their search for members of the incumbent political elite quickly turned into a general hunt for Beembe, a term considered to include southern ethnic groups in general whose members were considered to have profited more than others from the political system dominated by Pascal Lissouba. Militiamen used their own knowledge to identify which houses to loot, which was possible because most of them lived in these same neighbourhoods and knew which houses belonged to supporters of Lissouba. They also made inquiries of neighbours. They considered that an unoccupied house constituted evidence that the owner had chosen to join the camp of the enemy.

A change in the course of the conflict thus entailed an alteration in the tests applied by fighters to their victims. The enemy was not someone clearly identified by reference either to geographical location or to a particular period of time. Today's ally could be tomorrow's enemy. The actors thus constantly construed identity in function of the current context, while the credibility of people's actions was gauged as the result of a range of possible negotiations with the militias. Once the conflict had been transformed in this way, the roadblocks became, above all, for a period of four months, places to blackmail and rob the general population. It became normal practice for a militiaman to charge a fine of 500 CFA francs as a contribution to the war effort, on any person holding the wrong identity document in circumstances where, a short time before, death would have been the punishment for the same offence. Everybody was aware of this unofficial rule. Quite often, a person questioned in this way would begin a process of bargaining, claiming to have 200 or 300 francs available instead of the 500 francs demanded. This was often successful, and the possibility of such negotiation demonstrated that the use of violence was more than simple aggression of one person against another. For their part, the militiamen quickly realized that manning a roadblock was now the most profitable activity from the point of view of the risk run and the profit to be gained. The fighters could be more sure of procuring an income through levying informal taxes 'to finance the war' than they were of receiving the daily wages promised to them for manning the front line of battle.

Looting

The widespread practice of looting is an indicator of the ambiguity of the fighters' political engagement. This procedure was known as 'slaughtering the pig' ('*tuer le cochon*') in the northern part of Brazzaville and 'N'Kossa, everyone gets his share' ('*N'Kossa, chacun aura sa part*') elsewhere. N'Kossa, we may note, is the name of the largest of the Congolese oil fields controlled by the oil company ElfAquitaine. These two expressions, both of which refer to the idea of distribution or largesse, were intended as a criticism of the failure by the political elite to redistribute the wealth of the nation. The militias reasoned that the people were justified in taking their part by force in order to be able to live decently. In this sense, the partition of the city by different militias and by some inhabitants of Brazzaville was a consequence of this same criticism of the failure to redistribute.

Looting began immediately after the outbreak of hostilities. The speed with which this occurred bears a direct relationship to the experience of 1993 and the various promises made at that time. The Cocoye and the Zulus, considering themselves inadequately rewarded after their efforts in 1993–4, at once began looting the Batignolles district of Brazzaville, where many PCT dignitaries lived, and very soon attacked their own leaders. Another reason for the speed with which looting developed was a perception that hostilities would not last for long, and that it was advisable to use the opportunity while it existed. The logic of looting is well illustrated by the following testimony gathered from a militiaman who was defending himself verbally against someone who had accused him of theft:

> You call that stealing? When they incite us to kill, they call it 'human folly', then afterwards they drink champagne together. That's called 'national unity'. While this is going on, we get nothing. Have you ever seen any of the national leaders losing one of their own children in this war? Why is it always us? This has gone beyond a joke. We're going to loot all their houses and tomorrow, when we rebuild the country, perhaps we'll finally have a job to go to.[10]

Thus, the looting constituted a trial of the older generation, collectively held responsible for the everyday failures, the misfortunes and the frustrations of those who considered themselves the younger generation. The writer Joseph Tonda has shown how, in the provincial towns of Congo, these practices are an indicator of what he calls the 'orphaning' of the actors.[11] Tonda demonstrates how looting took on a sense of taking goods by force from relatives, people deemed to be kin by virtue of family or village or regional affiliation. This was so, for example, with the activities of the

Cobras in Talangaï – a district of Brazzaville – and in northern towns such as Etoumbi, Mbomo, Makoua, Owando, Mbama and Ewo. The Cobras pillaged the houses, shops and warehouses of people they considered to be of the same ethnic or kinship group as themselves. In some places, the looting was accompanied by the destruction of population registers, a gesture which wiped out, both symbolically and literally, family relations and the record which permitted such relationships to be formally determined. Comparable acts were committed by the partisans of the Presidential Coalition.

Amid the massive incidence of looting, there were two particularly notable targets: four-wheel drive vehicles and expensive houses. A fine house was considered to be the receptacle of the political power held by an individual, the symbol of his status in the city of Brazzaville. There was no distinction made between a private sphere and a public sphere, so that violence inflicted on the person of a politician or on his residence was considered tantamount to violence inflicted on his public persona. Possession of an expensive house was itself proof that an actor wielded real political power, and since domestic space had been politicized, political punishment entailed the destruction of the residence. In the course of time, all empty houses, whether or not they belonged to a political leader, became liable to being sacked. In the space of just one week in June 1997, every part of Brazzaville was systematically looted by fighters in combination with a good part of the urban population. The Cobras actually began to dance when they learned of a wave of looting carried out by their enemies.[12]

The pattern of looting indicated a certain political awareness on the part of the militias in the sense that it represented the emergence of a distance between themselves and the political leaders whom they had hitherto been protecting. We should not, however, overestimate the importance of this phenomenon, nor draw too many conclusions from it, since to some extent it was merely an ideological justification for actions taken for other reasons. Certain looters acted, naturally enough, for reasons of another type altogether. But in time, looting had a destabilizing effect on the political class itself, since politicians came to fear that their own militias might turn against them. This is well illustrated by an anecdote concerning the Cocoye militia, a group of whom were manning a roadblock close to the house of the Minister of Finance, one of the strongmen of the regime. The militiamen did not view kindly the seduction of a young woman from the neighbourhood by one of the minister's bodyguards. The militiamen went to complain to the minister's security officers, outraged that they had to fight while others were enjoying the good things of life. The minister's guards chased them off with a barrage of shots, at which point the militiamen returned, equipped with heavy weapons, and began an assault on the house. The minister's bodyguards promptly fled, leaving the militia to loot the premises.

The fact that young militiamen generally sent some of their booty to the smaller towns and villages of Congo is an indication that, in the culture of war, they retained a certain esteem for these places. Far from hiding the source of their fortune, the young fighters openly used the goods they had looted for the refurbishment of their villages. For them, it was an honour to introduce the trappings of modernity into this rural universe. It is no exaggeration to say that the last phase of the combat in Brazzaville was the occasion for certain city-dwellers to develop new ties of affection with the provinces and most particularly with the villages, which they saw as havens of peace and tranquillity. They calculated that the day might come when they would need to take refuge in a village, and by sending goods there they were taking precautions to ensure that they would be well received if they were to go there. The looters also sold their goods on the various city markets or on the streets in the various urban neighbourhoods. In the east of the city, the two key outlets for the sale of looted goods were the Diata market and the market at the Mfilou railway station. In the south-western district, the looters sold their goods at the Total market in Bacongo, at Bifouiti and at Madibou. In the north, the favoured spots were at the Intendance market or simply on street corners.

The militiamen spent their profits immediately, especially in bars and on women. A slogan often heard on the south side of the city was eloquent about the style of life to which the fighters aspired. They would say to young women that 'to refuse a Cocoye is to refuse money'. The opportunity of spending a lot of money at least once in a lifetime was a mark of social prestige and gave a young man a reputation. All this amounts to what Brazzavillois call 'living the good life' ('vivre'), signifying, at one and the same time, the accomplishment of a feat of kudos and, through spending, the acquisition of social recognition. Young men who lived through these times of intense excitement now remember them with great emotion, sometimes recalling 'I've done things and I've lived'. The equation of 'living' with ostentatious spending is an indication of the importance of instant gratification. Spending was the militiaman's way of becoming a social being in Brazzaville.

The relationship between the control of a city and the looting of its inhabitants is a sign of the existence of a complex system for the collective regulation of violence. In this sense, the development of the sale of looted goods could have brought an end to the war by July 1997 since these activities encouraged members of different militias to develop social relations with one another through commerce. These events were also shown on national television. As a result of a series of interviews, I have reconstituted the manner in which this fraternization developed, beginning with events in the commercial centre of Brazzaville, which was shared between the Cobras and members of the presidential militias. Each group of heavily armed fighters pillaged the shops in its area while avoiding the enemy. On one occasion, two hostile groups encountered each other and, in great nervousness, began a dialogue. 'Masta, masta, ndengue nini, ndengue nini?' ('Brother, brother, how are you?'). 'Why are we fighting? Why are we killing each other? We must stop this.' These contacts were not accompanied by any shooting. Each group then informed its allies of the contact and invited them to a peace meeting. A similar event occurred the next day in another troublespot, the Plateau des 15 ans. But the political leaders did not make any use of this fraternization, since they still preferred a military solution. From the time when the fighters developed the habit of systematic looting, it was difficult to mount any sustained offensive. In the first place, after a bout of looting, combatants needed to retreat with their booty to store it in a safe place, which allowed the opposition forces to retake the positions they had just lost. In any event, the militiamen lost any desire to advance into enemy territory where there was a chance of getting killed.

Young people and political violence

The initiation into political violence of thousands of young people was the result of a dynamic which both created and gave meaning to various collective movements. This process, occurring as it did at a time of transition to democracy, contributed to a larger recomposition of the body social after the elections of 1992 and the first round of hostilities in 1993–4. A certain number of social practices could be said to have entered the political arena, amplified by the various organs of propaganda and mass media, and were subject to a process of reinterpretation or elaboration. For present purposes we shall concentrate on two practices which contributed to the production of the militias in 1997: the reconfiguration of ethnic and regional identities and the growth in importance of provincial towns.

Most Congolese explain the political violence of recent times by reference to ethnic or regional factors. We certainly would not wish to deny the relevance of these as modes of representation and, above all, as mechanisms for assigning an identity to victims. As explanations, however, they require some further nuance. Ethnic identities in Congo are not primordial realities but social constructions, products of specific historical processes, which accompany struggles for the control of the state. Only by taking these political processes into account can we avoid the suggestion that collective identities are preordained and appreciate the specific manner in which they were constructed and transformed in the course of the battles.

When Congolese are discussing ethnic or regional affiliation, they commonly use six terms of identification organized into three dualistic categories which have succeeded one another over time: Kongo/Mbochi; later, northerners/southerners; and finally, Nibolek/Tchek. The first of these clusters refers to two precolonial ethnic groups; the Kongo and the Mbochi. These identities became politicized as a result of the multi-party rivalries of the immediate postcolonial period, when the presidency was held by a Kongo man.[13] This representation of political conflicts declined in popularity after 1968, following the coup which brought an Mbochi to power.[14] The new political context, characterized mainly by the militarization of political life, was based on a mode of domination effected through a single-party system established since 1963. In the popular view, a new dualism emerged based on geography in the form of northerners against southerners. The first was roughly equivalent to the identity of Mbochi, the second to Kongo.

When in 1991 Congo became one of many African countries to adjust to a wave of democratization, a one-person one-vote electoral system brought about a new development in the popular view of identity. The main actors in the multi-party system, in conformity with established practice, represented themselves as southerners, the most numerous group. This then split into two new blocs: Nibolek and Tchek. Nibolek is an acronym formed from the initial syllables of the administrative areas NIari, BOuenza and LEKoumou. Public opinion considered only people from the Pool region to be Tchek. These identities thus refer solely to territorial units created as a result of administrative measures taken by the state.

The hostilities of 1997 show a marked change in these ethnic and regional identities. Wherever fighting occurred, there was a tendency to reproduce the categories of northerner and southerner, with a further division of the latter into Nibolek and Tchek. As we have seen, fighting was concentrated in certain districts, such as Poto-Poto, Ouenzé, Talanga and Moungali in the north of the city, held by Sassou-Nguesso's Cobras, and Mfilou in the south-east, largely inhabited by Nibolek and controlled by partisans of Pascal Lissouba. The south-western suburbs of Bacongo and Makélékélé, dominated by Tchek and controlled by the MCDDI, having declared their neutrality, remained calm until 10 October 1997. The northerner-southerner distinction implies a larger conception than that between Nibolek and Tchek, since the former covers the whole country, and the latter only four administrative areas.

These changes in perception were also connected to the rise in importance of provincial towns, a significant factor contributing to the spread of violence. This may be seen if we recall that the trigger of the violence was an incident which took place in Owando, and not in Brazzaville itself.

Congo is divided into 10 administrative regions.[15] If we take as a frame of reference the settlements containing between 2,000 and 20,000 inhabitants, the country contains, excluding Brazzaville and Pointe-Noire, 18 secondary towns, 34 small or medium-sized towns and 39 smaller administrative centres, such as district capitals. The population of these secondary towns has increased rapidly over the last twenty years, passing from 5 per cent of the population in 1960 to 12 per cent in 1980. Moreover, these places receive migrants from rural areas, especially in connection with education. For this reason they form concentrations of school drop-outs and unemployed school or college graduates. The last census, in 1984, indicates that 20.4 per cent of the population of these secondary towns is under 15 years of age, 59.26 per cent aged between 15 and 59, and 1.2 per cent aged 60 or more. Their economic life is marked by great uncertainty and a lack of diversity. The secondary towns contain as many as 75 per cent of the total number of unemployed and a high percentage of adolescents over 15 who are still in the educational system. The active population is employed in the sectors of agriculture (55.2 per cent), services (18.3 per cent) and trade (12.5 per cent).

The politicization of the frustrations felt by the semi-urbanized population was already reflected in 1992, in the form of the proposals which were made at that time for an ethno-regional electoral system. This model was used in local, regional and legislative elections.[16] Support for the UPADS was strongest in the three regions of Niari, Bouenza and Lekoumou; for the MCDDI, it was in the Pool and Brazzaville; for the PCT, in Brazzaville and Likouala. Other regions were shared between the rival parties. Election figures clearly show the importance of provincial towns in Pascal Lissouba's victory in the 1992 elections since his support base was principally outside the capital city whereas, until 1990, political power had been largely confined to various interests in Brazzaville. The results of the 1992's elections thus underlined the relative decline in the political power of the capital, even though it remained the main site of political conflict in the sense that representatives of the various regions were obliged to travel to Brazzaville to defend their interests.

The fact that most militia members in 1997 were not actually inhabitants of Brazzaville offers a partial explanation for the manner in which hostilities unfolded. In the first place, it meant that rival leaders could not easily use their own militias to invade enemy positions since many militiamen had only an imperfect knowledge of the city. Having no real affection for the city, fighters were more ready than Brazzavillois themselves would have been, in similar circumstances, to participate in the destruction of the city. These two factors combined to induce the militias to attack their enemies from a distance, by means of artillery bombardments.

The massive enlistment in the militias by young people from secondary towns began especially after the first looting in Brazzaville. The commerce in goods looted from Brazzaville with the rest of the country then played an important role in the recruitment of new militiamen, especially among the Mambas, who anticipated the opportunity of acquiring booty of their own.

Violence and the new political order

The process of democratic transition in Congo in the early 1990s had a marked effect in disseminating the use of political violence throughout a large section of society. This had a consequent effect on relations between civilians in general and the armed forces. The militias asserted that they were 'real' soldiers since they were the ones who bore the brunt of actual fighting, and they despised professional soldiers who, for the most part, deserted from their posts. Hence an analysis of the violence of the period, considered in terms other than as a dysfunctioning of the democratic process, can reveal much about the way in which political practice in Congo has been transformed. This amounts to a redefinition of common social experience and popular conceptions of social status, the true subject of the various conflicts which have been so tragically militarized.

Notes

[*] This article has been translated from the French by Stephen Ellis.

[1] On the controversies surrounding the Lissouba presidency, see Patrice Yengo, 'Questions autour d'une guerre', *Rupture* (Pointe-Noire) 10, 2 (1997), pp. 45–59.

[2] Various publications offer a description and an analysis of these events. See e.g. the special number of the journal *Rupture* entitled 'Brazzaville des violences', 10, 2 (1997) Marc-Eric Gruénais, 'Le Congo: la fin d'une pseudo-démocratie', *Politique africaine*, 68 (1997), pp. 125–33; and the reconstruction based on press agency reports by Elisabeth Dorier-Apprill, 'Guerre des milices et fragmentation urbaine a Brazzaville', *Hérodote*, 86/87, 3–4 (1997), pp. 182–221.

[3] Studied in Rémy Bazenguissa, *Milices politiques et bandes armées à Brazzaville: enquête sur la violence politique et sociale des jeunes déclassés* (Les Etudes du CERI no. 13, Centre d'Etudes et de Recherches Internationales, Paris, 1996).

[4] This information was not collected under absolutely identical conditions. Data on the Cocoye were collected in September and October 1997, in interviews conducted during a period of hostilities; I was able to interview Cobra members only after the fighting was over.

[5] The following testimony, given by a doctor who took part in numerous burial parties, illustrates the point well: 'Around the Palais de Justice, we were told that someone had found a body in one of the gutters by the Palais.... The body was still warm; death had occurred less than an hour previously. The victim had been found in possession of several identity documents with his photo which, in the opinion of the militiamen manning the area, was sufficient grounds for his execution.' Jean-Claude Moudzika, 'Morts sans sépulture', *Rupture*, 10, 2 (1997), p. 36.

[6] Not all Mbochi in fact supported Sassou-Nguesso. Moreover, the Cocoye and Zulus considered that some northern ethnic groups, such as the Konyou and Mkwa, were not included in the enemy camp.

[7] I have been unable to find any indication as to how and by whom these lists were created and how many names figured on them.

[8] Joachim Mbanza, 'La guerre comme un jeu d'enfants', *Rupture*, 10, 2 (1997), p. 12.

9 Mhanza, 'La guerre comme un jeu d'enfants'.

10 'Conscience de ... pilleur', *Rupture*, 10, 2 (1997), p. 43.

11 Joseph Tonda, 'Esprit de désespérance sociale et guerre civile permanente', *Rupture*, 11, 3 (forthcoming).

12 This transformation is described in the following testimony: 'It was after the first three-day ceasefire, from Friday 13 June to Sunday 15 June, that the Cobras learned of the looting spree carried out by their enemies the soldiers, the Zulus and the Cocoye. They began to dance, not wanting to be left out. The signal to commence was received on Sunday 15 June during the afternoon. From then on, the war was also a campaign of looting. But in theory, it was a selective looting: supporters of the President and Beembe only.' Mambou Aimée Gnali, 'Bonjour! Nous sommes les Cobra!', *Rupture*, 10, 2 (1997), p. 41.

13 Jean-Marie Wagret, *Histoire et sociologie politique de la République du Congo* (LGDJ, Paris, 1963).

14 More details are to be found in Remy Bazenguissa, *Les voies du politque au Congo: essai de sociologie historique* (Karthala, Paris, 1997).

15 Likouala, Sangha, Cuvette, Cuvette-Ouest, Plateaux, Pool, Niari, Bouenza, Lékoumou and Kouilou. On secondary towns, see Robert-Edmond Ziavoula, *Villes secondaires et pouvoirs locaux* (Nordiska Afrikainstitutet, Uppsala, 1996).

16 For the election results, see Fabrice Weissman, *Élections presidentielles de 1992 au Congo: entreprise politique et mobilisation électorale* (CEAN-IEP, Bordeaux, 1993); Ziavoula, *Villes secondaires et pouvoirs locaux*.

3 The Local & the Traditional

MITZI GOHEEN
Chiefs, Sub-Chiefs & Local Control

Reference
Africa, 62/3, 1992, pp. 389–411

When I lived in the Nso chiefdom in western Cameroon from 1979 to 1981, I spent quite a bit of time with one of the sub-chiefs, the Fon Nseh.[1] I became a regular visitor at his palace and spent many an afternoon drinking palm wine in the courtyard while Fon Nseh, a calm and stately presence, entertained visitors and petitioners for favours, settled disputes, and in general conducted the business of his chiefdom. One afternoon during the rainy season as I slid down the muddy path and stood dripping in the entryway to the palace, Fon Nseh, unusually agitated and upset, motioned me to follow him into a small interior courtyard where a number of important lineage heads – the 'landlords' or, more accurately, the [A] *Taa-Ngwoen* ('men who own the fields') of Nseh had gathered. I watched them fill a ceremonial calabash or *shoo* with palm wine from the palace. Swearing an oath to their ancestors that the ritual they were preparing would seek the truth, each man spat into the *shoo*.[2] The lineage heads then exited *en masse*, clambered into a waiting Land-Rover, raised their umbrellas and headed out to complete the ritual. Fon Nseh and I headed back to the relative dryness of the palace.

Soon we were seated sipping palm wine in the interior of the palace in a small private audience room. A dim light seeping in from the high narrow latticed windows cast shadows of the figures carved into the Fon's throne against the dank walls, evoking images of a Mongo Beti novel. Fon Nseh, still upset but now somewhat calmed by both the wine and the ritual preparation, proceeded to explain the events of the past half-hour. It seems his relationship with the Fon Nso, the paramount chief of Nso, had been strained for some time. The day before it had been stretched to breaking point when the Fon Nso took hoes away from Nseh women working in fields over which both rulers claimed jurisdiction. (The women had been using hoes on an Nso 'Country Sunday' – a ritual day set aside by the appropriate ruler and the 'landlord' of the field on which hoes are not to be used, as a sign of fealty and respect to the ritual leader and his ancestors.) Not quite knowing how to respond, I took a gulp of palm wine and stared at my cup. Graciously ignoring my lack of response, Fon Nseh continued his story. 'We in Nseh are in the right; it is our land. We perform the rituals for the land and the Fon Nso is a trespasser.' The lineage heads were at this moment travelling to the land in question to pour the contents of the ritual calabash on the earth and swear an oath that this was true. Furthermore, the Fon Nseh went on to inform me that he was not a subject of the Fon Nso, by emphasising the fact that he was

walking together with the Fon Nso as an equal, as a brother, using my own power. We helped Nso fight the Bamoun and the Germans. Now he [Fon Nso] says he owns us. How can that be when we were moving together as equals? The Fon Nseh was never captured [by Nso]. So the Fon Nso has a very big head. If you go to meet him now he will not tell you the truth.

By focusing on the estrangement between these two rulers and explaining this single event in one relatively obscure chiefdom in the highlands of Cameroon, I will try to clarify some of the many complexities involved in describing relations to the land in modern Africa. An account of the estrangement between these two men who, according to the Nseh, 'became David and Jonathan' in the early twentieth century[3] must include an understanding of two core symbols in Nso: the significance of the Earth in Nso cosmology and the related meaning of stewardship of the land as a symbol of political (and religious) leadership. It must also include two relatively recent processes: a growing scarcity of arable land brought about partially by population growth, but also by the ambiguous tenure situation created by contradictions between traditional tenure arrangements and national land ordinances – contradictions which have been exacerbated by a propensity toward privatisation of land and land use, and an accompanying tendency to treat land as a commodity, a resource with a cash value assigned to its use and ownership (see Goheen, 1988). Clearly, the present disaffection between these two men cannot be understood without reference to history, keeping in mind that the present, while a product of history, is not simply a continuation of the past. The critical task here is to discover just how cultural meaning is reordered by the historical process. The aim of this study is to unravel the meaning of this event and trace the various threads backwards and forwards in time to reveal how the reproduction of particular structures and relationships ends up instead as their transformation.[4]

The changing meaning of land in Nso

Land shortages are rapidly becoming a serious local issue in the Nso chiefdom of highland Cameroon. Old hostilities between Fulani herders and local agriculturalists have worsened, and newer tensions between constituencies of the chiefdom have emerged and intensified. The meaning of control over land as symbolic of legitimate political authority has, however, changed less rapidly than the practices associated with the exercise of this control. According to customary tenure, all people in Nso have rights to farm land by virtue of citizenship in the chiefdom. The Fon Nso is the titular owner of all land, but this is symbolic of his political control. Actual allocation of land is in the hands of a number of lineage heads called the [A] *Taa-Ngwoen*, or the 'men who own the fields'. Their rights are symbolic of their ability to manage a large kinship group, and they are under obligation to give out farm land to all their dependants. Land is 'begged' with a prestation consisting of a calabash of palm wine and a fowl; all people working on the land of a particular lineage head also owe him respect and fealty, and occasional labour on his mensal farm. In the precolonial era, and in most of Nso before the introduction of coffee in the 1940s, the lineage head (and not a man's heirs) inherited his property when he died. Women most often farm on the land of their husband's lineage, although they have had rights through their mother's family too (Kaberry, 1952; Goheen, 1984, 1988). In the subchiefdoms of Nso the Fon Nso has allocated his political control over land to the sub-chiefs in their respective villages.

Figure 1 North West Province, with Bui Division, Cameroon.

Access to land has been viewed as a right of citizenship in Nso; today that right has been put in jeopardy. As land becomes scarce and begins to have a commodity value attached to it, conflicts over the control of rights of access to and allocation of its use have sharpened between the paramount Fon Nso and his subchiefs. These conflicts have become particularly acute between the Fon Nso and Fon Nseh, whom we met at the beginning of this article, the latter being the chief of a village in the northern reaches of Nso. Both rulers have claimed the right to allocate land lying on the Nseh side of the border, between Nseh and Nso proper, each appealing to a different set of rights and a different interpretation of history. As we shall see, their dispute revolves primarily around rights in people as opposed to rights in territory, focused here on control of access to land, and around different historical legitimations of these rights.

Struggles over land and over the meaning of its control have accelerated rapidly since the national government passed land ordinances in 1974 encouraging 'rational development' through privatisation (Cameroon, 1974). These land ordinances have enabled an emerging rural elite to acquire large tracts of land under individual title. I have argued elsewhere that they have effectively encouraged not agricultural development but rather growing land scarcity and conflict (Goheen, 1988). The dispute between these two rulers is just one, albeit an important and public one, among many such disputes as people invoke various rules of each, and sometimes both, systems of tenure to secure access to land.

In looking at the negotiations over the right to control land, and the shifting relationship of different social actors to this control, I have assumed certain perspectives:

First, I read the history of the relationship between Nso and Nseh not simply as a chronology of events, but rather as what Jean Comaroff (1985) has called a 'dialectic in a double sense'. It needs to be seen on the one hand as the structural interplay of socio-cultural order and human practice, and on the other as the historical

articulation of dominant and subordinate systems. This double dialectic is played out both in internal centreperiphery relationships within the chiefdom and in external relationships between the chiefdoms and the colonial and postcolonial governments. These relationships and different interpretations of their meaning held by various people from Nseh and Nso proper, including the two fons, lead to conflicting and often contradictory practices on the part of different categories of people. These practices both reproduce and transform the structure of relationships within the chiefdoms.

Second, I see a shift in the nature of productive relationships and the social relations of land tenure, which have historically been relations of dependence – mainly lineage- and kinship-based – but which under present circumstances are increasingly characterised by the growing importance of national politics and accumulative economics. Land has become a form of accumulation as well as a means of subsistence. Negotiations over these shifting relationships have been largely contained and reproduced in the superstructure, although changing material conditions have recently intensified these struggles. The terms of the discourse have contained several historically changing, and sometimes contradictory, themes as different people contest interpretations of what is actually happening. Ideology, or control of the dominant discourse, is then itself an aspect of the social relations of production.[5]

Finally, I see continuity in the cultural meaning of control over land as a symbol of political leadership even in the context of growing privatisation. The cultural meaning of stewardship of land as a symbol of political leadership is reinforced by the symbolic significance of the earth, as well as by the tendency for new elites to invest in the symbols of traditional Nso leaders and to participate actively in traditional politics.

Regional and historical background

The Nso say that 'before foreigners came, Nso was in the earth [*naasy*] and the earth was at peace' (Chilver, forthcoming). This may not be precisely accurate in historical terms but it is suggestive of the connection the Nso make between their physical and social environment. The Nso belong to the earth just as the earth belongs to them; it is the place of the important dead, the ancestors, who are believed to have power over the living. The earth can become 'hot' and punish those who transgress against the moral code, and can be called upon to make judgement in disputes. The Nso physical and social worlds are inextricably interconnected, and it is within this context that we need to understand the connection the religious and political connotations of stewardship of land in Nso cosmology.

Nso is the largest chiefdom in the Bamenda Grassfields of what is today the North West Province of Cameroon. The borders of the chiefdom closely follow those of Bui Division. Bui Division straddles the south-east arc of the Ring Road, the laterite-surface road connecting the main towns of Cameroon's North West Province to the provincial capital of Bamenda. From Bamenda a well paved highway connects the province with Bafoussam, Nkongsamba, and Douala, Cameroon's major commercial city, on the Atlantic coast. By the latter half of the nineteenth century Sem II, Fon Nso, through both conquest and the adroit manipulation of a palace-based title system, was able to consolidate his power to create a regional hegemony which has remained salient up to the present. Renowned as fierce warriors and described by their German conquerors as greatly feared slave hunters, the Nso are today often spoken of by their neighbours as arrogant and stiff-necked. The emphasis of local peoples on regional cultural identity, common in Cameroon, reaches its most pronounced expression in Nso. Nso elites in the national capital in Yaounde can be heard telling their francophone colleagues that they (the colleagues) are fortunate that the Germans came, because otherwise Nso would have conquered them.

With a population of some 200,000 and an area of 2,300sqkm, Nso is heavily populated for an agricultural region, with an average density of some eighty-five per square kilometre (compared with an average of twenty per square kilometre nationwide; the national population is 9.5 million) (Delancey, 1989). The Grassfields in which Nso is situated constitute a distinct culture area comprised of a number of chiefdoms of various size and complexity. They range from the small village chiefdoms of Widekum to the expanding conquest states like Nso whose population was estimated at 20,000–25,000 by the Germans who fought and finally subdued them in the early twentieth century (Chilver and Kaberry, 1967). While these chiefdoms are linguistically and ethnically diverse, they share a number of features in common, including the centrality of chiefship, the importance of men's secret societies and an emphasis on title and rank as significant political attributes. The Nso also share the region with two groups of Fulani graziers, the Mbororo, who arrived in the early 1900s, and the Aku'en, originally occupants of the high Jos plateau, who migrated into the area in the 1950s in the wake of a cattle epidemic from what was then the Benue Province of Nigeria.

At one time in the distant past the Grassfields were a forest zone occupied by hunting and gathering peoples (Nkwi and Warnier, 1982). Many cultural features of the current populations indicate some historical connections with the forest peoples south of the highlands. Today the forests have almost disappeared and the most distinctive vegetation is the tall savanna grass after which the region is named. The Grassfields lie east to west between the 4th and 7th parallels. They are essentially a high lava plateau surrounded by a series of lower plains and valleys, broken by volcanic peaks. Ecological conditions are diverse, encouraging the production of both temperate and tropical-zone crops. Altitude within the Grassfields varies substantially, ranging from a low of 500m in the north to the high plateaux around Bamenda and Nso at 1,400–1,700m. The plateaux are traversed by mountains with steep slopes, often cut by deep valleys. Largely as a function of altitude, temperature and rainfall vary widely. The high plateau around Nso receives over 3,000 ml of rainfall annually, while lower regions in the Grassfields average between 1,000 and 2,000ml. Average temperatures around Nso range from a mean annual maximum of 66°F to a mean minimum of 51°F. The cold, damp nights during rainy season can chill even Europeans and North Americans who are used to cold, almost arctic northern winters. Lower-lying areas are much hotter, and less pleasant to trek around or travel through in a crowded taxi, with a mean annual maximum of 95.5°F and a minimum of 72°F. There are, generally, a six- to seven-month rainy season from April to October, a cool dry season from October to December, and a hot dry season from January to March. Nso lies in the fertile crescent extending from Bamenda north-east to Nkambe and south to Bafoussam in the neighbouring Ouest Province. This region is targeted by the national government for development as a breadbasket for the growing national urban centres.[6]

According to local oral tradition, the founders of the dynasty travelled to Nso in the distant past from the north-east, and succeeded in securing the allegiance of a number of local groups.

Figure 2 Nso chiefdom and Nseh.
(Based on a map by Mrs E. M. Chilver, reproduced in *Africa*, vol. 62, no. 3,1992.)

Their migration probably began some 300 years ago, although in the absence of documentary evidence it is difficult to pinpoint the exact time or number of people involved. Movement into the region was often initiated by slaving razzias. Population pressure and intra-group feuding also played significant roles.[7] When the chiefdom expanded and became increasingly centralised in the nineteenth century, the Afon[8] of Nso incorporated various conquered chiefs and important lineage heads into national political life. The pattern was to grant lesser chiefs rank, titles, and participation in centralised decision-making, along with symbolic and economic privileges, in return for political fealty. The chiefs of larger villages were accorded the title 'Fon' and allowed to retain their hereditary dynasties and autonomy in the management of local affairs in return for political support and tribute (*nshwi*). Two principles came to be stressed in the system of dues and tribute: local derivation of tribute from the sub-chiefs and generalised redistribution from the paramount Fon Nso, emphasising mutual rights and

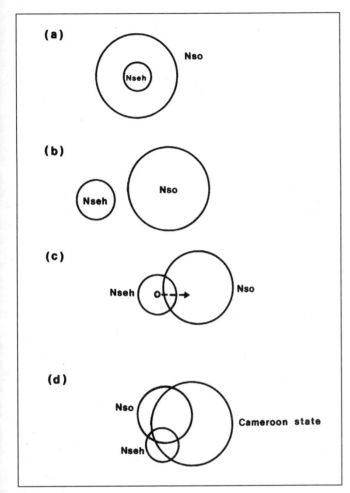

Figure 3 The different views of the relationship. (a) Fon Nso's perspective: inclusion, marked by symbols at German surrender. (b) Fon Nseh's perspective: same level of classification, different interpretation of the Nso-German war and surrender. (c) The individual Nseh perspective: membership depends on the context. (d) perspective from the 'outside': inclusion/membership depends on the context.

obligations. 'We take from Nkar [a sub-chiefdom of Nso] and give to Nkar,' says the Fon Nso.

Nseh occupies a special position in relation to the paramount Fon Nso. The Fon Nseh is neither related to the Fon Nso nor was he ever conquered, and Nseh was never invaded or attacked by Nso. In fact Nseh helped Nso with its military conquest of other small chiefdoms in the late nineteenth century. In addition, Nseh helped Nso defeat Bamoun, its neighbour and largest rival, in the second half of the nineteenth century, and fought with Nso against the Germans in the early twentieth century.[9] According to both Nseh and Nso people, the Fon Nseh gave a white fowl, honey, and grain to the Fon Nso upon their defeat by the Germans. They were

subsequently given to the German commander as a sign of surrender.[10] But the interpretation of these gifts differs today. The Fon Nseh insists that he and Fon Nso were fighting together as equals and that he never became a subject of Nso. The Fon Nso, on the other hand, claims that Nseh voluntarily became tributary to Nso; that the fowl and honey were symbols of submission, not merely gifts given to an equal to help pay tribute to the Germans. The Fon Nso complained to me that 'the Nseh people now want their freedom, but I cannot give it. They [and people in several other sub-chiefdoms] no longer love me or want to live in peace with me. They no longer bring food and firewood.'[11]

The Fon Nso marshals several pieces of evidence to prove the claim that the Fon Nseh voluntarily accepted a tributary relationship with Nso. He points to the fact that Lam Nso, the language of the Nso people, has replaced Limbum, the original language of Nseh, as the language of everyday discourse (although Nseh rituals are still performed in Limbum). A white fowl is the traditional gift of surrender, and it was given by Nseh direct to Nso. In return the Fon Nseh was granted the right to retain all his royal trappings, along with autonomy of rule over his territory. Indeed, Nseh people, while stressing their ties with the Limbum-speaking Nsungli chiefdoms to the north, acknowledge their citizenship in Nso (Fjellman and Goheen, 1984). (See Fig. 3 for the different views espoused by various players in this scenario.)

'From tribute to tax'

Although most Nseh people agree that they are citizens of Nso, today they stress their differences with and estrangement from the Fon Nso and assert their independent status. In a pamphlet distributed during Nseh Cultural Week in 1977 a whole page is devoted to 'Dissimilarities in the Nseh and Nso Traditions'. This publication, put out by a local committee headed by the Fon Nseh, stresses early cooperation and equality between the two rulers. Although it is vague about the origins of the rift between them, it is quite clear about the fact that a rift exists:

> friendly ties between the Fons of Nseh and Nso increased after fighting the Germans. It came to a peak when both Fons agreed to work hand-in-hand. This cordial relationship continued until the last days of Fon Minglo [the Fon Nseh before the present Fon].... Since then these two friends are apart, their dispute whose solution is basically traditional still remains unsolved till today. [Nseh Week Council 1977: 3]

By the late 1970s relations between the two rulers had deteriorated to the point that the Fon Nseh began to assert heatedly and publicly that he was not a subject of the Fon Nso, stating angrily that:

> You [Nso] never captured me, I was travelling with you, using my own power, and then we were captured in several places – so why should you treat me in such a way? Because he [Fon Nso] just wants tokens, because the population of Nseh is so small, that is why he treats us so.

If we look at the time when people say friction between the two rulers began, we can see that it was at a point when two core principles of governance between the centre (Fon Nso and his government in Kumbo) and the periphery (village sub-chiefdoms) – the principles of local derivation and generalised redistribution – began to be seriously undermined by the changing policies of the colonial system of taxation and tax collection.[12]

Until the 1920s the sub-chiefdoms owed tribute (*nshwi*), consisting primarily of surplus production, to the paramount Fon Nso. The larger part of tribute and prestations given to the Fon Nso was, however, redistributed either on an on-going basis through hospitality at the palace or when, in times of food shortage, the palace storehouses were opened up for distribution to all villages of Nso. The Nso saying 'The Fon takes from Nkar [one of the Nso sub-chiefdoms] and gives to Nkar' means that the Fon Nso is owed tribute from his sub-chiefs but is expected in turn to look after the needs of all the people of Nso.

When taxes in the form of a head tax on all adult males (men eighteen years and older) were imposed, first by the Germans in 1911, and then after 1917 by the British colonial administration, they were collected by the colonial office through the Fon Nso as Sole Native Authority; the commission retained by the Fon was viewed as a form of tribute. The sub-chiefs were relieved of the burden of tribute by Fon Bifon (the Fon Nso) around 1923 in exchange for their portion of the tax receipts. From the time taxes were imposed until the early 1930s, the colonial administration collected all taxes direct through the paramount Fon Nso. However, beginning in the 1930s, a new plan was instituted, creating a civil service which collected taxes from each sub-chief. Sub-chiefs then received direct from the Native Authority a percentage of the taxes paid from each of their villages.

The important point here is that the tax commission retained by the Fon Nso was viewed as a substitute for tribute from the sub-chiefdoms. When the Native Authority allowed the sub-chiefs to collect taxes and retain a portion of the revenues, the sub-chiefs believed that this conferred on them a new status and a far greater degree of politically sanctioned authority than the administration intended to give. As early as the late 1940s the sub-chiefs, now relieved of tribute payments and receiving a tax commission direct from the Native Treasury, began to question the overlordship of the paramount Fon Nso.

Around the same time that the colonial administration re-organised tax collection, it also set up a financial council in Nso with the Fon Nso as head. Monies for public works and local develop-ment were distributed through this council. The Fon Nso did not have the same control over the redistribution of taxes that he had had over the redistribution of tribute. The capital at Kumbo was developed by the colonial government, while village chiefdoms did not receive roads, medical facilities, and schools. The sub-chiefs came to believe that the Fon and people in Kumbo were profiting unduly at their expense and hence began to campaign vigorously for autonomy.

By collecting taxes through the sub-chiefs the colonial adminis-tration supported them to an extent not initially intended. Their direct relationship with the colonial office weakened the Fon Nso's authority over his sub-chiefs. Equally damaging was the fact that taxes, unlike tribute, could not be redistributed through the Fon Nso's largesse. Local derivation was stressed now in a new context: the redistribution of taxes through implementation of local services and public works. But the Fon Nso no longer had ultimate control over this generalised redistribution. When proposals from the sub-chiefs to the Nso Advisory Council were turned down – actually by colonial administrators but symbolically by the Fon Nso – the sub-chiefs claimed he was pocketing the tax receipts and developing the capital at Kumbo without adequately redistributing goods and services to his people in the sub-chiefdoms.

Colonial tax policies undermined the credibility of the paramount Fon in his sub-chiefdoms. But otherwise his close relationship with the colonial administration in the context of indirect rule supported and perpetuated his superior position. Upon independence in the 1960s, the policies of the national government did the same. Local offices of the national government work closely with the Fon Nso; he plays a prominent role on divisional development councils and is a member of the divisional lands commission. He must approve – at least symbolically – all allocation of land in the division, both according to customary land tenure rules and according to the national land ordinances instituted in 1974. While we can trace the beginnings of conflict between Nso and Nseh back several decades, the dispute has sharpened owing to pressure on land. The estrangement between the two rulers today is predicated upon a conflict between rights over people and rights over territory, the latter by virtue of ritual responsibility for the land in question. This argument is illustrated by the current dispute over Kuvluv, a village on the Nseh side of the Nseh-Nso border. It is this dispute which occasioned the ritual scene with which the article opened.

Fealty, land and the ancestors: arguments over Kuvluv

By the 1960s, and perhaps earlier, people from Kumbo had been moving into Nseh villages – Ngondzen, Boninyar, Mbarang, Kuikov or Kuvluv. Whether or not he became tributary to the Fon Nso aside, these villages were in the Fon Nseh's domain, and he and his lineage heads were responsible for performing the rituals for the land and the people working on the land in these areas. While there were numerous disputes caused by extensive crop damage due to the numerous cattle inhabiting the area, especially around Ngondzen, there were, until the 1970s, few disputes about who controlled access to the land in and around the villages. Kuvluv constitutes a part of Nseh and the Fon Nseh was given rights of local control in his territory. As land became scarce around the capital at Kumbo, people from Nso proper 'begged' land in outlying areas, including Kuvluv. While the Fon Nseh is not pleased that people from Nso proper are farming in Kuvluv, the dispute is not about the farming of the land as much as it is about control over the symbols of authority over the people farming on the land.[13] The Fon Nso maintains that he is the supreme Fon and thus ultimate overlord of all land in the division. He claims that this position entitles him to control any area where Nso people have acquired land. Therefore, he insists, people who have settled in Kuvluv should observe his 'Country Sundays' and pay taxes directly through him. But since Kuvluv is viewed by the Fon Nseh as part of his territory he insists that people living in Kuvluv – both Nseh people and those who have moved there from Nso proper – should pay taxes directly through him and observe the Country Sundays of Nseh.

Depending on the meaning assigned to various symbols and acts, each argument has an interpretation which gives it customary legitimacy. As Raymond Williams[14] has argued, most versions of 'tradition' can quickly be shown to be radically selective. From the past, which presents multiple meanings and practices with a variety of interpretations in relation to the present, certain meanings and practices are selected to have meaning and efficacy and others are discarded. Such selection is then passed off by the dominant group as 'the tradition' and 'the significant past'. Therefore any tradition is an aspect of contemporary power relationships; it is that aspect which is meant to connect with and ratify these relationships in the interests of a dominant group. Particular events always happen in time, and become part of different versions of history, which can then be used to buttress arguments about relationships in the present. The Fon Nseh points to the fact that the Fon Nso will not perform the traditional wine-drinking ceremony with him to swear the validity of his claim. He presents this as evidence that the Fon Nso knows the land really belongs to Nseh and, knowing he is in the wrong, is afraid to perform the ritual.

The Fon Nso counters this argument by claiming that he does not fear the ritual, but it is simply beneath his dignity to submit to the Fon Nseh's request. It is important here to re-emphasise the significance of the meaning of the earth (*nsaay*) in Nso cosmology. Legitimate authority is based on descent and the ancestors, and the earth of the dead is the repository of religious moral values which are given legitimacy by referring to them as ancestral values.[15] The earth can be called upon to punish offenders. The earth is viewed as the place where the important dead, the ancestors, reside; they sleep underfoot and can be awakened. If an act occurs which is considered to be a trespass against moral values, the earth of the dead may get 'hot' (angry) and refuse to grow crops and otherwise afflict the area. An act of appeasement is then required so that the earth is 'cooled' and sleeps again.[16] The Fon Nseh and his lineage heads emphasise the fact that they perform rituals for the land at Kuvluv. They view the area as part of Nseh and claim the fealty of people living there – and invoke their ritual obligations for the land as proof.

Since tax is seen as a form of tribute, the debate has centred on which ruler people pay taxes through, but the real issue is much more complex. It is also, and more crucially here, a conflict between the ideal of control over people as opposed to control over territory as a justification for controlling land. As land becomes both scarce and expensive, people on all levels are trying to hold on to as much land as possible. Both the Fon Nseh and the Fon Nso believe they are in the right – and in a sense both are. They are merely applying different interpretations and resting their arguments on different principles of right and obligation – the Fon Nso emphasising the ideal of rights in people, and the Fon Nseh stressing rights in territory. When asked how the dispute would have been settled in the past, elders in Nseh claimed that the disputes would not have arisen in the past; the 'land was not so difficult [to get] then' and the land was 'blank'. We could add that the presence of a higher court of appeal, the national government, has probably strengthened the resolve of the Fon Nseh to hold his ground, so to speak, against the more powerful paramount Fon. It is not surprising that the principles of rights in people and rights in territory should have come into conflict at this time, since historically land was abundant and direct control over people the key to power and wealth, while today land is becoming scarce, and people more abundant, and no longer do traditional leaders have direct control over their dependants' lives and fortunes.[17] Given the current practice of some Nso landlords of demanding an 'under the table' cash payment for the use of land and the cash value the government has recently attached to urban land (Goheen, 1984, 1988)[18] as well as the national government's emphasis on privatisation, these values were bound to come into conflict in Nso, whose core values stress freely available farmland for all its citizens. An unexpected twist to this particular dispute lies in the fact that, from one vantage point, it could be argued that the Fon Nseh's claim is the more orthodox. One might expect a claim to rights in territory to be buttressed by more recent or imported values.[19] What is clear here is that, for the Nso, control over land remains a central symbol of leadership, both historically and today.

The judgement: between orthodoxy and heterodoxy

The inability of these two rulers to come to a compromise finally led to intervention by the District Officer and his staff – men who are seen and who see themselves as part of a new Nso elite. Their decision, while not entirely satisfactory to the paramount Fon, favoured his position.[20] Attempting, and failing, to emulate the wisdom of Solomon, the judges opted for the status quo, and divided the land between the two rulers. All people farming around Kuvluv who were not originally from Nseh were to pay taxes to the Fon Nso and observe his Country Sundays, while Nseh people would continue to pay taxes directly through the Fon Nseh and observe his ritual day of rest. Given his close relationship with the government bureaucracy, it comes as no surprise that the decision favoured the Fon Nso. Yet while the decision favoured the Fon Nso, it did not discount the claims of the Fon Nseh entirely. To have ignored the claims of the Fon Nseh would not only have increased the hostility, it would have gone against what has commonly and widely been perceived as tradition or 'correct fashion' throughout Nso, wherein the justification for control over access to land has been associated with the ritual obligations of a ruler for the land in question.

If we step back and look at the position of the new bureaucrats, it is clear that it would be in their interests neither to cross the Fon Nso nor to declare publicly an unorthodox position – one which would go against what are commonly seen as valid traditional relationships. While the Fon Nso decries the commoditisation of land in Nso, he also plays a key role in allocating national lands to individuals for development schemes, and is thus a key player in furthering the process of privatisation of land. Many of these new elites, whom I have called 'modern big men' (Goheen, 1984, 1988), use their access to the state and their knowledge of the new land ordinances to acquire access to the allocation of national lands on an individual basis. Access to the state is necessary but often not sufficient to establish a successful claim to land as private property. The approval of the Fon Nso and two of his councillors, who sit on the land commission, must also be solicited. The new elites must also be sensitive to traditional politics – indeed, most of them assume prominent roles in traditional politics and often acquire titles and offices in secret societies (Goheen, 1984, 1988, 1991).

By acquiring the symbols and roles of traditional Nso leaders, these men validate the legitimacy of their claims to land and leadership within the chiefdom. In assuming the personae of traditional lineage heads they reproduce a social, not an individualised, identity,[21] for these are social and not individual roles, with obligations as well as rights attached. Traditional rulers in Nso, once enstooled (put 'on the stool' or enthroned), are no longer called by their given name, but rather by the title of their office. Rights, obligations and property belong to the title, not the title-holder, so that when a man 'takes over the stool' as lineage head he inherits his predecessor's name, his wives and his property. If a lineage head is deposed for not fulfilling the obligations of his office, his cap is removed by a messenger from *ng'werong*, the palace regulatory society, who then calls him by his given name as a sign that he has become a commoner.

The current tax dispute is mainly a symbolic one over the recognition of political allegiance, since the actual tax revenue accruing to either Fon from this area is fairly minimal. It is not surprising that the collection of taxes, seen as a sign of fealty and tribute, should have become a source of dispute and tension, as the nexus of control over people begins to change from direct relations of fealty based primarily on kinship to control through ownership and redistribution of resources, including land. The fact that the Fon Nso's credibility in his sub-chiefdoms was eroded when he lost the power to redistribute the surplus, now in the form of tax monies used for development projects, demonstrates the degree to which generosity and redistribution are important political principles and symbols of leadership in Nso society, both historically and today.

As title-holders and big men in Nso, the new elites must have an 'open hand' – they must redistribute the wealth. And they continue to do so. New forms of access to power and control via the modern state have broadened the base of control from an ascribed kin-based form to a more open one which includes an assortment of kin and clients.[22] It is still essential that the modern big men redistribute wealth, for staying in the political limelight depends on the ability to dispense favours and goods, not only at politically expedient times but always.

There is, however, a significant difference in the structure of redistribution by the new elites. Resources which are redistributed are gained primarily through knowledge of and access to the national bureaucracy. New forms of redistribution include access to jobs and higher education. Papers for traders' licences, applications for building and development projects, for access to national lands and national agricultural loans are facilitated through the system. In short, redistribution by the new elites includes more or less openly many practices their counterparts in western countries try to hide so as not to be accused of graft or nepotism. These practices all share an important attribute. By drawing on personal networks and political connections, rather than on individual wealth, the new elites are able to redistribute without giving up their ability to accumulate. Unlike traditional lineage heads, the new politicos in Nso can gain clients, support kin and accumulate a significant amount of personal wealth at the same time.

By taking an active role in traditional government, and paying attention to customary law and local opinion when making national decisions, the new elites secure the co-operation of traditional authorities in their leadership and entrepreneurial ventures. They have become the mediators between the local and national arenas, the interpreters as well as the architects of the intersections between customary and national law. Importantly, by assuming these roles and often acquiring traditional titles, these modern big men assume a legitimate and culturally appropriate social identity.

The truth about the tributary nature of the relationship of Nseh to Nso may never be revealed – if, indeed, there is 'a truth'. Clearly the question cannot be resolved to the satisfaction of all parties concerned. But the dynamics of the contradictions between sets of institutions, as each group recalls a different history and differentially interprets a set of symbols, and the struggles over meaning and power in asserting rights to control access to land in this small region give us an idea of the complexities involved in trying to make sense of political and economic processes surrounding the control and meaning of land in Africa today.

Conclusions: land and social identity – conflict and contradictions

Many of the current conflicts over land in Nso can be explained by the contradictions which result from the interaction between state-promoted privatisation of land, emphasising individual accumulation, and the core values of Nso, which stress the right to land as a right of citizenship; which see the earth as a repository of lineage values; and which emphasise the moral commitment and generosity of lineage leaders. While there is a tendency toward individualism and privatisation of property, including land, there is a contradictory tendency stressing social identity. This latter stands in opposition to privatisation of individual identity analogous to the possessive individualism which accompanied the emergence of private property in Europe, with each individual seen not only as the proprietor of his property but also as proprietor of himself (MacPherson, 1962). Practices surrounding land tenure arrangements reflect the contradictory nature of a process which is at one and the same time fragmented and united as both privatisation and patronage increase in importance. The process is not unilineal. Nor is it easily separated into 'traditional' and 'modem' strategies or camps. Depending on the social identity of the people involved, and the nature of the dispute, the same individuals will appeal to both customary tenure rules and the national land ordinances, singly and sometimes in combination, and will invoke whatever ideology or cultural symbols are appropriate to substantiate the claim. Continuity and change merge together, being embodied not in different individuals but in the same people playing different roles in semi-separate contexts.[23]

As channels of access to land are redefined by the state, contradictions, paradoxes, and unintended consequences increase, and struggles over meaning and power intensify.[24] 'Throughout Africa,' Berry writes (1989: 46), 'where rights of access to land depend on social identity, people are investing in social identity … social identity and status have become objects as well as instruments of investment.' Investment in social identity and status as a key to economic wealth is not new; it has long been a strategy of advancement for ambitious men in Nso. By presenting gifts to the palace (called 'to *tang*' the Fon) and acquiring titles, these men could parlay wealth gained in local trade into access to the more lucrative precolonial state-controlled trade in ivory and slaves (Chilver, 1969; Nkwi and Warnier, 1982; Rowlands 1979). In the precolonial as well as in the colonial state, access to land and other resources has depended on social identity as well as on the ability to use wealth wisely. This continues to be true in the postcolonial state. What is new today, however, is the modern state and the accompanying potential for individual accumulation, for in the postcolonial period access to the state has become a precondition for individual economic success.[25]

This discussion has focused on conflicts and contradictions arising in struggles over the right to control land access and use in a context of increasing commoditisation and growing land scarcity. The argument between the two traditional rulers, the Fon Nso and the Fon Nseh, is just one level of the current discourse on land rights taking place in Nso. Struggles over rights to land in Nso today are on-going between various individuals and categories of individuals. These negotiations are intimately linked into social identity and the interpretation of this identity within the context of a historical discourse which includes several sometimes contradictory themes, a discourse which has been historically changing over time. The particular events which are recalled to validate claims to land have happened at particular points in time and have become part of different versions of history. No relationship is ever static. Relationships between social identity and land have always been intimately connected in Nso. As practices associated with control over land change, people recall different versions of history and assert various rights associated with social identity to validate their claims to land.

As tax replaced tribute in Nso the authority of the paramount Fon Nso was displaced by the authority of the colonial administration, and sub-chiefs began asserting their autonomy. The tax policies of the colonial office undermined the principles underlying the traditional system of dues and tribute, thus sharpening the discord between the centre and the periphery of the chiefdom. However, the paramount Fon's relationship to the colonial administration perpetuated his superior position. A growing land shortage focused the argument on control of land. Here the principle of control over territory was invoked by the sub-chief, Fon Nseh, while as paramount chief the Fon Nso invoked his rights of control over all people living in the chiefdom.

The solution to this conflict favoured the Fon Nso but stayed within the bounds of orthodoxy by taking seriously the Fon Nseh's arguments regarding his ritual obligations for the land in question. The decision did not rest on the land ordinances of the state; instead, with a bow to the *Realpolitik* of the chiefdom, it stayed firmly within the orthodox discourse. However, customary land tenure arrangements, part of the *doxa* before the introduction of coffee in the 1950s (Kaberry, 1950, 1960), are no longer orthodox. The universe of discourse within which negotiations about land take place has become increasingly heterodox, changing from one in which access to land (and other resources) is determined primarily by social identity to one in which social identity is often created by control over property, including land. The practices engaged in by the new elites reflect and reproduce this shift. The new elites have privileged access to the state. By adroit use of this political connection and some personal wealth, they can maintain a large network of kin and clients and feed wealth into the local redistribution system. They are active in traditional politics, and often assume the social identity of more traditional Nso leaders. Adept at playing both national and local politics, they have become the translators of received custom and national law into new practices.

In the customary tenure system, traditional land settlement and rights of various individuals to land are supported by relations based on kinship and by the Fon's and the lineage head's appeal to the legitimacy of the ancestors. There is a conflict set up then between traditional land settlement and individualised ownership as private property. This conflict is resolved by the investment of the new elites in traditional social identity. But the contradiction between traditional land settlement and the national laws which stress national control, development and privatisation is not resolved, and social identity is not going to continue to mediate the conflict as this contradiction deepens with increasing pressure on land.

The dialectical relationship between land settlement and appeals to kinship supports an internal hierarchy where legitimacy is based on the moral legitimacy of the earth and the ancestors. This comes into conflict with the secular legitimacy of the modern state, which supports individual ownership and privatisation. The contradictions set up by this conflict cannot be mediated by the new elite's investment in social identity as the state pursues its project of 'rational development' (Cameroon, 1974). It is the contradictions which drive change. These contradictions will ultimately create a transformation of the tenure system. But the ways in which the system changes are a matter of negotiation and struggles over the meaning of land. The struggles are informed by different interpretations of what is – and should be – happening on the part of various social actors. They are also informed by various relations of power both within the chiefdom and within the modern state.

'It is in the structure of practice,' Sahlins argues (1981: 72), 'that relationships themselves are put at issue, not just this or that cultural category.' The true meaning of practice can remain obscure and distorted, with consequences that often outrun individual conscious intentions.[26] Whether willy-nilly or by design, practices regarding land in Nso have radically altered the social relation of land tenure. The differential connections of the educated elites and the typical village farmer with the modern state have changed internal relationships in Nso in ways which are often more real than apparent. In the current political economy of land, everyone is scrambling, because land is quickly becoming scarce and expensive. This obviously leads to conflicts between various constituencies of the chiefdom, including, as we have seen, the paramount Fon and his sub-chiefs. To validate his claim, the Fon Nso appeals to old principles of control over people, while the Fon Nseh appeals to old principles of control over land by virtue of the ancestors and his ritual obligations. The new elites can appeal to new laws and the paraphernalia of the modern state as long as the Fon and some subset of his councillors will support them. New elites invest in the cultural symbols of political leadership and are active in traditional politics. They feed cash into the local distribution system and maintain large local kin and client patronage networks. It is ironic that the participation and investment of the new elites in traditional roles and their public adherence to custom have facilitated the ease with which they engage in practices which have led not to the reproduction but rather to the transformation of the structures and relationships of power in Nso. When the Nseh lineage heads, whom we met at the beginning of this article, call upon the Earth to pass judgement on the disputes over land in Nso today, which principles will endure and just what will that judgement be?

Epilogue

I returned to Nso in the summer of 1988 and again in 1991. There is now a new Fon Nso who has much graver problems than his dispute with the Fon Nseh. Unlike the late Fon Nso, his successor is said not to have an 'open hand', and both wine and conversation have dried up at the palace in Kumbo. There is a heated dispute between the two secret societies, *ngwerong* and *nggiri*, over the distribution of power, and each has denounced the support of the Fon Nso for the other. The hostility between the two rulers regarding the dispute over Kuvluv has remained unresolved, with neither Fon willing to resolve it in a culturally appropriate way, which – referred to as a *kimann* ceremony – requires that a goat be sacrificed. People in Nso say the Fon Nseh can (and should) give a goat to the Fon Nso to end the problem between them and make peace but the Fon Nso cannot give the goat because he is not under the Fon Nseh. They point to the fact that the Fon Nso ended up giving the hoes back to the women farming in Kuvluv and therefore took a step towards resolving the animosity between the two rulers. Nso notables claim that, if a goat is necessary to resolve the issue according to ancestral tradition, then the Fon Nseh should provide it; for the Nso the return of the hoes is already the *kimann*, or resolution, of the affair. Notables in the palace in Kumbo claim that, if the Fon Nso gives the goat, it means that the land is no longer part of Nso; therefore no goat can be given. Until the issue of the goat is resolved the death celebration of the late Fon Nso cannot be celebrated by *ngwerong* in Nseh. This has meant further estrangement between Nso and Nseh and has led the Fon Nseh to emphasise his ties to the national state rather than to the paramount

Fon. But it is telling that land in Nseh itself – a village of only some 4,000 persons, without good year-round road access, running water, or electricity, and few of the amenities found in larger villages – is currently being purchased for substantial amounts of money by absentee landlords – not on a large scale, but still an indication of the trend towards privatisation and the changing meaning of control over land.

Notes

1. The title 'Fon' is used for chiefs throughout the highland Grassfields of Western Cameroon. The Grassfields are a high-altitude savanna area which from the early colonial period was seen to possess a distinct political and cultural unity. The region was named by the German colonialists after the tall grass which is the predominant vegetation.
2. The Fon's wine is seen to have potent truth-finding power. See Chilver (forthcoming) and Mzeka (1980) for an analysis of Nso cultural symbols.
3. The quotation is from a pamphlet put out in Nseh for Nseh Traditional Week in 1977, quoted below in the text.
4. See Sahlins (1981: 7): 'the great challenge to an historical anthropology is not merely to know how events are ordered by culture but how in that process the culture is reordered. How does the reproduction of a structure become its transformation?'
5. See Friedman (1979), Godelier (1978), Althusser and Balibar (1970) and Williams (1977), all of whom argue in various ways that social relations are often contained and reproduced in the superstructure, that the relationships between production, distribution and exchange are often played out in the superstructure. They also see ideology as an aspect of the social relations of production. Ideology from this viewpoint is not a homogeneous or seamless whole, nor does it exist merely as a concealing and mystifying veil hiding the secret workings of society. To use Bourdieu's (1977) terminology, within any given habitus there exist struggles over meaning and the control of meaning, over orthodoxy and heterodoxy, which, while not separate from material reality, are neither a mere reflection nor an epiphenomenon of the material base.
6. Statistics from Scott and Mahaffey (Goheen 1980).
7. For historical accounts of Nso see Chilver and Kaberry (1967) and Jeffreys (1962).
8. *Afon* is the plural of *fon*. This process of incorporation was relatively long, beginning when the Nso first reached the Grassfields and accelerating in the second half of the nineteenth century, spanning the reigns of several *Afon*.
9. According to both the Nseh Week Council (1977) and various people in Nseh and in Nso proper, the Nseh aided the Nso when they were at war with Bamoun, Din and Ndu. After Nso had defeated Bamoun, the Fon Nso took the head of the Fon of Bamoun, who was killed in the war, and the Fon Nseh took his cutlass, his necklace decorated with frogs, and his cap, which are still in the keeping of the Fon Nseh today. According to the Nseh, that is why, during the reconciliation of Nso and Bamoun, many of the traditional activities were performed by the Fon Nseh.
10. It is worthy of note that the Nseh Cultural Week pamphlet does not mention this transaction but instead claims that 'The Fon Nseh presented the Germans with four bags of salt and one hundred calabashes of honey which he produced by means of witchcraft' (Nseh Week Council, 1977).
11. The word for love in Lamnso – [*kong*] – can be glossed in several ways, one of which means respect for a ruler or superior. Firewood and food are among the items of tribute traditionally owed by village chiefdoms to the Fon Nso.
12. Most of the following historical material was obtained from Chilver and Kaberry (1960) and Phyllis Kaberry's unpublished field notes from 1945-63 which were generously made available to me by Mrs Chilver. The remainder was collected during 1979–81, when I lived both in Kumbo and in Nseh for extended periods of time.
13. The distinction between control over resources by virtue of control over people as opposed to direct control over resources themselves is a familiar one in African customary legal systems. The distinction is outlined in detail in Gluckman (1965). In the 1970s the Fon Nseh directed Nseh lineage heads not to lend out land any longer to people from Kumbo. One lineage head who did so anyway was 'destooled' (removed from office) and fined twelve goats, twelve fowl, and twelve calabashes of palm wine.
14. Williams (1977: 115–19). The meaning depends importantly also on the configuration of the relationship of symbols to each other within varying interpretations of history, or, as Rabinow (1975) argues, 'Meaning is not found on the cultural level alone but in the partial and imperfect relation of symbols to the particular historical conditions in which they are situated.'
15. For an excellent analysis of power, legitimacy and moral order in the Grassfields see Rowlands (1987b).
16. See Chilver (forthcoming) for an insightful analysis of Nso religious beliefs.
17. The population of Nso went from 50,000 in 1953 to 105,000 by the mid-1960s to approximately 200,000 today. By the mid-1960s people from Nso proper had begun to move into the sub-chiefdoms and to farm in the Ndop plain, to the south-east. Lineage heads in the past had considerable control over their dependants, including arranging the marriages of the women of their lineage and the inheritance of all the material wealth of their male dependants, from which they derived their political power. See Chilver and Kaberry (1967) for population statistics. See Kaberry (1952) and Goheen (1984) for the relation of political power to control over dependants. The fact that rights in people rather than rights in territory or property formed the basis of power and wealth in precolonial Africa is common knowledge; see especially Goody (1976, 1979) and Rey (1975).
18. Although most landlords will deny that *they* charge anything beyond the traditional calabash of palm wine and a fowl for land use, they all know that others do. Those who do admit taking cash for access to farm land justify the practice in several ways. They point to the price the government has set on land in and around villages. They point to the practice of government officials, who demand a 'dash' for allocation of national land (all land that was deemed to be 'unoccupied' when the 1974 land ordinances came into effect). They say that formerly their dependants were farming the land to get enough food to eat but that now they are also farming for the market the lineage heads feel they should get a cut of the profit. And the lineage heads claim that the money they charge is compensation for handling the increasing number of land conflicts that are brought to them for adjudication.
19. It is usually although not necessarily true that population pressure in rural areas increases restrictions on access to land in African descent groups, but the development of relationships to the land in conditions of rural crowding is not always a simple, one-way process. See Shipton (1984).
20. I have argued previously that an understanding of the internal dynamics of Nso history is essential to an understanding of current relationships between Nseh and Nso. See Fjellman and Goheen (1984).
21. The various ways in which the self is conceptualised have been a subject of much interest and debate in recent literature. Several studies have sought to place more emphasis on the individual in analyses of those societies where previous scholarship had failed to do so. McHugh (1989) especially has argued that much previous scholarship has stressed societal and relational aspects leading to the exclusion of an autonomous self or self-awareness of individuals as effective actors. Others have dealt with cross-cultural variation in concepts of the self (Shweder and LeVine, 1984; Shweder and Bourne, 1984; Geertz, 1984; Errington and Gewertz, 1988). When I talk about reproducing individual rather than social identities I am not talking about concepts of the self or ignoring the fact that all identities are in some sense both individual and social. What I am arguing here is something quite different about social structure in Nso – and it is commonplace in many African chiefdoms where lineages play important roles in centralised government – namely, that for title-holders it is the office, and not the individual who holds it, which carries political, religious and economic significance. See Rowlands (1987a: 7): 'Many West African societies [are concerned

with] the jural definition of status. Here, persons are invested with offices which may be endowed with rights to wealth, knowledge and property. Kinship roles are defined as certain kinds of inheritable estates separate from the persons who hold them. This yields a hierarchy of positions rather than persons, based on the inheritance of offices (and regalia)....' It is perhaps of interest to note that the Western idea of the individual or self is unique, as will become germane later in this article. Here I quote Geertz (1984: 126): 'The Western conception of the person as a bounded, unique, more or less integrated motivational and cognitive universe, a dynamic center of awareness, emotion, judgment and action organized into a distinctive whole and set contrastively both against other individuals and against its social and natural background is … a rather peculiar idea in the context of the world's cultures.'

[22] This is a common African pattern within the modern state which is most pronounced among men in bureaucratic jobs who have moved to the cities. See Rowlands and Warnier (1988: 130): ' … urban dwellers earning a salary are compelled to house and feed young relatives from the village who come to town to attend school and to take idvantage of city life. Members of the urban elite are also expected to put their positions in the State apparatus or in the party to good use, to provide their villages with roads, a school, a dispensary, etc … and their kin with salaried jobs.'

[23] Den Ouden (1987) makes a similar point about the distinctions drawn between 'traditional' and 'modern' identity in the Bamileke chiefdoms in the neighbouring Ouest Province.

[24] Berry (1989) argues that this is the case for Africa in general, noting that, after independence in most African countries, 'access to the State became a precondition for doing business successfully'; this created a proliferation of channels and strategies for access to the state, along with conflict and contradictory practices regarding land acquisition.

[25] Access to the state is viewed by the majority of authors writing on related topics as perhaps the most critical mechanism for acquiring personal wealth and advancement in African countries today. See especially Hart (1982), Jua (1988), Kennedy (1988), Lubeck (1987), Nafziger (1988) and Berry (1989).

[26] Bourdieu (1977: 79) makes an argument regarding the conscious and unconscious production and reproduction of objective meaning, claiming that 'It is because subjects do not strictly speaking know what they are doing that what they do has more meaning than they know.'

References

Althusser, L., and Balibar, C. 1970. *Reading Capital*, trans. B. Brewster. London: Verso.

Berry, Sara 1988. 'Concentration without privatization? Some consequences of changing patterns of rural land control in Africa', in R. Downs and S. Reyna (eds.), *Land and Society in Africa*, pp. 53-75. Durham, N. H.: University of New England Press.

——. 1989. 'Social institutions and access to resources' *Africa* 59 (1), 41-55

Bourdieu, Pierre. 1977. *Outline of a Theory of Practice*. Cambridge: Cambridge University Press.

Cameroon, United Republic of. 1974. *State Lands Ordinances*. Yaounde: United Republic of Cameroon.

Chilver, Elizabeth M. 1961. 'Nineteenth century trade in the Bamenda Grassfields', *Afrika und Übersee* XLV, 233–57.

——. Forthcoming. 'Thaumaturgy in contemporary religion: the case of Nso in mid-century', *Journal of Religion in Africa*.

Chilver, E. M., and Kaberry, P. M. 1960. 'From tribute to tax in a Tikar chiefdom', *Africa* 30 (1), 119.

——. 1967. *Traditional Bamenda: the history and ethnography of the Bamenda Grassfields*. Buea: Ministry of Primary Education and Social Welfare.

Comaroff, Jean 1985. *Body of Power, Spirit of Resistance*. Chicago: University of Chicago Press.

Delancey, Mark 1989. *Cameroon*. Boulder, Colo.: Westview Press.

Den Ouden, J. H. B. 1987. 'In search of personal mobility: interpersonal relations in two Bamileke chiefdoms', *Africa* 57 (1), 3–28.

Errington, F., and Gewertz, D. 1988. *Cultural Alternatives and a Feminist Anthropology*. Cambridge: Cambridge University Press.

Fjellman, Stephen M. 1984. 'What Ramanujan didn't say: sociology and the discourse of order', *Current Perspectives in Social Theory* 5, 101–19.

Fjellman, S. M., and Goheen, M. 1984. 'A prince by any other name: politics and identity in the Cameroon highlands', *American Ethnologist* 11 (3), 473–86.

Friedman, Jonathan 1974. 'Marxism, structuralism and vulgar materialism', *Man* 9 (3), 444–9.

Geertz, C. 1984. 'From the native's point of view', in R. A. Shweder and R. A. LeVine (eds), *Culture Theory*. Cambridge: Cambridge University Press.

Gluckman, Max. 1965. *The Ideas in Barotse Jurisprudence*. New Haven, Conn.: Yale University Press.

Godelier, M. 1978. 'Infrastructure, society and history', *Current Anthropology* 19 (4), 763–71.

Goheen, M. 1984. 'Ideology and Political Symbols: the commoditization of land, labor and symbolic capital in Nso, Cameroon', Ph.D. dissertation, Harvard University.

——. 1988. 'Land accumulation and local control: the negotiation of symbols and power in Nso, Cameroon', in R. Downs and S. Reyna (eds), *Land and Society in Africa*, pp. 280–308. Durham, N. H.: University of New England Press.

——. 1991. 'Men own the fields, women own the crops: gender and accumulation in Nso', in P. Geschiere and P. Konings (eds), *Modes of Accumulation in Cameroon*. Leiden: University of Leiden.

Goody, Jack. 1962. *Death, Property and the Ancestors: a study of the mortuary customs of the LoDagaa of West Africa*. Stanford, Cal.: Stanford University Press.

——. 1976. *Production and Reproduction*. Cambridge: Cambridge University Press.

——. 1979. *Technology, Tradition and the State in Africa*. Cambridge: Cambridge University Press.

Hart, Keith. 1982. *The Political Economy of West African Agriculture*. Cambridge: Cambridge University Press.

Jeffreys, M. D. W. 1962. 'The date of the Bamun-Banso war', *Man* 62 (May), 70-1.

Jua, N. 1988. 'The Petty Bourgeoisie and the Politics of Social Justice in Cameroon', paper presented at the Conference on the Political Economy of Cameroon, Leiden, Netherlands, June.

Kaberry, P. M. n.d. Unpublished field notes, 1945–63.

——. 1950. 'Land tenure among the Nsaw of the British Cameroons', *Africa* 20 (4), 307–23.

——. 1952. *Women of the Grassfields*. London: HMSO.

——. 1959a. 'Nsaw political conceptions', *Man* 59 (August) 138–9.

——. 1959b. 'Traditional politics in Nsaw', *Africa* 29 (4), 366–83.

——. 1960. 'Some problems of land tenure in Nsaw, Southern Cameroons', *Journal of African Administration*, 12 (1), 21-8.

Kennedy, P. 1988. *African Capitalism: the struggle for ascendancy*. Cambridge: Cambridge University Press.

Lubeck, P. M. 1987. *The African Bourgeoisie*. Boulder, Colo.: Lynne Rienner.

MacPherson, C. B. 1962. *The Political Theory of Possessive Individualism: Hobbes to Locke*. London: Oxford University Press.

McHugh, E. 1989. 'Concepts of the person among the Gurungo of Nepal', *American Ethnologist*, 16 (1), 75–86.

Mines, M. 1988. 'Conceptualizing the person', *American Anthropologist* 90 (3), 568–79.

Mzeka, Paul. 1980. *The Core Symbols of Nso*. Agawam, Mass.: Jerome Radin.

Nafziger, E. W. 1988. *Inequality in Africa*. Cambridge: Cambridge University Press.

Nkwi, P., and Warnier, J. P. 1982. *Elements for a History of the Western Grassfields*. Yaounde: University of Yaounde Press.

Nseh Week Council. 1977. 'Nseh Cultural Week', mimeo. Nseh: Nseh Week Council.

Rabinow, P. 1975. *Symbolic Domination*. Chicago: University of Chicago Press.

Rey, P. P. 1975. 'The lineage mode of production', *Critique of Anthropology*, 3, 102–13.

Rowlands, M. J. 1979. 'Local and long-distance trade and incipient state formation on the Bamenda plateau in the late nineteenth century', *Paideuma* 25, 1-20.

——. 1987a. 'Centre and periphery: review of a concept', in M. Rowlands, M. Larsen and K. Kristiansen (eds), *Centre and Periphery in the Ancient World*, pp. 1–11. Cambridge: Cambridge University Press.

——. 1987b. 'Power and moral order in precolonial west central Africa', in E. M. Blumfiel and T. M. Earle (eds), *Specialization, Exchange and Complex Societies*, pp. 52–63. Cambridge: Cambridge University Press.

Rowlands, M. J., and Warnier, J. P. 1988. 'Sorcery, power and the modern state in Cameroon', *Man* 23 (1), 118–32.

Sahlins, M. 1981. *Historical Metaphors and Mythical Realities: structure in the early history of the Sandwich Islands kingdom*. Ann Arbor, Mich.: University of Michigan Press.

Scott, W., and M. Mahaffey (Goheen). 1980. *Executive Summary: marketing in the Northwest Province*, United Republic of Cameroon. Yaoundé: USAID.

Shipton, Parker. 1984. 'Strips and patches: a demographic dimension in some African land-holding and political systems', *Man* (n.s.) 19 (4), 613–34.

Shweder, R. A., and Bourne, E. J. 1984. 'Does the concept of the person vary cross-culturally?', in R. A. Shweder and R. A. LeVine (eds), *Culture Theory: essays on mind, self and emotion*. Cambridge: Cambridge University Press.

Shweder, R. A., and LeVine, R. A. (eds), 1984. *Culture Theory: essays on mind, self and emotion*. Cambridge: Cambridge University Press.

Williams, Raymond. 1977. *Marxism and Literature*. London: Oxford University Press.

JOHN HAMER
Commensality, Process & the Moral Order

Reference
Africa, vol. 64, no. 1, 1994, pp. 126–44

In this article I wish to examine how self-control and sharing in the exercise of socio-political power is connected with eating practices and ideological symbols in the everyday living of an Ethiopian people. It is necessary to begin with the term 'commensal', which, according to Webster, refers to people eating together and/or in a biological sense, organisms living together, sharing the same resources so that they may be 'benefited by the association' (1931: 448). So I wish to discuss how the sharing of food by persons in authority, in real life and as expressed in folk tales, consists of a metaphor for the acceptable distribution of power and order among the Sadāma of southwest Ethiopia.[1] The purpose is to suggest an analogy between these processes and a possible solution to the problem of ethnic diversity in African states.

Theoretical background

It is ritual, its connection with sacrifice, the distribution of food, and the metaphorical implications of these acts for the Sadāma people that will be examined in this article. It is my contention that these acts have to do with what Sahlins (1988: 42–3) has called a 'cultural code'. This code, or shared consciousness, is always threatened by the conflicting interpretations of people who come together to resolve the exigencies of everyday existence. For the Sadāma this occurs in historical events which lead them to re-examine their code in what constitutes '… a tactical interplay of different values and interests in specific pragmatic circumstances' (ibid.: 43). Sahlins considers this process in terms of the coming together of different cultures, but there is no reason why it should not apply to the conflicts arising out of ordinary daily events which cause people to debate the way in which the ambiguous attributes of a code must be interpreted to fit the continuously changing situation.

Thus people have accepted codes to which they commit their sentiments with the potential for creating an idealised sense of social cohesiveness. The latter, however, always remains a potential because of the inevitable conflicting interpretations of the code. In African societies in general, and among the Sadāma in particular, the ideal of cohesiveness is expressed through the rituals associated with consensual debate. That is, the disputes of everyday existence and crises in institutional structure bring people together with conflicting interpretations of the code which in the end must be consensually resolved. It is this historically continuous process of coming together to resolve conflicting interpretations that gives a society moral order. The symbolic representations often, although not invariably, involve rules and practices about commensality, which for the overall process of interpretative debate and consensus constitute a metaphor. It is a process generally lacking at the level of the nation state in modern African societies.

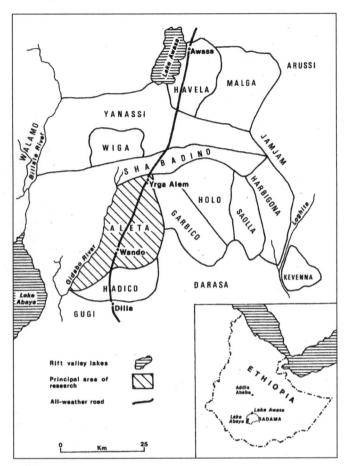

Figure 1 The Sadāma.

Who are the Sadāma?

The Sadāma are one of the Highland Cushitic-speaking peoples, numbering approximately 15 million according to the 1984 census (Hudson, 1976 Office of the Population and Housing Commission, 1984: 28). They have a subsistence production system based on the cultivation of *ensete ventricosum* and the herding of cattle, the two existing in a symbiotic relationship (Hamer, 1987: 14–19). The food staple *ensete* is referred to as the 'false banana tree' because the fruit is non-edible. And indeed it is a separate genus within the musa family, differing from the ordinary banana plant in terms of the pseudo-stem, seed, embryo, and chromosome number of the fruit (Bezuneh, 1972: 9, 12). It takes the plant three to six years to build up a sufficient store of carbohydrates to be utilised as food. During that time it requires large amounts of manure or it will exhaust the soil. Despite this disadvantage *ensete* will support a greater density of population than cereal grains, has high caloric yield per land unit, and is far more drought-resistant (Smeds, 1955: 38; Olmstead, 1974: 153). In addition to subsistence production in some parts of Sidamoland cash income is generated through the production of coffee.

The people are organised into patrilineages (*boselo*) that are subsumed by more inclusive patri-clans (*gurrī*) and integrated by cross-cutting classes of a generational class system, called the *lua* (Hamer, 1987; 31–9, 99–104).[2] It is the elders of these descent groups, who reach their position by promotion in the generational class system, who have the real authority in Sidamoland, settling disputes of everyday life, making policy rules about production, assisting the central government in collecting taxes, and performing the rituals that negotiate the changing meanings of the cultural code. Indeed, they are the ones closest to the influential dead elders who, through dreams, remind the living of their obligations to that code. And, as is not uncommon in societies of this nature, there is a group of specialist mediators who are leaders of the major clans (*mote*), the generational classes (*gaden*), and a few esteemed old men who have survived two cycles of the generational class system (*wōma*). In effect this is a social system which I have elsewhere characterised as a gerontocracy (Hamer, 1970).[3]

The charter for thinking and practice in Sidamoland is called *halōli*. When first hearing this term in the early stages of field research I came to gloss it in English as 'truth'. Later, as the term was expressed in different contexts, it became apparent that it had a much broader interpretation as 'the true way of life' and, depending on the context, could concern honesty in giving evidence, adherence to the principle of mutuality, generosity, and the avoidance of greed (Hamer, 1987: 82–3, 99).

The mythological origins of the concept are vague. It may date back to the Creator, but the mythology surrounding that deity is principally associated with a quarrel over human mortality (ibid.: 81–2). Nevertheless, Magano, the Creator, lived for a time on earth, instructing the people in how to conduct their daily lives. Following the departure of the Creator it is believed that succeeding generations of elders developed and elaborated *halōli*, in terms of defining truth, mutuality, and generosity. It is held that the concept was clearer and more closely adhered to in the past. And since the elders are the 'keepers' of *halōli* it follows that the dead elders are closer to the ideal condition of the concept than the living. Consequently, the former are in a position to use dreams to inform the living elders of deviations from the 'true way'. Thus the Sadāma themselves came to recognise *halōli* as a concept which was continuously unfolding under the challenge of changing conditions, which required reinterpretations by the elders leading to new forms of consensus.

Halōli has some resemblance to other African cultural codes, such as the *pulaaku* of the Fulani and the *mutumin kirkii* of the Hausa in West Africa. *Laawal pulauku* is broadly glossed as the 'Fulani way', which refers specifically to circumspection, technical virtue, and 'correct conduct' in personal relations (Stenning, 1959: 55–60). Technical virtue connotes consistency of commitment and skill in the care of cattle, the basic source of subsistence for this pastoral people. The ideal in personal behaviour is an endogamous marriage, preferably parallel or cross-cousin marriage, which establishes a linkage of co-operation between household and kin in the maintenance of the family herd (ibid.: 56–7). Marriage between close kin is considered a way of preserving 'moral purity', a means of distinguishing Fulani from other ethnic groups. The guardian of this moral code is the *moudo laawal pulaaku*, the senior member of a patrilineage, who is a ceremonial leader, presiding at youth initiations and marriages, as well as judge who can banish individuals deviating from the 'Fulani way'. To have flouted the code such stigmatised persons are considered mentally unbalanced or physically ill, hence indicating that moral attributes are to be associated with bodily organs. They can be readmitted to society only upon repentance, following a period of banishment in the bush.

Among the Hausa the term *kirkii* refers to kindness mixed with generosity, and *mutumci* is showing respect for others (Barkow, 1974: 5-7). These traits are basic to how the people define moral character (Kirk-Greene, 1974: 2-3). Thus *mutumin gaskiya* is the ideal 'man of truth' who is open and forthright, acts in a just manner, shows patience, is respectful of and generous to others (ibid.: 412). Such a person is also known for his faithfulness to Islam and attendance to religious duties. Unlike the *halōli* of the Sadāma, however, in which argument and debate are encouraged to determine specific applications, controversy and the possible occurrence of anger are discouraged in the interpretation of Hausa moral principles. Rather than being open to debate and sanction by councils of elders, the Hausa code is enforced indirectly through gossip and accusations of witchcraft. Nor are the moral principles, as among the Sadāma, believed similarly appropriate for all Hausa, but are considered more applicable to high-status men of wealth than to those of low status (Barkow, 1974: 11-12). Men in the highest positions of wealth and power are even exempt from evaluation for *mutumci* and *kirkii*. Nevertheless, like the Sadāma, the Hausa consider that wealth connected with generous redistribution is estimable, but, when combined with greed, can bring only low esteem.

There are similarities between several of the principles of these cultural codes, as well as divergences in meaning, methods of interpretation and the sanctioning of performance. Variation in meaning relates to the production systems and social structures of these three peoples. The Sadāma are extensive horticulturalists whose cultivation of *ensete*, until recently, has entailed movement across clan boundaries to expand garden and pasture land (Hamer, 1986). The generational class system eases this movement because the elders belong to classes which cross-cut clan boundaries and are responsible for the allocation of unoccupied land. Since *halōli* is applicable to all, and the elders are the guardians of this code, they are always in a position to interpret its implementation in disputes over land and clan affiliation, that inevitably arise out of these movements. Thus *Halōli* is always in the process of becoming, in which specific meanings must be established by consensual agreement. This is different from the 'Fulani way', which must be interpreted by a single arbiter when sanctioning nonconformists. The Fulani are pastoralists seeking to retain resources within lineage groups which pride themselves on their purity and superiority. Hausa are, in general, intensive horticulturalists and traders with a hierarchical social structure. Their code emphasises many of the virtues espoused by the Sadāma, but related to the ideals of individual character, rather than equally applicable to all under varying circumstances which must be interpreted by gerontocratic consensus. Given the stress on the individual character attributes of *mutumin kirkii*, without an institutionalised body for interpreting application to specific individuals, the only sanctions are informal gossip and witchcraft.

Socialisation of the code

Fundamental to *halōli* is the idea that self-worth is based upon wealth and power, which ironically can be obtained only through disciplined self-restraint and generous redistribution of food and material rewards to others. Thus the wealth and authority accruing to elders are based on the service and deference provided by the youth. But labour service is forthcoming from the latter as a result of the elders generously providing patrimony and bridewealth along with patient guidance and training (Hamer, 1987: 47–8). Thus fathers train sons to plant gardens and herd cattle. They seek to instil in them the principle of *agāino*, which implies the three attributes of planning, persistence and knowledge, all of which are directed toward attaining wealth and authority in elderhood, the measure of a man's true self-worth (Hamer, 1978: 48–9). There is even the encouragement of rivalry among siblings, in that parents pick favourite children on the basis of obedience and faithfulness in serving their elders These children are rewarded with extra food and praise. Nevertheless, at the same time that they are taught to excel over others there is a counter-emphasis on self-control and circumspection in the pursuit of personal gain. The technique involves an adult or older sibling offering a child a desirable object, or a food titbit, or suggesting an act of naughty behaviour. Then the person who has encouraged the act will withdraw the proffered item and/or respond punitively to the greed or misbehaviour of the youngster. So in this fashion a child soon learns circumspect self-control in interacting with others.

The balance of acquisitiveness and self-aggrandisement with sharing, avoidance of greed, generosity, and restraint, which for centuries has been the means by which elders appropriate surplus labour and production from the youth, has never been perfect. The competitiveness and chicanery of the youthful heroes in the clan origin myths, the rivalry between generational classes, and the historical struggle to oust others in obtaining land show the imperfections of the articulation between self-interest and the social affiliation ideals of *halōli*. Nevertheless, the symbolic representation of the latter principles in the oral literature of the people and the continuous reinterpretation of *halōli* by the elders in negotiating consensus help to overcome, or at least control, the negative aspects of greed and exploitation in the course of everyday existence.

The oral literature lends drama to the mundane admonishments of the socialisation process. Children's tales, known as *māto*, are usually told around the fire as the mother prepares the evening meal. The adventures of ordinary people, sometimes transformed into mythical cannibals or other villainous forms, invariably bring mixed responses of laughter, horror, and surprise, indicating the provocative stimulation of thought about the moral issues involved. Further, there are adult tales, which, unlike the children's, always end with specific moral dicta. These are told whenever adults gather for coffee and conversation as well as at critical points in making policy and settling disputes. *Tāugi*, as such stories are called, relieve the tension of partisan discussion and bring to the attention of all concerned transcending moral norms that have been lost in often acrimonious debate.

An examination of seventy-five of these oral narratives, collected in the mid-1960s, shows that thirty-five (47 per cent) contain themes concerning the importance of rules and restraint, generosity, avoidance of greed, and truth.[4] In terms of frequency it is clear that the emphasis is on creating an image of acceptable behaviour and the avoidance of avarice.

Rules and restraint themes are typically portrayed by showing conformity bringing rewards, nonconformity leading to disaster, and failure to be circumspect in evaluating a situation having nasty consequences. Typical of the rules and restraint theme is the *māto Ginānte Aināno* (Jealous Co-wife) in which a jealous stepmother kills her husband's favourite daughter. The husband goes on a pilgrimage to persuade the Creator to restore the life of his daughter. On the way he asks directions from two groups of children and a woman, all engaged in gardening and herding. They test him to see whether he accepts the correct attitudes for co-operative work, the appropriate division of labour, and proper use of resources. Thus he is told by the first group of children to disperse some grazing horses so that they run away. Instead he insists that they collect the horses and keep watch over their grazing. This correct adherence to the rules causes the children to give him the directions to the Creator's abode. Next he meets a woman weeding a spice garden, and she asks him to help her pull up the plants. But the man follows the correct practice of carefully separating the weeds from the herbs. Later, after she has sent him on his way, he meets some children who request him to help them chase and scatter their goats. He admonishes them that this is wrong, helps them to collect the goats, and then instructs them to watch the animals carefully to see that they avoid injury and stay out of the gardens. After meeting this test of moral judgement the children tell him that he is very near the Creator's household, but he must be careful not to become angry with the latter's stubborn mule, fierce dog, and shrewish wife. Further, he should not smoke the Creator's pipe or eat his food when requested to do so by the wife. And as a result of these instructions and his show of restraint the Creator receives him graciously, restoring his daughter to life and providing him with three additional children.

The jealous co-wife then decides to murder her own daughter and see if she can add to her household by following the same procedure. In fact she does the opposite of what is considered correct by following the false instruction of the children and the old woman gardener. So in the end she is punished by the Creator, who arranges for her to be devoured by a hyena and a leopard.

The numerous tales depicting the dangers of greed are well illustrated by Tako, a son who refuses to work for his mother. By contrast the seven sons of the latter's co-wife work hard at expanding their gardens and herds. The lazy half-brother devises schemes to cheat others out of their wealth, including his half-brothers. He concocts a dubious plan for gaining wealth which lures the unsuspecting half-brothers to their death. Then Tako acquires their gardens and cattle, but he eats so much of the fruits of their labour that he shortly dies of gluttony.

The theme of generosity comes to the fore in a mother-and-son story in which the former becomes upset with a son who gives some of their scarce food supply to wild animals. Since these are not domesticates they are considered to be totally outside the boundary of household dependants. But in the end the animals respond to the generosity of the son by bringing him and his mother great wealth.

Then there is the tale of the son of a courageous elder who aspires to the fame of his father. Before he succeeds in the brave act of killing a lion with his spear he commits several foolish and cowardly acts. So one day when he goes with his father to drink honey with other brave elders from the neighbourhood, the father asks him to tell the others what he has done that would entitle him to join this esteemed group. The son replies, 'I killed a goat while sleep was in my eyes. Then I killed a donkey, because I was so angry I didn't known what I was doing. At last I behaved like a brave man and killed the lion.' The father was pleased with his truthful admission of mistakes in judgement and restraint which led to the successful conquest of the lion, and welcomed his son to drink with the group.

There are several variations on these themes of morality, restraint, greed, generosity, and honesty (Hamer, 1990). The instruction of children by adults in the lessons of *halōli*, as to what is acceptable and unacceptable, has a specific and general reference; an application to a particular work, play, or relationship event which has broad, if ambiguous, meaning for future events of everyday life. In like manner the metaphors and symbolic, emotional markers of oral literature dramatically portray to both children and adults the general outline of what should constitute worthy social behaviour in Sidāmoland. But how may the necessary specific application of these broad principles be applied to the changing events of ordinary living? One way in which *halōli* is continually at risk and subject to reinterpretation is in the procedural debates of elders' councils.

Elders' councils

Despite the importance of the aforementioned leaders as sanctified mediators to whom the people are often devoted and whose assistance in settling disputes and performing rituals of harmony are frequently in demand, they are always subject to the controls of the collective will of the elders' councils (*sōngo*). These councils exist at the hamlet (*kāča*) and neighbourhood (*olau*) as well as the lineage (*boselo*) and clan (*gurrī*) levels of organisation. As groups for mediating and restoring peace between disputants they deal with different complexities of conflict and policy, with the clan *sōngo* constituting an appeal body from decisions of the other councils (Hamer, 1987: 112–28; 1972: 232–47).

At all levels the elders, by hearing evidence, seek to determine correct procedures, assess rightness or wrongness in a dispute, negotiate settlements, and impose sanctions. The procedure is always one of cajoling, encouraging, and scolding, in a process of seeking out consensus or getting recalcitrant disputants to accept a compromise that will help to reconcile a previously broken relationship. Sanctions involving fines, ostracism, or cursing are always imposed with negotiation in mind so that a disputant or a person violating council policy can recant, pay a token fine, and have a curse or ostracism removed. Acceptance and even eagerness to negotiate sanctions is not based simply on respect for the elders, but the continuous haranguing and social pressure of the latter lead obstinate people to believe that acceptance of a judgement and a plea for a forgiveness penalty is much preferable to the wrath of the council. Thus (and this is important) those who disagree with or have knowingly committed a deed that constitutes an affront to the elders' opinions regarding the principles of *halōli* are led to believe that acceptance of the elders' decision is preferable to the social disadvantages of further dissent. Throughout the settlement process there is always the element of a transaction, but one which must be negotiated within the limits of a compromise which tends to favour the elders as keepers of *halōli* (Hamer, 1980: 89-91).

In other papers I have dealt with the substance and procedures of policy and dispute settlement (1972: 232-47; 1980: 89-109; 1987: 112-28). Here the focus is on the rituals and symbols of food distribution pertaining to *halōli*. As will be shown, the symbolic representations associated with rites of unity and the distribution and sharing of food are more than simply internalised as a sense of collective consciousness; instead they constitute a process supporting continuous negotiation for determining what is consensually correct. It is the unfolding of this process among the Sadāma that provides a clue to how the African state in general might be restructured to become a more effective consensual society entity.

Ritual and food distribution as process

To the anthropologist, as an outsider, one of the earliest and most important impressions of the people is the ubiquitous presentation of food and discussion about its serving, about who should receive it, and about the correct adherence to precedent. How is one to interpret the pervasive concern with these matters? A short period of observation and questioning leads to the realisation that the production of food, especially *ensete*, corn meal, butter and milk, and its distribution to others are a measure of personal and community wealth, hence a way of indicating individual and collective worth. Moreover, the symbolic representations in the distribution process reinforce the importance of rules and restraint, the avoidance of greed and the privileging of generosity, so important to the code of *halōli*. Further, distribution within the context of the *sōngo* provides a process for symbolising the procedures for dealing with the ambiguities of unprecedented events and the means of representing the boundaries of the application of *halōli*.

The production of *ensete* and its symbiotic relation to cattle herding is of considerable historical depth, as is indicated in the mythology of the founding fathers. For in the original legend the founder of one of the two principal congeries of clans came into present-day Sidamoland from the south, searching for ideal soil fertility. The founder of the other large grouping of clans came from the same direction, but lagged behind, seeking optimum grazing conditions for his large herds. More prosaic old men, in discussing the origins of the emphasis on cultivating *ensete*, suggest that it was a cultigen natural to the environment, cultivated by people the Sadāma found on their arrival. The more poetic, however, claim that *ensete* was originally found growing out of a cow's horn. In any event there is a clear connection in legend between the development of a production system based upon a symbiotic relation between the plant and cattle. To maintain food production from these two sources requires intense co-operation and sharing between men, women, and children. Men and older boys must clear the land and plant the *ensete* seedlings annually, women must daily see that the cattle kraals are cleared of dung and that it is placed around the growing plants, and young children of both sexes herd cattle and assist their mothers in food preparation. At the apex of this system are the old men who are the keepers of *halōli*, the makers of policy, the settlers of disputes, and the preservers of the moral well-being of the community. As a consequence it is not surprising that proper forms of preparation and food sharing, elaborated into a system of rules, at the periodic meetings of these authorities become emblematic of how people should work and share together in the production system that sustains life.

To understand the moral significance of food for the ritual of council procedures it is essential to realise that presenting or withholding it is a sign of acceptance or rejection within the social order. Acceptance in a most poignant form is to be seen in the way in which people vie with one another to feed famous mediators or old men, in order to receive their blessing. The eagerness to pay a fine of persons who have offended a council is another indication of the importance of acceptance. Invariably there will be supplication for a lighter penalty than the onerous initial demand for a sacrificial animal to be fed to the elders.[5] The importance of the fine to the commensal enjoyment of the elders is as a signal that disruption of the social order has been repaired and the offender is once again a legitimate community member.

Avoidance of food sharing is one indication of the social distinction between cultivators (*wallabīčo*) and artisans such as potters (*hadīčo*), ironworkers (*tunfīča*), and leather workers (*hawāčo*). The latter provide essential services but are considered of less social worth than the cultivators who are exclusively producers of food (Hamer, 1987: 55–60).

Hence at one meeting of a clan council a member of the host neighbourhood (*olau*) came forward and claimed he had been insulted by another who had called him an *hawāčo*. Though it was considered by several an inappropriate time to take up such a matter, other elders considered it important, since they had already eaten food provided by the neighbourhood. If they had eaten food contributed by an 'impure' leather worker a planned sacrifice could not be performed. At this juncture the alleged name-caller admitted he had argued with the complainant but said that he had never had even the intention of calling him an *hawāčo*. The complainant being satisfied, the elders no longer felt threatened and the ritual could proceed.

The ultimate sanction of rejection, represented by withdrawal of commensal privileges, is a form of ostracism called *sīra*. It is reserved for the most recalcitrant offenders, those refusing to obey, or showing contempt for, the elders. The offender is placed beyond the social pale in that no one will share food with him or provide labour assistance, even avoiding his household altogether.

An interesting example of ostracism, from the author's experience, involved four elders sanctioned by the clan *sōngo*. This action was later to cause a dilemma for persons attending a mourning ceremony for a dead elder. Like other household heads they had brought food prepared by their wives to serve to the mourners. Now it is considered a great insult not to eat food brought by a household head to such rites, but it is also wrong to eat with or take food proffered by a formally ostracised person. At a mourning ritual it is tantamount to defaming the link between the legitimate food providers and the honoured. As a consequence some adhered to the hospitality rule and others shunned the sanctioned four. So commensal relations became linked to social controversy and there followed so much gossip and acrimony, directed at those who had eaten with the sanctioned four, that the latter appealed to the neighbourhood council. They argued that *sīra* had been improperly imposed by the clan elders, as the latter had met and proclaimed it in front of the house of a potter (*hadīčo*), a member of an impure artisan group. To have imposed so severe a penalty, placing persons beyond the pale of mutuality in sharing food and labour in a place of impurity and avoidance of food exchange, the neighbourhood council agreed, was clearly incorrect procedure. This decision resolved the dilemma, ending the contentious gossip and wrangling.

Food and commensality are also used in conjunction with sorcery accusations to symbolise social disorder, hence the antithesis of *halōli*. A sorcerer is invariably perceived as a person lacking in self-worth and thirsting after the esteem or wealth of others – essentially the garden produce or cattle of a more successful farmer. Hence the sign of a sorcerer is his/her presence in another's garden before dawn, an unusual cut in the tail of a cow, a dead frog or a lizard belly-up on a garden trail. The *sōngo* elders are often called upon to curse sorcerers by persons suspecting themselves to be victims.[6]

There are more subtle norms in which food and commensality become emblematic of rejection. People may, for example, joke about others as being too fond of food, as a thinly disguised suggestion that they are stingy. Thus the rule that the community must feed the elders' council becomes impractical, especially at the neighbourhood level, when it must meet frequently and on successive days. Nevertheless, when the neighbourhood elders are of different clans, members may jokingly accuse those of the hamlet (*kāča*) in which the *sōngo* is being held of '... liking food too well'. The latter are usually offended and apologetic, proffering the excuse that the *sōngo* was called too abruptly, leaving insufficient time for preparation.

A specific instance serves to illustrate how a failure of commensal obligations can be taken as a personal affront. An old man, Adani, was invited by a younger man, Bocaso, to come to his household for food and coffee after they had attended a nearby funeral.[7] In the course of participating in the events of the funeral-gathering Bocaso forgot about the earlier promise. Then later in the day, after the lineage council had met to discuss an important homicide case, food was served to all the elders. Adani, as the oldest, was by rule expected to take the first portion of food. When he refused the others were nonplussed. Upon questioning, Adani revealed the broken promise of Bocaso, which he considered a threat to his dignity as an elder. The matter was resolved when Bocaso came forward, apologised profusely, and kissed the head of Adani as a sign of respect.

Then there are the metaphorical implications of rules for sharing food within the context of the elders' councils. For the way in which food is presented and shared symbolises the order that is supposed to exist in everyday life, in accordance with the principles of *halōli*. Food must be presented in sequence by the husbands of the women who have prepared it. Therefore it is inappropriate to begin eating another person's food before finishing that of a previous donor. On one occasion, in the presence of the anthropologist, a group of elders had finished only a quarter of a bowl of *ensete* porridge before a second host came forward with another bowl. This immediately provoked a row between the first and second hosts, the former claiming that it was an insult to his wife's care and concern in the preparation of the food. Finally, the eldest man present intervened and insisted that the first bowl must be finished before the second was started.

Food must be provided at appropriate times and not at random intervals. Thus a community obliged to provide an evening meal cannot bring some food in the evening and the rest the next morning. For example, on one occasion a large pot of beer was offered to the elders at breakfast, after some had expressed surprise that it had not been served with the evening meal, as was appropriate at that particular time of year. There developed an almost acrimonious debate as to whether the beer had been proffered by the host of the household in which this particular group of elders was staying or by the host community. If the latter, the drink had been served too late at an inappropriate time and they should not drink it; if the former, it was a gift of which they could partake. Fortunately for the thirsty old men, it turned out to be part of their host's hospitality.

Rules are quite strict about the preparation of sacrificial meat. Thus at an important clan ritual it was discovered that a young man cutting up the carcass of the sacrificial bull had eaten some of the meat. Since the meat must first be presented to the elders who have made the sacrifice this inappropriate action nullified the efficacy of the ritual. In consequence the elders of the host neighbourhood were required to provide another sacrificial animal.

Rule ambiguity and *halōli*

In effect the rules of commensality involving communal authorities are a metaphor of the orderly life, representing generosity, mutuality and freedom from greed. But what of the extraordinary event when the ambiguities of *halōli* become subject to debate? In three instances the author was able to observe the process of adapting this moral order: a case of excessive generosity and rivalry for esteem, disputed interpretation of prestation rules, and a threat to the mutuality principle.

The matter of mixing generosity with prestige rivalry began at a meeting of the clan *sōngo* to settle disputes and perform a fertility sacrifice. After food and portions of the sacrificial animal had been distributed it was announced by one of the elders that members of his hamlet (*kāča*) had brought a bull to feed the visitors. Immediately one of the leading clan elders vigorously objected that it was not proper to slaughter and consume more than one animal on such a ritual occasion. It was carefully explained that the donors only wanted to show their generosity and esteem for the visiting elders. The latter, however, suspected there was more involved and demanded, in the name of *halōli*, that the donors should tell the truth. After much urging and discussion it emerged that rivalry between the three hamlets in the neighbourhood had led to a dispute.

To explain the circumstances of the rivalry it is useful to label the communities A, B, and C. It seems that at an earlier clan council, convened to settle a dispute in B, the latter had provided hospitality without any assistance from A or C. The elders of B later accused their counterparts in A and C of ignoring their obligation to feed the clan council. The matter was serious enough for a meeting of the whole neighbourhood council to be called, in the hope of effecting a settlement. Representatives of B however, refused to attend, and the elders of A and C decided the correct procedure was that, when a clan council met only to settle a dispute involving a single hamlet in the neighbourhood, the other two communities were not under an obligation to bring food. Full neighbourhood hospitality was required only when the clan was meeting to perform a sacrifice or settle a dispute affecting the whole neighbourhood. Further, since representatives from B had failed to attend this meeting of settlement, the elders sanctioned them with a fine and imposed ostracism until it was paid. Subsequently, B elders admitted their wrongdoing and paid the fine. So when the clan council agreed to meet in their neighbourhood to perform a sacrifice amity seemed to have been restored, with hamlets B and C agreeing to provide food while A would bring coffee and beer. On the day of the sacrifice the household heads from B failed to bring any food. To compensate and demonstrate a kind of one-upmanship, without consulting A and C, elders of B came the next day to feed the *sōngo* in style with a whole bull. Not to be outdone, elders of A and C brought their own animal on the third day, thus rekindling the original rivalry.

After several hours of often heated discussion the clan elders decided that A and C were wrong in their show of excessive generosity. Nevertheless, all three communities were admonished for failing to consult and coordinate their commensal obligations. To demonstrate a return to a state of harmonious cooperation, elders of B were required to contribute to the cost of the animal brought by A and C. As the course of the discussion showed, the old men recognised a dilemma between the virtues of generosity and the virtues of restraint associated with *halōli*. On the one hand it was clear that confusion had developed in the policy of distribution and timing between the three communities which should have been resolved by their respective elders. As a consequence of this failure, competition developed to see who could gain the most favour with the clan elders, which in turn would have caused the latter to break the rules of restraint concerning the slaughter of more than one animal to feed a council.[8] The council discussion and subsequent resolution were a commonsense solution to the ambiguities of the alternative principles.

The situation involving disruption of the proper order of presentation also occurred at a clan *sōngo*. As everyone was seated in a circle waiting to be served, a man stepped forward with the usual communal bowl of porridge. Suddenly he was jostled by a second man, who shouted that the first had no right to serve the food prepared by his (the second man's) wife. The first man, however, insisted that since they were both from the same hamlet it made no difference who served the food. After several minutes of heated argument which seemed on the verge of leading to blows, the elders intervened. They pointed out that even though the men resided in the same hamlet and were therefore 'relatives', the food had been produced and prepared in a single household. Therefore it was only fair to let the head of the household serve it, unless he delegated the role to another. It was a matter of broad *v.* strict interpretation of the rules, and the elders opted for the latter.

At another meeting of the same clan *sōngo* an altercation developed over the order of precedence in the serving of food and the status of the purveyors. The elders initially questioned why the neighbourhood in which a sacrifice was to take place was represented only by young men who had not yet been promoted to elderhood. But the youthful representative objected, claiming that their status should have been questioned the previous day when they arrived with the food the elders consumed that evening. Some councillors demanded an answer, and a rather raucous debate ensued. Finally, consensus was reached that they would not insist on an answer or impose a fine, but that the controversy should serve as a warning to the neighbourhood to increase the participation of the elders. This, then, was a case of conflicting rules in which the composition of the host delegation should have been questioned before partaking of their food. Nevertheless, the clan elders took the opportunity to express their concern about adherence to the attendance rules.

The threat to mutuality was a combination of communication error and failure of clan *sōngo* procedure. It began when a sacrifice was being planned in a distant neighbourhood. Elders representing the latter returned home and told the people to prepare for the feeding of fifty to eighty guests on the specified date. Much food was prepared, but shortly before the scheduled meeting and sacrifice a distinguished old man from another neighbourhood arrived with a message that the whole event had been postponed. He apparently conveyed this information to only a few and rumour did the rest. As a consequence only a few of the clan elders appeared at the scheduled time and much of the prepared food was spoiled. Meanwhile, some of the most senior clan elders set about remedying the effects of the false rumour by rescheduling the event several days later.

When at last the councillors assembled, the issue was raised immediately as to who had been responsible for the rumour. A long debate ensued about whether the messenger or the person who originally suggested cancellation was the culprit. One man suggested that all the clan elders who accepted the message were in the wrong. The failure to appear was discouraging to all those who had prepared food, threatened the respect of ordinary people for the elders, and the credibility of the clan *sōngo*. Eventually the assemblage agreed that the clan had erred, that a meeting to perform sacrificial rites could not be postponed or cancelled, and that they must apologise to the neighbourhood and beg not to be fined by the latter. It was not possible to discover how the rumour of postponement had started, but the elders had debated the issues, had overcome the inclination to scapegoat the messenger, and had proclaimed their own collective responsibility. By taking the latter approach they had supported the mutual equity aspect of *halōli*.

These rather mundane examples show how procedural rules regulating the commensal behaviour of the authorities who make policy and maintain peace constitute a metaphor for the *halōli* charter. The rules are in effect a symbolic guide to the elders in striving after the ideals of generosity, mutuality, and respect for personal worth. Further, these examples show that *halōli* is not static but a process involving reinterpretation to fit the changing events of everyday life. In this connection there is the question of what has happened to the metaphorical implications of commensality during the seventeen years of the 1974 socialist revolution. The widely established peasant associations with legislative, judicial, and police functions have reduced the elders' councils to a largely secondary role (Hamer, 1987: 230–3). Elders have come under pressure to observe the egalitarian aims of the revolution and not to discriminate in their behaviour, including eating practices, towards members of artisan groups. In practice, however, there are signs that the elders continue to follow the old practices and beliefs in regulating commensal behaviour towards artisans.[9]

But what are the boundaries of the application of these principles other than the outside force imposed by the now defunct socialist revolution? It is possible to see from examination of council meetings that there are commensal metaphors which imply the limits of *halōli*. This happens when food becomes a commodity, in situations where production and commensal sanctions can be ignored, and when *halōli* principles are used simply as a means of creating barriers between the Sadāma and other ethnic groups.

On one occasion the author was able to attend a clan *sōngo* during the election campaign of 1965, when the elders were addressed by a young Sadānčo standing for the Ethiopian parliament. There were several outside contenders who, regardless of true ethnic affiliation, were invariably stereotyped as 'Amhara'.[10] The Sidāmo candidate, in conformity with custom, used the offering of food and drink as a metaphor for gaining access to power. In effect, he suggested, the 'Amhara' would attempt to buy their votes '… with food and drink which will quickly disappear in your urine, as quickly as "Amhara" promises will vanish once they are in power'. He insisted that in reality his opponents wanted to seize their land rather than protect it as a Sadānčo would. Later questioning by the anthropologist revealed that this young man considered his character and clan affiliation more important in garnering votes than promises to upgrade schools, clinics, or communications systems, which tended to be the approach of the 'Amhara' candidates.

The Sidāmo candidate was suggesting that accepting food from non-ethnic candidates was more than a sign of agreeing to accept the authority of the latter. It involved a commoditisation of food and commensal arrangements in which personalised authority was being objectified into a system in which people, like land, could be bought and sold.[11] Thus a boundary was being created between the mutuality of *halōli* – in Sahlins' terms, 'generalised reciprocity', and the 'balanced', if not 'negative', reciprocity of outsiders (1972: 193–6).

Another way in which food and commensal relations served as a metaphor for boundary markers had to do with the circumvention of the ostracism sanction. Informants suggested a developing fear among the elders that imposing the sanction could lead an offender to accuse the former of harassment in an Ethiopian court. Though at the time no law existed against such sanctions – indeed, under the Ethiopian Code courts were supposed to be supportive of local custom – it was possible to bribe the 'Amhara' judges into imprisoning the elders.[12] Then it would take long and costly negotiations to obtain their release. And as to the suggestion that such attempts at circumventing elders' authority might lead the offender to be even more despised, it was indicated that people were more afraid of the courts and thus reluctantly accepted their verdicts.

There was also the view that the principles of *halōli* have no geographical boundaries, but apply to Sadāma regardless of position or wherever they may be. This was illustrated by the young parliamentary candidate who insisted that, if elected, his first priority would be to help his kinsmen and other Sadāma, with the general welfare of all Ethiopians a vague and distant concern. Thus even outside Sidāmoland he was first of all a Sadānčo bound by the code of *halōli* and secondly a citizen of Ethiopia, bound only by the very literal police power of the central government.

The commoditisation of commensal relationships, in comparison with personalised distribution and consumption as a metaphor for power and authority, becomes a marker for the in-group in opposition to a hostile outgroup. To break the rules of *halōli* and avoid sanctioning commensal behaviour and work assistance by appealing to a more powerful outside group is to maintain one's position in the community by force without the real acceptance of others. Nevertheless, this gives rise to social dissonance within the community, creating an ultimate threat to social control and order. An even greater threat to the national moral order is the attitude that Sidāmo well-being always takes precedence when one acquires authority at the national level. A further complication is that, if this personal commitment to *halōli* is retained, once outside the borders of Sidāmoland, the personalised controls of the elders' councils are non-existent.

Commensal behaviour is a metaphor for the acceptance or rejection of others. The presentation and sharing of food symbolise the fundamentals of *halōli* concerning restraint, generosity, truthfulness, and mutuality. These attributes acquire strong sentiments through their socialisation in children and dramatisation in the pervasive moralistic tales. As a consequence the metaphor is a part of everyday commensal activities but the focus in this article has been upon the political arena of the elders' councils with their rules for orderly commensal behaviour and ritual sacrifice. Just as the principles of *halōli* are not static, so the rules of commensality, aided by their ambiguity, must be adapted to changing events. Then the rules are always subject to debate and discussion until the elders reach a consensus, as shown in the examples involving uncertainty as to whether generosity had become an excuse for rivalry, a threat to self-worth in the presentation process, and a mistake by the elders threatening mutuality.

The limits to the effectiveness of the commensal metaphor as symbolising order and unity are evident at junctions where the Sidāmo socio-cultural system articulates with the nation state. It is a boundary of uncertainty and threatening disorder, as witnessed in the examples concerning the commoditisation of commensality, circumvention of sanctions, and giving priority to the principles of *halōli* outside the processual jurisdiction of the elders. For when the cultural code of the Sadāma is removed from the daily process of the community and from appropriate consensual debate as to its interpretation, it can be manipulated in favour of self-aggrandisement. If persons are involved in political and/or economic activities at the national level they are free to represent themselves or their constituent community solely on the basis of their personal interpretation of the moral code. There is seldom an overarching national code subject to discussion and the debate over changing events, which is accepted at both the national and local level. Even when there is a code, as in the form of Marxist–Leninist ideology in the Ethiopian state of recent years, there is no structure analogous to the elders' councils, their members representing varied interests, to discuss and interpret the ideals to fit changing historical circumstances. Under these conditions the parochial chauvinism, self-aggrandisement, and corruption that are so much a part of contemporary African states have every opportunity to develop.

Since the demise of the Marxist–Leninist government of Ethiopia in 1991 the Transitional Government has focused on dividing the country into ethnic regions, forming political parties, planning elections, and seeking retribution against officials of the previous regime.[13] There has been no attempt to develop an all-embracing set of values for a constitution that would transcend the boundaries of ethnic codes. Consequently, the first local elections have been fraught with ethnic and regional power rivalries, difficult to resolve without the precedence of a new, national, moral order.[14]

There are indeed constitutions and structural facades, in the form of parliaments without authority, in most African states. Seldom, however does provision exist for the continuous discussion, debate, and sanctioning by representatives of the general population, of what these constitutions imply for everyday policies and practices. Ironically, these one-party states seem to have fostered division rather than cohesion, because the members of a ruling party are in reality responsible only to a single leader and to their own personal ambitions of sustaining themselves in office. The latter is accomplished by interpreting the local codes to further their own ends, without the controls of either dialogue with, or the consensus of, leaders at the community level. Moreover, the widely expressed view of proponents of these states that debate would be divisive is contradicted by the Sidāmo experience, in which debate is the very process of arriving at consensual unity.

There is no accountability comparable to that of the members of the Sidāmo councils for members of African political parties. In the widespread patron-clientage system that has resulted, corruption develops because the socio-moral aspects of redistribution, based on rules and ritual, have been lost. Perhaps this is why there is so much demand throughout Africa for the establishment of multi-party systems, a '… new wind of change'.[15] The contention of candidates representing different interpretations of the ideological implications of national constitutions could stimulate grass-roots dialogue and discussion, as well as provide a more effective means of accountability. Further, competing political parties might provide the framework for on-going debate at the state level about the changing rules, procedures, and meanings of the various national codes, to the benefit of local constituencies.

Notes

Fieldwork among the Sadāma was carried out in 1964–65 and in 1973 under the auspices of the Ford Foundation, the Great Lakes Colleges Association and the Canada Council. Material on post-revolutionary events was gathered on a short visit to Ethiopia in 1984.

[1] *Sadāma* is the term people use to refer to themselves as a group, *Sadānčo* refers to the individual and *Sidāmo* is used as an adjective in this article.

[2] There are two broad groupings of these clans, referred to as the Āletā and the Yamaīčo. Among the Yamaīčo the clans are virtually autonomous, each being headed by a ritual chief and mediator of disputes known as the *mōte*. The Āletā cluster of clans have, for the historical reason of their relatively recent existence compared with the Yamaīčo, only a single *mōte*. All clans, regardless of cluster affiliation, have separate elders' councils.

[3] Elderly women, like their male counterparts, acquire prestige and authority among other women, but they do not make community policy, formally settle disputes, and participate in all community rituals. Nor are the dead women elders considered an influence on the living. Further, all women must have their cases presented before the councils of elders by male spokesmen.

[4] The tales were transcribed by the recorder in all of the major clan areas of Sidāmoland and then, with the aid of my research assistant, translated into English.

[5] Usually the elders will demand a bull, but a supplicant will plead poverty and beg them to accept a goat, sheep, or today even money as a fine.

[6] Some informants were of the opinion that sorcery was on the increase in the 60s and 70s because of the land scarcity that had become noticeable with the increase in population.

[7] The names are pseudonyms.

[8] Restraint in slaughtering cattle is important, considering the reliance on milk and butter, as well as the symbiotic relation between cattle and *ensete*, i.e. the dependence of the latter on manure from the former (Hamer, 1987: 18–19).

[9] Personal communication from Norbert Vecchiato, who did field research in Sidāmoland in the mid-1980s.

[10] Since the conquest of Emperor Menelik's armies in the 1890s all non-Sadāma, regardless of ethnic origin, have been referred to as 'Amhara'.

[11] According to time-honoured custom, land is not a commodity in Sidāmoland, but all Sadāma have usufruct rights of access, either through hereditary rights or through allocation by the elders (Hamer, 1987: 39-43).

[12] See, for example, Hamer (1987: 142-7).

[13] See especially *Africa Confidential* 32, No. 22 (1991): 7; *Friends of Ethiopia Newsletter* I, No. 4 (1992); p. 1; and the article by Paul Henze in ibid. I, No 5 (1992), pp. 2-3.

[14] See 'Special Edition on Ethiopian Elections', *Friends of Ethiopia Newsletter* (August 1992), pp. 118. This is a series of reports of the observers of *woreda* and *kebele* elections in June 1992.

[15] There are many articles and books on this issue, but a succinct account of the situation is provided by Rawnsley (1990: 25). In a recent article on the problems of the centralised state in Africa, James Wunsch has written, 'The shared values of individual obligation to community, reciprocity, social cooperation, and deference to tradition are formidable norms, and rich resources upon which social relations are built.... The success Africans have had in relating peacefully to members of other kin groups and ethnic communities suggests that such values can be used both to organise effective working rules regulating the relationships among members of differing communities' (Wunsch and Olowu, 1990: 285).

References

Barkow, J. H. 1974. 'Evolution of character and social control among the Hausa' *Ethos* 2, 111–14.

Bezuneh, T. 1972. 'Progress Report on Ensete Research Project'. Debre-Zeit Agricultural Experimental Station, College of Agriculture, Haile Selassie I University (mimeograph).

Hamer, J. 1970. 'Sidamo generational class cycles: a political gerontocracy', *Africa* 40(1), 50-70.

——. 1972. 'Dispute settlement and sanctity: an Ethiopian example', *Anthropological Quarterly* 45, 232-47.

——. 1978. 'Goals, status, and the stability of n-achievement: a small sample from southern Ethiopia', *Ethos* 6(1), 46–62.

——. 1980. 'Preference, principle, and precedent: dispute settlement and changing norms in Sidamo associations', *Ethnology* 19(1), 89–109.

——. 1982. 'Rivalry and taking kinsmen for granted: limiting factors in the development of voluntary associations', *Journal of Anthropological Research* 38(3), 303–14.

——. 1986. 'Hierarchy/equality and availability of land resources: an example from two Ensete producers', *Ethnology* 27(2), 215–28.

——. 1987. *Humane Development: participation and change among the Sadāma of Ethiopia.* Tuscaloosa, Ala.: University of Alabama Press.

——. 1990. 'Folktales as Ideology in the Production and Circulation of Wealth among the Sadāma of Ethiopia'. Unpublished manuscript.

Henze, P. 1992. 'Ethiopia in early 1992: preparing for democracy', *Friends of Ethiopia* I (5) 1–6.

Hudson, G. 1976. 'Highland East Cushitic', in M. L. Bonder (ed.), *The non-Semitic Languages of Ethiopia*, pp. 232–77. East Lansing, Mich.: Michigan State University.

Kirk-Greene, A. H. 1974. *Mutumin Kirkii: the concept of the good man in Hausa,* Bloomington, Ind.: Indiana University Press.

Office of the Population and Housing Commission. 1984. *Ethiopia 1984: Population and Housing Census Preliminary Report.* Addis Ababa: Government Printer.

Olmstead, J. 1974. 'Versatile ensete plant: its use in the Gamu highlands', *Journal of Ethiopian Studies* 12(2), 147–58.

Rawnsley, A. 1990. 'The new wind of change', *Manchester Guardian Weekly* 143 (12) 25.

Sahlins, M. 1972. *Stone Age Economics.* New York: Aldine.

——. 1988. 'Deserted islands of history', *Critique of Anthropology* 8(3), 41-51.

Smeds, H. 1955. 'The ensete planting culture of eastern Sidāmo, Ethiopia', *Acta Geographica* 13(4), 139.

Stenning, D. J. 1959. *Savannah Nomads: a study of the Woodaabe pastoral Fulani western Bornu Province, Northern Region, Nigeria.* London: Oxford University Press for the International African Institute.

Webster, N. 1931. *Webster's New International Dictionary of the English Language.* Springfield, Mass.: Merriam.

Wunsch, J. S., and Olowu, D. 1990. *The Failure of the Centralized State: institutions and self-governance in Africa.* Boulder, Colo.: Westview Press.

RICHARD FANTHORPE
Locating the Politics of a Sierra Leonean Chiefdom

Reference
Africa, vol. 68, no. 4, 1998 pp. 558–83

The chiefdoms of Sierra Leone were originally designed to harness 'native authorities' to British colonial rule. They were inherited by the Sierra Leone Republic, and remain key institutions of local government. The longevity of these institutions has prompted much academic analysis. For example, political scientists have drawn attention to the paradoxical role of Paramount Chiefs as state agents commissioned to exercise 'traditional' authority (Kilson, 1966; Barrows, 1976; Cartwright, 1978; Reno, 1995). They also reserve strong criticism for the Native Administration Scheme, introduced in legislation in 1937. The main aim of the scheme was to devolve the considerable economic and juridical powers formerly invested in Paramount Chiefs to a local assembly (Tribal Authority, later Chiefdom Council) directly representing, and funded by, local taxpayers (Kilson, 1966: 24–33; Clapham, 1976: 75–6; Barrows, 1976: 83–5). Yet little in practice was done to prevent Paramount Chiefs from continuing to collect payments for political and jural services, and appropriating tax revenue for private uses (Kilson, 1966: 53–68; Barrows, 1976: 98–142; Reno, 1995: 55–78).

It has been the avowed policy of successive governments of the Sierra Leone Republic to conserve the chiefdoms (Barrows, 1976: 98–142). All of Sierra Leone's parliamentary constituencies outside metropolitan areas follow chiefdom boundaries (Clarke, 1966). While all adult citizens are entitled to vote in parliamentary elections, many rural people remain unknown to the state except as chiefdom taxpayers and their dependants. Accordingly, government officials are reliant upon the Chiefdom Councils to supply them with the information necessary for compiling the electoral register, and parliamentary candidates are obliged to ally with local political factions in order to win votes. Furthermore, an amendment of 1972 to the Protectorate Land Ordinance of 1927 effectively left it to the Chiefdom Councils to determine the criteria of 'native' status which confer chiefdom citizenship (Tuboku-Metzger and van der Laan, 1981: 30). These developments have provided Paramount Chiefs with renewed opportunities – and power – to act as political brokers (Kilson, 1966: 219–80; Minikin, 1973: Barrows, 1976: 143–242; Reno, 1995).

The apparent inertia of successive Sierra Leone administrations towards the reform of local government has prompted scholars to voice their own moral judgements. For example, Kilson (1966) saw the chiefdoms as anachronistic barriers to political modernisation. Reno (1995), writing in more pessimistic times, claims that the post-colonial era merely saw the extension of corrupt patrimonial politics to the higher echelons of government. Noting the profound historical influence of the Atlantic trade, Reno also suggests that Paramount Chiefs are descended from a long line of local 'strongmen', for whom power was essentially a matter of securing alliances with foreign agencies (cf. Bayart, 1993). Yet this is not a view that many historians would share. A more general historical view is that the Atlantic trade fostered wide-ranging political and economic interaction in the Upper Guinea region, and that this was further facilitated by intermarriage, multilingualism and Arabic literacy. While state builders frequently had to contend with local rivals, the propensity of military coalitions to rapid and extensive formation had a regulatory effect on conflict. The most successful African rulers of the era were noted for their skill in diplomacy and jurisprudence as well as in warfare (Howard, 1972: 186–297; Lipschutz, 1973: 216; Wylie, 1977: 31–164; Abraham, 1976a, 1978: 4–41; Howard and Skinner, 1984).

Historians thus tend to mark the moral decline of Sierra Leonean politics by the imposition of colonial rule in 1896. The British created a multiplicity of small chiefdoms in order to facilitate tax collection, often dismantling large pre-colonial polities in the process (Abraham, 1976b). It has also been shown that British officials' assumption that pre-colonial chiefship was a hereditary estate, owned by 'ruling families' (or 'houses'), sometimes had little historical basis (Barrows, 1976: 80-2; Abraham, 1978: 274-80). Furthermore the early British administration was not averse to promoting men – and occasionally women – to paramount chiefship on the basis of willingness to collaborate rather than previous political status (Little, 1951: 176–9; Grace, 1975: 107–31; Wylie, 1977: 190–207; Abraham, 1978: 244–65). Such assessments have prompted the Sierra Leonean historian C. Magbaily Fyle to write a biography of Suluku, the ruler of pre-colonial Biriwa Limba (Fyle, 1979a). This explicitly celebrates Suluku's manifest economic, military and diplomatic successes as an example of the true achievements of indigenous Sierra Leonean political culture.

The colonial provenance of the chiefdoms, allied to the moralising thrust of many scholars' arguments, has tended to elide anthropological analysis of internal chiefdom politics. While anthropologists generally agree that chiefship has deep cultural roots in Sierra Leone, their analyses tend to focus on changes in the formal relationship between Paramount Chiefs and populace under colonial rule (Little, 1951: 175–215; Dorjahn, 1960; Finnegan, 1965: 14–51; Finnegan and Murray, 1970). Even then, anthropological analyses of 'traditional' politics are often open to criticism on historical grounds. For example, the argument developed by Ruth Finnegan in respect of the Limba is that their 'traditional concept' of chiefship (*hugbakaine*) stresses the personal attributes of generosity, jurisprudential oratory and social knowledge. In the latter regard, members of the populace constantly entrust personal and family news to the chief (Finnegan, 1963). In Finnegan's view, the pre-colonial Limba chief (*gbaku*) was essentially a 'big man' (Finnegan, 1965: 33). In the colonial era the title *gbaku*, and the attributes associated with it, became focused on the Paramount Chief. Yet Finnegan (1967: 12-13) observed at least one successful candidate for paramount chiefship striving to embody these attributes in an attempt to secure popular support. In a final contribution Finnegan and Murray (1970) point out that colonial administrators and local politicians alike have perpetuated a myth of unchanging Limba chiefship. In that regard, however, the 'traditional concept' of Limba chiefship begins to look like a modern construct. Its very silence on the question of power enables modern politicians to identify with their historical predecessors by emulating their putative personal qualities. To take another example, in northern Sierra Leone the concept of the chiefdom 'ruling family' passed into professional ethnography as a result of the work of the colonial administrator and Africanist scholar E. F. Sayers. It was Sayers who discovered that the principles of Manding clanship

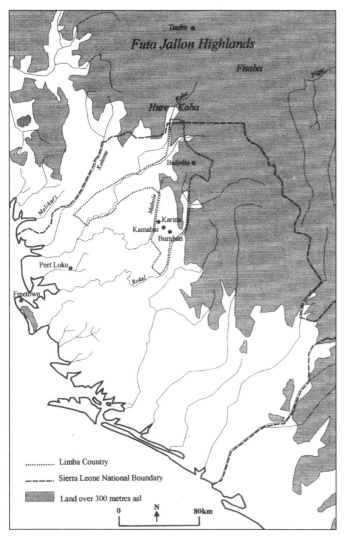

Figure 2 The Limba colonial chiefdoms. I Biriwa. 2 Safroko. 3 Mapaki (amalgamated with Temne Bombali Masabong chiefdom to form Paki Masabong chiefdom, 1949). 4 Kalantuba (amalgamated with Koranko Diansogia chiefdom to form Kalansogoia chiefdom, 1953). 5a Kasunko, b Kakiling, c Gbonkogbon, d Kayaka, e Tamiso. (5 a–e were amalgamated to form new Kasunko chiefdom, 1948–53.) 6 Warra Warra Yagalla. 7a Warra Warra Bafodia, b Kamuke (absorbed by 7a, 1940). 8 Sela. 9 Thonko. Black squares show chiefdom capitals, 1985; circles show other settlements.

Figure 1 Limba country.

are general to this area (Sayers, 1927; McCulloch, 1950: 54–65; Parsons, 1964: 125–9; Jackson, 1974). Yet in the Limba case the concept of an historic political estate consisting of ranked exogamous patriclans (Finnegan, 1965: 52–4, 147–9) tends to obscure other ethnographic evidence indicating that pre-colonial Limba polities were based upon initiation associations. Some of these were entered on a mutual basis (Hollins, 1925; Dorjahn and Tholley, 1959), others under the aegis of a ruler (Banton, 1955: 245).

In the final analysis, however, there is no reason to assume that debates about the moral authority of Paramount Chiefs, and the proper criteria of succession to political office, are confined to the realm of scholarship. In this regard at least, analysis of chiefdoms as local political arenas is long overdue. This article considers the role of historical discourse in the politics of Biriwa, a Limba chiefdom which took its name from the polity ruled by the above-mentioned

Suluku. It seeks to explain why debates over historical precedent, in many cases relating to events and personalities of the precolonial era, continue to play a central role in allocating rights in land, settlement and political representation. It is argued that historical precedent fills a lacuna created by the persistent failure of successive Sierra Leone governments to complete the extension of modern measures of citizenship (e.g. the registration of births and deaths, and written deeds and title to land) to the rural populace. The progressive localisation of social and political relations emerges here as a visibly historical process.

The Biriwa chiefdom

Limba country is located in the Northern Province of the Sierra Leone Republic. It is a rugged land, straddling the escarpment which divides the hill country of north-eastern Sierra Leone from the plains to the south and west (Fig. 1). Suluku remains a prominent figure throughout Limba country, and has featured in several historical studies (Finnegan and Murray, 1970; Howard, 1972; Lipschutz, 1973; Fyle, 1974, 1978, 1979a). He ruled from Bumban for almost forty years until his death in 1906. During this period Bumban formed a central link in trade networks connecting the Sierra Leone Colony with African states of the Futa Jallon highlands and the upper Niger plain. Suluku was at first regarded in the Colony as having authority over the whole of Limba country. In 1888, however, the British emissary Major A. M. Festing reported that Suluku was 'king of Biriwa-Limba only' – although he went on to note that his '*ipse dixit* is tantamount to law in the remaining Limbas, and has great weight both amongst the Susu and Temne tribes near to his border'.[1] A British document of 1899 confirms Suluku's status as the 'Paramount Chief of all the Biriwa Limbahs', although several of the subchiefs this allocates to him were later recognised by the British as independent Paramount Chiefs (Fyle, 1979a: 52–8).

The name 'Biriwa' was eventually attached to one of fourteen colonial chiefdoms in Limba country. Some of these were tiny, and amalgamations were later carried out under the aegis of the Native Administration Scheme (Fig. 2). Unaffected by the amalgamation process, the Biriwa chiefdom covers an area of just over 800 km² and now has a population approaching 30,000. Like much of northern Sierra Leone, it has become a relatively isolated area in which opportunities for secondary and tertiary employment are limited. The local population is now mainly engaged in small-scale farming and cattle herding. Migration to Freetown, and the Kono diamond mining district, is also a long established feature of local economic strategies (Finnegan, 1965: 123–43; Moseley, 1978).

There now follows a fairly detailed account of the complex social and political organisation of the Biriwa area. Analysis of the issues it raises is developed subsequently.

Administrative structure

In 1985 the Biriwa Chiefdom Council consisted of the Paramount Chief, the court president, two speakers, nine section chiefs and 201 village headmen. This body was formally established in 1950, when the Native Administrative Scheme was introduced to the chiefdom.[2] Under the scheme, the Tribal Authority (as it was then known) was empowered to elect the Paramount Chief and lesser officials by secret ballot. It also had control over a treasury funded by a poll tax levied on all adult males resident in the chiefdom. Yet the new arrangements conserved many elements of the earlier colonial political system they were designed to replace.

First, it was not until Suluku's death that the British authorities began to establish the constitution of the colonial chiefdom. In April 1907 District Commissioner H. C. Warren gathered local leaders together to elect the new Paramount Chief. Prior notice had been given to allow consultation, but Warren found that the sons of Suluku in Bumban had shut themselves away for several days without deciding upon a candidate. Ali, who had been appointed Regent Chief on Suluku's death the previous year, came forward as a brother of Suluku. Yet Warren found that Kalawa of Kamabai 'seems to have the greatest support amongst the big-men of the country', and duly installed him as Paramount Chief.[3] Warren's report goes on to identify Suluku and Kalawa as members of a ruling family that had been founded by Woseya 'about the middle of the last century'. Accompanied by his sons Sankelay and Bubu,

Woseya had 'claimed land from the Manko people'. Sankelay had succeeded Woseya, and his son Suluku had succeeded him. Kalawa was Bubu's son; his supporters told Warren that Bubu had in fact succeeded Sankelay, but, 'finding himself too old to rule, [he] handed back the chiefdom to the house of Sankelle, which was the late Suluku'. In their view, Kalawa was taking up Bubu's deferred inheritance.

Local informants now credit Woseya's father Sarawa with the foundation of Bumban, and tend to identify him as a Mandingo settler from Sankaran in the upper Niger plain (Finnegan, 1965: 14 16, 147–9; Howard, 1972: 154–6, 182 n. 143; Fyle 1979a: 3–8). Claims to external origins are general to the colonial ruling families of Limba country (Sayers, 1927: 87–94; Dorjahn and Tholley, 1959; Finnegan, 1965: 147–9), although this did not deter the British from designating them as 'Limba'. In Biriwa the British were concerned primarily with apparent conflict within the ruling family. One year after Kalawa's election, Warren committed the following entry to the Koinadugu District Decree Book:

> Since the crowning of chief Kallawah, the Bumban people have been making it very hard for chief Kallawah to govern his country in the way it should be governed. Kallawah has on several occasions complained that the Bumban people won't agree to any orders he may give to them. Consequently there is, and I'm afraid always will be, friction between these two houses.[4]

Warren went on to suggest that 'splitting up Biriwa country' might prove to be the only solution to this difficulty. But he believed that Ali, Kalawa's rival the previous year, was the chief instigator of this disobedience. Ali was subsequently 'deported' to Mende country.[5] Kalawa also met with dissent from other quarters. In 1913 Sub-chief Dikor of Karasa, and the headmen of five neighbouring villages (Karasa, Kabwita, Kasan, Katerina and Kamaron) were also fined for 'refusing to obey the lawful orders' of Kalawa. The Karasa headman and two others were later fined again for 'rebellious conduct'.[6] Antagonism between Bumban and Kamabai appears to have been alleviated by Kalawa's death in 1914 and the subsequent election of Suluku's son Pompoli as Paramount Chief. Thereafter the British encouraged rotational succession between the 'house' of Bubu in Kamabai and the 'house' of Suluku in Bumban.

After 1950 this system of succession was opened to greater democratic examination. In the Biriwa paramount chiefship elections of 1952, 1956 and 1963 candidates were required to state their claims before the Tribal Authority at meetings chaired by a District Officer and an Assessor Chief from a neighbouring chiefdom.[7] The records of the proceedings show that numerous candidates came forward. Some represented the established 'houses', but others represented indigenous Limba groups, and immigrant Muslim families who had retained their Mandingo identity. On each occasion, however, the Tribal Authority elected the leading candidate of the established 'house' whose turn it would have been under the old system. How far British officials influenced voting in 1952 and 1956 is unclear. Yet it is noteworthy that copies of DC Warren's original report appear in the official files on all three elections, together with notes assessing the strength of each candidate's claim in 'native law'. The 1956 election was in fact suspended because a split of the vote between Bumban candidates had allowed a Muslim Mandingo from Karina to poll the most votes. The Assessor Chief advised, without any discernible trace of

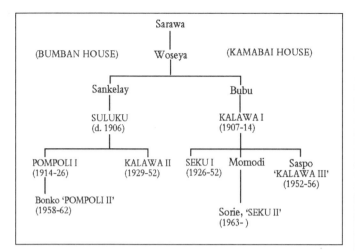

Figure 3 Genealogy of Biriwa Paramount Chiefs according to official colonial sources.

Source file: Death of Alimamy Pompoli II and election of successor

Figure 4 Biriwa chiefdom sections. I Kamabai. 2 Bumban. 3 Kayongaro. 4 Karasa. 5 Kagbangona. 6 Kasankhori. 7 Bumbandi. 8 Karina. 9 Balandugu. Black squares show section headquarters, 1985; white squares show former section headquarters.

irony, that 'Mandingo accession' was unacceptable in a Limba chiefdom. Two years were to pass before some of the candidates could be persuaded to step down so as to enable the leading Bumban candidate to overtake his Karina rival. Again, however, local political tension appears to have been alleviated by the death of the Paramount Chief, in 1962, and the subsequent election of a much younger Kamabai chief than had hitherto been customary. The latter, by now in late middle age, was still in office in 1985. Fig. 3 reproduces a dynastic chart of the Biriwa Paramount Chiefs that was found in the file on the 1963 election (see also Finnegan, 1965: 149). Its simplicity and symmetry belie the political struggles of the time.

Second, the new poll tax, like the old hut tax, was assessed annually with reference to a register of villages. Village registration had been instituted in the early colonial era as a measure to relieve Paramount Chiefs of personal liability to tax. Villages were grouped into districts (Sections), each having a sub-chief (later, Section Chief) charged with responsibility for collecting tax and maintaining the register (Cox-George, 1961: 70–5). After 1950 the Biriwa chiefdom retained its nine original Sections (Fig. 4). Two of these (Karina and Balandugu) had always been reserved for Muslim Mandingo, and their fragmentary appearance reflects the priority given here to ethnic affiliation over territorial integrity.

The Native Administration Scheme also promoted the formal recognition of village headmen as ordinary members of Tribal Authorities/Chiefdom Councils. In Biriwa this measure was also realised in a conservative fashion. A ratio of one council member per twenty taxpayers was settled by executive fiat in 1956. It was declared that, in addition to the senior officials, the council should consist of headmen of villages having more than twenty taxpayers, with one extra member for each additional set of twenty taxpayers. Villages with less than twenty taxpayers were expected to qualify for council representation by grouping themselves into units of not less than twenty taxpayers (Kilson, 1966: 194; Barrows, 1976: 83– 5). In 1965 the chiefdom tax assessment reported 3,946 taxpayers in 200 registered villages. The corresponding figures for the years

1974, 1980 and 1985 are 3,887 and 201, 3,990 and 203, and 4,263 and 203 respectively.[8] The recurrence of approximately 200 registered villages and 4,000 taxpayers in these assessments clearly honours the officially sanctioned ratio of one chiefdom councillor (i.e. village headman) to twenty taxpayers. Yet in 1965 68 per cent of villages appearing on the Biriwa register had less than twenty taxpayers; the corresponding figure for 1985 was 61 per cent. Instead of attempting to reorganise the local electorate, the Chiefdom Council evidently used the gross figures to calculate the total number of village headmanships permissible, then allocated these according to criteria lying outside the 1956 guidelines. Further examination of local political affairs indicates the nature of these criteria.

Settlement and social organisation

The main settlement form in Biriwa is the compact, nucleated village. A survey carried out by the aid agency Primary Health Care in 1978 found that the chiefdom contained 291 permanent villages, of which 199 were registered. Only twenty of these villages had more than 200 inhabitants, and only four had more than 500 inhabitants.[9] The latter group includes Bumban and Kamabai. My own survey of 1985 produced a figure of just under 1,500 for the resident population of Kamabai, which now serves as the market, administrative and service centre of the chiefdom. The corresponding figure for Bumban, now a comparatively isolated settlement, was just under 600.

In spite of the small size of modern Biriwa villages, the area displays a substantial degree of settlement continuity. In the second half of the nineteenth century Bumban was often visited by Krios and Europeans exploring the trade routes serving the Sierra Leone Colony. As I have discussed in detail elsewhere (Fanthorpe, 1994: 389–96), these surveys name fifty-three villages within a 30 km radius of Bumban, and often locate each village relative to its neighbours with careful recordings of compass directions and distances of intervening travel. In 1985 these historical sources still served to identify forty-seven existing settlements. Corroborative information was supplied by local informants and the most recent Directorate of Overseas Surveys maps. The latter are based on air photographs, but take their settlement and topographical nomenclature from a series published in 1928.

Most of the local Limba-speaking population answer to one of the following Manding clan names: Konteh, Koroma, Kamara, Sisay, Kargbo and Mansaray. Yet the simple fact that people may share the same name is not taken as a basis for social relationships (cf. Finnegan, 1965: 52–4). In Biriwa – nowadays, at least – it is the village rather than the patriclan which serves as the primary matrix of social group formation and self-identification. The Limba term for village, *meti ma*, literally means 'clearing'. This refers equally to the physical act of removing vegetation, and the application of human knowledge and perception to a locale. This act may be undertaken by an individual, two or more 'brothers', or a group of non-relatives forming a co-operative 'association' (*mathono ma*). The general aim is to make a *makwi ma* ('settlement', 'foundation') that can be built upon by succeeding generations. Prerogatives in respect of farm land allocation, ritual decision making and political representation tend to be reserved for the patrilineage (*lantha*, lit. 'root' or 'stem') of the putative founder(s). However, large village groups tend to divide into factions aligned with prominent individuals of intermediate generations. Descendants of 'strangers' who settled in the village after its foundation may also achieve prominence in the village group – even sometimes to the extent of obtaining the political deference of the descendants of the original founders. Village factions also tend to intermarry, even when they share some patrilineal ancestors – and thus the same clan name.

Historical criteria also serve to establish relations between villages. Farm hamlets (*konkosain*) – and also permanent villages lacking village headmen – tend to be classified for purposes of tax assessment and political representation as components of the registered villages in which the founders were born. Sometimes one or more registered village with its own headman will also recognise another village in their neighbourhood as the birthplace of its 'founder'. While maintaining their independence in matters of land allocation and political representation, such former 'satellite' groups still tend to give priority to requests from the 'parent' group for support in locating potential spouses, organising life-cycle rituals and handling disputes with third parties (cf. Finnegan, 1965: 55–61). Beyond the neighbourhood, village groups tend to establish relationships on the basis of common connections with centres which supplied political and/or religious authority in pre-colonial times. This factor underlies the division of the local population into ethnic and political groupings, and holds for both Limba and non-Limba.

Ethnic and political groupings

Fig. 5 plots the location and reported ethnic identity of 167 village groups from which data were collected in the field. Village groups calling themselves Biriwa Limba (*bibiriwan be*) tend to identify their founders, or sometimes later 'chiefs' (*gbakain*), as men who had gone to Bumban to receive social and ritual 'training' (*madinki ma*) under Suluku. Some of these were said to have been Limba men, others were said to have come from outside Limba country to settle under Suluku's aegis (Fanthorpe, 1994: 457–66). No such attendance on Biriwa Paramount Chiefs has taken place in recent times, although Bumban continues to maintain its reputation as one of the earthly abodes of Kumba, a spirit that has a central place in the Limba pantheon (Sayers, 1927: 91–4; Finnegan, 1965: 113–16). Rituals associated with this spirit are still held in Bumban, but participation is now restricted to men born there.

My patron during fieldwork in 1980-81 was the late Section Chief (SC) Yaya Biriwa Konteh of Bumban, a grandson of Suluku. He had served with the British army in Burma during the Second World War and later worked as a police sergeant in the Temne town of Mototaka. He had been an unsuccessful candidate in the 1956 election during that period of employment, retiring shortly before his election to the Bumban section chiefship in 1965. Like other senior men in Bumban, SC Yaya would not deny that his ancestors came from outside Limba country. Yet he emphasised that he was a Limba on the grounds that his mother tongue, like that of Woseya and Suluku, was Limba (cf. Finnegan, 1988: 47–8). For SC Yaya the key political issue arising from history was that many 'foundations' in the wider region had sprung from Bumban. His extensive social network reflected this claim. For example, he introduced me to the Kuranko Paramount Chief of Mabonto, a grandson of one of Suluku's daughters, while attending an initiation ceremony there. He also introduced me to the Paramount Chief of Bumbuna, another grandson of a daughter of Suluku, and a grandson of Gbebe, a Safroko Limba war leader who features in Fyle's biography (Fyle, 1979a: 16-17). For SC Yaya, Bumban was a moral capital, if no longer a political one. He applied the same principle to the Biriwa Limba villages, where he was constantly in demand as a guest of honour at initiation and other life-cycle ceremonies.

However, SC Yaya was less successful in his relations with some of the villages putatively founded by agnates of Suluku. Thirty of these are found today, and all but one are located within the borders of the Biriwa chiefdom (Fig. 6). Nine of the founders were Suluku's own sons, nine were his brothers and a further nine were his

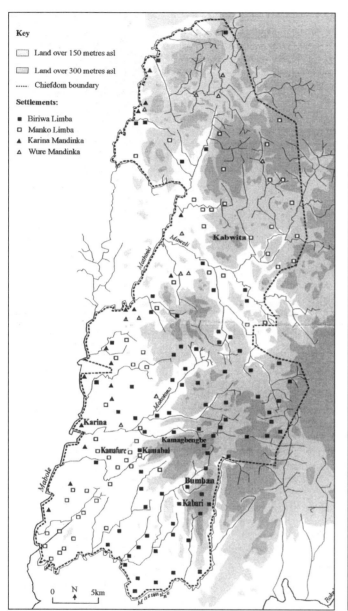

Figure 5 Biriwa chiefdom: land and settlement.

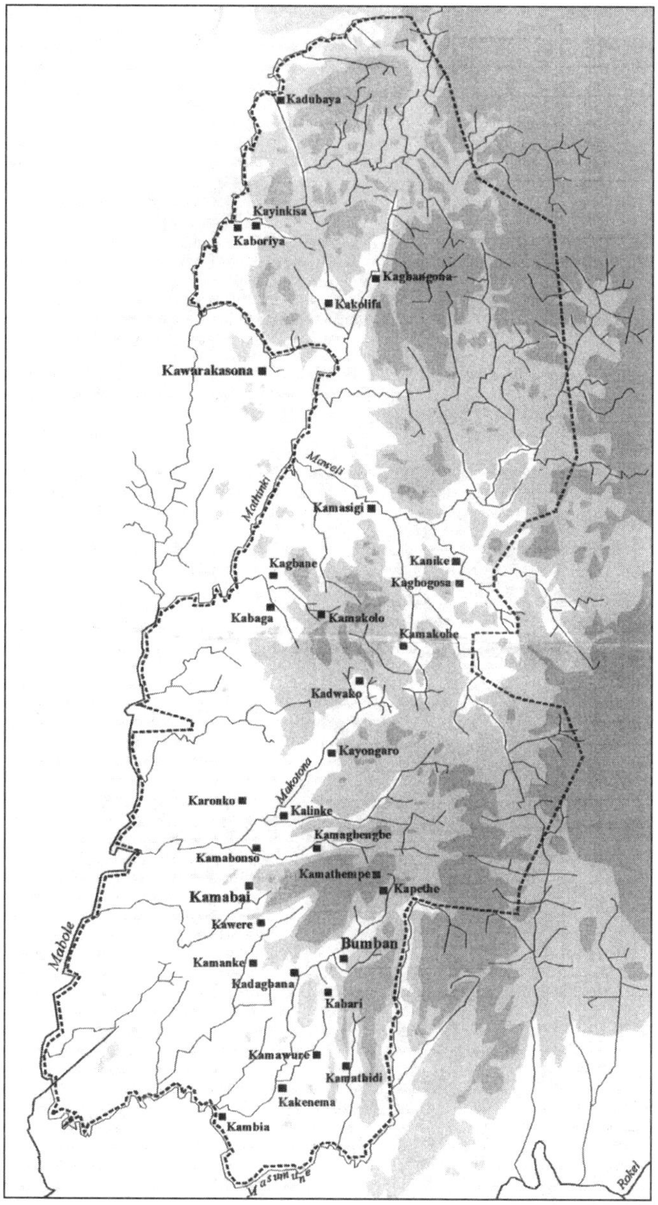

Figure 6 Settlements of the Biriwa Konteh.

brother's sons. The remaining three were sons of one of Suluku's father's brothers. The headmen of these villages tend to identify themselves as the *lantha* of Woseya, and use the name 'Biriwa Konteh' in order to distinguish themselves from the other Konteh who reside in the chiefdom (Fanthorpe, 1994: 270 83). In SC Yaya's view, all these village groups came from Bumban and thus represent 'one family' (*hunpo hunthe*) who should have 'one voice' (*tampa sinthe*). Yet some of the groups now see themselves as representing distinct (and intermarrying) 'foundations', and are

therefore inclined to challenge what they see as Bumban's one-sided view of their family obligations.

Informants in Biriwa Konte villages tend to recall a time when all the 'sons of Woseya' lived and worked together in Bumban. Suluku was supported by all as 'chief' (*gbaku*). Now that Suluku and his brothers are all dead, they see no reason why the Bumban people should have an exclusive right to lead the family – or to supply the Paramount Chief. This point is often established with reference to Suluku's 'covenant' (*lahaidi*) with his brothers. For example, in

Kamabai the Paramount Chief reprised the claims of his grandfather Kalawa's supporters in 1907: Bubu was older than Suluku, and ruled his own settlement of Kamawuray. However, war was troubling the country and the white men were close at hand. Bubu therefore decided that Suluku, a powerful warrior, was the best person to take responsibility for the country. He nevertheless made Suluku promise that Bubu's sons should succeed him. Kalawa was a powerful man in his own right, and had founded Kamabai from Kamawuray. He succeeded as Paramount Chief in 1907 because everyone in the country remembered Suluku's promise.

In Kamagbengbe, Suluku's 'covenant' with his brother Karankay – the founder – was established in a more allusive narrative featuring the spirit Kumba. Karankay's son was Ali, who stood against Kalawa in 1907. Two sons of Ali contested the 1956 election, and one of these narrated a story which I now paraphrase. Karankay was a hunter. One day he and Suluku were walking though the bush. There they met Kumba, which captured them and told them that it would grant any man the power of chiefship (hugbakuine) if it received a human life as a sacrifice. Neither Karankay nor Suluku could bring himself to kill any of his children, and as a last resort Karankay allowed Kumba to take him. The power of chiefship consequently fell into Suluku's hands. However, as Karankay died he made Suluku promise to treat his orphaned sons as his own. The informant refused to elaborate further, but the moral issue this story raises seems clear. Was Suluku's chiefship a personal property, to be inherited by his sons alone, or was it a family property that all descendants of Woseya should share?

Another informant narrated a similar story. He came from a Bumban family descended from a sister of Suluku, but was no longer resident in Biriwa. His father had contested the 1952 election on the grounds that his own father Kiampe had been 'the right-hand man and treasurer of Suluku'. This informant claimed that his family – the Kargbo – had been the founders of Bumban. Kumba was merely the 'wife' of the spirit Sogoduna, which lived on the inselberg overlooking Bumban. This couple had conceived the first Limba humans, and Sogoduna had performed the first initiation ceremony. It had marked the ground (biri, hence biriwa, 'that which is marked') with the blood of the human males, creating an estate which it charged them to share in perpetuity. When Sarawa arrived from Sankaran, he was incorporated into the estate after marrying a Kargbo girl. Their son was Woseya, and it was a daughter of Woseya, married in turn to a Kargbo man, who gave birth to Kiampe. This informant's explicit conclusion was that the Biriwa Konteh had yet to honour Sogoduna's 'covenant' by sharing the paramount chiefship.

These accounts also allude to Bumban's current social and ritual insularity. The settlement now has every appearance of an isolated farming community. While it has a state primary school and a Roman Catholic church, other external agents and agencies are notable for their absence. In 1985 81 per cent of Bumban's inhabitants lived in households headed by patrilineal descendants of Sarawa; half of these were also descendants of Suluku. Even so, many Bumban people have embarked upon successful professional careers outside Limba country. Recent examples include university graduates, schoolteachers, nurses, and army and police officers. In the early 1980s this group also included a chief police officer, an assistant to the Sierra Leonean ambassador to Italy and a Member of Parliament representing Bombali East constituency.

The Kamabai Konteh, to date the only successful challengers to Bumban's historic ascendancy, have pursued an opposite strategy.

Kamabai's development as the modern headquarters of the chiefdom seems to have begun with Kalawa's election in 1907. Suluku had always refused permission for Christian missions to station themselves in his country, but an American Wesleyan mission was established in Kamabai in 1908 (Turay, 1981). A branch line of the Sierra Leone railway reached Kamabai in 1915, and two European traders took out business leases there shortly afterwards (Tuboku-Metzger and van der Laan, 1981: 74–8). While this line was closed in 1930, a large 'strangers' quarter' had already become established in Kamabai (Singer and Baldridge' 1929: 84–5). In 1985 this quarter (Kamabai Serifula) accounted for just over 40 per cent of the town's population. Its Muslim Fula, Mandingo, Soso and Temne inhabitants are heavily engaged in wholesaling and retailing activities. Kamabai has also acquired a secondary school, three primary schools and a Roman Catholic mission. In 1985 39 per cent of Kamabai's population (including 33 per cent of Limba) were living in rented accommodation, many as a result of professional postings. The Kamabai Konteh still claim historical precedent for their accommodation of modern agents. In general, they are far more willing to acknowledge Sarawa's Mandingo origins than their Bumban counterparts. Furthermore, the Paramount Chief in 1985 was one of many Muslim descendants of Bubu. He claimed that his branch of the Biriwa Konte family had become Muslim after Woseya sent Bubu in his youth to the Futa Jallon highlands to receive an Islamic education.

Manko Limba (bimankoen be) have also made their voices heard in recent Biriwa politics. Many among this group claim to speak a purer dialect of the Limba language than the Biriwa, and regard themselves as the original Limba inhabitants of the area. They say that their ancestors made the escarpment the 'boundary' (biri) beyond which Sarawa was allowed to settle (Fanthorpe, 1994: 287–91). Kabwita, located in the upper Maweli valley, represents another earthly abode of Kumba. Even in Bumban it is acknowledged that Woseya visited Kabwita in order to receive ritual instruction. It is also said that aspiring politicians – especially candidates for paramount chiefship – still go there to purchase knowledge of the unseen realm. In some quarters this 'market' is looked upon with disapproval, but it is said that nobody who visits Kabwita for the purpose is allowed again to cross the river Maweli. In 1985 the Paramount Chief, investigating a land dispute in the far north of the chiefdom, had to make a detour through four neighbouring chiefdoms in order to avoid breaking this sanction. It may not be mere coincidence that SC Yaya of Bumban – who died in that year and so never had another opportunity to contest the paramount chiefship – married two women from villages across the Maweli, and regularly attended initiation ceremonies in that area.

The Manko Limba villages in the southern half of the chiefdom tend to look first to Bumbandi ('small Bumban'), and second to Kamafuray, as sources of their historic 'foundations'. Bumbandi is said to have been the capital of a powerful pre-colonial 'chief' (gbaku) called Mori Brima Koroma (cf. Fyle, 1979a: 6–7). Some informants cited Mori Brima as a contemporary of Sarawa, although in Bumban he is said to have been a contemporary of Suluku. Like Bubu, Mori Brima is said to have received an Islamic education in the Futa Jallon highlands, although his modern descendants are mainly Christian (Fanthorpe, 1994: 466–73). In 1985 these included the local Section Chief, who had served with SC Yaya in Burma. In his view, the Bumban and Bumbandi people were now 'one family', on the grounds that his own grandparents included a son of Mori Brima and yet another daughter of Suluku. One of his female relatives had also married SC Yaya.

Even so, his predecessor Section Chief, Yangba Konteh of Kamafuray, had mounted a vigorous campaign to win the Biriwa paramount chiefship in 1952 and 1956. He claimed that his ancestor Mori Brima had ruled over the country prior to the settlement of Sarawa. Yangba Konteh's campaign nevertheless appears to have died with him. His family in Kamafuray now draw attention to the fact that Kamabai, located 500m from their village, was built on land belonging to Kamafuray and three other Manko village groups. An informant in one of these villages narrated an almost identical story to the one I heard in Kamagbengbe, substituting his ancestor and Woseya for Karankay and Suluku. Kamabai indeed has very little farm land; the Paramount Chief's immediate family have to make their rice farms on land belonging to Biriwa Konteh villages 25 km distant from Kamabai. This seems to be the price the Kamabai Konteh have been obliged to pay for extracting themselves from Bumban's moral orbit.

The Muslim Mandingo population of the chiefdom represent the final element in this political pattern. They have been settled in the area since precolonial times, and their villages are mainly found in a narrow strip of land between the Limba settlements and the Mabole river. Today, as in the past, this group is heavily involved in wholesale cattle and produce trade. The Karina Mandingo, who head a Section of seventeen villages, are led by the Serifu (from the Arabic *sharif*, descendant of the Prophet). They are said to have come to Limba country from Fitaba in the Futa Jallon highlands during the time of Suluku (Fanthorpe, 1994: 473–6). Serifu men from Karina also mounted a strong campaign to win the paramount chiefship in the 1950s. The idea of a historical 'covenant' was again central to their claims. In the 1952 election Alhaji Seku Serif came forward to claim that the Limba were indebted to the Mandingo because they had secured the Mabole river as the frontier between Limba and Loko countries, and had furthermore negotiated peace between Suluku and the invading military forces (Sofas) of the Samorian empire in the 1880s (see Fyle, 1979a: 30–40). In 1956 Karina was represented by Alhaji Bobor Serif whose mother was a daughter of Suluku. He repeated Alhaji Seku's claims, adding that Suluku had promised that a Karina Paramount Chief would succeed him as a reward for Karina's diplomatic intervention with the Sofas. Alhaji Borbor was prevented from taking the Paramount Chiefship only by the suspension of this election.

The Wuray Mandingo have a Section of eight villages, and say that they came to Limba country from Hure Kaba, a region adjacent to Fitaba. Their founder was Momodu Balandugu, after whom their Section is named. He is said to have been a cattle trader who worked for Woseya, the latter giving him a daughter in marriage and granting land for his people (Fanthorpe, 1994: 478–9). It is noteworthy in this respect that the Wuray people did not contest the paramount chiefship in the 1950s. However, when the 1956 election was suspended they did add their names to Alhaji Borbor and Yangba Konteh's joint petition for 'transfer to a Loko chiefdom in preference to further subservience to Bumban'.[10] Many Karina and Wuray Mandingo now own houses and trading stores in Kamabai.

History, identity and localisation

There now follows an analysis of Biriwa politics in the light of the issues raised in the introduction. First, the most striking feature of recent Biriwa politics is that it remains orientated towards powerful pre-colonial personalities and their putative relationships. At first sight this is hardly surprising, given that the chiefdoms were designed to conserve history and tradition. Yet the modernising initiatives of the Native Administration Scheme appear to have had little effect upon this orientation, and these claims display a distinctive cultural logic that is not reducible to the prescriptions of the British colonial authorities.

As noted above, Limba patrilineal kin groups tend to regard themselves as the owners of villages on the grounds that they represent the primary physical embodiment of those 'foundations'. Yet, as Ottenberg (1984) points out in respect of the Limba of Bafodia, the prerogatives of patrilineal kin groups are always established *in relation* to others owning complementary statuses. Such groups consequently encourage the settlement of strangers, friends and affines, and also tend to tolerate their own members' pursuit of distinct professional and religious identities. Finnegan, writing about the Limba in general, also reports that the participation of *sesain* – relations through women – is essential for sacrifices to patrilineal ancestors (Finnegan, 1965: 57). A *sesa* – especially a sister's son – is seen as having a close and affectionate relationship with his 'mother's brother'. He is not a competitor for his patrimony, and is therefore an ideal person with whom to conduct life. Indeed, the stem *npo* in *hunpo* ('family' literally means 'carry on the back', as a mother does her child. The moral community of 'one family' (*hunpo hunthe*) may therefore include all those – affines and *sesain* included – whose presence is necessary for the conduct of social life and the creation of the next generation.

However, in a localised 'foundation' the distinction between those who share in the conduct of life (relations through women) and those who share a common patrimony (relations through men) inevitably becomes blurred by intermarriage. Finnegan alludes to this point when noting that in Limba villages 'those living together are thought of as being commonly descended from ancestors commonly prayed to' (1965: 113). In Biriwa this distinction is blurred further by the tendency of polygynous patrilineal groups to divide into intermarrying factions. Uterine kinship often establishes the basis of these divisions. Northcote Thomas, writing early in this century, reported that 'at Bumban, a man takes the farm and house that belonged to his mother, and younger sons get land from the eldest' (Thomas, 1916: 169). In this context, inheritance of a father's or grandfather's personal property (e.g. chiefship) is never clear-cut. Hence the importance attached, in Biriwa political discourse, to historical 'covenants' between 'brothers'. Hence also the political importance attached to descent through women. This simultaneously signifies incorporation within the historic political estate and the formation of a distinct identity providing precedents for current political competition (cf. Murphy and Bledsoe, 1989).[11] Candidates for paramount chiefship have not been alone in embracing these principles. For example, both the MPs representing the Biriwa area (Bombali East constituency) in the early 1980s were highly educated professionals. Yet the first was also a grandson of one of Suluku's daughters, and his successor, born in Bumban itself, was also a descendant of one of Suluku's sisters.

Second, the fact that modern Biriwa politics is amenable to ethnographic analysis does not in itself explain why local politicians seem to have found it necessary to locate their ancestors among historical groups which no longer exist as such, and to which they would not in any case claim further allegiance. However, the above-noted evidence of long-term settlement continuity in the Biriwa area suggests that village registration, a procedure instituted

Table 1 Comparison of field data and tax assessments for ten settlements in Biriwa chiefdom, 1985

Field survey settlement	Total population	Adult males counted	Tax assessment
Kamabai	1,461	193	153
Bumban	589	84	112
Kakenema	509	59	51
Mile 14	221	28	26
Kagbane	174	29	23
Kathantha	154	24	18
Kamafure	185	30	27
Kamanke	131	21	22
Kagbungbo	39	7	6
Kamadebe	31	3	3

Table 2 Tax assessments for ten settlements in Biriwa chiefdom, 1965–85

Settlement	1965	1970	1974	1980	1985
Kamabai	159	168	171	135	153
Bumban	102	111	115	102	112
Kakenema	55	51	54	52	51
Mile 14	21	21	25	20	26
Kagbane	26	21	32	24	23
Kathantha	16	20	18	18	18
Kamafure	30	33	31	26	27
Kamanke	17	16	17	20	22
Kagbungbo	8	6	7	4	6
Kamadebe	3	3	5	5	3

at the beginning of the early colonial era, has played a significant role in the localisation of political relations. Chiefdom tax registers prior to the election of the current (1985) Paramount Chief have not survived, but the first significant piece of evidence the surviving registers contain is that the four 'Biriwa Limba' Sections (Bumban, Kamabai, Kayongaro and Kagbangona) have slightly more village headmen than the Manko and Mandingo Sections put together (107 as opposed to ninety-seven in 1965). This illustrates how imperative it has been for politicians to retain the support of 'their' people, and for all parties to ensure that village groups are maintained so as to prevent the possible transfer of village headmanships to rival factions.

During the period 1965–85 nine new villages appeared on the register and nine others were deleted. Tables 1 and 2 compare the Chiefdom Clerks assessments with my own survey data for ten villages. These reveal a high degree of correlation when one considers the difficulties of assessing birth dates among a largely non-literate population. National census data confirm the tendency towards stasis in the adult male population of Biriwa chiefdom. The average annual rate of population increase in rural Sierra Leone between 1963 and 1974 was 1.8 per cent. Despite an expected net growth of 20–5 per cent in the rural population over the intercensal period, the chiefdom's population grew by just 4.3 per cent. The overall sex ratio decreased by 1.5 per cent to 85.7 males per 100

females, and males accounted for less than 39 per cent of the local 15–39 age group. This group had declined by nearly 6 per cent over the intercensal period, and the corresponding sex ratio by nearly 2 per cent (Thomas, 1983: 119–21; Karimu and Richards, 1980: 11–16). These figures suggest that out-migration absorbed much of the expected increase in the chiefdom's population over the intercensal period.

But the fact that the tax registers show little evidence of decline in the adult male population suggests that, while young men have tended to enter the migrant labour market in large numbers, many return to the rural villages in later life to take the places of deceased or otherwise departing men. This in turn implies that migrant movements are managed. Indeed, in Bumban in particular I witnessed cases where every departing household member was replaced by a return migrant of comparable age and gender (Fanthorpe, 1994: 312-35).

The balance of voting power in paramount chiefship elections has not been the only issue at stake in settlement conservation. In the absence of modern measures of citizenship, incorporation within the moral community of a registered village has always represented the best available means of establishing rights to land and legal and political representation. The socially and politically localising effects of this process are illustrated by the following case. Kabari village is located a few hundred metres from Bumban, and its leading resident in the pre-colonial era was Suluku's brother Faforay. In November 1980 the Kabari village headman led a delegation to Bumban to inform SC Yaya that they were going to the Chiefdom Court to claim compensation for damage done by Bumban cattle to their crops. SC Yaya tried to persuade them otherwise. He reminded them that Bumban and Kabari were 'one family' (*hunpo hunthe*), who should be able to settle disputes without the intervention of a third party. However, the compensation he offered did not satisfy the Kabari people, and a date was set for the hearing. Informants in Kabari later pointed out that the founder of Kabari was not a relation of Suluku. His daughter had married Woseya, and their son Faforay had settled in Kabari in order to farm his mother's land. They also recalled a time when the Bumban and Kabari people gathered together to make a sacrifice. Suluku was late for one ceremony, but Faforay insisted that they were all 'brothers', and so could take what they needed from Suluku's granary. When Suluku arrived he was furious, accusing Faforay of theft and shouting so loud that he could not hear Faforay's attempts at explanation. As with all historical stories of this kind, its 'truth' (*thia*) lies in its moral message: Suluku had played his part in the division of the Biriwa Konteh family, and the Bumban people could not now have it both ways by citing family unity as a pretext for avoiding payment of full compensation. Their voice was no longer the loudest.

This dispute did not prevent SC Yaya from acting as guest of honour at a Kabari male initiation ceremony a few months later. While the circumcision ritual itself takes place in strict seclusion, these ceremonies are also public festivals in which the neophytes are presented to the senior guests. SC Yaya attended five such ceremonies in the dry season of 1981, and it is unlikely that he would have remembered all the names and faces of the boys presented to him in the course of his career. Yet these occasions enabled him to renew acquaintance with local village headmen, and during the ceremonies I attended he was involved in much informal discussion about family and village history. It would therefore seem that SC Yaya, like his counterparts in other historic settlements in the area, established his political career as the representative of a 'foundation' (*Bumban*) which continues to serve as a repository and guarantor of the identities which establish the basic rights and properties of the rural population.

Third, and finally, scholars have differed in their assessments of the territorial integrity and level of centralisation of Suluku's pre-colonial polity (Finnegan and Murray, 1970; Howard, 1972: 154–6, 182n. 143, 286; Lipschutz, 1973: 39–44; Fyle, 1979a). Further consideration of this issue is beyond the scope of the present article, but even a brief survey of the historical sources suggests hitherto unacknowledged connections between Biriwa's pre-colonial past and political present. With the exception of Sarawa, all the pre-colonial Biriwa rulers shown on Fig. 4 can be identified in the reports of pre-colonial European and Krio travellers (Fyle, 1979a: 3–14). In the early 1870s the political situation in Biriwa appears to have been in flux. The Church Missionary Society expedition led by E. W. Blyden reached Bumban in March 1872. Blyden reported that Suluku, whom he identifies as the 'warrior-chief of Big-Boumba', was 'really the ruler of the Limba country'; Sankelay was 'only the nominal chief'.[12] Bumban was visited again in November 1872 by the Reverend I. M. Williams, originally a companion of Blyden's. Williams reports Sankelay's recent death. While he had dealings with Suluku, he identifies 'Gbubu, the chief of Kammawehreh' [Bubu of Kamawuray] as the 'nominated successor of Sankailey, deceased of Bombabah', and the 'king-elect of the Bilwah Limba'.[13] As Fyle (1979a: 11–12) has noted, reports reached the Colony the following year describing Suluku as the ruler of Limba country. It was in this capacity that he hosted a second Church Missionary Society expedition, led by the Reverend A. Shapira, in 1876.[14] Even so, Bubu does not drop from historical view. As Fyle (1979a: 12) has again noted, Bubu was a co-signatory to numerous Arabic letters sent by Suluku to the Colony in the ensuing decade. These recurrently identify Bubu as Suluku's 'older brother'. Festing passed through Kamawuray in March 1887, describing it as 'a town presided over by one Bubu, an older brother of Suluku by a different mother'.[15]

The first point to emerge from this evidence is that Bubu's involvement in the production of Suluku's Arabic correspondence may indeed indicate that he had been the recipient of an Islamic education. Bubu may also have been the 'elder brother' whose arrival Suluku was awaiting before granting permission to Shapira to read aloud from the Bible.[16] Fyle's dismissal of Kalawa as a colonial collaborator who 'would not possess the traditional principles of legitimacy' (1979a: 12–13, 56) now seems premature. The historical sources are not conclusive on the question of whether or not Bubu 'actually ruled', and in any case it was the British who instituted the 'rule' that Paramount Chiefs should be the patrilineal descendants of pre-colonial rulers. An indication of the local view on this matter can be found in a letter sent by some Biriwa men to DC Warren at the time of Kalawa's election. This letter was discovered by Lipschutz, and he quotes the following passage:

It has never been the custom in the Biriwa Country to crown a Chief before: it has always been the custom to recognise the biggest man in the country as our rulers ... but now we wish to have a crowned King. [Lipschutz, 1973: 146, 174 n.31]

It is of further interest here that the pre-colonial sources clearly identify Bubu as Suluku's older brother, not his father's brother, as reported by Warren in 1907. Local informants stated with absolute unanimity that Sankelay, Bubu and Suluku were brothers: sons of Woseya by different mothers (cf. Fyle, 1979b: 18–20). On this basis, the pre-colonial Biriwa Konteh begin to look less like a dynasty than the extended family their modern descendants claim them to have been. DC Warren and his successors may therefore have mis-interpreted the factional division into localised 'houses' that took place on Suluku's death as a dynastic division taking place a generation earlier.

Yet, as noted above, the most outspoken opponents of Kalawa's paramount chiefship appear to have been guardians of shrines to Kumba: Suluku's people in Bumban and the inhabitants of villages surrounding Kabwita. Suluku is still spoken of with awe in the Biriwa area as the 'son of Kumba' (Finnegan, 1965: 38, 113–16, 1967: 11), and, as I have noted elsewhere (Fanthorpe, 1998), rituals involving this spirit appear to concern control over rainfall. Such rituals still take place in Bumban, albeit in strict seclusion. Nathaniel Boston, a Krio companion of Shapira's in 1876, has nevertheless left us with an account of rituals taking place on the inselberg over-looking Bumban:

... their [the Limba's] national God is Mt. Casogoduna, once in three years the King [Suluku] and all the males repair to the top for a sacrifice ... on the previous day, the King repairs to the top, recounts all the chief matters of the land and begs for the aid of the mountain for the time to come – also before any war is undertaken, the assistance of the mountain is implored by sacrifice.[17]

Boston was told later that it was actually 'the Devil who resides in the mountain' who received the sacrifice. Festing reported in 1887 that Suluku personally owned all the land of his country, took charge of the produce and distributed it 'as food is required'.[18] Furthermore, whilst surveying the Sierra Leone Protectorate boundary in 1897, J. K. Trotter also remarked that Suluku ruled his subjects 'without the assistance of any executive' (1898: 25). Suluku's status as the Biriwa 'king', and 'trainer' of local men, may thus have derived from his role as Kumba's earthly mediator – as the guarantor of the fertility and security of the land upon which his protégés settled. Here one may find the historical roots of Bumban's recent role as a repository of historical knowledge and producer of human capital. Whether or not Bubu's Muslim affiliations disqualified him from acting as Kumba's earthly mediator remains uncertain on several counts – as does the question of whether the local shrine to Kumba was the property of the Biriwa Konte family or open to wider competition between 'big men'. Yet Kalawa's campaign to succeed Suluku may still represent a local initiative responding to new colonial conditions – an attempt to shift towards more cosmopolitan and Muslim-orientated political leadership. Recent history nevertheless suggests that such a political project has been subject to both spatial and moral containment. This in turn suggests that 'patrimonial' politics in postcolonial Sierra Leone may sometimes serve a higher purpose than corrupt self-aggrandisement.

Conclusion

The evidence presented in this article shows that anthropological analysis can illuminate aspects of local politics in post-colonial Sierra Leone. Biriwa politics is manifestly a local cultural product, with perhaps deeper historical roots than has hitherto been imagined. In that regard, the tendency of some scholars to make a division between a pre-colonial era of 'indigenous' politics, and a twentieth-century era of morally compromised 'colonial' politics, may ultimately prove to be unhelpful (cf. Peel, 1984; Lenz, 1994). Indeed, the recurrent presence of DC Warren's original report in later colonial files calls into question whether there was ever sufficient dialogue between British officials and local politicians to render the discourse of the latter 'substrate' (cf. Pels, 1996). The conservative nature of recent Biriwa politics, as displayed especially by the organisation of the Chiefdom Council and paramount chiefship elections, emerges as a pragmatic response to a perennial problem of uncertain citizenship. The roots of this uncertainty clearly lie in British colonial policies of 'indirect rule'. As long as village registration remains the primary means of establishing rural citizenship, rights and properties will continue to be tied to historical statuses and identities attached to villages. The recent civil war in Sierra Leone, leading to the virtual collapse of the state infrastructure, may only have served to place further emphasis on localised identities as a means of securing basic rights, properties, and protection.

Notes

1. Public Record Office (PRO), London: CO 879/24/318, Rowe to Holland, 23 February 1888.
2. Sierra Leone Government Archives (SLGA), Freetown: Bundle Assorted 1937–4, SPA 416/2, *Tribal Authority, Biriwa Chiefdom*.
3. Warren's report was originally filed under 'DC Kabala to Col. Sec., 6 May 1907, SPA 416/1'. Mimeos of this document were found in several files relating to the Biriwa chiefdom at the Sierra Leone Ministry of the Interior, Bombali District Office, Makeni.
4. SLGA, Freetown: *Koinadugu District Decree Book*, vol. 1, 38.
5. *Koinadugu District Decree Book*, vol. 1, 39.
6. *Koinadugu District Decree Book*, vol. 1, 77, 96.
7. The material in this paragraph is taken from the following files stored under reference SPA 416/1 at the Sierra Leone Ministry of the Interior, Bombali District Office, Makeni: *Death and Crowning of Paramount Chiefs: Biriwa Chiefdom* [1952], *Death of Alimamy Kalawa II and Election of Successor* [1956], *Death of Alimamy Pompoli II and Election of Successor* [1963].
8. I am grateful to Paramount Chief Seku 11 of Kamabai for granting me permission to consult the Biriwa chiefdom tax registers at the Chiefdom Clerk's office in Kamabai.
9. I am grateful to Father Angelo Aguerre of the Roman Catholic Mission in Kamabai for giving me a copy of the map upon which the Primary Health Care survey data are plotted.
10. Bombali District Office, Makeni: *Death of Alimamy Kalawa II and Election of Successor*.
11. Both principles feature prominently in the ethnographic literature on Manding societies of the upper Guinea savanna zone. Here, they are discussed in relation to *sanakuya*, a prescriptive alliance between two clans or between a clan and a caste (Labouret, 1934: 101–4; Dieterlen, 1951: 80–2; Paulme, 1973; Jackson, 1974; Amselle, 1977: 38). *Sanakuya* is not known among the Limba of Biriwa, but the prominence of these principles in political discourse may still tell us something about the cultural background of the local Limba-speaking population.
12. PRO, London: CO 267/316, Pope Hennessey to Kimberley, 1 September 1872.
13. SLGA, Freetown: Local Letters to Governor, 1872, untitled letter, 20 January 1873.
14. PRO, London: CO 267/330, Kortright to Carnarvon, 19 December 1876.
15. PRO, London: CO 879/24/318, Rowe to Holland, 1 July 1887.
16. Church Missionary Society (CMS) Archives, University Library, University of Birmingham: CA1 0189/24, 'The Journal of the Revd A. Shapira's Mission Expedition to the Interior of West Africa from Sierra Leone to the Limba Country from the 16th October '76'.
17. CMS Archives, Birmingham: CA1/051/6, 'Missionary Expedition to the Interior, 16th October–l0th November 1876'.
18. PRO, London: CO 879/24/318, Rowe to Holland, 1 July 1887.

References

Abraham, Arthur. 1976a. 'Mende warfare, settlements and states', in A. Abraham (ed.), *Topics in Sierra Leone History: a counter-colonial interpretation*, pp. 9–30. Freetown: Leone Publishers.
——. 1976b. 'Fragmentation and colonialism', in A. Abraham (ed.), *Topics in Sierra Leone History*, pp. 90–105. Freetown: Leone Publishers.
——. 1978. *Mende Government and Politics under Colonial Rule*. London: Oxford University Press.
Amselle, J-L. 1977. *Les Négociants de la savanne*. Paris: Editions Anthropos.
Banton, M. 1955. 'The Ethnography of the Protectorate: review article', *Sierra Leone Studies* (n.s.) 4, 240–9.
Barrows, W. 1976. *Grassroots Politics in an African State: integration and development in Sierra Leone*. New York: Africana.
Bayart, J-F. 1993. *The State in Africa: the politics of the belly*. London and New York: Longman.
Cartwright, J. R. 1978. *Political Leadership in Sierra Leone*. London: Croom Helm.
Clapham, C. 1976. *Liberia and Sierra Leone: an essay in comparative politics*. Cambridge: Cambridge University Press.
Clarke, J. A. 1966. 'Political constituencies', in J. A. Clarke (ed.), *Sierra Leone in Maps*, pp. 33-4. London: University of London Press.
Cox-George, N. A. 1961. *Finance and Development in West Africa: the Sierra Leone experience*. London: Dobson.
Dieterlen, G. 1951. *Essai sur la religion bambara*. Paris: Presses Universitaires de France.
Dorjahn, V. R. 1960. 'The changing political system of the Temne', *Africa* 30 (2), 110–39.
Dorjahn, V. R., and Tholley, A. S. 1959. 'A provisional history of the Limba, with special reference to Tonko Limba chiefdom', *Sierra Leone Studies* (n.s.) 12, 273–83.
Fanthorpe, R. 1994. 'Settlements and Networks in Biriwa Limba Chiefdom, Northern Sierra Leone'. Ph.D. thesis, University of London.
——. 1998. 'Limba "deep rural" strategies', *Journal of African History* 39 (1), 15–38.
Finnegan, R. H. 1963. 'The traditional concept of chiefship among the Limba', *Sierra Leone Studies* (n.s.) 17, 241–54.
——. 1965. *Survey of the Limba People of Northern Sierra Leone*, Department of Technical Co-operation, Overseas Research Publication 8. London: HMSO.
——. 1967. *Limba Stories and Storytelling*. Oxford: Clarendon Press.
——. 1988. 'Speech, language and non-literacy: the Limba of Sierra Leone', in R. H. Finnegan, *Literacy and Orality*, pp. 45–58. Oxford: Blackwell.
Finnegan, R. H., and Murray, D. J. 1970. 'Limba chiefs', in M. Crowder and O. Ikime (eds), *West African Chiefs: their changing status under colonial rule and independence*, pp. 407–36. Ile-lfe: University of Ife Press.
Fyle, C. Magbaily. 1974. 'Segmentation and succession in upper Guinea', *Africana Research Bulletin* IV (3), 55-60.
——. 1978. 'Almamy Suluku of Biriwa Limba: political and economic organization in a Limba kingdom', *Afrika Zamani* 8, 33-50.
——. 1979a. *Almamy Suluku of Sierra Leone, c. 1820-1906: the dynamics of political leadership in precolonial Sierra Leone*. London: Evans.
——. 1979b. *Oral Traditions of Sierra Leone*. Niamey: OAU Centre for Linguistic and Historical Studies by Oral Tradition.
Grace, J. 1975. *Domestic Slavery in West Africa, with particular reference to the Sierra Leone Protectorate, 1896–1927*. London: Müller.
Hollins, N. C. 1925. 'Précis of events in the Safroko Limba chiefdom, Sierra Leone Protectorate', *Sierra Leone Studies* (o.s.) 7, 35–8.
Howard, A. M. 1972. 'Big-men, Traders, Chiefs: power, commerce and spatial change in the Sierra Leone-Guinea plain, 1865-95'. Ph.D. thesis, Madison, Wis.: University of Wisconsin.

Howard, A.M., and Skinner, D. E. 1984. 'Network building and political power in north-western Sierra Leone, 1800-65', *Africa* 51 (2), 3-28.

Jackson, M. 1974. 'The structure and significance of Kuranko clanship', *Africa* 44 (4), 397–415.

Karimu, J., and Richards, P. 1980. 'The Northern Area Integrated Agricultural Development Project'. Unpublished consultancy report.

Kilson, M. 1966. *Political Change in a West African State: a study of the modernisation process in Sierra Leone*. Cambridge, Mass.: Harvard University Press.

Labouret, H. 1934. *Les Manding et leur langue*. Paris: Librairie Larose.

Lenz, C. 1994. 'A Dagbara rebellion against Dagomba rule? Contested stories of origin in northwestern Ghana', *Journal of African History* 35, 457–92.

Lipshutz, M. R. 1973. 'Northeast Sierra Leone after 1884: response to the Samorian invasions and British colonialism'. Ph.D. thesis, Los Angeles: University of California.

Little, K 1951. *The Mende of Sierra Leone: a West African people in transition*. London: Routledge.

McCulloch, M. 1950. *Peoples of the Sierra Leone Protectorate*. London: International African Institute.

Minikin, V. 1973. 'Indirect political participation in two Sierra Leone chiefdoms', *Journal of Modern African Studies* 11 (1), 129–35.

Moseley, K P. 1978. 'Land, labour and migration: the Safroko Limba case', *Africana Research Bulletin* VIII (2), 14–44.

Murphy, W. P., and Bledsoe, C. H. 1989. 'Kinship and territory in the history of a Kpelle chiefdom (Liberia)', in I. Kopytoff (ed.), *The African Frontier: the reproduction of traditional African societies*, pp. 123–47. Bloomington and Indianapolis: Indiana University Press.

Ottenberg, S. 1984. 'Two new religions, one analytic frame', *Cahiers d'études africaines* 96 XXIV 4, 437–54.

Parsons, R. T. 1964. *Religion in an African Society*. Leiden: Brill.

Paulme, D. 1973. 'Blood pacts, age classes and castes in Black Africa', in P. Alexandre (ed.), *French Perspectives in African Studies*, pp. 73–95. London: Oxford University Press, for the International African Institute.

Peel, J. D. Y. 1984. 'Making history: the past in the Ijesha present', *Man* XIX, 113–32.

Pels, P. 1996. 'The pidginization of Luguru politics: administrative ethnography and the paradoxes of indirect rule', *American Ethnologist* 23 (1), 738–61.

Reno, W. 1995. *Corruption and State Politics in Sierra Leone*. Cambridge: Cambridge University Press.

Sayers, E. F. 1927. 'Notes on the clan and family names common in the area inhabited by the Temne-speaking people', *Sierra Leone Studies* (o.s.) 10, 14–108.

Singer, C. and Baldridge, C. 1929. *White Africans and Black*. New York: Rudge.

Thomas, A. C. 1983. *The Population of Sierra Leone*. Freetown: Government Printing Department.

Thomas, N. W. 1916. *Anthropological Report on Sierra Leone* 1, *Law and Custom of the Timne and other Tribes*. London: Harrison.

Trotter, J. K. 1898. *The Niger Sources and the Borders of the new Sierra Leone Protectorate*. London: Methuen.

Tuboku-Metzger, F. C. and van der Laan, H. L. 1981. *Land Leases in Sierra Leone: a summary of leases granted under the Protectorate Land Ordinance of 1927*. Research Report 12, Leiden: African Studies Centre.

Turay, E. A. 1981. 'Suluku of Biriwa Limba and the Church Missionary Society expedition of 1876: an episode in Euro-Limba relations', *Africana Research Bulletin* XI (2), 81–91.

Wylie, K. C. 1977. *The Political Kingdoms of the Temne: Temne government in Sierra Leone, 1825–1910*. London: Africana.

STEN HAGBERG
Mobilisation of Rights through Organisational Structures

Reference
Between Peace & Justice:
Dispute Settlement between Karaboro Agriculturalists & Fulbe
Agro-Pastoralists in Burkina Faso
Uppsala University, 1998, ch. 10

In this chapter I shall focus on notions of 'rights' and justice' in dispute settlement and relate them to organisational structures for national intervention and ethnic mobilisation. These notions boil down to a reflection of the meanings of justice. Firstly, processes of regional and national intervention and local appropriation will be analysed. I shall explore principally interfaces in which official policy, informal networks and local politics interact. Here dispute settlement between farmers and Fulbe agro-pastoralists is talked about in a language of rights. I shall therefore analyse the discourse of rights in relation to 1) the Land and Tenure Reorganisation (RAF), 2) the Hunting organisation (*donsoton*), and 3) the Trade Union for Graziers (*Syndicat des Eleveurs*). Secondly, contrasting meanings of justice will be identified in the ethnographic account of these three organisational structures for socio-political mobilisation. To analyse the political shaping of dispute settlement in the Comoé Province I shall pursue my use of the analytical framework of a social field of relations and rights.

National intervention and local appropriation

To approach national intervention not only in terms of official policy but also in the interaction with informal networks and local politics may appear to be a risky and somewhat speculative enterprise. It is indeed extremely difficult to identify and estimate the relative importance of socio-political networks which transgress localities, societal levels and other boundaries. Yet I have chosen to concentrate on linkages to dispute settlement as a means by which to analyse these socio-political networks. Dispute settlement between Karaboro agriculturalists and Fulbe agro-pastoralists involves networks and politics far away from the specific dispute about a border of a sorghum field. But this inclusive approach of regional and national socio-political structures should not diminish analytical clarity. Therefore, I shall attempt to find the appropriate balance between what may be called the 'Burkinabe political culture' and the specific socio-political intricacies of dispute settlement.

'Le Burkina appartient à tout le monde'
The Land and Tenure Reorganisation (RAF) is a common reference in the local politics in the Sidéradougou Department. The RAF forms the legal foundation for the Agro-pastoral Management Scheme, or the Sidéradougou Project. This scheme was introduced by the state administration through the Ministry of Agriculture and Animal Resources (see chapter 4). The is closely connected with the Revolution according to most local actors.[186]

But despite the RAF's statement that all land belongs to the state, it is not implemented in rural areas, outside what is administratively defined as the 'urban' centre of the Sidéradougou Department.[187] I would therefore argue that to most rural people the RAF represents a general idea, more than a specific system of regulations. The different articles included in the RAF are not necessarily known to local actors – in fact, few in Sidéradougou, including government officials, seem to have read the law themselves – but the RAF is first and foremost interpreted by local people on the basis of statements made by government officials. The expression 'Le Burkina appartient à tout le monde' – i.e. Burkina belongs to everybody – is widely disputed in the Sidéradougou Department. It is used by government officials to stress that there must be a place for all Burkinabe citizens, even those who come from elsewhere (notably Mossi and Fulbe). Many local farmers find that this expression challenges the right of firstcomers. But few informants, including government officials. seem to question whether or not the expression 'Burkina belongs to everybody' actually summarises different articles of the RAF. Although it could be argued that few people in any nation state – except for lawyers – are likely to be familiar with the law, this expression represents a phenomenon of particular significance. It translates the idea that the state has the right to control the way that landed resources are managed.

State intervention is often justified by references to land degradation and conflict. Accordingly, the land-use of local herders and farmers is frequently described as *exploitation irrationnelle* and their settlements as *occupation anarchique*. In development discourse, the underlying assumption tends to be to increase state control over the use of landed resources. Swift argues, for instance, that '[d]esertification justified increasing control by natural resource bureaucracies' (Swift 1996:87). In this vein, discourse of land degradation and conflict trickles down to local settings, and becomes subject to local interpretations and is thereby appropriated. Similarly, the RAF has been conceptualised nationally, but is differently interpreted in local settings. In the following I therefore discuss three examples of local interpretations of the RAF through the expression 'Le Burkina appartient à tout le monde'.

The first example is an event that was narrated to me by a man belonging to the social category of 'sons of the village' (see chapter 7). This man (P) was heavily engaged in reconciling the parties during the violent conflict in 1986. In the heat of the violent conflict P was driving around by car in the Tiéfora Department (the neighbouring department to Sidéradougou) together with the head of the Gendarmerie from Bobo-Dioulasso. The purpose was to calm down the feelings of Karaboro farmers in villages. They met a group of Karaboro men and started to discuss with them. The head of the Gendarmerie stated that 'Burkina is Burkina'[188] in order to point out that the Burkinabe law should be applied even in this department. A Karaboro man then answered, 'Burkina is Burkina, but Tiéfora is Tiéfora'.[189] This statement is heavily loaded with undertones and catches the essence of many Karaboro farmers' reluctance to recognise the RAF. At one level it communicates the firm intention of rejecting imposed state law in Tiéfora. The norms of Tiéfora or any other village in Karaborola contradict overtly state law especially because it was stated in front of a powerful representative of the state. The perceived bravery of the Karaboro man conforms moreover to the kind of individual socio-political leadership so common in Karaboro communities. At another level the statement expresses that in Tiéfora things should

be done according to the way of the Karaboro, not to that of the state administration. The Karaboro men communicate the perceived right of the Karaboro to do what they want in 'their country' (*o ka jamana*) that is in Karaborola (*Kaye kulo* in Karaboro). The statement 'Burkina is Burkina but Tiéfora is Tiéfora' thus carries central 'Karaboro' notions of rights.

But such rights are differently perceived outside Karaborola. Accordingly, the Sidéradougou and Mangodara violent conflicts analysed in this study did not occur in Karaborola but in Tiefo and Komono 'countries'. There Karaboro farmers cannot claim any similar right to do what they want. A young Fulbe man once pointed out to me that there are no Fulbe pastoralists residing in Karaborola except in Tiéfora village which is the centre of the department. 'The only Fulbe you encounter in the bush [of the Karaboro] are herders employed by the Karaboro'. This man also claimed that no Mossi have settled in Karaborola either, 'there is no Mossi between Banfora and Noumousso'. The point raised here is that in Karaborola no important community of any other ethnic group resides, a fact which this young Fulbe saw as an expression of the reluctance towards strangers. An obvious down-to-earth objection is that Karaborola is densely populated and that most Karaboro farmers have left the area to farm elsewhere. There is simply no 'place' (i.e. arable land) for newcomers even if this young Fulbe probably exaggerates the nonexistence of Mossi in Karaborola. Yet I would argue that violent conflicts between Karaboro farmers and Fulbe agro-pastoralists of the kind that occurred in Sidéradougou in 1986 and in Mangodara in 1995 are not likely to take place in Karaborola. The Karaboro are not residing in their own 'country' (*jamana*), and not Masters of the Earth.[190] In Sidéradougou and Mangodara they cannot possibly claim to be firstcomers. In the absence of a legitimate right – that of firstcomers – Karaboro farmers living in the bush rather tend to defend their rights as farmers exposed to crop damage. In Karaborola Karaboro farmers claim rights as firstcomers, as well as those granted through colonial legacy (Karaborola *canton*).

The second example of local interpretations of the RAF is linked to the Agro-pastoral Management Scheme, commonly called the Sidéradougou project. In general, when discussing the RAF in offices in Ouagadougou or Bobo-Dioulasso, one easily gets the impression of a widespread reform that involves the entire national territory, rural as well as urban areas. In some areas specific activities have been carried out to implement the RAF; the Agro-pastoral Management Scheme is such an area. Yet, although the delimitation of sub-zones within the Agro-pastoral Management Scheme was physically done in the field at the beginning of the 1990s, people have not adjusted their farming and herding practices to the new tenure regime. Instead, there is an ongoing 'colonisation' of these zones by both migrant and autochthonous farmers (Barry 1996:18). Barry further argues that the distance between the state administration, the technical services and the rural producers has increased since the violent conflict in 1986. Today Fulbe agro-pastoralists do not hesitate to denounce the complicity of the state administration in the agricultural 'colonisation' of pastoral zones (ibid.). A veterinary surgeon in Sidéradougou said that the scheme had not been put into practice because of lack of funds for carrying out the delimitation. There was no project money left in his ministry for further development activities.

Discontinuity of development projects is common. Projects tend to have short-term perspectives (e.g. three years), but become rapidly arenas for competing local norms and interests. The

Sidéradougou project has been criticised for favouring Fulbe agro-pastoralists at the expense of farmers (Barry 1996; Hagberg & Berté 1991). A government official who served in Sidéradougou at the time of the violent conflict told me that the project only concerned its own project staff but none of the Agriculture Extension Workers.

> Not even the people of Sidéradougou were involved. They did not know in what direction the project moved. The Masters of the Earth were not involved.

This statement reflects a commonly held view of the RAF, the Revolution and the Scheme. It also reveals envy, because (as in most small localities) rumour and jealousy are important aspects of social life. Autochthonous farmers maintain an attitude of reserve to the Agro-pastoral Management Scheme. This is due to the fact that they have not been sufficiently involved. Barry reports that today there is a refusal among many people to redistribute land for herding or to give land to farming or herding migrants (Barry 1996:30), but unfortunately he does not substantiate this statement with any concrete data.

To local farmers, the RAF as articulated in the shape of the Agropastoral Management Scheme represents a top-down imposition made by the government, but its consequences are variably understood. Most autochthonous farmers perceive that strangers are those who benefit from the RAF. Whereas the expression 'Le Burkina appartient à tout le monde' has come to represent locally the general notion of belonging to the Burkinabe nation-state, the RAF is generally disliked in Sidéradougou.[191]

The third example demonstrates how local interpretations of 'justice' are intertwined with state law. Fulbe informants repeatedly revealed the frustrations they experienced (see chapter 7), because no judgement has been handed down after the two violent conflicts. Local government officials tend to agree with the idea that no judgement should be made. They argue that social peace is fragile, and a judgement would only fuel new outbreaks of violence. One government official stated this clearly:

> After the conflict, [in 1986], certain administrative measures were taken. But in legal terms, nothing should happen. In fact, there will be no sanctions.

Another government official argued that there will not, and should not, be any judgement. To promote peace, the argument goes, there should not be any judgement at all. Social peace must be maintained. But this also recalls the gendarme who said that 'we are sitting on a powder-magazine' (see also chapter 7).

Behind this plea for peace, however, is the idea that to maintain peace people need to forgive rather than to claim rights. In other words, social relations should come to the fore and rights should be played down. But this way of reasoning is increasingly challenged from different camps. Here the vague category of intellectuals (les intellectuels) play a crucial role. People of this social category are often closely attached to the state administration, but when they claim rights, they act from a platform of other loyalties. People are engaged in political parties and organisations (e.g. Syndicat des Eleveurs), work with media, especially journalists writing for independent newspapers. Others use their influence for supporting specific contenders in court or government affairs. In the two organisations discussed in the following sections, the social category of intellectuals is of utmost importance.

Claiming Fulbe rights

The revival of the trade union of graziers in western Burkina Faso (Syndicat des Eleveurs) since 1994 has introduced a specific dimension both to local Fulbe politics (see chapter 6) and to dispute settlement. The Syndicat des Eleveurs advocates a more outspoken attitude to defend herding interests rather than to 'arrange an affair'. The organisation is based on the occupational criteria and for the benefit of any grazier, but is first and foremost perceived as a Fulbe organisation. A Fulbe man, who is active in the organisation, narrated an event which illustrates this ambiguity. At the organisation's congress, there was a need to identify in what language to communicate.

> I suggested that we should use Fulfulde, Dyula and French, and not only Fulfulde [...] Even at the top, this notion of an organisation for the Fulbe remains. But we worked to include other ethnic groups in the board. [...] In the texts [i.e. the internal rules of the organisation], there is no discrimination, but in the facts.

The office of Syndicat des Eleveurs in Bobo-Dioulasso is located in the trade unions' building Bourse du Travail in front of the municipality. There is a permanent flow of people and information in the small office, which is in fact only one room with a couple of tables. The organisation intervenes in different cases both at the Regional Tribunal, i.e. La Justice, or in villages located anywhere in the Boho-Dioulasso region (the Comoé, Kénédougou, Houet and Léraba Provinces).

The organisation is, however, strongly criticised both by many government officials and by intellectuals supportive of the farmers' cause. The main reason appears to be that its leaders claim Fulbe rights. Instead of trying to 'arrange an affair' – i.e. mobilising relations to settle specific disputes – they position themselves in relation to state law. They carry out missions in villages that experience disputes, and on these occasions, they support their members in dispute settlement. The organisation thus acts at different levels: nationally, regionally, provincially, and locally. It has representatives in some departments (e.g. the Mangodara Department).

The most important public occasion on which the Syndicat des Eleveurs claimed the rights of graziers was when President Blaise Compaoré of Burkina Faso came to Banfora in 1995. The speech, which in fact was a letter addressed to the president, was given by one of its members. The general situation for animal husbandry was recalled. Four violent conflicts resulting in several deaths were also mentioned: Sidéradougou 1986, Lobi country 1987, Samorogouan and Sikorola 1994 and Mangodara 1995.

> Monsieur le Président, force est de constater que la Comoé est incontestablement un foyer de conflits constants entre éleveurs et agriculteurs, nous savons pouvoir compter sur la magnanimité de votre Excellence pour une intervention légale adéquate dans cette zone en vue d'y apaiser et assainir le climat social.
> (Letter from the General Secretary of Syndicat des Eleveurs de l'Ouest Burkina 15 April 1995)

In addition to this general phrasing, the organisation formulated some specific grievances. It requested that the state legal process follows its course in the Mangodara conflict, and that those having initiated and perpetrated this conflict should be judged and punished according to facts. Compensation should be paid to victims, those injured, and relatives of those who had been killed.

The speech of the *Syndicat des Eleveurs* to the President was badly received by local people supportive to the farmers' cause. Intellectuals supporting the farmers strongly criticised the attitude of the organisation. A local politician in Banfora said:

> The *Syndicat des Eleveurs* poisons the situation. The *Syndicat* should educate its members and then defend the interests of the graziers. But the *Syndicat* is directed by intellectuals. That is what is serious. The *Syndicat* wants to make the graziers understand that they have the right to graze the cattle on fields. In fact, the representatives [i.e. leaders] of the *Syndicat* enrich themselves from this situation. They get money from graziers. The *Syndicat* is based in Bobo, and led by retired Magistrates and Veterinary surgeons. Instead of understanding the case, the representatives rush at the legal level, even with corruption.

The central point raised here is that intellectuals leading the organisation are fuelling tensions in villages more than reconciling parties. They claim, according to this politician, even the right to graze on farmers' fields.

Understandably, Fulbe representatives challenge such statements. Intellectuals involved in the *Syndicat* argue for their part that Fulbe graziers should not be forced to pay money if they are not in error. The situation of the hunting organisation was, for instance, raised in the letter addressed to the president.

> Dans la Comoé, nous deplorons l'attitude du groupe de chasseurs qui s'organisent et se substituent en 'justiciers', appréhendant et 'rançonnant' des citoyens qui seraient plus ou moins suspecté par eux. (Letter from Secretaire Général du Syndicat des Eleveurs de l'Ouest Burkina 15 April 1995)

In March 1995, graziers were arrested and forced by the hunting organisation to pay 150,000 FCFA and 225,000 FCFA respectively (ibid.).

In villages, exaggerated claims for compensation made by the farmers are often mentioned by Fulbe agro-pastoralists to be a problem. They may accept that their cattle have caused crop damage and pay for it, even if only a few stalks remained in the field. The farmers are accused of demanding too much compensation, and in some villages they have become even more militant. They keep the herder and the cattle until money is paid. According to a Fulbe perspective, farmers claim compensation and the cattle-owner is forced to pay in order to maintain peace. If he refuses to pay, the dispute is likely to escalate.

The *Syndicat* requests graziers' rights to have the case tried objectively, and that they should not be forced to pay exaggerated sums to farmers. However, a Fulbe intellectual told me that to put the rights in the forefront is not always supported by Fulbe agro-pastoralists living in villages, because 'the Fulbe like the easiness'. It is easier to pay money and get rid of the problem. In other words, they prefer to mobilise social relations of neighbourhood, rather than to claim rights. In the aftermath of the Mangodara conflict in 1995, the *Syndicat* tried to raise funds in Fulbe communities to be able to hire an advocate to pursue the legal dossiers in court. Although Fulbe communities in rural Comoé raised funds to support the victims' families, many were not ready to engage an advocate.

The leadership of the organisation has been highly disputed, partly manifested in the competition between Boobolangôbe and Fulbemossi. There may be a difference in the kind of leadership which is promoted by respective groups but this is a sensible issue and partly outside the scope of this study. A Fulbe intellectual (Boobolangôbe) once said that Fulbe in Bobo-Dioulasso should not be led by a Fulbemossi. But a leader is, however, not only evaluated in terms of his traditional legitimacy but also of his socio-political networks. Both among Boobolangôbe and Fulbemossi, leaders appear to have important connections to top-level politicians, but it is difficult to establish the relative importance of these connections in specific cases. Rumours circulate intensely about leaders' connections to different politicians and ministers. A Fulbe leader originates from the same village as a top-level politician. Critics take for granted that he uses this common locality as a political resource. Yet, although I have recorded many statements on such connections, it would be a methodological mistake to take such information at face value. Such information could not be treated as more 'true' than other, even though it favours conspiracy theories among antagonists.

To sum up, the *Syndicat* is an organisation that defends the rights of graziers. It is highly controversial among intellectuals supportive of the farmers' cause. The membership of the organisation is based on occupational status, but the growing importance of the *Syndicat* also reflects the process of ethnification in the 1990s.

Defending Bambaraya

Recent expansion of the hunting organisation (*donsoton*) raises questions in connection to its ambiguous appearance manifested in two names, *Kondoro* for its traditional and *Benkadi* for its modern aspects. In chapter 5 I have related this expansion to the emergence of a recent Karaboro leadership. It is also important to remember that initiation frames the socio-political purpose of the organisation. In this section I shall rather analyse the *donsoton* from outside and see it as a vehicle for defending *Bambaraya*, i.e. the way of Bambara or Paganism.

The hunting organisation responds to a deeply felt need of fighting against theft in rural areas. The organisation transgresses the Ivorian and Malian borders and collaborates with brother-organisations there. The prevalence of hunting organisations playing a protective role against banditry has also been reported from the northern Ivory Coast (Bassett 1994; Diallo 1995). Doubts expressed about the competence and honesty of government officials have implied that disputes between peasants and graziers are settled locally with the help of hunters (Diallo 1995:40). Cattle thefts are regarded as the most important problem by the hunting organisation, and have contributed to raise farmer–Fulbe graziers tensions. Senufo claim that prior to the arrival of Fulbe and their hired herders, there were no cattle thefts (Bassett 1988:467). In 1996, many people in the Comoé Province referred to the hunting organisations in the Ivory Coast. Banditry was described as the principal problem in villages, especially cattle thefts. Most informants accused salaried Fulbe herders of committing cattle thefts. The inability of the state administration to deal with banditry in rural areas has definitely contributed to the expansion of hunting organisations. In the Ivory Coast, hunters collaborate with the state administration and protect transport-cars (*taxis brousse*) from attacks.

A police official said about the hunting organisation in the Comoé Province that it was a good thing, but that it is not legally competent to judge people. 'If they [the hunters] respect the texts, there is no problem'. Many farmers recognise that banditry has diminished thanks to the hunting organisation. But the organisation is simultaneously feared, especially by Fulbe. It is treated with suspicion and ambivalence by government officials.

The hunting organisation in the Comoé Province is led by a traditional hunter (*donso*) in Dakoro.[192] The organisation poses central dilemmas to the politics of the state in the Comoé Province. It raises questions concerning notions of justice in a socio-political realm located on the margins of the Burkinabe state, but with strong connections with top-level politicians in this same state. In the following pages I shall discuss the hunting organisation from three different angles. Firstly, the hunting organisation raises the problem of local legitimacy versus central strategies, here exemplified by hunters' participation in an environmental protection programme as well as the census of fire-arms in 1996. Secondly, the organisation provides the frame for a socio-political movement of becoming Bambara, i.e. to turn paganism into a positive criteria. Thirdly, the hunting organisation challenges central notions of justice as defined by state law. To defend *bambaraya* provides a means by which something significant is articulated about politics in the Comoé Province.

The first point to be discussed deals with the problem of legitimacy. According to the basic definition of any state, it should have the monopoly of violence. The 'armed forces' are perceived to stand ultimately under the control of national legislation and its representative bodies.[193] But the ambiguous character of the hunting organisation challenges the monopoly of violence of the state. The president of the organisation embodies the ambiguous character.

Within the discourse on 'participatory development', the Ministry of Environment has chosen to work directly with the hunting organisation in the Global Environment Fund supported programme Participatory Management of Natural Resources and the Fauna (GEPRENAF) in the Comoé Province.[194] The president of the hunting organisation travelled around the Province and also informed the organisation in the Ivory Coast that, firstly, the GEPRENAF intervenes in the border zone between the two countries (in Diéfoula and Logoniégué forest reserves), and that, secondly, the hunters should not allow poachers to enter the area. In fact, the hunting organisation appears to have been instrumental to diminish poaching. A forester said that formerly the relation between the hunting organisation and the Forestry office was 'dog and cat, but today it is dog and dog'. His point was to stress that today foresters and hunters work together.

The state administration nevertheless hesitates of how to handle this organisation [sic]. The organisation has not yet been officially recognised by the state. The constitutive assembly of the organisation *benkadi* took place on 5 April 1996 in Dakoro. A first version of the rules of the organisation (the modern aspects) was nevertheless rejected by the state administration, due to the fact that the organisation was said to provide 'protection' to any citizen (farmer, trader, grazier), and not only to its members. A government official told me that the organisation should not substitute the Police. The state administration therefore hesitated, because no-one wanted to be deemed responsible for having recognised an organisation that, at worst, could develop into an armed militia.

The official recognition of the hunting organisation is not necessarily more than a formal procedure. A police official confirmed in June 1996 that the official agreement of the organisation had been delivered on provincial level. The police official thus believed that the hunting organisation was officially recognised by the state administration. My interpretation is that locally the organisation had already been recognised in practice by government officials. It had become legitimate by means of the GEPRENAF and

the census of arms.[195]

Several sources report that the number of arms has increased dramatically in the Province. Often firearms enter illegally. A well-informed government official said that many firearms enter from Ghana. The Ministry of Environment and Water carried out a census of firearms in the Comoé Province in 1996. Attempts have been made to control the circuit. The Forestry Office chose to conduct the census through the hunting organisation. Instead of closing the eyes and pretending that illegal firearms did not exist, it was better to legalise ownership of fire-arms and make the hunters move toward the Forestry Office. The *rationale* was to gain control over the hunting organisation by governmental technical services.

The results from the census reveal an ambiguous image somewhat difficult to interpret. The departments in which Karaboro and different Senufo groups dominate numerically demonstrate high figures, e.g. Mangodara 201 firearms, Tiéfora 347 firearms, Sidéradougou 223 fire-arms, Loumana 191 firearms, and Sindou 237 firearms.[196] However, I have not been able to obtain the figures for some departments, e.g. the Dakoro and Niankorodougou Departments. The problem of interpretation is that in departments where the hunting organisation appears to be very dynamic, the figures of firearms are high and the question is to what extent these high figures are linked to the active participation of hunters in the census. Those departments may well coincide with real figures, because many organised hunters live there.[197] The financial contribution to be made by different departmental groups of hunters to the overall hunting organisation was established at the constitutive assembly in 1996. While four departments were charged to pay 100,000 FCFA to the provincial hunting organisation *Benkadi* (Dakoro, Sindou, Tiéfora and Sidéradougou) others should contribute less. Put together, the high rates of hunters and firearms in these departments confirm the dynamic character of the hunting organisation. The state administration has thus profitably used the hunters and their networks and influenced both to fight against poachers (GEPRENAF) and to carry out census of firearms, but these joint actions have equally provided the hunting organisation with a socio-political legitimacy.

The second point to ponder upon regarding the hunting organisation is its 'mystical aspect', as a government official put it. Whereas *Benkadi* (the modern aspect) is open to anyone who accepts the internal rules of the organisation, *Kondoro* is only open to those who are accepted by a senior *donso* (traditional hunter) and who will undergo initiation. In this sense the hunting organisation (*donsoton*) favours the emergence of a stronger identity as Bambara or Pagan. It follows the way of the hunters, and gives the impression of being an ethnic organisation. The overwhelming majority is composed of those classified as 'Senufo peoples', recalling the relationship between Pagan Senufo farmers and Muslim Dyula traders (Launay 1982). Becoming Bambara not only serves as a model of specific socio-political relationships but also provides a model for action. The president of the organisation consciously uses this model, arguing that 'we started from the origin of *donsoya*'.

Whereas a Muslim Dyula identity is usually employed to get a job or other advantages, *Bambaraya* represents the prohibited, and often oppressed identity of local farmers.[198] To borrow from Amselle (1990:186), I would argue that people at Bambara, first settlers or Pagan in relation to Muslims or Dyula conquerors. Yet, in the case of the hunting organisation, *Bambaraya* is celebrated as a virtue, and an authentic source. It essentialises local culture as *Bambaraya*, and opposes it to Muslim culture. To become a true member of *donsoton*, the individual must be initiated. But it is hard to conceive initiation for Fulbe or Dyula Muslims. Thus, in practice Muslims are excluded, and cannot join the organisation. By emphasising *Bambaraya*, the organisation demonstrates a strong ethnic exclusion, because it is mostly composed of the vague category of 'Senufo peoples'.

The strong ethnic character of the hunting organisation is criticised both from the inside and the outside. The local president in the Sidéradougou Department, who is an ancient Tiefo hunter, argued that he has become president only 'by name'.[199] He questioned why hunters of today are dressed in hunting dress everyday.

> They [young men] carry the hunting dress as a sign of adolescence, bravery [*cameliya*]. Formerly, if someone carried this dress, there was something going on in the bush. [...] Today they carry it to frighten, to intimidate people.

The local president argued that today the hunting organisation is the problem of the Karaboro (*Karaboroko*), but 'the Karaboro cannot make anything good'. Hence the hunting organisation has become a problem of the Karaboro due to recent politics rather than being grounded in any traditional attachment. The local president in the Sidéradougou Department rejected the ethnic character of the organisation.

> We were born to find that there were hunters among the Europeans, the Fulbe etc. Those who want to become hunters they confine themselves to someone [a *donso*] so that he teaches them how to become [hunter]. Others have it in the lineage [*buruju*]. All people may become hunter, there is no ethnic group [*sia*] that may not become hunters.

Similarly, ethnologist Youssouf Cissé describes in his early article on Malinké hunters that since the ascendance of the Mali empire of Sunjata in the 13th century, the politico–military organisation of hunters is given a status, which excludes 'toute notion de tribu, de classe et de caste' (Cissé 1964:176). Instead, the children of Sanènè and Kòntròn – the common cult of the hunters – are neither Malinké, Bambara, Senufo, Bobo, Fulbe, White nor Black (ibid.: 178).

In the Comoé Province, however, the hunting organisation could be interpreted as an attempt to gather different groups of people and reinforce the identity as 'peasants' or 'Bambara'. It gathers around a common cult and shared interests. In this vein, the organisation could be seen as a response to the dilemma of a decentralised socio-political structure of these rural communities and the importance of defending rights in contemporary Burkinabe political culture.

This relates directly to the third point to discuss with respect to the hunting organisation, that is, the politics of ethnicity in a regional and national political context. Many informants reported that politicians frequently render visits to the president of the hunting organisation in Dakoro. When they need support for rallying campaigns, the position of the president and his organisation is deemed to be of utmost importance. Hunters often participate in official ceremonies, e.g. the inauguration of a development project or the visit of the President. Hunters give status and prestige to the organisers. Jonckers reports from her study of the Minyanka in Mali that the power of the hunting societies goes beyond the village level, 'des autorités administratives s'entourent de chasseurs renommés. Tel commandant de Cercle, tel commissaire de police voit son prestige accru s'il est bon chasseur' (Jonckers 1987:42). A well-informed man in Bobo-Dioulasso said that 'the hunting organisation has a political support. These people [those of the Comoé Province] are very *wackés* [i.e. strong in using magical powers]'.

A top level politician in Burkina Faso, who originates from the Comoé Province, is said to be a member of the hunting organisation. He often performs in the hunting dress at official manifestations. He is widely appreciated for fighting for the western Burkina nationally. Critics argue that he was actively involved in the aftermath after the Mangodara violent conflict in 1995. People say that he went to Mangodara and promised that those Karaboro retained in prison should be released. Left aside whether this politician was involved or not, after about six months in prison these Karaboro 'rebels' were released. According to the language of state law, the release of the prisoners appears to have been possible as the court set them on 'preliminary liberty'. Locally, however, it was interpreted quite differently. A Fulbe agro-pastoralist in Mangodara said:

> what frightens us is that if someone makes bad to another, even before the judgement, we get to know that this law sets these people free. Without any judgement, we have seen these people return. Our people have been killed, we have lost them forever, as well as our cattle, motor-bikes and our things. We are here as losers, but with all this, they do not leave us in peace.

A well-informed man in Bobo-Dioulasso argued that the named national politician only had met the autochthonous farming population in Mangodara, and not the Fulbe agro-pastoralists. This meeting had compromised the legal dossier. Other informants provided similar accounts. It should be noted, however, that these informants did not actually participate at the meeting. Their accounts merely reflect local interpretations of what happened instead of eye-witness accounts (which do not necessarily need to be more 'true').

To sum up, all accounts and comments on events boil down to the conclusion that notions of 'justice' of the Karaboro farmers actively involved in the hunting organisation differ significantly from that of state law, or at least the way state law is locally implemented. State law and local normative orders constitute different logics. Documents made from the point of view of one logic with respect to another logic are likely to reveal something significant about the way the relationship between state law and other normative orders is shaped. State law and local normative orders are mutually constituent in the sense that both logics are articulated in specific disputes (or cases). But this should not obscure the power relations that are involved. Local interpretations of state law are crucial for understanding the ways by which local normative orders are shaped. Similarly, comments on tradition and local institutions influence the means by which state law is implemented. The hunting organisation is a case at stake. However, hunters put themselves in the place of Justice when they 'arrest' Fulbe herders and accuse them of thefts. Although the leaders of the hunting organisation insist that they 'work together with the armed forces', the organisation's dependence on these 'armed forces' is highly relative. The state administration has chosen to make 'the hunters come toward us'. It is better to incorporate them into a movement that is possible to control than to let them get marginalised.

Meanings of justice

In this section the ethnographic accounts of the RAF, the *Syndicat des Eleveurs* and the hunting organisation (*Donsoton*) will be brought into the analytical framework of relations and rights. In particular, contrasting notions of 'justice' are approached. I have demonstrated the importance of social relations in dispute settlement in chapter 9. These relations may be used 'to cool' the disputes. The disputing parties thus choose to drop the dispute thanks to the social relations that bind them together.

However, it is worth recalling that disputes are often not settled at all. The underlying conflict of interests may remain (despite an official agreement) and become articulated in specific disputes years later. In the study of land-use and conflict, this is not extraordinary *per se*, but the interesting point is the linkage between notions of 'peace' and notions of 'justice'. Elizabeth Colson points out that negotiation and adjudication can settle particular claims, but have much less success in convincing contenders that they are in the wrong.

> However much disputes and their settlement are conducted in a rhetoric of community values appealing to something like *communitas*, what people learn from them is much more pragmatic information: the limits of community tolerance for different kinds of behaviour under a variety of circumstances, an appreciation of how particular individuals respond to provocation, and some mapping of the changing alliances that form the basis for daily interaction. (Colson 1995:80)

Colson's emphasis on the 'limits of community tolerance' as well as 'mapping of the changing alliances' raises key issues for dispute settlement. Although the parties have reached an agreement of how to leave the dispute behind, they may still feel to have been treated unjustly. A farmer may accept to diminish compensation, not because he thinks that his claims are not fair, but because he prefers to acquire some money and maintain a good relation with the cattle-owner. The latter may from time to time provide the farmer with money when he is in need. Similarly, a Fulbe agro-pastoralist may find that crop damage is inevitable if the farmers grow crops around a water-course. Although he compensates the farmer, he may find that he has been unfairly treated.

Notions of 'justice' are central to dispute settlement between Karaboro agriculturalists and Fulbe agro-pastoralists. It could of course be argued that the term 'justice' should be reserved for state law, because it is ideologically loaded and intertwined with state legal language. The French term *La Justice* has clear connotations even for non-French speaking people in Burkina Faso. For the inhabitants of Djelgôdji (Djibo in northern Burkina Faso), the term *La Justice* does not signify an idea of moral rightness or the quest for the reason, but simply the mobile brigade of the Gendarmerie Nationale (Riesman 1974:36). However, although the term justice has strong connotations to state law, it would be inadequate to exclude other notions of justice, located outside state legal realm. Thus I find it appropriate to deepen the reflection of different meanings of justice in a more encompassing sense.

Terms such as community or popular justice have been used to grasp non-state forms of justice. Merry points out that popular justice occupies an intermediate space between state law and non-state forms of ordering. 'This space between state law and indigenous ordering is a contested space, in which state law and indigenous law struggle to establish control' (Merry 1992b:170). In a recent special issue of the *Journal of Legal Pluralism and Unofficial Law* (36/1996), the term popular justice is employed. The communitarian tradition of justice, or popular justice 'embraces an ideology and assumption set which promise a quality of justice and a range of related practical benefits that cannot be achieved or are difficult to achieve through the more conventional, formal justice apparatus of the State' (Depew 1996:23). The distinctive quality of popular justice 'is of a social rather than a strictly legal nature' (ibid.). However, a problem with a term like 'popular justice' is that it 'wears many hats and has become a catch-all phrase to denote anything not of the formal, adversarial criminal justice system' (LaPrairie 1996:1). There is thus a need to contextualise the use of the term 'popular justice'. My attempt is therefore to approach notions of justice in the ethnography of dispute settlement in the Comoé Province through two different angles. Firstly, I shall discuss socio-political organisation and legitimacy with respect to the RAF, the *Syndicat des Eleveurs* and the hunting organisation. In particular, the ambiguous membership of these three organisational structures and how the respective leadership attempts to speak on behalf of a collectivity will be focused. Secondly, I shall start out from principles and practices to reflect upon different meanings of justice articulated in dispute settlement.

Membership and leadership in organisational structures

In the first part of this chapter I have described three specific examples of organisational structures of national intervention and ethnic/local mobilisation in dispute settlement. The Land and Tenure Reorganisation (RAF) was first analysed in the way it is interpreted locally, expressed in the phrase 'Burkina belongs to everybody'. Secondly, the *Syndicat des Eleveurs* was related to public discourse of claiming Fulbe rights. Finally, the hunting organisation (*donsoton*) was analysed as both ideological and practical expressions of defending *Bambaraya*.

In this section I shall compare these organisational structures, because the RAF as well as the two organisations raise two inter-related questions with respect to dispute settlement between farmers and agro-pastoralists. The first question is to what extent the two organisations are mutually identifiable and regarded as entities of the same order, and explores local representations of the RAF. The second question analyses the local leadership in charge of negotiation, and discusses whether the different leaderships are regarded as legitimate, and to whom. One could object, however, that while the *Syndicat* and the *Donsoton* represent interest organisations for the respective social category, the RAF is a law and therefore of another organisational order. There is indeed a structural difference between the RAF on the one hand, and the two organisations on the other, but I find it useful to look at them as organisational structures which are articulated in local settings. Common to all three is the variable and ambiguous criteria for belonging (membership) and the struggle to speak on behalf of a collectivity (leadership).

The first aspect is the ambiguous criteria for belonging. The RAF addresses the issue of land and the right of Burkinabe citizens to get a piece of land to farm. Locally, it has often been interpreted and used as a tool for getting access to land without the permission of the Master of the Earth. Graziers' rights to cattle tracks and grazing land is stated in the RAF, but locally this is only evident in the case of the Agro-pastoral Management Scheme through which 'development' is to come. Yet, while the right to land has continuously been granted by the Master of the Earth, access to grazing land is – at least today – not regulated by this institution.

In the 1980s, the RAF officially treated all people – even the Masters of Earth – in the village simply as Burkinabe citizens. The political discourse at that time held the traditional leaders to be 'feudal'. In the heat of the outbreaks of violence in 1986, the Karaboro men in Tiéfora questioned the criteria for belonging defined by the RAF by stating that 'Burkina is Burkina, but Tiéfora is Tiéfora'. The Karaboro men thereby rejected the imposed state law in Tiéfora, in 'their country'. In the 1990s the Masters of the Earth are given some recognition, but the fact that 'Burkina belongs to everybody' is locally seen as the profound intention of the RAF.

The *Syndicat* has chosen to define membership on the basis of economic occupation. Although people of Fulbe origin dominate the organisation, other people join the organisation as well. A Fulbe agro-pastoralist that I met in the Mangodara Department experienced problems of emphasising the occupational criteria for the organisation.

> We agree upon the talking [*kuma*], but not in terms of work. Because if one talks about graziers, all graziers are included. But we have seen that our cattle are deprived of water, and that their cattle may drink. Our cattle are deprived of the remaining stalks on fields, but their cattle are left grazing without any comments. This is the situation.

To promote the interests of graziers rather than those of Fulbe ethnic category is controversial in the core of the *Syndicat*. Some Fulbe leaders even use the term 'genocide' when referring to violent conflicts, because all victims were Fulbe in Mangodara in 1995 (see chapter 8). A Fulbe intellectual recognised the dilemma to struggle for graziers on the one hand, and to claim Fulbe rights on the other. But he argued that ethnic questions could not be reduced to those of a trade-union. 'We have to take the risk of encompassing more people than only the Fulbe'.

The hunting organisation (*Donsoton*) is based on a dual membership criteria: the traditional *Donsoton* to which one must be initiated (the cult of *Kondoro*) and the modern *Benkadi* to which one must pay 1,000 FCFA to become a member. Both represent aspects of the hunting organisation. The criteria for membership was nonetheless questioned by a traditional Tiefo hunter (*donso*), 'it is a women's organisation, […] not a men's organisation'. This statement questions the fact that other people than traditional hunters (*donso*) now may join the organisation. Traditionally the hunting dress should only be carried by *donso*. But, according to this *donso*, today the hunting dress is carried by Karaboro youth, who have not even killed a rabbit.

According to Article 2, *Benkadi* is open to any hunter of at least 18 years old, who resides in the Comoé Province, and who is entitled with a hunting permission (*permis de chasse*) and has manifested the desire of joining the organisation. However, the president in Dakoro emphasised the sacred aspect of the organisation. In practice, membership is therefore radically circumscribed. Fulbe may pay 1,000 FCFA and become simple members. But they cannot become *donso*, because 'we do not shoot at their dog'. The president thus explicitly refused to initiate Fulbe to the cult of *Kondoro*.

The second aspect is the aspirations of all three organisational structures to speak on behalf of a collectivity. The RAF takes the issue of the right of Burkinabe citizens to get access to land,

irrespectively of birth, status and wealth. A government official originating from the Bobo-Dioulasso pointed out that:

> the administration has a tendency to protect the weakest. […] That is why one speaks about the agrarian reform [i.e. the RAF].

A local politician expressed himself even more radically. According to him, the RAF is a means for Mossi (the majority ethnic group) to conquer the area, because all migrants have heard that land belongs to the state. This solution to conflicts is that 'people in Ouagadougou' have to change their mentality of conquerors. This local politician thereby made allusion to the fact that traditional Mossi kingdoms have been expansionist states: 'Fulbe graziers are manipulated [by the people in Ouagadougou]'. In short, these two informants argue more or less explicitly that the RAF serves the interests of Mossi. In local interpretations, it gives strangers the right to settle without the permission of the autochthonous population. The RAF could then be perceived as a project for the Mossi majority, who dominate in national politics and thereby use the RAF to 'colonise' western Burkina.

The *Syndicat* is speaking on behalf of the collectivity of graziers, but is locally perceived as a Fulbe organisation. However, the legitimacy is sometimes questioned in practice. Many Fulbe agro-pastoralists residing in villages seem to prefer to 'arrange the affair' through *Kannankefulbe*, the chief of the Fulbe in Bobo-Dioulasso. The president of the *Syndicat* recognised that this is a problem. 'If the graziers themselves take the *Syndicat* in their hands, they will have much more success'. However, the struggle for Fulbe chieftaincy in the Bobo-Dioulasso region between Boobolangobe and Fulbemossi is not necessarily reflected in specific disputes. Even Boobolangobe graziers may prefer to act through the Fulbe leader of Fulbemossi origin. The retired Magistrate may be regarded as a better option than the traditional chief, whose legitimacy is merely grounded on tradition.

The hunting organisation (*Donsoton*) is to some extent speaking on the behalf of the collectivity of farmers, but are first and foremost acting in 'their name' and serving their immediate interests. However, people supportive to the farmers' cause may also be hesitant to the organisation. The local politician who accused the RAF for serving the Mossi interests, did not support the hunting organisation. 'I see a militia emerge. I disapprove it. I do not like violence. The republican state should have an army'. Others argue that the hunting organisation has been efficient to fight against banditry. It collaborates rather than competes with the 'armed forces'.

An influential Fulbe agro-pastoralist in the Sidéradougou Department criticised the hunting organisation for its biased membership.

> If a hunting organisation should be created, all ethnic groups must be part of it. An organisation starts, but if it only gathers agriculturalists, that is not good, or if it only gathers graziers, that is not good either. No graziers are part of the hunting organisation that has been created in the region. They are playing below (*o bi munu munu na duguma duguma*, appr. they turn on the ground, that is, they are conspiring].

This man further argued that hunters replace the *La Justice*. Hence the region is not good any longer. 'If you come and pass in front of my courtyard and I do not like you, I kill you and say that you were a thief. Could you, who is dead speak any longer?'

The hunting organisation grieves other than Fulbe in the

Sidéradougou Department. There is no Tiefo in this organisation, except the traditional Tiefo hunter, who criticised the organisation strongly for being a women's organisation. A Tiefo Master of the Earth said that all know that Tiefo are hunters (*donso*).

> We do not want to destroy the organisation, but they have to start again from the beginning and meet the hosts [i.e. Tiefo]. And then that the hosts become members of it and granted with responsibilities.

Common to both the *Syndicat* and the *Donsoton* is the references made to tradition. Yet, the nature and shaping of tradition differ significantly between the organisations. Whereas the hunting organisation is based on the sacred and is composed of traditional *donso*, the *Syndicat* is an entirely modern phenomenon in organisational structure. But the power struggle between Boobolangôbe and Fulbemossi over the commanding of Bobo-Dioulasso is possible to detect even in the *Syndicat*. The hunting organisation has a dual identity, clearly manifested in its two names: *Benkadi* and *Kondoro*. This is not only an issue of legitimacy among their supporters, but also among their antagonists. A Fulbe intellectual argued that 'the precolonial hunting organisation was behind the fall of Samory. [...] The Senoufo of Kénédougou took the name of the Malian [precolonial] Kénédougou. And behind Sikasso, we have Wassoulou'. The RAF emphasises modernity. Locally, however, the RAF is often perceived as a Mossi project to get access to land. It thus manifests a certain historical continuity of Mossi kingdoms based on the relationship between people of the earth and people of power (Izard 1985; Zahan 1967).

To sum up, in all three organisational structures there is an emphasis on 'rights' rather than on 'relations'. In the RAF, the right is to be granted to those who farm land and/or graze land. The *Syndicat* argues that graziers should not be forced to pay money, but to be granted rights by the government. The hunting organisation stands for the right of local farmers to defend themselves against thieves. Actors external to the local setting are nevertheless not only struggling for the right of their respective group, but could also be regarded as socio-political entrepreneurs. Whereas external actors are likely to have vested interests – whether economic, political or symbolic – in dispute settlement, local government officials remain, at least officially, reluctant to deal with disputes and suggest that disputing parties settle the dispute out of court. Lack of resources and fear for violent conflicts reduce the willingness of becoming involved in dispute settlement.

Justice and rights

Discourses of 'justice' and 'rights' dominate in debates among actors external to the local setting – here simply called external actors – who are based on provincial, regional or national levels but intervene in local dispute settlement. These debates are instrumental to the politics of difference. Specific disputes arc shaped by debates on rights and vice versa. People from the *Syndicat des Eleveurs* travel regularly to villages where there are problems to support the graziers. Similarly, a specific dispute in a village is used by them to demonstrate what they perceive as injustice and incorporate it in their struggle for their members' rights. A specific dispute thereby becomes a precedent of negotiation.

The three organisational structures described here relate to different notions of justice and rights. However, they share the underlying assumption that people living in local communities are incapable and badly suited to settle disputes themselves. Each dispute must be adjudicated by a third party. This is expressed as il *faut trancher l'affaire.*[200] Otherwise, the argument goes, the right of the party which the external actor supports is not likely to be granted.

To structure the analysis of justice and rights in dispute settlement between agriculturalists and Fulbe agro-pastoralists, I find that Gulliver makes a very important observation in reference to his distinction between negotiation and adjudication. Whereas adjudication is norm/rule-using and focuses on past behaviour, negotiation is norm/rule-making and concentrates on future behaviour (Gulliver 1979:15). The point is then that negotiation is an attempt to establish rules and codes of conduct between the parties, but adjudication judges past behaviour.

> In adjudication, there is more likely to be concern for values and a definition of disputes in terms of values, an emphasis on the application of norms, and a concern for all-or-nothing decisions, for acts (rather than actors) and past behavior, and for less multiplex relationships (Gulliver 1979:21).

In adjudication, values are forwarded rather than interests, or at least, the interests are verbally dressed in terms of values. Adjudication is 'essentially characterized by the fact that decision-making and the outcome of the issues in dispute are controlled by a third party exercising some degree of accepted authority' (Gulliver 1979:20-21). But a third party with 'accepted authority' is not necessarily what we observe in dispute settlement in the Comoé Province. External actors aspire to have the right to intervene in disputes, at best to *trancher l'affaire*, but this is the outcome of negotiation. Hence the distinction between negotiation and adjudication halts when confronted to external actors in this specific ethnographic context, but I find comfort in the fact Gulliver presents his model with 'a prudence characteristic of Gulliver's cautious adventures in theorizing' (Moore 1995:12). Thus I keep the distinction between negotiation and adjudication because it is still 'good to think with'.

The ethnographic account of the RAF, the *Syndicat des Eleveurs* and the hunting organisation (*Donsoton*) demonstrates that discourses of justice and rights in dispute settlement are as much attempts to define the dispute at stake and parties involved and to defend the perceived rights of the party one supports, as to fight for a socio-political platform to claim rights on behalf of a collectivity. Hence dispute settlement is a social field in which actors external to the local setting aspire to intervene. In the following I discuss, firstly, the dispute definition and the rights that are claimed in relation to each definition, and, secondly, external actors' relationship to the state administration.

The struggle for definitions of disputes and disputing parties was one principal point of departure for this study. Two local politicians with whom I discussed the problem of definition argued that 'l'éthnie n'a rien là-dedans, mais c'est l'acte qu les uns et les autres posent'. They claimed that people of the Comoé Province often are accused (at a national level) of being racists, regionalists and ethnicists, but that this is not true. Instead, one of them rhetorically asked why the Fulbe pose problems. All other ethnic groups try to see the Master of the Earth, but not the Fulbe. The politician specified that the Fulbe do not ask the permission to stay while grazing cattle in an area, but recognised that they ask permission to farm if they settle.

Formerly, even transhumant graziers passed to see the *Canton* Chief. Today, when there are problems, one says that graziers settle without asking for the advice and permission of anybody. It is the proliferation of land property.

The central issue raised by these politicians is that the Fulbe do not respect the 'normal procedures'. This gives the farmers the right to react against Fulbe exactions. Fulbe have no rights any longer due to their misconduct. This attitude toward the Fulbe is also reflected in expressions such 'the Fulbe is a traitor'.[201] Disputes are caused by Fulbe graziers, the argument goes, and farmers only defend themselves and their subsistence.

A Karaboro intellectual stated that if relations are bad between the agriculturalist and grazier, the state administration is contacted. If the agriculturalist is not compensated, he brings his firearm to the field. He shoots at the cattle, and then at the herder: 'Voilà le conflit arrivé'. According to this man, the conflict is caused by the bad behaviour of Fulbe and the state administration rather than by the competition for resources. The state administration is furthermore implicated, because they treat complaining farmers unjustly. However, the lack of judgement by the Regional Tribunal in Bobo-Dioulasso is not regarded as a problem. A local politician put this quite clearly,

> Je préfère qu'il n'y ait pas de jugements [des conflits de Sidérad-ougou et Mangodara]. Si l'Etat continue sa politique, si le système d'ethnification continue, on ne veut pas cette justice.

The *Syndicat des Eleveurs* officially promotes economic categorisation of disputing parties, but some members find this counterproductive, simply because the Fulbe are those targeted in violent conflicts. 'Only God supports the Fulbe', as a Fulbe elder put it. This contradiction needs to be handled by different Fulbe actors. A Fulbe intellectual said that certainly some people act badly, and that some herders purposely cause crop damage, but rights should still be granted to Fulbe. They have come and settled, but are still after generations defined as strangers. In Sidéradougou, some local government officials refer to Fulbe as Palestinians, i.e. people without land. In this vein, Fulbe need the support from the state administration to be granted rights over water, pasture and farmland. A Fulbe intellectual said that 'we want the law to be applied'.

Some Fulbe accuse farmers of not allowing them to stay more than a few years at each place.They have to leave, because farmers want to obtain access to the land that has been fertilised by the droppings of cattle. Fulbe agro-pastoralists argue that their right to land is weak. But to claim rights for Fulbe agro-pastoralists is highly controversial. Leaders of the *Syndicat* were for example accused by a local politician of enriching themselves through disputes.

The second point to discuss in this section is the external actors' ambiguous relationships to the state administration. Throughout this study I have treated the state administration as one but specific socio-political configuration among others. Ideally, the state is a body of organisational structures, but empirically the bodily metaphor halts. According to various local interpretations, the state is simultaneously the sum of the parts (both inherently contradictory and complementary) and the representation of power, force (*fanga*). Hence, the Burkinabe state is far from being a homogeneous entity, but is represented to local people through different 'services' as well as individual government officials. The RAF is, in turn, interpreted by every single official according to what he thinks is its intention or how he consciously manipulates it.

External actors are often in an ambiguous position vis-à-vis government officials. In many cases the people that I have referred to as intellectuals or as external actors are also employed by the state administration. A local politician who, in 1996, accused the state administration of having worsened the situation by the means of the RAF upheld, in the early 1990s, a high politico-administrative post in the Province. Other intellectuals criticising the state administration have also direct attachment to the same administration through employment. This is nothing extraordinary *per se*, but emphasises strongly that much public discourse revolves around the state administration. The most evident consequence is that state legitimacy is not generally questioned in violent conflicts. Instead it is the legitimacy of *local* government officials and their abilities to settle disputes which are questioned.

In the ethnic relations between Karaboro agriculturalists and Fulbe agro-pastoralists, Mossi farmers constitute a category of 'others' to both groups. More than any other ethnic group in Burkina Faso, the Mossi are locally seen as holders of political power. In most rural communities in the Sidéradougou and Mangodara Departments, there are Mossi farmers who reside. In Sidéradougou, the Mossi are ethnically represented by a *Naba*, i.e. the title for the political chief of the Mossi. In general, Mossi farmers are badly perceived by local farmers (e.g. Karaboro), but they are in a way 'untouchable'. In contrast to Fulbe agro-pastoralists, the Mossi farmers are strangers but demographically too numerous and politically too important. They are not explicitly targeted in outbreaks of violence against strangers. They are criticised, but feared for their 'long arms' into the state administration.

Local interpretations of the RAF serve Mossi farmers' interests, because it ensures access to land. 'Burkina belongs to everybody' has come to mean that access to land is open to all. The RAF seems to fit quite well into Gulliver's definition of adjudication. In official state discourse, the RAF is emphasising the rights (or values) of a national belonging. It is conceptualised as to grant the right to land primarily to those who farm it. However, the interests of the Mossi majority to get access to land are played down within this discourse. The RAF thus promotes rights rather than relations. But in muted discourse relations are central to translate these rights in practice. A government official brings a younger brother from his home-village to his duty-station in the Comoé Province. This brother gets a piece of land to farm and to settle in the Sidéradougou Department. Access to land is facilitated by the relations maintained by the elder brother. The RAF is therefore not the only enabling factor for Mossi migration toward western Burkina. Faure reports that in the 1990s, it rather organises itself in the form of a Muslim network. These Muslim communities (of *tidjanya* faith) invest the forests of Kénédougou and Bougouriba Provinces (Faure 1996:173).

For Fulbe agro-pastoralists, the government is Haabe, i.e. composed of Black Africans, and therefore not likely to serve Fulbe interests. This is clear at the level of principles. The main programme to implement the RAF is the Land Management Programme (*Programme de Gestion des Terroirs*). Yet, the *approche terroir* implemented in many Sahelian countries have been criticised, because 'notions of space, limits and control that are at the heart of the concept of terror are implicitly those associated with sedentary populations living in stable village settings' (Painter *et al.* 1994:450). At the more practical level, however, Fulbe agro-pastoralists may be supported by individual government officials. These officials may then be accused of having been bribed by Fulbe. It is very difficult to substantiate such accusations, but it should be noted that accusations may also serve farmers' interests. Such accusations may be a way to obscure farmers' actions to the detriment of Fulbe agro-pastoralists, e.g. farming close to cattle tracks.

But the economic interests vested in Fulbe agro-pastoralists go beyond those of individual government officials. Diallo reports from the northern Ivory Coast that while the state and urban interests (government officials, deputies, developers, etc.) are interested in Fulbe presence for various reasons, a peasant majority is increasingly embarrassed by this presence (Diallo 1995:42). Similarly, urban people often invest in cattle in Burkina Faso, which they confine to Fulbe agro-pastoralists. Economic interests in Fulbe presence among external actors may therefore not be limited to potential corruption, but coincide with important individual interests to invest in cattle.

Currently, Fulbe agro-pastoralists' claim for rights are also motivated by a regional movement of Fulbe returning from the Ivory Coast, Ghana, Benin or Togo (Sanon 1996:4). They return to their country of origin – in this case Burkina Faso – due to lack of pastoral space, or because they are chased by these states after conflicts with local farmers (ibid.). A Fulbe agro-pastoralist narrated his personal experience of being chased.

> We have come here [Mangodara], because the diseases are finished [i.e. animal trypanosomiasis recently eradicated]. Here there is grass. We left the Ivory Coast, because the Ivorians told us that the 'contract' has finished. Thus we were obliged to leave. [...] If it will heat here, we will go to the Ivory Coast or to Ghana. If people do not agree with us, we will go to Ghana. [...] Cattle are wealth for the country. We did not stay in the Ivory Coast, because they treated us like strangers [*boyorojan*, lit. those coming from far away]. But here they also diminish us [*o bun dogoya*, i.e. do not respect us].

In the scenario of Fulbe agro-pastoralists returning from the Ivory Coast, the expression 'Burkina belongs to everybody' takes on a new dimension. Burkina Faso is their country of origin in the eyes of the Ivorians. There they could claim the right to land, not in the Ivory Coast. But when they come back, Fulbe agro-pastoralists have difficulties in settling in strained socio-political environments.

Summary

In this chapter I have analysed existing linkages between national intervention and local appropriation through three specific organisational structures: the Land and Tenure Reorganisation (RAF), the *Syndicat des Eleveurs* and the hunting organisation (*Donsoton*). The main point discussed is that rights are expressed and interpreted through these forms in dispute settlement between Karahoro agriculturalists and Fulbe agro-pastoralists. Five specific points need to be recalled.

Firstly, these three organisational structures of 'intervention' in dispute settlement claim rights on behalf of a collectivity. But the criteria for belonging are ambiguous to all three. Consequently, issues of membership, legitimacy and representativity are located in the core of the politics of national intervention and local appropriation. The RAF is defined to concern all Burkinabe citizens, but serves particularly the interests of Mossi farmers migrating towards the western Burkina. The *Syndicat* struggles officially for the rights of graziers, but is internally as well as externally to a large extent perceived as a Fulbe organisation. The hunting organisation has a dual membership; whereas *Benkadi* is open to all, the sacred dimension of the organisation gathers around the common cult *Kondoro*.

Secondly, the analysis of notions of rights and justice demonstrates that state law and local administrative orders are mutually constituted, that is, both are locally constituted by the very interaction. In the Sidéradougou Department, state law such as the RAF is subject to local interpretations, which rapidly become more important than actual texts. The expression 'Burkina belongs to everybody' summarises the idea of a national identity of Burkinabe citizens with respect to land-use, but is used in radically different ways by different actors and for specific purposes. While autochthonous farmers challenge it and argue that the local normative order dominates in their 'country', Fulbe agro-pastoralists returning from the Ivory Coast perceive that they originate from Burkina and have the right to stay there.

Thirdly, all three organisational structures position themselves in the frame of modernity and tradition. Hence, no-one could be situated entirely outside neither modernity nor tradition. While the hunting organisation emphasises the 'sacred aspects', the organisation also conforms to the state administration. The syndicate is shaped in the form of a modern trade-union with a well-defined interest-group, but contesting claims to power are often grounded on tradition. The RAF is a modern project, but locally perceived to serve primarily the interests of Mossi farming expansion. It therefore resonates to history and continuity of Mossi kingdoms.

Fourthly, Mossi farmers residing in the Comoé Province constitute a category of 'others' both for Karaboro farmers and Fulbe agro-pastoralists. They are strangers who are criticised, but feared. The reason is that they are demographically too numerous and pull too much political weight in Burkinabe national politics. They thus remain 'untouchable'.

Finally, in chapter 9 I argued that relations are ideologically important for the maintenance of peace and prosperity in villages, but in practice, however, rights are defended. In this chapter I have on the contrary suggested that rights provide an ideological justification for external actors to defend a disputing party. In practice, relations are, however, important, but are played down in public discourse. I find that Gulliver's distinction between negotiation and adjudication applies sufficiently well to 'the social field of relations and rights'. In adjudication there is a concern for values, acts and past behaviour, but negotiation deals with interests, actors and future behaviour.

Notes

* Please note that original footnote numbering has been retained.
[186] The legal decision to create the Agro-pastoral Scheme was taken jointly by the High-Commissioners of the Comoé and Houet Provinces in June 1988.
[187] In general, the RAF is merely applied in specific 'pilot villages' supported by international aid. These villages are included in the Land Management Programme (*Gestion des terroirs*) which to a large extent are supported by international donors such as the World Bank and the UNDP. In 1990–91 I visited a 'pilot village', Diassaga in the Kénédougou Province, on several occasions. It was apparent that rural development oriented missions were directed to this village by local government officials in the provincial capital of Orodara.
[188] *Burkina ye Burkina ye.*
[189] *Burkina ye Burkina ye, nga Tiéfora ye Tiéfora ye.*
[190] The killings in Tiéfora (i.e. in Karaborola) in 1986 were tragic consequences following the spreading of the conflict over the region after the outbreaks of the violent conflict in Sidéradougou.
[191] As discussed elsewhere (notably chapter 4) the RAF has been modified on several occasions toward a larger recognition of Masters of the Earth whose rights thereby have been strengthened.

[192] Since the Decentralisation in 1966 (in practice since 1997), Dakoro belongs to the new Léraba Province. Today (1998) the president of the Comoé Province is a Karaboro hunter (*donso*) in Tengrela, a village about 10 kilometres west of Banfora. The traditional hunter in Dakoro remains president of the Léraba Province. However, I here discuss the hunting organisation as it was organised in 1996.

[193] However, Franz von Benda-Beckmann points out that if the right is based on the monopoly of legitimate violence, there would not be a pluralism of monopolies 'Mais nous admettons tous qu'il n'y a jamais de monopole, mais simplement des revendications ou des affirmations de monopole' (von Benda-Beckmann 1993a:50).

[194] *Gestion Participative des Ressources Naturelles et de la Faune.*

[195] When I made a short field-visit in February 1998, key informants told me that the hunting organisation was not yet recognised by the state administration and that the High Commissioner had transmitted the dossier to his superiors in Ouagadougou.

[196] Figures communicated by the Forestry office in Banfora in 1996.

[197] The interests of the individual hunter to register the firearms was that the census provided an opportunity to get the official permission to carry firearms.

[198] Young Karaboro men who go to the Ivory Coast often use a Muslim name. For instance, all men in the compound where I stayed had Muslims names in addition to the Karaboro names. Although I did not make any systematic survey, the general impression was that few Karaboro 'living in the bush' pray.

[199] During my field-visit in February 1998, I learned that this Tiefo hunter was no longer president in the Sidéradougou Department. Instead, the vice president – a Karaboro farmer – has become president.

[200] A similar expression is also used in Dyula: *ka kiti tige* (lit. to cut a decision).

[201] *Fula ye janfanti ye.*

References

Amselle, J.-L.1990. *Logiques Métisses: Anthropologie de l'Identité en Afrique et ailleurs.* Paris: Bibliothèque scientifique Payot.

Barry, H. 1996. 'Etude sur la gestion des conflits liés aux aménagements pastoraux: Cas de la zone pastorale de Sidéradougou Ouagadougou': Projet Regional d'Appui au Secteur de l'Elevage Transhumant.

Bassett, T. J. 1988. 'The Political Ecology of Peasant-Herder Conflicts in the Northern Ivory Coast' *Annals of the Association of American Geographers* 78, 453–72.

——. 1994. 'Hired Herders and Herd Management in Fulani Pastoralism (Northern Côte d'Ivoire),' *Cahiers d'Etudes Africaines* 34, 147–73.

Cissé, Y. 1964. 'Notes sur les sociétés de chasseurs malinké,' *Journal de la Société des Africanistes* 19, 175–226.

Colson, E. 1995. 'The Contentiousness of Disputes', in P. Caplan (ed.), *Understanding Disputes: The Politics of Arguments.* Oxford, Providence, USA: Berg.

Depew, R. C. 1996. 'Popular Justice and Aboriginal Communities: Some preliminary considerations', *Journal of Legal Pluralism and Unofficial Law*, 21–67.

Diallo,Y. 1995. Les Peuls, les Senoufo et l'Etat au nord de la Côte d'Ivoire: Problèmes fonciers et gestion du pastoralisme. APAD Bulletin, 35–45.

Faure, A. 1996. 'Pratiques et politiques foncières en milieu rural,' in R. Otayek, F. M. Sawadogo & J.-P. Guingané (eds), *Le Burkina entre révolution et démocratie (1983–1993): Ordre politique et changement social en Afrique subsaharienne.* Paris: Editions Karthala.

Gulliver, T. H. 1979. *Disputes and Negotiations: A Cross-cultural Perspective.* New York: Academic Press.

Hagberg, S. & D. Berté. 1991. *Etude des projets d'aménagement de terroirs dans les provinces de la Comoé et Kénédougou, Burkina Faso.* Rapport de Travail UNSO/BKF/90/X02. Banfora: Ministère de l'Environnement et du Tourisme/Programme des Nations Unies pour le Développement.

Izard, M.1985. *Gens du pouvoir, gens de la terre: Les institutions politiques de l'ancien royaume du Yatenga (Bassin de la volta Blanche).* Paris: Editions de la Maison des Sciences de l'Homme.

Jonckers, D. 1987. *La Société Minyanka du Mali: Traditions communautaires et développement cotonnier.* Paris: Editions L'Harmattan.

LaPrairie, C. 1996. Introduction. *Journal of Legal Pluralism and Unofficial Law*, 1–8.

Launay, R.1982. *Traders without Trade: Responses to Change in two Dyula Communities.* Cambridge: Cambridge University Press.

Merry, S. E. 1992b. 'Popular Justice and the Ideology of Social Transformation', *Social and Legal Studies* 1, 161–76.

Moore, S. F. 1995. 'Imperfect Communications', in P. Caplan (ed.), *Understanding Disputes: The Politics of Argument.* Oxford & Providence, USA: Berg.

Painter, T., J. Sumberg & T. Price. 1994. 'Your terroir and my "action space": implications of differentiation, mobility and diversification for the approche terroir in Sahelian West Africa', *Africa* 64, 447–464.

Riesman, P. 1974. *Société et liberté chez les Peul Djelgôbé Haute-Volta: Essai d'anthropologie introspective.* Paris: Moulton La Haye.

Sanon, Y. 1996. *Etude sur la gestion des conflits liés aux aménagements pastoraux: Cas de la zone pastorale de Samorogouan.* Ouagadougou: Projet Regional d'Appui au Secteur de l'Elevage Transhumant & Ministère de I'Agriculture et des Ressources Animales.

Swift, J. 1996. 'Desertification: Narratives, Winners & Losers', in M. Leach & R. Mearns (eds), *The Lie of the Land: Challenging Received Wisdom on the African Environment.* Oxford & Portsmouth (N.H.): James Currey & Heinemann for the International African Institute.

von Benda-Beckmann, F. 1993a. 'L'Etat et le monopole de la violence dans la perspective de l'anthropologie juridique', in E. Le Roy & T. von Trotha (eds), *La Violence et l'Etat: Formes et évolution d'un monopole.* Paris: Editions L'Harmattan.

Zahan, D. 1967. 'The Mossi Kingdoms' in D. Forde & P. M. Kaberry (eds), *West African Kingdoms in the Nineteenth Century.* London: Oxford University Press.

4 The Politics of New Social Forces

MAMADOU DIOUF
Urban Youth & Senegalese Politics

Reference
Public Culture, 8, 2, 1996, pp. 225–50

The extraordinary vitality of African youth in the political arena – the high visibility achieved by their spectacular demonstrations – is perceived as signifying that African societies have broken with the authoritarian enterprises inaugurated by the nationalist ruling classes. Youth has played a crucial role in the configuration of nationalist coalitions,[1] even if it has subsequently been swept aside through the invocation of African traditions that uphold rules of deference and submission between both social and generational juniors and seniors. The young have also been the first group in society to have manifested, in practical and often violent ways, hostility toward the reconstituted nationalist movement.

The young have produced a precocious reading of the nationalist movement's evolution, identifying the authoritarian drift of the postcolonial powers whose neocolonial economic and political orientations they denounce. This awareness seems to have been the basis for youth's resistance to the repression, *encadrement,*[2] and cooptation through which the state handles social movements.[3] Logics of exclusion based on tradition, like those of the postcolony's treatment of the young, render public space as an adult territory off limits to youth at the same time that it denies them a private space. As Claude Lefort remarks *à propos* of totalitarianism – defined as a regime in which power is not the object of open contestation, that is, a regime in which public space is devoid of exchange[4] – 'the effect of the identification of power with society is that society enjoys no autonomy by "right", it is contained within power as "private space."'[5]

The correspondence underlined here is accentuated in the African contexts where the subordination of the young is conceived as a traditional imperative. In this article, I analyze the social movements, in particular those led by young people (high school and university students, unemployed youth, members of political parties) that violently shook the Senegalese political scene at the end of the 1980s and the beginning of the 1990s. During this period youth marked their territory, painting the city walls throughout Dakar and its suburbs with representations that fashioned, in however hesitant a manner, a new way of being, of living – and a new rhythm. Their practices expressed a will to break with the historic memory that accompanied the nationalist generation's rise to power at the end of the Second World War.[6] It is this memory whose expressions, however rhetorical, still furnish the guidelines for the political discourse of consensus and unanimity and for public displays like commemorations as the convocations of memory and independence parades as institutional celebrations of the army and youth.

The sudden appearance of youth in politics is not exclusive to Senegal. Almost every West African country has experienced strikes resulting in a lost academic year or '*année blanche*';[7] the most recent case being Nigeria in 1987–1988. The recourse to violence, the symbolics of purification by fire, the destruction of the places and monuments of postcolonial munificence – as if to deterritorialise its inscription in space – constitute common elements of the social movements led principally by youth. The project of uprooting the ruling elite's postcolonial style of legitimating itself is legible in numerous developments: the riots orchestrated by Malian students (5 April 1993),[8] the absence, in districts of Lagos and certain Nigerian cities, of any authority on the part of administrators and politicians and their reliance on 'area boys';[9] and the crucial role played by 'disaffected youth' in the armed struggles in Liberia and Sierra Leone.'[10]

The *mise en scène* and the models for these violent demonstrations seem to have been images of rioting in South African townships and the Intafada uprising in Israeli-occupied Palestinian territories, widely diffused through audio-visual media, as well as Hollywood films such as *Rambo* and *Terminator*. Regarding the diffusion and consumption of this culture of the riot, P. Richards writes: 'Television does not, in any simple or unproblematic way, transcribe reality. More plausibly, it should be seen as a medium that enhances the scope of human image-making within the range of consumption of a mass audience.' [11] This youth is heterogeneous and its manifestations, like the ways it inscribes itself on the urban landscape, are plural. The city, as the scene of its actions, poses numerous problems that the young take into account as actors. Postcolonial urban sociology is dominated by a paradigm in which the rural peasantry is regarded as the fundamental expression of indigenous Africa. As a consequence, the city has long been thought exclusively in terms of the colonial ethnology of detribalization, rural exodus, and the loss of authentically African traits and values.[12] Before World War II, it was assumed that urban dwellers were rootless; having left their tribal homeland, they were supposed to have lost their traditional reference systems, qualities, and virtues. Colonial and postcolonial literature portray cities as sites of corruption, moral, sexual, and social deviance and as sites in which Africans lose their souls and their sense of community. Africans appropriated this colonial representation in their statement that villagers are the 'only' full-blooded 'Africans' and village values the only authentic ones. The political hegemony of the rural world was reinforced by its demographic domination which, although progressively diminishing, survives in the ruling classes' regime of truth as the popular legitimation of their power. In view of the democratic, essentially urban rooted contestation, and of the increased urban violence, they regard urban space as lacking both tradition and its logics of supervision and control.

In contrast to a highly legible rural territoriality, the city is a space of superimposed inscriptions and references which appeal to composite memories. The city asserts a cosmopolitan intermingling even as it organizes a geography of territories – simultaneously physical and identity-constituting spaces that continuously reconfigure allegiances, languages, and idioms. Urban territoriality defines itself in relation to a state geometry: the city is the seat of power, the terrain for expressing the imaginary of the ruling class and its ascendence. In this field, there are no possibilities other than confrontation and negotiation. The procedures employed are therefore those of circumvention and, more frequently, of feigned acquiescence and direct confrontation.

In view of the physical breakups and ideological fragmentation ensuing from the economic and political crises, African societies are experiencing major chasms through which new networks – economic, political, ethnic, women's, youth – are stealthily slipping through and enlarging their scope. These networks call for a variety of identity references such as locality, age, gender, common goals, promotion of former school and university classmates. Their fluidity, flexibility, and often uncertain origin strongly affect social demands and political modes of intervention in the public and private spheres.

With the unity of the missionaries of modernity fizzling out, each of the segments appropriated a specific discourse. Thus, in addition to the physical decay of the space in which power is wielded and displayed is the fragmentation of the ruling social groups (government, unions, students, pupils, entrepreneurs). The reduced capacity of these groups to flaunt themselves and assert their dominance has thereby jeopardized the ability of the ruling class to reproduce itself. Thus the African crisis has paved the way for opening new spaces while promoting deep upheavals which could be briefly summed up as follows: several beliefs including those regarding the homogeneous nature of the urban world and the capacity of cities to construct a homogeneous culture against specificities are being challenged by the ongoing demographic changes. This is related to the demise of the 'perception – heretofore unsuspected – of an elite with common interests and values by an urban population which felt that it was a strong minority vis-à-vis the mass of networks.'[13]

Thus a new generation emerged on the African political scene, a generation which came into existence in the wake of the foundational event for African nations, namely, independence. A combination of factors led to the invention by this generation of its own sociability which expressed itself in communal and religious enterprises.[14] These factors included the fact that, in addition to holding on tightly to reconstructed traditions mixed up with values of a global world, this new generation felt excluded from the postcolonial munificence and its sites of sociability, e.g., recognition, the rights to free speech, work, and education, and although a numerical majority, as youth, they were reduced to political silence. This youth is actually behind political violence, which ranges from urban riots to Islamic fundamentalist armies, and is spearheading armed conflicts and criminal actions of random violence, looting, students strikes; it uses violence to express its disillusionment with the outcome of the restoration of democratic rule.

Assessing the social conditions

Dakar and its suburb Pikine contain 19% of the total population of Senegal and close to 50% of the urban population.[15] Dakar accounts for 46% of this population, Pikine-Guédiawaye 42%, and Rufisque Bargny 12%. The Dakar metropolitan area is the principal destination for migrants. It was calculated in 1976 that 51% of 630,000 migrants took up residence in Dakar.[16]

The selective character of access to property and housing, one of the principal vectors of socialization and means of social differentiation, indicates the precarious situation of the young. The same figures prompted a research team to remark that 'the young are

under the control [in the total care] of their elders.'[17] High unemployment rates profoundly affect the youth of Dakar and reinforce their status as dependents. Newspapers not controlled by the government daily portray a state incapable of assuring a decent quality of life and education for its students or offering them work. The figures published by *Le Témoin* are a case in point: 100,000 young people enter the job market every year and 4,000 among them have advanced degrees.[18] According to Bocquier, 45.2% of the employed population of Dakar are younger than thirty years old.[19] This group includes only 15.6% apprentices in enterprises in the unregistered sector. He specifies that the unemployed who have never worked are clearly the youngest: 80.8% were younger than thirty.

Two component groups of Dakar area youth are markedly distinct. The members of one have been labeled social marginals (*encombrements humains*) by the official ideology.[20] This notion evokes social maladaptation, economic marginalization, and deviance. These social *déclassés* by the regime standards are equally products of the rural exodus, rejects from the school system, traveling merchants, and beggars. According to a clerk of the Dakar Tribunal,

> minors between 12 and 20 years are found every week of the calendar in the 'lockup' for the most varied infractions. Some fist-fight or steal in the markets. Others, girls between 14 and 16 years, are 'picked up' along the public thoroughfares. Still others are dedicated to itinerant begging on behalf of charlatan marabouts. Virtually all rural youth without qualifications who 'come up' to the capital live in the poorer districts and congregate around the port, the markets, and the stations.[21]

It is this population in particular that yields those labeled, on the one hand, as vandals and bullies by the militants of the reigning Socialist Party (PS) and, on the other, as thugs and mercenaries by the opposition in the wake of demonstrations or punitive expeditions by the PS.

The second group – school-leavers from the high schools, colleges, and universities – is better understood due to the large number of studies devoted to it.[22] The unemployed who have never worked are better educated than the actively employed; this category has more women than men.[23] Since 1980, this situation has been aggravated by a generalized crisis of the school and university systems. A. Sylla observes: 'A review of the state of the schools in 1990, with the diverse difficulties and problems they have had for a decade – the numerous protest movements and strikes that led to an *année blanche* in 1987–88 – makes their future appear quite uncertain, particularly if the causes of distortion and dysfunction are not thoroughly eradicated.'[24]

The consequences of this disastrous situation have been a fierce instructors' strike and a radicalization of the student movement, with a considerable increase in the number of university graduates out of work. The defeat of an operation by unemployed holders of master's degrees and the rising failure rate of students, and of unemployed university graduates, usher in new forms of struggle and new groups, e.g., the movements of young members of Muslim religious brotherhoods, in the school and university milieux.

These two categories of Dakar area youth – students and social marginals – have always been a central preoccupation of the Senegalese state apparatus and the class that runs it. Since 1966, the Economic and Social Council has considered that the essential problem of the urban youth – whether an intellectual or a manual laborer, employed or unemployed – is that of his social equilibrium.[25]

The Senegalese state uses two logics associated with cooptation, repression, and *encadrement* and has consistently attempted to design solutions which integrate the young into the social hierarchy by institutional means, whether political, economic, and/or legal. These strategies have evolved over the years in the attempt to adapt themselves to the plural and multifaceted procedures adopted by the young.

Political framing versus mass movements

There is extensive evidence which shows that the Senegalese state's handling of the youth question has been guided by a vision that, while being tied to the real, emerges more from the repertories of the imaginary and the ideological. Youth and the young are a key theme in the discursive project of nationalist ideology. Although the ideology itself is out of style, it still informs the Senegalese regime's interventions in the management of youth. It is based on the political harnessing of the 'vital forces of the nation' and on traditional social values. The ideology of political framing and the extension of the state's domain provide the key references for political, economic, and social activity. This ideology blurs the distinction between the state and the holders of power, on one hand, and the masses, on the other. It rests on the manipulation of traditions of submission to authority and to elders, thus circumscribing a social and political space from which youth is radically excluded. The monocentric orientation of power and the institutionalization of the de facto single party inspire the creation of public youth organizations.

These organizations are particularly directed at high school and university students and the more or less educated urban young. They have not enjoyed great success. The anti-imperialist trade union organizations were always capable of subverting spectacular demonstrations by the movements affiliated with power. Attempts at political institutionalization were designed to draw youth close to the party in power, and relied heavily on the Ministry of Youth and Sports with its exclusive preoccupation with advanced athletic competition and football (soccer). The failure of these attempts led to an intensification of oblique practices and militancy by the opposition parties, the majority of which were clandestine until political reforms in 1981, which removed restrictions on both the number and ideology of political parties and established integral multipartyism. It is at this stage that student organizations took up the task of spreading the messages of leftist groups, notably marxists. This same alliance was the beginning of the fragmentation of the student organizations themselves, in the image of the political left, from which they had difficulties distancing themselves in a context of political liberalization.

The Senegalese government has always advocated a political reading of student demonstrations by interpreting student demands as the result of manipulation by opposition parties or outside forces, more precisely maoist or communist parties or regimes.[26] As a consequence, since the violent student demonstrations in 1968, 1969, and 1971, the state has adopted operating procedures that oscillate between repression and corruption of the student leadership. However, the institution of integral multipartyism in 1981, in opening the public political arena to marxist parties, provoked a mutation in the student movement: the extraordinary political diversity and confrontations between leftist factions progressively expelled high school and university students from the political scene. The students, in turn, progressively demobilized in order to devote themselves to better defending their standards of living and education – and not only against the regime, but increasingly against the teachers unions and the opposition parties.[27] This tendency was intensified by the degradation of living and study conditions, with classroom overcrowding, increases in the failure rate, and the abolition of scholarships, grants, and the provision of books and educational materials. This effort to reorganize the student movement resulted in new practices adapted to organizational structures, new forms of struggle, and new modes of mobilization and intervention.

For the second group, those bypassed by the educational system – the unemployed, deviants, beggars, peddlers, informal sector apprentices – who constitute the vast majority of the youth population, the government has always reserved repressive treatment. This treatment has been legitimated by the persistence of the colonial ideology regarding public space and thoroughfares and the nationalist ideology's reading of the rural exodus and its baneful consequences. *Le Soleil* faithfully echoes the discursive complex of the regime:

> Senegalese society has known profound upheavals that occasionally have dramatic repercussions for familial structure The Senegalese family forms a very important social group in a strongly hierarchical agrarian society. Today, with all order of change, the family has been completely transformed and, with it, parental authority is lax, indeed permissive, if not gone altogether.[28]

The state assumes the right to substitute itself for parents who have abdicated their responsibilities and to restore traditional values fallen into disuse. With the same gesture, it expells the young marginals from its own space and from that circumscribed for tourism. The notion of 'social marginals' permits the state to rank each deviant person according to its own norms or in reference to the traditions it manipulates and continuously reinvents to sustain the total alignment and *encadrement* of society.

The decline of parental authority has become a recurrent theme in political discourses on youth. It is amplified by recourse to marabouts and brotherhood hierarchies and references to the Qu'ran and to the ancestors. Discourses with a high moral tenor support and justify repressive handling of youth. This orientation was aggravated by the surge of 'law and order' ideology at the beginning of the 1980s, an ideology that emanated from the ruling class and affected the entire society.

The failure of the policy of *encadrement* of the young by the party in power, the extremely low participation in government-sponsored youth organizations, and youth's extraordinary lack of interest in opposition parties have combined with the effects of the economic crisis to make the youth question the central political issue. Dakar area youth appear to have left the terrain of institutions and formal political organizations for agitational practices outside of conventional public frameworks.

Inscribing themselves in heterodox (*buissonières*) practices, youth have set about promoting new solidarities and producing new parameters, confronting the state, parents, and educators – or simply ignoring them. They invest their energies in reconstructing urban spaces and practices, challenging the state and municipality's authority over certain districts and their power to name streets and police them. Certain segments assign themselves the role of guardians of Muslim morality to justify their 'combing' operations and punitive expeditions against addicts, drunks, and thieves. Since 1988, *Le Soleil* daily relates the occasionally fatal incidents between 'youth gangs' and 'thieves or delinquents.' In certain parts of Dakar's working-class suburb, Pikine-Guédiawaye, youth gangs organize 'moral cleansing' operations in zones reputed to be 'places of prostitution, bars, and crime.'[29] The young thus become key players in political struggles and the driving force of urban social movements.

Political idioms: violence and heterodox practices

This section concentrates on the imaginary of the social movement that launched an assault on the ruling class and the history of its dominance as inscribed in urban space with sticks and stones (the electoral riots of 1988), violent pogroms against the Moors (Senegalo-Mauritanian conflict of 1989), and mural painting and clean-up operations (1990), clearing a path through the city and redefining the spaces and logics of sociability and public places.[30] These expressions were in no way violent ruptures, they attest to the long accumulation of heterodox (*buissonière*) practices that led the young to organize themselves in an autonomous and non-institutional manner.

The essential characteristic of the crisis of the 1980s is the defiant attitude of the young toward political, economic, social, and cultural institutions. This attitude was manifested in the tendency to create autonomous organizations with strong religious or ethnic connotations, often centered on common origin, region, or locale. This movement affected every segment of the young, rural as well as urban. Two new structures accurately reflect the new tendencies in the urban areas: the Cultural and Athletic Associations (*Associations Culturelles et Sportives*) and the new coordination between movements of high school students and university students.

Cultural and athletic associations

These associations promote a cultural, social, and athletic life of great intensity. They organize diverse activities such as clean-up operations and vacation classes for children. Faced with the temptations of the neighborhood political leadership to appropriate public playgrounds and to control the fire-hydrants, and especially in the wake of trash-collecting operations, the young increasingly engage in tests of strength against established public institutions (electricity, water, and transportation companies). Some of these associations are now experimenting with public libraries and professional training centers. The appearance of the *Groupement d'Intérêt Economique* (GIE) and *Petites et Moyennes Enterprises* (PME) attests to the evolution of a strongly economic orientation of some associations whose goal is increasing employment among the young.

Through their organizational structures, these far more democratic organizations escape the clientelist logics and the prebendal modalities that have continuously enervated the logics of political integration. They create fissures in which the young elaborate strategies of cooperation and confrontation with the state. In this way, they obtain better results in accomplishing projects and managing communal equipment. Involved with the emergence of a new social conscience and highly critical of governmental plans, the cultural and athletic associations are confronted with the resistance of political entrepreneurs who face the erosion of the effectiveness of their mercenary support. The associations have fostered the progressive dissolution of the logics of centralization and the

submission of social actors to the power of the state.

The neighborhood focus of cultural and athletic associations translates, to a certain extent, the search for a territorial inscription that defies a colonial and postcolonial spatial and institutional arrangement which emphasizes both the symbols of the colony (the builders of the colonial empire) and of the nation (the fathers of the nation). Renaming streets after local figures (football players or marabouts) in the Médina or in Gueule Tapée/Fann-Hock in the place of letters of the alphabet attempts to erase a certain memory. It also unveils self-definitional procedures that create the categories of a new sociability, distinct from those produced by the nation and the ethnic group. Finally, it attacks the state's modalities of management and dismemberment of urban space. The groups that have been founded in the course of the movement have produced private local memories, selecting their own past, their own 'founding fathers,' and etching their own signs on the sand and the stele. The new constellations of stars (those who have streets named for them) reveal a reconstruction of the past that is a socially revealing elaboration of the present and includes the ubiquitous absence of women being commemorated by this male-dominated movement.

One of the most spectacular forms of this new dynamic was the success of the Cairo '86 operation which made it possible to put the generous financial contributions of the public, and particularly the young, at the disposal of the national football team to finance its participation in the Africa Cup. The elimination of the national team and Senegal's exclusion from participation in the African competition for more than fifteen years, as well as the rumors of embezzlement, had provoked a collective hysteria. The year 1986 seemed to mark a turning point in the modes of expression of the young, first by resisting municipal recruitment for the *set weec* or *Augias* community service operations (1987),[31] and then by the progressive appropriation of certain governmental functions.

For example, in various neighborhoods they set up 'militias for self-defense and the security of property and the tranquillity of peaceful citizens in the "hottest" quarters of Dakar.'[32] In 1989, the youth of the Medina organized 'lynching parties' in the caves of the Corniche along the ocean;[33] these were directed against the thieves and addicts who are blamed for the reign of insecurity in the district bordering on this zone. The raids were designed to compensate for inadequate policing. In 1990 in the same quarter, following a morning assault on a muezzin, fundamentalist youth gangs launched a reprisal operation. Numerous bars and night clubs were burned. In September and October 1993, to fight against the nuisances and accidents caused by collective taxis, the residents bordering Valmy and Petersen streets in the center of Dakar blockaded them and then demanded the governor issue a decree forbidding the circulation of the vehicles, more specifically collective taxis whose drivers systematically disregard traffic rules.

High school and university student movements

The newest conjuncture of crisis (increasing failure rate, eroding infrastructure, discontinued scholarships) and the democratic opening found new forms of struggle at the heart of the movement of high school and university students. The movements developed an expertise that rendered their leadership less vulnerable to the manoeuvres of the authorities through the adoption of a rotating leadership. Their daily submission of negotiations to the sanction of the general assembly imposes a logic more of permanent confrontation than compromise. One of the student movement's most interesting successes is its skill in using the independent press to mobilize public opinion in its support and against the government.

Nevertheless, the students have to a certain extent deserted the terrain of partisan political militancy – at least this no longer exclusively determines their union practices. They have set up coordinating committees (Coordination of Senegalese High School Students and Coordination of Dakar University Students), whose flexibility is testimony to their independence. They present themselves 'as rejects of the state, marginalized by civil society, or simply as pawns in the hands of the parties on the political chessboard.'[34] The students mounted an intransigent defense of their demands, above all in the context of the massive unemployment of graduates. The slow restructuring of the student movement, its disarticulation from politics *stricto sensu*, has resulted in repeated strikes and the imposition of long and humiliating negotiations on the government. The regime's exasperation has led to a constant and massive utilization of repression. Beginning with the 1987-88 school year, the confrontation led to an *année blanche* and the total paralysis of the Senegalese educational system, with the exception of the private schools, attended by children of the elite.

Sopi: *Violence and political disillusionment*

The context is also that of Abdou Diouf's succession to Senegal's first president, Léopold Sédar Senghor in 1981 and the difficult democratic transition and contested elections of 1983, at a highly unfavorable economic conjuncture. The state had been progressively disengaging from the sectors of health, education, and sanitation. Public services and public and parapublic institutions 'trimmed the fat' and impoverishment ensued. At the same time, the government reinstated the municipal statute of the city of Dakar (1983) which involved the financial disengagement of the state from local structures. In its juridical translation, this returned the administration of public space to the local population, through the intermediary of its elected representatives.

The inefficiency of repression and corruption, the disqualification of social and political intermediaries (parents, teachers' union, marabouts), and the interference of the student demonstrations that began in 1987 with campaigning for the 1988 presidential and legislative election forced the government to negotiate with leaders of youth groups, who obtained concessions that had never before been accorded to social actors. The President of the Republic was obliged to give them an audience after they had repeatedly refused to negotiate with school and university authorities.[35]

In the difficult context of an electoral campaign, the student movement was able to link up with the *Sopi* movement without fear of manipulation.[36] They filled the streets with their own slogans, which they combined with slogans of the opposition party that had been recast as democratic demands. Their resistance and their autonomy vis-a-vis the political parties were interpreted as 'revenge on the state and civil society.'

The historic fabric of the electoral and post-electoral violence and the founding events of *Set/Setal* is woven from the threads of the school and university crises, the *année blanche* being the catalyst for a series of strikes, demonstrations, and riots in which students, unemployed youth, and marginals attacked urban symbols and the signs of power in the Plateau at the beginning of 1990, before the clean-up operations.[37] The violent assaults against alcohol sales in the Médina and on the fringes of the Plateau together with the operations against the social marginals (robbers, drug addicts, alcoholics) of the Corniche attest to the same movement, in its 'moral' and political aspects. The authors of the first work on the movement indicate very clearly this interweaving of motivations:[38]

The urban riots known as *Sopi* begin with the advance campaigning for the campaign and elections of February 1988. The announcement of the election results provoked violent riots that shook the principal cities of Senegal for days. The principal authors of the violence, destruction, and resistance to the forces of order were the young: high school and university students and social marginals. February '88 to April '89, Senegalese youth made a dramatic appearance on the political scene. Nobody expected them but they couldn't have cared less. Fear of the future expressed itself in a formidable destructive rage. Between throwing stones a 17-year-old *lycée* student spits out, 'We are going to tear everything down in order to rebuild.' Hot air? We shall see. Since July 1990, the juvenile violence has passed over into a sort of dense madness that remains an enigma. Under the eyes of transfixed adults, the erstwhile Mauritanian-hunters, groups of young people put into practice their new credo: order and cleanliness. The most horrible city on the continent, the most infested with squatters and traffic jams is cleaned from top to bottom. Public parks that were no more than sordid urinals are restored to their original role, rehabilitated and beautified.[39]

Sopi was the expression of the brutal irruption of these social categories into the tête-à-tête between political parties. It marked the failure of attempts to institutionalize models of political action and definitively consecrated youth as the 'accursed share' of Senegalese society. Both the violence of the clashes and the youth of those confronting the forces of order were surprising. It was recorded in the photographic coverage of *Le Soleil*, accompanied by the following account: 'Throughout the day yesterday, Dakar was in an uproar. Cars set on fire and overturned, stores ransacked, gas stations in flames.'[40]

The principal targets of the young rioters were symbols of the state: the center of the civil administration of greater Dakar was torched; eighty of the public transit company's buses and numerous telephone booths were damaged; government and administration cars were attacked and set on fire;[41] these 'Black Monday' rioters attacked the homes of militants and individuals close to PS power.[42]

The riots were the consequence of the logic of verbal excesses surrounding the Electoral Code and the partisan position of the administration, denounced by the opposition, and the threats directed at certain opposition leaders. The firm will of the opposition parties, including the recourse to violence, to bar the way to any attempt at electoral fraud, intimidation of PS women, and the closing of schools and universities by the Minister of the Interior all heightened the tension. It was in this 'very tense context' that 'the Senegalese state let loose in the street a fraction of the young submitted to difficult living and study conditions and to an uncertain future where they joined the ranks of the young unemployed.'[43]

The incumbent, President Abdou Diouf used pejorative and degrading terms to characterize the youth or one of its component parts – it has never been made clear which – as 'unwholesome pseudo-youth.' Youth responded to this insult with a total condemnation of the state and the ruling PS and massive support for the *Sopi* convoys of the electoral campaign. In the same spirit, they attacked and disrupted electoral meetings of the PS and affiliated movements.

A fringe of the urban youth organized the post-electoral riots.

The interviews obtained by a journalist from a French radio station during the event give a fairly exact impression of the attitude of this group .[44] These young people were generally between eleven and eighteen or nineteen years old. They expressed their total refusal to play the classic political game through their violence and in a language of explosive virulence – a language that not only rebelled against politics but even more surely against so-called traditional values. And, even as they clothed themselves in the discourse of the opposition symbolized by the *Sopi* slogan, they twisted the meaning and preached physical confrontation with the state, a state which, according to their terms, is a regime of robbers divested of its historical legitimacy and its function as principal actor in the building of the nation.

In fact, the irruption of youth into the political arena in such violent modalities establishes an investment in the present and the refusal of the deferment imposed by the nationalist historicity of the ruling class. The state's response to the social movements culminated with the declaration of a state of emergency and the deployment of police throughout Dakar, the goal being to isolate the Plateau and control the strategic points of access to this area along Avenue Malick Sy. The poorer neighborhoods, particularly the Médina, the HLM (Habitations à Loyer Modéré)-subsidized housing development district, and Colobane, were left to the young rebels and to the opposition.

The violence of youth's intervention attests to the furious response to the ongoing attempts at *encadrement* and authoritarianism. The revolt constituted a total refusal of the places assigned to youth not only by political power – first single-party rule and then multiparty democracy – but also, and throughout the revolt, by a tradition whose imperatives of submission to elders are endlessly repeated in radio and television broadcasts as a *crises de valeur* (in French) and an 'abdication by parents of the education of children' (in the national languages).

To defuse the crisis that followed the elections, President-elect Abdou Diouf committed his new five-year term to improving the conditions of youth. The constant oscillation in the discourse of the ruling class between a negative pole and a positive pole testifies to its ambivalence towards the practices of the young and its inability to take them in hand, as much in a social and economic register as in an ideological one. The violence seems to have been the sign of enormous distress, profound anguish, and fear in the face of a blocked future and a more and more unequal division of power and riches in a society in crisis.

The profound and lasting disruption by youth and urban marginals of the implementation of the mechanisms for the democratic transition since 1983 (symbolized by *Sopi*) inaugurated a new era: the refusal to allow the institutions established by the ruling class to direct the process of democratizing Senegalese society. It illustrated the expansive struggles for democracy and, above all, the demand for dialogue, for a hearing without reference to legitimation, henceforth to be backed up by violence on the part of social adults who refused the role of social junior which no longer offered any benefits in a changing society.

After the state's severe response to the electoral riots and its arrest and subsequent release of the principal opposition leaders, the negotiations of the opposition's most representative fractions and the politicking of *La Table Ronde* discredited the option of a change of political regime.[45] Thus was achieved the unlikely accession of the *Sopi* leaders to power. The controversies within and between the opposition parties and the regime's expert management of the post-electoral crises led to sectors of the opposition (PDS and PIT) joining the government in 1991. The stability of the political configuration, combined with the renewal of structural adjustment programs without political danger to the regime, definitively pushed certain political actors to take shortcuts to achieving a voice; theirs was a discourse refractory to postcolonial sociability and its logics of compromise and accommodation.[46]

The disappointment of the youth in the insignificant role that they were accorded in the post-electoral discussions found a violent outlet during the Senegalo-Mauritanian crisis, provoked by a scuffle between pastoralists and agriculturalists on the banks of the Senegal river. Dakar was the scene for the explosion of a murderous and irrational rage against the Moors. Dozens were mutilated or had their throats slit after Senegalese in certain Mauritanian towns met the same treatment. Youth unleashed an unheard-of violence and threw itself body and soul into campaigns of vengeance which were amplified by more or less fanciful rumors. Mauritanian-owned stores were looted. It required the intervention of the army, rounding up Mauritanians and repatriating them, to put an end to the torrent of violence and hatred.

This extraordinary murderous fury in a society proud of its hospitality (*teranga*) and pacifism seems to have surprised the Senegalese themselves. And, as if to purify themselves, the young threw themselves into the assault against filth, garbage heaps, and stagnant water, following the torrential rains of September 1990. The moral aspect of the movement is reconstructed in this commentary by a young leader: 'This massive rain is a sign of purification, so we must clear our neighborhoods, rid them of their recent memory, and of existential dramas of all kinds.'[47]

Set/Setal: *From the political arena to community territory and space*

In its most widely accepted definition, *Set/Setal* is the mobilization of human effort for the purpose of cleansing in the sense of sanitation and hygiene, but also in the moral sense of the fight against corruption, prostitution, and delinquency. The movement's primary concern was to rehabilitate local surroundings and remove garbage and filth. It also undertook to embellish these sites, sometimes naming them, often marking them with stele and monuments to bear witness by recalling moments or figures from local history or appealing to the private memories of families or youth associations. *Set/Setal* is clearly a youth movement and a local movement (in opposition to national movements and even to parties and urban sections of parties), that is to say, one centered on the neighborhood. It is a specific response to the accelerated degradation of the urban infrastructure and to the virtual absence of residential garbage collection in the poorer districts, and increasingly in the Plateau, because of the strained relations between the private garbage collection company and the new municipal administration. The new city hall's lack of technical capabilities and financial means lasted until the creation of a new semi-public, semi-private garbage collection company. The state's desertion of public service and the municipal authority's inability to replace it had plagued Dakar with a repulsive filthiness. Furthermore, political reconfigurations and feuding within the new municipal administration, as well as within the central government led to conflicts that were accentuated by the recomposition of the ruling class after the legislative and presidential elections of 1983 and again in 1988.[48]

These elements of political crisis were constantly renewed, both through the election of leaders for the majority Socialist Party (PS), and through the regular elections. The ways that violent pitched battles or the riots were brutally dispersed by the forces of order testify to the crisis between 1983 and 1990. And *Sopi* was the rallying cry and banner of these years; it expressed the debasement of political standards, the rise of a new, totally postcolonial generation, and a 'crisis of values' intensified by the liberal effect, which resulted from structural adjustment programs and multiparty rule.

Set/Setal possesses historical antecedents for its sanitation and human investment themes, and a genealogy that goes back to the nationalist and voluntarist episode of the first decade of the Senegalese postcolony. These activities were designated as *set weec*, the generic term for human investments, or the *Augias* operations.[49] The *Augias* operations had always been an occasion for the ruling class to affirm its munificence, its incontestable power, and its authority over a population hemmed in on all sides by political *encadrement*. They were the affirmation, at the local level, of the strength of the party in power, of its articulation with the legitimacies of localities and districts, and the expression of the centrality of clientelist constructions and their languages in Senegalese political trajectories. They provided proofs of magnanimity and a reaffirmation of the rule of the nationalists and their heirs.

These practices in the city demand an interrogation of the current political stakes in urban management, that of the worlds of work and of leisure, as well as in the history of the city and the traces left on it by social actors. The morphology of a city, its representation and production, effectively signify the trajectories of the individual and collective lives that unfold there. Does the context of the 1980s and 1990s, marked by the policies of structural adjustment, adequately explain the dynamics of which *Set/Setal* seems to be the most complete expression? Can we identify relationships between the stylistics of power and the style of *Set/Setal*? The logics induced by *Sopi* and the incomplete character of the process of democratizing Senegalese society are developments which proceeded hand in hand with the disengagement of the state and the appeal to continuously reformulated ethnic, religious, and regional identities. Can *Set/Setal* be read as a strategic syncretism, capable of creating an alternative space for social relations? Does it favor a redefinition of relationships among the state ruling class and the youth? Or is it simply a new tactic by Senegalese youth in the search for a fixed point of reference, as well as a referential matrix in which to ground itself within a changing urban landscape? *Set/Setal* expresses a harsh critique of the world of adults and politicians by the vast majority of youth. It is an attempt to overcome youth's dependent position and the lack of attention from the adults who provide for them:

> *Set/Setal* is in the hearts and souls of all young people. If people think that going *Set/Setal* is simply sweeping the streets and painting the walls, they are mistaken because there are people paid to do that. You can't make street-sweepers out of every one of us. The authorities haven't understood a thing. They don't know how to listen. To do *Set/Setal*, is to rid ourselves of this colonial heritage that regulates our way of being, of conceptualizing things. *Set/Setal* is an absolute obligation to find a way out and this necessity to express new concepts in a new language, in this struggle for life.[50]

Whatever the case, taking charge of clean-up and beautification required financial resources that the youth groups obtained either through the organization of public music and dance parties and demonstrations or through the more or less forced solicitation of motorists. According to one of the leaders of these groups, in the HLM district, 'The money gathered from the masses, that is to say door to door and by stopping vehicles, was solely designed to make the public participate in our activities, to be independent of the administration and the politicians.'[51]

The expression of urban malaise and the malaise of youth has never been experienced in Senegal in such plural and original forms, in this constant oscillation between violence, creativity, and practicality (*la débrouille*). The educated youth sustain their activities through the uncompromising political struggle to rid Senegal of the PS regime that 'prevents us from having a future.' During the 1993 elections, the same procedures were again taken up by youth in a different context. The entire political class adopted a consensual political code. Foreign observers were present for the first time to monitor the elections and prevent the PS from manipulating the voting. One of the Senegalese opposition's long-standing demands was thus met.

The youth's enthusiastic engagement in the cause of deposing the head of state, however, did not translate into a massive voter registration. As in 1988, they followed the electoral processions of the opposition, especially M. A. Wade, in large numbers. Students constituted the subgroup of youth which was most engaged in the electoral battle of 1993, in contrast to 1988 when they were less involved than unemployed and uneducated youth. To achieve their objective, the defeat of Diouf and the PS, students organized campus debates and created movements such as *La Jeunesse pour l'Alternance* (JPA) and *Coordination Laye Espoir* (CLE).[52] In contrast to the university students, high school students, and especially those from the *lycées*, demonstrated violently against the regime. The repression against them was ferocious, most notably on February 11, 1993 when Dakar *lycéens* clashed with the Mobile Intervention Group riot squad of the Senegalese police.

Despite recurrent violence since the elections of 1988 which is, from this point on, the privileged form of expression for youth, the emergence of a tradition of self-reliance on the margin of all systems (educational, economic, parental) is overriding attempts to change the regime through elections. The desertion of the political and of political modes of expression has been the outcome of the crises of *Sopi*, confirmed by *Set/Setal* and this explains perhaps the absence of drama in the 1993 elections.

The failure of *Sopi* has had contradictory consequences for the political behavior of Senegalese youth, notably affecting their political voice (*parole*). The most spectacular factor in this evolution is the utter refusal of postcolonial sociability and its logics of compromise and accommodation. The study of the success of this refusal is responsible for Senegal's reputation in West African scholarship.[53] This dissonance presupposes plural modes of expression, plural strategies, and above all, new readings of the city – more precisely a counter-history to nationalist fictions and fables of the radical alterity of African desires, needs, and practices. The dissonance between the style and the discourse of the ruling class, the ruses of democratic opening, and the living conditions of a population on the road to marginalization and impoverishment, provoked the activation and redeployment of powerful new symbolics drawn from both Senegalese nationalism and the globalism made possible by African world music and its Western references.

If political strategy requires an identification, the production of different references proves indispensable in order for those excluded from the political arena, those who express themselves in *Set/Setal*, to act and think as different kinds of political subjects. The action that aimed at shaking the foundations of the nationalist memory went hand in hand with a new treatment of space that celebrates local memory. *Set/Setal* expresses the proliferation of new idioms that rest principally on a refusal of traditional political action and assesses new forms and practices of citizenship. These idioms were not accounted for by African nationalist ideologies which forcefully argued for cultural restoration, including gender and age hierarchies. *Set/Setal* presents itself as an indigenous appropriation of the city. The human investment, the rehabilitation of neighborhoods, and the murals express a political challenge by the youth and their demand that the political class rethink its actions and its modes of intervention. Through a radical refutation of the modes of political framing, the young have enunciated a new sociability, contradictory to the norms that have presided over the postcolonial compromise.

Multiple paradoxes characterize the situation today. After its association with the government of President Abdou Diouf, the PDS is again in the opposition.[54] It is allied with a religious movement, the *Moustachidines wal moustachidati*. This religious association is led not by a fundamentalist leader but by Moustapha Sy, a young Tijani marabout who is today in prison for allegedly threatening the security of the state. The *Ligue Démocratique Mouvement pour le Parti de Travail*, another opposition party, rejoined the government after the 1993 elections. Currency was devalued despite salaries having been reduced by fifteen percent to prevent it. The disenchantment has become so widespread that the unions are unable to mobilise their militants.

This young marabout leads the *Moustachidines wal moustachidati* and symbolizes the opposition to the regime and its politics. His supporters inaugurate novel forms of expression and resistance, such as challenging judicial authorities. They chant religious poetry instead of responding to questions, thus thwarting the judicial ritual.[55] The young strike a violent blow against the languages of power through the production of synthetic idioms whose elements are borrowed from distant and heterogenous worlds. They are in the process of creating an urban culture, detached from the colonial and nationalist memories. From the violence of 1987 and 1988 to the flourishing heterodox (*buissonière*) style of *Set/Setal*, Senegalese youth express the impossibility of authoritarianism in the period of structural adjustment. And if the murals are the iconographic index of multiple ruptures, can't one discern their history lessons? Has a cultural projection that remodels the imaginary and historical conscience of the generation of independence already come to ill through technocracy and adjustment?

The murals, like *mbalax* (a form of popular music),[56] express the mobilization of new idioms to capture novel situations. One can support the hypothesis that the *Set/Setal* movement and its accompanying signs are the indices of a dynamism that was thought to have been suffocated by autocracy and the pervasive mediocrity of an unrealized 'democracy of the educated,' incapable of managing economic and social crises. The assumption of responsibility for the reconversion of space and its cleansing, as well as the reclaiming of indistinct territories and renaming of streets, have been the vectors for the reintroduction of an excluded youth into a space and a struggle over the city. The youth assumed responsibilities which encroached upon the prerogatives of public authority and insisted that accounts be settled. Their actions signify the recuperation of a power that founds and legitimates new discourses of identity. Inasmuch as these orientations are highly local, they are multiple and, therefore, capable of leading to sectarianisms that impede social cohesion.

In the same way, by intervening directly in the organization of space, *Set/Setal* called into question the subdivision of living spaces in the old *lebu* quarters of the Plateau – reexamining the spaces set aside not only for work but for innovation (*la débrouille*) and/or delinquency, spaces for which the city alone offers such diverse possibilities. Each time that the state 'unloads' a space, its pretensions to rule are diminished; the liberated space becomes a territory for invention, for dissidence, and for dissonance.

The neighborhood is substituted for the national territory as the canvas for elaborating the symbolic and the imaginary. Discursive and iconographic fables register a local memory that proclaims itself as such against the nationalist memory. This contestation also translates into commemorations and festive demonstrations, of which the music and dance parties and celebrations (*furël*) are the most obvious signs of the invention of new traditions. To the theatricality of power is opposed the theater of the street whose young actors and directors invent scenes and texts by drawing on a global repertoire. And, paradoxically, it is along this trajectory that traditional celebrations and games have been rediscovered and recreated, after the state had worn itself out promoting them in vain, in order (it was said) to restore traditional morality.

At stake is the relationship between the national memory and local memories. The new urban order is being elaborated through democratic innovation and the crises that today rock the African postcolonies. Through protests, clean-up campaigns, murals, and memorials, the imaginary and the conscience of the young and marginal of Dakar, who have become a social movement, mark their possession of urban spaces to oppose the state – its official nationalist history and its economic policies in the era of structural adjustment.

At stake here is a form of citizenship that disavows the biases of tradition and challenges authoritarianism, two outstanding features of the African postcolonial states.[57] Through their cold rejection of the modalities of membership in the nation, the youth are redefining the spaces of legal citizenship and erasing their nationalistic attributes and referents, thereby questioning the state's authority to define citizenship.[58]

Notes

The author is grateful to Molly Roth for translating this essay from French.

[1] On the nationalist coalitions, see P. Anyang'Nyongto, ed., *Thirty Years of Independence in Africa: The Lost Decades?* (Nairobi: Academy of Science Publishers, 1992).

[2] Deriving from *cadre* or frame, *encadrement* combines implications of state control and subjugation with those of spatial circumscription. The term *encadrement* will be used as it does not have an adequate English translation. (Translator's note.)

[3] For the francophone situations, see the studies and accounts of the Fédération des Etudiants d'Afrique Noir en France (FEANF): C. Diane, *La FEANF et les Grandes Heures du Mouvement Syndical Etudiant Noire* (Paris: Editions Chaka, 1990); A. A. Dieng, 'Histoire des Organisations d'Etudiants Africains en France (1900–1955),' 2 vol. (Dakar: mimeograph, 1986); S. Traoré, *La Fédération des Etudiants d'Afrique Noire* (FEANF) (Paris: L'Harmattan, 1984). On Senegalese students, see A. Bathily, *Mai 68 à Dakar ou la Révolte Universitaire et la Démocratie* (Paris: Editions Chaka, 1992).

4   On the notions of public and private space in totalitarian systems, see Claude Lefort, *L'Invention Democratique. Les Limites de la Domination Totalitaire* (Paris: Livre de Poche, Biblio Essais, 1983), 53–60. In 'Identité et Métissage Politiques,' Compte-Rendu de la Séance du 20 février 1991 (*Feuille d'lnformation No. 16 of Groupe de Travail Cartes d'ldentité*), J.-L. Amselle confirms that a group cannot exist socially unless it is able to achieve accreditation, emerging on the public scene through the recourse to spokespeople or proxies, thus creating its own public space.

5   C. Habib and C. Mouchard, eds. *La Démocracie à l'Oeuvre. Autour de Claude Lefort* (Paris: Edition Esprit, 1993).

6   On this subject, see M. Diouf, 'Représentations Historiques et Légitimes Politiques au Sénégal 1960–1987,' Revue de la Bibliothèque Nationale 34 (Winter 1989): 14–24.

7   An *année blanche* is an academic year that has not been officially completed because of the inability to organize year-end examinations and competitions, due to strikes and the resulting insufficiency of completed class hours. The consequence is a universal repetition of the school year.

8   For the Malian situation, refer to C. O. Diarrah, 'Les Ambiguïtés et les Difficultés de la Concrétisation Operationelle du Projet Démocratique du Mali,' report presented at the Atelier sur les Villes Ouest Africaines, Dakar, 15–17 November 1993.

9   On the 'area boys,' Abubakar Momoh writes, 'the area boys as a social category become preponderant, popularized and organised from about 1986 when the Structural Adjustment Programme took its full course. Hence today, any form of crime or criminal activity in the entire South-Western Nigeria is identifiable or traceable to the area boys. The area boys are the equivalent of "Yanbaba" in Hausaland, they are also called *allaayes, Omo oni ile* (sons of the soil or landlords), "street urchins," "government pickin," "untouchables," or "alright sir".' See Abukar Momoh, 'The South-Western Nigeria Case Study,' paper presented at the West African Long-Term Perspective Study, ADB-CINERGIE Conference, Lagos, 11–13 October 1993, 28.

10 P. Richards, 'Liberia and Sierra Leone,' in O. W. Furley, ed., *Conflict in Africa* (forthcoming).

11 Ibid., 2.

12 Colonial novels and the urban sociology of the first two decades of independence are the best illustrations of this point of view. See Camara Laye, *L'Enfant Noir* (Paris: Plon, 1953), and C. H. Kane, *L'Aventure Ambiguë* (Paris: Julliard 1961).

13 OECD/ADB, 'L'émergence de la compétition. Transformations et déséquilibres dans les sociétés ouest-africaines,' unpublished manuscript, 1994, 6. In terrns of the analysis of demographic issues, I benefited from being involved with the CINERGIE/CLUB SAHEL team which conducted the WALTPS surveys.

14 See O. Kane, 'Les Mouvements Religieux et le champ politique au Nigéria Septentrional: le cas du reformisme musulman à Kano,' *Islam Sociétés au Sud Sahara* 4 (Nov. 1990): 7–23. R. Marshall, 'Power in the Name of Jesus: Social Transformations and Pentecostalism in Western Nigeria,' in T. O. Ranger and O. Vaughn, eds., *Legitimacy and the State in Contemporary Africa* (Oxford: Macmillan, 1993), 213–246; R. Otayek, 'Une relecture islamique du projet révolutionnaire de Thomas Sankara' in J.-F. Bayart, ed., *Religion et Modernité Politique en Afrique noire. Dieu pour tous et chacun pour soi* (Paris: Karthala, 1993), 101–160; and L. Brenner, *Muslim Identity and Social Change in Sub-Saharan Africa* (Bloomington: Indiana University Press, 1993).

15 The data used in this chapter are drawn from: the IFAN/ORSTROM team, P. Antoine *et al.*, 'L'Insertion Urbaine: Le cas de Dakar,' Unpublished report, Dakar, March 1992; P. Bocquier, 'L'Insertion et la Mobilité Professionelles à Dakar,' Ph.D. diss., Demography, Université de Paris V, 1991; and Sénégal Ministère de l'Economie et des Finances, Direction de la Statistique, 'Recensement Général de la Population et de l'Habitat, Résultats Préliminaires,' September 1988.

16 P. Antoine, 'L'Insertion urbaine,' 118.

17 Ibid., 75.

18 *Le Témoin* 134 (23 February 1993), 3.

19 P. Bocquier, 'L'Insertion et la Mobilité Professionelles à Dakar,' 55.

20 *Encombrements humains*, literally 'social obstructions or clutter,' see R. Collignon, 'La Lutte des Pouvoirs Publics contre les Encombrements Humains a Dakar,' *Revue Canadienne des Etudes Africaines* 18, 3 (1984): 573–82.

21 *Le Soleil*, Senegalese national daily newspaper, special edition, *La Jeunesse au Coeur* (free /supplement), May 1990, 18.

22 See A. Bathily, M. Diouf, and M. Mbodj, 'The Senegalese Student Movement from its Inception to 1989,' in M. Mamdani and E. Wamba-dia-Wamba, eds., *African Perspectives in Social Movements and Democracy* (Dakar: CODESRIA, 1995), 368–407; and M. C. Diop, ed., *Sénégal: Trajectories d'un Etat* (Dakar: CODESRIA, 1992), 431–77.

23 P. Antoine et al., 'L'Insertion Urbaine,' 122.

24 A. Sylla, 'L'Ecole, Quelle Réforme?' in M. C. Diop, ed., *Sénégal*, 379.

25 Conseil Economique et Social du Sénégal, 'Essai sur la Situation Actuelle de la Jeunesse' (Dakar, 1966).

26 On the question of the political manipulation of student movements, refer to the interesting analyses of A. Bathily, *Mai. 68 à Dakar*, and to M. C. Diop, 'Le Syndicalisme Etudiant, Pluralisme et Revendication,' in M. C. Diop, ed., *Sénégal*.

27 On the questions of the political and union recompositions of the movement of university and high school students, see M. C. Diop, ibid.

28 *Le Soleil*, May 1990, 18.

29 On the geography of the bars and the violent relations in these troubled areas, see the excellent analysis and eye-witness account of J. F. Werner, *Marges, Sexe et Drogue à Dakar* (Paris: Karthala, 1994).

30 For the mural paintings and their geography, see Enda-Tiers Monde, *Set, Des Murs Qui Parlent … Nouvelles Cultures Urbaines à Dakar* (Dakar: Enda, 1991); and, for an initial analysis, see J. C. Niane, Vieux Savané, and B. Boris Diop, *Set/Setal. La Seconde Génération des Barricades* (Dakar: Sud Editions, 1991).

31 *Set weec* and *Augias* were voluntarist clean-up operations, e. g., cleaning streets and planting trees, organized by the Office of the Mayor and the youth branch of the ruling PS party. As such, they were official events and partisan expressions and were markedly unsuccessful in comparison to the community organized and controlled *Set/Setal* operations. *Set weec* is a generic Wolof term expressing the centrality of investments of human energy as opposed to the capital and technological investments which only developed countries can afford. *Augias* derives from the Augean stables of Herculean legend and, thus, French high culture.

32 The daily reading of *Le Soleil* provides a striking example.

33 Corniche is the designation for the area of the cliffs which run along the sea shore on the western side of the Dakar peninsula and contain numerous caves.

34 A. Bathily, *Mai 68 à Dakar*, 51.

35 M. C. Diop and M. Diouf, *Le Sénégal sous Abdou Diouf* (Paris: Karthala, 1990).

36 *Sopi* means change in Wolof, the dominant language in Senegal. It is the slogan of the Parti Démocratique Sénégalais (PDS), the principal opposition party whose leader, Abdoulaye Wade, is the principal rival of President Abdou Diouf. This slogan symbolizes the fight against the regime of the party in power, the Parti Socialiste (PS).

37 The Plateau is the affluent downtown Dakar area where European residences were formerly located.

38 For more details, refer to M. C. Diop and M. Diouf, *Le Sénégal sous Abdou Diouf*, chapter 12: 'Les Emeutes de Février-Mars 1988,' 335–54.

39 I. C. Niane, V. Savané, and B. B. Diop, *Set/Setal*, Foreword.

40 *Le Soleil*, Special Edition Urnes [election] 88, March 1988, 11-13.

41 *Le Soleil*, 2 March 1988.

42 M. C. Diop and M. Diouf, *Le Sénégal sous Abdou Diouf*, 337.

43 Ibid., 337.

44 Tropic FM, 'Elections au Sénégal,' radio broadcast on 28 February 1988.

45 *La Table Ronde* was the Senegalese formula for managing political differences following the electoral riots, which brought together leaders from all the political parties.

46 See, on this subject M. Diouf, 'Fresques Murales et Ecriture de l'Histoire. Le *Set/Setal* à Dakar,' *Politique Africaine* 46 (June 1992): 41–54.

47 A. Diallo, 'L'Experience de *Set/Setal* à Dakar,' in *Jeunes, Villes, Emploi. Quel Avenir pour la Jeunesse Africaine?* E. Le Bris and F. Chaveau, eds., Colloquium papers (Paris: Ministère de la Coopération et du Développement, 1993), 211.

48 On all these questions, refer to M. C. Diop and M. Diouf, *Le Sénégal sous Abdou Diouf.*

49 Enda-Tiers Monde, *Set, Des Murs Qui Parlent*, 7-8.

50 Interview in A. Diallo, 'L'Experience de *Set/Setal* à Dakar,' 213.

51 Ibid., 211.

52 *La Jeunesse pour l'Alternance* means Youth for Alternation (rotation of political leadership). 'Laye' is the diminutive for Abdoulaye, referring to Abdoulaye Wade, and *espoir* is hope (salvation).

53 Refer to the works of Donal Cruise O'Brien: *The Murides of Senegal* (Oxford: Oxford University Press, 1971); *Saints and Politicians* (Cambridge: Cambridge University Press, 1975); and 'Senegal' in J. Dunn, ed., *West African States: Promise and Failure* (Cambridge: Cambridge University Press, 1978), 173–188. See also J. Copans, *Les Marabouts de l'Arachide* (Paris: le Sycamore, 1980); and C. Coulon, *Le Marabout et le Prince* (Paris: Pedone, 1981).

54 In the period from 1991 to 1993, PDS leaders were members of the government. After the 1993 elections the PDS rejoined the opposition in an alliance with several parties uncompromisingly opposed to the PS (MSU, AJ, etc.), provoked in part by the arrest and detainment of Abdoulaye Wade, and joined in convening a national conference on the model of the democratic conferences being held in a number of West African states. Despite the recent radicalism of its stance, the PDS rejoined the government of President Abdou Diouf in March 1995, deserting its previous allies and provoking a crisis within the Senegalese opposition.

55 See A. L. Coulibaly, 'Evénements du 16 Févier au Tribunal,' *Sud Quotidien*, 19 November 1993.

56 *Mbalax* is a Senegalese contribution to World Music, diffused worldwide by Youssou N'Dour, Ismail Lo, and other musicians.

57 See Achille Mbembe and Janet Roitman, 'The Figure of the Subject in Times of Crisis,' *Public Culture* 7, 2 (Winter 1995): 323–352; and René Devisch, 'Frenzy, Violence and Ethical Renewal in Kinshasa,' *Public Culture* 7, 3 (Spring 1995): 593–629.

58 Lauren Berlant, 'The Theory of Infantile Citizenship,' *Public Culture* 5, 3 (Spring 1993): 395–410.

RONALD KASSIMIR
The Catholic Church in Uganda

Reference
N. Kasfir (ed.) *Civil Society & Democracy in Africa*
Frank Cass, 1998

This article poses the question of what kind of power civil society organisations possess, and argues that a key component of the answer lies in internal organisational dynamics. Scholarship that privileges the place of civil society in understanding political transitions, in Africa and elsewhere is now pervasive in the social sciences, and donor agencies are actively seeking to strengthen civil societies on the continent. While none of the proponents of civil society approaches would contest that the power resources and organisational capacities of civil society actors deeply condition their political possibilities, it is striking that such considerations enter into these approaches in an unsystematic manner (when they enter into them at all). This is not only a matter of putting the theoretical cart before the empirical horse, although it is clear that we lack a great deal of knowledge about civil organisations in Africa.[1] Without a way of theorising about the social power of organisations, scholars and donors may bet on the wrong horses, that is, focus on those organisations that, however 'civil', lack the capacity to effect political change.

Civil society organisations are often defined on an *a priori* basis, that is scholars identify them with categories taken from other (typically Western) societies. Alternatively, these organisations are identified by what their leaders say they are or claim to be in support of, rather than in terms of what they do and for what purposes. When these self-identifications and claims conform to standard conceptualisations of 'civil' organisations, their socio-political role is often presumed independently of an analysis of the social power of these organisations. To the degree that civil society is invoked as an independent variable in explaining democratisation and democratic consolidation in Africa, the failure systematically to incorporate the power resources of social organisations into the analysis greatly limits the claims of the civil society approach.[2] The consequences of ignoring organisational capacities are, it is argued, both the perpetuation of an inflated sense of the political efficacy of empirical 'civil societies' and the rendering of 'civil society' as a weak analytical tool. Indeed, it is worth asking why we should expect civil society, or any organisation that is part of it, to play an assigned role.

Below, I use the example of a Ugandan religious organisation to address this question. One observer has written of 'the immense influence that the Christian churches have over the majority of the population in Uganda'.[3] In the analysis that follows, I specify *what kind of influence* the churches have in Ugandan society and politics, and explore to what extent this influence correlates with the *a priori* assumptions of civil society approaches.

When applied to Africa, civil society approaches tend to focus on normative dimensions, while the social power of organisations is either assumed, ignored or treated as exogenous to its role in making civil society effective. For example, by insisting that civil society organisations are those that promote participatory values and a sense of political efficacy among their members or by stressing how they relate to the state – that is, that they engage the state but are autonomous from it[4] – these approaches divert attention from the politics going on inside organisations that contribute to their potential for political influence. But until we know what organisations can and cannot do – that is, what kind of power they hold – we can say little about their capacity to contribute to political change.[5] Here I argue that a focus on capacity, and especially *internal organisational dynamics*, can provide a handle for grasping the power of social organisations. By internal dynamics, I mean the relationships among organisational leaders as they attempt to define and pursue the goals of their organisation, and between them and their members or followers.

Without understanding the social power of civil society organisations, and especially their internal politics, the invocation of civil society as an analytical tool will continue to be asserted rather than demonstrated. Foley and Edwards have identified two basic variants of the civil society approach that make strong claims on behalf of the power of civil society. What they label 'Civil Society I' is associated with neo-Tocquevillian approaches and focuses on the 'ability of associational life in general and of the habits of association in particular to foster patterns of civility in the actions of citizens in a democratic polity'.[6] Viewed from the lens of social power, I call this the power of organisational leaders to *socialise* members by instilling participatory norms and a sense of efficacy in social and political life. What Foley and Edwards label 'Civil Society II' construes 'civil society as a sphere of action that is independent of the state and that is capable – precisely for this reason – of energizing resistance to a tyrannical regime'.[7] There is no necessary reason to privilege opposition in this version (though many civil society approaches do this). Thus, one could also include as possible action support for democratic regimes and/or an insistence on their accountability. Viewed through the lens of social power, I call this the power of organisational leaders to *mobilise* members to promote political change.

Foley and Edwards, in their critique, emphasise the contradictions between these two versions of civil society. I would add that, in practice, many conventional civil society approaches combine them through suggesting that socialisation may be necessary for mobilisation, that is, that norms and a sense of empowerment transform actors' identities and interests in ways that affect the nature and direction of mobilisation. Here, I will concentrate on mobilisation, incorporating the issue of socialisation when it influences the former. The broader point is that civil society approaches put mobilisation and socialisation at centre-stage, but their *a priori* lens lacks the tools for analysing these processes. By looking at civil organisations through the lens of social power and the ways in which internal organisational dynamics affect capacities for mobilisation and socialisation, I demonstrate the limits of putting current efforts at political reform in Africa in the frame of civil society.

The Roman Catholic Church in Uganda provides a revealing case study for exploring the power of an organisation to mobilise and socialise. The church is not a 'typical' example of a civil organisation, nor is Uganda typical of the contexts within which social organisations operate. Rather, the case demonstrates that a focus on organisational capacities, viewed through the lens of social power, has broad applicability to understanding social organisations

and the efficacy of civil society in the trajectory of political transitions on the continent.

Catholicism, civil society and organisational dynamics

One reason to focus on organisational capacities is that it offers a picture of what churches do 'on the ground'. This picture provides a means of assessing the predominant, although not unanimous,[8] view that African Christian churches are 'naturally' leading organisations in civil society and the democratisation process, destined to play out a role resembling the one attributed to Poland's Catholic Church in the 1980s. This *a priori* optimism for Christian churches in Africa tends to conflate the political stance of religious organisations with their political efficacy, and their relative autonomy from the state with their capacities to effect change.[9] Much of this confusion among the optimists is tied to the claims made by church officials regarding their own position, and thus the place of the organisation they lead, in political, social and moral reform. The Kenyan Catholic Church has declared itself the 'conscience of society',[10] while the Ugandan Catholic hierarchy dons the mantle of the 'moral conscience of the nation' and proclaims that 'the saving Gospel of Jesus Christ is *the most effective instrument* for a fundamental change of the human person and human society'.[11] However, whatever the intentions or degree of sincerity of these religious leaders, it is clear that they cannot, through the act of public discourse, will themselves into becoming the exemplars of civil society. Without the organisational capacities to take on the declared role of a leading institution, such pronouncements may only have the effect of creating expectations that are not met.[12]

Thus, scholarly discussions of the role of the African Christian churches in political reform tend to parallel the bold assertions of church leaders. Several examples can be found in the most detailed volume to date that describes this role. The editor, Paul Gifford, argues in his introduction that, while past accounts of African churches and politics construed religious organisations as passive or reactive, in the recent work '[t]he direction of influences to be traced has now been reversed; it is less how the churches have *responded* to political developments, than how they are *helping to shape* them'.[13] While creating analytical space for the agency of the churches is laudatory, this orientation risks making the same mistake as older approaches, that is, privileging one particular perspective. It also mirrors the same *a priori* assumptions of civil society approaches by deciding in advance that civil organisations are principally independent variables, and assigning them a role rather than analysing it.

While subscribing to the view that democratisation efforts on the continent constitute Africa's 'second liberation', Gifford is cognisant that there have been serious obstacles to the extension and consolidation of democratic rule. He adds that 'If any real change is to be effected, the contribution of the churches is therefore even more critical than ever'.[14] Such a formulation tends toward tautology. If democratisation succeeds, it is in large part due to the churches. If it fails or stalls, then the churches are needed more than ever. There is no room here for a scenario in which the churches' role is marginal, or where their inactivity is constructive for democratic rule. The point is not that the churches do not have a significant role. Rather, it is that this role cannot be assumed *a priori*.

Finally, the optimistic view endorses the image of a natural connection between civil society and democratisation, within which the churches are inserted:

> From this perspective of civil society, it is obvious why churches are seen as so important to Africa's democratisation. In so many one-party states, the churches were the greatest single element of civil society. The contribution of the churches to Africa's democratisation – and the ways in which this contribution could be increased – have become important areas of study.[15]

If this is the case, it is incumbent to show the precise *mechanisms* through which churches take a major position in civil society. However, not all church mechanisms for intervening in the democratisation process provide evidence of its 'civil' nature or qualities, at least if the concept of civil society is to have any specificity and avoid tautology. In other words, the intervention of churches on behalf of political reform is not necessarily through their location in civil society. In addition, churches are complex organisations with complex goals. A democratic political vision may be seen as a means to some other end – be it the protection or extension of institutional privileges or social justice for the masses – as well as an end in itself. It is thus crucial to see how organisations act to defend themselves as institutions in order to understand their capacities to play effective roles in confronting states and promoting democracy.

Religious institutions, and the Catholic Church in particular, have a diverse repertoire of mechanisms, only some of which are related to their 'civil' nature – as conceptualised by civil society approaches, these are neo-Tocquevillian socialisation and political mobilisation. But churches have other ways of intervening in the public sphere that need not rely on these 'civil' mechanisms: the participation of church leaders in elite social networks, formal and informal diplomacy, service provision and development projects. Even official church discourse addressing public matters would be a dimension of its 'civil' role only if these pronouncements are connected to socialisation and mobilisation capacities. Indeed, all of these mechanisms have been part of the church's repertoire for centuries, long before the emergence of civil societies in continental Europe.[16] None of them require the participation of the laity in order to be effective, although they may imply that, if the church does not achieve its ends or is threatened, a broader activation of the laity may ensue.

Civil society approaches can only bring specificity to the concept, and make an argument about its efficacy in political change, by demonstrating that the leaders of civil organisations connect with their members and the wider public via the mechanisms of socialisation and mobilisation. Only once it is established that these capacities are present does it make sense to worry about whether these organisations influence politics and the public sphere in 'civil' ways – that is, promote 'civil' values through 'civil' means in pursuit of 'civil' ends. In this regard, Gifford notes an important paradox in the present role of African churches. It has been the mainline Protestant and Catholic churches that have been most closely involved in political reform efforts on the continent, while African independent churches and newly established pentecostal churches have tended to be either quiescent or supportive of recalcitrant authoritarian regimes. Yet it is the latter churches that demonstrate an ability to socialise their members into a new sense of personal and social efficacy under trying conditions, and, on occasion, to mobilise them for both religious and other purposes. Gifford writes that *in theory* there is

no reason why the mainline churches should not play such a role; but in practice it seems that the newer pentecostal churches have been able to achieve these ends in a way that the mainline churches have not'.[17] Ironically, the African churches that evince the neo-Toquevillian attributes seen as the *sine qua non* of a 'civil' organisation in some approaches are the ones least disposed to support, and organise on behalf of, democratisation. At the same time, the mainline churches promoting democratisation have rarely done so through the civil mechanisms of socialisation and mobilisation. A clear example is the role of Catholic bishops as titular heads of national conferences in West Africa.[18] This has occurred through the long-standing church mechanisms of diplomacy and arbitration that do not require, and in fact did not involve, the mobilisation of members.

Of course, *in theory* there are reasons why the mainline churches do not play their assigned role. The problem is that the relevant theories lie outside the civil society approach. Concepts in organisation theory and the sociology of religion, especially the distinction between churches and sects, require an analysis of internal organisational dynamics that do not fit easily with *a priori* assumptions. In an instructive analysis of the Kenyan case where the mainline Christian churches did have some success in mobilising and socialising members against the Moi regime while independent and evangelical churches rallied to its support, Ngunyi shows how divergent church histories, internal modes of authority, intra-church conflict and organisational interests account both for religious mobilisation and the diverse purposes to which it is directed. Rather than construing the mainline churches as acting out their assigned role in civil society and the others as pathological deviants, he provides a far richer and empirically grounded analysis. For the mainline churches, Ngunyi argues that the protection of once privileged status, ethnic sympathies, state manipulation and support for lay empowerment and participation intertwine in explaining their challenge to the political *status quo*.[19]

Since the coming to power in 1986 of the National Resistance Movement (NRM) headed by Yoweri Museveni, the role of Uganda's Catholic Church has been quite different from its sister church in neighbouring Kenya. On the one hand, the Ugandan church appears to have acted in ways consistent with the expectation of civil society approaches, preaching and making formal pronouncements supportive of everything from democracy, clean and accountable government, human rights, women's rights and personal security. It has used its access to substantial donor aid to engage in an array of development projects, and encouraged church members to participate in the constitution-making process, elections, and serving in the local council system introduced by the NRM.

On the other hand, it is very difficult to measure the effectiveness of church leaders' statements, since they often coincide with the NRM's own political discourse. In many ways, church officials have had close and collaborative relations with the regime.[20] Moreover, it is striking that, on many of the most critical issues facing Uganda, the church has been relatively silent. It has not taken part in public debates regarding the acceptance of structural adjustment packages and economic reform in general, nor on other issues like land reform and the occasional arrest of journalists. On the controversial decision by the government to impose a value-added tax, which was protested against vigorously by local business people, the church did enter the debate, but only to oppose the tax's application to foreign donations.[21] Until 1996, it made little effort to press the NRM to seek a peaceful negotiation to the unending rebellion in northern Uganda. Even the government-run newspaper labelled the church's intervention as 'long overdue'.[22] The church's peace and justice programme, which was to establish offices across the country, has been moribund in most dioceses.

Thus, church leaders have played a strikingly ambiguous role in Ugandan civil society. I will examine this role by gauging the church's capacity for mobilisation and socialisation in several different arenas. First, I examine the fluctuating and divided position of church officials on what is perhaps Uganda's most contentious political issue, whether to maintain the no-party movement system of the NRM or return to a multi-party system. As support for and action on behalf of the latter is an important component of what a civil society organisation is 'supposed' to do, the church's role is hard to grasp via a civil society approach. A focus on internal organisational dynamics, the legacy of the church's past experience in political mobilisation and its present capacities provides a better angle from which to explain its current ambivalence toward multi-party competition.

Catholic organisation and political mobilisation

In Uganda, the connection between religious organisations and political mobilisation has been dominated by a rather unusual phenomenon in African politics: the rise of political parties whose base of support is rooted (or perceived to be rooted) in religious identities with the active intervention of church officials. This section analyses the role of Catholic Church leaders in partisan mobilisation, the relationship between church officials and lay leaders of the 'Catholic party', and the church's broader position in the debate on multi-party politics in Uganda under the NRM.

In 1989, a public statement by a group of Catholic Church leaders signalled a surprising shift in Ugandan politics that goes against the expectations of conventional notions of civil society. Only three years earlier, in the first pastoral letter issued by the Uganda Episcopal Conference after the capture of state power by the NRM, Uganda's Catholic bishops declared that 'a multi-party system of government is an expression of the fundamental freedom of assembly and association guaranteed by our National Constitution'.[23] The NRM came to power determined to replace the multi-party system which had characterised periods of civilian rule in Uganda's post-colonial history with a 'movement system', that is, non-party politics. It promptly banned party activity, especially during elections, although it allowed existing parties to maintain headquarters, hold private meetings and publish newspapers.

In 1989, as the NRM was initiating an elaborate process to construct a new constitution, the bishops issued a pastoral letter which dropped their insistence on the appropriate party system: 'As to the concrete question of what form of government Uganda should adopt, we must state clearly that the church does not advocate any one form.'[24]

This shift of the official church's political vision to, in effect, neutrality regarding the question of parties in Uganda is momentous not only because of its past advocacy of multi-partyism, but also because of past ties between Catholic religious identity and one of Uganda's leading political parties – the Democratic Party (DP) whose support was seen as predominantly Ugandan Catholic. From 1986 up to the present, the DP has been in the forefront in demanding that a multi-party system be included in the new constitution.

But in this it failed. Uganda's new constitution, which took force in October 1995, continues the no-party movement system of the NRM for five more years, after which a referendum on the future of party competition will be held.

The logic of conventional civil society approaches suggests a contradictory account of this watershed event. On the one hand, the church's abandonment of support for multi-partyism could be interpreted as problematic for freedom of association in civil society and prospects for democratisation. On the other hand, the church's abandonment of the DP's position could be understood as the de-linking of a 'primordial' political identity (that is, Catholicism) and its institutional representative (that is, the church) from the political arena, a positive development for civil society.[25] Looking at the shift in the church's position through the lens of social power, and particularly the organisation's mobilisational capacity, provides a richer interpretation – one that takes full account of intra-organisational dynamics, in particular, the relationship between church officials and lay elites. However, the church's role in Ugandan political mobilisation must also be viewed historically. It has often been asserted that church leaders were the primary agents of the mobilisation of lay Catholics in support of the DP. But a more nuanced reading of the party's history shows that efforts to mobilise Catholics by church leaders were not straightforward, or even central. Lay elites and activists were, in fact, the central actors in the formation and expansion of the party. Church officials were certainly allies of the laity, but never controlled the party. In fact, church leaders and party activists sometimes clashed; their interests intersected but were never identical.

The particular kind of religious pluralism that prevailed in Uganda prepared the way for the association of religious identities with parties. Under British colonial rule, the Anglican Church, despite its smaller membership compared with the Catholics, operated in many ways as a de facto established church, especially in the kingdom areas in the south and west of the Protectorate. Lay Catholics, and especially elite Catholics, experienced discrimination in public sector employment and in access to other forms of patronage under indirect rule native governments. This situation of Anglican privilege, and the grievance it engendered among Catholic clergy and laity, was the raw material used by DP leaders to mould a political support base.

The DP was launched in the mid-1950s as a response to court politics in the Buganda kingdom, where a leading Catholic chief was denied the prime ministership through backstage dealings by Protestant politicians and the Buganda king. Catholic chiefs and other elite Catholic Baganda organised the DP in response to this incident on the presumption that, with the Buganda parliament (lukiiko) ostensibly moving towards direct elections, they could take through the ballot box what was being denied them by established mechanisms of patron-client politics, which favoured Anglicans.

Catholic elites in other districts in the Protectorate, experiencing similar discrimination in their local governments, soon opened DP branches. By the late 1950s, the DP existed as a relatively decentralised party that began developing national-level structures as Uganda moved towards independence. Its building blocks were disgruntled elites who tapped into lay associations established by the missionaries under the rubric of Catholic Action, the primary mode of lay organisation developed by the church in Europe after World War I. They also reached out to Catholic professional organisations, especially the Catholic Teachers Guild.

To varying degrees, and with varying levels of openness, church officials supported the party through sermons, publications, and backstage exhortation.[26] At the time of the DP's formation, the church unambiguously applauded it: 'There is a new political association of Catholics in formation, and it is received with enthusiasm in all Catholic quarters.... It will be called the "Democratic party" and will allow non-Catholics to join.'[27]

As nationalist activity increased in the latter half of the 1950s, the church urged voters to support parties that guaranteed religious freedom and especially the rights of parents to choose the form of their children's education. The latter was a thinly disguised code for continued church control over their schools, which the DP supported. Connected to this was an attack on parties seen as communist or as 'fellow travellers' – a label applied to the populist Uganda National Congress (the first Ugandan political party) and its successor, the Uganda People's Congress (UPC). As the leadership of these parties was predominantly Protestant, Catholic Church officials denounced these parties both as serving Protestant interests and as Communist-influenced.[28]

Many Ugandan Catholics, whether or not taking the communist accusation seriously, did perceive the UPC as a party controlled by Protestants, just as many Protestants had come see the DP as a Catholic party.[29] Elite Catholics surely saw the UPC's goal, in part, as maintaining the system of Protestant privilege in most of Uganda's districts. DP leaders seemed to be largely successful, though varying from district to district, in mobilising ordinary Catholic voters. However, no exit polls exist that would confirm Catholic voting support for the DP in any election. In effect, elite Catholics established a potential alternate network of patron–client ties to the existing system from which many Catholics were shut out. It is certainly plausible that loyalty to the church influenced ordinary Catholics to support the DP, although this claim lacks solid evidence. In most cases it can be more persuasively hypothesised that this was secondary to the motivation that the interest of Catholics was best served by ending the system of Protestant privilege.

Thus, to the degree that the DP gained the support of ordinary Catholics, it was able to overcome the fluidity of Catholic social identity through constructing a sense of common political interest.[30] The existence of a political organisation founded by elite Catholics helped to 'create' a Catholic *political* identity and interest as much as a pre-existing interest led in some natural way to the formation of the party.[31] This interest was defined and mobilised by lay party leaders; the role of church officials, while present, was clearly secondary.

The DP's association with Catholicism is complicated by its putative ties to Christian Democracy. Some observers, such as Colin Leys, have argued, without offering any direct evidence, that the party's name was shortened from Christian Democratic Party.[32] The DP's 1984 official history, while playing down such connections and arguing against the claims that the DP was a 'confessional' party, hardly helps its own case since the volume was edited by a staff member of Christian Democratic International, was published in Rome, and includes photographs of party president Paul Ssemo- gerere with various European Christian Democratic party leaders and Pope John Paul II.[33]

The image of the DP as a Christian Democratic party in the European mode, while valid in some respects, obscures as much as it reveals, at least to the degree that it implies that support is based upon socialisation into a Catholic political vision rather than a form of machine politics.[34] Unlike Christian Democracy in western Europe (as well as Latin America), the DP was formed as a response to discrimination against Catholics in public sector employment and their treatment at the hands of Protestant chiefs, not in opposition to class-based secular movements (liberalism, Marxism) seeking to expunge the church and religious faith from the political arena. European and Latin American parties, in their origins, had more overt Catholic content regarding ideology, social values and safeguarding the status of the church. In the DP's political discourse, the only overt pro-church position was its support for continued church control over education. In general, the DP's *raison d'être* was far more the social mobility of lay Catholics than the promotion of a Christian world view or the protection of church privileges.

Church leaders seem to have been far more attached to the ideals of Christian Democracy than party activists. The most important point is that a distinction can be made between church support for the party and church control over its ideology and policies.[35] As Gingyera-Pincywa documents, the discourse on Christian Democracy that emerged in Uganda in the late 1950s was produced and disseminated by the church, not DP leaders. He also notes that in most instances the DP's policies were not easily distinguishable from the UPC, and in fact the DP promoted some policies not in accord with the tenets of Christian Democracy as it had been explicated by the church. Rather than supporting a party infused with Christian Democratic principles, the church was attempting to bring the DP, formed largely for other reasons, to these principles.[36] Church support was not the same as church control, and its relationship with the party was a marriage of intersecting rather than identical interests. Once formed, the DP consistently pursued its own agenda and, while remaining respectful to the institution, rarely took the church's priorities as its priorities.

Even this respectfulness had its limits, as two brief examples will illustrate. When the UPC, in coalition with the Buganda-based and Protestant-dominated Kabaka Yekka party, emerged victorious over DP in Uganda's 1962 independence election, it brought to power a government largely controlled by Protestants, exactly what the DP and the church had feared. In 1964, the UPC government announced a drastic nationalisation of church schools. While this affected both Anglican and Catholic institutions, it was protested against with much greater vehemence by the Catholic Church, not only because of its traditional concerns with autonomy and control over the socialisation of the laity, but because church leaders surmised (correctly, as it turned out) that Anglicans would, in many instances, be appointed as heads of Catholic schools. However, the degree of social protest against the nationalisation was quite muted among the laity and the DP.[37] Indeed, at the very moment when the Catholic Church was under its greatest threat since the early missionary period, large numbers of DP parliamentarians were crossing the floor to join the UPC.

The following year, a row developed between the bishop of the Catholic Diocese of Fort Portal and local DP leaders in Toro, largely because the latter accused the bishop of not standing by them in their battle against the UPC-dominated local government. The bishop ended the affair by dissolving the Toro Catholic Council, which the local administration had accused of being a DP front allied with a rebellion in the southern part of the kingdom. Apparently, church leaders in Toro could not accept an organised group of lay members claiming to represent Catholics who 'were constantly undermining Diocesan authority and causing friction in the diocese', thus disturbing 'the peace of the church'.[38]

Thus, Catholic Church leaders by the mid-1960s could literally not win for losing. When the church was under threat (the school issue), the supposedly Catholic DP not only attempted a meagre defence, but many of its leading members joined the party that implemented the policy. On the other side, lay Catholic leaders and DP loyalists in Toro were trying to pull church leaders closer to their cause, producing internal divisions and ultimately the decommissioning of the leading lay association in Fort Portal Diocese. Although this need not signify that church leaders had begun to regret their support for the DP, it does echo the dangers seen by late nineteenth-century European church leaders in lay mobilisation.[39] Once lay leaders gained some autonomy from the institution, and a base of support outside church channels, they developed interests of their own – their support for the church when it was under threat was not guaranteed, and a tendency to make representative claims on behalf of Catholics challenged the church's hegemony.

By 1966, Uganda first moved towards a one-party state under the UPC and then almost a decade of authoritarianism following the military coup led by Idi Amin. These devastating political conditions almost eliminated the DP's existence until 1979, when Amin was ousted by the Tanzanian army in alliance with Ugandan dissident groups. The party re-surfaced to contest the 1980 post-Amin election of that year as an organisation that still maintained roots in the lay Catholic community, but that had also taken on a regional cast as many Protestant Baganda and other Protestant southerners flocked to the DP to prevent the return of UPC.[40] Church leaders, who had made the institution available as a refuge for members during the Amin years but mostly avoided voicing public critique and opposition,[41] again supported the DP in this election, although less overtly than in the late 1950s and early 1960s, and with less unanimity. It is difficult to tell whether this support occurred because it saw the DP as a Catholic party, or because there was no alternative to preventing a UPC victory. Given what was now a more diverse social base for the DP, and the past experience described above, the latter seems more plausible.

Milton Obote and the UPC returned to power in the 1980 election, which most observers and many Ugandans believe would have been won by DP were it not for massive vote-rigging on behalf of the UPC. The rigging was the ostensible motivation for Museveni and his colleagues to start their guerilla war. The war may have sown the seeds for a further gap between the church and the party. Even in the 1980 elections, some Catholic priests in Western Uganda had forged connections to Museveni's fledgling Uganda Patriotic Movement party (UPM), which fared poorly in the 1980 elections. During the guerilla struggle in Toro, not only lay members, but some priests as well, supported and even joined the NRA. When Obote was overthrown in a military coup by northern army officers in 1985, the DP agreed to support the coup leaders. Even though these officers were Catholics, many southern Catholics (priests and laity) who were otherwise DP sympathisers saw this move as a sell-out. When the NRM defeated the military regime six months later, church connections with DP varied greatly across regions: fairly strong in the north (now seen as threatened and ripe for retribution under a southern-dominated NRM), mixed in Buganda and weakest in most parts of the west.

This is the historical trajectory within which to situate the church's turnaround from openly supporting a return to a multi-party system to neutrality. In 1990, one year after the bishops' declaration of neutrality, an all-Uganda meeting of priests to discuss the constitutional debate produced a formal recommendation in sup-

port of a multi-party system.[42] This opinion was far from unanimous, however. In Fort Portal Diocese, many priests supported the no-party movement system, with younger priests especially hostile to a return to multi-party competition. Fort Portal's bishop at the time, the late Serapio Magambo, had referred to 'cheap party politics' as one of Uganda's many ills.[43] Elsewhere he pronounced:

> And now what a pack of lies we hear, that religion divides people. If it divides people, what do politics and economics do? No, religion as a bond between God and his people unites people … It is *religionism* or the use of religion for selfish political or economic ends that divides people. It had better be banned from Uganda.[44]

Magambo was both defending the church against attacks made by NRM radicals on its past political role while accepting, in principle, the NRM's opposition to the politicisation of religious identities so strongly connected with political parties. In reviewing memoranda submitted to the Constitutional Commission by religious bodies, John Waliggo, a Catholic priest and the Commission's secretary, reported a general lack of consensus on the multi-party issue.

> On issues which were quite controversial throughout the country, the memoranda from the religious bodies were also sharply divided. Such issues included citizenship, the death penalty, the nature of the political system, the form of government, the electoral system, the traditional rulers and the national language. This was one indication that the gap between the institutional church and the members, the People of God, was becoming narrower in this democratisation process.[45]

By declining to provide unambiguous support for the DP, or even the more neutral goal of a return to multi-partyism, church leaders implicitly endorsed the position of the NRM's anti-sectarian policy and reflected the views of many (but not all) lay members that the politicisation of religious identities, and the role of the church in it, was inappropriate, 'un-civil' behaviour.[46] Ironically, this end was to be achieved, at least in the frame of civil society approaches, by decidedly 'un-civil' means – the banning of political parties. For the church, the old problem of lay members claiming to represent Catholics in the political arena was solved, at least for the moment.[47] However, church leaders were now reflecting the actual and diverse views of its members in their neutral public stance, rather than simply asserting their power to represent members' interests as they had typically done in the past.

Thus, the shift signalled that church leaders had abandoned past goals of political socialisation on the principles of Christian Democracy and the mobilisation of distinctly Catholic political interests. As I have argued, church officials were always more ambivalent about such mobilisation than has commonly been acknowledged, and less central to it than has often been asserted.

Lay organisation, socialisation, and social action

The question then arises of what other kinds of socialisation and mobilisation is the Catholic Church capable of effecting that could be coded as civil society practice? Waliggo, Uganda's leading Catholic intellectual and the church's most open advocate of elements of liberation theology, writes that

> given the immense influence that the Christian churches have

over the majority of the population in Uganda it is evident that they have not done enough to mobilise women, youth, workers, children and farmers to stand up to defend their rights. Yet tangible democracy can only be attained through organising such powerful sections of society to be promoters and defenders of democratic governance.[48]

This section will provide answers to why the churches (and in this case, the Catholic Church) 'have not done enough to mobilise' these social groups, or to engage in consciousness-raising forms of socialisation,[49] by analysing the *kind* of influence that the churches have over Ugandans.

Church-based organisations, of course, do not exist only or even primarily to act directly in the political arena. Lay associations have been established by the Ugandan church to assist in its pastoral and evangelical mission, and to socialise the laity into the values and beliefs of the faith, and obedience to the clergy. In principle, these groups could be called upon to mobilise in defence of the church when under threat by external forces, or internal schisms. More ambitiously, they might enter the public sphere with an explicitly Christian agenda, not in the sense of practising interest group politics, as with the DP,[50] but to imbue 'civil society' with Catholic values. The majority of these associations were created by Catholic missionaries in Uganda under the umbrella of Catholic Action, meaning that they were to be tightly controlled by the clerical hierarchy. In a social context where most Catholics, especially in rural areas, have limited contact with the institution's official representatives, mobilised Catholic Action groups were intended to supplement catechetical training, sustain the laity in the absence of regular access to the sacraments, and serve as a shield against 'backsliding'.

While associations like the Legion of Mary apparently flourished in the past, in recent years they have become stagnant, and virtually ignored by young Catholics and most males. Older groups such as the Legion reproduce themselves, but their composition is largely older women whose piety and good works are appreciated by others who rarely join their ranks.[51] Whatever their past capacity for socialisation, groups formed on the principles of Catholic Action only touch a minority of Catholics.

The majority of church members regularly violate many of the faith's norms and doctrinal rules, obviously a situation not unique to Uganda. This is largely a function of the Catholic Church's inclusionary membership criteria. The act of baptism, most commonly infant baptism, along with confirmation after training in the basic doctrines of the Catholic faith, are the only essential requirements for Catholic membership. These inclusionary criteria vastly expand the range of possible orientations to formal doctrine that do not contradict membership. In this sense the Catholic Church is like a 'family', whose sons and daughters remain members no matter how loyal or prodigal their actions become. Under such an organisational principle, the relevant question is less into what values most Catholics are being socialised than under what conditions any kind of socialisation is possible.

The church both creates the conditions for multiple interpretations of Catholic identity through its inclusionary criteria, and then defines this reality as a problem in need of solution. Church leaders across Africa recognised that their control over most of their nominal members was tenuous, and in the 1970s instituted a new priority in lay organisation: Small Christian Communities (SCCs). SCCs were modelled, in theory, on the base communities which had begun to take hold in Latin America, and which in some cases became the organisational locus of liberation theology. The idea was that lay Catholics needed to take more responsibility for their own socialisation through bible-reading, prayer and self-help groups based on residence. In the spirit of the second Vatican Council of 1962–65, the grip of the institution was to be loosened by the mobilisation of SCCS, with the goal of instilling a sense of efficacy and empowerment in members' spiritual lives, which might then spill over into more social and political pursuits (as in parts of Latin America, where members took part in oppositional social movements against authoritarian regimes). SCCs were to be vehicles of a Christianisation, evangelisation and socialisation from below, rather than from the top down. A recent report of the Association of Members of Episcopal Conferences of East and Central Africa (AMECEA) states that SCCs

> make a great contribution to the much needed decentralisation of power in the church. They are schools of leadership, where Catholics who are often afraid to chair a meeting or speak in public, learn self-confidence and basic leadership skills. In the long run, this experience may prove to be the most important contribution of the church to the process of democratisation of society.[52]

Thus, the church imagines SCCs in the way that de Tocqueville described Protestant congregations in nineteenth-century America and Putnam depicts the choral societies of northern Italy.[53] SCCs were to be schools in the 'art of association', and in the development of values, skills and self-confidence that nurtures democracy and civil society from below.

However, the bulk of the AMECEA report is a remarkably frank exposition on the limits of SCCs, indicating that, after 20 years of experimentation, the results have been uniformly meagre across Eastern and Central Africa. Almost all of what it has to say rings true for Uganda, based on my research carried out from 1989 to 1991. Like other churches in the region, the Ugandan church unambiguously endorsed SCCs as an organisational innovation designed for a new kind of lay socialisation and mobilisation. However, in discussions with clergy and lay members in Fort Portal, most combined an almost ritualised approval of the need for SCCs with a sense that it was a 'flavour of the month' without a genuine commitment to its aims. In a paper on SCCs presented at Fort Portal Diocese's Synod in 1989, the author (a lay person) reported that SCCs have failed to take hold in the Diocese, and those that started up disbanded rather quickly. He asks: 'Why would we have to think of SCC at this material time when we are holding this Synod? Is it because the church says we ought to have them or is it because Christ's faithful in this diocese deem it necessary to have SCC?'[54]

There have been a few exceptions. In the Diocese of Fort Portal, sections of Butiiti parish had several very active SCCs, holding prayer meetings and engaging in a variety of self-help projects. The parish priest of Butiiti, an American of the Holy Cross Mission order, played a key role in nurturing these groups and pushed very hard for these areas to be made into a separate parish.[55] It is no coincidence that a rare occasion of the flourishing of SCCs occurred under the guidance of a relative outsider who is more autonomous from the diocesan hierarchy and less threatened by the potential autonomy of these groups than local clergy. The same pattern was evident in Latin America, where base communities were often mobilised by members of religious orders, often foreign, outside the immediate control of the diocesan hierarchy.[56]

Four aspects of SCCs are most pertinent to our discussion. First, SCCs in Uganda were not structured as voluntary organisations, but as the lowest branch of the church's territorial administrative system to which all Catholics living in a village, or a portion of a village demarcated by a hill or valley, belonged. The AMECEA report states that many SCCs 'have started out on a wrong basis: as purely administrative sub-divisions of existing outstations'. Elsewhere, the authors observe that SCCs tend to see themselves 'as an administrative unit rather than as a community of life'.[57]

Second, the hope that SCCs might prove to be the key mechanism for the engagement of Catholics in the public sphere has been a misplaced one. 'The huge political, economic and social problems of the Continent (which the Bishops analyzed so clearly during the African synod) have not become the concern of the average SCC.'[58] Thus, even where SCCs may have contributed to a deeper evangelisation, this has not translated into 'Christian' action in the public arena. In 1986, Uganda's bishops noted this situation regarding Catholic youth, which has changed little in the ensuing decade: 'In this mission [for the youth] the church is facing grave difficulties. Many young people fail to see the relevance of the gospel message in their lives, and even those who are faithful to Sunday prayers, are failing to take up their responsibility in the social, economic and political fields *with a Christian identity*.'[59]

Third, the neo-Tocquevillian goal of SCCs as schools for the growth of participatory values in an institution dominated by hierarchical structures has been difficult to realise. While the leaders of SCCs are elected, 'the election process does not guarantee a participatory leadership style; leaders of SCCs can be very directive even authoritarian, copying … what they have seen in the parish priest or in politics!'[60] Rather than transforming the patrimonial relationships and styles predominant in Uganda's public sphere, SCCs may be prone to capture by a patrimonial logic, an observation made by several writers on NGOs in general.[61]

Finally, and as implied in the above comment from the report, priests themselves have not been easily reconciled to SCCs, which require them to shift 'from being the organiser of everything to being the animator and facilitator'.

> One of the major problems of the Church … is that on one hand the SCCs has [sic] become the pastoral option of the Church, on the other hand priests and seminarians are still largely training in the traditional image of priesthood and feel ill at ease and not competent in the role of animator. It is often not their fault as they have never been trained for it.[62]

Indeed, while SCCs are envisioned as looser components of the church system than lay associations established as Catholic Action, they were never intended to act independently of clerical leadership and monitoring. In their 1986 pastoral letter, the Uganda bishops wrote with regard to SCCs that 'when we come on Pastoral visitation we shall be happy to see the progress made by these groups'.[63] Here again, the reluctance of church leaders to grant autonomy to lay associations produces an outcome conducive neither to mobilisation nor socialisation. The authors of the AMECEA report are sociologically astute on this point, and are worth quoting at length.

> Hierarchy is part of the self-understanding of the Catholic Church which the Vatican Council counterbalanced with the concept of the church as people of God and of collegiality, a balance that is not easily maintained. The same balance is needed in the formation of SCCs. … If they do not have sufficient autonomy, their life can be stifled by too much control from the centre. If they are not embedded into structures and the life of the larger parish, they can take on a sectarian character.[64]

Thus, SCCs have not proved to be efficacious vehicles for socialisation or mobilisation within Catholic networks. In Uganda, most Catholics have not been socialised into obedience. Indeed, SCCs were intended to counter disobedience by fostering a greater sense of individual and community responsibility within the normative framework of Catholic doctrine. Nor have most lay members, although inactive in SCCs, abandoned the church. Instead, they maintain a partial loyalty, grounded in a partial acceptance of doctrine and a periodic reliance on the church as a means of social support. They strategically accept the trappings of institutional paternalism while seeking other forums for participation. These arenas have expanded greatly since 1986, when the NRM introduced the system of local councils. Many Catholics who are active in church organisations also participate in this evolving experiment in local democracy, but rarely with the agenda of advancing Catholic interests or Christianising the public sphere. While Catholics are socially and politically active, especially at the local level, socialisation and mobilisation has largely occurred outside official church organisations, networks and world views.

Popular religious mobilisation

To make the case for 'civil society' as the central analytical tool for understanding political change, proponents of this view must demonstrate the capacity of civil organisations for mobilisation and socialisation. However, in spite of the ostensible 'immense influence that the Christian churches have over the majority of the population of Uganda',[65] at least in the case of the Catholic Church, this has not translated into such capacities. If a 'civil organisation' with as pervasive a social presence as the church is constrained in this regard, this should give pause to granting explanatory power to other organisations, or to civil society more generally. However, the argument offered here, focusing on the social power of the Ugandan church leaders, does not maintain that Catholics do not mobilise as *Catholics* in contemporary Uganda. Rather, when this mobilisation occurs, it is typically outside the formal channels the church establishes to link officials with lay members, and for purposes that are unrecognisable by conventional civil society approaches.

The use of the term 'sectarian' in the above quote from the AMECEA report is not meant in the metaphorical sense, popularised by the NRM in Uganda, of political mobilisation along 'primordial' identifications, but in the more traditional sense of religious mobilisation outside the control of the church that incorporates heterodox religious practices. Ironically, while the figurative sectarianism of religious identities and institutions has been a relatively infrequent occurrence in post-1986 Uganda, literal 'sectarianism' within the church has been a growing phenomenon.

Perhaps not coincidentally, the increasingly moribund trajectory of old and new Catholic lay organisations has been accompanied by a dramatic increase in the expression of popular religious beliefs and practices in Uganda, and the public and organised nature of these expressions.[66] Many of these practices encompass popular concerns with witchcraft and spirit possession. Such concerns are prominent across Africa in the 1990s. As Monga colourfully notes: 'The idea of being possessed traverses all social classes, all "tribes." Exorcism, as a result, is a booming business.'[67]

It is certainly booming in contemporary Uganda, and Catholics are major participants. Lay members do mobilise for spiritual purposes, but often do so outside church structures, or use formally recognised associations for purposes radically different from their stated objectives. Church policy has been either to ignore or suppress such movements, both because of their perceived heterodox practices and because they validate a lay religious charisma independent of the church.[68] Thus, for the most part church leaders have been unable or unwilling to harness this energy, further limiting it as an organisational locus for mobilisation. More recently, however, they have given more consideration to co-optation strategies in order to establish a deeper linkage to popular concerns.

What do exorcism and witchcraft have to do with civil society? Primarily, the answer is that effective and accountable leadership is connected in popular conceptions with the maintenance of order, and witchcraft is perceived as one source of disorder in all of rural, and much of urban Uganda.[69] Witchcraft is also linked to unfair advantage in the accumulation of wealth and power, although perhaps less so in Uganda than in other African societies.[70] Indeed, it would not be too much of an exaggeration to say that popular notions of 'civility' are informed by the control of witchcraft and other manifestations of evil spirits and the devil.[71] When state institutions and important social organisations like the mainline churches do not take a leading role in this control, popular movements may emerge to carry it out.

One way to gauge the church's potential for accommodation with popular religiosity is to contrast two recent examples from western Uganda. First is the case of Dosteo Bisaaka and his exorcism movement in western Uganda. A former Catholic catechist, Bisaaka's movement swept the region in the late 1980s until it was banned by the government in 1991. Part of the reason for the banning was pressure on the NRM by the western dioceses of Fort Portal and Hoima, which had lost thousands of followers to the movement. One could interpret the church's response to this group as markedly 'un-civil' in that, although Bisaaka was accused of counselling group members not to seek modern medical care, the NRM's ostensible reason for its banning, the principal reason for the church's opposition was that Bisaaka was engaging in direct competition for members and publicly denouncing the church as irrelevant. Bisaaka followers whom I interviewed in 1991 argued that they were being denied freedom of religion, which the church should be upholding. In a sense, both the church and the NRM regime demonstrated their power to define organisations as 'legitimate' – in this case a 'legitimate' religion – and thus a legitimate member of civil society.

However, by the mid-1990s, the banning order was rescinded, and Bisaaka and his followers openly began to practise once again. In June 1997, the group threw a birthday party for their leader in his home *saza* (county) of Buyaga in Kibaale district. The *New Vision* reported that the event 'caused a temporary standstill ... when schools and some government departments closed to celebrate the local prophet's birthday'. In addition, the NRM-appointed Resident District Commissioner of Kibaale was reported to having thanked Bisaaka 'for having solved the witchcraft problem that had bedevilled Bunyoro Kitara Kingdom but more particularly BuYaga county which had become a no-go area'.[72]

The second example of popular religious mobilisation took place within the Catholic Church, where similar remedies for spirit possession and protection against witchcraft were sought. A once relatively inactive lay association in Fort Portal Diocese dedicated to the Uganda martyrs – *ekitebe ky' bakaiso*, or Uganda Martyrs Guild – began performing exorcisms and casting out evil spirits in 1991. At first, the Diocese reacted cautiously, inviting the group to hold its sessions in the diocesan meeting hall and sending priests to observe whether the group's practices were in accord with church doctrine. But over the next few years, and not long after the arrival of a new bishop, the church became more open to the group. According to the guild's president, Lawrence Kasaija, the diocese formally recognised the group in 1995, with guild leaders taking an oath of fidelity to the church and promising to stop their activities should the church re-consider its ruling.[73] Several priests have joined the movement, which now has thousands of members and conducts witch-finding operations across the Toro region and elsewhere in the country. Opinions about the group are not unanimous. Other diocesan priests are deeply opposed to the point of refusing to allow guild members to operate in their parishes. One priest stated: 'These things just don't happen. It is either the work of a trickster or of mentally unbalanced people.'[74] But, as a regional Catholic magazine article put it: 'The sale of rosaries has shot up, the prayers are firmly biblical in content and both the reception of the sacraments and the reading of the Bible have vastly increased. Who wants to quarrel with a movement of this kind!'[75]

The Martyrs Guild movement may be accomplishing many of the goals that other church lay associations are unable to, but in a very different way from that which church officials would have preferred, or even imagined. This is a movement begun by a layman who works as an equal with supportive priests in fighting evil. In the process, what the church had typically viewed as heterodox practices are being redefined as 'Catholic', enabled by the tradition of exorcism within the church that had been largely ignored until now.[76]

One obvious, and complementary, interpretation of the church's atypical co-optation of the movement is to counter the influence of Bisaaka (who had explicitly stated that Christianity had been superseded by the arrival of his movement), as well as the growing number of Protestant pentecostal churches in Uganda that have begun to attract Catholics. But it is worth considering who is being co-opted here: the guild or the church? The church's willingness to recognise lay charisma, and its compromise with popular notions of spiritual power, might imply a new capacity for mobilisation. To the degree that conceptions of accountability and justice are connected to the control of witchcraft, the church's engagement with popular religiosity may also evolve into augmenting the social power of the church in local 'civil' society, although here civil means something very different than in standard civil society approaches.

Of course, accountability and justice are certainly not defined at the local level solely in terms of the control of witchcraft. If the church's popularity and mobilisational capacity increases as a result of its compromise with popular religious concerns, it will have to contend with both the 'un-civil' vigilantism that such movements sometimes practise, as well as how such concerns connect with more material dimensions of governance and political participation. Local notions of 'the civil' are themselves fraught with multiple and contradictory definitions, something typically missed in most civil society approaches. But the larger point of this section is to suggest that without some kind of mobilisational capacity linking leaders to followers, the church's socio-political practice is not captured by a civil society framework for analysis. A focus on the social power of the church is a more effective analytical framework for understanding its actual practice, as well as its purposes.

Conclusion

This article has argued that an understanding of the role of social organisations in civil society is presupposed by an account of the capacities of civil organisations to act in the public sphere. Civil society approaches themselves see socialisation and mobilisation as two central 'actions' that civil organisations take in confronting or engaging the state. Without empirical verification for the capacity of organisations to socialise or mobilise, the justification for analysing them through the lens of civil society is weak. I have demonstrated the serious obstacles which the Ugandan Catholic Church leaders face with regard to the socialisation and mobilisation of its members, and thus the limits of a civil society approach in accounting for its role in Ugandan society and politics.

Of course, this does not mean that all African social organisations, or even all religious organisations, lack these capacities. Rather, I argue that we must first view organisations through the lens of social power to grasp their political influence, rather than an *a priori* determination to place them under the rubric of civil society. In examining the role of the Ugandan Catholic Church in political, social and religious mobilisation, the church lacks the kinds of linkages with its members that foster such mobilisation and the mechanisms for socialising members into new values and roles. Church officials' ambivalence toward mobilisation is both a cause and consequence of their actual capacities. In general, Catholic leaders view the reproduction of the institution not only as a priority that guides their political vision, but as the necessary condition for the organisation's action in realising this vision. This does not make the church any less of a member of civil society. It does, however, lend a distinct risk-averse quality to its socio-political role, reinforces its 'logic of maintenance',[77] and gives doubt to the utility of a civil society approach in accounting for its capacity to effect change.

Uganda is both a diffficult and an important case for thinking about the role of civil society actors, both the churches and other organisations, because whether it is in a 'phase' of democratisation or of democratic consolidation is an issue debated both by scholars and Ugandans themselves.[78] Clearly, the current political system under the NRM falls short of the definition of democracy commonly accepted by civil society approaches, with critics pointing not only to the unfair electoral advantages of the NRM in a no-party system, but also to restrictions on associational rights in civil society itself.[79] An ambiguous outcome has emerged where opposition parties promote multi-partyism but not broader reforms in associational life, while most civil society organisations have not taken sides on the multi-party question. This situation has been to the advantage of the NRM regime, which has proved to be quite adept at manipulating it by presenting the image that Uganda is already in a phase of democratic consolidation. This raises another kind of critique of civil society approaches not discussed here – that is, the way in which party structures, state policies and the broader political context shape the structure and direction of civil society.[80]

In linking the issue of consolidation to the role of civil society, it is apparent that once the political situation has moved from, or at least is defined as other than, a simple matter of opposition to authoritarian rule, the question of how civil society actors work within a system is a thorny one. For religious organisations, Archbishop Desmond Tutu has described the conundrum of once-activist churches in post-apartheid South Africa with great eloquence: 'We knew what we were against, and we opposed that fairly effectively. It is not nearly so easy to say what we are for and so we appear to be dithering, not quite knowing where we want to go nor *how to get there*.'[81] For once-activist Catholic churches under authoritarian rule, in the shift to ostensibly liberal democracies in eastern Europe and Latin America, their role has also become decidedly more ambiguous: the Polish church has taken strong public stances, and used its political clout, in favour of 'illiberal' causes, while the Latin American churches, if not exactly retreating from the public sphere, have had difficulty defining their role in a more open political context.[82] This implies that the kind of organisational capacities conducive to mounting an effective challenge to authoritarian regimes may not be equally propitious in the consolidation of democracies or of civil societies.

The Ugandan Catholic Church has been on a different trajectory; whether it is able to move from its role as a refuge under political chaos to an effective socio-political actor in a new political situation remains to be seen. In the 11 years since the rise of the NRM, the results have been ambiguous at best, and many church leaders, while proclaiming the important place of the church in civil society, have been ambivalent in practice about whether to take on this role. I argue that, while church leaders think about 'how to get there', scholars must systematically consider organisational capacities and internal organisational politics to see how civil society actors got to the place they currently occupy.

To repeat, the point here is not that the Ugandan church lacks social power or that it has no political influence. Rather, the kind of power that the church possesses, and the mechanisms it deploys to achieve influence, are not best understood through the lens of civil society. In Uganda's political struggles not only to identify the appropriate institutions of democratic rule, but to define the content of democracy itself, the church may have a role to play. But by asserting a leading role without the capacity to play it, church leaders run the risk of building up expectations which cannot be met. Civil society proponents, by conflating the power of a normative idea with an analytical tool, run a similar risk.

Notes

This article is a revised version of a paper prepared for the workshop 'Rethinking Civil Society in African Politics' held at Dartmouth College on 25 October 1997. The author wishes to thank Irving Leonard Markovitz, Aili Mari Tripp, Roger Tangri, and especially Nelson Kasfir for their comments.

[1] One author rightly states that there is 'a wide gap existing between theory and concrete investigation. That is, little empirical work has been undertaken by the champions of "civil society" to substantiate or elaborate their theoretical assertions'. M.G. Ngunyi, 'Religious Institutions and Political Liberalisation in Kenya', in P. Gibbon (ed.), *Markets, Civil Society and Democracy in Kenya* (Uppsala: Nordiska Afrikainstitutet, 1995), 122.

[2] In a superb study of the political orientation and organisational power of NGOs in Kenya, S.N. Ndegwa 'treats civil society actions as the *dependent* variables that need to be explained rather than as the causal variables of political reform', *The Two Faces of Civil Society: NGOs and Politics in Africa* (West Hartford, CT: Kumarian Press, 1996), 110, emphasis in original.

[3] J.M. Waliggo, 'The Role of Christian Churches in the Democratisation

Process in Uganda 19801993', in P. Gifford (ed.), *The Christian Churches and the Democratisation of Africa* (Leiden: E.J. Brill, 1995), 224.

4   For typical cases, see J.W. Harbeson, 'Civil Society and Political Renaissance in Africa', in J.W Harbeson, D. Rothchild and N. Chazan (eds.), *Civil Society and the State in Africa* (Boulder, CO: I.ynne Rienner, 1994), 1-29, L. Diamond, 'Rethinking Civil Society: Toward Democratic Consolidation', *Journal of Democracy*, 5, 3 (1994), 4–17; and N. Chazan, 'Africa's Democratic Challenge', *World Policy Journal*, 9, 2 (1992), 279–308.

5   See Ndegwa's savvy discussion of the 'organisational power' of NGOs in *The Two Faces af Civil Society*, chapters 2 and 6, and M. Bratton's analysis of the relationship between organisational autonomy and organisational capacity in 'Peasant–State Relations in Postcolonial Africa: Patterns of Engagement and Disengagement', in J.S. Migdal, V. Shue and A. Kohli (eds.), *State Power and Social Forces: Domination and Transformation in the Third World* (Cambridge: Cambridge University Press, 1994), 231–54.

6   M.W. Foley and B. Edwards, 'The Paradox of Civil Society', *Journal of Democracy*, 5, 3 (1996), 39.

7   Ibid., 39.

8   For example, J. Haynes, *Religion and Politics in Africa* (London: Zed Books, 1996), chapter 4.

9   Examples of this optimism can be found in some of the essays in P. Gifford (ed.), *The Christian Churches and the Democratisation of Africa* (Leiden: E.J. Brill, 1995); and H. Assefa and G. Wachira (eds.), *Peacemaking and Democratisation in Africa: Theoretical Perspectives and Church Initiatives* (Nairobi: East African Educational Publishers, 1996).

10 This is the title of a recently published collection of the pastoral letters of the Kenyan Episcopal conference: R. Mejia, SJ (ed.), *The Conscience of Society: The Social Teaching of the Catholic Bishops of Kenya* (Nairobi: Pauline Publications Africa, 1995). Interestingly, the title is taken from a speech given by Jomo Kenyatta to a gathering of East African Catholic Bishops in 1976: 'The Church is the conscience of society, and today society needs a conscience. Do not be afraid to speak.'

11 Catholic Bishops of Uganda, *With a New Heart and a New Spirit* (Kisubi, UG: St. Paul Publications-Africa, 1986), 69, 10.

12 At a 1993 conference of East African religious leaders, Gifford reports that 'some delegates actually argued that the church was Africa's "only hope for social change".' P. Gifford, 'Introduction: Democratisation and the Churches', in Gifford (ed.), *The Christian Churches and the Democratisation of Africa*, 9.

13 Ibid., 11, emphasis in original.

14 Ibid., 13.

15 Ibid., 8.

16 S. Kalyvas, *The Rise of Christian Democracy in Europe* (Ithaca, NJ: Cornell University Press, 1996).

17 Gifford, Introduction', 6, my emphasis.

18 See Haynes, *Religion and Politics in Africa*; Gifford, 'Introduction'; and P. Gifford, 'Some Recent Developments in African Christianity', *Afncan Affairs*, 93 (1994), 513–34.

19 Ngunyi, 'Religious Institutions and Political Liberalisation in Kenya'. The role of churches in Kenya has attracted much attention from scholars. See A.C. Abuom, 'The Churches' Involvement in the Democratisation Process in Kenya', in H. Assefa and G. Wachira (eds.), *Peacemaking and Democratisatian in Africa: Theoretical Perspectives and Church Initiatives* (Nairobi: East African Educational Publishers, 1996), 95-116; M. Bratton, 'Civil Society and Political Transitions in Africa', in Harbeson, Rothchild and Chazan (eds.), *Civil Society and the State in Africa*, 51–81; G. Sabar-Friedman, 'Church and State in Kenya, 1986–1992: The Churches' Involvement in the "Game of Change"', *African Affairs*, 96 (1997), 25–52; and D. Throup, '"Render unto Caesar the Things that are Caesar's": The Politics of Church-State Conflict in Kenya, 1978–1990', in H.B. Hansen and M. Twaddle (eds.), *Religion and Politics in East Africa: The Period Since Independence* (London: James Currey, 1995), 143-76.

20 R. Kassimir, 'Ambiguous Institution: The Catholic Church and Uganda's Reconstruction in the First Five Years of the NRM', in Leonardo Villalón and Philip Huxtable (eds.), *The African State at a Critical Juncture* (Boulder, CO: Lynne Rienner, 1998).

21 *Uganda News Bulletin*, 26 Aug. 1997.

22 *New Vision*, 18 June 1996.

23 *With a New Heart and a New Spirit*, 77. Elsewhere in this document, the bishops wrote that 'the leaders of the church, represented by the hierarchy and the clergy, will not identify themselves with any particular political grouping', 68.

24 Catholic Bishops of Uganda, *Towards a New National Constitution* (Kisubi, UG: Marianum Press, 1989), 19. They continued: 'The Church does not censure any government, *of whatever form*, provided that the whole governmental system is constituted in such a way that it is able to guarantee the common good, that is the respect of human rights and the welfare, both spiritual and material, of the citizens', 20, my emphasis.

25 For an argument against seeing religious identity in Uganda as 'primordial', see R. Kassimir, 'Catholics and Political Identity in Toro', in Hansen and Twaddle (eds.), *Religion and Politics in East Africa*, 120–40.

26 For the only detailed case study, See A.G.G. Gingyera-Pincywa, *Issues in Pre-Independence Politics in Uganda: A Case Study on the Contribution of Religion to Political Debate in Uganda in the Decade 1952–62* (Kampala: East African Literature Bureau, 1976).

27 Uganda National Council of Catholic Action, *Memorandum on the Situation of the Catholic Missions by the Uganda Protectorate* (1956), 7.

28 'The Protestant approach to life, in Uganda, and its tendency to consider Protestantism as a step-stone [*sic*] to wealth, social superiority and power, is not alien to the spread of radicalist ideas', Uganda National Council of Catholic Action, *Memorandum*, 63.

29 The acronyms for the two parties were popularly satirised as religious emblems. DP became *Dini ya Papa* (Swahili for 'Religion of the Pope') while UPC became United Protestants of Canterbury.

30 See Kassimir, 'Catholics and Political Identity'. In a sense, this is the reverse of Laitin's case study of the Yoruba, where fairly well-defined and relatively stable notions of Anglican and Muslim identity did not evolve into a sense of common political interest and organisation. See D.D. Laitin, *Hegemony and Culture: Politics and Religious Change Among the Yoruba* (Chicago, IL: University of Chicago Press, 1986).

31 Kalyvas discusses a similar process of Catholic political identity formation in nineteenth-century Europe in *The Rise of Christian Democracy*, chapter I .

32 '[T]he fact that it was originally to have been called the Christian Democratic Party indicates the analogy with European Democratic parties which guided the thinking of the founders of the DP.' C. Leys, *Politicians and Policies: An Essay on Politics in Acholi, Uganda 1962–5* (Nairobi: East African Publishing House, 1967), 5–6. Even if the first part of this claim is true, it is not proof that Christian Democracy 'guided the thinking' of the DP's founders.

33 See R. Muscat (ed.), *A Short History of the Democratic Party 1954–1984* (Rome: Foundation for African Development, 1984). To make matters more complicated, the volume was ghostwritten by a Makerere University History Professor who is a Protestant DP supporter.

34 In his landmark study of Christian Democracy, Michael R. Fogarty identified the DP as a Christian Democratic movement, noting in a new preface to his book 'the victory in the Uganda elections of 1961 of the Democratic Party, of primarily Catholic inspiration and with encouragement from the clergy and Catholic Action'. *Christian Democracy in Western Europe, 1820–1953* (Westport, CT: Greenwood Press, 1957, 1974), xxvi. It is also true that over the years the DP has received advice and financial support from international Christian Democratic organisations, and particularly parties in Germany and Italy. Of course, these parties, and especially the latter, have become better known for machine rather than ideological politics.

35 Michael Twaddle writes: 'But had the DP really been established quite so firmly as a confessional party on the European Christian Democratic model in the early 1950s, one would expect more philosophical underpinning than just a few unfriendly remarks by one expatriate priest and just one pastoral letter ostensibly designed more to protect Catholic interests in schools than to foster the development of any one political

party.' 'Was the Democratic Party of Uganda a Purely Confessional Party?', in Edward Fashole-Luke et al. (eds.), *Christianity in Independent Africa* (Bloomington, IN: Indiana University Press, 1978), 260.

[36] At times, the church appeared to believe that the DP was already a Christian Democratic party. Thus, Gingyera-Pincywa is correct in referring to this as 'wishful thinking or an attempt to read into the Party's policy something it did not have'. *Issues in Pre-independence Politics*, 205.

[37] Kathleen G. Lockard writes that most teachers, including Catholics, welcomed the nationalisation. 'In general the teachers felt that their own self-interest lay more on the side of government control, since the churches as employers had traditionally demanded high standards of Christian morality of their teachers, particularly on the question of monogamous marriage.' 'Religion and Political Development in Uganda 1962–1972' (Ph.D. Dissertation: University of Wisconsin-Madison, 1974), 336.

[38] *Annual Report, Lay Apostolate in Fort Portal Diocese*, 1966. A new association, set up to take the place of the Toro Catholic Council, contained within its constitution: 'no Catholic Association can be tolerated or allowed in a Diocese if its aims and actions as well as its procedures disturb the peace of the Church.' For more details, see Kassimir, 'Catholics and Political Identity'.

[39] See Kalyvas, *The Rise of Christian Democracy*, Chapters 1 and 2.

[40] In his autobiography, Yoweri Museveni claims that this caused consternation for older DP leaders who felt that the influx would dilute its ability to pursue Catholic elite interests. 'Frightened by the new members, the old Catholic originals [of DP] starting talking of themselves as the only legitimate members of the parly, *banasangwaawo*, and referring to the newcomers as upstarts.' *Sowing the Mustard Seed: The Struggle for Freedom and Democracy in Uganda* (London: Macmillan Publishers, 1997), 118. This is echoed even today by the Mobilisers Group, which emerged from within the party in the early 1990s to criticise the DP leadership's occasional alliances with the NRM and to purify it back to its roots (although it never framed the matter as Catholic roots.)

[41] M. Louise Pirouet remarks that, under Amin, 'The churches found themselves dragged, against their will, into becoming foci of opposition, until eventually they became feared by those in power'. 'Religion in Uganda Under Amin', *Journal of Religion in Africa*, 11, 1 (1980), 13. This is notably different from the pro-active stance taken by the mainline Kenyan churches in opposition to Moi, making it remarkable that Sabar-Friedman would state that in relation to the Kenyan churches 'It is interesting to note that, although significantly different in [their] historical background and [their] political affliation, both the Anglican and Roman Catholic Churches of Uganda have taken upon themselves a similar role' under Amin and Obote. 'Church and State in Kenya', 29.

[42] *New Vision*, 6 Aug. 1990.

[43] Bishop S.B. Magambo, *The Life and Mission of Lay People in Uganda* (Kisubi, UG: Marianum Press, 1988), 9.

[44] Bishop S.B. Magambo, 'A Critique of Ugandan Christian Education', in *Proceedings of the Catholic Teacher Guild Seminar* (Kinyamasika, Fort Portal Diocese, 3–12 Dec. 1988), 12, my emphasis.

[45] Waliggo, 'The Role of Christian Churches', 220. Although he does not say so explicitly, Waliggo clearly implies (in ways that are consistent with my own observations) that these divisions were as pervasive within churches as they were across them. In an editorial, the independent newspaper *The Monitor* stated that during the 1996 presidential elections, 'The Churches must face the fact that they failed to set the moral tone for the campaigns … in the last 16 years, the Church has often seemed at sea; with sections of it hob-nobbing with the regime of the day and abandoning their duty to fight for Justice, and only a few tenacious ones speaking out against wrong. At the beginning of this year, both the main Churches the Catholic and Protestant, and the Islamic leadership split in factions supporting the main presidential candidates'. 31 Dec. 1996. However, it should be noted that during the campaign, the Catholic Archbishop of Kampala, Cardinal Emmanuel Wamala, publicly criticised the behaviour of candidates and irregularities in the electoral

system, an intervention denounced by some NRM supporters although not by Museveni himself. Still, the Cardinal's statements did not endorse the opposition or its stance of returning Uganda to a multi-party system.

[46] This both in spite of, and because of, the fact that religion did emerge as the basis for political rivalry during several elections under the NRM, mostly in the two southwestem districts of Kabale and Bushenyi.

[47] It should be added that there is little evidence that the DP would explicitly play the Catholic card if it was allowed to compete openly. The question is more whether old alignments would re-constitute themselves under a multi-party system that would replay the old Catholic-Protestant divide.

[48] Waliggo, 'The Role of Christian Churches', 224.

[49] Indeed, there is a strong sense, both among more conservative clergy and populists like Waliggo, that education – whether consciousness-raising or the more traditional forms of evangelism – leads directly to mobilisation and is thus the main mechanism to be employed in order to achieve it. In the sentence that immediately follows his call to organise the social groups he mentions, Waliggo writes: 'Civic and political education cannot be left to government agencies alone', privileging education as the primary tool for mobilisation. 'The Role of Christian Churches', 224.

[50] For an account of religious identities as interest groups in Uganda, see D.M. Mudoola, *Religion, Ethnicity and Politics in Uganda* (Kampala: Fountain Publishers, 1996).

[51] See Kassimir, 'Catholics and Political Identity', and R. Kassimir, 'The Politics of Popular Catholicism in Uganda', in T. Spear and I. Kimambo (eds.), *African Expressions of Christianity* (forthcoming).

[52] 'Small Christian Communities: 20 Years Later', *AMECEA Documentation Service* 472 (1997), 15.

[53] R.D. Putnam with R. Leonardi and R.Y. Nanetti, *Making Democracy Work: Civic Traditions in Modern Italy* (Princeton, NJ: Princeton University Press, 1993).

[54] J. Aduta, 'The Laity and Small Christian Communities', Fort Portal Synod, Position Paper No. 7 (1989), 2.

[55] He finally succeeded in 1994, when the parish of Kyarusozi was erected by the bishop who 'officially handed it over to the congregation of the Holy Cross'. Reported in *Pact Bulletin* [a publication of Fort Portal Diocese], October 1994.

[56] See J. Burdick, *Looking for God in Brazil: The Progressive Church in Urban Brazil's Religious Arena* (Berkeley, CA: University of California Press, 1993); D.H. Levine, *Popular Voices in Latin American Catholicism* (Princeton, NJ: Princeton University Press, 1992); and C. Smith, *The Emergence of Liberation Theology. Radical Religion and Social Movement Theory* (Chicago, IL: University of Chicago Press, 1991).

[57] 'Small Christian Communities', 16, 14.

[58] Ibid., 11.

[59] *With a New Heart and a New Spirit*, 57, my emphasis.

[60] 'Small Christian Communities', 14.

[61] See, for example, A. Fowler, 'The Role of NGOs in Changing State-Society Relations: Perspectives from Eastern and Southern Africa', *Development Policy Review*, 9, 1 (1991), 53–84.

[62] 'Small Christian Communities', 15.

[63] *With a New Heart and A New Spirit*, 52.

[64] 'Small Christian Communities', 17.

[65] Waliggo, 'The Role of Christian Churches', 224.

[66] Kassimir, 'The Politics of Popular Catholicism'.

[67] C. Monga, *The Anthropology of Anger: Civil Society, and Democracy in Africa* (Boulder, CO: Lynne Rienner, 1996), 140.

[68] Kassimir, 'The Politics of Popular Catholicism'.

[69] While not discussing witchcraft, Mikael Karlström makes a very persuasive case for the connection between local conceptions of civility with order, and even hierarchy, in Buganda. 'Imagining Democracy: Political Culture and Democratisation in Buganda', *Africa*, 66, 4 (1996), 485–505.

[70] See P. Geschiere, *The Modernity of Witchcraft: Politics and the Occult in Postcolonial Africa* (Charlottesville, VA: University of Virginia Press, 1997).

[71] Thus, while Fatton is correct in bringing concerns about witchcraft into the discussion of civil society, he misses the connection between witchcraft eradication and popular notions of what might be called civility, focusing instead on the allegedly 'obscurantist' nature of such practices. 'Witchcraft and counter-witchcraft rituals are deeply embedded in the private practices of daily existence; they are personal remedies to the overwhelming presence of evil, and they pervade civil society with a supernatural aura. Civil society is thus not all enlightenment, it is also the domain of profoundly inegalitarian and obscurantist institutions and lifestyles. Nor does its opposition to the state automatically spell freedom, as "witches" – self-seeking predatory rulers and aspirants – can easily subvert it into corrupt and cruel ends.' R. Fatton, 'Africa in the Age of Democratization: The Civic Limitations of Civil Society', *African Studies Review*, 38, 2 (1995), 76–7. I cannot imagine anyone who believes in the 'reality' of witchcraft disagreeing with this last sentence, but it confuses the point, which is that it is 'witch-cleansing' that can spell freedom, or, at minimum, order.

[72] *New Vision*, 17 June, 1997. In interviews conducted in June 1997, several church leaders stated that Bisaaka had forged ties with the NRM, and that some of the regime's officials were now followers of his movement.

[73] Interview with Kasaija, I July 1997.

[74] In Fr. Raphael, 'Driving Away Evil Spirits', *Leadership*, 357 (1996), 17.

[75] Ibid.

[76] 'The Guild is and remains an offcial movement of the Diocese, and, as is usual in the Catholic Church in such circumstances, no official pronouncement is made on the out-of-the-ordinary side-shows of the movement as long as what they teach is not heretical.' Note that the danger is what is taught, not what is practised. Ibid.

[77] The term is from J.A. Coleman 'Raison d'Eglise: Organizational Imperatives of the Church in the Political Order', in J.K. Hadden and A. Shupe (eds.), *Secularization and Fundamentalism Reconsidered: Religion and the Political Order, Volume III* (New York: Paragon House, 1989).

[78] Michael Bratton and Nicolas van de Walle have coded Uganda as a 'blocked' and 'managed' political transition in their recent comparative study: *Democratic Experiments in Africa: Regime Transitions in Comparative Perspective* (Cambridge: Cambridge University Press, 1997).

[79] See M. Mamdani, 'Pluralism and the Right of Association', in M. Mamdani and J. Oloka-Onyango (eds.), *Uganda: Studies in Living Conditions, Popular Movements, and Constitutionalism* (Vienna: JEP Books, 1994), 519–63. Mamdani points out that the NRM did not create these restrictions, which have been in place since the colonial period, but have not acted to remove them.

[80] See Ndegwa, *The Two Faces of Civil Society*; and Foley and Edwards, 'The Paradox of Civil Society'.

[81] D. Tutu, 'Identity Crisis', in Paul Gifford (ed.), *The Christian Churches and the Democratisation of Africa* (Leiden: E.J. Brill, 1995), 96, my emphasis.

[82] For the latter, see C.A. Drogus, 'Review Article: The Rise and Decline of Liberation Theology: Churches, Faith, and Political Change in Latin America', *Comparative Politics*, 27, 4 (1995), 465–77.

AILI MARI TRIPP
Everyday Forms of Resistance & Transformations of Economic Policy

Reference
Changing the Rules: The Politics of Liberalisation & the Urban Informal Economy in Tanzania
University of California Press, 1997, ch. 6

You can't make people go along one narrow road. People have their own minds. They aren't going to go along with force.
CCM ten-cell leader, Dar es Salaam

As the economic crisis deepened in the early 1980s, the conflicts between the government and those involved in the informal economy over how the self-employed were treated, over legalizing their small businesses, and over other policies that were perceived as threatening ordinary people's pursuit of a livelihood reached a new intensity. Urban dwellers' options had become more limited; resources and jobs, more scarce. In the early 1980s the authorities initiated a series of measures targeting people they labeled loiterers, unproductive elements, and economic saboteurs. These and other inflexible policies forced increasing numbers of people to pursue strategies of noncompliance, refusing to abide by laws that violated popular notions of justice.

Meanwhile, the slowdown of the world economy and world trade and the concomitant pressures from external donors and international agencies like the IMF and the World Bank put enormous pressures on governments of low-income countries like Tanzania to respond in ways that weakened their own internal legitimacy. The economic crisis, coupled with these external pressures for restructuring, occurred at the same time that domestic pressures in the form of massive noncompliance with government and CCM regulations became more apparent. This chapter, however, is about changes that were mainly consequences of internal pressures, many of which had little to do with donor conditionality.

After the mid-1980s, open repression of small entrepreneurs gradually gave way to legalization, liberalization, and privatization. Small-business operators who had previously been considered engaged in illegal occupations were now able to apply for licenses. Trade of foodstuffs that had been channeled through parallel markets could now make its way through liberalized open markets. Bus transportation, banks, and medical practices, which had been monopolized by the government, were opened to private ownership. Sometimes, however, the authorities either did not have the capacity to enforce their policies or were not prepared from an ideological standpoint to sanction various practices officially. In these cases they continued to ignore certain illegal economic activities.

The activities discussed in this chapter affected not only the self-employed but also employees in the public and private sectors and their household members. These struggles over the legitimacy of self-employment as a means of obtaining a livelihood and other such conflicts were the main source of tension in the 1980s between those in power and the urban dwellers, including workers and civil servants. With the deepening of the crisis and the state's simultaneous growing inability to maintain adequate wages, the battleground for workers shifted from the official workplace to areas in which the state encroached on people's key sources of income: informal income-generating activities.

People's persistence in their informal income-generating activities in defiance of government restrictions became a form of opposition. These forms of resistance were not formally mobilized, but the collective impact of hundreds of thousands of individuals' resorting to similar kinds of measures clearly was not lost on those in power. They had to respond, often by making policy changes of the kind described in this chapter.

James C. Scott forcefully argued that such 'everyday forms of resistance' can be effective, widespread, durable, and highly coordinated, even though they are not formally organized and do not seek 'self-consciously' broad policy goals (1987, 421). Although he was referring to peasant resistance, the same conceptualization could equally apply to resistance in the urban setting.

The Tanzanian state's responses to noncompliance were rarely direct. Instead, they involved tacit compromises. The leadership's gradual shift in policy with respect to these small-scale enterprises came about primarily through societal pressures. These pressures initially did not directly threaten the ideological underpinnings of a state that had sought legitimacy from upholding populist and socialist goals of egalitarianism, self-reliance, and communalism. As Scott argues, direct challenges to rulers are more likely to face suppression than are quiet strategies, because a concession to direct challenges necessitates a permanent and acknowledged response, whereas a concession to a quiet pressure can be made informally, without any symbolic or official change in policy. Moreover, the concession can always be retracted. As such, resistance that follows the path of least resistance is often the most effective (Scott 1987, 423). Many of the initial government responses were tacit, but mounting pressures eventually led to policy changes that did, in fact, involve shifts in ideological orientation, as seen in the dismantling of the Arusha Declaration (see chapter 7).

Although forms of noncompliant resistance are sometimes termed passive, empirical analysis of the Tanzanian experience shows that such resistance is by no means characterized by passivity in the literal sense. By pursuing their various survival strategies, people were not just responding to necessity, they were actively remolding their own destinies. They were not only seeking new and innovative ways of obtaining an income, they were consciously and vigorously resisting the state. In the course of defying various anachronistic state policies, they were reshaping the political and economic structures that surrounded them.

People of every class were involved in the informal economy. The poorest vendors might carry out their business in unauthorized locations. At the same time, the upper ranks of civil servants evaded the Arusha Declaration Leadership Code by owning sideline projects and hiring workers to assist them in these businesses. Middle- and upper-income people kept chickens, cows, and pigs in their backyards at a time when city ordinances outlawed such practices. Doctors would illegally moonlight after putting in their hours at the government hospital.

Involvement in projects was characteristic of most classes, but government repression of informal economic activities was not uniform. City Council militia harassed the poorest women, youth, and child vendors on a daily basis, while leaving alone the well-to-do who had sideline incomes and were not paying taxes. During the 1983 Nguvu Kazi repatriation campaign to move so-called loiterers – most of whom were self-employed – to the countryside to farm, one resident of Pemba wrote to the *Daily News* editor: 'I would like to question those in authority of their indiscriminate arrests of pedestrians and cyclists in the streets between 10 A.M. and 2 P.M. is legal and constitutional. … People using cars and trucks during the so-called work hours are not harassed. Why? Can't someone loiter with his car for petty personal business during work hours? Are we creating two classes of citizens in this country – the oppressed and the privileged ?'[1]

Examples like this show that although the tactic of non-compliance can be used by many sectors of society, the consequences are not borne equally by all. Rather, the poorest members of society are most likely to suffer the severest consequences, for they generally do not have 'friends in the right places' or the mechanisms through which to defend their interests.

The following discussion focuses on some examples of how people involved in various aspects of the informal economy defied government policies through non-compliance and brought about small but important changes. Non-compliance became so pervasive that the cost of coercive enforcement became excessive. The authorities responded by ignoring the activities or by eventually changing the rules in order to give legal sanction to practices that had already, de facto, been in existence. These changes indicated the beginnings of some long overdue adjustments in state–society relations that made the state more responsive to societal needs.

It is important to recognize that non-compliance was not restricted to economic strategies. Other, equally important issues evoked similar non-compliance to government policies. The expansion of unplanned housing settlements is a case in point. Settlement in unplanned areas has mushroomed ever since the city began to expand significantly in 1963, when all freehold land became state land (Stren 1982, 80). For ten years after independence, the government attempted a policy of clearing so-called slums and squatter settlements through the National Housing Corporation.[2] Having had little success with this policy, Tanzanian authorities started a scheme in 1972 to upgrade these areas, and it provided several thousand newly surveyed plots with basic services in planned areas for low-income families. There were some beneficiaries of this plan, but the majority of new urban dwellers continued to settle in unsurveyed and unplanned areas. A 1982 estimate placed the number of illegally built houses at five times that of legally built houses. Town authorities had little choice but to recognize the new illegal settlements as full and recognized town districts (Kulaba 1989, 224–28; Lindberg 1981, 133; Stren 1982, 80).

Richard Stren suggests several reasons why people did not build in surveyed plots in the initial years after independence, even though with a legal plot they had a better chance of obtaining water, garbage-disposal services, and community facilities. Steep legal fees and complex, time-consuming bureaucratic processes involving a maze of paperwork deterred most of the urban poor (1982, 80–81). This was compounded in later years by other disincentives, including the general decline in urban services and officials who were prone to demanding bribes for various necessary certificates. Moreover, the abolition of urban councils during the 1972–1978 period spurred the growth of these settlements, because there was no institution to regulate the informal building of houses (Kulaba 1989).

In housing settlements, as with informal income-generating activities, people resisted government policy because the plans had been made not with their objectives as a starting point but with other preconceived notions of what constituted desirable development, because they had to engage a complicated bureaucracy in order to obtain legal recognition, often requiring the payment of numerous bribes at each step of the way, and, perhaps most importantly, because the urban dwellers did not believe that compliance would result in a fair bargain; that is, their financial input would not result in an exchange for adequate government services.

Legalization

Defining productive work

Both the colonial and postcolonial states made numerous attempts to remove so-called unproductive elements from the city and to repatriate them to the countryside. Often these elements included the self-employed, whose basic conflict with the state thus became one of determining not just how they would obtain a livelihood but also who would control their very means of survival. The resettlement schemes of the postcolonial state had their origins in British vagrancy laws, which date back as far as 1349. They were vigorously enforced by authorities in eighteenth- and nineteenth-century England as a means of securing cheap labor for industry and to round up alleged criminals. These laws were transferred to the colony of Tanganyika in the form of the Penal Code, which targeted prostitutes, beggars, gamblers, suspected thieves, 'rogues,' and 'vagabonds.' In addition to this code, the colonial government introduced the Townships (Removal of Undesirable Persons) Ordinance in 1944, which is still in force. Under this ordinance, a district commissioner can order an 'undesirable' person who has no regular employment or 'reputable means of livelihood' to leave the town (Shaidi 1987).

Another colonial ordinance still in force is the 1923 Destitute Persons Ordinance, which pertains to people found without employment or unable to show that they have a 'visible and sufficient means of subsistence.' The magistrate can order such 'destitute persons' to find work, detain them, or return them to their original place of residence. One of the main aims of these vagrancy statutes was to provide cheap labor for settler communities and to keep people in the rural areas, where they could continue the cash-crop production that was so crucial to the colonial state. In the 1930s the police commissioner and the provincial commissioner (Eastern Province) initiated the first forcible removal of unemployed people from Dar es Salaam to the countryside (Shaidi 1987).

The independent government attempted a number of operations to resettle urban dwellers in the nearby villages, the most important of which was in 1976. It was not long before the majority of the resettled people had returned to the city, some only a few hours after being moved out (Shaidi 1987, 12). In another such initiative the government enacted a Penal Code Amendment in 1983 that banned people involved in so-called unproductive activities from the cities because they were considered 'idle and disorderly persons.'[3]

Soon after the Penal Code Amendment was enacted, the Human Resources Deployment Act was passed in May 1983, requiring all urban Tanzanians to be registered and issued labor-identification cards.[4] Under this act, also known as Nguvu Kazi, those who could not produce proper identification were to be resettled in the countryside. In the Dar es Salaam region all unlicensed, self-employed people, including fish sellers, shoe repairmen, and tailors, were considered idle and disorderly and treated like loiterers. President Nyerere ordered the prime minister to be 'bold' in implementing the Nguvu Kazi act, saying: 'If we don't disturb loiterers, they will disturb us.' Nyerere compared the 'loiterers' with economic saboteurs and racketeers, 'whom the nation has declared war on' and depicted this campaign as a strong vehicle for promoting economic production.[5] The leadership justified the operation by the need 'to increase productivity and make the country self-sufficient in food.'[6]

Immediately after the Deployment Act went into effect on 15 October 1983 the police, national-service soldiers, and people's militia started rounding up thousands of suspected loiterers on a random basis. Even an employed person found walking the streets during working hours could be charged with being 'engaged in a frolic of his own at a time he is supposed to be engaged in activities connected or relating to the business of his employment.' During the early 1980s Tanzanians experienced severe shortages, and workers frequently left their jobs during work hours to stand in lines to obtain food.

Detainees were taken to one of three centers in Dar es Salaam and had to provide documentation that they were employed and, in the case of women, that they were married. Those who were declared unemployed were sent back to their home villages or to state-run sisal plantations. Three months after the campaign started, 15,611 people had been detained (Shaidi 1984, 86).

The campaign was especially problematic regarding women. The authorities required married women to produce official marriage certificates within seven days of being detained to indicate that they had husbands who were providing for them (Kerner 1988, 53; Shaidi 1984, 86). This policy contained numerous questionable assumptions, including the notion that all women who did not fall into the category of officially married – that is, women who were single, divorced, or widowed or women in common-law marriages – could be suspected of being loiterers and unproductive elements. Moreover, it assumed that the wives were dependent on their husbands, disregarding the fact that married women might have been supporting their families through their own projects.

For a brief period, food vendors and shoe shiners disappeared from the city streets, employed people did not venture away from their jobs during the day, and children going to and coming from school rode buses in groups (Kerner 1988, 49). But it quickly became clear that the campaign was a failure. No sooner were truckloads of people dropped off in rural areas than most of them returned to the city to resume their small-scale enterprises. The illegal trade in identification papers boomed, so that virtually anyone could come up with some form of documentation.

The Nguvu Kazi enterprise had its parallels in other parts of Africa in the late 1970s and early 1980s as various countries sank deeper into economic crisis. In July 1984 Nigeria's military rulers launched a War against Indiscipline, involving the arrests of vendors and the destruction of their stalls along main roads of urban areas. A day or so after the state action the vendors returned to resume business as usual (Eames 1988, 87; Trager 1987, 247–48). In Zambia police attempted to control price hiking during the period of shortages in 1982 by arresting and destroying the wares of women street vendors (Hansen 1989, 148). In Ghana the military government of the Armed Forces Revolutionary Council sought to do away with hoarding and price hiking by market traders during a period of shortages. Soon after their takeover in June 1979, they literally dynamited the central market in Accra to the ground and sold off the trader's stocks at the Kumasi central market. Market sellers continued to sell their goods through friends and from their homes, however. The heightened risk factor meant that the prices of the goods skyrocketed (Clark 1988, 61; Dolphyne 1987 ,27).

In Tanzania the Nguvu Kazi campaign was destined to fail when the government resorted to coercion in an offensive against city dwellers, with little regard for the realities faced by the urban poor. It is ironic that while the Nguvu Kazi enterprise aimed at forcing urban dwellers into 'productive' agricultural production, by the late 1980s those with farms outside the city or on the outskirts of the city were in an enviable position of having this additional means of livelihood. In principle, most people had no objection to farming and would have welcomed a viable scheme that gave them land and a means to cultivate. As one cigarette vendor who was born and raised in the city told me, 'The government just collected us young men and dumped us in the forest to farm. They gave us plots but no capital, no houses, no food. ... We had no choice but to come back to the city and continue selling cigarettes. If I had a place to live and the means I would have stayed to farm.'[7]

Today it is widely recognized that rural life may hold more promise than urban life does, for in cities, in order to eat, one needs cash, which is difficult to come by. As one textile worker who purchased a 1.6-hectare farm in 1976 said: 'If I do statistics in my head, life in the villages is better than city life. One has a plot and can sell one's crops. You have no problem if you rely on the crops that you grow. Life in the cities is harder. Where I work many have left their jobs since 1982 and many more since 1985. They have decided to go back to the villages or be self-employed.'[8]

The absurdity of the Nguvu Kazi policy was underscored by reports like the one of twenty-two shoe shiners who were arrested on the grounds of being unproductive. Several of them were physically handicapped, and half of them were students at a nearby vocational school who were trying to support their studies through this sideline activity. A city official told them to find jobs and warned them against turning to shoe shining. He announced that people with leather shoes needing regular polishing should learn to do it themselves. The official added, 'Otherwise you have to buy safari boots or canvas shoes.'[9]

Public response to this campaign was by no means indifferent. The notion that these activities were not productive made little sense to most people. The Tanzanian *Daily News* carried a series of interviews with self-employed people and asked them about the illegal and unproductive nature of their activities.[10] One fishmonger said, 'I regard this activity as being gainful. Every day I make a profit of at least 100 and 200 shillings or more at best. I have a wife and five children who are dependent on me. It is a good thing that people should be involved in some gainful activity or other. But there are people who have their businesses who will be harassed for no good reason. I don't see how you will convince me that a certain job is better than what I am doing now. Even if you give me employment in your company, I won't accept it. I just couldn't survive on a monthly salary.' A peanut vendor responded, 'I tell you I have been able to keep a wife and four children by doing nothing but selling groundnuts. My children are now in school and I rent a house. I have saved 3,000 shillings in a bank. I have even helped people who are employed in offices who came to me to borrow money when in financial trouble.' And a knife sharpener answered, 'It would not be fair to dismiss this as a useless activity since very

many people depend on us. Shopkeepers, hoteliers, butchers and even other individuals bring their knives and *pangas* [machetes] for sharpening. The government should instead give us licenses and a place where we can conduct our activities.'

Not surprisingly, rounding up these so-called unproductive elements proved far beyond the capacity of the government. Moreover, it merely served to antagonize the majority of the city's population. It was implemented at a time when virtually no new jobs were available and informal projects had become the main means of subsistence for most urban dwellers. The campaign failed because people simply refused to comply, continuing their daily income-generating activities as they always had. They ignored the new policy because their survival depended on their continuing these activities.

The government was forced to back down from its campaign. By 1984 the mass detentions were curtailed significantly. That same year the City Council began to register people through the ten-house-cell system to verify employment (Kerner 1988, 44). One top City Council official explained to me why the local government changed its position: 'The City Council decided to change the 1983 government policy after analyzing the situation. The government could not provide work for all and could not repatriate the people in the countryside. We failed to send them into the regions, and then we failed to send them even to villages near the city.'[11]

In 1985, at about the time the new president, Ali Hassan Mwinyi, came to power, the policy softened further, and the government began to license small businesses, thus giving official recognition to them. By the late 1980s, however, there remained disagreement among authorities over whether small projects constitute gainful work. The regional director of administration, who was in charge of seeing that the City Council carried out development policies like Nguvu Kazi, told me: 'Some are against such work. They say such jobs could be done by the disabled, the old, not by strong men.'[12]

Nevertheless, after 1983 the government began to recognize, even if only minimally, the importance of the small-scale enterprises to the national economy. It 'reinterpreted' the Human Resources Deployment Act to see the informal sector in a more positive light. A 1985 study sponsored by the government in cooperation with the ILO Jobs and Skills Programme for Africa explored the possibility of using the Human Resources Deployment Act as the basis for a national human resources scheme to deal, as the author put it, with the 'failure of the modern sector to absorb an increasing proportion of the labour force.' The new policy toward the informal sector would make it essential that special attention be given to its role in creating employment because of its ability to do so at low levels of capital investment (Aboagye 1985, 1).

The change from 1983 was also evident in the remarks of the director of the National Vocational Training Programme, Morgan Manyanga, who said in a 1986 speech to Parliament that the 'informal sector' is a 'hidden sector.' Services, he said, are provided without valid training licenses, work contracts, or taxation. He urged that such groups come out of 'hiding' so that they could greatly help the nation by undertaking productive ventures. Although there is an element of absurdity in the notion that 95 per cent of Dar es Salaam's population should 'come out of hiding,' this official's stance indicates a greater legitimation of these activities than the tone exhibited in 1983.[13] Referring to this change in policy, one young man we interviewed said, 'Up to now the government has failed because it wants people to work, but it fails to provide work. They arrested people and sent them to the villages without capital. Even in the past we were not loiterers, we had small businesses, but the government did not want to recognize what we were doing. Now at least they have considered that.'[14]

At the national level, the emphasis had clearly changed by the 1990s. The government was beginning, if only haltingly, to assist the informal sector and was encouraging donor support for such activities. By the early 1990s the Human Resources Deployment Act itself was under review. The Ministry of Labour and Youth Development, which was to implement the act, had taken a few concrete measures to address the needs of young people who did not have access to formal education (International Labour Organisation 1992, 7, 8). The Ministry of Industries and Trade had established a Small Scale Industries Promotion Unit to improve the business climate for small-scale industries, and the ministry's Small Industries Development Organization (SIDO) began to address the needs of informal sector operators in 1988, though budgetary constraints limited the impact of SIDO activities.

By 1994 the government had come up with a national policy to assist informal-sector activities in both rural and urban areas, focusing on the provision of financial services, appropriate technology, markets, and the development of skills. Encouraged by such positive gestures, international donors stepped up their support for the sector. The ILO, for example, launched a major initiative to support the informal sector. This project especially targeted women, children, and youth engaged in low-productivity activities outside 'formal regulatory and social protection mechanisms and who have limited access to credit, skills or training.' The initiative focused on policy and regulatory reforms and on improving access to credit.[15]

Whereas the 1980s saw a basic acceptance of the right for small businesses to exist, in the late 1980s and 1990s the debate shifted to issues of how municipal authorities dealt with problems of licensing, health violations, and relocating businesses to prevent overcrowding. In particular, small-scale traders were concerned about the abuses that occurred in the enforcement of various laws regarding this sector. In the mid-1990s the City Council militia were continuing their harassment and roundups of street vendors to move them to different business locations. The vendors, whose numbers had swelled in the city center, continued to charge City Council employees with seizing their goods for personal benefit.[16]

Licensing small businesses
The key piece of legislation affecting informal-sector operators has been the Urban Authorities Act (1982), which gave the district councils the authority to determine how operators should function. Moreover, it gave them authority to collect revenue and to determine additional fees, such as for garbage collection. In Dar es Salaam two kinds of licenses were issued to small businesses and to market sellers. After 1985, fifty-six different kinds of small-business activities required licenses under the 1985 Dar es Salaam City Council (Hawking and Street Trading) Amendment to the 1982 Local Government (Urban Authorities) Act (see Appendixes D and E).[17] The 1985 law revoked a 1963 law that abolished the urban trading licenses in response to pressure from shopkeepers (Bienefeld 1975, 67).

According to the City Council licensing authorities, only 252 people were found guilty of violating the licensing law in 1987, and all had been fined. Many more, however, had been detained for such violations. They were rounded up by militia hired by the Inspection Committee of the City Council's Manpower Depart-ment. The City Council had six inspectors who decided daily where the militia should go. They concentrated on the central part of the city, Kivukoni, Kisutu, and Mchafukoga (Mnazi Moja), rounding up license violators and taking them into custody. In other parts of the city, each ward had its own inspectors who organized similar kinds of raids. Although micro-entrepreneurs considered legalization of informal-sector activities an improvement over the policy that branded their businesses unproductive, regulation of these small businesses through licensing posed a new set of problems.

City Council officials stated that their concern was making sure that vendors sold their wares in approved locations, yet the officials had no documentation that would indicate precisely where the off-limits areas were. Similarly, they claimed that they were concerned with meeting city health regulations. Yet this was at a time when there was little concern for other, more pressing citywide health issues. For example, shop owners and other people freely dumped large quantities of garbage into downtown streets; drainage systems remained clogged throughout the city; and control of malaria-carrying mosquitoes was virtually nonexistent, although in the past, vigorous campaigns to remove standing water and to spray the city had been undertaken regularly. These factors, along with the harassment of unlicensed small entrepreneurs (rather than the wealthier ones), made urban dwellers suspect that the issue of licensing the entrepreneurs was more than a question of keeping the city clean. Rather, it was aimed at keeping various patronage networks lubricated by extracting bribes from vendors. To a lesser extent, it was a response to shopkeepers' complaints about vendors' selling in unauthorized locations in front of their stores. The actions of the militia did not indicate any real effort to suppress the vendors but, rather, an attempt to intimidate them day after day into handing over a portion of their goods or earnings. It was clearly in the militia's interests to see the vendors return each day.[18]

In 1987–1988, for example, 6,082 small-business licenses were granted out of 10,000 requests. (In Buguruni 325 people out of roughly 30,000 self-employed applied for licenses in 1987.) In 1987 these businesses brought in TSh 3.6 million, or 1 percent of the entire City Council annual revenue. When I asked why licensing of the smallest entrepreneurs was so important, given the unpredictability of their income and the fact that most were just barely feeding their families, a top City Council official responded emphatically, 'But how are we going to control them if we have no licensing system?' He cited the cleanliness of the city and public health that would be jeopardized if people sold wherever and however they pleased. Moreover, he added, the City Council would not be able to do its job properly if it could not control and manage entrepreneurs in this way. City Council officials also suggested to me that people did not obtain licenses because they were selling stolen goods and because they were dishonest.[19]

The self-employed people with whom I spoke had a considerably different perspective on all of these issues. In a country where wages were not adequate, where there were few government welfare provisions, and where the people had to care for their own sick, elderly, disabled, and unemployed, licensing regulations were often seen as an affront to popular notions of economic justice or to the norm of fairness (see Levi 1991). Virtually all of the hundreds of residents and ten-house party-cell leaders we spoke to about this issue saw the licensing of small projects, especially women's projects, as unjust. Many said they had no objection to the licensing of business people engaged in lucrative projects like the sale of charcoal (wholesale), shopkeeping, or operating a restaurant. But for a poor person just trying to get by, they believed, licenses were an injustice because their sources of inputs and markets were too unreliable to make it worthwhile to obtain a license.

Most self-employed in Dar es Salaam operated their businesses without licenses. Ninety-nine percent of all self-employed workers were not licensed in 1988, according to my calculations based on City Council records and the 1988 census. In our survey, 87 percent openly admitted to not having licenses.

Popular sympathy for the self-employed was evident in confrontations between the militia and vendors. Passersby would frequently relay messages to vendors, warning them of the impending arrival of the militia. In May 1991 the *Daily News* reported an incident in which the militia came to arrest vendors who sold meals to workers in downtown office buildings. Passersby joined hands to protect the vendors. Fighting broke out, and the police had to come to the rescue of the militia, who were overpowered by the crowd, which booed the militia and called them thieves.[20] Popular sentiment was underscored in a letter to the *Daily News*, which stated, 'The sympathy of the public is always with these … people when they are almost daily chased away by guys in the City Council uniforms.'[21]

Many City Council officials denied that the militia extracted bribes from the self-employed. Living in the center of the city, I observed the daily cat-and-mouse games of the militia in their pursuit of vendors. I often interviewed the sellers after the raids to find out who had been caught and detained, how much bribe money had been extracted, and whether the militia had confiscated or stolen their wares. Because the militia sometimes came in street clothes, vendors warned each other of an impending raid. Such typical occurrences may explain why City Council officials were so sensitive about the activities of the Nguvu Kazi office in charge of enforcing the purchase of licenses. In fact, they were under orders not to talk to any outsiders (such as journalists or academics) regarding their work and were to refer such people to the city director himself. Only after we interviewed the director did the Nguvu Kazi officials agree to talk to us.

Although the cost of a license was an important factor in explaining why people did not obtain licenses, perhaps even more significant was their rejection of state regulation of a part of life that was considered their own. The most basic right for the urban poor was the right to control their means of subsistence. For this reason, any outside attempts to regulate their means of subsistence was seen as an invitation to further interference, which could prove disastrous at a time when survival was so precarious.

At the same time, the arbitrary assignment of various fees by City Council officials to small businesses only compounded the general frustration with licensing. No study had been made to assess the income obtained from various enterprises. This accounted for the obvious incongruences in the fees relative to the value added of different kinds of enterprises. A woman with eighteen cows making TSh 120,000 a month from milk sales was required to pay the same license fee as was a woman who fried buns and earned TSh 6,000 a month. Tailors, carpenters, and masons, generally at the upper end of the informal-sector income bracket, paid the same license fee as did someone who made and sold paper bags, a low-capital, low-income project. The income of women running hairdressing salons depended on whether they braided hair or used chemicals to treat the hair. These incomes also varied with the size of their clientele, the location of their business,

and other factors, yet they were all required to pay the same rate.

Another factor mitigating against obtaining licenses was the fact that in order to pay the license fee one often had to go through the bureaucracy and pay bribes amounting to three or four times the cost of the license itself. As one self-employed carpenter, who in 1982 left employment with the government-owned electricity company, put it:

> Licenses only bring problems. Bribery is so common it isn't even worth mentioning. I have a license, but I had to pay a 10,000-shilling bribe to get it from the City Council. I just paid it because I got tired of coming back day after day and being told that they had not filled out the forms. The militia harass a carpenter for not having a license, but we make more income than they do. A clerk at the City Council makes 2,000 shillings a month. Such authorities know that if they arrest you, you will pay a bribe. It is their means of obtaining revenue. Those in top posts are not hungry because they squeeze the people below.[22]

In addition to the problem of bribery in obtaining a license, many in Buguruni and Manzese reported that they had applied for licenses but had waited for months with no response from the licensing officials. The cumbersome application process for a business license served as an effective deterrent to most potential applicants. The applicants were to first fill out forms obtained from their local ward office, submit the forms to the ward office, and wait until the forms were returned to them. The applicants would then take the forms to a Councillors Committee of the City Council, which would then evaluate the applications. The applicants would have to secure signatures from the responsible City Council Nguvu Kazi officials after having met personally with them (which could require several visits to the downtown City Council offices). In order to obtain a business license, individuals would first have to show evidence of having paid their taxes, of having a building permit, and of having had their business premises inspected for proper hygiene by a health officer (under the 1950 Health Act and the Factories Ordinance). Failure to obtain a license carried a penalty of TSh 2,000 ($20 at 1988 exchange rates) and/or imprisonment for six months.[23] However, it was not uncommon for the application process to take as long as six months. One frustrated applicant applied for a business license, and by the time his forms were processed the license period had expired. When he asked that his application be applied to the following year, he was told to start all over again.[24]

Widespread refusal to obtain licenses eroded the government's credibility and revealed a split among different levels of the government regarding the self-employed. One conflict emerged between local leaders and the City Council; a second, between national and local governments.

Conflicts between levels of authority

Payment for small-business licenses was an issue that was vigorously taken up by local CCM leaders and patrons at the lower levels of the party. Historically, the role of local leaders, especially at the cell level, had been to serve as a buffer between the higher state authorities and the people to whom they were accountable (Samoff 1973, 74). Numerous studies have shown how local leaders accommodated their constituents' preferences rather than complying with directives and policies from above (Hyden 1980, 114; Molloy 1971; Samoff 1973). One reason for this greater affinity between ten-cell leaders and local people is that their socio-economic interests do not differ significantly from those of their neighbors, whom they represent.

Virtually all of the hundreds of CCM cell leaders we spoke to saw the licensing of small projects as unjust for the same reasons citizens opposed the licenses. Although the self-employed opposed payment for licenses for small businesses through quiet non-compliance (that is, refusal to pay), local cell and branch leaders were more vocally against licensing small businesses and, in particular, against the militia harassment of people without licenses. Some branches had sent complaints to ward and district levels of the party, to the City Council, and to Parliament.

One CCM branch leader said that he had taken all steps within his power to raise the issue of licensing with the City Council. Nothing had come of his efforts to try to abolish the licensing of small businesses. He explained that 'Those who can't farm have to do small businesses, but they have to do these with difficulty and without freedom. The City Council militia can come and harass them for not having licenses and then take away their wares from them. If I know the authorities, it won't be easy to get them to do away with licenses. These small businesses should not be licensed. The local governments should find another source of revenue and leave the people alone. They don't get much revenue, but still the City authorities harass them.'[25]

Local CCM leaders were especially impassioned about this issue because many had small businesses themselves and had experienced harassment. One cell leader said that her children, who sold pastries for her, had been harassed three times by the militia. 'We have to run because we can't bribe them always. You run, leave your goods, everything, to save yourself.'[26] Another cell leader in Manzese who sold coconuts at the market said: 'We pay 200 shillings a month to the City Council for the market space and 500 shillings a year for the license, but the City Council does nothing for us. All we have is what God has given us and boards to build a stall. There is no medicine in the hospitals, and you end up going to the private hospitals anyway. If you do not have a license the militia come and harass you and take away your goods and money. We get angry when they come. What kind of government do we have? Where is our freedom?'[27]

Local party organizations were all too often the recipients of orders from above rather than forums for expressing interests that were filtered up to higher levels of leadership, as they were intended. Nevertheless, these organizations were the main forum urban dwellers attempted to use, not only in settling local issues but also in attempting to confront higher bodies within the party and the government.

Urban dwellers also sought local patrons to defend them against militia raids and other encroachments on the interests of local people by the authorities.[28] In fact, some of our most critical comments of party policy came from these patrons, many of whom sought positions as local party-cell leaders or on the elders' council of the party branch. They saw themselves as champions of the poor and the disadvantaged against the intrusions of the party and the government. The patrons' flexibility and willingness to lend money and provide other social and economic arrangements made them indispensable in the community.

One such patron we interviewed was a Zaramo cell leader and businessman who had established a thriving wood trade. He had a little office with a desk and two chairs at the end facing each other, just like the local CCM offices. On the wall he had hung a party calendar and two large pictures of the then party chairman,

Nyerere, and President Mwinyi. Outside the office, from which he ran his wood business, he flew the green CCM flag. He proudly explained to us that when the City Council militia came to harass the women selling pastries along the side of the road, they ran to his office with their pots and pans to hide. Thus, while surrounding himself with the symbols of the CCM, this patron was at the same time perpetuating another set of power relations.[29]

In another CCM branch, a hotel owner established himself as a patron. Although he was active in the CCM, he was also critical of it and put distance between himself and the CCM and the government. He remarked, 'If they change the [top] leadership of the party, life will be better. My life goes on because I don't sleep. I am a businessman and don't depend on the government. I have a hotel, so I don't wait for the government to help me.'[30] The CCM secretary of this branch said that when she needed help in party matters she went to the hotel owner because she respected him and 'considered him her father.' The terms of kinship are frequently extended to nonfamilial patron-client relations as a means of further solidifying these relations. Clients often refer to the patron as 'father' and to themselves as 'his children.'

The City Council was not only at odds with local leaders over the harassment of vendors without licenses. It also had differences with the national government on the issue. Since 1986 national leaders have won popular support in criticizing the City Council for its harassment of vendors, especially of women. In the late 1980s President Mwinyi several times openly decried the harassment of street vendors 'whether licensed or not.' In spite of his appeals, City Council representatives continued their harassment of unlicensed entrepreneurs, reflecting, perhaps, some of the competing interests between local and central governments. In one of the appeals, Mwinyi vowed that 'stern action' would be taken against any police or militia found harassing vendors. The president said that 'the traders were actually engaged in *legal* activities, trying to struggle against harsh economic conditions facing everybody. ... He said that all urban councils should help the people engaged in petty businesses because that was one way of easing their economic burden.'[31]

After Mwinyi's November 1987 condemnation of the City Council militia harassment, I heard vendors express enthusiasm for his statements. The *Daily News* quoted one woman who sold buns as saying: 'We have been saved by the President from the hands of the City Council militiamen who have been a constant menace.'[32] Vendors also had their reservations, skeptical that this appeal would be heeded by the City Council. Their suspicions were confirmed a few days later when the militia resumed its raids.

Other national leaders also decried the harassment of street sellers. Cleopa Msuya, when he was minister of industries and trade, addressed a 1994 seminar of small-scale women entrepreneurs in Mwanga, which I attended. He responded to their concerns about militia raids on businesses and property to check on licenses and location: 'It is something negative to destroy these huts without informing the people. First, after all, these businesses must be allowed, period, because they help people. Second, people must be clear about where they should carry out their business. There must be well planned areas where people can run their businesses. Third, there must be an effort all the time to make sure that people are not interfered with in their places of business and that we should avoid the idea of going and breaking their huts and taking their license payments.'[33]

For some leaders, appeals to the rights of street vendors became a quick and shrewd way of gaining popularity. One controversial national figure, Augustine Mrema, became a vocal champion of the causes of the urban street sellers and women. As former deputy prime minister and home affairs minister, he was one of the fiercest critics of corruption from within the CCM. He defended street hawkers from attacks by the City Council and personally intervened with husbands who beat their wives. When he was thrown out of his ministerial post in February 1995, he joined the opposition National Convention for Constitution and Reform (Mageuzi) and became its presidential candidate. His popularity increased, and for the first time the opposition was able to pose a credible threat to CCM's dominance.

The fact that common city dwellers saw the national leaders as allies against the City Council on this issue was evident after an intense period of raids against vendors in 1986. In one particular incident a group of vendors who sold in and around the Kigamboi fish market formed a demonstration and marched to the State House to register their grievances with the president. They told reporters that the City Council was threatening their 'struggle to survive.' Police diverted the march to the Central Police Station, where the vendors were told to bring their complaints to the City Council or the party.[34] The national government's concern in keeping City Council militia from harassing poor vendors was a way of responding directly to the problem of not having the resources to adequately pay workers. The continuation of these projects became a means of garnering greater legitimacy.

The differences between the national leaders and the City Council authorities appear to stem from the different interests they hoped to appease. National leaders were responding to pressures from labor to ease the conditions under which workers and their household members carried out projects. The City Council itself was probably divided. On one hand, there was concern to increase council revenue and to maintain good ties with the official business community by keeping vendors off their property. At the same time, the continuing practice of bribery by the militia and by people in charge of granting licenses suggests that the council had individual interests to satisfy within the institution itself.

Dodging the Development Levy

Refusal to obtain business licenses is related to the issue of tax evasion, for licensing and registration require the payment of taxes. Tax evasion has been one of the classic forms of non-compliance worldwide, according to Scott. He argues that although taxes were one of the most frequent causes of riots and revolts in early modern Europe and elsewhere, the main form of tax resistance was through 'flight, evasion, misreporting, false declarations, and so on' (1987, 423). Certainly these quiet forms of opposition characterize resistance to taxation in urban Tanzania, where city dwellers have always been artful tax dodgers.

J. A. K. Leslie, writing about Dar es Salaam in the late 1950s, observed that new migrants during their first few days in town made it a priority to visit relatives and meet new people who could, among other things, provide a place to hide from tax clerks. People often used several names in order to make it difficult for the authorities to trace them in the event that they would be sought for not paying their taxes. Moreover, in the colonial period Leslie was describing, people commonly withheld their names or someone else's name from a foreigner or government representative for the same reason. Colonial authorities eventually set up tax drives because voluntary payment had failed. They blocked off streets,

asking comers for evidence of payment. Even here, tax dodgers had little difficulty finding back routes to their homes (1963, 58, 60, 250). Those who were caught faced prison or labor camps, where they worked to pay the tax.

As in the 1950s, urban dwellers dodged the collection of the Development Levy, the poll tax of the 1980s and 1990s. The Development Levy, in fact, had its antecedents in the poll tax. The British colonial administration created this tax under the Native Authorities Ordinance of 1926, which established indirect rule through local African institutions and leadership. Under this ordinance, local authorities collected taxes for the use of central government. The poll tax, known as local rates, was a flat rate collected from all adult men over the age of eighteen. Women were exempted from the tax unless they were employed or had an independent source of income. The tax had the effect of forcing Africans into wage-earning jobs in order to pay the tax. Later ordinances gave local authorities the authority to collect taxes for their own use (Bukurura 1991, 77–78).

The local rates were abolished in 1969, partly in response to public opposition to harsh tactics used by authorities in collecting the tax but also because of the association of the tax with colonial practices (Kulaba 1989, 219). The abolition of the tax left local governments completely dependent on the central government, without a major independent source of revenue This move to eliminate independent sources of revenue was followed by the disbanding of local governments in 1972. Although the dissolution of local governments was heralded as a move to decentralize government, it in fact placed greater decision-making power in the hands of the central government. Regional- and district-level authorities, funded by the national treasury, gained power but were now accountable to the central government rather than to the localities, which had little control over personnel or the way in which funds were allocated. Conditions in the urban areas deteriorated quickly, including the provision of basic services like water and electricity, sewage disposal, and garbage collection (Kulaba 1989).

In 1982 two measures were enacted to rectify this situation. The Local Government Act was passed to reestablish the urban councils that had been abolished in 1972, and the Local Government Finances Act No. 9 was enacted to empower local councils to collect revenue. The passage of these acts meant that the central government dealt with taxes that were easy to collect, such as income taxes, duties, and licenses for larger businesses, whereas the local authorities were responsible for collecting fees that were more difficult to collect from an administrative and political standpoint (Kulaba 1989, 221, 231).

The Development Levy was instituted soon thereafter, though by a narrow margin of two votes in parliament and after much heated debate.[35] This law required all individuals between the ages of eighteen and sixty-five to pay a flat rate if they were low-income earners or farmers, while wage earners paid a graduated rate that was deducted automatically from their paychecks. Self-employed workers in Dar es Salaam were required to pay a personal Development Levy and a Development Levy on their enterprise the first year they were in business. After that they paid only the business Development Levy, which was a percentage of their yearly business license (30 percent in Dar es Salaam).

People whom I interviewed bitterly resented the Development Levy, regarding it much like the colonial poll tax. They designed means of evading it that were as surreptitious as those of the evaders of the colonial taxes.[36] In some instances, tax collectors resorted to tactics reminiscent of colonial practices, such as road blocks, massive swoops, and detainment of defaulters.[37] Even employees who had the Development Levy automatically deducted from their pay-checks were subject to harassment.[38] In July 1987 local governments began to use ten-house cell leaders and village governments to collect the levy in order to minimize confrontations between the people and the authorities, which had at times become violent, especially in urban areas. But this practice often backfired because it was not only taxpayers who evaded payment but also the local authorities assigned the task of providing lists of taxpayers who refused to comply because of the responsibility they felt to their constituents.

Some have argued that the major evasion of the Development Levy has been due to the inability to pay and to a lack of clarity regarding duties, obligations, and reasons to pay. They argue that the government has not done a good job of educating people about the purposes of the Development Levy and convincing them of the necessity of paying the tax (Bukurura 1991, 91). Certainly these factors have contributed to the massive non-compliance in paying the Development Levy. However, it is also instructive to consider what people themselves have to say about the levy, especially given the fact that although for some the fee is too high, for most self-employed urban dwellers the sum is relatively small. The objections I encountered were varied but hinged around the issue of the lack of state legitimacy.

First, residents believed that they received little from the government in return for payment of the levy. They saw few tangible benefits, while the very poorest individuals were forced to meet the most basic welfare provisions on their own.[39] Moreover, residents strongly resented what they believed were excessive mis-appropriations of funds by government authorities.[40] Second, they feared that one tax would lead to endless demands for money by the government and the CCM. Income tax, house tax, tuition fees, and contributions for school and various fund-raising campaigns of the CCM were mentioned most frequently in this regard. People feared that agreeing to pay for one state tax was an invitation to raise taxes and to find new reasons to demand money from citizens. They made no distinctions between local governments and the central government with regard to these various taxes. Yet another concern was the harassment that accompanied the collection of the levy. In the Coast Region, residents appealed in 1988 to regional authorities to halt mistreatment of people in checking for payment of the levy. The government responded by passing the Local Government (Collection of Rates Procedure) Rules to reduce and eliminate default and do away with harassment by having village and cell leaders collect the levy (Bukurura 1991, 88–89).

Finally, the issue of women's paying the levy was especially controversial. Supporters of the levy on women argued that they were equal to men according to the law and theoretically could own their own property. Opponents argued that women in the rural areas rarely owned their own property and therefore should be exempted. In fact, prior to 1969 most women were exempted from paying the levy, and only those who had their own earnings were required to pay (Bukurura 1991, 80–81). In urban areas, low-income women argued that the tax was unjust because the economic crisis had placed heavy burdens on women and because they had thus been shouldering on their own the burden of caring for the young, old, and sick and of feeding the employed members of the household with income from their own small enterprises. As

Table 1 Local sources of Revenue of Tanzanian Urban Councils, 1985–1986

Source	Amount in TSh	Percentage
Development levy	246,690,000	55
Taxes on dwellings	73,244,400	16
Trading licenses	60,915	0
Market dues and fees	29,923,900	7
Other taxes	96,713,900	22
Total	446,633,115	100

Source: Kulaba 1989, 222.

one woman I interviewed in Manzese, a low-income part of Dar es Salaam, put it, 'Life is hard, but they don't understand that these fees just harass us. They are very strict with the Development Levy in the rural areas. A woman with a one-month-old baby was arrested for a whole day because of the Development Levy. Other women like Mrs. Kawawa [former chairperson of the Union of Tanzanian Women] and Kate Kamba [former secretary general of the Union of Tanzanian Women] and the rest marched in support of Development Levy. They do not know the problems of ordinary women. I am just an ordinary citizen.'[41]

Clearly the Development Levy brought to the fore the conflicting perspectives of low-income and wealthier, better-educated women, who were concerned with gender equality and the implications of exempting women from the levy. The issue was hotly debated in Parliament for years, with some members of the National Assembly arguing that women need not pay the levy because they are 'naturally weak.' Women members of Parliament firmly opposed the exemption, but they were overridden by Prime Minister John Malecela when he announced in 1991 that the local councils could exempt women from the tax and look for other sources of income. Still, the conflict between upper- and lower-income women over the levy reflected how women experienced their alienation from the state in different ways (Tripp 1994b).

Local authorities fared even worse with the small-business tax (Kulaba 1989, 219, 231). Self-employed producers avoided registration not only to evade the Development Levy but also so that they could operate their businesses without being subject to sales taxes and price controls. Taxes on produced goods ranged from 25 to 200 per cent, and no differentiation was made with respect to the size of the production unit. Thus a small-scale industry paid the same tax as did a large-scale one. Because the sales tax is the most important source of domestic revenue for the government, it is doubtful that these laws will be changed (see Tables 1 and 2). Nevertheless, small-scale industries were so vulnerable financially that even simple taxes could make or break them. For most cooperatives and smaller production units the only way to survive was to avoid registration and hence taxation altogether (Havnevik 1986, 280).

The battle over grounds

Part of the conflict over small businesses centered on the issue of business locations. Selling in an unapproved location was one reason the City Council militia harassed vendors. Sometimes they were acting at the behest of shopkeepers who did not want vendors positioned in front of their stores. More often, however, the militia were only interested in the vendors' location as an excuse to harass

Table 2 Domestic sources of Revenue of the Tanzanian Central Government, 1989–1990

Source	Amount in millions of TSh	Percentage
Customs duty	13,547	14
Excise duty (imports)	2,683	3
Excise duty (local)	11,140	11
Sales tax (imports)	10,445	11
Sales tax (local)	20,200	21
Income tax	19,123	20
Other taxes	6,940	7
Nontax revenue	13,044	13
Total	97,122	100

Source: Calculated from data in a report of a Ministry of Finance and Planning Commission published in 1991 in *Tanzanian Economic Trends* 4 (2) 80.

and extract bribes from them. No one in the Nguvu Kazi office or any other department of the City Council knew where the authorized or unauthorized locations were because they had never been determined. This meant that it was left up to the militia and the inspectors to decide arbitrarily whether people were selling in approved locations. These conflicts continued into the mid-1990s. In 1995 organizations like the Organisation of Small Businesspeople (FESBA) and the Dar es Salaam Kiosk Owners' Association criticized the City Council for failing to find places to which street vendors could relocate after the City Council cracked down on them in the central Kariakoo market in February 1995. The association chairman, Issa Mnyaru, said in a statement issued to councillors that they were fed up with false promises by the government: 'We are in a multipartyism era. You are required to listen to the people who voted for you.'[42]

Indiscriminate militia attempts to move vendors from certain locations by and large failed. For example, the plans to move the central Kigamboni fish market to a less accessible location at Msasani met with little success. The market remains the main fish-auctioning center in the city. The City Council was, however, more successful in moving wood carvers who had set up kiosks along Bagamoyo Road to a central location in Mwenge in 1984. At the time, the City Council demolished some of the carvers' kiosks without prior notification and threatened to demolish more if people did not comply.[43]

One important conflict over location had to do with City Council attempts to channel the wholesale trade through a central market at Kariakoo. The downtown Kariakoo market was rebuilt in 1975, after which all wholesale fruits, vegetables, certain staples, and dried and smoked fish were to be channeled through this City Council-operated market. Its aim was to bring the Dar es Salaam parallel market under its control, because it was believed at the time that only 50 percent of the wholesale trade was going through official channels (Sporrek 1985, 74–82). However, the centralization of the wholesale trade in Kariakoo did little to stem the parallel-market trade in the years that followed. The majority of produce coming into the city continued to be sold through markets like Manzese, which is the largest unofficial wholesale grain market in Tanzania.

The issue of location also concerns those with projects involving the keeping of poultry, cattle, and pigs because animal husbandry had initially been forbidden within townships (Kulaba 1989, 213). Urban dwellers relied on people with such projects for their chickens, eggs, ham, and milk, however. A 40 per cent increase in registered livestock was reported in the city between 1987 and 1989 (Stren, Halfani, and Malombe 1994, 191). So pervasive was the practice of animal husbandry in the city itself that the City Council conceded to the practice but told owners to keep their livestock strictly within compounds to engage in zero grazing in 1989. The policy was revised in 1990, when livestock owners were permitted to keep no more than four animals at home zero grazing.[44] Further impetus was given to such practices by Mwinyi's call on workers to start farm, animal-husbandry, and other projects.[45] Nevertheless, small herds of cattle continued to roam the city streets despite numerous City Council warnings, ultimatums, petty fines on cattle owners, and roundups of 'loitering' cattle, as they were referred to by the authorities. As many as 2.3 per cent of all reported road accidents in Dar es Salaam were caused by these animals (Kironde 1992, cited in Stren, Halfani, and Malombe 1994, 191). Although from time to time the City Council would round up 'loitering cattle and goats,' as it did in a 1995 raid,[46] for the most part this was one of the least enforced regulations. Because the majority of animal owners within the city belonged to the class of administrators and professionals, it is conceivable that the authorities in the City Council were more hesitant to enforce strictly a law that would impinge on themselves and their friends and families, who depended on these projects for their sustenance.[47]

Privatization

The Daladala bus wars

Another indication of policy change toward the informal economy was the privatization of sectors that had previously been controlled by state monopolies. Bus service was one of the first privatization moves. Up until 1986, only government-owned buses could operate legally, and the transport needs of the population far exceeded the available services. Around 1983, as the transport problem began to reach crisis proportions, informal buses called *daladala* or *thumni* came into greater use. The name of these minibuses comes from the price of a ride, which in 1983 was TSh 5, or the equivalent of one dollar; hence the term *daladala*. Individuals also began to use their private vehicles as illegal taxibuses, giving people rides for a small fee. Both the drivers of these vehicles and the passengers were liable if caught.

Nyerere had been adamant that the government-owned buses retain their monopoly status, but the desperate economic situation and the existence of the informal sources of transport forced the government to legalize the *daladala* in 1986. Three hundred buses were registered with the government bus company. After 1986, even private transporters like owners of pickup trucks were allowed to carry passengers for a fee if they obtained a contract from the public-transport authority and met various safety requirements (Stren, Halfani, and Malombe 1994, 195). By 1988 only 100 government buses were operating, while the legal *daladala* had dwindled to 183 due to the high agency fee they were required to pay. Both public and private buses were often badly in need of repair. The city, according to experts, needed a minimum of 750 buses to meet the needs of its residents in 1988 (Kulaba 1989, 241).[48] By 1991 the number of passengers using government-owned Usafiri Dar es Salaam (UDA) had dwindled to 13 per cent of the number in 1982 (Stren, Halfani, and Malombe 1994, 192).

In sharp contrast, by 1991 the number of *daladala* had increased significantly, but approximately 450 out of 600 were operating without licenses. The government then temporarily suspended registration of *daladala* buses, because they had put the government-owned UDA buses virtually out of business. There were only 50 government buses in operation, and their operating costs by their own admission were higher than those of the *daladala*. The *daladala* were favored by passengers because they would go almost anywhere passengers were heading and did not follow strict routes (partly to avoid being caught). Another type of bus that became popular in the early 1990s was known as *chai haharagwe* (tea and beans) because these dangerous open buses contained long benches that reminded people of seating arrangements in local restaurants.

Vehicles like the *daladala* were legalized in other parts of Africa as well, notably in Kenya, where in 1984 the informal *matatu* buses were licensed after being public carriers for twenty years (Kapila 1987, 21). In Nairobi the initial demand for 'pirate taxis' mushroomed from 400 buses in 1970 to more than 2,000 buses by 1982 and possibly up to 10,000 in 1987 after privatization.

Doctors and chickens

The health sector was another area in which privatization occurred in the 1980s in response to popular pressures. Although the majority of employees affected by party and government policies regarding second incomes and informal economic activities were low-income workers, the policies also impinged on the welfare of professionals and semiprofessionals. One dramatic turnabout in policy resulted from the controversy over sideline incomes in the field of medicine. The conflict eventually led to the lifting of restrictions that had prevented physicians from practicing medicine privately. Physicians had been forbidden to practice medicine privately while off duty from serving in government hospitals and clinics. Most physicians were involved in agricultural production or animal husbandry on the outskirts of the city to supplement their income. They often hired local villagers to tend their farms. Nevertheless, a large part of the doctors' time was taken up in their sideline activities. As one Asian woman physician told me, 'When I studied to be a doctor, I never thought I'd learn so much about chickens or end up doing so many other things.'[49] Other doctors quietly carried out private practices during their off hours (Joinet 1986).

Many doctors believed that it was a waste of the country's resources to be spending so much time cultivating and doing other projects unrelated to medicine, when they could have been practicing medicine privately and legally after hours. Between 1984 and 1989, 196 physicians had left Tanzania to work in hospitals in neighboring countries (Shaidi 1991, 128). The movement for privatization was spearheaded by the Medical Association of Tanzania (MAT), which argued that the association's intention was not to do away with public service but to allow physicians to engage in private practice on the side.

The then-president of the MAT, Dr. Philemon Sarungi, said at a conference of the association that preventing public-service doctors from having private practices during their free time forced them to divert their energy and professional knowledge to non-medical pastimes such as rearing chickens or pigs.[50] The minister of health and social welfare at the time, Dr. Aaron Chiduo, opposed the move to permit private care on political grounds, saying that the poor would suffer and not have access to health provisions.[51]

The debate made its way into Parliament, where member of Parliament Dr. Zainab Amir Gama argued forcefully that the ministry would 'do justice to both the doctors and to the profession if it allowed doctors to practice on a part-time basis instead of going for poultry keeping.' She said that 'it was an open secret that some doctors were working with private clinics and hospitals on a part-time basis, although it was illegal. Others engaged in poultry projects so as to augment their "meager" salaries.'[52]

Doctors at Muhimbili Medical Centre struck in mid-1990 (and again in the beginning of 1991) because the government failed to follow up on its promise to increase doctors' allowances. To placate the doctors, the government had allowed them to practice medicine privately during their hours off duty. Doctors employed in government hospitals were allowed to work part-time in private clinics and hospitals, although they were not permitted to operate private hospitals and clinics. The prime minister even admitted that the decision to ban private medical practice in the 1980s was out of tune with the present situation in Tanzania.[53] By 1994 health expenditures accounted for only 5 per cent of the government budget, as compared with 30 per cent in 1984.[54] With the public-health system in disarray, the government finally lifted its twenty-eight-year ban on private medicine in 1993. By 1995 the number of private hospitals and dispensaries had mushroomed to around 950, making up 38 per cent of the country's health facilities, catering to about half of the country's outpatient population, and accounting for 30 per cent of all hospital beds.

Government monopolies in the provision of basic services like medicine and transport were privatized reluctantly, slowly, and only when the crisis had grown to the point where continuing the monopoly would seriously undermine government legitimacy.

Economic liberalization

Supplying the city with food

The liberalization of food markets was another arena of micro-level impact on macro-level policy, as Benno Ndulu describes it (Ndulu and Mwega 1994). By the early 1990s the liberalized trade market was no longer an issue of debate and was taken for granted as being an improvement over the controlled markets of the 1970s and 1980s (Amani and Maro 1991–1992, 36). In this latter period, parallel markets gained in importance, thus creating linkages between rural producers, traders, and urban retailers. Parallel markets provide channels for the sale of crops outside the official state-run crop authorities.

Maliyamkono and Bagachwa (1990) made a useful distinction among the different kinds of informal food-marketing arrangements. The first arrangement involved trade between members of one village or of nearby villages. A second was characterized as a shuttle food market, in which family members took one to three bags of grain by bus or truck to a nearby town where they could fetch higher prices than in their own village. A third arrangement was based on inter-regional trade, in which food commodities were transported from one region to another by unlicensed traders, either on a regular basis or occasionally on their way back from transporting other goods to a certain locale.[55] A fourth arrangement involved urban open markets, in which urban dwellers sold produce they had grown or grain obtained from regional or national food distributors or from the National Milling Corporation (NMC). Finally, a fifth arrangement could be described as the export market, in which crops were smuggled out of the country. Smuggling occurred mainly in border regions. In all of these cases, the forms of trade were not new, but the scale of activity increased significantly in the 1970s.

The extent of parallel-market activity has always been determined, if not defined, by the official marketing system. Even in the 1960s more food crops were being sold privately and illegally than through official markets. At this time the newly independent government, however, expanded the functions of cooperatives to crop marketing and credit, input supply, and other programs. The cooperatives quickly became overloaded with functions beyond their capacity, while corruption was rampant. Nevertheless, their role was expanded even further after the 1967 Arusha Declaration and especially after the nationalization of wholesale trade in 1969 (Coulson 1982; Raikes 1986).

The cooperatives' inefficiency and corruption increased, so that by 1975 the government found sufficient justification to replace them with crop authorities, which were under direct state control. These crop authorities took over the purchasing, processing, and selling of crops and the provision of extension services. This additional centralization only compounded the inefficiency, corruption, waste, and cost overruns that had plagued the cooperatives, as the crop authorities accrued enormous deficits. In 1982 the cooperatives were reinstated, but they were kept under considerable state supervision. Meanwhile, in the 1970s parallel markets had clearly become an institution in the Tanzanian economy as the inefficiency of the foodcrop authority, the NMC, was compounded by food shortages (Raikes 1986, 116–20). For example, a study by Peter Temu (1975) estimated that in the early 1970s twice as much maize was being sold in parallel markets as through the official markets. This unofficial trade expanded in the early 1980s, and the Marketing Development Bureau estimated that by 1983–1984 only 25 per cent of the marketed surplus of maize was sold through official channels (Ödegaard 1985, 156).

Only a small portion of the food market was channeled through the NMC. Smallholder subsistence producers, who account for most of the country's food supply, bypassed the marketing systems altogether. In fact, the trade in vegetables and some fruits had always been part of an unregulated, well-organized and effective trade system.

Unofficial producer prices were generally higher than those of the NMC (except during bumper harvest seasons or in areas where there were no competing government purchasers) (Temu 1975). These prices were more flexible, varying with the season and from year to year according to supply and demand, whereas NMC prices were fixed before the season began. Crop authorities also suffered from delays in collecting the harvests, lack of storage facilities, and delays in paying for the produce (Raikes 1986).

The purpose of official markets was to bring food supplies to the urban areas and public institutions. Although parallel markets favored rural producers, the traders had the most to gain. Traders charged urban dwellers exorbitantly high prices for agricultural commodities in scarce supply through official channels. Even so, the profit margins were smaller for private traders than for official marketing authorities (Ndulu and others 1988, 9–10). In some instances the open-market consumer prices were higher than official ones, but for key staples like maize, sorghum, and cassava,

they were lower than official prices in 1986–1987.[56] For those commodities for which the official price was lower, it should be noted that most city dwellers did not have access to commodities at the official price because of the shortages in the official marketing system and because people with connections frequently diverted the goods to sell at *ulanguzi* (hiked) prices.

Evidence of the increase in urban purchases from the open market are overwhelming. In the early 1980s per capita official food deliveries were about 15 to 20 per cent of the 1970 level (Raikes 1986, 116). Obviously, urban dwellers had not reduced their food requirements by 85 per cent during this period. If anything, the food demands of Dar es Salaam increased due to population growth. There is little doubt that the difference between officially marketed produce and consumer needs was met by the parallel markets, even though it is difficult to gauge the actual quantities traded unofficially. According to a Marketing Development Bureau study, 90 per cent of marketed maize and 75 per cent of marketed rice, the major staples under government control, were sold through parallel markets from 1980 through 1987.

Parallel markets also affected the export sector. Cash-crop producers often favored selling their goods on the unofficial markets because their prices were higher than what the government was offering. One of the biggest changes in agricultural production since the 1970s was the shift from export crops to food crops. The general understanding has been that official prices of government-run crop authorities favored food crops since the mid-1970s, hence this drop in export production. However, economists have more recently noted that the real reason for the shift is the gap between the low official prices for export crops and high unofficial prices for food crops (Raikes 1986, 122).

The policy of pan-territorial pricing accounted in large measure for the regional differences in sales through official channels. In Tanga, Kilimanjaro, and Morogoro regions, NMC purchases of maize grain accounted for 28 per cent of its regional purchases in 1976–1977; five years later, NMC purchases from these regions amounted to only 1 per cent of its regional purchases. Meanwhile, per capita maize production increased in all three regions. In effect, those regions that had the lowest transport costs were subsidizing regions with the highest transport costs. This meant that unofficial prices looked much more attractive to producers in these regions and that they were able to obtain twice the price in informal markets than through formal channels. Meanwhile, sales through official channels in more remote, high-transport-cost areas increased (Maliyamkono and Bagachwa 1990, 75).

The pervasiveness of unofficial marketing made regulation virtually impossible. Ultimately it resulted in the liberalization of food markets. Local markets in staples were recognized in the 1982 National Agricultural Policy. Liberalizing measures included the removal of the 500-kilogram restriction on interregional movement of food in 1984; the abolition of permits to move food inside the country in 1986; the decontrolling of pricing and marketing of millet, sorghum, and cassava at the cooperative level in 1987; and the 1988 measures to make the NMC into a commercial enterprise. Maize was also decontrolled at the cooperative level, and private traders were permitted to trade maize after purchasing it from the cooperatives.[57] Other measures included lifting consumer subsidies, especially for maize, to reduce budgetary deficits arising from official food trade; raising producer prices at a yearly rate of 5 per cent; reducing impediments, like roadblocks, to private trade; and, in March 1987, doing away with restrictions on the quantity of crops that could be transported. Unofficial regional trading was forbidden until 1986–1987, when the government began to move toward acceptance of a trading system that combined the NMC, cooperatives, and the open market. The measures had positive results almost immediately, with significantly increased production, especially for maize and rice. Open-market consumer prices resulted in the subsequent stabilization of prices for rice and a decrease in prices for maize after 1983-1984. Moreover, the gap between open-market prices and official prices narrowed significantly (Ndulu and others 1988, 12–16). Another important function of the liberalization of internal trade was to erode the high-scarcity premiums of some traders.

The primary impetus for this particular policy change came from internal developments at the micro-level. Although these domestic factors were directly responsible for the liberalization of internal food markets, it is important to note that they occurred against the backdrop of pressures on Tanzania to sign an agreement with the IMF, which undoubtedly played a role in speeding up the process of loosening restrictions on domestic trade.

The limits of government concessions

Government accommodation to many issues made it easier for people to engage in small private enterprises or trading. On other issues the government tried to exert some control, but it clearly was not strong enough to stem the pervasiveness of various activities. For example, a debate emerged within the teaching profession over whether teachers could legally tutor students after school hours. The Ministry of Education had from time to time issued warnings against the prevalent practice of teachers' holding tutorials, called 'tuition,' after school because it privileged wealthier students who could pay the extra fees. After years of ambiguity in policy and a tacit acceptance of 'tuition' by school principals, the practice of tutorials was finally banned in 1991 by the Ministry for Education and Culture. The ban drew immediate protests by angry parents and teachers, who called or visited the official newspaper *Daily News* to voice their complaints. One columnist who supported the ban nevertheless described it as having touched 'a raw nerve' among parents and teachers. 'This is the only way we can subsidize our earnings,' one teacher told a *Daily News* reporter. Another said: ''We cannot survive without tuition.'[58] In an opinion poll taken by the newspaper, the majority of people interviewed in Dar es Salaam opposed the ban.[59]

In interviewing students and teachers from seven Dar es Salaam secondary schools and teachers and principals from primary schools in Manzese and Buguruni prior to the ban, I found that the practice of holding tutorials was widespread. In secondary schools it was not uncommon for students to take as many as six hours of tutorials a week, paying around TSh 100–200 a month for classes like math, French, Swahili, biology, and English, while physics tutorials could run as high as TSh 400 to 680 a month. The teachers could double, triple, or quadruple their monthly salaries, depending on how many students they had and the number of tutorials they held.

Students gave a wide variety of reasons for taking tutorials. In some instances, they reported that teachers would come to the regular classes but do little in the way of instruction. This left students who wanted to pass their qualifying exams with little choice but to attend tutorials, where the same instructor made a concerted effort to teach well. Some students sought other teachers for tutorials because the quality of teaching was so poor in their regular classes. Other students had difficulty in certain classes and believed they needed extra help. Still others were competitive and wanted an edge over their fellow students so that they would be admitted to secondary school or university.

In effect. a private educational system had emerged within the public school system. Teachers paid little heed to the ministry's various directives and continued the tutorials at home, while school principals overlooked the practice. Teachers openly disagreed with the ministry's action. They had their own justifications for holding tutorials. One primary-school teacher explained, 'Tutorials help a lot, both for the teachers and the students. In the past, classes had 25 to 30 children and it was easy to teach them. Now with the Universal Primary Education there are 100 students to one teacher. So you can't teach them well. But with tutorial classes you have a few, 10, 12, 15, and it is nice because you have peace and quiet and can teach them well.'[60] In this teacher's school the practice of tutorials started in about 1984. She said she used to enjoy teaching but that, after thirty-five years, her salary was only TSh 3,000. She continued, 'We have no books or textbooks to use in instruction. My students have no desks or chairs. In an effort to cut back costs, the Government laid off the school watchmen and then all the desks and chairs were stolen. Then the Government lost more money on that.'[61] Many teachers like this one felt that the satisfaction and money they obtained from teaching tutorials was some compensation for the frustrations and low wages they faced on the job.

Teachers had many other ways of supplementing their income, too. It was a common practice for them to sell ice cream, soda, *maandazi* buns, peanuts, embroidery, homemade envelopes, and paper bags to students. One teacher rented out school chairs for outside functions at TSh 25 a chair. Some had students selling their products for 10 per cent commission. These sales on school premises were forbidden, along with the use of students as intermediaries.

As with the tutorials, teachers refused to curtail their projects, while the local school authorities looked the other way, knowing they could do little until the government was in a position to pay the teachers adequate salaries. Given these realities, it was unlikely that the government ban on tutorials would be honored and in all likelihood larger number of teachers simply moved their tutorials from school premises to their homes or some other location. These examples of teachers' strategies show quite vividly the incompatibility between the reality of survival and the egalitarian aspirations of the government. The alternatives are quite stark. The tuition system perpetuates inequalities, denying access to better education to the poor. At the same time, without significant pay increases, teachers will continue to conduct tutorials to support themselves. Were parents to fund schools more directly, perhaps the 'tuition' system could be eliminated, but then it would require government's relinquishing greater control to parents. Either way, the solution to the dilemma is far from simple, and it highlights the difficult choices that emanate from the lack of resources.

Conclusions

In the mid-1980s the Tanzanian government found itself responding to sharp pressures from international financial institutions and foreign donors to engage in various economic reforms. In some instances, structural-adjustment policies worked at cross-purposes with the interests of urban residents; in other contexts, pressures from the informal economy resulted in reforms that were incorporated into structural-adjustment policies; and, finally, there were informal-sector interests that were distinct from those addressed in the economic-reform packages

After the mid-1980s, open repression of small entrepreneurs and employees involved in informal sideline activities gradually gave way to legalization, liberalization, and privatization. Small-business operators who had previously been considered as engaging in illegal occupations were now able to apply for licenses. The internal trade of foodstuffs that had been channeled through parallel markets could now make its way through liberalized open markets. After 1993, medical doctors could practice medicine privately. Significant policy changes had been implemented in areas that directly affected the day-to-day survival of both urban and rural dwellers.

As the crisis deepened and as economic-adjustment policies pushed the cost of living even higher, people's persistence in informal economic activities led to debates within Parliament and the CCM over the suppression and restriction of various survival strategies. The government initially ignored many of these practices, either because it did not have the capacity to enforce its restrictions or because it was not prepared to officially sanction various practices for ideological reasons.

People's persistence in their informal income-generating activities in defiance of government restrictions became a form of opposition and of non-compliance. The massive scale of these evasions raised the cost of securing compliance for the government to an extremely high level. In the 1980s, to a greater degree than before, the authorities began to recognize various activities as legal. But in the process of transition they adopted a number of different policies: They often insisted on policies that preserved their ideological commitments yet did not have the capacity to enforce the policy, as the case of tutorials reveals. In the end, however, domestic pressures forced the authorities to dispense even with these key ideological principles. The authorities looked the other way when people violated government regulations that lacked any logical correspondence with reality (such as the ban on sideline activities of doctors prior to 1991). At times they made open accommodation (as in the shift from the 1983 Human Resources Deployment Act to the encouragement of small-scale entrepreneur-ship in the 1990s). At other times they exerted open opposition to various economic activities and attempted to enforce them (as was the case with the 1991 restrictions on illegal *daladala* buses). The authorities also quietly encouraged other illegal activities like militia bribery of vendors because they provided a source of revenue for government employees. These varied government responses clearly reflect the ambiguity of non-compliant economic resistance, as well as its potential transformative power.

Notes

[1] *Daily News*, 10 October 1983.
[2] Even the use of terms like *slum* and *squatter* by authorities, like their use of *loiterers and unproductive elements* for the self-employed, belies the profound gap between government understanding of who these people are and the nature of their experiences, problems, and objectives.
[3] The Penal Code amendment expanded the categories of 'idle and disorderly persons' to include:
    a. any able-bodied person who is not engaged in any productive work and has no visible means of subsistence;
    b. any person employed under lawful employment of any description who is, without any lawful excuse, found engaged in a frolic of his own at a time he is supposed to be engaged in activities connected or relating to the business of his employment (Shaidi 1984, 82).
[4] The minister of labour, assisted by the labour commissioner and advised by the National Human Resources Deployment Advisory Committee, was in charge of enforcing the act, but the actual implementation was left up to the local authorities (Shaidi 1984, 85).
[5] *Daily News*, 26 September 1983.   [6] *African Business*, December 1983.
[7] No. 1.6, interview by author, 21 August 1987, Mnazi Moja, Dar es Salaam (DES).
[8] No. 6.54, interview by author, 11 November 1987, Manzese, DES.
[9] *Daily News*, 17 November 1983.   [10] Ibid., 2 October 1983.
[11] No. 7.18, interview by author, 21 June 1988, DES.
[12] J. B. Kitambi, regional director of administration, Coast Region, interview by author, June 1988, DES.   [13] *Daily News*, 9 June 1986.
[14] No. 1.6, interview by author, 21 August 1987, Mnazi Moja, DES.
[15] Alpha Nuhu, 'Tanzania-Labour: ILO Comes to the Rescue,' Inter Press Service, 31 May 1995.
[16] 'War on Hawkers to Continue,' *Daily News*, 6 June 1995.
[17] The other piece of legislation regulating small businesses is the Licensing and Registration Act of 1967, which stipulates that all enterprises employing ten or more workers are required to obtain an industrial license from the Commercial Law, Registration and Industrial Licensing Department, Ministry of Trade and Industries (International Labour Organisation 1992, 21). Few informal-sector operations are large enough to fall into this business category.
[18] One person wrote the following letter to the editor of the *Daily News* (3 June 1990): 'If the Council is hard up why do they spend whatever little they have (in terms of money) to endlessly chase around the so-called unlicensed street vendors? (By the way is it not a wrong war in the wrong battlefield, and what happens to the "War Spoils").'
[19] No. 7.17, interview by author, 24 June 1988, DES.
[20] *Daily News*, 16 May 1991.   [21] Ibid., 16 July, 1985.
[22] No. 6.72, interview by author, 18 November 1987, Manzese, DES.
[23] Government Notice No. 765, 30 October 1987. The Dar es Salaam City Council (Hawking and Street Trading) Amendment, Section 80, No. 8, Bylaw 15.   [24] *Daily News*, 23 July 1985.
[25] No. 6.61, interview by author, 13 November 1987, Manzese, DES.
[26] No. 6.153, interview by author, 8 December 1987, Manzese, DES.
[27] No. 7.13, interview by author, 26 October 1987, Manzese, DES.
[28] Patron–client relations in Tanzania are rooted in the traditional headman or chief–subject relationship. These local patrons gained prominence in a number of different ways: through the social standing of their families; by marrying into a prominent family; by making a pilgrimage to Mecca and becoming an Al-Hajj; or by becoming a *shehe* (a Muslim sheikh) or *imam* (prayer leader). Their financial status was usually derived from owning boats, hotels, buses, or taxis or by engaging in trade (M.-L. Swantz 1986, 8–9, 37).
[29] Seleimani Chamgulia, interview by author, 9 January 1988, Buguruni, DES.
[30] No. 6.46, interview by author, 10 November 1987, Manzese, DES.
[31] *Daily News*, 3 May 1989, emphasis mine.   [32] Ibid., 14 November 1987.
[33] Comments made at a seminar on 'Women Entrepreneurs in the Local Economy,' hosted by the Small Entrepreneurs Association of Mwanga, 7–10 March 1994.
[34] *Daily News*, 4 November 1986.
[35] *Africa Research Bulletin*, 15 July–14 August 1982, 6525.
[36] Collection of the levy varied from year to year. For example, targets were exceeded in 1984–1985 by many towns, and by the following year, only 53 per cent of the targeted amount was collected. Since then, revenue from the development levy has continued to fall (*Daily News*, 7 August 1991).
[37] Ibid., 4 January 1985, 3 April 1986, 9 October 1986.
[38] Ibid., 25 April 1986.
[39] A typical comment by a Dar es Salaam resident: 'When it comes to the Development Levy we have … seen nothing as a result of the levy we pay. Take Dar es Salaam as a [case in] point: the city is very dirty and the situation is deteriorating day in and day out. Our hospitals in the city are low in standards, [they have] poor hygienic conditions, no soaps, no insecticides and no mosquito nets in the hospitals. What we want to see is how such taxes are being spent' (*Daily News*, 9 June 1985).
[40] One Dar es Salaam businessman commented: 'The Government is all the time raising taxes. Okay; it needs more revenue, but it has not plugged its own misappropriation of millions of shillings' (ibid., 9 June 1985).
[41] No. 6.80, interview by author, 17 November 1987, Manzese, DES.
[42] *Daily News*, 8 May 1995.   [43] Ibid., 24 January 1984, 31 January 1984.
[44] Ibid., 19 December 1990.   [45] Ibid., 2 May 1987.   [46] Ibid., 5 June 1995.
[47] One satirist, Adam Lusekelo, in the government newspaper *Daily News*, had this in mind when he offered the following tongue-in-cheek observation

about animal owners in the Oyster Bay suburb populated by professionals, civil servants, and administrators: 'Supposing "City" [Council] is simply ignored by the Oysterbay Ranching Inc. What then? I don't imagine a scenario whereby our personages of great consequence are taken to court. Besides, who will dare take them to court? You can take the Tandika [a poorer area of the city] livestock keepers to court for letting their animals "fertilise" our roads with their dung. But not kraal owners of Oysterbay. You risk a serious paralysis of Party and Government organs' (ibid., 9 August 1987).

⁴⁸ Ibid., 3 August 1988.   ⁴⁹ No. 2.9, interview by author, 16 August 1987, City Center, DES.   ⁵⁰ *Daily News*, 18 September 1986.   ⁵¹ Ibid., 8 April 1987.
⁵² Ibid., 29 July 1987.   ⁵³ Ibid., 19 September 1991.
⁵⁴ Inter Press Service, 6 February 1995.
⁵⁵ A 1988 study of Manzese traders provides a useful profile of the traders I encountered in Manzese, one of the two locales in Dar es Salaam where I carried out fieldwork. In the study, Henry Gordon and Paul de Greve found that most trading businesses were single proprietorships run by men, ranging in age from 32 to 49. The lack of younger traders can be attributed to the fact that it takes time to establish contacts and to gain the trading expertise necessary to maintain and expand the business. The largest number of traders were from the Morogoro area. The sale of maize as a grain and of rice and beans was the main source of income for the traders; vegetables and fruit were of secondary importance. Maize and kidney beans are the most heavily traded items at the Manzese market. As is usually the case, the traders did not own transport or storage facilities themselves. For this reason, traders are confined mainly to purchasing the produce at rural markets and bringing it to the urban markets. Similarly, transporters rarely engage in trading. Instead, they are hired by wholesalers and agricultural producers, both in rural and urban areas. The traders surveyed reported an increase in trade after 1985, some attributing it to changes in the political climate. They also noted that the trade had become more competitive since 1980 (*Tanzanian Economic Trends* 1, no. 3 (1988): 25–33). One Manzese trader I interviewed had been employed as a guard at Tanzania Breweries but had left in 1985 because his salary of TSh 600 was insufficient. He began trading in 1983, while he was still working at the breweries. He traded with his younger brother and another hired youth, bringing tomatoes, oranges, coconuts, and pineapples three times a month from Morogoro to the Manzese market. His main concern was timing; for example, getting the tomatoes to Dar es Salaam before they went bad. He was saving to build a house, and he felt his business was going forward.
⁵⁶ *Tanzanian Economic Trends* 1, no. 1 (1988): 35.   ⁵⁷ Ibid., 1, no. 3 (1988): 26.
⁵⁸ *Daily News*, 1 March 1991.   ⁵⁹ Ibid., 4 January 1991.
⁶⁰ Yusa Lui, teacher, Kilimani Primary School, interview by author, 23 January 1988, Manzese, DES.   ⁶¹ Yusa Lui, interview by author.

References

Aboagye, A. A. 1985. 'An Analysis of Dar es Salaam's Informal Sector Survey', Addis Ababa: Jobs and Skills Programme for Africa, ILO.

Amani, H.K.R., and W.E. Maro. 1991–1992. 'Policies to Promote an Effective Private Trading System in Farm Products and Farm Inputs in Tanzania.' *Tanzania Economic Trends* 4 (3–4): 36–54.

Bienefeld, Manfred. 1975. 'The Informal Sector and Peripheral Capitalism: The Case of Tanzania', *IDS Bulletin* 6 (3): 53–73.

Bukurura, Lufian Hemed. 1991. 'Public Participation in Financing Local Development: The Case of Tanzanian Development Levy', *Afrique et Développement/Africa Development* 16 (3–4): 73–99.

Clark, Gracia. 1988. 'Price control and Local Foodstuffs in Kumasi, Ghana, 1979' in Gracia Clark (ed.), *Traders versus the State: Anthropological Approaches to Unofficial Economies*. Boulder, CO: Westview Press, pp. 57–80.

Coulson, Andrew. 1982. *Tanzania: A Political Economy*. Oxford: Clarendon Press.

Dolphyne, Florence.1987. 'Market Women of West Africa', *CUSO Journal*, December 26–28.

Eames, Elizabeth A. 1988. 'Why the Women Went to War: Women and Wealth in Ondo Town, Southwestern Nigeria', in Gracia Clark (ed.), *Traders versus the State: Anthropological Approaches to Unofficial Economies*. Boulder, CO: Westview Press, pp. 81–98.

Hansen, Karen. 1989. 'The Black Market and Women Traders in Lusaka', in Jane L. Parpart and Kathleen A. Staudt (eds), *Women and the State in Africa*. Boulder, CO: Lynne Rienner Publishers, pp. 143–61.

Havnevik, Kjell J. 1986. 'A Resource Overlooked – Crafts and Small Scale Industries', in Jannik Boesen, Kjell J. Havnevik, Juhani Koponen, and Rie Odgaard (eds), *Tanzania: Crisis and Struggle for Survival*. Uppsala:

Scandinavian Institute of African Studies, pp. 269–91.

Hyden, Goran. 1980. *Beyond Ujamaa in Tanzania: Underdevelopment and an Uncaptured Peasantry*. London: Heinemann.

International Labour Organisation. 1992. *Policies for Informal Sector Activities in Tanzania: Analysis and Reform Perspectives*. Dar es Salaam, ILO.

Joinet, Father Bernard. 1986. '*A Letter to My Superiors, No. 8*', Dar es Salaam.

Kapila, Sunita. 1987. 'The Matatu of Nairobi', *CUSO Journal*, December 21–2.

Kerner, Donna O. 1988. '"Hard work" and the Informal Sector Trade in Tanzania', in Gracia Clark (ed.), *Traders versus the State: Anthropological Approaches to Unofficial Economies*. Boulder, CO: Westview Press, pp. 41–56.

Kulaba, Saitel 1989. 'Local Government and the Management of Urban Services in Tanzania', in Richard E. Stren and Rodney R. White (eds), *African Cities in Crisis: Managing Rapid Urban Growth*, Boulder, CO: Westview Press.

Leslie, J.A.K. 1963. *A Survey of Dar es Salaam*. London: Oxford University Press.

Levi, Margaret. 1991 (1990). 'A Logic of Institutional Change', in Karen Schweers Cook and Margaret Levi (eds), *The Limits of Rationality*, Chicago and London: University of Chicago Press, pp. 402–18.

Lindberg, Olof. 1981. 'Development of Settlement in Dar es Salaam, 1967–72', *Fennia* 159 (1): 129–35.

Maliyamkono, T.L. and M.S.D. Bagachwa. 1990. *The Second Economy in Tanzania*. London: James Currey.

Molloy, J. 1971. 'Political Communication in Lushoto District, Tanzania.' Ph.D. diss., University of Kent at Canterbury.

Ndulu, Benno J., and M. Hyuha. 1988. *Impact of Government Policies on Food Supply in Tanzania*, Dar es Salaam: Department of Economics, University of Dar es Salaam.

Ndulu, Benno J., and Frances W Mwega. 1994. 'Economic Adjustment Policies', in Joel D. Barkan (ed.), *Beyond Capitalism vs. Socialism in Kenya and Tanzania*, Boulder, CO: Lynne Rienner Publishers, pp. 101–78.

Odegaard, Knut. 1985. 'Cash Crop versus Food Crop Production in Tanzania: An Assessment of the Major Post-Colonial Trends', *Lund Economic Series, no. 33*. Lund: Studentlitteratur.

Raikes, Philip. 1986. 'Eating the Carrot and Wielding the Stick: The Agricultural Sector in Tanzania', in Jannik Boesen, Kjell J. Havnevik, Juhani Koponen and Rie Odgaard (eds), *Tanzania: Crisis and Struggle for Survival*, Uppsala: Scandinavian Institute of African Studies, pp. 104–42.

Samoff, Joel.1973. 'Cell Leaders in Tanzania: A Review of Recent Research', *Taamuli* 4 (1): 63–75.

Scott, James C. 1987. 'Resistance without Protest and without Organisation: Peasant Opposition to the Islamic Zakat and the Christian Tithe', *Comparative Studies in Society and History* 29 (3): 417–52.

Shaidi, Leonard P. 1984. 'Tanzania: The Human Resources Deployment Act 1983 – A Desperate Measure to Contain a Desperate Situation', *Review of African Political Economy* 31: 82–87.

——. 1987. 'Legal Control of Surplus Labour in Tanzania's Urban Centres', Paper presented at the Workshop on Social Problems in Eastern Africa, Arusha.

——. 1991. 'The Leadership Code and Corruption', in Jeannette Hartmann (ed.), *Rethinking the Arusha Declaration*, Copenhagen: Centre for Development Research, pp. 125–31.

Sporrek, Anders. 1985. 'Food Marketing and Urban Growth in Dar es Salaam', *Lund Studies in Geography, Series B, Human Geography*, Malmo: Gleerup, vol 51.

Stren , Richard E. 1982. 'Underdevelopment, Urban Squatting, and the State Bureaucracy : A Case Study of Tanzania', *Canadian Journal of African Studies* 16 (1): 67–91.

Stren, Richard, Mohamed Halfani and Joyce Malombe. 1994. 'Coping with Urbanization and Urban Policy', in Joel D. Barkan (ed.), *Beyond Capitalism vs. Socialism in Kenya and Tanzania*, Boulder, CO: Lynne Rienner, pp. 175–200.

Swantz, Marja-Liisa. 1986. 'The Role of Women in Tanzanian Fishing Societies: A Study of the Socioeconomic Context and the Situation of Women in Three Coastal Fishing Villages in Tanzania.' Unpublished report commissioned by the Royal Norwegian Ministry of Development Cooperation (NORAD).

Temu, Peter. 1975. 'Marketing Board Pricing and Storage Policy with Particular Reference to Maize in Tanzania.' Ph.D. diss., University of Stanford.

Trager, Lillian. 1987. 'A Re-Examination of the Urban Informal Sector in West Africa', *Canadian Journal of African Studies* 21 (2): 238–55

Tripp, Aili M. 1994b. 'Rethinking Civil Society: Gender Implications in Contemporary Tanzania', in John W. Harbeson, Donald Rothchild and Naomi Chazan (eds), *Civil Society and the State in Africa*, Boulder, CO and London: Lynne Rienner, pp. 149–68.

BESSIE HOUSE-MIDAMBA
Gender, Democratization & Associational Life in Kenya

Reference
Africa Today, 43, 3, 1996, pp. 289–306

The quest for democracy is the quest for freedom, justice, equality and human dignity. … It is a far-reaching and wide-ranging movement, encompassing the liberation of citizens from local despots and tyrants, women from domestic and social subjugation and nations from foreign domination and exploitation.[1]

The role of African women in political development has received increased attention from researchers, policy analysts, and Africanist feminist scholars over the past three decades.[2] Although current research interest in democratization movements in Africa has been spurred to some extent by increasing domestic dissent and unrest, it is also attributable to some degree to the 'winds of change'[3] that have recently swept throughout the continent of Africa. As Guy Martin has so eloquently articulated, 'After three decades of authoritarian one- (or no) party rule characterized by political repression, human rights abuses, economic mismanagement, nepotism and corruption, democracy is spreading like bushfire throughout Africa.'[4] Consequently, a large literature has developed on democratization movements on the African continent.

The literature on the democratization movement in Kenya has encompassed several major themes. These include (1) conceptualizations of democratization and political liberalization and explications of the types of strategies that need to be incorporated to establish an effective governance realm;[5] (2) discussions about conditions that need to pre-exist to make a successful transition to a democratic society;[6] (3) analyses of the ongoing dynamic, interplay, and problematic of state and civil society in the transition period;[7] and (4) feminist analyses of the role of the state as arbiter of gender struggles as they relate to issues of gender equity, equal access, and competition over scarce resources in the society.[8]

This article examines the role of Kenyan women in the recent democratization movement. Several key questions provide the cornerstone of this study. First, what contributions have women made, both individually and collectively, in the recent transition from single-party to multiparty rule? Second, what avenues exist at both the formal and informal levels of society to bolster more political participation by women? Third, what role have women played in pressuring the state for political reforms and more accountability? Fourth, what can we predict about the relationship between women and the state as we move toward the year 2000? And last, do current debates on civil society and associational life really address or speak to the specific needs of women?

The basic premise of this article is that women's voluntary associations affect the transformation of society by articulating visions and goals that promise to link the state more effectively with civil society. As Joel Barkan and others have posited, voluntary associations

Not only provide links between the state and societal interests, but also perform an important mediating role whereby the macro-policy objectives of the state and the particularistic interests of society's groups are adjusted to each other by the process of bargaining. Expanding the sphere of 'civil society' increases the likelihood of a more pluralistic and democratic political order.[9]

The argument advanced here is that although in theory women's associations are apolitical entities, they have, in the context of a developing civil society in Kenya, played a significant role in helping to undermine antidemocratic forces. The central role of voluntary associations in the democratization movement has been acknowledged by a number of scholars. As Stephen Ndegwa has emphasized,

In recent times, among the most vocal proponents of authoritarian regimes in African countries have been voluntary and associational groups such as the churches, organized labor, professional associations, and grassroots movements. From this mix of civil actors, formidable oppositions have arisen against settled authoritarian regimes.[10]

Women's associations are not monolithic, however, and at times they have exhibited an ambivalent posture with regard to their relationships with the state. This ambivalence has been manifested on several different levels, with its most obvious manifestation illustrated by some women's groups' adoption of a reactionary posture against the state, whereas others have been more supportive of state policies.

Here, I analyze strategies used by individual women and women's organizations that have had a catalytic or transformative effect on Kenya's recent change from single-party to multiparty politics. To be sure, the democratization movement has greatly expanded the debate over the political and economic directions for Kenya's future, and in the process, new avenues and political spaces have emerged for Kenyan women to voice their concerns.

Amazingly, Kenyan women have not been passive actors but instead have taken strategic advantage of the new circumstances in which they find themselves. With the repeal of Section 2a of the constitution, which successfully paved the way for Kenya's recent multiparty reforms, many changes occurred that were to some degree attributable to the actions of women. A number of new organizations were formed with the aim of further mobilizing women and articulating their concerns in the broader debates about political life. Some groups that were organized initially as apolitical entities began to engage in activities that can only be characterized as overtly political. Although much of this activity occurred under the auspices of educated and upper-class women in Nairobi, it has increasingly encompassed poor, rural women as well.[11] When analyzing the role of African women in the recent democratization movements taking place on the continent, Gwendolyn Mikell recently noted that

Women appear aware that the present climate of political experimentation and 'democratization', whether resulting from Western pressures or internal shifts within cultural/religious communities, offers them unique political opportunities to alter their sociopolitical positions. Even in the Muslim communities of Nigeria and Sudan, some women are making use of the political spaces that national crises and elections have created in order to mobilize women to achieve increased status in many areas of life.[12]

Thus, a number of factors, both internal and external, are important in understanding the constellation of forces that crystallized to precipitate the push for democratization. Domestic opposition movements were clearly influenced by economic decline, increased government corruption, intimidation of the press, the proliferation of human rights abuses and tortures, and the increase in the number of pro-democracy movements in various regions of the world. Nonetheless, one of the most important catalysts for change was undoubtedly the pressure brought to bear on Kenya by the external donor community. Therefore, this article places particular attention on the decade of the 1990s, because it was during this time period that the real impetus for change reached unprecedented proportions. For example, President Moi's decision in December 1991 to finally allow multiparty elections to take place was precipitated in large part by the fact that the Paris Consultative Groups planned to withhold $350 million in foreign aid unless significant progress was demonstrated in the areas of economic and political reforms.[13]

The development of associational life in Kenya

Kenya, like many other countries in sub-Saharan Africa has a vibrant history of self-help organizations. The first self-help groups were founded by the Kikuyu during the late 1930s and the 1940s to develop schools, which were not provided by the colonialists, and as a way to declare their African independence. Hence, the development of the Kenya Independent Schools and the spirit of voluntarism it engendered proved to be important because it ultimately paved the way for the establishment of a grassroots organization movement that promulgated principles of self-reliance.[14]

Self-help organizations also emerged among the Luo, who founded the Luo Thrift Association and the Kavirondo Taxpayers Association during the 1940s. When Kenya received its independence from the British in 1963, Jomo Kenyatta, Kenya's first independent president, encouraged all rural Kenyans to participate in self-help projects. Voluntary associations continued to proliferate and develop under the broader umbrella of the *harambee* movement, which literally means 'let's pull together' in Kiswahili. These groups assisted in reducing citizen demands on the government for rural services, although these demands increased dramatically around independence. Thus, through *harambee* efforts, rural dwellers were strongly encouraged to develop self-help strategies and to ask for assistance from their elected leaders, whereas leaders were allowed to develop a political base through the assistance they provided to citizens. In the process, politicians were forced to focus attention on the needs of their local constituents rather than on issues relating to policies of the central government.[15] In other words, '*harambee* became the nexus where civil society in rural Kenya met the state.'[16] By the mid-1980s, it is estimated that between 15,000 and 20,000 *harambee* self-help groups existed in the country. Although the Kenyatta period (1963–1978) was characterized by authoritarian rule, particularly during his later years in office, it was perhaps less repressive than the administration of his successor and Kenya's current leader, President Daniel Arap Moi, who came to power after Kenyatta died in office.[17] As Maina Kiai has pointed out,

Kenya's human rights record has been dismal. Political assassinations, deaths in police custody, detentions without trial and police brutality have been prevalent in Kenya ever since the reign of Kenya's first president, Jomo Kenyatta … [and after Moi took power in 1978], government critics were harassed and intimidated through brief arrests and interrogations. By 1980, however, the regime had severely circumscribed freedom of expression and a culture of silence and fear began to permeate society.[18]

In spite of the use of authoritarian tactics during the Kenyatta era, scholars generally agree that the political climate was nonetheless conducive for the development of a wide variety of associational organizations that included, among others, the Kenya Farmers Association, the Central Organization of Trade Unions, church groups, the Law Society of Kenya, non-governmental organizations (NGOs) such as Maendaleo Ya Wanawake, the National Christian Council of Kenya, the Kenya Manufacturers Association, ethnic associations, self-help *harambee* groups, and the Chamber of Commerce.[19]

The Moi era

J. B. Mugaju has postulated that, at least in theory, 'A democracy should express the sovereignty of a country's adult population through a system of representative and accountable institutions, competitive party politics, periodic elections, and free and open dissent. All parties are supposed to abide by the rules of the game and accept the electorate's verdict.'[20] The implementation of these principles of democracy into practice has been particularly problematic, especially during the Moi era (1978–present), because he took a number of steps to reduce avenues for open political debate. Even though Kenya had been a *de facto* one-party state since 1969, a constitutional amendment was passed in 1982 to make Kenya formally a *de jure* one-party state. In general then, rule under Moi has led to a deterioration of both the strength and effectiveness of a host of voluntaristic associations, and their autonomy has been seriously reduced.[21]

The high level of dissatisfaction that accompanied the results of the 1988 elections crystallized into a demand that Kenya's one-party system be dismantled so that political pluralism could be reintroduced. A number of opposition forces for change pressured the state for reform. The Kenya African National Union (KANU) government was also struggling to contain the fallout from the rather controversial and politically explosive issue of the mysterious assassination of Robert Ouko, the former minister for foreign affairs, following the findings of a judicial commission of inquiry that implicated the government in his death. These findings eventually set off violent antigovernment protests that led to demands for the resignation of the government, including the president.[22]

Eventually, the state made a number of concessions that included an end to expulsions from the party and to the rather controversial policy of queue voting, as well as to the 70 per cent preliminary elections rule, which had been severely criticized by the citizenry. As stated earlier, in the aftermath of the repeal of Section 2a of the constitution, Kenya reluctantly reintroduced multipartyism, in the interim period, several new political parties have been registered. These include the Forum for the Restoration of Democracy (FORD), the Democratic Party of Kenya, the Labour Party Democracy, Kenya National Congress, the Party of Independent Candidates of Kenya, Kenya National Democratic Alliance, and the Social Democratic Party.[23]

The politicization of Kenyan women

Kenyan women's involvement in the political realm is not a new phenomenon; on the contrary, their participation in politics can be traced back to the colonial period. Although they have rarely been analyzed or discussed in any of the major studies of Kenyan nationalist movements, women played extremely important roles in both the organization of anticolonial strategies and the dissemination of political ideas. Kikuyu women were actively involved in all aspects of the nationalist movement and served as members of gangs in the forests. As Cora Ann Presley so skillfully reminds us, like their male counterparts, women were incarcerated in detention camps and jails, processed through 'pipelines,' and forced into barbed wire-enclosed villages during the 'Mau Mau' emergency.[24] The gradual politicization of Kikuyu women was influenced by a number of factors, including concern about forced labor of women and children on the coffee estates and government road projects, disagreements between the Kikuyu and the colonialists over the issue of female circumcision, the expropriation of Kikuyu land,[25] and the detention of Harry Thuku.[26]

Women developed political power through both formal and informal processes. On the informal level, women utilized avenues through which their vocal protests could be heard. Women sang protest songs; about chiefs, government policies, and retainers who forcibly used their labor. On the formal level, women split from the male-dominated Kikuyu Central Association and formed their own political organization, the Mumbi Central Association.[27]

In the postindependence period, women have continued their political activism. The United Nations First Decade for Women (1975-1985) and the End of the Decade for Women Conference, which was held in Nairobi, were particularly fortuitous for Kenyan women in that they provided a political platform for those women to articulate and concretize goals and strategies that could be used in their relations with the state to improve their position in society vis-à-vis that of men. Elsewhere, I have analyzed the extent to which Kenyan women were empowered politically in relation to the goals articulated by the United Nations during its recent decade for women. The data from my earlier study clearly indicated that a number of barriers still exist with regard to women's unequal status in the country.[28] The fourth world conference on women held in Beijing, China, in 1995 refocused global attention and awareness on the plight of women cross-culturally.[29]

One way to measure the impact of democratization would be to assess the extent to which women have been able to penetrate the formal political realm in terms of their participation in key decision-making institutions and their ability to exercise power over final policy outcomes. Unfortunately, thus far women's gains in these crucial areas have been marginal. Although a few women have been elected or appointed to serve in key political institutions at the local and national levels of politics (i.e. mayoral races, local branch offices of the Kenya African National Union, Parliament, and the ministries), their overall participation has been minimal.

Women comprise more than 50 percent of the country's total population, but in 1985 they made up only 1.16 percent of the total membership in Parliament. There were only two women cabinet members or ministers and only two female judges sat on the High Court. Moreover, in spite of conscious efforts by a number of female lobby groups such as the National Committee on the Status of Women, the League of Women Voters, Mothers in Action, the Anti-Rape Organization, and others to encourage more women to run for political office in the 1992 elections, they fell far short of their original goal, which was to achieve 30–35 percent female representation in Parliament. Although more than 250 women ran for civic and parliamentary seats, only 6 were elected to serve in Parliament. Furthermore, only 45 women were elected to civic posts and none were appointed to cabinet positions. Although women who participated in the National Capacity Building Workshop for female candidates selected Professor Wangari Maathai as their presidential candidate, she decided not to run for office.[30] To quote Maria Nzomo, 'The modest number of women elected into political office in the December 1992 elections is an important political achievement but is not enough. ... Furthermore, outside the political arena many of the gender concerns women identified and lobbied for still remain on the drawing boards.'[31]

Women's rather meager participation in some of the formal political institutions in society might suggest that the mere presence of multiparty democracy alone may not necessarily be a palliative for all of the problems that continue to plague Kenyan women. Other areas of society must also be dealt with to enforce principles of gender equity and fairness. For example, the legal sphere continues to pose almost insurmountable obstacles for women. In this regard, the existence of multiple legal systems in Kenya – that is customary, statutory, and religious laws – has in some cases exerted a negative effect on women's roles and status. African societies like many others in the world, have shown a strong proclivity toward male domination. As I have suggested elsewhere,

> Perhaps nowhere is this principle so deeply ingrained in the social fabric of African society as in the area of inheritance and property relations. Historical data has demonstrated that rights in the area of landholding and inheritance have generally not favored Kenyan women, particularly those who reside in rural areas.[32]

But it is not only in these areas that women have experienced acute difficulties. Other problem areas include women's rights in marriage, divorce, spousal abuse, custody of children, and reproduction.[33]

Women and the state in Kenya

At this juncture, I address the critical issue of what strategies women have used, either individually or collectively, to engage the state in an attempt to pressure it for important political reforms and more accountability. In what ways have women been able to make the state more accountable to the civil society, particularly with regard to gender-based issues and concerns? This concern is germane because no matter how civil society is defined, whether 'as a collection of individuals as an array of interest groups defined in many ways from economic to communal, as social classes in conflict, or as some combination of all three, it is widely assumed that civil society is the ultimate guarantor of the democratic process.'[34]

The issue of state-civil society relations is also important to Kenyan women because it focuses on how the state can accommodate their needs in the democratization process. The issue focuses attention on what Joel Barkan and colleagues refer to as 'the political bargaining process' in which adjustments are made with regard to interests and needs of the state in relationship to those of the citizenry.[35] To what extent have women been able to influence the final policy outcomes in the political bargaining process, as well as the exercise of political power, and how has the state responded to their demands?

In the aftermath of the introduction of multiparty politics in Kenya, the political reality is that the state continues to exercise inordinate control and power in determining the manner in which interaction occurs between citizens and the government. This has become a serious concern during the Moi era, because the rules of the game are not always clear and are subject to be changed without notice. For example, on several occasions Moi has suddenly announced drastically new directions in policy without consulting the Kenyan people, his advisers, or the heads of departments who were supposed to implement the new plans. The decisions to provide free milk and to restructure Kenya's educational system are only two well-known examples.[36]

These stark realities also speak to the much broader issues of political legitimacy and efficacy, as well as to the ability of the state to engender political loyalty and respect from the populace at large. To quote Barkan,

> The existence of a governance realm is dependent on a regime's adherence to a predictable and legitimate set of procedures that regulate the exercise of political authority and the competition between claimants for state resources. Procedures that are frequently changed are never institutionalized. Procedures that do not provide for a significant measure of bargaining and reciprocity between the rulers and the ruled, and between competing claimants, will never be regarded as legitimate.[37]

In spite of the repressive political conditions in which they find themselves, women have not stood idly by but have continued to advance their struggle for women's rights and, in some cases, have emerged victorious. Much of this action has taken place under the umbrella or aegis of women's organizations. It is important to note that the development of contemporary women's organizations in Kenya has been derived in part from a transformation of indigenous cooperative groups that was based on the need of rural women to mobilize effective means for acquiring resources to support their activities. It also developed from a model popularized and introduced by European women to teach African women about Western health care and home economics.[38] Although scholars have defined self-help or voluntary associations in various ways, I use the term to refer to groups that organize individuals to engage in collective action to ameliorate their conditions and, concomitantly, to change the social arena in which they operate. There are a number of reasons voluntary associations have become more prevalent in Africa. First, they help to lessen the large gaps that exist with regard to government provision of needed social services, as well as the effects of the relatively small number of formal institutions within the developing civil society. Second, in far too many cases, repressive political regimes often use questionable political tactics and strategies to suppress traditional, sometimes conflict-ridden social organizations. Hence, activists for change are often labeled seditious and a threat to internal political stability. Third, self-help associations have been viewed by the international community and by large multilateral financial institutions as extremely credible entities in terms of their ability to implement relief and development programs for the citizenry. In this capacity, these organizations have provided substantial financial support, other types of resources, and publicity to expand the parameters of collective action, particularly at the grassroots level.[39]

The three women's organizations I focus on here are Maendaleo Ya Wanawake (MYWO), the National Council of Women of Kenya (NCWK), and the Green Belt Movement (GBM). The first two groups were selected because they are the top national women's associations in Kenya, whereas the latter is a grassroots environmental organization. Maendaleo Ya Wanawake (Swahili for Women's Progress) is the largest women's voluntary association in Kenya and the only one that has a countrywide group of clubs within its network. As such, it has enabled women to form a power base largely around issues relating to gender and underdevelopment. Developed by a small group of European women in 1952 under the framework of the Colonial Government's Department of Community Development and Rehabilitation, MYWO was founded to advance the status of women and to raise African living standards through self-help activities.[40]

Through the years, the organization has provided instruction in farming methods, nutrition, hygiene, handicrafts, and sports activities and has encouraged the development of traditional handicrafts such as basketwork, pottery, palm leaf work, and needlework. Although the organization suffered a serious decline in membership after independence, in the late 1970s it was revitalized and has emerged as Kenya's leading NGO. By 1985, it was estimated that the organization had more than 300,000 members divided among eight thousand women's organizations.[41]

MYWO was much more militant during its early years, as it popularized women's issues and supported marriage and divorce reform laws aimed at uplifting the legal status of women. It also pressured the government for more economic assistance to finance its programs. In recent years, however, the organization has experienced serious problems amid charges that it was controlled by a new urban elite. It has also been accused of being unresponsive to its rural constituents. Further, the general public has not been sympathetic to the rather flamboyant lifestyles of some of its leaders.[42]

In 1986, MYWO was deeply embroiled in a financial scandal. The chair of the organization was dismissed after a report by a government-appointed probe committee found evidence of financial mismanagement and corruption. The government took advantage of this strategic opportunity to constrain MYWO's autonomy by formally dissolving its executive committee and placing it under the control of the Ministry of Culture and Social Services. As explained earlier, during the 1980s the KANU government under Moi was not very receptive to independent activities of civil society and continued to take whatever steps it could to further consolidate the power of the state. Thus, the overt action of actually amalgamating MYWO with KANU can be interpreted as a step by Moi to increase his power by seriously jeopardizing MYWO ability to criticize the government. After the amalgamation, MYWO relationship with the state became much more accommodative. Perhaps in response to the new 'pro-government' stance of MYWO, President Moi canceled an income tax debt of 6 million shillings in 1988, which the organization owed on its city-center building.[43]

MYWO's 'pro-government' position was also undoubtedly a significant factor in Moi's attribution of many of the achievements in the improved status of women during the United Nations First Decade for Women to the work of MYWO rather than to the NCWK, perhaps in part because the NCWK had called for legislative actions on behalf of women that were unacceptable to the government. MYWO was formally demarcated from KANU in 1992. This means the group was thrust rather unceremoniously back into the ranks of civil society.[44]

The NCWK, founded in 1964, was established to coordinate other women's groups in Kenya, including MYWO. The basic purpose of the group is to stimulate women's interest in good citizenship and obligations to family and society and to encourage their participation in all relevant national organizations. Through the years, the NCWK, like MYWO, has experienced a gradual decline in its effectiveness. Several factors have contributed to this state of affairs. First, some critics have argued that the organization is dominated by the Kikuyus, the largest ethnic group in the country. Second, the Women's Bureau has usurped many of the functions originally delineated for NCWK. Third, through the years a power rivalry emerged between NCWK and MYWO. This rivalry reached its apex during the 1970s, leading to the withdrawal of MYWO from affiliation with the NCWK in 1981. Finally, the resignation of Wangari Maathai as the group's leader in 1987 had an affect on the NCWK's visibility and effectiveness.[45]

Founded in 1977 by the NCWK as part of 'Save the Land Harambee,' the GBM was developed to deal explicitly with the serious and ominous threat of desertification in Kenya. The head of the GBM is Wangari Maathai, a biologist and former professor of veterinary medicine at the University of Nairobi. Under her able leadership, to date the GBM has planted more than 10 million trees and has received international praise for its environmental activities.[46]

In addition to its concern about the environment, the GBM has also focused on income generation for women and on training women to cultivate seedlings. There appear to be at least two major reasons that the GBM has had difficulty confining itself to the apolitical arena. First, one of the most important objectives of the group is to empower women. Consequently, in trying to achieve this goal, the GBM has found out the hard way that it must often challenge the political and social institutions in society that provide the cornerstone for gender inequality.[47]

Second, the GBM has found itself in a confrontational posture with the state more than once because many of the issues it focuses on emanate from political or policy decisions such as damming a river, evicting forest dwellers, or clearing up forestland. Therefore, Maathai has adopted a confrontational strategy that necessitates actively engaging the state whenever necessary in an effort to halt environmental decay. Although the government initially supported the establishment of the GBM because it viewed the group as relatively harmless, in recent years, as the GBM has dared to openly challenge the state, it has been increasingly perceived as a threat.[48] Ndegwa posits that

In the Kenyan NGO community, the Green Belt Movement under Wangari Maathai stands out as a vehemently political NGO that has spared no opportunity to challenge the state on issues that it considers within its purview or within the broader public interest. Apart from mundane tasks of its permanent tree-planting campaign, the GBM has been a prominent actor pursuing advocacy and protest from the late 1980s to the present.[49]

On another level of collective action, Kikuyu women continued their history of political activism when they incorporated a number of nonviolent tactics to force the Kenyan government to release their sons from prison when they were incarcerated in October 1990 after being accused of plotting to overthrow the Kenyan government. In response, the women held a hunger strike, delivered a signed petition to the government demanding their sons' release, held meetings inside All Saints Cathedral, and stripped

naked in front of police officers to advance their cause. According to Kikuyu beliefs, *Guturamira ng'ania* (stripping) is meant to place a curse on those who perpetrate violence. In this case, the curse was a response to police brutality against the mothers who began their hunger strike on Freedom Corner in Uhuru Park in Nairobi. The mothers fought the system and won, because their sons were eventually released from prison.[50]

In other cases, lone Kenyan women have singlehandedly confronted ubiquitous state actions. In this regard, the individual actions of Maathai are worthy of brief discussion. Although it can be argued that Maathai has always been concerned about political issues, many believe it was her campaign against the government's plan in 1989 to erect a $200 million sixty-story skyscraper with a thirty-foot statue of President Moi in front of Uhuru Park in Nairobi that put her on a head-to-head collision course with the state. Angered primarily by the environmental issues associated with the proposed project, Maathai filed a lawsuit with the High Court asking for an injunction to halt the construction of the project. In retaliation, Moi strongly criticized Maathai and others who did not support the project and accused them of 'having insects in their heads.' He also wondered why Kenyan women did not ostracize Maathai. MYWO, which at this time had adopted its 'pro-government' posture, responded to the president's suggestion by insisting that Maathai be expelled from the political party, KANU. Furthermore, the GBM, which occupied a government-owned office, was given twenty-four hours to vacate the building. Nevertheless, Maathai persevered and lobbied the international donor community for support. Her crusade finally ended in victory, and the project has not yet been implemented.[51]

More recently, Maathai's activities have focused more on issues of political reform and human rights. She was arrested in January 1992 and, along with other members of FORD, charged with 'rumormongering' because they called a press conference apparently to question the government about plans to give power to the military. Her arrest brought strong condemnation and criticism from members of the international community. Maathai has also been a strong critic of the system of queue voting, which was recently scrapped by Moi, and she was seriously injured by police brutality when she participated in the hunger strike staged by the mothers of the political prisoners discussed earlier. As cofounder and a member of the steering committee of the Forum for the Restoration of Democracy, Maathai has played a significant role in the transition to multiparty rule. After receiving numerous death threats and much intimidation, she went into hiding for two months in 1993. On 17 March 1993, eight well-known Kenyan female politicians asked Moi to stop the intimidation tactics against Maathai.[52]

The internationally known saga over the remains of S. M. Otieno catapulted his widow, Wambui, to the forefront of the legal arena in 1987 as she battled the Luo clansmen in the Kenyan courts over the disposition of her deceased husband's remains. Although S. M. Otieno had died intestate (without a will) and had apparently indicated to his wife that he wished to be buried in Nairobi, his Luo clansmen argued that according to Luo customs and tradition, he was to be buried in his tribal homeland in western Kenya. Although the case involved a host of complex issues, some of which have yet to be resolved, one critical question revolved around determining who was his next of kin. His wife argued that under the new Law of Succession Act, she was his personal legal representative, or his next of kin. The Luo clansmen vehemently disagreed and claimed that, in reality, they were the next of kin. In the end, Wambui won only a partial victory. The clansmen buried her husband, but she did get access to his estate.[53]

Although Wambui Otieno is a leader in the Kenyan women's movement, having held positions in both of Kenya's major national women's organizations (MYWO and the NCWK), ironically neither group seriously challenged the court's findings in the case. In other words, whereas Wambui argued that the decision of the court reflected gender discrimination and bias, the women's movement was clearly divided on the issue. Some women supported the position of the clan, and others sympathized with Wambui. A number of female politicians were apparently afraid to support Wambui publicly. especially because Moi sided openly with the Luo. Eventually, perhaps as a result of her increasing politicization and the level of awareness that was raised during her challenge within the legal system in Kenya, Wambui ran for Parliament under the auspices of the opposition party, FORD-Kenya, in the 1992 multiparty elections. Although she did not win the election, she popularized the cause of more equitable participation for women in the political process.[54]

Conclusion

This article has analyzed the important role of women in Kenya's recent movement toward multiparty rule. Analyzing women's actions on both the collective and individual levels, the data indicate that women have successfully created new avenues of expression and spaces for themselves within the context of the changing political realities in the society. Moreover, although in theory women's voluntary associations are apolitical, they have increasingly challenged the state in a number of ways on issues that have impinged on the political realm.Thus analyses that situate women within the context of a burgeoning civil society and associational life inform our analysis by specifically explicating the types of strategies women have used to foster democratic values. Although the state continues to exercise inordinate sway over the rules of the political process in Kenya, the political order is not static. On the contrary, the rules of the game are still very much subject to renegotiation and political bargaining.

As we approach the year 2000, we can expect to see more political activism by Kenyan women from all walks of life. The data indicate that women have become much more sensitized to gender issues They are also beginning to understand the interrelationship among political, economic, cultural, and social phenomena. More important, women have demonstrated that they have the ability to confront unpopular state actions, and in some cases they have emerged victorious.

Notes

Bessie House-Midamba wishes to thank Dr. Toyin I Falola, Dr. Gilbert Khadiagala, and Dr. Lisa Aubrey for their suggestions on this article.

1 Afrifa K. Gitonga, 'Introduction," in Walter Q Oyugi, Atieno Odhiambo, Michael Chege, and Afrifa K. Gitonga, eds., *Democratic Theory and Practice in Africa* (Portsmouth, N.H.: Heinemann, 1988), p. 2.

2 See, for example, Bessie House-Midamba, *Class Development and Gender Inequality in Kenya, 1963–1990* (Lewiston, NY.: Edwin Mellen Press, 1990), pp. 107–124; Bessie House-Midamba, 'The United Nations Decade: Political Empowerment or Increased Marginalization for Kenyan Women?' *Africa Today*, vol. 37, no. 1 (1990), pp. 37–48; and Maria Nzemo, 'The Impact of the Women's Decade on Policies,

Programs and Empowerment of Women in Kenya,' *Issue: A Journal of Opinion*, vol. 17, no. 2 (Summer 1989), pp. 9-17.

3 Guy Martin, 'Preface: Democratic Transition in Africa,' *Issue: A Journal of Opinion*, Special Double Issue, vol. 21, nos. 1-2 (1993), p. 6.

4 Ibid.

5 Joel Barkan, 'The Rise and Fall of a Governance Realm in Kenya,' in Goran Hyden and Michael Bratton, eds., *Governance and Politics in Africa* (Boulder, Colo.: Lynne Rienner Publishers, 1992), pp. 167–192.

6 Makau wa Mutua, 'Human Rights and State Despotism in Kenya: Institutional Problems,' *Africa Today*, vol. 41, no. 4 (1994), pp. 50–56; and Githu Muigai, 'Kenya's Opposition and the Crisis of Governance,' *Issue: A Journal of Opinion*, Special Double Issue. vol. 21, no. 1–2 (1993), pp. 26–34.

7 Frank Holmquist and Michael Ford, 'Kenya: State and Civil Society the First Year After the Election.' *Africa Today*, vol. 41, no. 4 (1994), pp. 9–15.

8 Bessie House-Midamba, 'Rethinking Gender, Ethnicity, and Economic Development in Kenya,' *African Rural and Urban Studies*, vol. 2, no. 1 (forthcoming in 1996); Maria Nzomo, 'The Gender Dimension of Democratization in Kenya: Some International Linkages,' *Alternatives*, vol. 18 (Winter 1993), pp. 61–73, and Maria Nzomo, 'The Status of Women's Human Rights in Kenya,' *Issue: A Journal of Opinion*, vol. 22, no. 2 (Summer 1994), pp. 17–20.

9 Joel Barkan, Michael L. McMulty, and M. A. O. Ayeni, '"Hometown" Voluntary Associations, Local Development, and the Emergence of Civil Society in Western Nigeria,' *Journal of Modern African Studies*, vol. 29, no. 3 (1991), pp. 457–458.

10 Stephen N Ndegwa, *The Two Faces of Civil Society: NGOs and Politics in Africa* (West Hartford, Conn.: Kumarian Press, 1996), p. 2.

11 Alexandra Tibbetts, 'Mamas Fighting for Freedom in Kenya,' *Africa Today*, vol. 41, no. 4 (1994), p. 30.

12 Gwendolyn Mikell, 'African Feminism: Toward A New Politics of Representation,' *Feminist Studies*, vol. 21, no. 2 (Summer 1995), pp. 409–410.

13 Gilbert M. Khadiagala, 'Kenya: Intractable Authoritarianism,' *SAIS Review* (Summer-Fall 1995), pp. 45–54; see also Holmquist and Ford, 'Kenya,' pp. 5-7.

14 Barkan, 'The Rise and Fall of a Governance Realm in Kenya,' p. 176.

15 Ibid., pp. 176–177.

16 Ibid. p. 177.

17 Ibid. p. 176.

18 Maina Kiai, 'Putting People over Politics: Reforming Aid Policy Toward Kenya,' *Harvard International Review*, vol. 15, no. 1 (1992), pp. 14–15.

19 Barkan,'The Rise and Fall of a Governance Realm in Kenya,' p. 175.

20 J. B. Mugaju, 'The Illusions of Democracy in Uganda, 1955-1966,' in Oyugi et al., eds., *Democratic Theory and Practice in Africa*, p. 86.

21 Barkan, 'The Rise and Fall of a Governance Realm in Kenya,' pp. 180, 185.

22 Muigai, 'Kenya's Opposition and the Crisis of Governance,' pp. 26–27.

23 Ibid., p. 29.

24 Cora Ann Presley, 'Kikuyu Women in the Mau Mau Rebellion.' in Gary Y. Okihiro, ed., *In Resistance: Studies in African, Caribbean, and Afro-American History* (Amherst: University of Massachusetts Press, 1986), pp. 54–69.

25 Ibid. See also Luise White, 'Separating the Men from the Boys: Colonial Construction of Gender in Central Kenya,' *International Journal of African Historical Studies*, vol. 23, no.18 (1990) pp.1–26; and Tabitha Kanogo, *Squatters and the Roots of Mau Mau, 1905–1963* (Nairobi: Heinemann, 1987), pp. 8–17, 143–148.

26 Harry Thuku was a supporter of many women's issues. He was one of the founders of the Young Kikuyu Association in 1921, which was later renamed the East African Association.

27 Presley,'Kikuyu Women in the Mau Mau Rebellion,' pp. 54–69.

28 House-Midamba, 'The United Nations Decade,' pp. 37–48.

29 Ibid., p. 40.

30 Maria Nzomo, ed., *Empowering Kenya Women: Report of a Seminar on*

Post-Election Women's Agenda: Forward Looking Strategies to 1997 and Beyond (Nairobi: Committee on the Status of Women, 1993), pp.1–3.

31 Ibid., p. 9.

32 See Bessie House-Midamba, 'Legal Pluralism and Attendant Internal Conflicts in Marital and Inheritance Laws in Kenya,' *Africa: Rivista Trimestrale*, vol. 49, no. 3 (September 1994), p. 387; See also Bessie House-Midamba, 'The Legal Basis of Gender Inequality in Kenya,' *African Journal of International and Comparative Law*, vol. 5, no. 4 (December 1993), pp. 854–868; and Nzomo, 'The Status of Women's Human Rights in Kenya,' p. 17.

33 House-Midamba, 'Legal Pluralism,' p. 367.

34 Holmquist and Ford, 'Kenya,' p.9.

35 Barkan, McNulty, and Ayeni, ' "Hometown" Voluntary Associations,' p. 460.

36 Barkan,'The Rise and Fall of a Governance Realm in Kenya,' p.179.

37 Ibid. p. 167.

38 Monica Udvardy, 'Women's Groups Near the Coast: Patron Clientship in the Developing Arena,' in David W. Brokensha and Peter D. Little, eds., *Anthropology of Development and Change in East Africa* (Boulder, Colo.: Westview Press,1988), p. 219.

39 Marc Michaelson, 'Wangari Maathai and Kenya's Green Belt Movement: Exploring the Evolution and Potentialities of Consensus Movement and Mobilization,' *Social Problems*, vol. 41, no. 4 (November 1994), pp. 540–543.

40 Audrey Wipper, 'Women's Voluntary Associations,' in Margaret Jean Hay and Sharon Stichter, eds., *African Women South of the Sahara* (London: Longman, 1984), pp. 77–78.

41 Ibid. See also Audrey Wipper, 'The Maendaleo Ya Wanawake Organization: The Cooptation of Leadership,' *African Studies Review*, vol. 18, no. 3 (December 1975), p. 99.

42 April Gordon, 'Gender, Ethnicity, and Class in Kenya: "Burying Otieno" Revisited,' *Signs: Journal of Women in Culture and Society*, vol. 20, no.41 (1995), p. 900; and Wipper, 'The Maendaleo Ya Wanawake Organization,' p. 99.

43 Patricia Stamp, 'Burying Otieno: The Politics of Gender and Ethnicity in Kenya,' *Signs: Journal of Women in Culture and Society*, vol. 16, no. 4 (1991). p. 831; see also Ndegwa, *The Two Faces of Civil Society*, pp.94–96.

44 Nzomo, 'The Impact of the Women's Decade on Policies,' p. 11.

45 Ibid.

46 Ndegwa. *The Two Faces of Civil Society*, p. 84.

47 Ibid., pp. 84-96; see also Michaelson, 'Wangari Maathai and Kenya's Green Belt Movement.' p. 548.

48 Ndegwa, *The Two Faces of Civil Society*, p. 96.

49 Ibid., p. 97.

50 Tibbetts, 'Mamas Fighting for Freedom in Kenya,' pp. 27–40.

51 Michaelson, 'Wangari Maathai and Kenya's Green Belt Movement,' pp. 552–553.

52 Ibid.

53 Gordon, 'Gender, Ethnicity and Class in Kenya,' pp. 883–887, see also David William Cohen and E. S. Atieno Odhiambo, *Burying SM: The Politics of Knowledge and the Sociology of Power in Africa* (Portsmouth, NH.: Heinemann, James Currey: London 1992), pp. 1–17.

54 Gordon, 'Gender, Ethnicity and Class in Kenya,' pp. 884, 892, and 907.

5 Political Change

JOCELYN ALEXANDER
The Local State in Post-War Mozambique

Reference
Africa, 67/1, 1997, pp. 1–25

In recent years, Mozambican intellectuals and officials (as well as international donors) have increasingly looked to decentralisation as a means of making the state more efficient and responsive to local needs. Mozambican debates over rural society have also shifted, broadly moving from a Marxist concern with class to a focus on chieftaincy, culture, ethnicity and 'civil society'.[1] The Law of the Municipalities,[2] passed in September 1994, encompasses both these concerns: it calls for a wide range of state functions to be decentralised to elected district institutions, and for a greater role to be played by 'traditional authorities'.

The law comes at a time of wider academic and political debate over the failures of African states in which a strong civil society, democratisation and decentralisation are cast as remedies. Such debates tend to posit a fairly firm distinction between state and society, and to assume an oppositional relationship between them. 'Civil society' is imbued with a democratic character, and its leaders with a desire for (if not capacity to achieve) democratic reform. Much of this literature tends also to have an urban, elite and macro-level bias.[3] The history, and current forms, of political practices in the rural areas where the majority of southern Africa's people live receive short shrift, while democratic aspirations are assumed rather than investigated.

As this article explores, state and society are rarely clearly distinguished, while leaders of 'civil society' may well want to ally with – even become part of – the state, not oppose or reform it. Nor are democratic aspirations necessarily common, particularly where violent conflict and authoritarianism have long moulded political practice, as in Mozambique. I argue that an exploration of the interaction and connections between local representatives of the state and rural society is central to understanding processes of political reform. My account thus focuses on the rural grounding of the state, the points at which its capacity is tested, policy is put into practice, and attitudes to official authority are produced. I develop an historical perspective on the ways in which the state has been established and justified in the rural areas, and how its representatives have acted, as well as an interview-based picture of how people think and talk about authority, and what they believe to be politically possible.

A case study of Manica Province in central Mozambique provides the basis for my investigations. Manica was one of the most hotly contested provinces in Mozambique's lengthy post-independence war. It presents difficult challenges both to the exercise of state authority and to democratisation in the post war era. Two four-month periods of fieldwork were undertaken in 1993 and 1994, focusing on both government and opposition-held territories in Sussundenga, Macossa and Báruè Districts. My analysis relies on government records and interviews of salaried officials as well as of a range of 'local leaders', e.g. political party leaders, deputies of assemblies, chiefs, church leaders, businessmen and women's leagues.[4] I start with an account of political and administrative changes introduced by the Frelimo (Frente de Libertação de Moçambique) government from 1974 to 1975 in Manica, and then by the opposition military movement, Renamo (Resistência Nacional Moçambicana).[5] Subsequent discussion turns to local political developments in the period following the signing of the peace accord between Renamo and Frelimo in October 1992, and then to views on current decentralisation initiatives.

Frelimo: construction, destruction and transformation

Frelimo's leaders inherited a country characterised by inequality, poverty and little experience of other than authoritarian rule. The new leaders retained aspects of the existing state structure while introducing a programme for dramatic change.

Continuities included the strong centralisation of political and administrative power, and the pivotal role of district administrators in rural areas. Officials also maintained an attachment to the strict hierarchies, labyrinthine bureaucratic procedures and material accoutrements of power which had marked Portuguese rule. In Manica Province, administrators regularly retained the houses and to some extent the style of life of their predecessors, often treating the illiterate and those who could not speak Portuguese with disdain.[6] Attempts to break with the past were, however, ambitious. Frelimo sought to create a nationwide political and administrative presence, and to transform social and economic relations along Marxist lines. Frelimo leaders envisioned a united and modern nation state in which there was no place for social and cultural difference (see Cahen, 1985, 1990; Geffray, 1988). Frelimo prohibited chiefs from participation in the new structures of state and party and condemned beliefs and practices deemed 'traditional' or, in the parlance of Frelimo, 'obscurantist' or 'feudal'. This exclusion and condemnation took little note of the wide variations in authority and popularity of chiefs or other holders of ritual power.[7] Religious groups also faced condemnation: churches were closed, religious paraphernalia burned, believers sent for re-education. In the economic sphere, Frelimo sought to supplant the largely Portuguese and Indian trade and shop network with state-run people's stores, and to restructure settlement patterns and relations of production through the introduction of communal villages, or concentrated state-planned settlements with a nucleus of co-operative production. Large, usually abandoned, farms and some factories were taken over by the state.

Frelimo set out the new structures of state and party over the 1970s. In Manica Province, dynamising groups were established from the *bairros* of the cities to rural villages in 1974 and 1975. After its conversion from a front to a vanguard party in 1978, Frelimo introduced a more formal hierarchy of party cells, circles, zones and districts, each headed by a secretary.[8] In 1977 and 1978 administrative, executive and judicial structures expanded. Administration followed the Portuguese hierarchy, with district administrators and, beneath them, *chefes* of posts. In 1986 the post was subdivided into localities.[9] Executive councils, constituted of Ministry representatives and headed by administrative officials, replaced their colonial predecessors, while people's assemblies, which were intended to act as representative bodies, were a new addition (Sabonete, 1994). Frelimo also sought to institute popular tribunals from village and *bairro* on up. Party and state were at every level closely linked: the highest-ranking administrative official at district and post level was also the first secretary of Frelimo, and president of the assembly; the provincial governor sat as president of the provincial assembly and was the ranking party official in the province. Party leaders prepared the lists from which assembly deputies were nominated; directors of state enterprises and farms, provincial Ministry representatives and military commanders were almost always party leaders as well as deputies of assemblies.

The realisation of these momentous and not necessarily pragmatic or popular institutional and policy initiatives faced severe obstacles, in part due to popular opposition and lack of state capacity. In Manica, Frelimo sought to overcome such obstacles through mobilisational campaigns or 'offensives' in which party-state officials, or brigades organised by them, travelled through the countryside or to urban centres in order to introduce and enforce new policies (see, e.g., GPM, 1979). Meetings were so numerous that provincial reports complained they prevented people from engaging in 'productive work' (e.g. GPM, 1984b). These campaigns had some strengths, such as in rapidly spreading party structures, politicising society and expanding social services. They were, however, authoritarian in style. In the districts, party-state officials had little capacity to influence policies, instead simply receiving 'orientations' from on high. Tribunals, assemblies and executive councils were only weakly institutionalised and were dominated by higher levels. They spread slowly in the countryside and lacked resources and skills.[10] In practice, executive and administrative organs dominated representatives institutions, and were themselves dominated by their superior counterparts.

The Frelimo party-state's attempts to build new institutions were authoritarian from the outset, and constrained by the lack of material support received by local institutions and the rural economy at large. These factors combined with the spread of war to produce an uneasy marriage of militarisation, on the one hand, and compromise with only recently vilified social categories on the other.

Frelimo's militarisation
Frelimo inherited a military ethos from the war for independence (de Brito, 1988, 1991). Many Frelimo leaders, from Samora Machel on down, began their political careers as military commanders. After independence the experience of the liberated zones in the north of the country was a much cited model for transformation, and a military vocabulary ('campaigns', 'offensives', 'enemies', etc.) pervaded official discourse. The military legacy was, however, much more than simply discursive.

In Manica Province the first direct experience of Frelimo was through contact with its guerrillas in the early 1970s (Alexander, 1994; Borges Coelho, 1993). Though their operations were largely limited to the northern third of the province, guerrillas and other military detachments played an important role in 1974 and 1975 in organising and running meetings at which leaders of dynamising groups were chosen. Soldiers were often perceived as threatening, and their pronouncements as unquestionable.[11] The

post-independence war spread early in Manica Province, owing to its proximity to the then Rhodesia.[12] From the late 1970s the rural representatives of the Frelimo party-state were armed and stood in the front line of defence. Local officials were organised into, and themselves organised, popular militias, self-defence commands and popular vigilance groups. These were used in the service of political goals, as well as of military defence proper. In a context marked by fear and suspicion, coercion became an ever more important component of mobilisation and discipline. Hanlon (1984: 262) notes 'the sharp increase in arbitrary orders and punishments' from the early to mid-1980s, such that Manica's provincial governor 'was forced to publicly order a halt, at least, to "the practice of flogging people who criticise incorrect officials"'.

For many local officials, military considerations were at the heart of their daily lives, and the threat of 'losing' people, literally, or in terms of allegiance, to Renamo was keenly felt. Discussions about wartime administration with *chefes* of posts (the highest party officials, and the presidents of assemblies at that level), and with the Frelimo secretaries who acted as their subordinates, often devolved into debate over strategies of defence. Renamo targeted party-state leaders for attack; communities became divided between the two sides as people joined, or were kidnapped into, opposition. (Ironically, the poorly equipped popular militias were one of the groups which proved amenable to recruitment by Renamo.) People were afraid to take up party positions, and some were forced into positions which had become near suicidal to hold.[13] The war thus forced those who remained in office into the military roles, while Renamo offered a voluntary or involuntary 'exit option' from the party-state.

Rural rule: hierarchy and compromise
The party-state's militarisation interacted with other factors to create a political practice which was authoritarian and coercive but which also relied on local compromises that undercut Frelimo's official intentions regarding the composition of new political structures in ways little recognised in the literature but clearly demonstrated in provincial documents and interviews.

One set of obstacles lay in the difficulty of creating a basis for the authority of village Frelimo secretaries. Frelimo's stated criteria for choosing secretaries were largely negative: chiefs and their subordinates, polygamists, religious leaders, economic 'exploiters', etc., were to be excluded. Positive criteria were generally limited to participation in the *Luta Armada* and literacy or at least a command of Portuguese, which tended to benefit the younger and better-off. Though there was a constituency for such change, it created strong resentment among broad and influential segments of rural society. Party positions became part and parcel of local struggles over state patronage, access to land, and over authority between youth and elders and among lineage leaders.[14] The position of Frelimo's secretaries was further undercut by their use as enforcers of policies which were unpopular, and which many secretaries themselves resented. These included the denial of the existence of witchcraft, bans on religious activity, and the introduction of communal villages and co-operative production.

The exclusionary aspects of Frelimo policy were not easy to enforce. Provincial, never mind central, officials had little knowledge of who constituted rural party structures.[15] People could disguise the backgrounds of Frelimo's secretaries, while post and district officials' views tended to be pragmatic, opportunistic and often more sympathetic to local beliefs than to Frelimo dicta.

Figure 1 The province of Manica in central Mozambique. Districts and posts officially under Renamo: Macossa district, Buzua post, Mavonde post, Dombe post. No data available on Báruè, Guro or Machaze.

Practice with regard to chiefs was particularly interesting. Official tolerance of chiefs in Manica was most commonly dated to 1987 and associated with Joaquim Chissano's rise to the presidency,[16] but some officials openly abrogated Frelimo dictums much earlier. Sussundenga's district administrator from 1980 to 1988, for example, regularly consulted chiefs and incorporated them or their children or relatives into Frelimo committees. Under war conditions, he argued, it was far preferable to offend his superiors than to offend influential royal families: 'If I wasn't liked, I would have been killed,' as he succinctly put it (interview, Chimoio, 8 August 1994). This administrator was instrumental in holding large parts of a heavily besieged district: he was awarded the 'Second Degree Medal for Valour and Patriotism' in 1985, and was later appointed provincial first secretary of Frelimo, an indication that his success in holding on to territory was more valued than adherence to the party line.

There were other reasons behind a softening of attitude towards chiefs. They lay in Portuguese precedents, as well as in a conviction on the part of party-state officials that they had neither the capacity nor the knowledge to confront a range of problems, from unexplained outbreaks of disease to witchcraft and drought. In the late 1980s and early 1990s the Ministry of Agriculture involved

chiefs in solving disputes over land, and district magistrates gave their blessing to chiefs' courts in some areas (Alexander, 1994, 1995: 15).

The Frelimo party-state in Manica's rural areas thus relied on diverse alliances and practices which reflected the exigencies of survival and control, as well as sympathy for local beliefs. Though the state was authoritarian, hierarchical and militarised, local officials in particular interacted and allied with, even drew into semi-official capacities, groups which had been officially condemned. As the character of Frelimo rule increasingly diverged from that originally envisaged, so did the extent of its influence. Far from building a united and modern nation-state, Frelimo was driven out of large swathes of territory, and failed to deliver social or economic goods within them.

The geography of war and the capacity of the state
By the end of the 1980s Manica Province's government was restricted to a network of main roads and urban and district centres. Military considerations dominated its priorities.[17] New institutions – assemblies, executive councils, tribunals, and the party at local level – ceased to function (if they ever had) in many areas. Officials simply could not reach much of the province as Renamo expanded. Rural centres which remained in government hands lost staff and people to the cities of Chimoio and Beira and to Zimbabwe, further centralising the locus of decision-making, ironically at a time when Frelimo was first calling for decentralisation, in 1983. Some administrations were wholly displaced: in Báruè District, Catandica became home to the district administration of neighbouring Macossa, while the locality offices of Chuala were relocated to Honde, and Chôa's post administration moved to Nhachigo. In Sussundenga District, Dombe post's administration was displaced to the district centre, while Tambara's district administration was moved from Nhacolo to the better defended Nhacafula. Large population movements accompanied each displacement.

Obviously linked with the spread of Renamo control was a reduction in the state's ability to provide and protect social services and marketing networks. The early spread of health and education services crumbled, while people's stores and the state marketing board were a disaster from the beginning. People's stores were quickly abandoned in favour of a half-hearted return to reliance on private traders (Cravinho, 1995). The supply of basic necessities to outlying areas often became an emergency operation; rural livelihoods were threatened, as was Frelimo's military capacity as supplies to soldiers in siege towns failed to get through.[19]

The government's loss of control over territory did not, however, entail a proportionate loss of control over population. Communal villages played a key role in this respect, and became a violent locus of contestation between Frelimo and Renamo. Their rapid expansion in Manica coincided with an escalation of war. Senior officials cast entrance into villages as a test of loyalty; militias and the army were increasingly used to force people into them. Communal village inhabitants perceived the villages as intended solely to increase security and control, and then only variably to good effect. In all cases, the villages were portrayed as bearing a range of other costs, including increased social conflict, losses in production and the spread of disease.[20]

Nearly a third of the province's population lived in communal villages by the end of 1981, but the villages came under ferocious attack as Renamo, now under Afonso Dhlakama's leadership, benefited from the upgraded support of South Africa.[21] Much of the work on communal villages in 1982 and 1983 was directed towards reconstruction (GPM, 1982b, d, 1983) and, in later years, so-called communal villages were initiated explicitly for the purpose of accommodating displaced people and refugees. These were little more than concentrations of people, usually near administrative centres and roads, under military protection and within reach of aid distributions.[22] They were accompanied by increased restrictions on movement introduced by the *guia de marcha*, a letter of permission necessary for travel (Hanlon, 1984: 262). The term 'communal village' was eventually replaced by 'accommodation centre'. These were camps of *deslocados* – displaced people – and *recuperados*, people forcibly moved from areas vulnerable to, considered sympathetic to or under the control of Renamo.[23]

The provincial party-state's interventions were thus restricted to the most modest of social goals, and dominated by military imperatives: communal villages became counter-insurgency devices, people's stores were abandoned, the spread of health and educational services was severely limited, and party-state structures devoted their energies to defence and 'vigilance'. The party-state acted not as a developmental agent but as an embattled agent of control, and this fact would strongly shape popular perceptions of the role of the state, as discussed below. More subtle – and little recognised, either in academic writing or in Frelimo discourse – change occurred in terms of local officials' alliances with social groups and leaders initially condemned by Frelimo. Thus chiefs played an important role, as did private traders.

While the impetus towards change sometimes came from local officials who found themselves under tremendous economic and military pressures, reforms also originated from central levels, and were the product of combined international pressure, self-criticism and necessity. Notably following Joaquim Chissano's assumption of the presidency in late 1986, important reforms were introduced, ranging from the adoption of a (long prefigured) structural adjustment package to the warming of relations between church and state and changed views with regard to chieftaincy and 'tradition'. The new constitution of 1990 enshrined a turn to multi-partyism, heralding a gradual distancing of party and state.

In some ways there seemed to be a convergence between Renamo and Frelimo. Frelimo had adopted many of Renamo's putative demands (multi-partyism, market reforms, tolerance of chiefs and religion) and shared to a limited degree Renamo's militarised authoritarianism. However, popular perceptions in government areas – most strongly urban but also rural – of the difference between the two remained strong: Frelimo was cast as literate, civilised, urban; Renamo as brutal, uncivilised, poorly educated and dressed, from the bush. A conversation with a truck driver with whom I had caught a lift into Renamo-held Macossa in 1993 is illustrative. He was from Maputo and had been hired to deliver food aid to Maringue, Renamo's 'national' headquarters. As we travelled he admitted his greatest fear was to break down in a Renamo zone. The reason for his fear was not that he would be killed or his truck stolen. 'You see,' he explained, 'when Renamo people see a truck they don't think of it as a truck. They look at the tyres and they think, shoes. They look at the sides and they think, roof.' He feared his truck would be cannibalised by people in a world so divorced from the 'modern' that it saw use values only in its component parts. The truck driver's tale, and the popular stereotypes it reflected, call for a discussion of Renamo.

Renamo governance up to 1992

Renamo was first and foremost a military organisation: the weakness of its political programme and its brutality have been widely noted (Hall, 1990). As far as Renamo is credited with one, its ideology has been described as a 'traditionalist' inversion of Frelimo's modernist goals, and as holding particular appeal for the economically marginal (Roesch, 1992; Geffray, 1991). Renamo certainly did reverse some of Frelimo's initiatives, but it also paralleled Frelimo, and some divergences were due more to military imperatives than to ideology. Renamo, like Frelimo, was forced to compromise with the societies over which it ruled – with implications for its choice of allies.

At the end of the war, people in Manica most often distinguished Renamo administration from that of Frelimo by reference to Renamo's reversal of policy towards churches and chiefs and its dispersal of communal villages. The 'traditionalist' reliance on chiefs certainly constituted an important ideological plank for Renamo, but it was also a pragmatic step: Renamo had little option but to reject Frelimo structures and to rely on chiefs for a skeletal administration. It was a choice which drew as much (if not more) on colonial administrative precedents – i.e. using chiefs as tax collectors and mobilisers of labour – as on pre-colonial ideas of chiefly rule. Nor, as discussed below, was Renamo's reliance on chiefs always restorationist, conducive to ritual, or more appealing where people lived at the economic margins. As for communal villages, the dispersal of their populations was not solely aimed at returning people to their 'traditional' homes: it was as much a military as a political tactic, just as the villages had become a counter-insurgency device for Frelimo. Moreover, Renamo increasingly paralleled Frelimo as its expanding control over territory required more elaborate means of civilian administration and service provision. Its growing cadres of civilian officials aspired not to a 'traditional' life but to the accoutrements of 'modern' authority which they associated with Frelimo, or with Portuguese rulers. Renamo also adopted practices which it had condemned as among Frelimo's worst crimes – forced agricultural labour and controls on movement which mimicked Frelimo's *guias de marcha*, for example.

Renamo's wartime strategies of rural rule cannot be considered as a coherent whole. There were radical differences over time and space and between areas where more or less control was exercised (Vines, 1991). There were also differences between areas which were fairly strongly controlled by Renamo for long periods. I briefly compare two of these, the post of Dombe in Sussundenga District and the district of Macossa. Both Dombe and Macossa town centres came under attack fairly early, and both were reduced to siege towns in which a government military force, supplied by air or convoy, sat amidst Renamo-controlled countryside. Renamo considered both areas strategically important: Dombe became Renamo's 'provincial' headquarters for its version of Manica Province, i.e. the area between the Beira corridor and the river Save, while Macossa stood at the western gateway to Maringue, Renamo's 'national' headquarters. In both areas, Renamo relied on a system of civilian control and extraction built on chieftaincy, and bolstered by the Renamo police and intelligence agents, the *mujhibas*.

The two areas also differed in a number of respects: dry, remote and heavily forested Macossa was sparsely populated and had historically been poor in terms of services, churches, infrastructure, trade links and local production, while Dombe, a heavily populated, well watered and fertile area, was once a site of settler investment and cash-cropping as well as missionary development of schools, churches and clinics. Dombe also shared a border with Zimbabwe. The two sides were linked by trade, kin and labour migration, and the border offered the opportunity for raiding. These differences shaped Renamo's ambitions and relations with local people.

In Macossa, chiefs saw Renamo's practices not as a radical break with the past but as yet another round of coercive and disruptive rule in a long tradition of the same. Macossa had been home to *prazo* war lords and the Báruè rebellion (Isaacman, 1976). It had become a semi-liberated zone during the war for independence and was an early area of Renamo infiltration. Chiefs cited parallels with Renamo's *mujhibas* in the *sipaios* (administrative police) of the colonial era; with the forced recruitment of soldiers in the practices of Frelimo guerrillas and the Báruè kings before them; with forced labour, organised through chiefs, in colonial *mutarato*. Renamo's arrival had sparked the flight of, particularly, Frelimo representatives, but also civilians and chiefs. The establishment of a chieftaincy-based administration was far from a mere resurrection of a colonial, never mind pre-colonial, hierarchy, as many chiefs (and mediums) fled, or were removed in offensives by either side, and their relatives or others had to be pressed into service (Alexander, 1994: 60–3).

Though Renamo placed sometimes 'invented' chiefs in positions of authority and paid tribute to ritual, Macossa's chiefs deeply resented Renamo's demands for food and porters. Subsistence, notably during droughts, was threatened, as was chiefs' ability to carry out rituals, which had long become reliant on access to markets for, e.g., sugar and cloth, as well as the ability to travel to regional mediums. Chiefs were able to exert only very limited control over Renamo soldiers, principally, though not only, on spiritual grounds (Alexander, 1995: 28). In peacetime the memory of Renamo was deeply ambivalent: Renamo had been only weakly accountable to local leaders, had posed a dangerous threat to production, and had largely failed to deliver social services.[24]

In Dombe, Renamo officials were more often local people, recruited from the missionary-educated men. Greater effort was made to expand services, particularly schools, again drawing on an existing supply of educated people as teachers, and bolstered by the possibility of raiding for materials across the Zimbabwean border (interviews, Dombe centre, 26–7 August 1994). Renamo's civilian hierarchy in Dombe was elaborate and modelled on Frelimo structures, with modifications drawn from colonial administration. A great deal of attention was also paid to promoting the many local churches, a popular tactic, as the previous persecution of religious leaders was a much cited source of anger against Frelimo. Extraction was perceived as less burdensome than in Macossa, largely thanks to higher and more secure levels of production – people under Frelimo control in Dombe centre (until its fall on November 1991) had had, at any rate, to feed a large number of government soldiers when supplies failed, as they regularly did. Chiefs still played a key role in organising labour and food, but they tended to perceive Renamo as a liberating force, not as yet another form of domination. In the mountainous countryside around Dombe, Renamo had in fact arrived before Frelimo had established a presence, and it was Frelimo that was seen as the aggressor. Chiefs also received donations of cloth from Renamo for rain ceremonies, a gesture made possible by the proximity of Zimbabwe's shops. Both chiefs and church leaders in this area compared Renamo favourably with the Portuguese and with Frelimo (interviews, Dombe centre, 26–7 August 1994).

Nonetheless, in both areas the war was blamed for disastrous devastation of the local economy. If Frelimo had failed to deliver economic progress, Renamo certainly did not either: the inability to migrate to jobs, to go to town to purchase goods and sell produce, the destruction of shops, were angrily voiced complaints. The devastation of market relations contributed to the popular stereotype of Renamo as an overseer of backward, traditionalist areas. However, members of these rural societies had aspirations which were in no way restricted to subsistence production, and it would be a grave mistake to see them as happily ensconced in a supposedly traditional way of life. The war, in fact, undermined key aspects of what chiefs saw as their ritual duties, notably ceremonies dependent on marketed commodities, travel and surplus production. Nor, as we shall see further below, were Renamo officials' aspirations traditionalist: they wanted the accoutrements of authority associated with Frelimo and the Portuguese, and clung to the same notions of hierarchy dependent on wealth and education, on access to clothes, radios, cement houses.

Divided administration and crises of authority, 1992–94

Following the signing of Mozambique's peace accord in October 1992, perceptions of rural authority in Manica Province built on the war years, as well as on a longer historical memory. The late colonial period constituted one key point of reference, particularly with regard to chiefs' role as tax collectors and labour mobilisers in the state's employ. Older ideas of traditional authority were also important: chiefs', mediums' and healers' role in regulating social conflict and in re-establishing a much disturbed natural order was much debated. Drawing on both colonial and post-independence periods, a strong association of authority with wealth, education and privilege also persisted. No historical period, however, seemed to offer a model of democratic practice: fear and coercion were, instead, the norm. Below I consider these issues in the course of discussing peacetime challenges to Manica's divided administration before turning to the prospects of decentralisation.

In the period after the peace accord and prior to the national elections, the territory of Manica Province was divided between government and Renamo administrations, with only tenuous connections between the two. Administration and access were hotly debated issues in the run-up to the peace accord and afterwards. The hastily concluded agreement on administration was ambiguous: Renamo agreed that public administration would conform to the national laws then in force, while the government conceded that those employed in administration in Renamo areas must be local residents and that 'traditional authorities' who exercised administrative powers would continue to do so (Hume, 1994: 134–7, 142–3). Renamo was eventually allowed to nominate administrators in areas where it controlled the district or post seat, as well as to nominate three 'assessors' to work with each provincial governor. In Manica that left Renamo with administrative control of Macossa District (three posts), as well as the posts of Mavonde in Manica District, Dombe in Sussundenga, and Búzua in Tambara (Commissão Provincial do Plano, 1993). The somewhat specious criteria used to determine control – the physical occupation of administrative centres – disguised the very patchy nature of either side's jurisdiction.[25] I consider first government-administered and then Renamo areas.

Frelimo areas

In the post-war period, government administration was marked by a severe dearth of resources, by disorganisation, demoralisation and corruption. It was undermined by Renamo's territorial control on the one hand and by donor control of resources on the other: the sense in which it 'governed' was very narrow indeed. In Manica, the provincial government's budget sufficed for little more than paying salaries and maintaining vehicles and buildings. Low salaries, coupled with insecurity over the future and the 'opportunities' of economic liberalisation, created conditions in which corruption and the diversion of energy and time into alternative economic activities were common.

District officials worked under particularly arduous conditions. Many people simply moved beyond officials' reach as they left the main roads and so-called communal villages: 'Where there are no roads, there is no government presence,' as one assistant administrator put it (interview, Catandica, 1 September 1994). Others exploited the dual administration for asylum from one side or the other. District officials struggled to muster the support of institutions such as the party (which, where it functioned, was increasingly drawn into campaigning), assemblies, judges or police, and complained particularly about their inability to mobilise unpaid labour for projects or tax collection. A district magistrate explained that word had spread 'that people working in government have to be paid – and those who aren't can stop working and no one will arrest them' (interview, Catandica, 30 August 1994). Coercive power, along with institutional and economic capacity, was thus weakened.

Ad hoc means of administration were developed as a result. In a step to extend directly the state's reach, salaried employees of district administrations were, from as early as 1986 sent out to localities to act as 'presidents' where the unpaid assemblies had broken down. A provincial official explained, 'The president of the locality represented the popular assembly in theory, but there were gaps in functioning, so we would send someone from the administrative offices to be the "president". ... Those at the locality receive salaries as functionaries of the state, not as presidents of localities' (interview, Sussundenga, 5 August 1994). *Chefes* of posts developed variable practices of relying on Frelimo secretaries, chiefs or newly invented 'official' positions to perform a minimal set of tasks such as calling people to meetings, tax collection (where it was attempted), reporting newcomers and disputes, and organising labour for road maintenance. Some *chefes* directly appointed 'deputies' and 'village presidents'; others relied entirely on Frelimo secretaries. Where the party was weak, and the chiefs were influential, some *chefes* relied primarily on chiefs, justifying this step with reference to colonial administrative practice, or simply appointing chiefs as Frelimo secretaries. However, where Renamo successfully competed for the loyalty of chiefs, party secretaries were explicitly cast as part of the state.[26]

The confusion engendered by political campaigning and the shadow of Renamo presence in areas formally under government control further complicated the difficult task of administration. One of Renamo's most effective tactics in government areas was to lobby against the payment of tax or the provision of unpaid labour, arguing that under its rule, tax would be abolished and labour remunerated. Remarking on the difficulty of mobilising labour and other resources, one *chefe* of post said, 'People aren't understanding because things are mixed. We try to get people to contribute but other parties come and say, "If you elect me, you won't have to pay". In the Frelimo and colonial periods we could do it, but now you can't tell people what to do, you can't give orders' (interview, Rotanda, 17 August 1994). Another *chefe* explained, '[Renamo] has

a way of destroying government ... They say, "There's no government, don't pay tax, the government in power isn't leading, the party in power doesn't have the capacity to work for the country"' (interview, Nhampassa, 2 September 1994).

Though multi-partyism undermined administrative capacity, its promise of the separation of party and state was viewed positively by many officials. At district and post levels, most administrative officials had given up work as Frelimo first secretaries in 1992, though some still acted as presidents of assemblies; district administrators had given up party and assembly posts in 1990. *Chefes* of posts in particular held that the elision of party and state was, and had been, one of the major obstacles to efficient administration. 'I like to have things separate. Previously things were not clear – so many jobs for one person. ... There were problems of taking a case that should have been solved by law and solving it by politics instead,' said one *chefe* of post (interview, Mouha, 18 August 1994). Arguing that they only represented a neutral state had also helped some administrative officials in coping with the challenges of Renamo strongholds within their areas. Such officials looked forward to the day when party politics would no longer impinge on administration. They imagined a modified colonial model in which chiefs, not Frelimo secretaries, would act as their apolitical subordinates. For their part, village Frelimo secretaries wanted either to become part of the administrative structure, and thus be paid for their work, or a cessation of the demands placed upon them. District Frelimo secretaries sought to avoid responsibility for meeting the demands of their constituents: 'We are only the party, not the government, so people can't come to us with all their problems,' as one put it (interview, Catandica, 31 August 1994). However, party and administrative officials warned that official authority in the rural areas was still often seen as 'the party', and that it would be a difficult perception to change.

In government areas, mobilisational capacity, lost during the war in many areas, reached an all-time low as people refused to work without pay, moved beyond the limited reach of the state, and no longer necessarily regarded Frelimo as the sole, unquestionable authority. Party and state had begun to distance themselves for a range of reasons, and chiefs often fell into the breach. Chiefs inhabited a special position in that they were envisaged as having an historical grounding for the resurrection of a lost authority which could be used to bolster administrative capacity.

Renamo areas

I now turn to consideration of efforts to bring Renamo-controlled areas under one administration, and Renamo's attempts to build a civilian administration and political party. In the post-peace period there were extreme obstacles to Renamo's exercise of authority: it had been primarily a military organisation with a rudimentary administration and had no claim to the state's resources, a situation perpetuated by the failure of efforts to reintegrate Renamo zones. The Minister of State Administration's recruitment tour in the Renamo areas of Manica, Sofala and Niassa in June 1994 proved a largely symbolic exercise. The initiative was not, at any rate, particularly ambitious, as it only involved nominating one administrative official in each area, and did not extend to other fields such as health or education. In mid-September 1994 Manica's provincial governor simply stated, 'Reintegration with Renamo has not been effective' (interview, Chimoio, 15 September 1994). Both sides had reasons for opposing reintegration: Renamo feared a loss of control, and worried over the fate of its civilian officials; Frelimo officials held Renamo representatives in disdain, feared travelling into Renamo zones, and were concerned that if services were re-introduced therein Renamo would claim credit.

What Renamo managed to do in the period between the cease-fire and elections was nonetheless dramatic. Most notably, it transformed itself from a powerful military threat into a weak political party and administration. Party work was particularly derisory within Renamo zones, perhaps because of the (largely correct) assumption that they would by definition vote Renamo. In Dombe and Macossa political delegates rarely left the administrative centres, and had little familiarity with outlying areas. Their energies were mobilised only where Frelimo sought to campaign and then usually entailed little more than (sometimes violent) harassment.[27] Renamo administration, as it was formally established in 1992 and 1993, mimicked Frelimo's in that it was based on creating 'national' (i.e. Maringue) down to post-level hierarchies for administration, health, education and agriculture. Renamo and Frelimo officials even shared the same titles. Below the post, however, Renamo relied solely on chiefs. The often recently recruited administrative officials (many of them educated young men from urban areas) at first competed with the military for authority, and subsequently found themselves hamstrung by an almost total lack of resources. Administrative officials and health and education directors operated without salaries, transport or materials of any kind save for modest and late aid contributions, which themselves became a source of tension as different groups – administration, military, chiefs – competed for their control.

While administrations were stronger where there had been a more elaborated and locally recruited wartime structure such as in Dombe, Renamo officials everywhere complained bitterly of their lack of material support. Some held that conditions had deteriorated with the end of the war, as they could no longer rely on plunder. Renamo officials had often expected to live under the conditions enjoyed by their government counterparts – they wanted salaries, vehicles, houses, suits and ties. Instead, they had to make do with a few pens and notebooks, the occasional piece of clothing acquired in town or from aid distributions, the odd radio; they lived in poster-adorned mud huts, or the roofless and windowless cement relics of former administrations and shops. As the peace wore into its second year with no change they became demoralised. Much as Frelimo, Renamo lost its capacity to mobilise unpaid labour. 'We are all waiting to receive salaries,' said one Renamo director of education as he bemoaned his inability to keep teachers at work (interview, Dombe, 26 August 1994). Moreover, as the military capacity to enforce compliance was lost with demobilisation (in Dombe and Macossa not until 1994) chiefs became more autonomous. Renamo officials had none of the assemblies or village party structures which supported their government counterparts, however weakly. Their dependence on chiefs was greater, while their ability to circumvent them, or entice them with promises of material or other reward, was weaker. Some chiefs, particularly those with a strong popular base and claim to ritual authority, were notably more assertive and critical of Renamo in mid-1994 than they had been a year earlier. They had quickly realised how limited was the reach of Renamo administration, and were keenly aware of the withdrawal of soldiers.

The issue of divided administration went unresolved up to the elections, and has continued so to the present in some areas. In Dombe, for example, little progress has been made in establishing government structures of any kind: according to press reports from mid-1995, government police were driven out of Dombe (for the fourth time) by Renamo officials and chiefs, backed by *mujhibas*. Chiefs called for their own integration into the state, for salaries or at least compensation for their work in wartime administration, for uniforms, and for information on who had really won the 1994 elections.[28]

Implications for decentralisation

Decentralisation and the concern with promoting 'civil society' came amidst the changes outlined so far, but gave little recognition to the vested interests, political practices and attitudes towards official authority which would have to be confronted. The Municipalities Law, passed just prior to the national elections, drew heavily on colonial precedent (Grest, 1995) and contained many gaps and vagaries.

The most important changes introduced by the law fell at district level, where (in rural areas) there will be an elected administrator and assembly, a municipal council appointed and headed by the administrator, and provision for some role to be allotted to 'traditional authorities'.[29] The jurisdiction of these bodies is very wide, including responsibility for social welfare, health, education and roads, the promotion of development, protection of the environment, the management of land, public and private markets, civil protection, control of fire and calamities, and compilation of the civil register (article 4). The municipalities have powers of self-organisation, planning and budgeting; the power to acquire, administer, tax and alienate resources, as well as to pass and enforce Acts, to contract with public and private entities and to litigate (article 6). They may establish administrative delegations at post and locality level (article 12), and are advised to co-ordinate their activities in a range of fields with 'traditional authorities' (articles 8–9). In addition, the municipality is to be subject to supervision, particularly regarding finance and the legality of decisions, by higher levels of the state (articles 37–9).

Major gaps in the legislation concerned some of the most important and controversial aspects of decentralisation. Sources of finance, the level of support from central government, the relationship between the new municipalities and line Ministries, the terms of service of municipality members, the nature of the supervisory powers given to higher levels of government and the timing of elections were all left for later clarification at the time of the law's enactment (see Hanlon, 1995). These issues were of great concern to provincial government officials interviewed in 1994. They were worried particularly about staff and finance, as well as about the control to be exercised over aid agencies, some of which wielded larger budgets than the provincial government. The issues of finance and staff are key to successful decentralisation anywhere (Tordoff, 1994). Also important, though not so frequently discussed, are the attitudes to reform held by those whom decentralisation will affect. I focus on attitudes to two aspects of the Municipalities Law: the election of a district administrator and the role to be played by chiefs.

Electing an administrator

Many officials, as well as others, expressed misgivings about electing district authorities. Incumbent administrative officials feared for their jobs, and saw the idea of electing an administrator as a recipe for disaster: an elected official was considered inappropriate to executive decision-making or implementing policies, and might not have the proper qualifications. One administrator commented, 'The one who will be elected is the one who greets everyone in the road, who drinks beer with people. The adminstrator has to force people to work – people are lazy and they won't do anything unless they are forced.' He drew a distinction between someone who was elected – a representative – and the executive: 'The representative should only receive people like you [myself and my research assistant] and preside over ceremonies. The executive is what does things' (interview, Sussundenga, 5 August 1994). Such views were firmly rooted in the existing relationship between assemblies and administrators, and between them and their 'constituents'. Renamo administrators stressed that people qualified to hold the position of district administrator were simply not to be found in the rural areas. Lower-level officials – *chefes* of posts and presidents of localities – added other concerns. They regularly expressed the fear that competition for elected posts would create instability, even lead to violence, and repoliticise administration at a time when the opposite was needed. However, some *chefes* welcomed elections as an opportunity to bolster their authority. One explained, 'This is now a time of trouble. The government has no force, it is weak, it isn't legitimate. We at the post have to work with people. If we are chosen by the people we are legitimate, we can't be rejected. ... I would very much like the chance to be elected – it would give me a stronger position to work from' (interview, Rotanda, 17 August 1994).

Among others, such as church leaders, party leaders, deputies of assemblies, and chiefs, views regarding the merits of electing a district administrator provided sobering insights into local assumptions about the exercise of authority and perceptions of the possibility of reform. The idea of electing an administrator was often first met with frank disbelief. On further discussion, it was deemed positive because it meant that the administrator could not be arbitrarily transferred and protected by higher-level officials. As one assembly president remarked, 'If the adminstrator is nominated, he doesn't care because he has the support of the provincial level and so he doesn't do anything' (interview, Catandica, 31 August 1994).

In many interviews a debate developed over the qualifications of an elected administrator. People sought a careful balance, seeking to mute, though not overturn, the characteristics they associated with official authority. The administrator should be local in the sense that he should speak local languages, but not too local, as he might then engage in nepotism or be subject to witchcraft. He should be kind, and should have pity for people, but must also be educated, things which were taken to be contradictory almost by definition: an education implied a high-handed manner and disdain for rural people, their languages and culture, and the need for a high standard of living. He should be rich, but not too rich – a poor man would not command respect and would steal from public goods; a man who was too rich would not understand people's suffering, or might be jealous of others' success. A group of church leaders in Báruè District explained that 'All people steal when they are in power – the secretaries, the chiefs. ... [But] the way a rich person steals is different from the way a poor person steals: he will steal, but not too much' (interview, Catandica, 1 September 1994). Distrust of all holders of authority was commonplace, as was the association of education and relative wealth with authority.[30] In some interviews, concern over education extended to questioning people's very ability to *choose*, let alone *be*, an administrator: some only wanted the right to reject an administrator nominated from above. There was

also widespread fear that instability would follow from competition for the elected posts. Renamo representatives envisaged a situation in which Renamo won the district elections only to be hamstrung by continued Frelimo control at provincial level.

In short, locally identified problems with an elected district body were significant: existing officials feared job loss and doubted the efficacy of an elected official, though some welcomed the chance to enhance their authority through elections. 'Local leaders' often felt unable or ill equipped to take up a position of authority themselves, or even to choose others to do so, owing to their poverty and ill education. The legacy of previous years entrenched the view that everything was decided from above, and by those with access to education and wealth, to suits and cars. Moreover, competition was considered destabilising, and sparked fears of the repoliticisation of the state. It was unclear to people how someone could rule (and 'rule' was the only term used, not 'represent,' etc.) in such a context. Finally, economic conditions were partly behind the idea that development, however it was defined, could not proceed without coercion. These attitudes also shaped views regarding the role of chiefs under the new law.

'Traditional authority'

An aspect of the Municipalities Law which has been much vaunted in Mozambique as a means of ensuring that local interests are better represented is the role offered to 'traditional authorities'. Though not giving chiefs official status, and allowing local variation, the law does elaborate with great specificity the areas in which municipalities may like to 'collaborate' with chiefs (article 9). The law combines an idealised vision of chiefly authority with a set of duties which might have been drawn from a Portuguese manual on administration. Suggested roles ranged from the vague 'maintenance of harmony and social peace' and 'preservation of the physical and cultural inheritance' to a long list of duties such as the management of land, the collection of taxes, opening and maintaining secondary roads, census taking, preventing epidemics and infectious diseases, the control of illegal fires, hunting and fishing, policy implementation and the promotion of productive activity.

Officials' views (both government and Renamo) on chieftaincy offered little comfort for worries that chiefs were more likely to act as enforcers of state intervention than as representatives of 'communities'. Almost without exception, officials expressed great nostalgia for a late colonial era model of administration. Frelimo district administrators tended to claim that chiefs were weak and held pernicious 'obscurantist' views but that they could, nonetheless, be easily reinstated in their colonial roles, and that this would be invaluable in reviving effective administration. They cited chiefs' potential (and sometimes actual) utility in collecting tax, locating criminals, solving disputes, acting as messengers. They wanted chiefs to be paid, and so beholden to the administrative hierarchy. Some officials called for a return to the use of administrative police, the *sipaios*. One *chefe* of post remarked that, in the colonial era, 'when the administrator or *régulo* went out, he always went out with police. Now we only have the general police for all crimes. We want police for the administration itself, like the *sipaios*' (interview, Nhampassa, 2 September 1994).

However, some officials, particularly at post level, had reservations regarding chiefs. They noted that chieftaincy was much disrupted, that there were conflicts over territory, over hierarchy and titles, that chiefs had their own personal interests which might not reflect those of a wider community. Conflict was, in fact, often a consequence of early initiatives to give chiefs responsibilities. In some areas an entirely new hierarchy would need to be created as chiefs had fled or died during the preceding twenty years. *Chefes* of posts saw benefits in chiefs gaining recognition largely (and in contrast to district administrators) in terms, first of their access to spiritual knowledge considered beyond the ken of officials and Frelimo secretaries, particularly regarding rain but also the control of disease, evil spirits, and witchcraft and the enforcement of rules regarding sacred places. Second, they regarded chiefs as politically neutral, and thus as a good replacement for Frelimo secretaries.

Chiefs themselves, in both Renamo and Frelimo areas, also invoked a colonial model, focusing on their need for the accoutrements of officialdom – houses, uniforms, police and salaries – and prominently setting among their appropriate roles tax collection and labour mobilisation. However, they often feared to make claims to authority, many stating that they had to wait for officials to give them back their powers, since they had taken them away. The memory of Frelimo's denunciations was a bitter one, even where there had been collaboration with chiefs. In Renamo areas, chiefs were also concerned to distance themselves from their recent work in organising food and labour; some were more than sceptical of an alliance with Renamo officials. Chiefs were nonetheless exercising authority in a number of ways, such as settling disputes, solving cases of, e.g., witchcraft or adultery, engaging in disputes over titles or territory or access to aid. In southern Mozambique chiefs were reportedly demanding taxes, and fees from migrant labourers, as they had in the colonial period. They cited the Municipalities Law as authority (Hanlon, 1995: 6). In other respects, chiefs' practices in 1993 and 1994 indicated that their role as community representatives should not be taken for granted: they represented claims to authority and control over resources by specific groups, usually elders of autochthonous lineages, and could threaten the interests of others such as those defined as outsiders or those who had participated in their earlier marginalisation.

Chiefs were also far from politically neutral. Some were openly allied with either side, or found themselves vigorously courted by party leaders in the run-up to the 1994 elections. Frelimo party leaders defended chiefs' importance, a line strongly backed by Manica's provincial first secretary. Renamo leaders resented Frelimo's courtship of chiefs, seeing it as an opportunistic transgression of their political programme. In the post-election period Renamo leaders have sought to prevent or preempt government lobbying of chiefs, while national leaders of the Frelimo government have held high-profile meetings with chiefs in an effort to extend their influence into areas where government structures are weak or non-existent.[31] Conundra such as that noted above in Dombe are likely to multiply as competition for chiefs' allegiance and, in effect, efforts to use them as an extension of the state, continue.

Among the range of local leaders other than chiefs – from presidents of villages to deputies of assemblies to businessmen and Frelimo secretaries – views of chiefs again had a strong colonial resonance, as well as commonly causally linked problems of production, drought and witchcraft (or in Macossa a plague of rats) with Frelimo's treatment of the chiefs and the ancestors. Even women's organisations – both the former Frelimo Organisation of Mozambican Women (OMM) and Renamo's League of Women – strongly backed the chiefs. Rather than seeing them as oppressive patriarchs, they saw in chiefs a means of reestablishing control over youth, of inculcating a lost sense of morality, in terms particularly of sexual relations and respect for elders.[32] However, the women's groups, as well as others, were sceptical of an alliance between chiefs and the state, arguing it would distance chiefs from their communities. They also saw economic reconstruction as a prerequisite to the proper execution of a range of ceremonies, particularly those for rain: poverty, not only Frelimo's denunciations, undercut ritual.

Finally, it bears noting that chiefs' knowledge and authority were far from unchallenged either within their numbers or by other social groups. Disputes within and between royal lineages were common, a function of displacement, the years of repression, and competition sparked by new promises of recognition. In addition, the prolific and rapidly expanding Apostolic and Pentecostal churches in Manica's rural areas sometimes rejected chiefs' and *n'angas'* (diviner-healers) explanations of evil and of the spirit world more widely. To some church leaders the idea of chiefs exercising administrative powers was problematic, while some chiefs viewed the churches with hostility. Moreover, church leaders and *n'angas* alike were regularly subject to accusations of corruption, particularly as regards their efforts to solve what was widely described as a dangerous proliferation of evil spirit possession.[33] The commonly expressed distrust of spiritual authority, and lack of consensus regarding who, if anyone, could control life-threatening evil spirits, indicated a crisis of authority that went well beyond the state.

In short, there was a widespread desire for chiefs to resume various roles, and a strong popular belief that their previous ill treatment had contributed to a range of hardships. However, granting official authority to chiefs had already become controversial, and did not appear likely to address the wider challenge of transforming an authoritarian political culture. For officials, chiefs seemed to offer a cheap, willing and apolitical means of extending state authority, and thus redressing the quandaries produced by multipartyism and an inability to mobilise resources or labour by other means. They often invoked a colonial model, as did chiefs and others. However, chiefs were not always above party politics, nor did their interests necessarily reflect those of a wider community. Moreover, conflicts were common within and among royal lineages. Such conflicts were brought to the fore by official efforts to recruit chiefs as a means of extending the state, and may well become more severe.

Conclusion

The Mozambican state, and Mozambican society more widely, is experiencing a profound crisis of authority. The nature of the crisis is rooted in the practices and pressures of previous years. It is a product of the post-independence state's failure fully to transform Portuguese notions of authority, its coerciveness and militarisation, its blurring of distinctions between state and party, attacks on spiritual authority, and inability to deliver or protect economic progress. Renamo was effective in undermining Frelimo's mobilisational capacity, its territorial control and its efforts to deliver services. As an administrative or political organisation, however, it did not offer viable economic alternatives or opportunities for democratic participation. Neither Frelimo nor Renamo inculcated a political practice which prepared the way for democratic demands, or for an independent 'civil society'. In the post-election period, rural leaders, including those of Renamo, sought to become part of the state, or at least its favoured allies, more often than they sought to restrain or reform it.

Overcoming the crises of authority in Mozambique is certainly a pressing task. The limbo of Renamo areas inhibits reconstruction and, for the Frelimo government, the demoralisation of its officials, its reliance on less than efficacious forms of mobilisation, and its dependence on aid are debilitating. An exploration of local views regarding the Municipalities Law's formula of district elections and collaboration with chiefs, however, provides a sobering insight into the potential obstacles to political reform. The fear of renewed politicisation of administration and further instability, the perception that the vast majority of rural people could not exercise official authority, and the possibility of chiefs becoming a coercive and self-interested extension of the state, were all important issues. In addition, the context of extreme poverty and Renamo's continued influence focused the Frelimo government's energies on means of cheaply extending the state's reach, not on improved representation. Local-level administrative officials worried particularly over the difficulties of mobilising resources and labour. Transforming perceptions of the state as a coercive mobiliser of unpaid labour, as a structure to be avoided if it cannot be joined, will depend upon economic gains, as well as changing notions of authority which, through their association with wealth and education, are by definition beyond the reach of the vast majority.

Notes

[1] For example, see the official and academic views in Guambe and Cuerenia (n.d.), and papers presented to the 'Conferência sobre Moçambique pós guerra: desafios e realidades', Instituto Superior de Relações Internacionais and Centro de Estudos Estratégicos e Internacionais, Maputo, 14–18 December 1992, especially those by Magode and Khân, Lundin, Guambe and Machel.

[2] Assembly of the Republic of Mozambique, Law 3/94. The law is known as the *Lei dos municípios* or the *Lei do quadro institucional dos municípios*. See Grest (1995) for the series of seminars which led up to the law.

[3] Ranger (1992) surveys the varying role given civil society by southern African intellectuals. For recent critiques of, and alternative views to, the literature on civil society and democratisation see inter alia Lemarchand (1992); Bratton and van de Walle (1992); Robinson (1994).

[4] Conditions were difficult in terms of both logistics and negotiating the political tensions of the time. Many officials and chiefs were interviewed more than once, but other interviews could not be repeated.

[5] Renamo is sometimes also known by its English acronym MNR. I do not intend to go into the movement's origins as they are well documented elsewhere. See Flower (1987); Hall (1990); Vines (1991); Young (1990).

[6] This characterisation of continuities in official privilege and arrogance was regularly depicted by local leaders. The official hierarchy and the privileges that went with it obviously varied over time and among individuals. See Hanlon (1984); Egero (1987).

[7] The colonial three-tier hierarchy of 'traditional authority' (*régulo, chefe de grupo, chefe de povoação*) was imposed whether or not it fitted, and some leaders were excluded for political or other reasons. Those recognised as traditional authorities did not necessarily include all claimants to (or holders of) authority and were not necessarily (though they could be) popular with their constituents. Local terms for traditional offices vary. I generally use the term 'chief' as shorthand for *régulos* and *chefes de grupo*, for simplicity's sake and because the latter tend to act fairly autonomously. Officials usually use the term *régulo* to mean any level of the hierarchy, while chiefs and others (outside Macossa and Báruè) use the term *mambo* for the top two levels and a range of other terms (*sagauta, samwendo, sabhaka, mfumo*) for lower levels. In Macossa and parts of Báruè the hierarchy is topped by a *nhacuaua*, followed by a *tsapanda* and *mfumo*.

[8] In Manica the leaders of dynamising groups sometimes became Frelimo secretaries, and at other times existed parallel to them after 1978. Party

structures also proliferated on state farms and in factories. See GPM (1979) on party structures generally and Direcção Provincial de Indústria e Energia (1986) on the spread of party structures in 'production units'. The chronology and nature of the spread of party structures varied among provinces. Here I refer only to the experience of Manica Province.

[9] The initial administrative hierarchy within districts had only two levels: district and locality. There were usually three or four localities in a district. Confusingly, in 1986 the localities were renamed posts and were subdivided into localities, each headed by the president of the assembly at that level. I refer to the pre-1986 locality as 'post' throughout to avoid confusion.

[10] See provincial government and assembly reports for the 1970s and 1980s. GPM (1984a) contains a frank discussion of the problems faced by assemblies, including a strong critique of district assemblies by their provincial counterpart for failing to address the 'problems of the people', instead limiting themselves to 'rituals of obedience to the protocol rules followed by the hierarchically superior organs'. The charge might also have been made of the provincial assembly. I discuss these issues at greater length in Alexander (1995).

[11] E.g. interviews, Sussundenga centre, 30 November 1993; Nhaurombe, 2 November 1993; Lundin (1992b).

[12] On the early spread of war in post-independence Manica see especially GPM (1979), which enumerates and describes attacks in 1978, including the early Renamo's not unsuccessful attempts (in Frelimo's assessment) to mobilise popular support through attacks on and denunciations of unpopular officials, communal villages, low pay, labour on state farms, collective production, etc. For Rhodesian incursions see Martin and Johnson (1981).

[13] That people joined Renamo both by choice and involuntarily was uncontested by rural Frelimo officials, who stressed the complications of meeting a relative or neighbour who had crossed to Renamo. Nor was the common perception of official positions as dangerous and undesirable controversial, e.g. interviews, Chuala and Nhampassa, 3 September 1994; Nhaurombe, 2 November 1993; Rotanda, 17 August 1994.

[14] See Alexander (1994: 43-5); ARPAC (1993); Englund (1994); Geffray (1991); Xadreque and Americo (1990).

[15] E.g. see complaints to this effect in GPM (1982a, c).

[16] A stronger change in official attitudes towards chiefs, and towards what had been condemned as 'obsurantism', dated from around 1990, coinciding with the introduction of multi-partyism and organisations such as Ametramo, the officially recognised traditional healers' organisation. The Ministry of State Administration and Ministry of Culture openly discussed the issue of chieftaincy in the late 1980s and 1990s. See Ministério da Administração Estatal (1991, 1993); ARPAC (1993); Xadreque and Americo (1990).

[17] The emphasis on military concerns in Manica was not to the exclusion of other goals. In other provinces where the war arrived later different concerns dominated. E.g. Alice Dinerman (personal communication) argues that the imperative of production remained central in Nampula.

[18] Provincial government and assembly reports for the 1980s chronicle the reduction of control over territory and the number of functioning institutions.

[19] I deal with the government's reduced ability to provide social or economic services in some detail in Alexander (1995: 17-20, appendix one).

[20] On communal villages in Manica see Alexander (1994, 1995: 22); Hanlon (1984: 129); Raposo (1991).

[21] The loss of Rhodesian backing as a result of Zimbabwe's independence in 1980 caused Renamo a severe crisis but the movement emerged stronger than ever in the early 1980s, thanks to South African support.

[22] See provincial assembly reports for the 1980s.

[23] A full eighty-five accommodation centres existed by the end of 1989, with a population of 117,102 people. These centres were supported by a range of aid agencies. See GPM (1990). Also see Human Rights Watch (1992: 78-83) on the sometimes terrible consequences of these camps

and of 'recuperations'.

[24] Clinics were reserved for use by soldiers, while schools were introduced, on a very limited scale, and with almost no materials, only in the last year of war (interviews with people displaced from Macossa, Macossa Cruzamento, 2 September 1994).

[25] According to UN reports (UNOHAC, 1994), of thirty-seven administrative posts, Renamo controlled the majority of, or all, schools in thirteen posts (one-third of all schools), while the government held a majority of or all schools in twenty-four posts (just over half of all schools). Well over a third of posts, and nearly half if we exclude the urban locations of Chimoio city, were divided between the two sides. (Just over 10 per cent of all schools were not identified with either side.)

[26] Interviews with *chefes* of posts and locality presidents, Rotanda, 17 August 1994; Mouha, 18 August 1994; Nhampassa, 2 September 1994; Chuala, 3 September 1994; Catandica, 1 September 1994, Chôa, 5 September 1994. And see Administração do Distrito do Tambara (1994); Administração do Distrito de Manica (1993a).

[27] My impression from interviewing in Renamo areas was that, in comparison with administrative officials, political delegates were extremely unpopular. They were usually recently posted single men with no connection with the areas in which they were based, who often had a military background. Outside Renamo-administered areas, political delegates seemed more popular and were certainly more active.

[28] See *Noticias*, 16, 26, 27, 29 June 1995; 3, 7, 8, 13, 14 July 1995; *Domingo*, 2 July 1995. Other cases of Renamo, in alliance with chiefs, refusing to yield to government administrators were cited in Gondola District of Manica (*Noticas*, 28 June 1995). Dombe has remained a particularly vexed case, in part owing to allegations that Zimbabwean insurgents, dubbed '*Chimwenjes*', are living there under Renamo protection.

[29] The assembly will have between thirty-five and sixty-one members, and both the assembly and the administrator will serve for five-year terms. The municipal council is an executive body made up of five to twelve people who enjoy the administrator's 'personal and political' confidence. At least half their number must be members of the assembly. See articles 25, 26 and 27.

[30] See Bratton and Liatto-Katundu (1994) for interesting parallels with and divergences from voter attitudes in Zambia.

[31] For example, *Noticias* 10, 13 July 1995 reported President Chissano's meeting with chiefs in the Renamo stronghold of Sofala and Renamo's strenuous attempts to prevent the same. There were also reports from Nampula of Renamo and government officials competing to get 'their' candidate recognised as chief (*Noticias*, 10 July 1995).

[32] Renamo's league went further than the OMM, working with chiefs to reintroduce, or introduce, previously banned practices such as tattooing. There was, however, irony in the defence of 'tradition' by some members of Renamo's league who came from areas far from their current postings. For example, the head of the league in Dombe was from Zambezia, where notions of tradition were very different, and she was still struggling to learn Chindau.

[33] This is a complicated question which I have not the space to deal with adequately here. For a more detailed discussion see Alexander (1995: 561).

References

Administração do Distrito de Manica. 1993a. Acta No. 01/93. Manica
——. 1993b. Acta No. 02/93. Manica.
Administração do Distrito de Tambara. 1994. 'Diário de serviço do Mês de Julho de 1994'. Tambara.
ARPAC (Ministry of Culture). 1993. 'Analise do momento actual do ponto de vista da problemática socio-cultural e o papel da autoridade tradiçional africana neste contecto'. Beira: ARPAC.
Alexander, J. 1994. 'Terra e autoridade politica no pós-guerra em Moçambique: o caso da provincia de Manica', *Arquivo* (Maputo) 16, 5–94.
——. 1995. *Political Change in Manica Province: implications for the decentralization*

of power. Maputo: Friedrich Ebert Stiftung.
Borges Coelho, J. P. 1993. 'Protected Villages and Communal Villages in the Mozambican Province of Tete, 1968–82: a history of state resettlement policies, development and war'. D.Phil. thesis, University of Bradford.
Bratton, M., and Liatto-Katundu, B. 1994. 'A Focus Group assessment of political attitudes in Zambia', *African Affairs* 93 (373), 535-63.
Bratton, M., and van de Walle, N. 1992. 'Popular protest and political transition in Africa', *Comparative Politics* 24 (4), 419–42.
de Brito, L. 1988. 'Une relecture nécessaire: la genèse du parti-état Frelimo', *Politique Africaine* 29, 15-27.
——. 1991. 'Le Frelimo et la construction de l'État national au Mozambique: le sens de la reference au marxisme, 1962–1983'. Thèse de doctorat, Universite de Paris VIII, Vincennes.
Cahen, M. 1985. 'État et pouvoir populaire dans le Mozambique indépendent', *Politique Africaine* 19, 36–60.
——. 1990. 'Le Mozambique: une nation africaine de langue officielle portugaise?' *Canadian Journal of African Studies* 24 (3), 315–47.
Comissão Provincial do Plano. 1993. 'Balanço das actividades realizadas no primeiro semestre'. Chimoio.
Cravinho, J. 1995. 'Mozambique: modernizing, marketing and maize growing'. MS, Oxford.
Direcçao Provincial de Indústria e Energia. 1986. *Relatório das actividades desenvolvidas durante o penodo de 1975 a 1985*. Chimoio: Ministério de Indústria e Energia.
Egero, B. 1987. *Mozambique: a dream undone. The political economy of democracy, 1975–84.* Uppsala: Nordiska Afrikainstitutet.
Englund, H. 1994. 'Which Peasant, which War? From revolution to Renamo in a Mozambican village'. MS, Manchester.
Flower, K 1987. *Serving Secretly*. London: John Murray.
Geffray, C. 1988. 'Fragments d'un discours du pouvoir, 1975–1985: du bon usage d'une méconnaissance scientifique', *Politique Africaine* 29, 71–86.
——. 1991. *A causa das armas: antropologia da guerra contemporânea em Moçambique*. Oporto: Edições Afrontamento.
Governo da Provincia de Manica. 1979. *Relatório anual, 1978*. Chimoio: República Popular de Moçambique.
——. 1982a. *Relatório anual, 1981*. Chimoio: República Popular de Moçambique.
——. 1982b. *Relatório mensal*. Chimoio: Republica Popular de Moçambique.
——. 1982c. *XIII Reunião da Assembleia Provincial*. Chimoio: República Popular de Moçambique.
——. 1982d. *14a Reunião da Assembleia Provincial*. Chimoio: República Popular de Moçambique.
——. 1983. *XVIII Sessão da Assembleia Provincial*. Chimoio: República Popular de Moçambique.
——. 1984a. *XIX Sessão da Assembleia Provincial*. Chimoio: República Popular de Moçambique.
——. 1984b. *XX Sessão da Assembleia Provincial*. Chimoio: República Popular de Moçambique.
——. 1990. *Relatório anual, 1989*. Chimoio: República Popular de Moçambique.
Grest, J. 1995. 'Urban management, local government reform and the democratisation process in Mozambique: Maputo city, 1975–90', *Journal of Southern African Studies* 21 (1), 147–64.
Guambe, J. 1992. 'The Problems of Structuring Government in a Democratic Process: central government/local government'. Paper presented to Conferência sobre Moçambique pós-guerra: 'desafios e realidades', ISRI/CEEI, Maputo, 14–18 December.
Guambe, J. and Cuerenia, A. nd. *O processo de descentralização em Moçambique e seu enquadramento no actual sistema de administração pública*. Maputo: Ministério da Administração Estatal.
Hall, M. 1990. 'The Mozambican National Resistance Movement (Renamo): a study in the destruction of an African country', *Africa*, 60 (1), 39–68.
Hanlon, J. 1984. *Mozambique: the revolution under fire*. London: Zed Press.
——. 1995. *Mozambique Peace Process Bulletin* 15. Amsterdam: AWEPA.
Human Rights Watch. 1992. *Conspicuous Destruction: war, famine and the*

reform process in Mozambique. New York: Human Rights Watch.

Hume, C. 1994. *Ending Mozambique's War: the role of mediation and good offices.* Washington, D.C.: US Institute of Peace.

Isaacman, A. 1976. *The Tradition of Resistance in Mozambique: anti-colonial activity in the Zambezi valley, 1850–1921.* London: Heinemann.

Lemarchand, R. 1992. 'Uncivil states and civil societies: how illusion became reality', *Journal of Modern African Studies* 30 (2), 177-91.

Lundin, I. B. 1992a. 'The Concept of Democracy: the transformation of a given model into a standard model'. Paper presented to Conferência sobre Moçambique pós-guerra: 'Desafios e Realidades', ISRI/CEEI, Maputo, 14–18 December.

——. 1992b. 'Relatório de trabalho de campo nas provincias de Sofala e Manica. A autoridade/poder tradiçional e suas bases de legitimidade'. Maputo: Ministério da Administração Estatal.

Machel, G. 1992. 'Energizing the Civil Society in Mozambique: the role of NGOs in development in Mozambique'. Paper presented to Conferência sobre Moçambique pós-guerra: 'Desafios e Realidades', ISRI/CEEI, Maputo, 14-18 December.

Magode, J. M., and Khan, A. 1992. 'The Unitary State and the National Question'. Paper presented to Conferencia sobre Moçambique pós-guerra: 'Desafios e Realidades', ISRI/CEEI, Maputo, 14-18 December.

Martin, D., and Johnson, P. 1981. *The Struggle for Zimbabwe.* London: Faber.

Ministério da Administração Estatal. 1991. 'Reforma dos orgãos locais'. Maputo.

——. 1993. 'Reforms dos orgãos locais e o papel da autoridade tradiçional'. Maputo.

Ranger, T. O. 1992. 'Legitimacy, Civil Society and the State in Africa', first Alexander Visiting Professorial inaugural lecture, University of Western Australia, 2 December.

Raposo, I. 1991. *0 viver de hoje e de ontem: aldeia e musha.* Maputo: Documento de Trabalho.

Robinson, P. 1994. 'Democratization: understanding the relationship between regime change and the culture of politics', *African Studies Review* 37 (1), 39-68.

Roesch, O. 1992. 'Mozambique unravels? The retreat to tradition', *Southern Africa Report* (Toronto), May, 27-30.

Sabonete, C. L. 1994. 'Administração pública moçambicana: resume histórico'. Paper presented to the Seminário sobre decentralização, Movimento Pela Paz, Friedrich Ebert Stiftung, Governo da Província de Sofala, 8–9 February, Beira.

Tordoff, W. 1994. 'Decentralisation: comparative experience in Commonwealth Africa', *Journal of Modern African Studies* 32 (4), 555-80.

UNOHAC. 1994. *Província de Manica, Sector da Educação. Inventário de instalações e pessoal* (EPI). Chimoio: UNOHAC.

Vines, A. 1991. *Renamo: terrorism in Mozambique.* London: James Currey.

Young, T. 1990. 'The MNR/Renamo: external and internal dynamics', *African Affairs* 89 (357), 491-509.

Xadreque, A. and Americo, M. 1990. 'As Autoridades Gentílicas de Beira: segundo relatório provisório de investigação'. Beira: Núcleo de Projecto ARPAC (Ministry of Culture) de Sofala.

Acknowledgements

Research for this article would not have been possible without funding from the Friedrich Ebert Stiftung – Maputo and the co-operation of the Mozambican Ministry of State Administration. I also draw on earlier research supported by the University of Wisconsin's Land Tenure Center and Mozambique's Ministry of Agriculture. Thanks to Alice Dinerman, João Cravinho, JoAnn McGregor, Alberto Mourata Silva, Bernhard Weimer, Harry West and the *Africa* referees for comments on earlier versions. For his research and translation skills, as well as his inexhaustible patience and ingenuity, I am indebted to Leo Chikodzi. Thanks also to Luis de Menezes for help in the initial stages of research in 1994.

SALLY FALK MOORE
Post-Socialist Micro-Politics

Reference
Africa, vol. 66/4, 1996, pp. 587–605

'Modernity in Africa' is a theme that evokes visual images. From the public processions of shiny official cars in town to the cherished bicycles of less prosperous urbanites all the way to the plastic pails in rural homesteads, there are hundreds of recognisably 'modern' objects to be seen everywhere. They all have meaning in the exhibition of up-to-date respectability, let alone in the competition for prestige (Warnier, 1993). The hierarchical layers of society are clearly marked. At a beer drinking party in the countryside, bottled drink is for the elite; locally produced calabashes of home-brew are for ordinary villagers. Big gold watches and new briefcases are masculine status markers for administrators. There is a ubiquitous system of conspicuous consumption. It is easy for the observer to play Thorstein Veblen in town and in the bush.

But there are other, less visible, forms of the modern, recognised both from an African point of view and from that of outsiders. The way the arenas of status competition are organised, even the prizes, are notably subject to significant transformation. Now, with the Cold War over, the location and terms of competition have once again shifted in many parts of the world. Africa is no exception. This article will describe a few recent instances of energetic political striving over newly available resources. These seekings of power and goods were in process when I visited Kilimanjaro in 1993. Events around that time at four different levels of organisation will be sketched here, each involving different political aims. The action in these social fields ranged from polite strategising to lethal violence. Disquietingly enough, the violence, in fact, succeeded in its political aims.

At roughly the same time all of the following things were happening. (1) There was a bid for national power, epitomised by the founding of the local branch of a new national party. (2) A violent structural dispute inside the Lutheran Church erupted over control of assets. This led to destruction of property and a number of deaths. (3) A factional fight took place in a sub-village involving both witchcraft accusations and the authority of the village leader. (4) There was a significant quarrel within a divided patrilineage over the proposed fusion of its two major segments. The leader who advocated fusion wanted a larger constituency under his leadership. Over a period of a year, embellishing his arguments with pious references to the ancestors, he managed the political manoeuvring that ultimately enabled him to win.

The rhetoric and rationale of the struggles in each of these arenas were quite different. Political modernity on Kilimanjaro is no single, uniform, communal way of being. Some of the prizes in the four arenas have just become available, and there is much in the style of the effort to get hold of them that is new. But, as we shall see, there also are plenty of old stories incorporated into the new games. Particular local histories are being fused with new national circumstances. Recent changes in the global order of things set political liberalisation in motion. There were considerable repercussions in Tanzania.

Because the restructurings that are going on are part of an ongoing historical process, it is not altogether possible to predict which local shifts will he durable and which evanescent. There is nothing especially African about that. Many of the ideas that surround political activity anywhere have a limited shelf life. What is politically current and up-to-the-moment may be as time-dated as any carton of milk from an American supermarket. In Tanzania in 1961 Nyerere's brand of socialism was 'in'. Now the post-Cold War policies of the World Bank and the International Monetary Fund supply the current rhetoric as well as the credit. A free market, privatisation, and multi-party democracy have been designated as 'in'.

Preparing the same kinds of ideological sandwiches for Africa that it creates for home consumption, the industrial part of the world packages objects and ideologies 'to go'. But it would be a signal error to think of what is contemporary in Africa today as simply made up of such foreign exports. On Kilimanjaro there is also an ongoing local production of 'how to': how to be, how to think, what to have, what to do, how to organise things, all within the parameters of possibility set by happenings on the large scale. Continuously under construction, being invented, is a locally formed version of how to proceed, individually and collectively.

The attempt is to bring the new objects and the new rules of the political game under local control, to integrate them into local affairs as far as can be managed. That is the local 'domestication' of modernity. As far as possible it is done without giving up everything that was there before. The question is, how to be *au courant* without losing what you have invested in, who you are, what has already been put into self and relationships, into arrangements and things, into accumulated knowledge. The issue for the ambitious is how to gain ground, how to mobilise others, what to invent, and, of the resources that are already there, how to retrofit them for use in the new social machinery. That is always the game, full of risky attempts and complications, and not only in Africa, and not only today.

To try to communicate a sense of the multiplicity of forces in motion, I have set myself the task of looking at several separate but contemporaneous mini-fields of political action. Such a project is inherently analytically challenging. The question that must be addressed, along with the details, is whether there is any logical coherence to this aggregate of instances. The distinctiveness of each is partly a consequence of tracing a particular theme through all of the narratives. Tracing the way preexisting local identities and old commitments were deployed in each arena tends to particularise each situation. But, despite the particularities, there is an obvious overarching causal coherence involved. Certain common conditions surround competition in Tanzania today. The national party is much less powerful than it was. Some of its former assets are in the reach of others. Much greater freedom of assembly and expression exists than has been possible for decades. The open pursuit of material gain and political power has new legitimacy. Everyone is under relentless economic pressure doubtless intensified by the continuing rapidity of population increase. The list could go on. How is one to think about these myriad components, conjunctures, and combinants? How is analysis to proceed? In trying to describe and reflect on the many odd-shaped pieces of this puzzle, one can understand the aptness of Rabinow's comment that 'Post-modernist pastiche is both a critical position and a dimension of our contemporary world' (1986: 252).

A new political party: World-Bank-speak on Kilimanjaro

In Tanzania the shift from a one-party to a multi-party system was officially approved in July 1992. Six months later I was told that by that time twenty-three parties had already been formed. One of these new parties, under the acronym Chadema (*Chama cha Demokrasia na Maendeleo*), was in the process of launching itself on Kilimanjaro at the time of my 1993 winter visit. The party's charter was an unremarkable exemplar of standardised international donor discourse.

A prospectus for the Chadema party stated its 'Basic Principles and Objectives'. The document overtly demonstrated the globalisation of a certain post-socialist political rhetoric. Needless to say, the socialist rhetoric of the previous regime had also originated in an international movement. Like the great world religions, the philosophical styles of national political legitimation today tend to be derived from a supra-national discourse.

Almost all the right-thinking international donor watchwords were in the Chadema document: 'freedom and democracy', 'rights and freedom of every individual', 'accountability on the part of public officials'. 'Non-governmental organisations' were to be encouraged, as was the 'private sector'. A regime of private property was to be installed. Words were not minced about the negative effects of 'corruption' or about the 'fear of nationalisation' as an obstacle to economic development. Recent governments were castigated for everything from their financial and economic policies to the Preventive Detention Act. All this was to be changed. Health, housing, water, agriculture, commerce, industry, communication, transport, and education were slated for restructuring. The abolition of the teaching of an ideologically prescribed form of 'politics' in schools was underlined. The size of the army was to be reduced. The police were to be retrained. A variety of other agendas were outlined, including a call for a national body to be formed to address women's issues. As far as its text went, the Chadema charter could have been written in Washington.

How could this depersonalised statement acquire a locally meaningful set of referents? Who really read it through? For the Chagga people on Kilimanjaro, it was not the declarations of virtuous intention but what they knew about the leadership that gave the party its identity. The construction of the organisation was in Chagga hands.

Chadema was under the national leadership of one Mtei, a Mchagga who had once been prominent in the CCM (Chama cha Mapinduzi, the Revolutionary Party, which was in effect the renamed TANU, the old Tanzanian African National Union). At a much earlier time he had been Finance Minister in the central government and had known all the major CCM figures. I was told by several people on the mountain that, formal universalism of membership aside, Chadema was really a Chagga party, and that, at that moment at least, many of the new political parties were 'ethnic parties', despite claims to the contrary. If that was so, the emergence of such politicised ethnicities in the aftermath of a one-party regime was another Tanzanian phenomenon with parallels in many other parts of the world.

In the Vunjo area of Kilimanjaro it was well known that one of Mtei's high-level associates in Chadema was the son and grandson of a line of famous Chagga chiefs. He was a son of Petro Itosi Marcalle, whom I came to know in the late 1970s. The father, Petro Itosi, had been a prominent and powerful political actor, both under the British colonial regime and in Nyerere's government after independence. In the 1950s, when TANU was beginning to be a political force in Tanganyika, Petro Itosi was reputed to be no great friend of Nyerere's party. He knew Nyerere, having met him for the first time in London in 1951. However, ten years later, after independence, when Nyerere was firmly installed in power, Petro Itosi put out a characteristically canny story to cover up his original opposition. He said that even before independence he had always been a secret member of TANU. He maintained that he had kept his membership under wraps only to stay out of trouble with the colonial government.

What is impressive is that this clever Petro Itosi was sufficiently powerful to survive politically after independence despite the abolition of chiefship, and despite his scepticism regarding TANU-type socialism. As Petro Itosi explained it, President Nyerere had appointed him to a high central government office because the President preferred to have Petro Itosi in Dar es Salaam, where he could be watched, rather than on Kilimanjaro, where he might mobilise and lead a political opposition.

The time ultimately came when Petro Itosi had occasion to call in the debt Nyerere owed him for not trying to stir up such an opposition. In 1974 rumours spread that Petro Itosi's son (the high-ranking ex-army officer who is now prominent in Chadema) was plotting with several of his brother officers to mount a *coup* to overthrow Nyerere. Petro Itosi told me in 1979, with a wink, that it had all been just playful. 'They were simply army fellows drinking together and joking around. The talk of a *coup* was not serious.' Needless to say, Nyerere took it seriously. But, partly because of Petro Itosi, and partly because of his own unusual political character, Nyerere did not take the kind of extreme action that many an African head of state might have taken. Petro Itosi's son was neither shot nor imprisoned. Instead the colonel was sent safely into exile. He was assigned a diplomatic post in China and was barred from returning to Tanzania for a substantial period. After some years in China the colonel was moved to Japan for four years. He was not suffering. During those years he managed to send six Japanese cars into Tanzania in the diplomatic pouch, thus duty-free. His father was riding around in one of them when I knew him.

After the Japanese phase of his exile the colonel spent some years in England, where he was in the weapons business. His father, always politically conscious, assured me that the son sold arms only to 'freedom fighters'. In time the son was allowed to return to Tanzania for short 'family' visits, and eventually to return for good. By the winter of 1993 he had enjoyed a substantial period of residence in Tanzania, and was in possession of a luxurious modern house in Marangu on Kilimanjaro, on the very site on which a famous chiefly ancestor had lived. When, in the 1980s, the government of Tanzania changed, its new policies open to the agenda of the West, the colonel's personal history had ceased to be a liability and had become a political asset. The reputation he had acquired in connection with the rumours of a projected *coup* were now a political plus.

In 1993 the ex-colonel appeared on the mountain only inter-mittently, spending most of his time in Dar es Salaam. His wife, however, remained on Kilimanjaro, and undertook a very active role in Lutheran Church-associated women's organisations and their various 'development' efforts. She was a vice-chairman of the Church women's organisation of the province, a substantial notch above the parish prominence which she also enjoyed. A rather ebullient and accomplished organisational operator herself, she denied that any of this Church-related activity was political. She

was also closely involved with the opening of the first Chadema party office. It was located in a tiny shop-front off the Marangu market.

Serious campaigning was not allowed to start until August 1995. The first national multi-party elections were held in October. There seem to have been substantial irregularities in the voting and the counting. The national party declared that it had won, and continued to govern. Ten of the opposition parties, including Chadema, brought a lawsuit to challenge the validity of the election. They did not succeed in reversing its effect.

Chadema did not do as well in the elections as some had expected. In fact the Wachagga had more than one Mchagga presidential candidate to choose from in the elections of October 1995. A very prominent Mchagga member of the Revolutionary Party (CCM) who had been in President Mwinyi's government in 1993 subsequently left the government and, shortly before the elections, joined another opposition party, NCCR-Mageuzi. This man, Augustine Lyatonga Mrema, had been President Mwinyi's Minister of Home Affairs, and in January 1993 had been elevated to the position of Deputy Prime Minister. He will reappear in that role in another of these political vignettes as a presidential emissary sent to put out political fires in the Kilimanjaro region.

Ethnicity has certainly found a new niche in Africa in the framework of multi-party politics insisted on by the international donors. There is an irony in all of this. In socialist Tanzania, at the time of independence, 'detribalisation' was considered a matter of the highest priority in the project of nation-building. The policy of 'detribalisation' was not supposed to imply the prohibition of *private* folk practices at the level of family and neighbourhood. What was barred was any *political* expression of ethnicity in the *public* domain. It remains to be seen whether that conception of detribalisation, and the institutions built around it, such as the officialisation of Swahili as the national language, will nevertheless have a durable effect on the future of Tanzania.

What is clear at present is that, for many citizens, ideas about their own ethnic identity, and associated ethnic network connec-tions, remain an important ingredient in personal loyalties. But does that mean that the politicisation of ethnic categories that has been intensifying worldwide should be interpreted as a continuation of cultural 'tradition'? I think not. The game has changed, and the context of the game has changed. I propose instead that today's ethnic politics is an old cultural costume in which a new form of political 'modernity' shows itself.

The Church as a resource

During the period of high socialism in Tanzania the state did what it could to disempower the Christian Churches. It removed Church schools from Church control and turned them into state schools. It confiscated Church lands, limited what Churches could do to increase their revenues, and restricted Church activities in the domain of 'development' projects. The public activities of priests and pastors were carefully watched, and clergy were often asked to use the authority of their office to deliver government messages from the pulpit. All of that seems to be over. Since the Churches have sponsors in other countries, the donations they receive help to support them. In addition to meeting ongoing costs, some of the money is used for investment. Churches can now participate in small local businesses, and can take a share of the income to finance their own charitable and other activities. There is a direct mix of

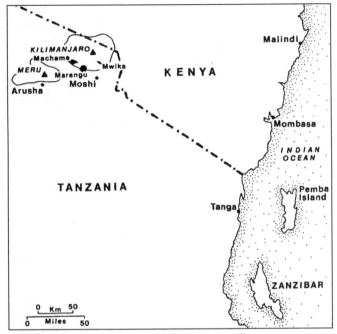

Figure 1 Mount Meru, Mount Kilimanjaro, some 'villages' on Kilimanjaro, and the towns of Arusha and Moshi.

international and local interests at work in Church affairs. This mix touches on everything from economy to organisation, to doctrine.

From the beginning, the Churches on Kilimanjaro have had to support themselves, since the assistance from the metropole has never been sufficient for their needs. In the colonial period they were allocated land on which they planted crops. Resident Chagga tenants constituted their major labour force. It was partly through the Church need for income that the production of coffee was introduced to the mountain. After independence, when Church lands were confiscated, the land was redistributed to local 'peasants'. For a long while restrictions on the secular operations of the Churches greatly limited their income and capacity to innovate. But there has been a change in their fortunes. The Churches have become NGOs, in the current political language of the international donors, and are enjoying a certain renaissance in their new state of freedom. Dioceses are supposed to be self-supporting and can now work more actively in their own cause.

Given the new push toward a free market, the Lutherans on Kilimanjaro have begun to participate in certain new, agriculture-related businesses. For example, in July 1991, parishioners from one Lutheran parish received several machines ordered from West Germany for processing sunflower seeds and extracting the oil. The commercial growing of sunflowers for oil is a profitable recent development on the flat lands of the plain below the mountain. The Church is obviously alert to such business opportunities, since it contributed toward the project and will receive a percentage of any profits. This is by no means the only 'development' enterprise in which Church groups are involved, some of them income-producing. Thus the Church receives contributions from members, income from its investments and monies or other help from foreign

donors. The links with Lutheran communities outside Tanzania have remained strong since the days of German colonial rule. Lutherans from Minnesota to Finland continue to maintain ties with Tanzania.

What, then, could be more desirable than to control a diocese and its sub-organisations and finances? That is exactly what a faction of Meru Lutherans thought. They wanted a diocesan reorganisation that would give the area local financial and administrative autonomy within the structure of the Church. They had an aggressive leadership that mobilised support for pressing such a demand. Meru is a mountain west of Kilimanjaro. It is occupied by two language groups. On the west side are people known as the Arusha who are Maasai-speakers. On the more easterly side are the Meru whose language is a form of Kichagga, related to that spoken in Machame, on Kilimanjaro. In 1992 the Lutheran Meru were included in the Northern Diocese of the Church, and were thus under the administrative control of Bishop Erasto Kweka of Machame (a Kilimanjaro ex-chiefdom). A faction of Meru were not happy with this arrangement and demanded an independent diocese of their own.

Kweka was disliked not only in Meru but in other parts of Kilimanjaro as well. Under his aegis the age-old practice of beer-drinking at weddings and at other ceremonies in which the Church was involved was prohibited. No one I knew in Vunjo liked this anti-drinking rule, though nominal compliance was instituted. But there was a more serious bone of contention. Kweka was accused of financial favouritism in relation to the people of his own section of the mountain, the people of Machame. Some said that contracts for the construction of the Church centre in Moshi (the nearby town and administrative centre at the foot of Mount Kilimanjaro) were all awarded to Machame people and not shared with other districts of Kilimanjaro, that Kweka kept all foreign contributions intended for the whole of the diocese exclusively for Machame projects, buildings, and vehicles. Some Marangu people told me that, when the Finns wanted to build a new hospital in Marangu, Kweka opposed the idea and demanded that it be built in Machame. The Finns were said to have been adamant about the Marangu location, and the change was not made. How much of all this is true, how much gossip, is not something I am in a position to verify, but I heard the same stories from several sophisticated and responsible people. Certainly many of the Meru believed something of the sort, since they disregarded all normal bureaucratic Church procedures and chose violence instead as their means of getting an independent diocese. Meru people who did not side with those who demanded a Meru diocese were attacked. Crops were torched. Church coffee trees were destroyed. Cattle were killed. Houses were burnt down. Five people died in the turmoil.

The matter was deemed serious enough to require national governmental attention. The Minister of Home Affairs, the very same Augustine Lyatonga Mrema of whom we have already heard (because he later became a presidential candidate), was sent north to try to work out some kind of peaceful compromise. As a result of Mrema's intervention matters were settled. The Meru got their independent diocese. Mrema, in turn, subsequently became Deputy Prime Minister (*Mwananchi*, 25–31 January 1993, p. 2).

In the speech-making connected with the announcement of this appointment Mrema was extolled for bringing about a settlement of the dispute, and Satan was blamed for the division of opinion in Arumeru. The rioting was deplored, since it had destroyed much valuable property and left some children orphaned. People in general were exhorted to discuss their differences and never to use violence, since it not only caused damage and injury but played into Satan's hands. The moral lesson was emphatically drawn. Yet, inspecting this instance at a distance, it appears to be one in which violence paid off, as did the political publicity for the peace-maker.

What can be gleaned from this brief sketch of one event in the politics of post-socialist modernity? This was a fight for local, sub-organisational autonomy inside the Lutheran Church. In more general terms, it was a struggle over the control of newly restored resources, organisational and financial. Many state restrictions on the Churches had been lifted. The old Church had emerged as a custodian of new resources, valuable enough to fight over. Yet it was only because the central state stepped in that the Church was obliged to yield to the demands of the rebellious Meru and ultimately let them have their own diocese.

A sub-village chairman and his war against witchcraft

Many 'sub-villages' on Kilimanjaro are very old units, often dating back to pre-colonial days. In the period of high socialism they were redesignated cooperative villages. Nominally integrated into an administrative design of the ruling party, they were subject to its rules. Nowadays sub-village leaders are less tightly supervised and are behaving accordingly. Thus, though the sub-villages are formally part of a supra-local bureaucratic structure, they have a life of their own which is now more unfettered than it was. The sub-villages are not nucleated concentrations. They consist of hundreds of contiguous garden-farm compounds.

In 1992 some residents of Kinyamvuo, in Mwika, complained to the sub-village chairman, a Revolutionary Party elected/appointee, that there was a lot of witchcraft going on in the village. Long ago, it is said, the chiefs used to protect people against witches, and used to find them and punish them. That ended during the colonial period, when the administration refused to lend any credence to witchcraft complaints and prohibited witchcraft trials. The post-independence government has adopted an equally disbelieving public stance, and has continued to maintain colonial anti-witchcraft statutes.

In socialist days it would have been difficult for the chairman of Kinyamvuo to take public action against a witch. Party higher-ups would have found out about it and might have removed him. But in 1992 the village chairman apparently felt free to side with the people of the village who were complaining. He agreed to allow two witch-finding diviners from Tanga to be brought to stay in the village until they had located the trouble and something had been done about it. Tanga is a coastal town well known on the mountain as a place where witchcraft objects can be bought when needed. Other witchcraft 'things', including formulas and spells, are said to be inherited in families.

The chairman held a big village meeting. Many people attended, not only from Kinyamvuo but from neighbouring sub-villages. He made a speech, saying that many villagers were angry about the witchcraft troubles that had beset Kinyamvuo. He named a day when anyone with a complaint about witchcraft could go to the two diviners. They were to present their grievance and to disclose their suspicions about who might be causing the problem. The village chairman also called on anyone who possessed witchcraft objects to bring them to the village office. He said he would form a collection and they would be put on public exhibition. I was told by someone who had seen the display that the things brought to the

village office were not objects ordinarily bought in Tanga. They were items like the hair of dead persons, or bones from human skeletons. Needless to say, once collected, the objects attracted a great deal of attention, and many people went to see them.

However, a faction of villagers refused to do so, and went instead to the Church office and complained about the chairman. The pastor was indignant. He subsequently warned his congregants not to go and see such things and that anyone who was caught doing so would be excluded from the Church.

That did not discourage many of the villagers. In fact, their witch-finding fervour encouraged someone to accuse a particular man of having concealed a dead body in the eaves (*daria*) of his house, which he was said to be using for witchcraft purposes. The village chairman gave the two young diviners permission to go and investigate. They went to the accused man's house and asked him to produce the dead body. The man said he was not a witch and had no corpse. The diviners said they would search his house anyway for witchcraft objects or instruments. Some people were only too ready to join them. But others were on the side of the accused and tried to bar the way. A violent fight ensued, involving about thirty people. No one was seriously injured, as they fought with bare hands, not with pangas.

Two sons of the accused were working at Dodoma. When they heard of the frightening threats to their father they came back to the village and soon went to the police. The police came and arrested the village chairman and the two diviners but none of the people who had been fighting. The case was sent to the District Court in Moshi, the town that lies at the foot of the mountain and is the administrative centre for Kilimanjaro. The chairman was found guilty of violating the witchcraft statutes. However, he appealed, and was allowed to return to the village and continue in the role of chairman. The appeal was still pending when I left.

The question of a secular modernity is not at issue. I have yet to meet a Mchagga who denies that witchcraft is possible or who argues that dead spirits have no power over the living. Priests and pastors and other enthusiastic Christians say that some of these other-worldly goings-on are a pernicious manifestation of the devil, but they do not doubt that they happen. The less devout have other explanations but are equally sure that witchcraft is practised locally.

The person who told me about the events came from an adjacent sub-village and is a friend of the chairman of Kinyamvuo. He hoped the conviction would be reversed. He said that the chairman was much liked and that 'He was just trying to end the trouble in the village.' Liked by some he surely was. But plainly there were factions that did not like him. His bid for a quasi-chiefly role, his attempt to enter into competition with the pastors as a witch-chaser, his self-serving use of the witchcraft artefacts and of the witchfinders, all bespeak an attempt to enhance the basis of his local power.

I know nothing of the history of the internal politics of the village that preceded this event, but I am sure there is more to the story than has been told here. Even in the absence of a fuller account one thing is clear, that in part of the Kilimanjaro countryside at a very recent time a minor political figure did not hesitate to use a witchcraft idiom publicly to show how diligent he was about protecting the citizens in his care. He was probably trying to enhance his political viability in the local elections or other political challenges that were ahead. What is also politically interesting is the recourse of his opponents to outside agencies, the Church and the police. The Wachagga have long played local official agencies against one another, but for a time the party hierarchy was sufficiently in control, and sufficiently united in policy, for the undermining of a party village chairman to have been difficult. And then, too, in that period, the village chairman probably would not have resorted to such exotic techniques of power maintenance.

Competition for the senior leadership of a lineage and out-migration by much of the younger generation

In the older areas of Kilimanjaro many households live in patrilineal clusters. Such patrilineages are surely one of the oldest forms of local organisation. Their definitions of membership have been durable and so have many of their cultural practices. But for all their long-standing cultural trappings, and their traditionalist claims, Chagga lineages have actually been endlessly transformed by an unrelenting flow of change. Change is taking place (and has taken place for as long as we know anything about them) not just around the lineages but in them. Many of the details of that historical process are available. The tale I shall tell here is of a recent intentional and self-conscious 'modernising' lineage reorganisation. It took place against the background of a radical process of out-migration by the younger generation. That out-migration will, in time, doubtless work other, more radical, transformations in the constitution of the lineages that remain locally resident on the mountain.

One might assume from theoretical models that kinship ties, ritual obligations to dead ancestors and the whole 'enchanted world' mode of thought that we associate with a kin-based way of life would have faded out on Kilimanjaro, given the kind of modernity and commercial activity long visible there. In this case the model contrasting commerce and secularism versus kinship and spirits, so much relied on by Bourdieu (1977: 172, 177, 183) and others, is a false dichotomy. There is much less inconsistency and incompatibility between the conceptions associated with what Bourdieu has called the 'self-interest economy' of capitalism and the ideas linked with the 'good faith economy' of kin-based society than Bourdieu's model presupposes. As we shall see, some activities on Kilimanjaro suggest the convertibility of the social structures of the good faith economy to the purposes of a self-interest economy. Surely, at this historical moment in Africa, the assumptions of an anthropology that defines modernism as the very opposite of the kin-based need to be seriously rethought.

At roughly three-year intervals since 1968 I have been following closely the affairs of a particular local lineage. In addition, in 1968–69, with the dedicated help of a Mchagga assistant, a household-by-household survey was undertaken of some 300 families living in the same sub-village. In 1993 a resurvey was started of the present state of the same households. It has not been completed, but I have detailed material on my closely followed lineage and some comparative material regarding the broader sub-village census. Fifty households in an entirely different sub-village in a different ex-chiefdom were also checked 1993 to see whether the current trend in Mwika regarding the exodus of the younger generation was in any way unique. It was not.

What is our baseline? In 1968–69 there were thirty households of the M— lineage. Their individual houses and gardens, most of them contiguous, were in a sub-village of Mwika. Seventeen of the thirty were fathers and sons. That is to say, four senior men had fathered thirteen sons who were married and had independent households in the local lineage territory. Most of the thirty were

subsistence farmers. About a third of the men, most of them in the younger generation, had salaried jobs. The work of half of these employed men took them far from the mountain. They saw their families only on holiday leave. The others were employed close enough to home so they could come back to their up-mountain homes on many weekends. The women-folk attached to these men made a few shillings from time to time by selling produce in the market.

At that time the wives and young children of all the salaried men continued to live in (and subsist on) the husbands' Mwika garden plots. There was no question of the wives and children moving closer to the towns where many of the men worked. Was this because of anxiety about losing land rights under socialist Tanzania's land-to-the-tiller policy? Or because it was much less expensive for the employed person to go alone? I do not know. Thus, in 1968, to accept a job away from Kilimanjaro was just that, an opportunity of paid work. It was not treated as an incentive to the permanent out-migration of a household.

By 1993 many things had changed. Fifteen of the original thirty household heads had died. A few had moved to other land on Kilimanjaro. But nine survivors of the original thirty household heads continued to live on the lineage lands where they had lived in 1968–69. Now most of them shared their plots with adult offspring, and, of course, the deceased were succeeded by sons. But, by 1993, the thirty household heads on the site in 1968 had sired an impressive total of about eighty-one sons. There was not enough land to support them. Given the shortage, what had become of them? Deducting the thirteen who already had plots of land and were part of the original thirty leaves sixty-eight sons. In 1993 fifteen of the sixty-eight were still schoolboys. *Of the remaining fifty-three, twenty-seven had left the mountain to work. They had moved to Tanzania's towns and cities.* They were located everywhere from Mwanza, Moshi and Arusha to Dar es Salaam. Of the remaining twenty-six adult sons, all lived on their fathers' plots of land, either where the thirty original heads of household did and/or nearby where their wives resided. Those twenty-six, plus the nine locally resident survivors from the original thirty, made up *the thirty-five resident male adults of the patrilineage who were locally resident in 1993.* Thus there is the illusion that the same way of life that existed before continues. However, continuity has been managed at the cost of the out-migration of half the younger generation of men. (Table 1).

In the 1980s the leader of this lineage became ill with cancer. He died in 1991, after many trips to the hospital and after making many sacrifices at the graves of his ancestors. His successor was chosen in 1990. Using the vocabulary of party organisation, he calls himself 'lineage chairman'. He was the previous leader's youngest half-brother.

No sooner was he selected than he proposed to reorganise the lineage. He wanted to fuse the lineage branch to which he belonged with another geographically close branch that had long been autonomous. (He also planned to include a few other scattered satellite households in his superlineage.) This move toward consolidation would considerably augment his constituency. From being 'chairman' of roughly thirty-five households he would instead head about seventy households. The close kinship links between the two lineage branches were recognised by everyone, and there had always been visiting between families in the two. However, during the socialist period, formal organisations other than the party and a few other entities, such as the Churches, were

Table 1 Employment and residence of adult males of the lineage

1968	
Married adult males	30
Living on Kilimanjaro (families there)	30
Employed away	11
Schoolboys or younger	15
Adult males living on original patrimonial land area	
Adult males	30
*Localism and delocalisation of marriages of males**	
All wives from Kilimanjaro	35
From same ex-chiefdom	23
From adjacent ex-chiefdom	8
From more distant ex-chiefdoms	4
*Localism and delocalisation of marriages of daughters**	
All adult daughters married on Kilimanjaro	
*Female employment in the formal sector**	
None	
1993	
Sons (post-1968 progeny)	68
Working in towns (families with them)	27
Living on original Kilimanjaro land plots	26
Adult males living on original patrimonial land area	
Adult males	35
*Localism and delocalisation of marriages of males**	
Origins of fifteen wives of sons	15
Same ex-chiefdom	2
Adjacent ex-chiefdom	5
More distant ex-chiefdoms	5
Non-Kilimanjaro spouses	3
*Localism and delocalisation of marriages of daughters**	
Daughters married[†]	30
In same ex-chiefdom	2
In other ex-chiefdoms	13
Non-Kilimanjaro spouses	13
Location unaccounted for	2
*Female employment in the formal sector**	
Teachers, nurses, cierks living away from Kilimanjaro	8

Notes

* Data for 1993 incomplete.

[†] Eleven live in towns with their husbands.

not allowed any prominence. Even meetings of large kinship groups were looked on with suspicion. Official permission to hold them had to be obtained and such meetings were attended not only by kinsmen but by party functionaries to make certain they had no politically subversive purpose. Now that socialism had faded, freedom of assembly is evident, and organisational possibilities are very different from what they were, hence the bold move of trying to unite the two related lineage communities. Both branches agreed to the consolidation.

Very shortly thereafter the new 'lineage chairman' was confronted with what constituted a scarcely disguised rebellion. A kinsman proposed that the newly consolidated lineage of seventy families be redivided into two branches, on the grounds that it was unmanageably large. He asserted that the line of fission should be between the descendants of two brothers who lived approximately four generations ago. Descendants of both brothers were interspersed in the two local communities. Implicit in this proposal was the scarcely disguised probability that the rebel would become the leader of one segment on grounds of genealogical correctness, leaving the existing 'lineage chairman' as the leader of the other. This would have shrunk the ambitious 'lineage chairman's' fused constituency to about half of what he had in mind.

In addition to creating and formalising this consolidated seventy-household lineage, emulating village chairmen of the socialist period, the lineage chairman made a written list in a notebook of all the household heads' names, and imposed a kind of internal tax on every man and wife. The men were to contribute 500 shillings a year, the women 300, to a common lineage fund, for which fund, of course, the chairman would be responsible. He opened a bank account for the lineage, the first bank transaction he had ever entered into. He collected not only from the locally resident but from relatives in the towns whom he knew to be prosperous, and tried to get them to give more than the requested minimum amount. He announced that the monies would be spent on funding vocational apprenticeships for the primary school leavers who did not pass the exams for secondary school and whose parents could not finance the training themselves. They could become bricklayers, carpenters, or tailors, or whatever. Of the first two young people to be funded, one came from the lineage cluster in the chairman's natal sub-village and one from the cluster in the sub-village that he had just annexed. He was a consummate politician. And he was plainly aware that out-migration was the only solution for many of the junior people in the lineage. This training programme would give the offspring of poor relatives a chance to earn a living elsewhere.

His rival, the man who would have preferred lineage fission to lineage consolidation, did not contribute to the fund and boycotted the chairman's lineage meetings. In retaliation the chairman held a meeting to persuade all kinsfolk to join him in ostracising his rival from all lineage sociability. A letter was sent to the rival, who was told he would be banned from any rituals, feasts, or celebrations, or beer-drinks held by lineage members and that he was formally expelled from the lineage. The chairman legitimated his policy by arguing that the division the rival was proposing was an act that violated the fraternal bonds of the ancestors, that it was a kind of sacrilege. He said the ancestors would have desired the consolidation of the two lineage branches that he proposed. A fused, super-lineage would reiterate the original connections between the ancestors themselves, and thus make them happy that their descendants had not forgotten the past relationship.

The rival bore up under his exclusion for a year but eventually could not bear his isolation. By 1991 he was ready to make amends. The chairman allowed him back into the lineage's good graces provided he would prepare a *pombe*, a ritual offering of beer for the whole lineage by way of public apology and admission of guilt. The rival did so and was reinstated.

This vignette shows in what complex forms fragments of a kin-oriented social life are interwoven with new practices and new exigencies. Political organisation and tax registers are used as models of an updated lineage organisation. Rationales grounded in ancestral ties legitimate the local ambitions of a leader to enlarge the domain of his influence. But the self-same leader, without any risk of being found inconsistent, is helping to attenuate and even sever lineage connections by feeding the stream of outmigration.

Concluding remarks

Untangling the vignettes, these intertwined glimpses of four levels of organisation have a gently subversive purpose. The events are of our time; thus they are modern in their chronological contemporaneity. But in what analytic sense are the founding of the new national party, the fight over the new diocese in the Lutheran Church, the anti-witchcraft measures in the sub-village, and the reorganisation of a lineage 'modern'? The periodisation of history is a motivated one. There is always a political framework within which different times are given their labels. In a factual sense, one could easily argue that the burst of innovative organisational activity described here occurred when it did as part of the immediate response to a post-socialist liberalisation in Tanzania. But is that manifestly new competition for control of resources illumined by any of the current philosophical or sociological conceptions of 'the modern'?

In any one of these instances can one talk (in the Habermas vocabulary) about the formation of a political 'collective will'? Was an overarching vision of political 'modernity' involved for the people in these social fields or was there a myopia born of activisim in which only immediate objectives were in focus? It would be difficult to answer such a question from the evidence in this article, so mixed are the indications of motivation. What is clear is that none of the organisations described could have operated in 1973 as they did in 1993. Each event shows individuals using the groups of which they were members to increase their own influence and power. But it is also plain that, in the process, the same individuals saw fit to design or redesign the organisations. They did so either by explicitly changing the rules in existing groups or, in the case of the national party, by issuing a prospectus of new policies to be implemented by a new organisation.

On the modern scene it is normally the state that empowers organisations to exist. Laws and regulations set the general terms of their legitimate operation. The state can also prohibit organisational formation. That this power is used very restrictively in one-party states is well known. Organisations are recognised as features of the political landscape. Left to self-invention they are almost certain to become dangerous to authoritarian political centres. The capacity to act collectively is a major liberty.

It is no accident that in 1993 all four organisational milieus described here were in an active condition of creation or trans-formation. They were all taking advantage of Tanzania's emergence from the highly constraining period of one-party rule. Surely, in considering such shifting forms of collective 'will formation', as much weight should be given to the organisational entrepreneur as is normally given to the economic entrepreneur. In trying to make his/her influence durable the organisational entrepreneur inscribes his/her ambitions on the very form and practice of collectivities.

The stories of such shaping acts and group-mobilising contexts are of critical importance if the process of change is to be under-stood. Models that overemphasise individual choice as if all of politics were a version of vote-casting are disassembling the very entities and processes that need examination. Overemphasis on modernity as individualism makes it impossible to see what is going on in the arenas where collectivities weigh in. Some of the enabling or constraining possibilities are in the surround. They may be embedded in the economy and/or in laws and policies crafted at a great distance from the scenes whose outlines they presume to generate. However, local social action also has its own imperatives, and its own designs. No one knows this so well as aspiring local leaders in Africa, some of whom now have completely new spaces in which to go public with their ambitions. Others must settle for reshaping collectivities that are already in place. What is being seen is the explicit imprinting of plans on structures.

To discover what is doing in rural African politics, what the latest is in organisational modernities, there is nothing so revealing as contests for directing organisational milieus. Incident by incident, local designs for personal and collective futures are jockeyed around and put in place. They face in a specific direction. That is the direction in which some intend the process of change to flow. For the minute? For the long term?

All the vignettes of events described here involved either legislation by the state or changes in the internally enforceable rules of an organisation. Legislation was necessary to make the new multi-party politics of Tanzania possible. In the Lutheran Church the recognition of a new diocese required either internal legislation or internal executive action (and, in this instance, external executive intervention). In the sub-village where the chairman made the rule that the harbouring of witchcraft objects was unacceptable, and that such objects would have to be surrendered, he said he was making a new, modernising administrative regulation. That it also had a variety of old precedents behind it did not, from his point of view, detract from his own modernity and progressiveness in pressing the matter. The lineage chairman who consolidated two lineage branches and taxed their members was effecting internal legislation in the interests of modernising the lineage. In all these cases, either the formal legal system or formal internal corporate rulemaking (or both) was involved. The rules were an explicit, consciously adopted, authoritative technique used to form or reform parts of the social order. In each instance there was an attempt to create something new, or reshape something old, and it was associated with the persuasive authority of particular persons.

Embedded in compressed narratives of events, such 'modern-ising' efforts have been presented here in situationally focused forms. All were clearly associated with recent national liberalisations. However, except for the new political party, the organisational reforms and quasi-legislative measures in each mini-arena were not described to me as parts of a grand vision of a new polity. Are general abstractions about what constitutes 'the modern' an object of lively intellectual contestation on Kilimanjaro? I doubt it. But in Western academe ideas of modernity and postmodernity are part of an ongoing debate about the history of the West. Multiple definitions have accumulated like barnacles on the boat-bottom of academic discourse. This is no doubt why Ernest Gellner could say of postmodernism that 'It is not altogether clear what the devil it is' (1992: 22) or David Parkin could say, 'There is no one thing we can call post-modernism, but in fact a number of intellectual stances' (1995: 146).

The question what is meant by 'the modern' from which 'postmodernism' sprang is only slightly less opaque. From Weber to Habermas there have been grand-scale attempts to characterise a generalised 'modern' order that contrasts with the 'traditional'. The 'traditional' supposedly existed in earlier societies and, by implica-tion, is presumed to continue in some non-Western ones

(Habermas, 1979: 157–8; Weber, 1978: 226–1). Foucault speaks of a modern epistemology, 'a certain modern mode of knowing' (1973: 250). Giddens, in the evolutionist vein, says, 'Modernity is essentially a post-traditional order' (1991: 20). But in other works the critical contrast now emphasised is between 'modernity' and an emergent postmodernism, rather than modernity being compared with 'traditional orders' (Benhabib, 1992; Rabinow, 1986: 23–61).

The central locale of reference, modern and postmodern, is Western. The content emphasised varies with context and authorship, sometimes focusing on the political, sometimes on cultural, literary or artistic issues, sometimes on individual identity. Thus in one essay Habermas defines modernity as follows:

> The modern age stood above all under the sign of subjective freedom. This was realized in society as the space secured by civil law for the rational pursuit of one's own interests: in the state, as the in principle equal rights to participation in the formation of political will; in the private sphere, as ethical autonomy and self-realization … [1992: 83]

In some writings on modernity the commentary on the non-Western is obvious though implicit. Thus Giddens says that:

> Modern institutions differ from all preceding forms of social order in respect of their dynamism, the degree to which they undercut traditional habits and customs and their global impact. … One of the distinctive features of modernity … is an increasing interconnection between … globalising influences … and personal dispositions. [1991: 1]

He continues:

> Modernity institutionalises the principle of radical doubt and insists that all knowledge takes the form of hypotheses. [1991: 5]

> The reflexive project of the self … takes place in the context of multiple choice. … Reflexively organised life-planning … becomes a central feature of the structuring of self-identity. [1991: 5]

What is smuggled into this sketch of modernity is its foundational contrast with a presumed opposite. Traditional social types are alluded to as if they were founded on obedience to unquestioned cultural dictates (see also Weber, 1978: 226–41; Habermas, 1979: 95–178). A condition of general conformity to tradition is postulated with an associated absence of individual choice. In such a system, as imagined, there is no conscious construction of the self. The lack of a sceptical consciousness is its characteristic mentality. But surely actual so-called 'traditional' societies have been in history, and history is not a tale of stasis, and not a story without rebels and reformers. History is everywhere a narrative of unending change and transformation. Certainly that is as much the African political and economic story as the history of any other part of the world (Bayart, 1989: 19–61). In this connection, a look at modernity in Africa today is an instructive exercise. It raises questions about the generalisability of the categories commonly used by certain avant-garde thinkers in the West to characterise our 'modern' or 'postmodern' selves. The description here of recent events in one corner of Africa invites greater attention to the way the narrowly local and historically specific is intertwined with broad trends. It invites attention to the question of the conjunction of causes, and raises questions about the appropriateness of models grounded in European history.

Not only looking at Africa, but considering eastern Europe today, it is quickly evident that the world is much more diverse in respect of local conceptions of how to pursue a desirable 'modernity' than is allowed for by either the evolution-oriented or the postmodern theoretical accounts. As Seyla Benhabib says:

> while the cultural and political ideals of modernity … have become suspect to the humanistic and artistic avant-garde of western late-capitalist societies, political developments in Eastern Europe and the Soviet Union have given these ideals a new purchase on life. While the peoples of Eastern Europe and the Soviet Union have taken to the streets and defied state police as well as the potential threat of foreign troops in the name of parliamentary democracy, the rule of law and a market economy, the academic discourse of the last decades, particularly under the label of 'postmodernism,' has produced an intellectual climate profoundly sceptical toward the moral and political ideals of modernity, the Enlightenment and liberal democracy. [1992: 1–2]

The implications of the post-socialist moment in eastern Europe and in the ex-Soviet Union have been much written about, but the situation in Africa, the aftermath of the one-party state being much more recent, has had much less fieldwork attention. Accordingly some aspects of the situation unfolding on Mount Kilimanjaro in 1993, however micro and special to that setting, have larger implications. The new freedoms, the new political open spaces, are being intensively appropriated. It remains to be seen what the long-term result will be of this momentary, but impressive, political free-for-all. The events described amply justify the argument that in Africa there are political-organisational versions of 'the domestication of modernity', that they matter, and that Eurocentric models may need some rethinking.

References

Bayart, Jean François. 1989. *L'État en Afrique: la politique du ventre*. Paris: Fayard.

Benhabib, Seyla. 1992. *Situating the Self*. New York: Routledge.

Bourdieu, Pierre. 1977. *Outline of a Theory of Practice*. Cambridge: Cambridge University Press.

Foucault, Michel. 1973. *The Order of Things*. New York: Random House.

Gellner, Ernest. 1992. *Postmodernism, Reason and Religion*. London and New York: Routledge.

Giddens, Anthony. 1991. *Modernity and Self-identity*. Stanford, Cal.: Stanford University Press.

Habermas, Jurgen. 1979. *Communication and the Evolution of Society*, trans. Thomas McCarthy. Boston, Mass.: Beacon Press.

——. 1992. *The Philosophical Discourse of Modernity*, (trans. F. G. Lawrence). Cambridge, Mass.: MIT Press.

Parkin, David. 1995. 'Latticed knowledge', in Richard Fardon (ed.), *Counterworks*. London and New York: Routledge.

Rabinow, Paul. 1986. 'Representations are social facts: modernity and postmodernity in anthropology', in James Clifford and George E. Marcus (eds.), *Writing Culture*. Berkeley and Los Angeles, Cal.: University of California Press.

Warnier, Jean-Pierre. 1993. *L'Esprit d'entreprise au Cameroun*. Paris: Karthala.

Weber, Max. 1978. *Economy and Society*. Berkeley and Los Angeles, Cal., and London: University of California Press.

WIM VAN BINSBERGEN
Aspects of Democracy & Democratisation in Zambia & Botswana

Reference
Journal of Contemporary African Studies, 13,1 1995, pp. 3–33

Introduction [1]

In this paper, I shall draw attention to background aspects of democracy and democratisation in two African countries, Zambia and Botswana, by exploring not the topical developments at the national political scene (a task for which others are much better qualified), but the political culture at the grassroots, to which my prolonged participant observation as an anthropologist has given me access. Before we arrive at the specific ethnography, I shall raise a number of methodological and theoretical points without which, I feel, my argument would remain in the air. This takes us to a discussion of democracy, globalisation and the dangers of Eurocentrism, and leads us to distinguish three modes of defining democracy. After having identified constitutional democracy as only one particular variant among others, and as an item of political culture which has been relatively recently introduced to Africa, we will discuss the recent democratic positions and processes among the people of Kaoma district, Zambia, and of the medium-sized town of Francistown, Botswana. The purpose of the paper is, beyond a descriptive one, to help define the wider setting and the boundary conditions within which the more specific discussion of the democratisation process in Africa since the late 1980s can be situated; that discussion itself, however, to which our African colleagues have made such major contributions, remains outside my present scope. [2]

Democracy, globalisation and possible Eurocentrism

Our social and political life is involved in an ever-accelerating process of globalisation. [3] Through formal education and literacy, through electronic media which have developed their own *lingua franca* of images which is more or less understood wherever there is media reception, and through mass consumption which spreads the silent language of standardised manufactured objects packed with meanings across the world, globalisation has produced a situation where a varying percentage of the inhabitants of all continents are familiar with and situationally adopt the global discourse, with its particular selection of symbols and meaning. In the process, the discourses specific to their local, regional and national sociocultural environments are far from lost, but are situationally accommodated (with varying degrees of integration, conflict, subordination or dominance) to the global discourse.

In the contemporary global discourse, 'democracy' has come to occupy an important place. It often carries deep emotional significance. It has acquired great mobilising power. In the course of the 20th century, many thousands of people have been prepared to die in struggles legitimated by reference to this symbol; many more people have admired others making such sacrifices in the name of democracy, and have spurred them on. Democracy has become a major export item of the USA and NATO. Ideologically (without denying the economic, political, religious and ethnic factors involved) the globalising concept of democracy was the force that breached the Berlin Wall and exploded the communist empire of Eastern Europe and North Asia. The global percolation of media images documenting this process has also contributed to the current democratisation movement in many parts of Africa.

The social scientist or historian reflecting on this African movement faces dilemmas that, phrased only slightly differently, are only too familiar from the study of world religions, mass consumption, styles of trade unionism, formal legislation by the nation-state, cosmopolitan medicine, and so many other aspects of the 20th century transformation of the African continent. These dilemmas address the extent to which North Atlantic models can acquire global relevance, and force us to explore the limitations of both Eurocentrism (which claims only one model to be valid) and cultural relativism (which claims all possible models, including those found outside the North Atlantic, to be equally valid and equally worth preserving for the future).

(1) The dilemma of *cultural imperialism*: is the institution of democracy, which we have seen spreading all over Africa, merely a *submission to alien* (viz. North Atlantic) forms which therefore will only fit like the proverbial square peg in the round hole of African cultures and societies; or is it, on the contrary, the awakening to *a universal heritage of mankind*, which has outgrown its being tied to a specific culture of origin (West European, North American, or whatever), so that Africans adopting it are merely coming into their own? In this light, the post-colonial vicissitudes of democracy in Africa would not imply any qualitative disability for democracy on the part of African societies and their members, but would be equivalent to the (much longer) formative stage of the same institution in the North Atlantic region itself (see below).

(2) The dilemma of *localisation*: even if considered global or universal, institutions invariably develop a local form; who is to say whether that local form is a regrettable deviation from abstract global standards?

(3) The dilemma of *wrongly claimed universality*: given the distribution of economic and military power in the modern world (*a basic state of affairs which the paradigm of globalisation does not take sufficiently into account, rather tending to obscure it under (illusory) postulates of cultural convergence and equality*), could members of a relatively powerful nation-state resist the temptation of claiming that their own culture-specific institutions have in fact supra-local, global relevance and truth? African democratisation gains interest and support outside Africa since it appears to liberate local African populations from the poor constitutional and economic performance of the post-colonial states in that continent. But if this amounts to furthering the *North Atlantic* model of formal democracy (disguised as universal), does it not at the same time imply the superiority of the north, and reinforce the relations of subordination which have existed between north and south since the 19th

century? Could democratisation mean that local African communities get rid of a failing state, but at the same time are more effectively subjugated (ideologically, institutionally and, since local democratic performance is increasingly a consideration in intercontinental donor relations, even economically) to unequal global power relations under northern hegemony? Is that the hidden agenda of the democratisation process?

(4) *The social price of relativism*: as social scientists we can afford to take our distance from, for instance, the Christianity of our ancestors (a North Atlantic institution whose spread outside Europe is well comparable to that of democracy), but we make ourselves unpopular and politically suspect in our own socio-political environment if we try to adopt the same stance with regard to democracy.[4] After all, who would not hope (especially in a secularising world of fragmented meaning, when absurdity has become the stock in trade of 20th century philosophy, art and literature) that such democratic principles as human rights and general elections, far from being culture-specific, would turn out to be universally applicable, to be 'true'? With the contestation by students and workers in Western Europe and North America in the late 1960s, the semantics of 'democracy' has moreover developed so as to include not only the constitutional level of the nation-state, but also participation, responsibility, initiative and competence in one's *immediate micro-political environment* (for example, on the shop-floor, social organisation or urban residential area). Democracy has become an important standard of evaluation for the legitimate managing of all power relations in which we are involved, and by implication for the propriety and meaning of all social action. The production of knowledge about democracy therefore is much more subject to social control (and thus far more prone to Eurocentrism) than many other respectable fields of cross-cultural social enquiry, for instance, concerning weaning practices, conflict settlement in polygamous households, or manuring techniques in peasant agriculture.

As an anthropological field-worker I have participated for long periods, and with as much existential commitment as I could summon, in four African societies[5] I was not born in, and there I have often encountered – and have lived – principles and procedures for the exercise of social power very different from the democratic ideas of my home society (Dutch urban society); in the latter, however, I consider myself a democrat. Against this background I cannot offer easy solutions for the dilemmas listed here. Meanwhile it is my contention that the current discussion on democratisation in Africa sometimes runs the risk of becoming myopic and Eurocentric in not paying sufficient attention to the analytical and methodological implications of cultural imperialism, localisation, wrongly claimed universality, and the social price of relativism – all of which are not exactly conducive to our objectivity as analysts.

Three modes of defining democracy

We also need to sharpen our conceptual tools and bring them into historical perspective. Democracy is a number of things at the same time, so that the term democratisation, as the process of bringing about or enhancing democracy, may refer to distinct and quite different phenomena. I propose to distinguish three modes, designated A, B and C.

Philosophically, 'democracy' denotes a specific answer to the question as to the source, within a collectivity of human beings, of the legitimate exercise of power through legal and political institutions. In the case of democracy, that source is not a supernatural being, a king, an aristocracy, a specific gender or age group, a priestly caste, a revealed unchangeable text or shrine, but 'the people' (A). Statements about 'the people' are sufficiently flexible and gratuitous to allow the philosophical label of democracy to be applied in numerous settings where in fact, through complex symbolic, ideological, legal and military means, voluntary or forced representation and usurpation have dramatically narrowed down the range of those who actually exercise the power. Examples would include not only the recently dismantled oligarchy of the German *Democratic* Republic, but also classical Athens – where women, and (for both sexes) slaves, children and youths, resident migrants (*metoikoi*), and citizens banished abroad, could not participate in the 'democratic' process.[6] After a succession of imperial, monarchical and theocratic options in the course of two millennia, democracy once more became the dominant legal-philosophical concept in the European tradition, and was pruned of its biases of inequality, in the American Declaration of Independence and subsequently the French Revolution, in the 18th century; the lists of basic human rights formulated in that context, still constitute the basis for the legal philosophy of democracy today.[7]

What marked these developments since the Enlightenment was the translation of the legal philosophy of democracy into constitutional and organisational arrangements that stipulate, in controllable and enforceable detail, the specific practical steps through which the ideal source of power is translated into concrete actions, offices, and personnel. It is these *constitutional* arrangements, rather than their philosophical elaboration, which have since characterised modern democracy (B).

Direct democracy through a plenary meeting (for which a *pro diem* was paid) with secret ballot was the ancient Greek formula at one stage, and archaeologists have pondered over the potsherds and the curious many-slotted stone slabs (anticipating our ballot computers of today) used in the process. Plenary meetings with formal voting procedures (or oath-taking, or other communication methods aimed at consensus) were found in many other historic societies, around the Mediterranean and beyond, organised on the basis of relatively small-scale local communities. For instance, the democratic thrust of the Dutch struggle for independence from Spain in the 16th century derived inspiration not only from philosophical, or rather theological, reflection on the ultimate source of legitimate power by early Protestant thinkers, but also from a much older tradition of village communities collectively administering their irrigation works (polders and dikes).

It is important to appreciate the factor of scale. Village communities conducive to direct political participation at the local level still exist all over the world. Moreover, a broadly comparable level of face-to-face interaction and ensuing direct interests on a day-to-day basis is, paradoxically, found among many members of urban mass society, in so far as these spend much of their working and leisure time in relatively small operational groups as defined within formal organisations and institutions (schools, churches, factories, government departments, sport clubs, etc.). Here the issues tend to be concrete and immediately appealing, and the often informal structures for individual participation in the decision-making process may have far greater relevance in the people's consciousness, than the formal and infrequently used constitutional arrangements for democracy at the national level.

Contemporary mass society as organised in nation-states at the national level no longer allows for direct democracy (although the current state of technology would make this a dated position, now that telephone lines and other electronic information carriers capable of instantaneous two-way communication extend into the majority of residential areas and even households). The standard formula has, of course, become that of representative delegation of 'the power of the people' through individual secret ballot by each eligible citizen registered as a voter. This is so much the accepted pattern that the organisation and international inspection of general elections has become the test *par excellence* of democracy. In discussions of democratisation in Africa, democracy is often equated with the presence of these very specific formal requirements.

The lexical and philosophical roots of the concept of democracy are far older than the specific accepted constitutional practical arrangements of democracy. In current discussions about democratisation in Africa we often forget that *the constitutional form of democracy as representative government empowered through general elections is only a recent phenomenon in the north*, and had far from materialised in its present form by the time of the Scramble for Africa which started the colonial period. *For most West European countries which effectively colonised most of Africa as from the late 19th century, the colonial period in part coincided, domestically, with a prolonged struggle for democratic rights on the part of the middle classes, workers, women, and youths.*[8]

The constitutional rights (summed up by the maxim 'one man (person) one vote') which Africans came to demand for themselves in the 1950s, thus belong to a package of modernity which, also in Western Europe, is 20th century rather than 19th, let alone earlier.

Meanwhile, the formal constitutional model of democracy has certain built-in features which would be self-defeating, unless other, less formal additional arrangements come to its rescue. For instance, the distance between the voter and the resulting national government under this model is so large, and the intervening stages and procedures are so complex, that the constitutional procedures of formal democracy may in themselves scarcely foster, in the ordinary voters, a sense of political competence, of actively shaping the present and future of their lives by participating in the decisions that most affect them; or, if they would still have such a sense of participation, it would often be based on illusion.

The negative effects of this distance can, however, be reduced in a number of ways, including:

- active participation in political parties organised on a mass basis;
- the development of a political culture of information and accountability, where citizens are aware of their constitutional rights and duties and where formal constitutional rights and politicians' performance are effectively tested by independent courts;
- the development, both in a formal bureaucratic form and through networks of lobbying, canvassing and opinion-making, of transparent links between the realms of direct participation at the grassroots level (not necessarily in political parties, but also in schools, churches, development committees, tenants' committees, co-operatives, union branches etc.) and the national political centre. People do not necessarily apply the same norms and procedures to (a) their immediate day-to-day environment

and (b) more distant national issues, and whereas a rigid divorce between the local and the national (in terms of political participation and identification) would amount to withdrawal, disenchantment, estrangement, of individuals vis-à-vis the political centre, a properly democratic system would succeed in effectively linking the local and the national.

- direct personal accessibility of those in power through networks of patronage, nepotism, regionalism, ethnicity and co-religionism; this is not exactly an option stipulated by the global democratic model, but it happens to be the only one that is found all over Africa;
- the existence of an open and general political discussion in the wider society, furthered by the overall accessibility of the written and electronic media, freedom of the press, widespread literacy, and a level of affluence enabling people access to the media.

All this amounts to a comprehensive political culture of democracy, which cannot be reduced to an abstract legal formula 'the source of all legitimate power is the people' (A), nor to the specific constitutional procedures including general elections (B). Its essence would appear to be that *people actively and responsibly participate, and have the sense of participating, in the major decisions that affect their present and future, in such a way that they see their major values and premises respected and reinforced, in a political process that links the local and the national* (C).

To sum up, we have identified a philosophical (A), a constitutional (B) and a sociological (C) definition of democracy. All three agree that democracy is 'something of the people'. As an anthropologist I flatter myself that I have learned something of the ordinary life and the private world-view of 'the people' who were my research participants. However, working through participant observation in local settings of face-to-face relations I have only obtained glimpses of the national level to the extent to which national level happens effectively to interpenetrate and link up with the local level. Since the 1970s anthropologists have struggled, and not vainly, to incorporate the state and the global political economy into their discourse. Therefore, if from the local level, the national political centre becomes visible only in a fragmented and problematic way, I submit that this is because the local/national relations are in fact problematic in the local situations under study, and not because anthropology has difficulty in addressing such situations. All the same, while local/national relations will be highlighted in my discussion of democratisation among peasants (generally identifying under the ethnic label of 'Nkoya') from Kaoma district in Zambia's Western Province (formerly Barotseland), and among working-class townsmen (most of whom identify ethnically as 'Kalanga' or as belonging to any of the various Tswana groups, mainly 'Ngwato', 'Kwena', 'Ngwaketse', 'Kgatla') from Francistown, Botswana,[9] my actual research was conceived in such a way that it does not enable me to make valid general pronouncements concerning democratisation in these countries at the national level.

But before we turn to the ethnographic detail there is one more general hurdle to take. If constitutional democracy (B) has sprung from the dynamics of the North Atlantic societies, how must we visualise its reception in African societies? The current wave of democratisation in Africa since the late 1980s appeals to, and seeks to restore, constitutional rights and procedures which allegedly have gone dormant under the failing performance of the post-colonial nation-states. But when and how were they planted on African soil in the first place?

Constitutional democracy (B) as a recently introduced item of political culture in Africa

At independence, African post-colonial states emerged as the continuation of the bureaucratic apparatus of the colonial state, but now increasingly staffed with African personnel, and defined by a national constitution. The constitution was, in most cases, and initially at least, highly reminiscent of that of the former colonial metropole. The exercise of state power by this bureaucratic apparatus was legitimated by constitutionally well-defined patterns of popular participation through the general franchise. In the background, the constitutional process would be supported by international and intercontinental treaties ensuring the post-independent nation-state of a respected place among the world's nations upholding fundamental human rights. Usually these rights were specifically summed up in the constitution.

The specific constitutional pattern thus stipulated in the new nation-states of Africa in the 1960s could boast only a shallow time-depth on African soil. The roles, statuses, rights and organisational forms, the concrete procedures of candidacy, individual vote, loyal opposition etc., as defined by that pattern, were alien to the indigenous structures of legitimate political power which had prevailed in most parts of Africa through most of the 19th and early 20th century. In other words, the pattern was not in continuity with modes of participation and legitimation which Africans from a village background would spontaneously apply in their immediate face-to-face social environment. If constitutional democratic features were already part of the political culture of the colonial metropole, the colonial state was built on the principle that they should not be extended to the vast majority of African 'subjects'.

How did this essentially alien and imported political culture take root in the minds, actions and institutions of 20th century Africans?

Conversion to world religions, especially Christianity, the concomitant access to literacy and formal education, and the adoption of positions as workers, foremen and clerks within capitalist relations of colonial production, made Africans share in aspects of the same societal experience (typically embedded within formal organisations such as schools, churches, mines, manufacturing enterprises, the police, the army, local government) that had prompted the democratic process in the North Atlantic region up to about half a century earlier.

The African experience was not just one of humiliation, although there certainly was an infuriating amount of that. Participating in a missionary organisation as an African evangelist, in a local government structure as a *boma* (district administration) messenger, in a school as a junior teacher, in a mine as a driller or 'bossboy', also involved (precisely while being humiliated) learning about the exercise and manipulation of power in a context of formal organisations; learning about an impersonal legal authority that derived not from God or from personal charisma through birth or achievement (e.g. kingship), but from the abstract written word of law and regulation; learning about rigid and intricate patterns of the organisation of time and space which had come in the trappings of colonialism and peripheral capitalism but which even more fundamentally defined the 20th century societal experience both in the north and in the south. In the latter part of the world they were manifested in the layout of the residential space – segregated in

Figure 1 South Central and Southern Africa

terms of 'race' and status – and the rhythm of time between work and off-duty, Christian Sunday and secular weekday, not to mention the legally-defined periods of time involved in the payment of poll tax, of notice when fired, and the contractual spells of migrant labour. All this against the background of a hidden premise of West European modernity (which settlers and other colonialists struggled in vain to prevent from seeping through to the colonised subjects): the human individual as essentially equal to other individuals, i.e. as interchangeable in a manner similar to manufactured products (and workers) in the Industrial Revolution; but also, more positively, in the sense that each human individual could be taken as exemplary in the manner of biological species, chemical elements and physical laws which post-Renaissance natural science had come to define; essentially equal, despite differences in status and power (related to class and race), and as equals converging theologically in the original sin and the Christian salvation of mankind according to the missionaries' preachings; and, in a secularising society increasingly organised along bureaucratic lines, equal before the letter of impersonal legal authority. Under the circumstances it could only be a matter of time until such premises of equality were also applied in the constitutional sphere, in the sense of universal franchise for Africans restored to competence and initiative over the political and social institutions that governed their lives.

In the struggle for de-colonisation and independence a crucial role was played by varieties of *self-organisation* (trade unions, political parties, welfare societies, burial societies, rotating credit associations, ethnic and dancing groups, women's movements, and such churches as welcomed popular participation and initiative) which were soon to be patterned after the same model of formal organisation. Until quite late in the colonial period, however, only a minority of the African population was sufficiently deeply involved in imported organisational structures to internalise the attitudes and values that would make them articulate democrats in the global, constitutional sense.

The African independence movement of the 1950s was not only about a vocal and educated African elite wrenching constitutional power from the hands of the colonialists, but also about a *broad social transformation which, through communication, mobilisation and mass organisation, made the tenets of constitutional democracy come to life for large numbers of Africans irrespective of their mode of livelihood, urban or rural residence, level of education or religious creed.* The leaders of the struggle for independence were political brokers canvassing for position, and planning a new nation-state. They were also the prophets, at least temporarily honoured in their own lands, of a brand-new democratic political culture.

They were not the only ones to offer a blueprint of a meaningful and attainable future to African populations which had seen their cosmologically structured, coherent universe fall apart in the turmoil of the 19th and early 20th century. As pedlars of meaning, organisational structure and restored competence through effective action, the independence politicians with their secular and constitutional message were in stark, often violent competition, over their following among the African masses, with witch-finders, prophets, church leaders, who locally or at a grander scale offered their own interpretations of current misery and future redress.[10] In many of these attempts at symbolic or ritual salvation, there was a large amount of bricolage, the various distinct movements arriving at specific recombinations of elements derived from the traditional world-view as well as from Christianity. The democratic movement around independence mainly sought to explore the mobilising potential of the common men's experiences of peripheral capitalism and colonialism in the propagation of a democratic and constitutional political culture which – certainly in the 1950s – was West European far more than it had already become localised and African. By contrast, the religiously-orientated alternatives to the democratic movement showed far greater continuity *vis-à-vis* the ideological and organisational orientation that had largely informed African life in the 19th century, and that was still a formidable force in the rural areas and in the kin networks of migrant workers in town. From one point of view there was, between the various political and ideological options at the time, a struggle for or against continuity of the village-based traditional world-view; from another, complementary viewpoint, various contesting categories within the changing local society manipulated alternative world-views so as to re-define the political and economic interrelations between these social categories. Chiefs, headmen, and elders in general derived much of their power over young men and over women from a traditional world-view that made these elderly men the main intermediaries between the villagers and cosmological forces (ancestors, spirits of the wild, the High God, royal spirits), and as such the indispensable mediators in the relations (sexual, conjugal, judicial) even between young men and women. For young men, particularly, this world-view hardly answered the existential questions related to their experience as migrant workers, and it denied such independence from elders as they had aspired to, and often actually enjoyed, at their distant places of work; the youth's adoption of new secular political or Christian ideologies helped them to take a relative view of the elders which had so far dominated their lives.[11]

Thus the continuity of a cosmologically-anchored local world-view with its own conceptions of legitimate political power and procedure; the interaction between on the one hand traditional leaders and, on the other, those of their subjects pursuing modern careers outside the village settings; the prominence of religious alternatives for the symbolic restructuring of local society: the explicit formulation, and the transmutation, of democratic political values in the mobilisation process of an independence struggle; and the specific relations to develop between local and national level at, and since, independence. All these would seem to be important factors in the production of a democratic political culture in the global sense. With this in mind, let us now turn to our two ethnographic examples.

Democracy versus ethnicity in Kaoma District, Zambia

The dynamics of democracy and democratisation in Kaoma district, Zambia, must be understood against the background of its traditional and neo-traditional political structure and its colonial experience.

The fertile, well-watered lands of Nkoya (now largely coinciding with the Kaoma district, on the Zambezi/Kafue watershed, at roughly the same latitude as Zambia's capital Lusaka but 400 km west) was the scene of dispersed communities of hunters, fishermen and agriculturalists organised on a basis of localised clans, when, from the middle of the 8th century, a number of kingdoms emerged here under the influence of long-distance trading opportunities and of political ideas derived from the Lunda empire in southern Zaïre. Around 1850 most of these kingdoms became incorporated in the Kololo/Luyana state which has since been known as Barotseland, with the Barotse or Lozi as the dominant ethnic group. Barotseland became the Protectorate of Northwestern Rhodesia in 1900, and even after Zambia's independence maintained a special status within the new republic until 1969 (Caplan 1970). Under the Lozi king, whose official title is *Litunga*, only two Nkoya royal titles (*Mwene Kahare* and *Mwene Mutondo*) managed to survive through the colonial period, as recognised and subsidised senior members of the Lozi aristocracy.[12] Nkoya traditional politics, concentrated on the Kahare and Mutondo capitals, has displayed a highly articulate ceremonial culture, involving, in addition to the royal family, a Prime Minister (*Mwanashihemi*), other titled court officials including judges, and court priests, musicians, executioners and slaves (the latter two statuses have been re-defined in recent times). Along with the senior court officials, about a dozen senior village headmen constituted the *Mwene*'s royal council, where[13] cases involving protocol and royal matters were handled, land was issued to locals and strangers who so requested, and the *Mwene*'s diplomatic relations with other Myene, with the *Litunga*, and the colonial, subsequently postcolonial government were deliberated. In exceptionally important situations (e.g. death of a *Mwene* or election of a successor, the visit of a major outside official, or cases involving witchcraft accusations of royals or otherwise reflecting on the entire kingdom) the council's session would be held not in the *Mwene*'s audience hall but outside, and then all subjects of the *Mwene* (regardless of gender and age) had a right to attend, whereas mature men (well over 40 years of age) and – but rarely – women of the same age group would take the floor, displaying their skills at the formal Nkoya rhetoric. A strong sense of protocol and procedure permeates Nkoya traditional politics and constitutional law. The

Mwanashihemi is usually co-opted (by the *Mwene* and the royal council) from another kingdom so as to ensure impartial application of these rules.

Political office is within the reach of many, and coveted. The bilateral kinship system with endogamous tendencies makes lines of descent frequently merge, so that kin groups are defined by *ad hoc* micropolitical dynamics hingeing on co-residence. It is these kin groups of shifting composition which own titles of kingship and village headmanship – the proper names or praise-names of their ancestors – and whose senior male members, after secret deliberations, confer a vacant title upon a candidate of their choice by a ritual of name inheritance called *ushwana*. An honoured title as headman is therefore within the reach of many men who live to attain middle age, and even the pool out of which royal candidates could be selected used to be quite large until, under Lozi and colonial influence, patrilineal descent was imposed; but even so there are still a number of rival royal candidates at every succession. And far from being considered obsolete, the competition for offices as headman, senior headman and *Mwene* is still very lively and sometimes (in a society where poison and sorcery are common-place) even deadly – these offices have continued to represent the highest form of career achievement, not only for those who have spent most of their lives in the village but also for labour migrants who have returned to the rural areas after living in town for decades and attaining stable and even senior positions there.

The *Mwene* ultimately derives descent from the demiurge Mvula, i.e. Rain,[14] and while Mvula's relationship *vis-à-vis* the High God Nyambi is not totally clear, the kingship is explicitly legitimated by reference to Nyambi's status as the first *Mwene* and as *Mwene of the Sky*. In terms of symbolic legitimation Nkaya kingship presents a Janus face: on the one hand the *Mwene* represents celestial beings and as such he is the incarnation of the cosmic order on earth; on the other hand his office is surrounded with connotations of sorcery and physical violence which are absolutely abhorred in the context of Nkoya non-royal village life. This presents an interesting puzzle for historical, symbolic and theoretical analysis, but we cannot present the details of its solution here (Van Binsbergen 1992a, 1993c). Suffice to say that there is a notion of legitimate power (*ngovu*), which is cosmologically anchored and of which the Mwene by virtue of a very elaborate enthronement ceremony[15] is the central representative, but only in so far as his actions remain within the dignity (*shishemu*) of his office and are underpinned by the advice from the royal council, which tends to be quite vocal. *Mwene mwene na bantu*: 'a *Mwene* is *Mwene* by virtue of the people', is the Nkoya maxim. In addition to his title and regalia, followers are the *Mwene*'s most important asset, and he is in practice dependent upon public opinion for his continuation in office. Just like the village headman, the king is dependent upon his followers' continued support, in the form of loyalty, respect and residence within his realm; formerly also in the form of tribute and tribute labour – a *Mwene* cannot engage in productive labour and would starve to death without tribute – as happened to the impeached *Mwene* Kashina in the mid-19th century. Since people have latent rights of membership and residence including use of land and other natural resources in a number of villages beside the village of their actual residence, a failing village headman sees the ranks of his followers dwindle by their moving to different villages until the village may be completely depleted; a failing royal *Mwene* may even be killed by the senior councillors. Regicide, forced abdication and impeachment of *Mwene* are documented in the

region's history throughout the 19th and 20th century. For fear of being poisoned therefore, no *Mwene* would drink beer that is not tasted first by a trusted kinswoman or cupbearer.

The Nkoya political system as it has existed since the 18th century (incorporating many elements from a clan-based pre-kingship system that is considerably older)[16] thus reflects interestingly on the three definitions of democracy presented above. There is a notion that high political office, however exalted a status and surrounded by taboos separating the *Mwene* from his subjects, and however underpinned by cosmological references, could not afford to dissociate itself from the people (A). There was a pattern of effective participation within the kingdom, in principle open to all subjects but in practice usually delegated to senior headmen and to mature men in general (C). But the constitutional procedures stipulating the election to high office and the exercise of power were completely different from those of the global democratic model (B), and defined for mature men a secluded realm of constitutional competence in a way which (through the exclusion of youth and women) reinforced gender and age cleavages in the local society.

Perhaps one would expect that such a historic political system offered fertile ground for the adoption of the global democratic model, also in terms of constitutional procedures. The opposite, however, turned out to be the case, as is clear from developments in this region in the 1950s and early 1960s, when Zambia was involved in the struggle for independence.

For most Nkoya at the time, colonial rule was not much of an issue. Incorporation in the global capitalist economy through labour migration had started early (late 19th century), but until well after independence it took the form of circulatory labour migration which kept people's social and conceptual dependence on their rural society of origin largely intact. The Nkoya (certainly those of the eastern Mashasha kingdom, that of *Mwene* Kahare) hardly had an option, since until *ca.* 1950 they had very little access to missionary education and therefore no basic skills that might have launched them on a stable urban career. The same lack of education, particularly illiteracy, made it difficult for the global democratic model to be absorbed by them at an early age. The imposition of colonial rule had reinforced the hold of the Lozi indigenous administration in the region, and it was the Lozi, far more than the British, who were perceived as oppressors. The seething of protest and contestation throughout the Federation of Rhodesia and Nyasaland in the second half of the colonial period, in the Nkoya region, at first took the form of symbolic reconstruction of society through witchcraft eradication (which often had anti-Lozi overtones, and was supported by the *Mwene*), followed in the 1950s by an outbreak of blatant sorcery practices (Reynolds 1963) as if new forms of power, meaning and redress could only be found in the mystical sphere and not in secular constitutional change. Only when democratic independence pioneers in the centre of Barotseland (the Wina brothers, Princes Nakatindi) turned out to challenge the Lozi aristocratic establishment, did the Nkoya become interested in modern politics, but the Litunga managed to prevent the registration (Mulford 1967) of a Nkoya branch of Mr H. Nkumbula's ANC – the Zambian independence party from which Mr K. Kaunda's ZANC (soon to be called UNIP) broke away in 1958. A few Nkoya young men who meanwhile, against many odds, had managed to get some formal education and had embarked on urban careers, featured in the various political parties on the Northern Rhodesian scene around

1960. Some even started an ethnically-orientated, but abortive, party called Mankoya Fighting Fund, and in the first general elections the Nkoya massively supported UNIP, but still the issue as perceived by the Nkoya was anti-Lozi far more than in favour of independence and constitutional democracy. When at independence the Lozi turned out to have occupied powerful positions in regional and national government, while not a single Nkoya operated at these levels, and when moreover the UNIP government stopped labour migration to Zimbabwe and South Africa which had been the Nkoya's main source of cash for many decades, the interest in modern politics dissipated entirely, and the Nkoya withdrew within the confines of the neo-traditional local politics.

During my first fieldwork in the region in the early 1970s, it was shocking to see how little the local population considered themselves to be part of post-independent Zambia. Zambia was the name for a country 'out there', along the 'Line of Rail' that crosses Zambia from north to south and along which its towns were concentrated. The principles and procedures of Zambia's constitutional organisation seemed largely unknown among most villagers, and commanded even less loyalty. Democratic voting procedures were considered morally and cosmologically obscene, for implying that political office could be bought for promises, favours and money rather than being a high responsibility entrusted to the best candidate on the basis of the elders' secret deliberations, and the legitimating *ushwana* installation ceremony which guaranteed ancestral support for the new incumbent. Incorporation in the wider world had so far only produced a conceptual boundary *vis-à-vis* that world, not a sense of wider relationships and responsibilities, let alone a new sense of power and competence at the national level. Even the Kaoma district centre, with its administrative and judicial offices and UNIP headquarters, was an alien place, where no Nkoya occupied any position in the political and administrative hierarchy above messenger, driver or cleaner; Nkoya were also conspicuously absent among local entrepreneurs. Paradoxically, the most conspicuous local link with the UNIP government was in the person of *Mwene* Kahare, whose subtle manoeuvring in the struggle for independence had gained him the honour of being nominated a party trustee. Besides, he was made a member of the national House of Chiefs, and although this did not give him any tangible power at the national level, it gave his subjects in the rural areas the illusory satisfaction that when their *Mwene* was summoned to Lusaka he went there, using government transport, in order to rule Zambia! Lozi oppression was felt to continue as before independence, and there was widespread nostalgia for the blessings of the colonial period, when blankets and clothing had been cheap and migrants' cash earnings had not been subject to income tax at source.

In the early 1970s, a local branch of UNIP existed nominally but it was virtually invisible at the village level. Rather more visible was a UNIP Youth branch, largely composed of sons and clients of senior headmen who were the *Mwene*'s main rivals with regard to traditional office. With very little feedback from national and regional headquarters, the youths' activities did not consist of political instruction or mobilisation. At the time when UNIP Youths elsewhere in Zambia created havoc with their violent card-selling and card-checking practices, the Nkoya Youth made themselves occasionally useful as a work-force for communal projects (emulating a historic pattern of tribute labour). They were particularly conspicuous when they organised a mass trial where *Mwene* Kahare and his staff were accused of the kind of ritual murder that had always been part and parcel of the kingship. In the process the youths presented a list of demands that, if implemented, would have made them the *de facto* authorities in the kingdom. This challenge of the traditional establishment misfired (ultimately the *Mwene*, subsidised and officially gazetted, had much more backing from the outside world than the self-styled UNIP Youths), but what is particularly revealing is that the youths' attack was completely inward-looking and failed to adopt the idiom of the national democratic model. The *Mwene*, on his part, could not convert his basic loyalty to the UNIP government and the post-colonial state into political education for his subjects, since his relationship with his subjects was determined by constitutional principles which were totally alien to the global democratic model.

The Nkoya participated in the struggle for independence on the basis of their own ethnic priorities, and did not yet learn much about constitutional democracy in the process. Thus the first opportunity, around independence, of turning the Nkoya into participants in the national democratic process, was almost completely lost. But not quite. I have passed over the urban experience of Nkoya migrants at the time. In the second half of the 1960s, Zambian towns were in the throes of conflict between ANC and UNIP, which was only resolved by the creation of the second Republic, under UNIP, in December 1971.[17] Nkoya urban residents had participated in this process as inhabitants of urban residential areas siding with one particular party, as street fighters etc., but only a handful of them had actually taken up office in either political organisation and thus had been exposed to the inner organisational structure and procedures of the democratic process. One of them, Mr J. Kalaluka, had even stood as an ANC parliamentary candidate in the 1968 elections, but had lost. The forced amalgamation between ANC and UNIP enabled him to be a UNIP candidate in the 1973 elections, and then he became the MP for Kaoma East. When, within a few years, he managed to add a ministerial post to his seat in parliament, the Nkoya had finally found the link to the centre that was to teach them how to appreciate and make use of modern constitutional forms.

Three additional factors facilitated this process: the Lozi's decline at the national level, successful rural development in Kaoma district, and the Nkoya's ethnic self-organisation.

(a) In 1969 President Kaunda had terminated the special status of the former Barotseland within the Republic of Zambia, and the 1970s saw the decline of Lozi power at the national level. In the process, the president and his administration missed few opportunities to curry favour with the Nkoya.

(b) In 1971, moreover, the powerful parastatal Tobacco Board of Zambia had initiated a major development scheme in the eastern part of Kaoma district. Few local villagers could lastingly benefit, as tenants, from the new opportunities this scheme offered, and the farms were largely occupied by ethnic strangers. Yet within 15 years the very sparsely populated forest turned into a rural town of nearly 20,000 inhabitants, Nkeyema, with schools, clinics, a thriving UNIP party branch, etc. (Nelson-Richards 1988). For a number of political brokers of Nkoya background, including Mr Kalaluka, the scheme offered both personal economic advancement and a platform for active mobilisation along ethnic and regional lines. Here, for the first time, UNIP songs and the Zambian national anthem were sung in the Nkoya language, whose legitimate existence had so far been denied by the Lozi and the central state.

Nkoya gradually awoke to the idea that the modern state and its institutions were not necessarily inimical, either to the ethnic identity they had developed in the context of Lozi incorporation, or to the kingship that had become the central expression of that identity. While Zambia as a whole saw a period of steady economic decline in the second half of the 1970s and throughout the 1980s, the relative economic situation in what had used to be a stagnant labour reserve, Kaoma district, began to look less bleak. Realising that the state had little to offer, economically, beyond the mixed blessings of the Nkeyema Scheme, Nkoya/state contacts increasingly concentrated on a non-material deal: the exchange of the Nkoya citizen's loyal support and participation, for state recognition and consolidation of their ethnic identity and traditional leadership.

(c) This process was formalised when in the early 1980s, after diffuse preparations from the mid-1970s, a few middle-class urbanites from a Nkoya background founded the Kazanga Cultural Association. This society has since linked urban and rural sections of Nkoya life, particularly through the organisation, since 1988, of the annual Kazanga cultural festival, where the Zambian state has always put in an appearance through a delegation at ministerial level. The festival (one of the five of its nature in the country, to be announced and reported on Zambia television) is an enormous source of pride to the Nkoya, and generates all sorts of further activities and innovations in the cultural, organisational and economic fields.

As a result of these developments over the past 20 years, the Nkoya people of Kaoma district have become far more effectively incorporated in the post-colonial state. The misery, bitterness, indignation and estrangement from the state under the Kaunda administration, which marked the 1980s for particularly the urban populations of Zambia, were here attenuated somewhat by the rural economic opportunities, but to a much larger extent by the ethnic revival the people went through, which restored a sense of meaning and competence to their rich cultural life, and created contexts in which this heritage was no longer self-consciously cherished and fossilised within a local universe increasingly sealed off from an inimical outside world, but could be communicated to that outside world, in forms (particularly media coverage) which have great prestige in that outside world, and which generate further innovation.

Interesting innovations are now taking place in the kingship. In the early 1970s the Nkoya neo-traditional court culture was marked by a rigid splendour. The emphatic maintenance of nostalgic historic forms of protocol and symbolic, particularly musical, production (which no longer corresponded with any real power invested in the kingship under conditions of incorporation by the Lozi indigenous state and by the colonial and post-colonial central state) reflected the fact that the need for boundary maintenance vis-à-vis the outside world was at its peak. All this contrasts strikingly with the laxity of court life today. It is as if the focus of articulation of Nkoya ceremonial court culture has now shifted from the day-to-day protocol at the secluded traditional capitals controlled by traditional councillors, to the annual public performance at the Kazanga festival, before central-state dignitaries and a massive audience of spectators, and controlled by the Kazanga association executive. Of course, the kingship, based on a local vision of the political and cosmological order, could only lose out when the subjects came to participate more effectively and whole-heartedly in a national democratic order based on very different constitutional

principles. However, at the same time a fervent reconstruction process is going on, where the Kazanga Cultural Association effectively negotiates between the state, the kings and the villagers, insisting on a new symbolic and ceremonial role for all four[18] Nkoya kings together along lines which, while ostentatiously appealing to tradition, in fact constitute recent innovations, rather at variance with established historical patterns, but which do result in restoring the kings to a level of emotional and symbolic significance perhaps unprecedented in 20th century Nkoya history. During the 1992 Kazanga festival, *Mwene* Kahare Kabambi, who used to be a somewhat pathetic, stammering figure dressed in a faded suit with ragged shirt collar, appeared covered in leopard skins and with a headband adorned with regal *zimpande* (Conus shells), and formidably brandishing his royal axe and broadsword, and after drinking from the sacred pit with beer made of the year's first harvest, for the first time in living memory performed the *kutomboke* royal solo dance which kept the audience breathless and moved them to tears. After his death in 1993, his successor *Mwene* Kahare Kubama kept up this pattern at the 1994 festival.

Having greatly invested in the UNIP administration in the last decade, and feeling that they had been given a fair deal, the Nkoya were certainly not in the forefront of Mr Frederick Chiluba's Movement for Multi-Party Democracy (MMD), when this materialised in 1990 out of the political contest against the failing Kaunda administration. Even though Mr Kalaluka had lost his parliamentary seat, and hence his ministerial post, in the 1987 elections to a non-Nkoya contender from Kaoma district, the links to the political centre had become sufficiently open, and the sense of political competence sufficiently developed, to take a maturely democratic stance. Recalling the lack of democratic knowledge and attitudes which I found in the area in 1973, 1 am now amazed by the ease with which ordinary villagers, men and women, talk about the national political issues of today, and define their own position within what is essentially a democratic constitutional framework. I grant that a considerable part of the credit must go to the inspiration of the democratic movement which swept over Zambia since the late 1980s; but this would have fallen on completely infertile ground, had not a gradual process of Nkoya/state accommodation over the 1970s and 1980s, under UNIP, already turned the people into democrats with a realistic national outlook. One recognised the unmistakable need for change, and was prepared to give majority support even to parliamentary candidates (such as Mr Mandande and Mr Tumbila, the present MMD MPs for the district) who were new men both at the national and the regional level, and of whom the former did not even qualify nor identify as Nkoya. Realising that the Nkoya group had come to carry a certain weight at the national and regional level, the political and symbolic brokers that make up the Kazanga association's executive lost no time in trading Nkoya support for organisational and logistic facilities under the new government. Needless to say, the promise of innovation and restoration which constitute MMD's main appeal tied in very well with the local reconstruction the Nkoya were already involved in on their own impetus. Again, the crucial inspiration appears to have been local and ethnic rather than national and democratic – but now at least within a framework of open and viable local/national relations.

However, the Nkoya have learned not to put all their eggs in one basket. Only a few months before the elections of October 1991 (cf. Sichone 1991–92; Baylies and Szeftel 1992) which brought Mr Chiluba's victory and Mr Kaunda's political demise, the latter had personally intervened in an attempt by the *Litunga*[19] to downgrade or even abolish the kingships of Kahare and Mutondo. Perhaps somewhat alarmed by the prominence, in MMD, of Lozi politicians such as Mr Arthur Wina and Mr Akashambatwa Mbikusita-Lewanika (both of whom have since left MMD, however), established Nkoya community leaders, both in modern and traditional office, tended to continue siding with UNIP. Even after Mr Chiluba's installation as President of Zambia, massive UNIP rallies have continued to be held in Kaoma district, with Nkoya party officials in prominent positions. Of course, this is to be expected under a multi-party democracy, and it is regrettable that, barely one and a half years after the change-over (April 1993), the first UNIP activists had to be made political prisoners in MMD Zambia. Most recently, the National Party's success in Western Province as a whole, at the expense of MMD, is also reflected in Kaoma district, and without destructive friction the national and regional executive of the Kazanga association continues to encompass the various party-political options such as exist at the national level. Local ethnic reconstruction continues to take precedence over national party allegiance.

The nature of my data does not allow me to make pronouncements about MMD and the recent democratisation process in general at the national level (cf. Mudenda 1992). My story about one ethnic group in one rural district should not be misread to imply an interpretative pattern for Zambia as a whole, or for rural Zambia as a whole. Having not started the post-colonial period with a great deal of knowledge or illusions about the democratic constitutional process and of their own role therein, having fared much better under UNIP than could be expected, and tapping a source of revitalisation at the local ethnic rather than the national democratic level, the Nkoya could scarcely muster the great sense of frustration and anger that characterised the seasoned trade unionists, politicians and intellectuals at MMD's centre (cf. Mbikusita-Lewanika and Chitala 1990; Kamwambe 1991).

The Nkoya story is only a footnote to the specific recent history of the MMD in Zambia. But it suggests that MMD in itself cannot be understood unless against the background of the total, and uneven, picture of the emergence of a global democratic political culture in Zambia, a process in which traditional leadership, religious alternatives, and local/national relations constitute important dimensions.

Glimpses of democracy in Francistown, Botswana

From this point in my argument, and from Zambia, it is only a short step to Botswana, a neighbouring country which appears to have remained untouched by the African democratisation movement of recent years. If the Nkoya case in Zambia brings out regional politics, ethnic reconstruction and the partial survival of a local, ancient political culture as limiting conditions to the reception of the North Atlantic democratic model, the Botswana case would suggest that further boundary conditions lie in the quality of the state's economic performance, and in the ideological construction of a sense of historic continuity in the local political culture, so that the state elite can pose as emulating, rather than providing an alternative to, political traditions as perceived by the state's ordinary citizens.

Botswana is a most interesting case among African countries, since to the outside world it has presented the image of one of the very few African democracies that has survived intact since independence; moreover it is one of the few African economies that has avoided the stagnation so common in the continent during the 1970–1980s. So the most obvious answer to the question as to why there is no conspicuous democratisation movement in Botswana, would seem to be: 'because no further democratisation is needed – the country is a viable democracy and the state delivers what the citizens expect'.

My research, since 1988, in Botswana's second largest town, Francistown has, however, convinced me that this answer is only partially correct. The Botswana state does deliver, albeit far from lavishly, and in ways which (as the Batswana[20] workers often complain) compares poorly with the income situation and standard of living in neighbouring South Africa, with which many Batswana are familiar from labour migration, personal contacts and the media. At the same time, Botswana is far from a totally convincing democracy.[21]

The political scene is dominated by the ruling Botswana Democratic Party (BDP). Of the handful of other parties, only the Botswana National Front (BNF) and Botswana People's Party (BPP) are sufficiently organised to win a few parliamentary seats in the general elections, which are held regularly at five-year intervals, the last in 1989. The weakness of the opposition is not due to lack of politicians of great capabilities, but to lack of funds (whereas the ruling party is at least logistically facilitated by the government), fragmentation, a low degree of grassroots organisation, and the circumstance that the ruling party's powers of co-optation and appeal for peace and unity cut across political boundaries. Among the tactics which the ruling party uses in order to perpetuate its position of dominance, are the appointment of additional members of elected political bodies whenever the opposition threatens to take a majority, and persuading opposition members to cross the floor to the ruling party (a case in point is the Francistown Town Council in 1987). Another strategy is that of postponing the implementation of unpopular decisions such as the demolition of a squatter area until after elections, especially if the area in question has a high proportion of BDP supporters.[22] A related and even more general strategy is securing public support in exchange for such facilities as the state (controlled by the ruling party) has to offer: junior secondary schools, clinics, boreholes. Comparable is the government's handling of many millions of Pulas[23] of arrears incurred in the country's ambitious and praiseworthy Self-Help Housing Association (SHHA) programme: on the basis of repayable loans and monthly service levies, this programme provided adequate, occupant-owned housing for tens of thousands of town dwellers, but until well after the 1989 general elections the BDP administration chose not to take legal action concerning the arrears for fear of estrangeing the vast majority of beneficiaries that had often run into very considerable arrears.

The electronic media in Botswana are government-controlled and so is the only daily newspaper, although there are a number of private weekly periodicals which maintain considerable independence from the ruling party. The Botswana constitution (Republic of Botswana 1983) guarantees the usual human rights, and its extensive limiting clauses in the interest of peace and order are fairly standard by comparison to other constitutions. In practice these clauses mean, for example, that people are not allowed to use any language other than English and Tswana in court and parliament (although about 30 per cent have other languages as their mother-tongue), and that hardly any periodicals or books in these languages are published, partly because people are under the impression that this would be illegal. The use of private printing presses is subject to a licence which every printer is at pains not to forfeit.

'Freedom squares', which are open spaces set aside for public meetings of a political nature, exist in every residential area and village and are open to whatever political party applies for a permit to use them, but all political meetings taking place there are attended by uniformed police who tape the proceedings. There are no political prisoners in Botswana, but individuals who during questioning time at such meetings bring up awkward issues have occasionally been known to be taken for questioning. Similarly, opposition politicians and ethnic activists have opted for careers of self-employment in the awareness that they would be likely to be penalised by thwarted promotion opportunities, if not actual dismissal, if they pursued their activities from positions as civil servants, teachers, etc. In places like Francistown where a garrison is stationed, and especially in border areas, people have learned to fear the soldiers, whose conduct is not always subject to the kind of control one would expect under the rule of law.

With the rapid post-independence quantitative expansion of education, and the existence of oppositional politics since the 1960s, constitutional knowledge is considerable in educated and middle-class circles. However, among the general public the level of democratic awareness and actual political participation, including voting, are low. Certainly in Francistown the majority of the population would give the impression of taking the government for granted, even in the *de facto* one-party form it has assumed in Botswana, without taking great interest and, especially, without being keen on change.

Here I refer to the distinction I made earlier between national-level political participation and immediate democracy at the grass-roots level of village, urban residential area, workplace, school, etc.. Batswana, both in town and in villages, do take a keen interest in their immediate social environment, and actively seek to structure it through organisation and participation. The social environment need not coincide with the direct physical environment, and often extends far beyond. In newly-settled residential areas many people find it difficult to establish flourishing dyadic, informal ties with the strangers that happen to have become their neighbours, but they actively maintain ties with people from their home village, their ethnic group, their church and their workplace (Van Binsbergen 1991, 1993a). And whenever dyadic relations can be embedded in a lasting collective organisational setting involving a number of people on a more or less permanent, formal and predictable basis, Batswana show great eagerness and creativity in the pursuit of public responsibility. Voluntary associations (especially independent churches and sport associations) are a dominant feature of social life, not only in towns but also in rural areas. The model of serious and candid consultation between equals informs the pattern of interaction at the village assembly (*kgotla*), where basic values of sociability, respect, and inclusiveness are brought out in a way which makes proceedings take on a social significance far exceeding that of the adjudication of petty individual cases. So much is the *kgotla* model the standard for ideal social behaviour, that it is immediately emulated whenever the diffusion of information, the need to arrive at a decision, or the settlement of a conflict necessitates the appeal to a common framework of interest and a shared model of action: in family matters, on the work-floor, in formal organisations, etc. In these contexts the everyday rhythm of activities including the bureaucratic division of labour and group boundaries are time and again punctuated by informal, impromptu but extremely effective ceremonies of consultation which are the

hallmark of Botswana political culture. For Batswana, the test of appropriate public behaviour, decision-making and 'democracy' lies in principle in this type of practical consultation, far more than in the remote letter of any modern or traditional constitutional legislation.

As such, the *kgotla* model, as pivotal in the national culture, provides a welcome instrument in the hands of the Botswana state elite seeking to legitimate and perpetuate its position of power. Emphatic public reference to, and artificial emulation of, the *kgotla* model can produce, in the mind of common Batswana, a sense of historic continuity and legitimation where in fact there is dis-continuity, transformation and unchecked elite appropriation of societal power. The skilful manipulation of the *kgotla* model in Botswana thus produces what we might designate, somewhat floridly, as 'populist authoritarianism through symbolic engineering'. Today, proceedings at village *dikgotla* and especially at Urban Customary Courts are claimed to be in accordance with the time-honoured *kgotla* model which – as the elite never tires of reminding the population – is at the heart of the Botswana tradition; but in fact uniformed police officials and clerks have appropriated the judicial process even at the village level, and even more so in town, where no cross-examination by ordinary members of the public is allowed, the slim volume of the Penal Code is applied rigidly and mechanically without reference to customary law even in the latter's codified form, and where sessions are even closed to the public. By the same token, the open-air Freedom Squares and the political meetings which the ruling party and its weak rivals organise there emulate the *kgotla* pattern, so much so that people may take their own traditional *kgotla* stools there for seats, or use make-shift seats of rocks; but we have seen how the actual proceedings during these meetings greatly deviate from the spirit of the *kgotla* pattern. More examples could be cited, for example, the sphere of traditional leadership (where the chiefs – *dikgosi*, of old the central figures at *dikgotla* – have been turned into salaried petty officials), or the state's authoritarian management (through the Registrar of Societies) of people's self-organisation in voluntary associations (Van Binsbergen 1993b). In these fields, and many more, the same elite-engineered suggestion of cultural continuity in combination with authoritarian state control along the lines of a non-traditional bureaucratic logic can be pinpointed.

In the Zambian Nkoya case traditional rulers, the Myene, appeared as original foci of a local political culture which, while allowing for certain forms of sociological democracy (C), could not and would not be reduced to the globalizing idiom of constitutional democracy along North Atlantic lines (B), – so that the trajectory of democratisation in that context revolved on the process of interplay between a local and a global political model, each accommodating to, and reinforcing rather than annihilating the other. In the Botswana case the situation is very different (Gillett 1973; Roberts 1972; Silitshena 1979). The *kgotla* pattern does imply the role of the traditional ruler, whose co-ordinating presence structures the *kgotla* proceedings, leads them to a conclusion, and legitimates them with the mystical sanctions of his office. Under indirect rule, *dikgosi* did continue to be the principal conspicuous political authorities in Bechuanaland throughout the colonial period, and since indepen-dence (1966) the post-colonial state has derived much of its authority in the eyes of its citizens from the skill with which it has encapsulated the *dikgosi*. In many ways it would be true to say that the central state is felt by its subjects to be the legitimate heir to the *dikgosi*. Besides, the BDP was founded by Sir Seretse Khama, heir apparent to a major royal title (that of the Ngwato), and son of the internationally famous *kgosi* Khama III. In other words, in the Botswana case we do not find a dynamic juxtaposition between local tradition and globalizing modem state structure, but the selective subjugation, appropriation and manipulation of local tradition by the state elite.

Some impression of political attitudes and behaviour can be gleaned from the following selected results of a questionnaire survey I conducted in Francistown in 1989.[24] The relevant questions as presented here were embedded in a far more extensive questionnaire dealing with household composition, social contacts, economic activities, health behaviour, sexuality, media consumption and church life. This resulted in highly personal and relaxed in-depth interviews each extending over several hours, taking every possible care that the questions were clear and neutral, and building in cross-checks.

(a) Did you register as a voter? Yes (73%); No (27%). *More than one quarter of the respondents claim not to have registered as a voter, although less than one tenth did not qualify for reasons of age and citizenship.*

(b) Which party do you support? None (10%); BDP (43%); BPP (27%); BNF (20 %). *Barely two fifths of the respondents claim to support the ruling party BDP, although in the 1989 elections the BDP carried as many as seven of the 11 Francistown wards.*[25]

(c) What do you think about the following statements?

1. 'In a democratic country like Botswana, every citizen is free to form a new political party and to try and get the majority vote.' Agree (76%); Don't know (11%); Disagree (13%). *As many as one quarter of the respondents turn out not to know their basic political rights.*

2. 'Botswana would be better off if the chiefs get the powers back they had before independence.' Agree (36%); Don't know (22%); Disagree (42%). *Only one third of the respondents claim to be dissatisfied with chiefs' position in post-independent Botswana, whereas many more approve of the current situation in which the state has effectively appropriated chiefs' powers.*

3. 'It is sinful to criticise the govement of Botswana'. Agree (35%); Don't know (21%); Disagree (44%). *More than one third of the respondents hold the view that it is morally wrong to criticise the government.*

4. 'It is all right to break the laws of the government as long as you are not found out'. Agree (18%); Don't know (9%); Disagree (73%). *Three quarters of the respondents give evidence of having fully internalised the state's authority.*

5. 'The government of Botswana makes sure that nobody needs to go without food, clothing, shelter, education and medical services.' Agree (49%); Don't know (12%); Disagree (39%). *Nearly half of the respondents claim that the Botswana state takes excellent care of its citizens, although almost two-fifths are of the adverse opinion.*

6. 'The people who talk about apartheid and oppose the political system of South Africa, are just troublemakers.' Agree (37%); Don't know (12%); Disagree (51%). *More than one third of the (Black) respondents reject the anti-apartheid movement in South Africa, most probably – cf. statement (3) – because political contestation is abhorred no matter how justified the cause.*[26]

7. 'Our traditional culture is just a thing of the past – it must disappear and be replaced by the international culture which we see on TV, in the magazines, and from the expatriates.' Agree (21%); Don't know (13%); Disagree (66%). *Two thirds of the respondents claim to insist on cultural continuity between the past and the future.*

(d) Do you know your ward councillor personally? Yes (55%); No (45%). *More than half of the respondents claim to know their ward councillor personally.* (This official acts as a reference when applying for the application of a self-help housing plot, but is hardly involved in informal conflict regulation between residents at the ward level).

What these responses suggest (but of course far more data and analysis are needed in order to substantiate this point) is that – at least at one level of formal and normative consciousness, such as is elicited in formal survey interviews – the average urban Motswana view even the post-colonial state not as a structure of democratic negotiation which is ultimately empowered and controlled by himself or herself, but as a sacrosanct outside entity, which nurtures and protects but should not be challenged, and which is essentially in continuity with the colonial and pre-colonial past.

This conception of the state as beyond civil control and criticism was even projected onto neighbouring South Africa, at a time when Mr Mandela was still imprisoned, and nothing hinted at the democratic developments which were to take place after 1990. The migratory exposure to South Africa has had a tremendous impact upon life in Botswana in the course of the 20th century, and it certainly has a political effect. The first political parties were founded in Francistown by returning migrants deeply involved in the South African ANC (Murray et al 1987; Nengwekhulu 1979); the Kalanga-oriented BPP retains that influence, but, at least in terms of election results, has lost out locally to the populist Tswana-oriented BDP, which claims continuity (through Tswana, the national language), with the Botswana traditional culture. The consequence is the dissimulation of social contradictions in the guise of an ideology of peace and progress. From a democratic perspective, church independence, with the political acquiescence and aloofness it has implied for ordinary churchgoers throughout Southern Africa, has proved a more significant, although negative, South African export.[27]

In such a setting, there is not much incentive for a drive for more democracy at the national level, given the skilfully-manipulated traditional *kgotla* model, illusory as it might be.

In the final analysis, it may not be the alleged continuity with the past (through language, the *kgotla* model, the encapsulation of traditional authorities, etc.) and with notions pertaining to the handling of power in face-to-face settings, which explains the majority's lack of interest in greater democratisation in Botswana at the national level, but rather the internal contradictions within the package of globalisation that has come to control Botswana today. And this is true of Botswana more than any other African country of my acquaintance with the exception of South Africa. As one would expect in a country like Botswana, it is not democratic political participation but mass consumption along incipient class lines which represents the part of the global culture which has the greatest mass appeal. Probably this selection partly reflects a concern with wealth, its circulation and accumulation, which was built into the pastoral economy and the patrilineal kinship system long before the advent of colonialism and capitalism; many centuries ago, the great Zimbabwe and Torwa state systems that once encompassed part of Botswana, already thrived on the circulation of wealth (Tlou and Campbell 1984). When consumption within a cash economy has become a basic standard of self-esteem and social prestige, as is very clearly the case in urban Botswana today, one would hardly expect to encounter democratic initiative and courage to a level higher than that found in the North Atlantic region where the damning effect of affluence on radical political attitudes has been the subject of a considerable literature.

The Batswana's fundamental satisfaction with the *material* performance of the post-independence state must be an important, perhaps even crucial factor in explaining their lack of opposition and the absence, in recent years of a democratic movement. The dynamics of the prevailing political culture would appear to be a very significant additional factor, for it engenders political acquiescence and dissipates foci of contention with civil society, producing the suggestion of cultural continuity between actual state performance and popular notions of legitimate power hingeing on the *kgotla* model, which in fact is only a manipulated neo-traditional facade for an authoritarian elite state based upon participation.

Conclusion

I have stressed that the global model of democracy is a very specific, and far from universal, form of political culture, which needs to be learned before it can be expected to be applied, and which operates in the context of alternative, more indigenous views of participation, legitimation and constitutional procedure. In order to appreciate the substantial local variations within this process, national level analyses can be fruitfully complemented with anthropological insights into the way people structure their local political life-worlds and interpret globalizing national politics within a particularist local framework of expectations and concerns. The democratisation movement in Africa since the late 1980s is often portrayed as the return to a model of national democracy that allegedly was already there at national independence but that had merely been eroded or become dormant in subsequent years. My argument, selectively based on ethnographic evidence from the grassroots level in two very different contemporary situations in Southern Africa, suggests, however, that the democratisation movement is only another phase in the ongoing political transformation of Africa, in the course of which, by an interplay between local and national (ultimately global) conceptions of political power, indigenous constitutional, philosophical and sociological alternatives for political legitimacy are tested, accommodated or discarded as obsolete. The capricious and contradictory outcomes of this process at the local level need to be taken into account, particularly by those who hope that the modern democratic model can yet transcend its North Atlantic origins and become the cornerstone of a new and better world.

Notes

1. An earlier version of this paper was presented at the seminar on Democratisation in Africa, African Studies Centre, Leiden. 24 September, 1993. I am indebted to the organisers, my colleagues Robert Buijtenhuijs and Elly Rijnierse, for creating a stimulating environment for the production of this paper, and to the present journal's anonymous reader for stimulating comments.
2. For an incisive, up-to-date summary of that discussion, cf. Buijtenhuijs and Rijnierse 1993.
3. Cf. Colás 1992; Hannerz 1987; Featherstone 1990; Van Binsbergen 1994b; and references cited there.
4. In this respect, adopting a detached, culturally relative view of the North Atlantic concept of democracy falls under the tantalising category of tabooed ideas in international social science, to which my teacher Köbben (1975; 1991) has devoted illuminating discussions.
5. Khumiri village society, highlands of north-western Tunisia, 1968, 1970; Nkoya rural society, Kaoma district, Zambia, and its urban extensions along the Zambian line of rail, 1972 to present; Manjak rural society, north-western Guinea-Bissau, 1983; Francistown urban society, Botswana, and its urban–rural ties ramifying into surrounding Kalanga, Tswana and Ndebele villages, 1988 to present.
6. Glover 1927; Forrest 1966; remarkably, Plato and Aristotle (e.g. Bierens de Haan 1943) criticised the *demokratia* of their time, not for being insufficiently democratic but for being over-democratic, for having become *oclokrateia*, or mob rule.
7. De Tocqueville 1954; Mannheim 1940; Doornbos *et al* 1984 and references cited there.
8. The following summary of Dutch constitutional history illustrates this point: 'Before 1848 the franchise in the Netherlands was very limited indeed. Even after 1848, at first the vast majority of the population were deprived of the franchise. Until the Constitutional Reforms of 1887, the right to vote depended on the amount one had to pay for taxes (the so-called census franchise). The Constitution of 1887 made provision for the extension of the franchise to certain, not clearly defined, categories of persons, by introducing the criterion of 'attributes of appropriate status and wealth', which attributes were further elaborated in the Franchise Bill of 1896. At that stage categories of voters included 'tax voters', 'dwelling voters', 'salary voters', 'savings voters' and 'examination voters'. Under this system in 1916 only 70 per cent of Dutch males had the right to vote. The Constitutional Reforms of 1917 introduced the general franchise for males, and in principle made provision for women's franchise. In 1922 women's franchise was enacted in the constitution. … Invariably, the passive franchise accrued to all Dutch mates who possessed the active franchise. Until 1917 women were explicitly excluded also from the passive franchise' (Winkler Prins 1974, my translation: cf. Oud 1967; Van der Pot & Donner 1968).
9. Anthropological field-work among the Zambian Nkoya, alternating between the Kaoma district and migrants in the national capital city of Lusaka, was undertaken in 1972–74, and during shorter visits in 1977, 1978, 1981, 1988, 1989, 1992 (twice) and 1994 (twice). Anthropological field-work in Francistown and surrounding rural areas was undertaken in 1988–89 and during shorter visits in 1990, 1991 and 1992 (twice) and 1994. I am indebted to the African Studies Centre, Leiden, for the most generous encouragement and financial support since I joined the centre in 1977; and to research participants, to assistants and government officials in both Zambia and Botswana and to members of my family, for invaluable contributions to the research.
10. A case in point is *African Watchtower* throughout South Central Africa from the 1910s; cf. also the Lumpa church of Alice Lenshina; Van Binsbergen 1981 and references cited there. For Botswana the rise of church independence as a major form of contestation preceding by several decades the formation of political parties (Lagerwerf 1982; Grant 1971; Chirenje 1977) is a case in point. For a general perspective on these points, cf. Gluckman 1971. For a critique claiming that views such as mine or Gluckman's amount to underplaying the contribution of villagers to the independence struggle, cf. Van Donge 1986.
11. A common assumption in the literature on the articulation of modes of production in Africa is that young men went to work so that, via a monetarisation of bride wealth, elders could continue to exercise their kinship-based power in new forms; in fact however, it was often intergenerational conflict at the village level (where youths have tended to regard all elderly men as sorcerers, and often wandered from one kin patron to another in a long chain of disappointment and distress) which propelled youths into a career as labour migrants. The comforts of the old African cosmologies ought not to be exaggerated.
12. Outside Barotseland, two more Nkaya royal chiefs survived: *Mwene* Kabulwebulwe of Central Province and *Mwene* Moomba of Southern Province.

[13] Even after the state's creation of Local Courts (which were nominally independent from the *Mwene*) in 1965.

[14] The *Mwene* is thus one of the Tears [or, less anthropomorphically, Drops] of Rain which feature in the title of my main book on the Nkoya (Van Binsbergen 1992a).

[15] Which is largely an exalted version of the enthronement ceremony of village headmen, and even of the ordinary name inheritance ceremony by which a surviving junior kinsmen takes a deceased's name.

[16] I cannot go into the peculiar gender dynamics of high political office among the Nkoya. Clan heads and early kings tended to be women, but there have been no female *Mwene* since the middle of the 19th century. Cf. Van Binsbergen,1986, 1992a.

[17] At the time political parties and the church provided virtually the only organisational structure for the rapidly growing squatter areas where Nkoya urban migrants used to live.

[18] A fifth Nkoya royal chieftainship has now been revived: in October 1994, *Mwene* Pumpola of Dongwe/Lukulu will be ceremonially installed before delegations of all other royal courts and with a substantial participation of the Kazanga association executive and its ceremonial dancing troupe.

[19] Who had meanwhile been restored to government esteem, and was even made Member of the Central Committee, i.e. UNIP's highest representative in the province, and a member of parliament. Under the Chiluba administration, meanwhile, state–Litunga relations are steadily declining again, while the Lozi aristocracy tends to retreat in delusions of territorial secession.

[20] In line with national usage, Batswana is taken here in the sense of 'Botswana nationals', rather than that of 'people identifying as members of the Tswana cluster of ethnic groups'.

[21] Cf. Holm & Molutsi 1989; Picard 1987; Molomio & Mokopakgosi 1991; Charlton 1993; Bernard 1989; Crowder 1988; Good 1992.

[22] As happened with the Francistown PWD squatter area situated in the Government Camp ward no. 58; Van Binsbergen and Krijnen 1989; Krijnen 1991.

[23] P1 = US$0.45.

[24] The results are based on a statistically representative sample survey of 175 adults (18 years of age and older) of both sexes, resident in Francistown in 1989; of these, seven per cent were under the legal voting age of 21 years. Of the 175 respondents, 98 per cent claimed to be Botswana citizens, and 87 per cent claimed to be in the possession of a national registration card ('O Mang').

[25] 'Government Notice No. 326 of 1989, L2/7/98 XX', in: Republic of Botswana, Government Gazette, 27, 59, 27th October, 1989, pp. 1398–1402 – the Francistown returns being listed on p. 1399. These data have been corrected in the light of 'Government Notice No. 354 of 1989, L2/7/126/II', in Republic of Botswana, Government Gazette, 27, 63, 17th November, 1989, p. 1504, according to which ward 67 was carried not by BPP but by BDP.

[26] This was more than half a year before Mr Mandela's release from prison, when nobody could foresee the imminent dismantling of the apartheid state. However, the response was more positive to a related but differently phrased question: 'The political system of South Africa is wrong and must he changed'. Agree (79 per cent); Don't know (12 per cent); Disagree (9 per cent).

[27] Cf. Schoffeleers 1991; church leaders and church committees present a rather more oppositional picture, cf. Van Binsbergen 1993b.

References

Baylies, C. and Szeftel, M. 1992. 'The Fall and Rise of Multi-Party Politics in Zambia', *Review of African Political Economy*, 54:75-91.

Bernard, St. 1989. 'Botswana: Un Multipartisme Fragile et Menacé?', *Politique Africaine*, 36:125–28.

Bierens de Haan, J. (ed.) 1943. *Politeia: Groote Mannen Over Staat en Maatschappij – van Plato tot Kant*. Amsterdam: Elsevier.

Buijtenhuijs, R. and Rijnierse, E. 1993. *Democratization in sub-Saharan Africa (1989–1992): An Overview of the Literature*. African Studies Centre research reports no. 51, Leiden: African Studies Centre.

Caplan, G. 1970, *The Elites of Barotseland 1878–1969*. London: Hurst.

Chariton, R. 1993. 'The Politics of Elections in Botswana', *Africa*, 63, 3: 330–70.

Chirenje, J. 1977. *A History of (Northern) Botswana 1850–1910*. London: Rutherford.

Colás, S. 1992. 'The Third World in Jameson's Postmodernism or the Cultural Logic of Late Capitalism', *Social Text*, 31–32: 258–70.

Crowder, M. 1988. 'Botswana and the Survival of Liberal Democracy in Africa'. In Gifford, P. and Louis, W. (eds.) *Decolonization and African Independence, 1960–1980*. New Haven: Yale University Press, pp. 461– 76.

De Tocqueville, A. 1954. *Tocqueville's 'Democracy in America'*, Bradley, P. (ed.) 2 vols., New York: Vintage Books. Translation of *De la Démocratie en Amérique* (1835).

Doornbos, M., Van Binsbergen, W. and Hesseling, G. 1984. 'Constitutional Form and Ideological Content: The Preambles of French Language Constitutions in Africa.' In Van Binsbergen, W. and Hesseling, G. (eds.) *Aspecten van Staat en Mautschappij in Africa: Recent Dutch and Belgian research on the African state*. Leiden: African Studies Centre, pp. 41–100.

Featherstone, M. (ed.) 1990. *Global Culture: Nationalism, Globalisation and Modernity*. London/Newbury Park: Sage.

Forrest, W. 1966. *The Emergence of Greek Democracy*. New York: McGraw Hill.

Gillett, S. 1973. 'The Survival of Chieftainship in Botswana', *African Affairs*, 72, 287: 179–85.

Glover, T. 1927. *Democracy in the Ancient World*. Cambridge University Press.

Gluckman, M. 1971. 'Tribalism, Ruralism and Urbanism in South and Central Africa.' In Turner, V. (ed.) *Profiles of Change (Colonialism in Africa 1870–1960, part iii*, general editors Gann, L. and Duignan, P.) Cambridge: Cambridge University Press, pp. 127-66.

Good, K. 1992. 'Interpreting the Exceptionality of Botswana', *The Journal of Modern African Studies*, 30,1: 69–96.

Grant, S. 1971. 'Church and Chief in the Colonial Era', *Botswana Notes and Records*, 3.1971.

Hannerz, U. 1987. 'The World in Creolisation', *Africa*, 57: 546–59.

Holm, J. and Molutsi, P. (eds.) 1989. *Democracy in Botswana*. Gaborone: Macmillan.

Kamwambe, N. 1991. *Frederick Chiluba: Is He Riding a Tide of Fortune?* Lusaka: Shelley's Printers.

Köbben, A. 1975. 'Taboes', *Vrij Nederland* [Amsterdam], issue of 19 April,1975.

Köbben, A. 1991. 'Taboes in de Wetenschap.' In Kobben, A. *De Weerbarstige Waarheid*. Amsterdam: Prometheus, pp. 9-26.

Krijnen, E. 1991. 'PWD: Een Squatterwijk Tussen Staat, Stad en Platteland: Verslag van Een Onderzoek in Francistown, Botswana.' M.A. thesis, Erasmus University: Rotterdam.

Lagerwerf, L. 1982. *'They Pray For You…': Independent Churches and Women in Botswana*. Leiden: Interuniversity Institute for Missiological and Ecumenical Research (IIMO).

Mannheim, K. 1940. *Man and Society in an Age of Reconstruction*. London: Routledge and Kegan Paul.

Mbikusita-Lewanika, A. and Chitala, D. 1990. *The Hour Has Come: Proceedings of the National Conference on Multi-Party Option Held at Garden House Hotel, Lusaka, Zambia, 20–21 July, 1990*. Lusaka: Zambia Research Foundation.

Molomio, M. and Mokopakgosi, B. 1991. *Multi-Party Democracy in Botswana*. Harare: Southern Africa Political Economy Series (SAPES) Trust.

Morton, F. and Ramsay, J. (eds.) 1987. *The Birth of Botswana: A History of the Bechuanaland Protectorate from 1910 to 1966*. Gaborone: Longman.

Mudenda, G. 1992. 'MMD Two Years Later', *Southern Africa Political and Economic Monthly*, p. 5.

Mulford, D. 1967. *Zambia: The Politics of Independence, 1957–1964*. London: Oxford University Press.

Murray, A.; Nengwekhulu, H. and Ramsay, J. 1987. 'The Formation of Political Parties.' In Morton & Ramsay 1987: 172–86.

Nelson-Richards, M. 1988. *Beyond the Sociology of Agrarian Transformation: Economy and Society in Zambia*, Nepal and Zanzibar. Leiden: Brill.

Nengwekhulu, H. 1979. 'Some Findings on the Origins of Political Parties in Botswana', *Pula*, 1,2: 4776.

Oud, P. 1967. *Het Constitutioneel Recht van het Koninkrijk der Nederlanden, i*, 2nd impression. Haarlem: Tjeenk Willink.

Picard, L. 1987. *The Politics of Development in Botswana: A Model for Success?* Boulder and London: Lynne Rienner Publishers.

Republic of Botswana. 1983. *Laws of Botswana: The Constitution of Botswana*, n.p. [Gaborone: s.n. [Government Printer].

Reynolds, B. 1963. *Magic, Divination and Witchcraft among the Barotse of Northern Rhodesia*. Berkeley: University of California Press, London: Chatto and Windus.

Roberts, S. 1972. 'The Survival of the Traditional Tswana Courts in the National Legal System of Botswana', *Journal of African Law*, 16:103–29.

Schoffeleers, J. 1991. 'Ritual Healing and Political Acquiescence: The Case of Zionist churches in Southern Africa', *Africa*, 61, 1: 1–25.

Sichone, O. 1991–92. 'Zambian Elections – An Example for Africa to Emulate', *Southern African Economic and Political Monthly*, Dec/Jan 1991–92.

Silitshena, R. 1979. 'Chiefly Authority and the Organisation of Space in Botswana', *Botswana Notes and Records*, 11: 55–67.

Tlou, T. and Campbell, A. 1984. *History of Botswana*, Gaborone: Macmillan.

Van Binsbergen, W. 1981. *Religious Change in Zambia*, London/Boston: Kegan Paul International.

——. 1986. 'The Post-Colonial State, "State Penetration" and the Nkoja Experience in Central Western Zambia.' In Van Binsbergen. W., Hesseling, G. and Reijntjens, F. (eds.) *State and Local Community in Africa/Etat et Communauté Locale en Afrique*. Brussels: Cahiers du CEDAF/ASDOC geschriften, pp. 31–63.

——. (With Krijnen, E.) 1989, 'A Preliminary Quantitative Analysis of Plot "Owners" in the PWD Squatter Area, Francistown, 1989', Francistown: Applied Research Unit Ministry of Local Government and Lands, Republic of Botswana/ African Studies Centre, Leiden.

——. 1991. 'De Chaos Getemd? Samenwonen en Zingeving in Modern Afrika.' In Claessen, H. (ed.) *De Chaos Getemd?* Leiden: Faculteit der Sociale Wetenschappen, Rijksuniversiteit Leiden, pp. 31–47.

——. 1992a. *Tears of Rain: Ethnicity and History in Central Western Zambia*. London/Boston: Kegan Paul International.

——. 1992b. *Kazanga: Etniciteit in Afrika Tussen Staat en Traditie*. Inaugural lecture, Amsterdam:Vrije Universiteit. English version in press in African Studies.

——. 1993a. 'Making Sense of Urban Space in Francistown, Botswana.' In Nas, P. (ed.) *Urban Symbolism*. Leiden: Brill, pp. 184–228.

——. 1993b. 'African Independent Churches and the State in Botswana.' In Bax, M. and De Koster, A. (eds.) *Power and Prayer: Essays on Religion and Politics*. CentREPOL-VU Studies 2, Amsterdam: VU University Press, pp. 24–56.

——. 1993c. ' "Geef Hem Dan Maar Aan de Krokodillen": Stastsvorming, Geweld en Culturele Discontinuïteit in Voor-Koloniaal Zuidelijk Centraal Afrika.' Contribution to a special issue on state formation, Dahles, H. and Trouwborst, A. (eds.) 1993. *Antropologische Verkenningen*, 12, 4: 10–31.

——. 1994a. 'Minority Language, Ethnicity and the State in Two African Situations: The Nkoya of Zambia and the Kalanga of Botswana.' In Fardon, R. and Furniss, G. (eds.) *African Languages, Development and the State*. London: Routledge, pp. 142–88.

——. 1994b. 'Dynamiek van Cultuur: Enige Dilemma's van Hedendaags Afrika in Een Context van Globalisering.' Contribution to a special issue entitled 'De Dynamiek van de Cultuur', Brouwer, L. and Hogema, I. (eds.) *Antropologische Verkenningen*, 13, 2: 1733.

Van der Pot, C. and Donner, A. 1968. *Handboek van het Nederlandse Staatrecht*. Zwolle: W.E.J. Tjeenk Willink.

Van Donge, J. 1986. 'Religion and Nationalism in Zambia.' Paper presented at the conference on 'Culture and Consciousness in Southern Africa', Manchester 23–26 September 1986.

Winkler Prins. 1974. *Grote Winkler Prins: Encyclopedie in Twintig Delen. Deel 11*, Amsterdam/Brussel: Elsevier. Anonymous article 'Kiesrecht', pp. 62–3.

MIKAEL KARLSTRÖM
Imagining Democracy

Reference
Africa, 66/4, 1996, pp. 485–504

Despite the recent resurgence of interest in democratisation in Africa, the systematic study of local understandings of democracy on the continent has barely begun. An earlier academic and African nationalist consensus held that Western-style liberal democracy was ill suited to African societies and cultures, which contained alternative forms of democratic practice rooted in traditional communalism, and that economic development was a higher post-independence priority than the maintenance of democratic institutions.[1] By the 1980s, however, Africa's 'one-party democracies' had proven both politically and developmentally disastrous, and the earlier consensus which seemed to justify them was abandoned. But the rush to renounce the older perspective has obscured the element of truth contained within it. For if Africans have shown themselves by no means uninterested in democracy, the democracy which they envision often does differ significantly from Western liberal conceptions.

While the earlier orthodoxy produced surprisingly little detailed research into local understandings of democracy and its assimilation to existing political cosmologies and practices, the new departures have provided an even weaker impetus toward such enquiry.[2] In this article I hope to contribute to a nascent literature which does take seriously the implications of local conceptions and practices for the prospects of democracy in Africa.[3] I examine the way democracy is understood and enacted by Baganda, the one-time subjects of the king of Buganda, which was the largest of Uganda's old kingdoms. My emphasis is on the complexity and dynamism of the process of articulation whereby elements of Western and global democratic discourse and practice have been selectively assimilated to an existing political cosmology, while also transforming that cosmology in important respects.

'Democracy' in Luganda

Although the concept of democracy has played some role in Ugandan political discourse since at least the 1940s, its popularisation has largely been due to the political rhetoric of the National Resistance Movement (NRM) government which came to power in 1986. By 1992, when I began my fieldwork, the English word 'democracy' was familiar to most rural Baganda, even those who spoke little or no English.[4] Their comprehension of the word, however, was organised around its standard translation into the Luganda language. This translation deserves careful analysis, since it effects a significant semantic shift in relation to the Western conception of democracy as 'rule of the people'.[5]

Like 'democracy' (from the Greek *demos* and *kratia*), the Luganda translation, *eddembe ery'obuntu*, is a composite term. The meaning of *eddembe*, however, is much closer to 'liberty' than to 'rule' or 'power' (*kratia*). It is generally used in the sense of having the freedom or liberty to carry out some particular activity without constraints imposed from above, for instance in the phrases *eddembe ery'okwogera* (freedom of speech) and *ebiseera eby'eddembe* (free/leisure time). It also carries the connotation of 'peace', and is cognate with the noun *emirembe*, meaning 'peace' and also 'royal reign', with which it is sometimes used interchangeably.

Obuntu, which is the abstract noun form of *muntu/bantu*, (person/people), may seem to correspond relatively well with the notion of 'the people' (*tiemos*). Its emphasis, however, differs from that of the contemporary Western inclusive and quantitative notion of 'the people' as comprising an entire citizenry on the principle of the political equality of individuals. This is evident from the most important idiomatic usage of the word, in the expression *obuntubulamu*. *Obuntubulamu* (healthy humanness) is a crucial term of public morality, connoting 'the possession of courtesy, compassion, good breeding, culture' (Murphy, 1972). *Obuntu* is thus less a politico-demographic category than an ethical and civic ideal. It reflects a notion of humanity which is differentially rather than uniformly conceived; a pan-human aim, perhaps, but by no means a pan-human achievement. As such, it is perhaps best translated as 'civility' in the somewhat archaic sense of the word which combines the senses of good governance and collective advancement on the level of polity with an emphasis on morality and 'good manners' at the level of individual conduct.[6]

Eddembe ery'obuntu can thus be taken to mean something like 'civil liberty', but in a sense which inherently establishes 'civil' limits not only on the exercise of authority but also on the exercise of the liberties themselves. In addition to its usage to translate 'democracy' it is also, and more accurately used to translate 'human rights'. What interests me here, however is precisely the semantic shift involved in its use as the standard translation of 'democracy'. This translation both effects and reflects the assimilation of the imported notion of 'democracy' to an historically anchored local constellation of conceptions of authority and the proper relationship between rulers and subjects.

Freedom from oppression

The first impulse among my informants was often to specify the meaning of democracy and *eddembe ery'ubuntu* in terms of freedom from oppression. At one level, this focus was undoubtedly an outcome of Buganda's longstanding and disastrous conflict with the Ugandan state. Accustomed to favouritism under colonial rule, the Buganda kingdom, situated in southern Uganda, was politically outmanoeuvred after independence and unilaterally abolished in 1967 by Uganda's first President, Milton Obote. Idi Amin's 1971 coup was greeted with jubilation in Buganda, but his regime quickly deteriorated into a brutal military dictatorship. The 1979 liberation from Amin brought Obote back to power and set the stage for a protracted and murderous civil war fought largely on Buganda soil, which resulted in the eventual victory of the NRM under the leadership of Yoweri Museveni in 1986. Acceding, albeit reluctantly to popular royalist sentiment in Buganda, the new government sanctioned the restoration of the Buganda monarchy in 1993. Although it is led primarily by western Ugandans, the NRM is thus the only Ugandan government since independence which has not taken on the aspect for Baganda of a foreign occupation.

While the oppression endured by Ugandans since independence is thus a brute enough fact, its local interpretation is less self-evident. My informants did not conceive of oppression as a consequence of unregulated or excessive state power. Rather, they conceived of it as the consequence of a disordered state, of authority which has lost its anchor. In this context, it is worth emphasising the close link between *eddembe* and *emirembe*, meaning 'peace' but also, inextricably, 'epoch' or 'royal reign'. In the pre-colonial kingdom the death of a king was followed by a period of both symbolic and material violence and disorder, which came to an end with the ritual installation of a successor to the throne (Roscoe, 1911:103; Ray, 1991:109). With the new reign came the return of order and freedom from arbitrary violence and oppression. In 1993 the coronation of Ronald Mutebi, ending an interregnum of nearly a quarter-century, was discussed in similar terms by royalist Baganda. Liberty in its most basic sense is thus a concomitant of a rightly ordered polity oriented around a properly and firmly installed ruler.

Freedom of speech

When I asked them to specify the positive liberties which they counted as central to *eddembe ery'obuntu*, most of my informants focused on the freedom of speech.

'Democracy'[7] is granted when a person has his/her freedom [*eddembe*] and can be heard if s/he has something to say regarding his/her affairs. [Young Muslim man, petty trader]

From what I understand, [democracy] means that under that form of rule I can have my ideas and they are taken into consideration. That's the main thing. I can get what I need provided that I ask for it. [Middle-aged Protestant woman, schoolteacher]

'Democracy' is *eddembe ery'obuntu*, each person speaking for himself, without reprisals, saying what you care about the most and saying it openly, and having it answered properly. [Middle-aged Protestant man, well educated]

Presently we can say there is democracy, because we can stand up and say something and the authority listens to it. [Young Catholic man, teacher, interviewed in English]

One of the most consistent characteristics of these equations of democracy with the freedom of speech is the implied orientation of that speech. It is not speech directed toward a general audience of equals, but rather the speech of subjects directed toward their ruler. In an interview recorded by Tidemand (1995: 125) this framework is used to contrast Uganda's two longest-serving Presidents:

Obote's government did not allow any speaking. ... If Obote wanted to remove someone from parliament, it was simply done. But it isn't like that now. If Museveni wants to reshuffle the Cabinet he consults the people. ... For example, Museveni passed an order to stop charcoal burners from cutting down trees. The ordinary people raised the alarm and when Museveni was on his way back from a visit to Luwero they stopped him .[near Kampala] and raised their complaint. They asked him: Do you want the townspeople in Buganda to die? Ever since we were young we have relied on charcoal. He later agreed with them and issued a statement allowing charcoal burners to continue their work, but selling charcoal at a reasonable price.

Today a common man can speak, but during the Amin and Obote regimes you could simply be killed by the soldiers of the special forces. [Informant No. 20: translation altered[8]]

The image evoked here, of Museveni as a ruler who consults the people he rules, does not in any way qualify his power or authority. There is no conception of a reversal or equalisation of authority relations between subjects and rulers. Museveni does not obey his subjects' wishes as their representative; he listens to their complaints and judges the case by vinue of his position as a ruler. He also does not merely withdraw his moratorium on charcoal burning, leaving the people free to do as they like; instead, he replaces it with another command, purportedly regulating the price of charcoal – a command which is all the more revealing in that it was never actually issued.

The conception of legitimate authority as hinging on open lines of communication bctween a ruler and his subjects is codified in the most widely told story about the pre-colonial kingship. The story tells of Muteesa I (1856–84), who succeeded to the throne under the name Mukaabya, meaning 'He who makes people cry/scream'.

Mukaabya made people cry/scream [okukaaba] for his own amusement and that of his fellow royals. He forced them to carry bundles of reeds so that the sharp ends cut into their heads. He planted sharp needles in the ground so that when people prostrated before him their hands would be punctured. Soon his people began to flee. When he realised that they were abandoning him, he was persuaded to change his manner and he began to discuss [okuteesa] matters with them. To show his change of heart, he took the new name Muteesa – 'He who discusses'.[9]

Despite the fact that a number of pre-colonial Ganda kings actually were deposed or overthrown, the possibility of rebelling against the king was not raised in any of the versions of this story told to me. The implicit model here is of the king as the immobile centre of the political order; it is the people who come and go, and who use their mobility to sway their rulers to better conduct and freer communication.

The Ganda concern with freedom of speech thus differs from a general Western liberal conception in that it is rooted, not in a model of politics as competition for power among the plural representatives of various political views, but rather in a model of legitimate unitary authority as founded on the willingness of power-holders to hear the voices of their subjects. Freedom of speech is a principle which does not stand in conceptual opposition to the singularity and transcendence of power, but rather presupposes it. The specification of 'democracy' as 'freedom of speech' thus further assimilates the concept to a local ideology of political order.

Justice and equity

Another central element in the Ganda conception of legitimate authority and, by extension, of democracy, is the fair and impartial judgement of disputes and court cases.

The way I understand 'democracy' is that it contains truth and justice/fairness [obwenkanya]; if you are a leader you have to be honest and you have to be fairminded [onwenkanya]. [Middle-aged Catholic man]

'Democracy', I would say, is like eddembe, and from what I can

tell you, eddembe ery'obuntu is to judge fairly when something is not as it should be. [Cited by Tidemand, 1995: 125]

This conception of fair judgement frequently came up in discussions of the monarchy:

What made us love the king in this way is that he was a good man who really loved the ordinary people down below without discriminating [tasosola] against anyone, and when there was a conflict he would judge by taking a middle position and deciding correctly. [Middle-aged Muslim man, RC3 chairman]

The concepts of justice (obwenkanya) and impartiality (obutasosola) were used by informants in explaining both the importance of free speech and their sense of justice. Obwenkanya is an abstract noun derived from the verb kwenkana, 'to be equal/similar', and can be loosely translated as 'fairness' or 'equality.' The equation of democracy with obwenkanya may seem to indicate something akin to Western egalitarianism. What is implied here, however, is narrower: a situational equality of subjects before a powerholder and decision-maker rather than an ontological equality of persons. Hence the centrality of the implied audience of decision-makers in statements like the following:

I understand 'democracy' to mean obwenkanya, like when you give an opinion and it is not ignored but is also considered and a decision is made taking it into account. [Cited by Tidemand, 1995: 127; emphasis added]

Such situational equality is an important element in contemporary royalist political consciousness. If power equalises, then the king himself is the greatest of equalisers. He does not acknowledge, but rather creates, equality by '[loving] the ordinary people down below without discriminating against anyone'. The principle is most dramatically demonstrated in the prostration before the king which is a virtual requirement of all his male subjects on public occasions, and which one young man at a post-coronation ceremony in 1993 enthusiastically explained to me as showing that 'before the kabaka there is no rank'.

Democracy as eddembe ery'obuntu, while predicated on the absence of oppressive constraints upon people's behaviour, thus presupposes the existence of a legitimate authority capable of dealing judicially with violations of certain basic norms and rights.

Civility and hierarchy

I have suggested that the phrase eddembe ery'obuntu may be most accurately rendered into English as 'civil liberty'. This is because the qualification of eddembe by obuntu points away from a sense of intrinsic individual freedoms or rights and toward an understanding of freedom as guaranteed by a rightly ordered polity, a society where both rulers and subjects conform to standards of civility which are inseparably ethical and political.[10] Indeed, several of my informants were quick to warn against the dangers of an individualistic interpretation of eddembe:

When eddembe is taken too far it is a bad thing. … Someone might refuse to work, to pay taxes, to dig wells, saying: I have my freedom. [Young Protestant man, sub-county chief, well educated]

Others insisted on a communal conception of liberty itself:

Q. What do you understand the word 'democracy' to mean?
A. I think it is the freedom [*eddembe*] which a person should have.
Q. Freedom to do what?
A. The freedom to work with your friends as you like and as they like, not just to get yours and keep it for yourself. We are all equal [*twenkanankana*] in our freedom, and we should share it together.
[Young Protestant woman, secondary-school leaver]

A few even linked democracy directly to standards of conduct:

I understand 'democracy' as self-governance [*olwefuga*]. That is, you have to have good manners/habits [*empisa*] in order to govern yourself. You have to change your manners/habits so you are doing good things, and then you can call yourself 'democratic'. [Young Protestant woman, primary-school teacher]

Ganda standards of civility, manners and proper conduct are deeply imbued with hierarchical elements. One of the main reasons given by my informants for their enthusiasm for the restoration of the monarchy was that it would revive such 'customs' or 'manners' (*empisa*) as obedience and respect for parents and elders, proper (i.e. deferential) greetings on the part of children and women, and unquestioning fealty to the king. The transmission and maintenance of such norms are felt to be the responsibility of the clans, and the abolition of the kingship is considered to have deprived the clan system of its coherence and moral authority. Indeed, the system of clans and king serves as a kind of hierarchical template for Baganda. Many attribute Uganda's descent into political turmoil in large part to the moral decay attendant upon the weakening of this system and the absence of a king.

There are several features of Ganda hierarchism which are central to understanding how the concept of 'democracy' has been assimilated to local conceptions of civility: the view of hierarchy as constructed from the bottom up; the singularity of power; regulated competition; and the unifying force of nested solidarities. Each feature can be viewed as based upon, or at least exemplified by, the system of clans and king.

When asked to describe the clan system, Baganda invariably begin with the household and recite the ascending levels of lineage, sub-branch, branch and clan. Each level has its head (*omutaka*), culminating in the 'roof' head (*omutaka ow'akasolya*), who is the linear descendant and living incarnation of the founding ancestor of the clan. This recitation is thus simultaneously a recitation of descent, and echoes the standard form of lineage recitation which is required of participants in clan gatherings. At the summit of all these hierarchies of *bataka* stands the king as *Ssaabataka*, or Superclanhead, who is conceived, as the leader (*omukulembeze*) rather than the ruler (*omufuzi*) of the fifty-two 'roof' clan heads. This conception of the hierarchical structure thus emphasises the allegiance of subordinates to superiors rather than the power of superiors over subordinates, and highlights the nested structure of hierarchically arranged solidarities.

Alongside the bottom-up conception of this system, there is a seemingly contrary sense that the system hinges upon the singularity and transcendence of its head. Ganda kingship is monarchical in the strongest sense. The king is the *Nnamunswa* (Queen Termite) around whom the termite mound revolves. He is also the pinnacle (*entikko*) of his realm, and his installation is really an 'empinnaclement' (*amatikkira*).[11] Hence the impulse to assert that *kabaka yekka*

(the king stands alone) in 1961 in response to the post-independence prospect of an elected party leader assuming powers comparable to those of the king (Hancock, 1970). This insistence on singularity is echoed at other levels of social organisation as well: every household has a single (prescriptively male) head; every public ceremony must be graced by a single guest of honour (*omugenyi omakulu*); and, most important, every Muganda is 'replaced' upon his or her death by a single successor (*omusika*) who takes over his or her structural role, regardless of any division of the material inheritance, and is installed in a ceremony which closely parallels the royal installation (Ray, 1991).

While the singularity of power is central to Ganda hierarchism, there is a relatively weak emphasis on the fixed ranking of groups or individuals within the hierarchy. The clans are not formally ranked in prestige or precedence, even though some are considerably older and larger than others. There is no particular preference for the firstborn in either royal or commoner succession, so that the sons of a living father stand in constant structural competition with one other. Where established ranking does figure prominently, the assignment of individuals to ranks is generally done by the single power-holder, whose prerogative it is to rearrange the hierarchy at will. In the pre-colonial kingdom, chiefships were held by royal appointment, and even hereditary ritual functions were often reassigned by the king based on the exploits or loyalty of particular clan members. Competition and competitiveness were thus fundamental to the pre-colonial Ganda political order (Fallers, 1959; Richards, 1964).

A similar, if somewhat depoliticised, competitive ethic is evident in the contemporary centrality of sporting competitions and competitive gift-giving to public occasions of all sorts. No local festivity is complete without a bicycle race, a plantain-peeling contest, a football match, or the like, all presided over by the guest of honour. Indeed, much of the recent royalist revival has been oriented around various clan-based competitions, such as the annual clan football tournament, which was revived in 1987. While these activities demonstrate the valorisation of competitiveness, it is equally significant that they constitute distinctly regulated forms of competition. They are invariably presided over by the king or a visiting dignitary, the single 'guest of honour', who serves as the situational 'pinnacle' of power toward whom the competition is oriented as its audience and who distributes the prizes. They cannot in principle involve competition *for* that pinnacle itself. In fact the pinnacle is the immovable condition of the possibility of the competition, the creator of a level playing field: 'before the *kabaka* there is no rank'. The singularity of power and the value of competition are thus interdependent rather than contradictory principles.

This compatibility of competition and hierarchy, and the internal dynamic that arises from it, is illustrated particularly well by popular attitudes towards the political advancement of women during the last ten years under an explicitly 'pro-women' NRM policy (Boyd, 1989). The majority of my informants, regardless of gender, were enthusiastic about this development, citing the achievements and competence of those women who had risen to prominent positions, and often noting their superiority to the general run of male politicians. But most of them, again regardless of gender, also insisted that the political advancement of women should not and would not change the established relations of domestic hierarchy between husbands and wives.

Taken together, these features – a bottom-up structure of nested allegiances, the singularity of power, and regulated competition –

constitute a local model of social solidarity and unity in diversity. More concretely, the embodiment of these features in the system of clans and king is viewed as the foundation of a 'civil' and unified socio-political order. Such unity (okwegatta) is regularly advanced as a prime political value and as the underlying reason for clan activities and even the existence of clans. Less well educated Baganda were often surprised to discover that in my homeland there are no clans and would ask me, 'How can you be united without them?'[12]

As in any hegemonic socio-political cosmology, Ganda hierarchism is differentially interpreted and enacted by social agents based upon the position they occupy in the social order to which the cosmology pertains. Elite Baganda and senior men, for instance, tend to emphasise the primacy of obedience or discipline (obuwulize), while women, younger men and non-elites stress the values of communication, justice and accountability. Yet there is little if any systematic divergence of this sort with regard to understandings of democracy. While subordinate groups certainly infuse their understandings of democracy with a preferential emphasis on accountability over obedience, they do not seem to have embraced the concept more enthusiastically than their social superiors, nor do they seem to give it a more egalitarian or anti-hierarchical interpretation. The potential counter-hegemonic leverage which the popularisation of the concept of democracy might be expected to afford these groups has thus by and large yet to be realised.

Democratic practice

So far, I have tried to show some of the ways in which the concept of democracy has been assimilated to local conceptions of civility, authority, legitimacy and the accountability of ruler to subjects. Democracy, however, consists not only in political conceptions but also in political institutions and practices. Baganda now have nearly a half-century of intermittent experience with the key institutions of Western representative democracy – elections, political parties and representative government. It is revealing that, when I asked my rural informants to tell me the meaning of democracy, these institutions virtually never figured in their answers. But if elections, parties and representation do not figure at the same level of priority as justice, communication and civility, this does not necessarily mean that Baganda are indifferent to these institutions.

Parties and elections: historical experience

By comparison with most other African colonial territories, no strong nationalist political movement or party emerged in Uganda during the late colonial period.[13] Uganda's first political parties were formed in Buganda in the wake of violent popular protests against commercial domination by Asian traders and the ensconced and unresponsive Ganda chiefly oligarchy in 1945 and 1949, but they were relatively unsuccessful at taking advantage of these dissatisfactions. When the British administration partially acceded to their demands for the introduction of elected representatives to local and regional councils, the ensuing elections were virtually ignored by the general population, with voter turn-out in the 1950s of only 5–10 per cent (Southwold, 1964: 239). Popular support for the parties did swell when they fought for the return of King Muteesa after the British had exiled him in a bungled attempt to force through a set of controversial reforms, but waned again following Muteesa's return.

One of the most important reasons for the relative weakness of Uganda's first political parties was that they were perceived from the start as a threat to the existing political structure in Buganda. In fact it was the refusal of the ruling chiefs in 1958 to allow direct elections and the institutionalisation of parties within the Buganda Council (Lukiiko) which undermined and eventually destroyed the Uganda National Congress (UNC), then the leading political party. But the chiefs were not alone in mistrusting political parties. Despite their continued dissatisfaction with the chiefs, the general population remained relatively reluctant to support the parties. This situation, where neither the chiefs nor the parties were able to depend upon popular backing, led to a political vacuum in Buganda in the late 1950s, just as the delicate issue of Buganda's status in relation to an independent Uganda was being worked out. It was exacerbated by the formation of the Catholic-dominated Democratic Party in opposition to the Protestant-dominated UNC,[14] and by the disintegration of the UNC into pro- and anti-Buganda groups – the beginning of a tendency for parties to exploit religious and ethnic antagonisms which continued to plague Ugandan politics well into the post-colonial period.

In 1961 the political vacuum in Buganda was filled by a sudden rush of popular royalism and anti-party sentiment. Beginning as a popular movement independent of both the political establishment and the existing political parties, Kabaka Yekka (The King Alone; KY) was a sort of anti-party party emphasising undivided loyalty to the king and the threat posed by political parties (Hancock, 1970). They based their campaign on the image of the king as the Nnamunswa who kills the red ants (parties) which are trying to destroy her termite mound. KY won a huge majority of Buganda votes in the 1962 independence elections, but was soon taken over by organised political interests and outmanoeuvred by Milton Obote's Uganda People's Congress (UPC), with which it had entered into an opportunistic alliance. Nevertheless, it contributed during its brief existence to transforming an existing distrust of political parties among Baganda into a more pronounced hostility.

In the more than thirty years since independence Uganda has had only one subsequent multi-party national election. Its first elected government, under Obote's UPC, imposed a new custom-made constitution on parliament and moved toward one-party rule in the late 1960s. Amin did not allow parties to operate in the 1970s. The elections following Amin's removal, in 1980, were widely regarded as having been rigged in the UPC's favour, and Obote's second presidency was dominated by a brutal civil war. When the NRM came to power in 1986 they suspended party political activities, allowing party members to speak and publish freely and stand for political office as individuals, but not to hold party meetings or rallies, or to stand as party candidates. Their argument for this policy, that Uganda's political parties had proven divisive and destructive, struck a deep chord with Baganda, and the conduct of local and parliamentary elections on a non-party basis during the past decade has been widely popular among them.

The problem with parties

Political parties were profoundly unpopular among Baganda when I conducted my research. Virtually every informant who offered me an explanation of Uganda's troubles since independence blamed them primarily on political parties. A recurring charge against political parties was that they tend to disrupt even the most fundamental of solidarities, pitting father against child, brother against brother, and neighbour against neighbour:

> Political parties [*ebibiina eby'obufuzi*] brought divisions among us, so that children differed with their fathers, and relatives parted ways over parties. Because if I am KY, that one is UPC, and you are DP, we cannot sit down together and talk things over. [Older Protestant man, landowner]

> We don't see any use for these parties. Because there is only quarrelling in them. Someone can hate his neighbour just because he dresses differently. [Older Muslim man, land surveyor]

> Political parties make each man the enemy of his fellow man. They just kill each other. [Middle-aged Muslim man, bus driver]

The general condemnation of political parties extended to a pejorative conception of politics itself:

> Wherever there is politics [*eby'obufuzi*] things get spoiled. Because with politics, for instance if I am your father, and you are DP, another is UPC, and another one ..., that is to say, we can all be mixed up together, and then this system comes in and [clap, clap] we all end up dead. Parents lose all their children. [Elderly Catholic man, carpenter, RC3 representative]

Parties were accused of promoting an ambition for power so excessive, so unregulated, as to render compromise and communication impossible:

> For my part I don't want them back because I've seen what they do. A party supporter can't allow anyone else to rule. Instead he fights for the seat of power [*entebe*], and if he doesn't get it there is trouble. They create divisions because you see DP or UPC sticking to themselves as if they were born divided. They don't want anyone to make even the smallest comment because of the power they have [*olw'entebe gy'alimu*]. [Middle-aged Protestant man, primary-school headmaster]

> What every party member wants is only for his own party leader to be President. [Elderly Muslim man, landowner and former teacher]

> I would not want [the parties] back at all, since those people have a political greediness. [Young Muslim man, petty trader]

These descriptions of political parties cast them as the very antithesis of the principles of legitimate authority and civility outlined in my earlier discussion. Central to this portrayal is the sense that parties violate the regulated hierarchy which anchors the 'democratic' political virtues. By contrast with the positively valorised forms of competition discussed earlier, parties do not compete for limited power within a regulated hierarchy which encompasses the social totality. Instead they form totalities of their own, competing to capture the pinnacle of power itself and thus dominate the entire hierarchy, excluding everyone else from access to it. As totalities of exclusion rather than inclusion, they interpret free speech as a threat to their authority, rendering communication and discussion impossible. And, since a party which acquires power has no transcendent anchor or status, it is destined to remain mired in partisanship and unable to judge conflicts impartially.

This fundamental coherence of the vilification of political parties with local conceptions of political legitimacy demonstrates that Ganda hostility towards parties is no historical accident. It should not, however, be taken to imply that it was inevitable, or that it is necessarily irreversible. Historical events such as the formation of Kabaka Yekka and Obote's abolition of the kingship served to inflame and consolidate the initially uneasy reception of parties and party-based elections. The NRM's successful implementation of a non-party political structure and its propagation of an anti-party ideology during the past decade have further reinforced it.

A democratic alternative

When it came to power in 1986 the NRM instituted throughout Uganda a new form of local government developed during the civil war in the areas under its control. The Resistance Council (RC) system was composed at the local level (RCI) of the entire adult population of a given village, which elected nine-member executive committees to run local affairs. Village executives combined as parish (RC2) councils to elect RC2 executives, and so on up to the district (RC5) level and the National Resistance Council (NRC; parliament). Candidacies were based strictly on individual merit and repute – not (at least explicitly) on affiliation with the suspended political parties. Voting was public, by queuing behind the candidate of one's choice. Positions on each executive were reserved for historically marginalised groups: women and youth. At the local level in particular, these councils took over many of the administrative and judicial functions of the civil service chiefship, and served as a check upon its remaining functions. The RC statutes also included the right of popular recall of lower-level elected officials.[15]

The RC system was praised by most of my informants, and was certainly judged 'democratic' by their standards. Their praise, however, was virtually never based on the fact that RC executives were democratically elected. In fact, when asked to compare the old chiefship system under the monarchy with the RC system, most insisted that the two were identical, since their functions and hierarchical structure were the same.

> [These systems] seem very similar. Because in the old form of rule we had village chiefs and parish chiefs, and higher up there were sub-county and county chiefs. When you compare with the RCs you can see that the RCI chief is like the village chief, the RC2 is the parish chief, RC3 the sub-county chief, and upwards like that. You can see that their tasks and workings are very similar. [Older Catholic man, well-to-do, private surveyor, RC2 chairman]

> It seems there isn't much difference, because the chiefs were there too, ruling their villages, and they called people to court when there were charges, and they decided cases, and if a case was too difficult they would send you to the magistrate's court. [Middle-aged Catholic man, tenant farmer]

Informants frequently described both systems as constructed in the bottom-up manner which I have identifed as a central ideological characteristic of the Ganda clan system and of Ganda hierarchism in general:

> The councils are likely to co-operate with royal rule, because the *kabaka*'s government appointed the village chiefs from the bottom and up to the parish and sub-county, but when you look closely you see that these things are practically the same. [Older Muslim man, tenant farmer]

There is no great difference. In the *Kabaka*'s time they would also choose [*balonda*] a local person … to rule the village. And it seems to be the same nowadays. [Older Catholic man, tenant farmer]

[The councils] are very similar to the rule of the kingship, since they are chosen [*balondebwa*] from below and reach up to the top. Just like under the *Kabaka* the village chief began at the bottom and was chosen because he was known within the parish. And likewise with these councils, when they see that someone is capable they choose him. [Older Muslim man, prosperous tenant farmer]

There has evidently been a fusion in popular consciousness between these two systems of local government, both viewed as highly legitimate by contrast with the centralised and oppressive administrative system during the two decades from 1967 to 1986. Both systems have in turn been assimilated to the valorised conception of structural hierarchy, with its core features of bottom-up construction and regulated competition.

There is a further distinction whose absence is even more crucial here: that between election and selection. The fact that both, in Luganda, are *okulonda* makes it possible, as in the last two statements above, to speak of the old chiefs and the current RC executives as 'chosen' without adverting to the fact that the former were appointed from above, whereas the latter are popularly elected. The expression meaning 'to vote' (*okutuba akalulu*) was rarely if ever used by my informants in discussing these issues. Such systematic inattention to the manner in which officials are selected speaks, once again, to the assimilation of democratic practices to existing conceptions of legitimate governance with their prioritisation of the values of communication, justice and hierarchical civility.

But if the manner in which chiefs and councillors are chosen is not central to the way in which rural Baganda conceive of relations of power and authority, this is not to say that they are unaware of the distinction between election and selection. When pressed specifically on the issue, most of my informants expressed an unqualified preference for popular election. This was generally true even of those who had initially insisted most strenuously on the identity of the two systems and praised the old chiefship system most unequivocally:

Q. There is no difference between these systems at all?
A. There is no difference, they are the same.
Q. And in the way they are selected [*ennonda*]?
A. This *ennonda* is good.
Q. Is it better than the old one?
A. That one was also good.
Q. But do you think this *ennonda* is better than under the kingship?
A. This *ennonda* is better for the current age [*mulembe*], which is how we measure things now, because in the old days they would just tell us we were still children, but now that we have seen this system we see that it is better. [Middle-aged Protestant man, RC2 chairman, well educated]

Q. Do you prefer one system to the other?
A. No. They are equal because they rule in the same way.
Q. Is there any difference in the *ennonda* of the old chiefs and that of the RCs?

A. The old *ennonda* was somewhat oppressive. In that one it was just 'I am giving you this parish.' But now they sit down together first.
Q. Which is better?
A. The best system is for people to be satisfied. They could bring someone you didn't know at all and just impose him on you, but now you choose someone you know. … Nowadays the person who rules ought to be chosen by the people. [Elderly Muslim cleric, minimal schooling]

This general but rather weakly articulated preference for democratic elections suggests an emerging contradiction. Whereas elections and democratic political representation figure only marginally among the political values to which rural Baganda express a commitment, these institutions have evidently gained considerable popular allegiance at a more pragmatic level. While the legitimacy of the RC system has not been *conceived* as founded primarily on their democratic election, such election has nevertheless for the first time been *experienced* as a viable means of achieving the predominant political ideals of justice, communication and civility. This experience has generated widespread support for democratic elections without, thus far, elevating democratic representation to the status of a core political value in its own right.

This contradiction may or may not produce lasting changes in Ganda political culture, either undermining its hierarchism or creating a new amalgam of democratic and hierarchical elements. What I find particularly significant is the fact that the new standing of electoral democracy in popular political consciousness is at least partially the product of government policies which have created a new and unusual democratic space in Uganda during the past decade – policies which articulate in a variety of ways with popular political concepts, ideals and expectations.

Democracy without parties: the NRM experiment

Chief among the NRM's democratic reforms has been the RC system. Despite the much longer history of sporadic elections in Uganda, it is only with its introduction that elections have become a reliable feature of Ugandan political life. For the first time since independence, elections have been held at regular intervals, first with the formation of RCs in 1986, then nationally in 1989 and 1992, and with frequent local by-elections to fill vacant posts or reconstitute dissolved or recalled executive committees.[16] Since previous Ugandan governments ran local affairs through centrally appointed civil service chiefs, it is also the RC system which has provided Ugandans with their first significant experience of democratic governance at the local level. As I have tried to show, this pyramidal system of indirect representation is eminently assimilable to the Ganda model of legitimate authority as constructed from the bottom up and founded on nested solidarities. It is also the first electoral system to resonate with the local preference for regulated, as opposed to total, competition. Within it, competition is simultaneously promoted and contained within certain boundaries. More specifically, since political parties are excluded from it, the RC system has not been perceived as a vehicle for the manipulation and exacerbation of religious and ethnic divisions. Virtually all my informants were adamant about the incompatibility of political parties with the RC system and the local unity and solidarity that it has produced.

In its pursuit of an alternative to multi-party democracy the NRM has in some respects evolved in accord with local political conceptions at the national level as well. Upon coming to power the NRM insisted on its status as an inclusive 'movement' and invited prominent political figures of virtually all stripes to participate in a 'broad-based' government. Since no Ugandan could be excluded from participation in the movement as initially defined, and leading figures from each of the old parties did join the new government, the NRM was interpreted as a hierachy of inclusion rather than exclusion. The NRM's adherence to the principle of free speech (particularly with regard to the press) also resonated with popular priorities, while its suspension of the freedom of association aroused few objections among a populace for whom this freedom does not figure as a central political value. The NRM also embarked upon a massive project of popular consultation in the process of formulating a new Ugandan constitution. This involved the appointment of a Constitutional Commission which conducted seminars at subcounty level throughout the country, collected some 25,000 submissions, and produced a draft constitution based on popular views. Subsequently a Constituent Assembly was elected by direct ballot in 1994 to debate, amend and ratify the commission's draft (Hansen and Twaddle, 1994; Regan, 1995).[17]

If certain democratic practices have gained a new popularity in the past ten years, it is partly because they have been implemented more systematically and with greater genuine commitment by the NRM than by any previous government. But it is also in part because the form of their implementation articulates significantly with local political values and conceptions.[18] Elections under the RC system make sense to ordinary Baganda in a way that previous electoral practices did not, and certain of the NRM's national policies have endowed them with a frame of legitimacy which previous regimes never possessed in Buganda. This has been a democratisation programme running with the grain of local political culture rather than against it, demonstrating that even a broadly undemocratic culture contains elements which can be deployed in a democratic direction.

The future of the NRM's experiment with no-party democracy, however, is now in some doubt. The success and legitimacy of many of the above-mentioned policies and institutions were based on the NRM's relatively consistent adherence to its own no-party philosophy. In its party-style campaign for the 1994 Constituent Assembly elections, in its subsequent claim to have 'won' them, in its 1995 purge of most prominent non-NRM politicians from the Cabinet, its majoritarian unwillingness to compromise on controversial issues in the (Constituent Assembly, and its unabashed skewing of the electoral rules for 1996, it has acted in rather stark contradiction of its own stated ideology (Kasfir, 1994; Regan, 1995).

Nevertheless, the NRM's non-party political system and ideology remain convincing among Baganda. In the Constituent Assembly elections Buganda (like much of the rest of the country) endorsed them by electing a decisive majority of delegates in favour of extending the system for another five years and conducting the 1996 presidential election under the same stipulation of individual candidacy. Despite a subsequent rift in the NRM–Buganda alliance over the issue of Buganda's administrative autonomy ('federalism') in the 1995 constitution, and the emergence of the Democratic Party leader Paul Ssemogerere (himself a Muganda) as the joint candidate for the pro-party opposition in the 1996 presidential contest, there appears to have been no significant increase in enthusiasm for political parties among Baganda during the past two years. President Museveni won an unexpectedly high 79.5 per cent of the Buganda vote in the May 1996 election, and my follow-up interviews indicate that enduring scepticism towards the old parties was one of the primary reasons for this outcome.[19]

Conclusion

I have argued that the reception of democracy in Buganda, both in conception and in practice, must be understood with reference to an existing socio-political cosmology. While the *concept* of democracy has been largely assimilated to local conceptions and thereby purged of some of its emancipatory content, there is also evidence that recent experience with democratic *practice*, particularly democratic elections, is beginning to challenge and change some of those conceptions. This impact has been made possible in significant part by the government's implementation of innovative democratic reforms and policies which articulate with local values and understandings. Their relative success suggests that whereas much academic analysis pins its hopes of democratisation in Africa to the emergence of Western-style institutions of civil society and an attendant Western-style democratic culture, equal attention, at the very least, should be paid to the compatibility of democratic reforms with existing political cultures.[20]

If democracy based on periodic elections contested by political parties is unlikely to take root, at least in the near term, in Uganda and perhaps elsewhere in sub-Saharan Africa as well, the countries of the subcontinent may seem destined to remain relatively undemocratic. But such a conclusion rests on an untenably universalist conception of democracy.[21] Because the democratic project is everywhere emergent and incomplete, the West, despite its historical priority, can claim no monopoly of its current and future forms or definitions. Contemporary African reluctance to reduce political communication to party-based elections speaks to challenges currently faced by even the oldest democracies, and some of the recent innovations in Uganda open up novel possibilities for addressing them. In a time of apathy and disillusionment in many older democracies, perhaps it is only mildly quixotic to suggest that African political ingenuity may help us re-ignite our own democratic imaginations.

Notes

[1] See Nursey-Bray (1983) and Staniland (1986) for overviews of this earlier consensus.
[2] In a recent review of this literature Robinson emphasises the neglect of 'norms, customs, and symbols of power, ... culture, local knowledge and their impact on participation' (1994a: 62).
[3] Miles (1988), Owusu (1992), Schatzberg (1993), Robinson (1994b), van Binsbergen (1995), Schaffer (1994); the emerging attention to political culture among proponents of the civil society paradigm (Chazan, 1993; Bratton and Liatto-Katundu, 1994), while salutary, is vitiated by reliance on Almond and Verba's (1963) approach.
[4] Interviews were conducted at two main sites during an eighteen-month period in 1992-93 – in Ngando sub-county, Mpigi District, a primarily Muslim area, and in Katabi sub-county, near Entebbe town, in Mpigi District, with a religiously mixed population – and during shorter visits in 1993 to Nakaseke sub-county, Luwero District (predominantly Anglican), and the rural environs of Masaka town (Catholic). Approximately 100 recorded interviews were conducted, all with ethnic Baganda, and all in Luganda unless otherwise noted.
[5] Western conceptions of democracy are of course complex and historically variable (Williams, 1983), but for my purpose here the core

elements of 'rule of the people' (or majority rule), egalitarian conceptions of citizenship and political representation via party-based elections are most salient.

6 The Oxford English Dictionary dates each of the usages of 'civility' which interest me here – good governance, conduct becoming a citizen, collective advancement, and courtesy, decency, good breeding – to the sixteenth century.

7 I use single quotation marks to indicate English words used in a Luganda context.

8 Per Tidemand and I conducted research simultaneously in Buganda and shared a concern with conceptions of democracy and popular political participation. I am grateful to him for much stimulation in the field and for access to the original text of this passage.

9 This is the standard telling of the story. According to Ssemakula Kiwanuka, a leading historian of precolonial Uganda, it is apocryphal aside from Mukeabya's adoption of the name Muteesa soon after consolidating his hold on the throne, and his occasional acts of public cruelty (Kaggwa, 1971: 144-5).

10 As Azarya (1994: 88-90) points out, this ethical dimension has been almost completely ignored by the proponents of 'civil society' in African studies.

11 This notion connects etymologically and conceptually with that of a bottom-up structure as well, since the root of enfikto and amatikkira is okutikka (to carry, especially on the head), which is what the Buffalo clansmen quite literally do for the king in hoisting him on to their shoulders during his installation.

12 The centrality of clanship in modelling these elements of Ganda hierarchism should not be taken as a reflection of the real salience of clanship in ordering social relations, which was already eroding during the nineteenth century, and was found by Richards (1955) and Southwold (1959) to be largely a nostalgic myth by the 1950s. Nor should the projection of contemporary conceptions of the clan king system on to the pre-colonial past be taken at face value: in pre-colonial Buganda there was an element of structural opposition in the relationship between the clans and the king (Southwold. 1961) which was eliminated under colonial conditions. These caveats notwithstanding, I think Welbourn (1965: iv) was right in criticising Fallers et al. (1964) for underestimating the enduring importance of clanship in Buganda, since its weakness as an organising sociological principle does not negate its conceptually orienting role.

13 The following discussion relies on Apter (1961). Low (1962). Welbourn (1965), Mamdani (1976). Kasfir (1976) and Young (1977).

14 Religion was established as one of the central axes of social cleavage in Uganda and Buganda at the very start of the colonial period.

15 The fullest recent discussions are Ddungu (1994). Brett (1992: chapter 3). Barya and Oloka-Onyango (1994) and Tidemand (1995); Mamdani (1994) provides an incisive analysis of the democratic potential and limitations of the RC system. Under the 1995 constitution the RCs have been renamed Local Councils (LCs).

16 See Kasfir (1991) on the 1989 elections for the most extensive analysis of any of the RC-based elections.

17 This process also appealed to the contractarian element of Ganda political culture emphasised by Kokole and Mazrui (1988).

18 It should be emphasised that Museveni and the NRM do not by any means conceive themselves as adopting indigenous political forms or idioms. In fact their attitude to popular political culture is distinctly dismissive.

19 I spent the month of May 1996 in Uganda as part of an election observation mission.

20 While Africa is a highly heterogeneous continent some recent literature suggests parallels elsewhere with elements of Ganda political culture and the reception of democracy in Buganda. Among Senegalese Wolof there is a similar stigmatisation of 'politics' as divisive and destructive. and a strongly consensualist approach to elections (Schaffer, 1994). In the Nokoya kingdoms of western Zambia there has been resistance to elections as 'morally and cosmologically obscene for implying that 'political office [can] be bought for promises, favors and money' (van Binsbergen, 1995: 17). Miles (1988) documents considerable ambivalence towards political parties in northern Nigeria. Schatzberg (1993: 449–50) cites Kenyan and Zairean conceptions of power as singular and indivisible. Botswanans remain deeply committed to political communication in the kgotla (village assembly) and continue to view multi-party elections and open political contestation with considerable suspicion despite Botswana's record as one of Africa's more successful liberal democracies (van Binsbergen 1995; cf. Comaroff, 1994: 35; Somolekae 1989: 85). In fact, Botswana is perhaps the one exception to my generalisation about the failure to craft locally coherent forms of democracy (Holm, 1988), although there is some question as to the genuinely democratic thrust of the state-sponsored kgotla system (van Binsbergen, 1995: 24); Ghana has also made a few attempts in this direction (Owusu, 1992).

21 The limitations of both universalist and relativist approaches to the study of democracy outside its historic homelands are set out very clearly by van Binsbergen (1995: 4–6).

References

Almond, G. A., and Verba, S. 1963. The Civic Culture: political attitudes and democracy in five nations. Princeton: Princeton University Press.

Apter, D. E. 1961. The Political Kingdom in Uganda: a study of bureaucratic nationalism. Princeton: Prineeton Uuiversity Press.

Azarya, V. 1994. 'Civil society and disengagement in Africa',]. W. Harbeson, D. R. Chazan and N. Chazan (eds.), Civil Society and the State in Africa. Boulder and London: Lynne Rienner.

Barya, J.-J., and Oloka-Onyango, J. 1994 Popular Justice and Resistance Committee Courts in Uganda. Kampala: Friedrich Ebert Foundation.

van Binsbergen, W. 1995. 'Aspects of democracy and democratisation in Zambia and Botswana: exploring African political culture at the grassroots', Journal of Contemporary African Studies 13 (1), 3–33.

Boyd, R. E. 1989. 'Empowerment of women in Uganda: real or symbolic', Review of African Political Economy 45/46, 106–17.

Bratton, M., and Liatto-Katundu, B. 1994. 'A focus group assessment of political attitudes in Zambia', African Affairs, 93, 535–63.

Brett, E. A. 1992. Providing for the Rural Poor: institutional decay and transformation in Uganda. Kampala: Fountain Publishers.

Chazan, N. 1993. 'Between liberalism and statism: African political cultures and democracy', in L. Diamond (ed.), Political Culture and Democracy in Developing Countries. Boulder: Lynne Rienner.

Comaroff, J. L. 1994. 'Democracy, fried chicken and the atomic bomb: a brief reflection on the "new" South Africa', Cultural Survival Quarterly summer/fall, 34–9.

Ddungu, E. 1994. 'Popular forms and the question of democracy: the case of resistance councils in Uganda', in M. Mamdani and J. Oloka-Onyango (eds.), Uganda: studies in living conditions, popular movements, and constitutionalism. Vienna: Journal für Entwicklungspolitik (JEP) Book Series.

Fallers, L. A. 1959. 'Despotism, status culture and social mobility in an African kingdom', Comparative Studies in Society and History (2), 11–32.

——. (ed.). 1964. The King's Men: leadership and status in Buganda on the eve of independence. London: Oxford University Press.

Hancock, I. R. 1970. 'Patriotism and neo-traditionalism in Buganda: the Kabaka Yekka ("The King Alone") movement, 1961–62', Journal of African History, 11 (3). 419–34.

Hansen, H. B., and Twaddle, M. (eds.). 1994. From Chaos to Order: the politics of constitution-making in Uganda. Kampala: Fountain Publishers, and London: James Currey.

Holm, J. D. 1988. 'Botswana: a paternalist democracy', in L. Diamond, J. J. Linz and S. M. Lipset (eds.), Democracy in Developing Countries II, Africa. Boulder: Lynne Rienner.

Kaggwa, A. 1971. The Kings of Buganda, translated and annotated by M. S. M. Kiwanuka. Kampala: East African Publishing House.

Kasfir, N. 1976. The Shrinking Political Arena: participation and ethnicity in African politics, with a case study of Uganda. Berkeley: University of

California Press.
——. 1991. 'The Uganda elections of 1989: power, populism and democratisation', in H. B. Hansen and M. Twaddle (eds.), *Changing Uganda*. London: James Currey.

——. 1994. 'Ugandan politics and the Constituent Assembly elections', in H. B. Hansen and M. Twaddle (eds.), *From Chaos to Order: the politics of constitution-making in Uganda*. Kampala: Fountain Publishers, and London: James Currey.

Kokole, O. H., and Mazrui, A. A. 1988. 'Uganda: the dual polity and the plural society', in L. Diamond, J. J. Linz and S. M. Lipset (eds.), *Democracy in Developing Countries* II, *Africa*. Boulder: Lynne Rienner.

Low, D. A. 1962. *Political Parties in Uganda, 1949–62*. University of London Institute of Commonwealth Studies Commonwealth Papers, No. 8, London: Athlone Press.

Mamdani, M. 1976. *Politics and Class Formation in Uganda*. New York and London: Monthly Review Press.

——. 1994. 'Pluralism and the right of association', in M. Mamdani and J. Oloka-Onyango (eds.), *Uganda: studies in living conditions, popular movements, and constitutionalism*. Vienna: Journal für Entwicklungspolitik (JEP) Book Series.

Miles, William 1988. *Elections in Nigeria: a grassroots perspective*. Boulder and London: Lynne Rienner.

Murphy J. 1972. *Luganda–English Dictionary*. Washington, D.C.; Catholic University of America Press.

Nursey-Bray, P. 1983. 'Consensus and community: the theory of African one-party democracy', in G. Duncan (ed.), *Democratic Theory and Practice*. Cambridge: Cambridge University Press.

Owusu, M. 1992. 'Democracy and Africa – a view from the village', *Journal of Modern African Studies* 30 (3), 369–96.

Ray, Benjamin C. 1991. *Myth, Ritual and Kingship in Buganda*. New York and Oxford: Oxford University Press.

Regan, A. J. 1995. 'Constitutional reform and the politics of the constitution in Uganda: a new path to constitutionalism?' in P. Langseth, J. Katorobo, E. Brett and J. Munene (eds.), *Uganda: landmarks in rebuilding a nation*. Kampala: Fountain Publishers.

Richards, A. 1. 1955. 'Ganda Clan Structure – some preliminary notes'. Unpublished paper presented at the Makerere Institution for Social Research.

——. 1964. 'Authority patterns in traditional Buganda', in L. A. Fallers (ed.), *The King's Men: leadership and status in Buganda on the eve of independence*. London: Oxford University Press.

Robinson, P. T. 1994a. 'Democratization: understanding the relationship between regime change and the culture of politics', *African Studies Review* 37 (1) 39–67.

——. 1994b. 'The national conference phenomenon in francophone Africa', *Comparative Studies in Society and History* 36 (3), 575–610.

Roscoe, J. 1911. *The Baganda*. London: Macmillan.

Schaffer, F. C. 1994. '*Demakaraasi* in Africa: what Wolof political concepts teach us about how to study democracy in Africa'. Doctoral dissertation, University of California at Berkeley.

Schatzberg, M. G. 1993. 'Power, legitimacy and "democratisation" in Africa', *Africa* 6:1 (4), 445–61.

Somolekae, G. 1989. 'Do Batswana think and act as democrats?' in J. Holm and P. Molutsi (eds.), *Democracy in Botswana*. Athens, Ohio: Ohio University Press.

Southwold, M. 1959. 'Community and State in Buganda'. Doctoral dissertation, Cambridge University.

——. 1961. *Bureaucracy and Chiefship in Buganda*. East African Studies, 14, Kampala: East African Institute of Social Research.

——. 1964. 'Leadership, authority and the village community', in L. A. Fallers (ed.), *The King's Men: leadership and status in Buganda on the eve of independence*. London: Oxford University Press.

Staniland, M. 1986. 'Democracy and ethnocentrism', in P. Chabal (ed.), *Political Domination in Africa: reflections on the limits of power*. Cambridge: Cambridge University Press.

Tidemand, P. 1995. 'The Resistance Councils in Uganda: a study of rural politics and popular democracy in Africa'. Doctoral dissertation, Roskilde University, Denmark.

Welbourn, F. B. 1965. *Religion and Politics in Uganda, 1952-62*. Nairobi: East African Publishing House.

Williams, R. 1983. *Keywords: a vocabulary of culture and society*. Revised edition, New York: Oxford University Press.

Young, C. 1977. 'Buganda', in R. Lemarchand (ed.), *African Kingships in Perspective: political change and modernisation in monarchical settings*. London: Frank Cass.

Acknowledgements

The research upon which this article is based was made possible by a Fulbright-Hays Doctoral Dissertation Abroad Fellowship. Subsequent visits to Uganda in 1995 and 1996 were made possible by a research grant from the Harry Frank Guggenheim Foundation and by the International Foundation for Electoral Systems. The article was written under dissertation funding from the Jennings Randolph Program of the US Institute of Peace and from the Center for Advanced Study of Peace and International Security at the University of Chicago. Earlier versions of the article were presented at the 1994 African Studies Association meetings in Toronto and at African Studies workshops at the University of Chicago and Yale University. I have benefited from detailed comments on various drafts by Holger Hansen, John Comaroff, Ron Kassimir, John Rowe, Michael Tuck, Bo Karlström, Per Tidemand, Fred Schaffer, Dan Ottemoeller, Movindri Reddy and David Laitin.

ADAM ASHFORTH
Witchcraft, Violence
& Democracy
in the New South Africa

Reference
Cahiers d'Etudes africaines, 150–52, XXXXVIII-2-4, 1998,
pp. 505–32

Witchcraft, broadly conceived as the capacity to cause harm or accumulate illicit wealth and power by supernatural means, is a central feature of African life in South Africa.[1] Since the first democratic elections in that country in 1994, witchcraft is commonly thought to be rapidly increasing. Witchcraft is not currently on the political agenda as the South African state is being remade in the image of a modern liberal democracy. In local African communities, however, it ramifies into every aspect of that agenda. For witchcraft is a central aspect of the insecurity of everyday life and a great deal of time, energy, and money is spent combating its dreaded effects. Morever, witches are typically understood to be engaged in a form of action akin to violence in the bringing of harm to innocent citizens – perpetrators of a form of crime and a threat to the community as a whole. People are beginning to ask: What is the Government doing about witches? This paper begins a discussion of the ways in which questions about witchcraft and the state are being discussed in local communities in Soweto.

South Africa is now governed as a modern liberal democratic state which is in the process of being reintegrated into the 'international community' with its global circuits of people, capital and culture. Dominant discourses of jurisprudence, public administration and political and economic management in this world leave little space for considerations of witchcraft as anything other than primitive atavism – a system of 'beliefs' mired in ignorance and backwardness. Witchcraft *beliefs* may be real enough, according to this perspective, and may provide a potent source of motivation to action, but the witches and their powers are deemed purely 'imaginary' – that is, not real. Yet amongst ordinary African people, even in the 'modern' cities of the new South Africa, witchcraft remains a vibrant concomitant of everyday life. Life is lived on the assumption that the powers of witches are real, indeed, enormous. Their actions are experienced as assaults akin to crimes. Witches are implicated, moreover, in causing large-scale problems such as unemployment with which the state must grapple. Witchcraft, then, constitutes a sort of ontological fault line within the contemporary South African state, revealing discontinuities between the principles governing politics at the level of public institutions – imbricated as they are in global circuits of power and meaning – and those operative at the level of everyday life in African communities. Underpinning this paper is the question: what is at stake in the contest between these two schemes of being, acting, and meaning?

This paper, offered in the spirit of a report from the field, is part of a larger project seeking to plot some of the lineaments of this fault line in the political landscape of the new South Africa by means of a detailed political ethnography of Soweto. My general aim is to examine the ways in which witchcraft is affecting the creation of a new state, as well as the ways in which the new state is understood as shaping the contexts within which witches work. In this paper I suggest that while for the present there does not appear to be any explicit involvement by political authorities in issues relating to witchcraft in Soweto, there is a good deal of pressure for such involvement. Moreover, Sowetans with whom I have discussed this matter in recent months consider it obvious that the government *should* be involved in solving the problem of witches in their community. The question, simply, is *how*? I will argue that the answers to this question that I have found to be emerging in Soweto hinge upon understandings of basic principles of democratic governance such as governmental responsiveness, collective action, and the role of expert knowledge in policy making. In the long-term, the paper suggests, the legitimacy of the democratic regime in South Africa will be solely challenged by the response of political authorities to issues concerning witchcraft in places such as Soweto.

Why Soweto?

I focus on Soweto because it is the principal black urban settlement in South Africa. Located beyond the generic suburbs of the drab modern city built upon the mines that a little less than a century ago drew the armies of the British Empire to this part of Africa – thereby bringing South Africa into the world – Soweto is in many ways a world unto itself. It was built as a dormitory for the black working people of Johannesburg; a conglomeration of segregated black townships that grew, one after the other, to become the largest black urban settlement in southern Africa. Owned, administered, and policed – until recently – by white authorities within a racially-discriminatory state, Soweto has long had the character of a distinct city with a distinctive ethos overlaying complex patterns of socio-economic and ethnic diversity. People there call themselves Sowetans; they speak of 'Soweto Style' drawing inspiration from diverse African, European, and American sources.

Estimates of Soweto's population range from one to four million, although the counting is inaccurate and the districts that are typically thought of as Greater Soweto are not the same as the more restrictive administrative subdivision that once upon a time was named the South Western Townships.[2] Yet while the place is like a city of several million strangers, it remains in many respects a web of interconnected villages populated by kin and neighbors who have known each other for generations. It is within these sorts of networks that witchcraft is considered to operate most powerfully.

I have been living in Soweto off and on since 1990 – since shortly after the release from prison of Nelson Mandela, the unbanning of the liberation movements, and the beginning of negotiations leading to the new constitution; In this engagement with Soweto I have slowly come to appreciate the significance of issues of spiritual insecurity in everyday life and the unseen domains within which all relations of power resonate. Witchcraft is always a consideration in everyday life, even if just for jokes and gossip. Yet it is not the only thing in life, nor is it experienced in the same way by all Sowetans. Stories of witchcraft are mostly recounted with the warm convivial malice of good gossip. Witchcraft is also jokingly invoked as the cause of trivial mishaps when we are confident that malice is not really at work and to show that we are not afraid of such nonsense. Sometimes, however, and this has been the case at least once in the last five years in every family to whom I am connected, witchcraft is a matter of the most deadly seriousness.

As the oppressive system that was apartheid has come to an end, two profound transformations in everyday life in Soweto occurred. On the one hand, the greater opportunities afforded to Africans in government and the economy have opened rapidly growing inequalities in populations that in previous generations were compelled to live in conditions of relative socio-economic parity. Yet while opportunities were greatly expanded for the new black middle classes, the expected benefits of democracy failed to materialize for the majority of the population. Unemployment remains high and as the economy has been liberalized the value of the currency has fallen, resulting in a steep rise in the price of the imported consumer goods so essential to marking status. These factors are widely seen as expanding the prospects for jealousy and envy. On the other hand, interpreting the meaning of misfortune has become more complex. Hithertofore, the misfortunes of individuals and families could be reckoned not only by reference to particular causes, but also to a general name hanging over the suffering of all black people – 'apartheid'. Now the sorrows of an unfair fate can only be measured, case by case, against the conspicuous 'progress' and good fortune of particular relatives, colleagues, and neighbors. Both of these developments feed into registers of witchcraft.

Soweto in the late 1990s seems submerged in a sea of consumerism. When I first came to this place in 1990, everyone was obsessed with politics. We discussed the political situation endlessly. Political rallies were the great social events. On June 16th, 1990, fifty thousand people crammed into Jabulani Amphitheatre to commemorate the anniversary of the Soweto Uprising and celebrate the freedom that seemed close at hand. Everyday speech was peppered with political slogans. Young people addressed each other as 'Comrade' – 'Com' for short. Any gathering of friends would provide an occasion for singing the then unofficial national anthem *Nkosi Sikelele* and the hundreds of 'struggle songs' that everyone knew by heart. Over the years of negotiations after 1990, the political fervor slowly died. It was reawakened somewhat by the election of 1994. In the celebrations following the ANC victory and Mandela's inauguration, though, when the people of Soweto took to the streets in their thousands, the songs they sang were the old ones, still calling for Mandela to be released from prison. Nowadays, only the worst political phonies use the honorific 'Com' and you can go for months without hearing *Nkosi Sikelele*. But everyone knows the price of everything. If a supermarket is opening in Soweto tens of thousands of residents will gather for the bargains and festivities. A Score supermarket opened near our place in June. The line of shoppers waiting patiently for hours in the sun stretched hundreds of yards in an eerie echo of the lines queuing on voting day, April 27th, 1994. Fifty-five thousand people attended the opening of the new Deon electrical goods store on the outskirts of Soweto. A week earlier, three hundred attended the official June 16th rally.

Political organizations in Soweto are moribund. By far the majority of voters supported the African National Congress in the national elections of 1994 and the local elections of 1995 and will probably do so again in the future, though with little enthusiasm. Of the hundreds of activists in my area of Soweto who were busy building the organization when it returned from exile in the early 1990s I know of none who are still members in 1997. Like most 'mass parties' the ANC is mostly the province of political careerists;

there is nothing political now for the masses to do. Periodically, the national or provincial government announces some mass campaign or other – most notably the *Masakhane* [Let us build together] – which falls on deaf ears. Elected officials of the national and provincial governments have no significant local presence in Soweto. Although representatives were elected on a national list system, the ANC has required its Members of Parliament to establish constituency offices and make themselves known locally. Only the most dedicated activist in Soweto would know who these people are. Generally, voters are resentful and apathetic. One long-time ANC supporter told me in June that she would never vote again. She only voted in the local government elections when she conceived the idea that with the new voter's rolls the government would be able to keep track of who didn't vote and would probably penalize them if ever they required assistance.

For the local government elections of November 1995, Soweto was divided between the southern and western 'Metropolitan Sub-Structures' of the Greater Johannesburg area in an effort to increase the black presence in the formerly segregated white suburbs of the city. Some local Council members were elected on a party list system, others were elected to represent specific local wards. From the discussions I have had with councillors and residents in my area of Soweto, it seems clear that ward councillors are being transformed into mini-chieftains, acting as brokers for council-provided services and intervening in disputes among residents and between residents and the council. For example, to start an 'informal' business in this area, it is necessary to get informal permission from the councillor. Councillors, whatever their credentials as ANC militants, are almost universally perceived as being in politics for their own financial gain, just as in the old days of apartheid councils. And while Mandela along with some others of the 'stalwart' generation stand above this suspicion, the movement of prominent national politicians into business careers has further fostered the perception that politics these days is business by other means. For local councillors, this means that their long-term future will depend upon their ability to build networks of patronage. It also means that as the local government struggles to impose measures such as compulsory payment for services, councillors will find themselves subject to the same repertoire of political action as of old when houses were burnt and councillors necklaced as collaborators. They are also being exposed to all the local forces of envy and intrigue that are said to inspire witchcraft in the less fortunate. When the first democratically-elected mayor of Soweto died in childbirth earlier this year, for example, it was assumed here in kitchen table gossip that her political colleagues should be suspected of witchcraft along with the usual suspects of relatives and neighbors.

Social life in Soweto seems to have changed, too, in subtle ways as if the barometer marking community fellow feeling and solidarity was steadily falling. A rapidly spreading township fashion, for example, has householders building high brick fences reminiscent of the white suburbs in front of their homes, obscuring the dwellings from view and allowing access only through heavy steel gates. A few years back, such walls were unheard of here. Not only would they be frowned upon as anti-social, but the consensus was that while fences (usually of chain-link wire) and lockable gates were essential for the nocturnal security of households possessing cars, the general security of the family was better preserved by having the property open to scrutiny at all times by concerned neighbors. A house obscured by walls or trees was also considered to be a house where witches were free to work without hindrance. Regardless of their occult proclivities, no-one would want to advertise themselves thus. Now the walls serve both to mark status and secure protection from neighbors who cannot be trusted.

My friends in Soweto, like most others, strive to resist the pull of witchcraft explanations for misfortune, knowing that such obsessions only increase fear and paranoia. Moreover, it is commonly known here that just as faith can heal, so too can fear strengthen the evil powers of witches. In the context of Sowetan life, however, resisting the fear of witches can be enormously difficult. This is not because people are ignorant and superstitious, although that can also be the case. Rather, from earliest childhood lives are lived in relationship with invisible beings and forces responsible for misfortune – and there is a great deal of suffering and misfortune to be accounted for. These evil forces are many and various, and every bit as important as those tutelary ancestral powers supportive of the good at work beneath the all-encompassing eye of God. The larger set of issues I am interested in concerns the ways in which these forces interrelating the innermost reaches of the self – the 'soul' – with the highest planes of the cosmos – the heavens – connect with those forces and entities governing the legal subject in a modern state. While I have some experience of matters relating to witchcraft in the private domains of everyday life in Soweto, neither I, nor anyone else, has studied these issues emerging into public domains as a new African state comes into existence in the south of Africa.

Three dialogues on witchcraft and the state

As a prelude to a proper investigation of witchcraft and the state in Soweto, I offer the following accounts of three sets of conversations with Sowetans conducted between June and September, 1997. The first is with an old friend of mine, a member of the so-called 'lost generation' of South African youth whose lives and prospects were disrupted by the struggles against apartheid of the 1980s. In this conversation, my friend raises the problem of the power of *inyangas* ('traditional healers' or 'witchdoctors' a.k.a. *sangomas* and *ngakas* – usage is extremely flexible) in relation to the common good of a democratic polity as he struggles to come to terms with his personal misfortunes in the post-apartheid era and strives to find a way of lifting the curse of witchcraft from his life. The second, with an *inyanga* practicing in the Mapetla district of Soweto where I stay, reflects upon the healer's work combating witchcraft in the area over the past sixteen years and the question of the proper relation between political power and divinatory expertise. Finally, I present a verbatim transcript of part of an interview with the Mayor of Soweto (technically, the Mayor of the Southern Metropolitan Local Council – which includes a large part of what used to be the South Western Townships). In the interview, the Mayor considers, for the first time, the question of the role of the newly constituted local government in relation to problems caused by witchcraft.

My purpose in presenting these three accounts is to show some of the ways these issues are beginning to bubble to the surface of community life in the new era. These conversations represent three perspectives on these issues which, while not scientifically sampled, are typical in revealing what might be termed a structure of plausibility in the consideration of these matters. They present a sense of the sorts of connections that are considered obvious in contemporary Soweto. In the conclusion I will suggest that what we are witnessing here is the birth of a question, a fundamental question about the nature and purposes of state power in relation to social evil with profound implications for the legitimacy of the political regime of democracy in South Africa.

One: A man afflicted

Three days after the Choku family buried their mother in 1996, following several years of nursing her chronic ill health, a prophet of the Zion Christian Church told the youngest son that the death was an 'inside job' – witchcraft perpetrated by a family member staying in the same house. Madumo, the middle of three sons, was immediately suspected and accused of killing his mother with *muthi* (herbs), magic medicines. Two aunts staying in the same house during the period of the funeral endorsed the accusation. Madumo, then thirty, was unpopular with his relatives because he had been unemployed for years, was rarely able to contribute to household expenses, and had begun a correspondence course of university study. Life became intolerable for the accused. He was forced to leave his family's home, wherein by right he should have expected to find shelter for as long as he required. Two days before sitting for his annual exams at the University of South Africa, Madumo was on the street struggling to survive by means of petty crime.

When Madumo consulted an *inyanga*, he discovered that his misfortunes were actually the result of another relative taking soil from his mother's grave, mixing it with herbs supplied by an unscrupulous witchdoctor and burying the mixture in a bottle in Madumo's yard to bewitch the whole family, thereby bringing about the initial accusation of witchcraft flowing from the Zionist prophet's divination. The fee for the *inyanga*'s services to rectify the problem (after an initial twenty Rand consultation fee and not including the cost of sundry chickens, candles, and sorghum beer) amounted to 650 Rands, the equivalent of six months' rent for the room Madumo was occupying. Although he consulted a number of other *inyangas* and prophets who presented him with a variety of different stories, Madumo decided the grave-soil diagnosis was correct. To get his life back of track, he had no alternative but to find the money for the *inyanga*, by any means necessary.

Compounding Madumo's problem was the fact that like that of many – perhaps most – young Sowetans, he was never really taught the proper procedures for communicating with his ancestors, who remain the principal source of ameliorative power. He has no solid grasp of 'tradition', that which Sowetans refer to, in English, as 'culture'; moreover, being estranged from his family and living alone, he is in a position for which, traditionally, there was no accounting. His father abandoned the family before Madumo was of an age to be taught the main rituals. The custodians of tradition in his family, the people who can speak authoritatively of the ancestors, their wishes, and the proper ways of relating to them, live far away in the rural areas and have no regular contact with their relatives in the city. Madumo has no money to travel to their place or to sponsor the expensive feasting that would re-establish communion with his ancestors. Madumo's mother, although she was 'spiritually inclined' and engaged in ceaseless commerce with the unseen worlds, died without passing on the traditions and rituals that would appease her side of the family. Madumo is thus left to stray alone through a world littered with spiritual and supernatural perils, a world where the ordinary hardships of life in a poor and violent place are exacerbated by the works of evil forces in unseen domains.

By engaging the services of an *inyanga* Madumo was voluntarily entering a relationship of physical and spiritual submission. The treatment was intense. For one long grueling month, in order to straighten out his relations with the spirits, my friend was put through the whole purgative repertoire of bleeding, vomiting, shitting, and sweating that the human body is heir to. At the climax of the treatment he came perilously close to kidney failure and death. By following the treatment, however, Madumo was able to deepen his faith in his *inyanga* and strengthen his confidence in dealing with the workings of unseen powers. As well as being something like a doctor, his *inyanga* was also a teacher, not to say priest. For Madumo was relying on the authority of the *inyanga* to reestablish the broken connections with his ancestors and teach him proper rituals to use in the future. These rituals were significantly different both from those previously witnessed in Madumo's home, and those which are more common in other households in Soweto. If his *inyanga* had been mistaken, or if Madumo messed up, he risked the wrath of the ancestors. At the end of his 30-day course of treatment, which the *inyanga* adjudged successful, Madumo was restored to square one, so to speak. That is, the curse of witchcraft was removed. Now, if he continues to have problems – getting a job, say, or troubles with his landlady – they will be simple consequences of his lack of qualifications or other objective factors, not a result of witchcraft.

Madumo was convinced that he was not alone in falling victim to witchcraft in the 'new' South Africa. In his view, most families in Soweto these days are suffering the ill-effects of witchcraft. And it is getting worse. You just have to be able to read the signs.

— 'When would you say it started increasing?' I asked him one afternoon as we were lounging in his room behind MaDudu's shebeen.
— 'I would reckon from Ninety Five', he said, 'January. When Africans, South Africans, black South Africans, thought that they were free from the hands of the white man, everybody just told himself that 'Oh, we don't have any grudges with Whites, they're our brothers and all. Now we are going to face each other since we are all free now. We're going to face each other.' And one other thing that has caused this high volume of witchcraft is lack of jobs. When other families are going well, their lives are compared. They [families who are not doing well] become jealous to them and cause this harm. It's lack of jobs.'
— 'So it's freedom and democracy that has caused this?' I asked. 'People are coming face to face with each other because they are no longer oppressed by the White Man?'
— 'Ya', my friend replied, 'direct confrontation. Like: Who owns this? Who's having this? I don't know how to put it. In fact, at first there was this thing of We want Freedom. Everything was blamed on the National Party. So, when everything was gone off and black leadership took over, society has had to make a direct confrontation. So with all these bad fates now, misfortunes and all, we are pointing fingers to each other. There's no more of that old story of, I'm sore because of apartheid, because of a white man. Now it's: I'm like this because of my neighbour. It's turned around.'

Moreover, as Madumo explained, those who used to sit back and say 'the White Man has destroyed us' are now not in a position to establish themselves under the new dispensation – 'unlike the other blacks who have accumulated education and equipped themselves with diplomas and all'. The major problem of witchcraft is emerging from the losers in the struggle for advancement: 'they are challenging the others with *muthi* [magical medicines].'

As Madumo explained, the 'lack of jobs' has also caused the 'high volume of witchcraft'. This is because people are suffering and are thus more inclined to turn upon their neighbors. But this same lack of jobs has in itself been partly caused by witchcraft. Few people would attribute the structural weakness of the South African economy entirely to the workings of witches. Nor would every unemployed person attribute their joblessness solely to witchcraft in every instance. But at the same time, it is extremely difficult to avoid the conclusion that witchcraft is not implicated in your plight when you lose a job while others don't or fail to find one when others do. Obviously, then, at least part of the underlying problem of unemployment – that is, not just the distribution of a given quota of social misfortune – must be caused by witches. For Madumo, it is this aggregative aspect of the evil work of witches that demands collective restorative action. And it is *inyangas*, traditional healers, who should be responsible for this work.

While prepared to place his complete faith in his own healer to restore his personal good fortune, Madumo harbored a residual resentment against *inyangas* in general. The presence of large numbers of *inyangas* at the President's inauguration on May 10th, 1994, made a big impression upon my friend, as it did on many others. But it also raised many questions: 'If we've got so many traditional healers', he asked, 'why do we have to suffer by becoming victims of evil forces? Who paid those thousands of healers at the Union Buildings? Why can't these healers protect our communities voluntarily?'

It was obvious to Madumo that while the witches were busy causing havoc, the *inyangas* had been standing idle. He had no doubt that the problem was a lack of will, rather than capacity:

'They can't just let our community to be destroyed by this evil monster that is not seen', he said, 'since they are in a position of curing it'. His view is that *inyangas* should stop operating simply on an individual basis, treating cases like his own as they come, one by one: 'They should form a club. Like when they went to the Union Buildings for Mandela's inauguration and danced and burnt all the herbs for all South Africans – Blacks, Whites, Indians and all. They should go from location to location and pour *muthi* on boundaries to keep out the witches. They should make rallies in the locations to sniff witches out, they should drive them out. They should protect the community by pouring their herbs in the street. We've got trucks and all. They should load in drums and drums of those herbs and pour them in the street. Sniff these people out. Definitely. I'm sure if they are going to protect us, witches won't be strong. If they just burn their substances, witches won't be strong.'

In other words, *inyangas* should seek to preserve the common good. As a child of the era of mass action in the 1980s, Madumo was transposing onto the *inyangas* and their work of healing the principles of organization and collective action learnt in the struggle against apartheid: 'They should make rallies.' Most young men of his generation in Soweto are convinced that it was their battles with the police in the streets, their struggle and resistance, that toppled the regime of the Boers. Surely the same must be possible for *inyangas*. All that prevents such combination of *inyangas* in the interests of the community as a whole is their jealousy of one another and their abiding interest in the continuation of witchcraft as the source of the ailments that drive their businesses. But while the autonomous action of individual witches can produce a situation of collective malaise such as unemployment, the individual actions of healers are proving ineffectual. In Madumo's view, the *inyangas* should combine their powers to counteract large social-structural woes such as unemployment and bring forth the good fortune South Africa so desperately needs:

> 'Why can't these people help us with foreign investment, they've the power to help with high escalating crime, help the police, in fact help the miners to produce more gold and prevent mines collapsing, and help fishermen down in wild seas. Help wineries in the Cape. Help with the different types of sickness that are found in the whole African continent, sniff all the witches and destroy them from the society, since these witches are really cruel and destructive.'

Furthermore, he argued, the *inyangas* should stop their business of supplying political parties and organizations with the *muthi* that strengthens them in their fights: 'Both sides had *muthi*, *inthelezi*, it's meant for killing. 'Madumo', I replied, 'if *inyangas* are so powerful why couldn't they find that little girl in the East Rand?'.

Interlude: Inyangas *come to the aid of police*   At the same time as Madumo was undergoing his treatment for witchcraft in the winter of 1997 a major police operation was underway in the East Rand, the first official joint operation of police forces and traditional healers. A child was missing. On March 25th, the day before she was due to testify in the trial of the man accused of raping her, seven year old Mamokgethi Malebane disappeared. By July, as a result of the usual incompetence of the police, the child had still not been found and the case became a *cause célèbre* in the Johannesburg press. The girl's mother, with the assistance of SANCO, the congress of civic associations, engaged a *sangoma* (diviner) to find her. No luck. A reward of ten thousand Rands for information was offered by the police. On July 5th, the investigating officer, Sergeant Themba Mazibuko of the Child Protection Unit, convened a rally of diviners and prophets at the Vosloorus Stadium to determine Mamokgethi's whereabouts. They came in their dozens, with thousands of onlookers. Finding things is one of the specialties of such people. Indeed one of the tests culminating the rituals of *ukuthwassa*, when diviners graduate from their apprenticeship (or are 'initiated', or 'ordained' as some would have it), is the search for objects hidden by the senior *inyanga* presiding over their training. On July 5th, and throughout the following week, members of the South African Police Service at the behest of ancestral spirits acting through diviners searched houses, rivers, and swamps in diverse parts of South Africa in quest of the little girl.

My friends in Soweto, like the rest of South Africa, were particularly amused by the story of poor Vusi Masondo, a *sangoma* from the East Rand, who made himself a laughing stock before a crowd of five thousand spectators when, insisting that the girl was in a river near Nyoni Park despite the failure of police divers to locate her, he was forced to enter the water himself to retrieve her. Bodies of water such as that river are often thought to be the sanctuaries of magical snakes, and Masondo was terrified that entering the water without appeasing the snake would put him in peril. The crowd had no sympathy, less patience. Masondo tossed a fifty cent coin into the waters in lieu of a sacrificial goat and began his search. After he leapt from the water in alarm, chased by the snake, the police divers, burly Afrikaners, fished out a rusty exhaust pipe. The crowd was merciless; Masondo was miffed: 'We do not need white people to interfere with this', he is reported to have said. 'This is a black thing and needs the support of our people. All *inyangas* must come and coax the mamba so that we can take the child.'[3]

Two weeks after the spectacle of *sangomas*, the man accused of raping the child, a neighbor of the family named Dan Mabote, was rearrested and, under the impression that he could apply to the Truth and Reconciliation Commission for amnesty, confessed to murdering the girl, leading the police to a grave miles from anywhere pinpointed by the diviners. The first joint effort of police and diviners thus ended in a flop. Media reports of the diviners' efforts, especially the story of the hapless Vusi Masondo and his exhaust pipe mamba occasioned much mirth in Soweto at the time. Sowetans, in my experience, typically combine a deep faith in the general possibility of the divinatory enterprise with a hearty skepticism about particular diviners. This derives from the common experience of false revelation at the hands of diviners (frequently with unpleasant results for those falsely accused) and a recognition that divination is an easy way to take money from the gullible. Coupled with the embarrassing fiasco of Hintsa's head in 1996, the Mamokgethi Malebane affair suggested the profession of divination was under siege.[4] Their failure to find the child, however, was generally interpreted not as evidence that the procedures of divination were false and futile, but rather that the flock of *inyangas* who turned out to chase the reward money were phonies.

Two: A healer and his craft
Above a small tin shack in the open ground in front of Merafe Hostel, a hand painted sign nailed to two knobbly-kneed posts announces, in Zulu and English with a Biblical twist, 'Brothers and Sisters, we are able to cure any sick, please come to us.' Outside the shack, on a table fashioned from an old packing crate, a collection of 'ready mades', murky brown liquids in recycled half-pint liquor bottles, also advertises the business within.

The healer's shack is divided into two rooms, an ante-room, where patients wait on coarse wooden benches, and an inner consulting room. An apothecary of roots and barks lining the far wall, piled loose on shelves and in a variety of jars, bottles, and recycled shopping bags, imparts to the shack the distinctive odor of South African herbalism, an odor that manages at the same time to be earthy, cloying, bitter and yet somehow sweet – utterly unlike any of the scents of antisepsis and cologne clinging to my memories of clinics and pharmacies. The healer waits in the inner room behind a table carefully overlaid with a covering of newspaper next to a window rescued from a wrecked kombi taxi. Mr Zondi is his name. He rose to greet us. He had been expecting us.

In 1981 Mr Zondi moved to Johannesburg and took up residence in Merafe Hostel in Mapetla near the railway station, where he opened his business. At first he operated out of his room, or, more accurately, the room he shared with fifteen other migrant workers. Then he built a shack outside the hostel to make his practice more accessible to local residents. Township residents always had an ambivalent relationship with the hostel and its population of several thousand single men. Residents used to enjoy the performances of traditional dances mounted by the hostel dwellers on Sundays in the sports grounds outside the hostel. Local men used to frequent hostel shebeens and occasionally use the showers there as most of the township houses had no bathrooms. But women, especially, often felt threatened by this enormous convocation of masculinity and were sometimes assaulted by envoys therefrom. Young people born and bred in the urban world of Soweto disdained the backwardness of those with rural roots living in hostels. Typically, young Sowetans treated migrants from rural areas such as populate hostels, as ignorant bumpkins. They still do.

The hostel men viewed the local youths as vicious and degenerate, particularly lacking that defining quality of African culture – respect for elders. Since 1976, periodic explosions of political conflict between hostel dwellers and surrounding residents have not helped relations. In one respect, however, the rural areas overwhelm anything the city can offer: they are home to the most powerful witchdoctors – and to the most dreadful of witches. That Mr Zondi still works out of the hostel speaks well for his power, signifying rural roots in an urban domain. And although the hostels are no longer exclusively male, men predominate there. For many, this would be considered an added guarantee of the power of Zondi's herbs – they are unpolluted by the presence of women.

I asked Mr Zondi if the problems patients were bringing him in 1981, when he began practicing here in Mapetla, were the same as those he was seeing today. 'It's getting worse, worse', he replied. 'Witchcraft?' I asked. 'Too much, too much.' The problem, as Mr Zondi explains it, is not only that the volume of witchcraft is increasing, but the witches themselves are becoming more sophisticated. 'They are becoming more and more professional', he said. They cause the same problems as before: illness, death, misfortunes such as accidents, unemployment, infertility, discord and hatred in families, and so on. But these afflictions are becoming more difficult to cure. And the witches have assistants. When one witch dies, there is always an assistant to take over their work. They study hard. Sometimes the witch will hand on their secret knowledge to a son or daughter and the craft will pass down through families. Other times the assistant is not related. Always, in Mr Zondi's view, the secret to their power lies in their knowledge of herbs. *Inyangas* depend for their powers upon ancestors, so they cannot reproduce themselves so easily.

To make matters worse for the *bona fide* practicing *inyanga* such as Mr Zondi, the 'professional witches' are virtually indistinguishable from legitimate *inyangas*. Anyone can go to them and purchase deadly herbal weapons. They keep their practice totally secret, however, so that only those with evil in their hearts know how to find them. I have no doubt that such people exist and conduct a trade in *muthi* for purposes of witchcraft. Periodically, for example, local newspapers will carry reports of court cases involving the procurement and sale of human body parts. I understand this commerce of 'professional witches' as being analogous to that of drug dealers in western cities. Every city in the world possesses an underground commerce in illicit drugs. Most decent citizens probably imagine this commerce to be more extensive than it is (and, certainly in the United States, political and civic leaders have long had an interest in exaggerating its scale), yet if one of these decent citizens suddenly decided to purchase a kilogram of cocaine, they would probably not be able to do so. Nor are their sworn agents, the police, ever able to eradicate the trade. Yet, miraculously almost, the trade persists, and those who desire the illicit substances find their way to those who can sell. Something similar probably happens with Mr Zondi's 'professional witches' and their clients in Soweto. Except in one crucial regard: while I have heard many people described as 'witches', and sat in on endless speculative discussions of the probable source of apparent witchcraft, I have never heard anyone recommend the services of a reliable 'professional witch' with a high-quality product.

Legitimate 'traditional healers' like Mr Zondi are regularly importuned by clients seeking herbs, *muthi*, to cause destruction. I want to see so-and-so dead by sundown, they might say. Sometimes such people can be simply turned away with the advice to look elsewhere for the herbs they need. Other times they won't take No for an answer. Mr Zondi chuckled as he told the story of a man who came to him looking for witchcraft herbs. Thinking to discourage him, Mr Zondi told him such herbs would cost five thousand Rands – a princely sum in these parts. Three days later, the man appeared with three thousand Rands in his pocket. Mr Zondi told him that he had been unable to locate his colleague who specialized in mixing such herbs. Come back later, he said. The man reappeared several days later with the full five thousand. According to Zondi's telling, he said to the man that the specialist was still unavailable so he should go elsewhere.

The career of an *inyanga* depends entirely on reputation: reputation for power and reputation for integrity. It Mr Zondi sold the man the herbs and they didn't work, he could become known as a dud, a 'fake' *inyanga*. (After wasting five thousand Rands, the client would be sure to denounce him, although he would most certainly not admit his malicious intention in buying the herbs in the first place.) If, however, misfortune befell the person against whom the herbs were directed – which is not at all unlikely in this place of poverty, violence, and suffering – Mr Zondi might find himself with the dubious reputation of being a powerful witch, even though the *muthi* was bogus. Moreover, the reputation upon which *inyangas* depend is not only a matter of talk amongst neighbors and clients in the hostel or location. He has to think of his own ancestors. Their opinion matters more than anyone's. If he should defy the ancestors, or misuse the gifts they have given, he risks losing his powers and, consequently, his reputation. Were he to become known in the neighborhood as a witch, he may even be killed.

There are two kinds of *inyangas,* then: those who practice witchcraft, and those who heal witchcraft. Nobody would ever admit publicly to being of the first group. And every *inyanga* that I have encountered vehemently asserts their place amongst those combating witches. Nor do they claim a capacity to turn evil forces to good ends. Their powers, they will say, come from ancestors and are intrinsically good. For this reason, some people get extremely agitated when *inyangas* and *sangomas* are referred to as 'witch-doctors', insisting that they are really healers, not witches. But the more vigorously *inyangas* deny their witchcraft and the importance of their healing practices, the more they invoke the figure of the powerful witch, possessor of arcane knowledge, secretive practitioner of an evil craft. Secrecy is the essence of this whole business. Whereas the healer's knowledge is private – inspired by personal revelation from his or her ancestors – the witch's knowledge is strangely public albeit derived, in principle, from a secret source. The way Mr Zondi speaks of these matters, the witch's knowledge is essentially scientific, in the sense that it is, if only among witches, publicly verifiable, based on experimentation, and transmitted by means of study and instruction. Witchcraft is often referred to colloquially as 'African science'. For healers such as Mr Zondi, the professionalization of witchcraft means that they must be constantly on their toes in the battle against the swiftly-evolving tricks of the evil doers. Moreover, the healer such as Mr Zondi, who operates as a 'traditional healer', stands alone with his personal ancestors against legions of witches with their professionalized science. A further problem the legitimate healers face is that the witches are gaining access to ever more varied sources of herbs. *Muthi* is being drawn from all around the country although not, in Mr Zondi's experience, from outside. The more complicated the mixture is, the more powerful it is; and with the witches' pharmacopeia increasing in diversity, the challenge of counteracting their herbs grows and the more quickly the healer must adapt. Do not expect to find any practitioners of ancient unchanging wisdom in this place, then. Where witchcraft is concerned in Soweto, the healer's struggle is to adapt or die.

The obvious solution to the problem of 'professional witches' posing as legitimate *inyangas* is the old device common to all professions seeking to keep out interlopers: the centralized Register of Practitioners and the Code of Conduct. When the Ralushai Commission inquiring into witchcraft violence and ritual murders, for example, produced its recommendations these were the central ideas drawn from the Zimbabwean system of Registered Traditional Medical Practitioners.[5] On the wall of Mr Zondi's consultation room, as on thousands of other walls, a framed certificate from the South African Council of Traditional Healers hangs. Such certificates are not difficult to obtain. An American woman describing herself as the 'Cosmic Gypsy' tells a breathless story in her web-page memoir *Igubu, The Sangoma Series* about how her mystical powers of healing were instantly recognized on a visit to South Africa by a *sangoma* she identifies as MT who was the Chairman of the local branch of the association: 'Your eyes [are] really bright. [he said] Would you like to be member of our healers and herbal association? T/Dr K O [*sic*] from Motherwell suggested you already, but it's me that is the Chairman, so I have to decide.' The Cosmic Gypsy bought twelve years membership for three hundred Rands and received a certificate to hang on her wall in America next to her Ph.D.[6]

The major problem with registration and accreditation for traditional healers is that their authority to practice comes directly from their ancestral spirits and the spirits recognize no higher authority in the form of government ministries or professional associations. Mr Zondi himself told me the story of how, as an apprentice undergoing *ukuthwassa*, his great-grandfather appeared to him in a dream and commanded him to discontinue the ritual singing which is the usual practice of apprentice *sangomas*. He was also instructed to use a certain gourd for divination rather than the more commonplace *astragalus* bones. Both of these innovations outraged the senior *sangoma* who was leading the young Mr Zondi through the process of becoming a healer. But the senior's authority was nothing compared with that of the dead great-grandfather. Mr Zondi ignored the senior man and went his own way. And thus it will be if the state tries to interfere with the will of the ancestors.

I asked Mr Zondi again whether witchcraft was increasing, as many people had been telling me recently. He replied that indeed it was. Why? I asked. Jealousy.

This is the stock answer in these parts for the motivation of the witch: jealousy. In seven years I have never heard another reason given for witchcraft. It is nicely circular: jealousy causes hate, hate drives witchcraft; witchcraft (as evidenced by its effects) must have been caused by hate. Why does anyone hate? Jealousy. The word names the original source of all ill will, and is usually cited in its English form. It is the fuel driving the engine of witchcraft (it is also cited as the main reason why men beat women). 'Jealousy' in Sowetan usage encompasses both the resentment of another's good fortune that is usually spoken of in English as 'envy', and the desire to restrict one's good fortune and prevent others from enjoying the same. If you are prospering, people who are less fortunate will be jealous and will strive to take you down; if you are not prospering, those who are more fortunate will jealously guard their advantage and strive to keep you down. Jealousy is that which needs no

further explanation. 'Why would they be jealous of us?' I have asked when witchcraft seemed to be coming our way. 'They just are', was the reply. Enough said.

Seldom is jealousy displayed openly for all to see, for its natural habitats are the dark secret recesses of the heart where it feeds off 'bitterness'. Friends who truly care for each other in this place will work hard to combat 'bitterness in the heart' before it grows into hatred and jealousy. For people can appear to be friends while still nurturing hate. The commonplace assumption is that others see your good fortune as something taken away from them. Except for your closest and most trusted friends, you must assume that everyone else is actually, or potentially, jealous – and prepared to act upon it. To assume otherwise is to take untoward risks in opening yourself to attack by witchcraft. Some people are presumed more susceptible to jealousy than others. Older women top the list, for they have no productive or reproductive capacities of their own and are dependent upon the success and status of their children and grandchildren. Hence old women are most commonly associated with witchcraft not because they have intrinsically greater powers (although they have had the time to accumulate more evil knowledge), but because they are thought to have the greatest occasion for jealousy.

Mr Zondi told me that he was quite puzzled about the recent increase in jealousy. 'The way things are now', he said, 'when a person buys furniture, the other one gets jealous and wants to destroy him. You've got cows? They'll kill you. You can't buy a pair of trousers. You can't buy a car. You can't do anything with your life. They don't want any progress. This jealousy is too high, and it causes the witches to be more active.' Mr Zondi's view was that jealousy seems out of control in recent years since there has been freedom.

Certainly the 'objective' conditions for an increase in jealousy are everywhere present in Soweto these days. Some people are prospering conspicuously while others are not. Most families are in the same sort of financial position that they were before the end of apartheid. At the same time, as I suggested earlier, the quickened sense of consumer desire is palpable and the drive to mark status through commodities intense.

'So what should be done about this increase in witchcraft resulting from the increase in jealousy?' I asked Mr Zondi. He had a solution: 'The witches must be eliminated from the community.' From his standpoint as an *inyanga*, Mr Zondi explained, the problem of witchcraft has two dimensions. The first is the actual suffering inflicted upon particular individuals and families. It is the *inyanga*'s task to remedy this, and he does so by virtue of enlisting the support of the ancestors and directing the powers of healing herbs. But curing the effects of witchcraft leaves the perpetrator of the evil untouched and free to strike again. Of course, most of the treatments for witchcraft use *muthi* with the object of sending the curse back upon the one who had despatched it as well as protecting the victim from further harm. But this can only be done on a case by case basis and cannot disable the perpetrator completely and permanently unless the object be to kill them. If death be the object, is that not witchcraft in itself? And, if so, why not just kill the witches outright? A further problem, Mr Zondi told me, is that the witches are getting too clever and have found ways of protecting themselves against the reversal of their spells. So the problem of the witches, the individuals responsible for harm and misfortune, is a problem for the community.

From Mr Zondi's perspective, Madumo is mistaken to think that a convocation of *inyangas* could combine their spiritual forces in order to create a power capable of counteracting the cumulative effects of the multiple individual acts of witches. For the ancestors of one *inyanga* cannot transfer their capacities to another, nor is there any evidence in the contemporary urban context of ancestors working one with another or of certain founding ancestors reigning superior over others.[7] Rather, in this view, the *inyangas* need to combine their expertise with the power of secular authorities to root out this evil at its source. The *inyangas* would act as policy advisers. Mr Zondi's solution would be to convene a community forum to 'sniff' out the witches. Each and every location in Soweto should establish such a forum and elect a committee of *inyangas* to oversee the process of elimination.

'How would the witches be identified?' I asked. Mr Zondi replied that if someone is a powerful witch around the community, the community knows it. Moreover, there are people who have *muthi* in their houses but who are not involved in healing people. Under the direction of the community forum, in Mr Zondi's view, the police should round up these people and force them to drink their own *muthi*. If they are legitimate healers, they will be fine. If they are witches, the *muthi* will kill them. If someone refuses to eat their own *muthi* it simply means that he or she is a witch and should be punished. Unfortunately, the new constitution makes it difficult to deal with witches. In Shaka's day, Mr Zondi says, the witches were simply killed: 'Now they have these human rights, so you can't just kill them.' But he is adamant that these scourges of the community should be imprisoned for life, and locked up away from other prisoners where they cannot get their hands on *muthi*. For the bottom line is that witchcraft is a crime.

I asked Mr Zondi about the role of the local council in all of this. In November of 1995, local council elections were held in South Africa, with Soweto being divided between two jurisdictions of the Greater Johannesburg Metropolitan region. Each location of Soweto now has its own ward councillor. If witchcraft is as big a problem as Mr Zondi insists it is, surely these people, sworn to serve the community's interests, should be doing something about it? I put this proposition to Mr Zondi. He agreed. 'It is a good suggestion', he said.

So Mr Zondi was keen to take on the idea that the local council should play a part in the control of witchcraft and the eradication of witches in Soweto. He considered that they could play a role, although they would have to be properly 'procedural', convening an elected council of *inyangas* to oversee the whole process. The danger is that people will just point out anybody, such as neighbors whom they hate, and accuse them of being witches. Even though the community does know when there is a real witch in its midst causing real harm, false accusation can easily be fabricated. Everybody in these parts who was around during the political struggles of the 1980s knows how easy it is for innocents to be targeted as enemies of the community.

I asked Mr Zondi about the Council of Traditional Healers, whose membership certificate hangs framed upon the wall of his consultation shack and whose leaders have the power to intuit whether a diviner is for real or not. The main reason he displays the thing, it turns out, is not to proclaim authoritative accreditation in the way an orthodontist might who nails a degree to a surgery wall, but rather to ensure that if someone under his treatment dies he can certify himself to the police as a healer, not a murderer. It might also serve in his defense one day should someone in the community feel so inclined as to sniff him out as a witch.

Three: The mayor

With Mr Zondi's concern to root out witches fresh in my mind, I decided to talk to the Mayor of Soweto, Mrs Nandi Mayathula-Khoza, about the council's role in witchcraft control. It took several weeks before I was able to get an appointment with Mrs Mayathula-Khoza, partly because she had to attend a meeting on local government and development at the United Nations in New York. We met in her office in the Council offices in Jabulani, built during the days of apartheid when councils and councillors were denounced as 'puppets'. For the first half hour or so of our meeting, Mrs Mayathula-Khoza told me about the work of the new Southern Metropolitan Local Council in 'development' – building roads and installing streetlights in Soweto. We discussed the problems of administrative reorganization and the difficulties of creating local democratic administrations. We discussed the problems of the so-called 'culture of non-payment' and the difficulties the council was experiencing in its efforts to persuade residents to pay for the services they consume. Then I raised the question of witchcraft:

AA. Let me ask you a slightly different question. You might find it somewhat unusual. ... When I came back this year I found that people of many different kinds of backgrounds have said to me that witchcraft is much worse than ever that it's going out of control almost: that since the elections of 1994, the levels of witchcraft are rising continuously. ... I was having a discussion with an *inyanga* at Merafe Hostel last week about this, and he was suggesting that each community – Phiri, Mapetla, Senacane, and so on – should call upon the police to assist them in tracking down and dealing with witches. Now, in this sense, if that is a community problem that people talk about and see as facing the community, do you find as councillors, or at the level of the council that there has ever been any suggestion that part of your job should be to address this evil that is afflicting the community?

NM-K. No, I haven't really heard of any discussion. or I haven't been involved in any discussion about that. Um. I don't know. I don't know, really. I'm not well conversant with this subject. But I know one thing for sure that witchcraft is there. Okay. But I haven't been personally inflicted with this problem as such. But if it is generally a problem experienced by members of the community and if the community wants to bring it up to council level, I'm sure council would be more than willing to address that problem and listen to people as to what kind of solution do they want to this problem. And if we can make any contribution towards that, in particular working with the police, because communities are now working with the police, council is working with the police and if they want the problem to be taken up by council, I'm saying we would be more than prepared to deal with that. But the kinds of problems basically that people have been experiencing and putting forward are developmental kinds of projects. Yes, there is witchcraft as a problem, but I'm saying so far, since I've been involved in council, since 1994, I haven't really been involved in a discussion dealing with that problem.

AA. You haven't heard of anyone else that's been asked to deal with aspects of this problem?

NM-K. Not within this council, not within the Greater Johannesburg Council or the Southern Metropolitan Local

Council. … But like I said, I really haven't been personally inflicted, and I haven't really personally experienced that. But I know one thing for sure. Even members of my family have experienced similar problems. And they've shared those problems with me and at that level then I know it's taking place and I know it's the biggest problem. But unfortunately it hasn't come through to the council. But I'm saying that if it's a community problem, and the community's interested, or wants the council to be involved, I think Why not?

AA. What sort of response do you think you would get from the white councillors?

NM-K. There are white councillors, some from the National Party, Democratic Party, but we don't have DP here [in the Southern sub-structure] and there are some white councillors as well within the ANC movement, the democratic organization. And I believe that witchcraft happens every-where. It happens also in the white community, it happens in the black community. And there are *sangomas* who are white as well as *sangomas* who are black. So it happens almost everywhere.

AA. So if it came up at Council you'd be able to run a discussion in the Council Chamber that would be worthwhile?

NM-K. Yes, I think it would be worthwhile. But now the problem is that we are confined by the Ordinance, which actually defines the sorts of functions that we should carry out. And I'm beginning to think, and wonder, if the ordinances would actually allow us to embark on such discussion. But I'm saying if it's a community problem then the council should really entertain a discussion of such. Because we have terms of reference as well for the council, terms of reference for various committees within the council. We also have caucuses. Probably it may be well taken, first at caucus level. Then if the caucus for various parties can actually decide that 'Let's take this up to the council', then I'm sure we can be able to do it, even if the ordinance doesn't spell out that we can actually entertain such problems.

AA. One of the things I've been doing is spending time with the local police. I drink at a shebeen there in the flats near the barracks and the police come after work. And discussing this issue with them. they find themselves caught in the position where officially witchcraft doesn't exist according to the law. There's the Suppression of Witchcraft Act, but that doesn't address witchcraft, it addresses witchcraft accusations. So it's illegal to accuse somebody of being a witch, but the actual practice of witchcraft is something else. And the police get caught in situations where they have to intervene, and often it comes down to private and unofficial action by them which is beyond the law. It's unofficial and informal policing.

NM-K. [chuckles] Yeah. And sometimes you'll find in some communities, people deal with that problem themselves and they get to kill you know a witch, a person who's considered to be a witch in a particular community. And again, that is considered as taking law into your own hands and it's just not allowed.

AA. I know in Senaoane there was a woman killed last year, do you remember that?

NM-K. I remember there was some case.

AA. It was the mother of this gangster, Chafunya.[8]

NM-K. Yes, yes, the Chafunya gang. It's true. But then that was not a witch-related problem, it was crime-related.

AA. But after the schoolboys got Chafunya, *she* was killed because they believed she'd been giving him *muthi* to strengthen him as a thug.

NM-K. Okay, to be involved in the criminal activities that he was involved in. No, you are correct. I remember very well. And that also she was allowing those children to carry on the evil work that they were doing. I remember, it was mainly the youth who stoned that mother to death … that lady, they'd taken the law into their hands. Yeah, it's a big problem. You know, one realizes that it's a big problem when you discuss it with somebody else. Yeah.

AA. This is what I was talking about with the police. In such a situation where you have a crowd, especially when it's usually schoolchildren at the forefront of these things [mmm] who are targeting a witch. If you step in as police and protect this mother, because she has a right to live under the constitution and your duty is to uphold the constitution, in fact from the point of view of the community, you are protecting a witch. And the witch is a source of evil to the community.

NM-K. To the community.

AA. And this is a problem that the police, the councillors, and the government are supposed to represent the community and to solve problems facing the community. It's potentially very difficult.

NM-K. It is very difficult. You know, now that we've spoken about it, I think I'll just discuss with other councillors informally and hear what their opinion is about this problem. And probably we could then take it to various caucuses and discuss it and see if we can't really give quality time to it in terms of discussing it and working with the community in coming up with means and ways of resolving this problem. … No, we will look at that. Definitely. It's interesting.

When the Mayor of Soweto and her colleagues on the Council do get around to talking about what is to be done about witchcraft, it is difficult to imagine what they can say – beyond putting forward proposals for eradicating the belief in witches – that will not seem ridiculous to their colleagues who represent the suburbs and do not live in worlds with witches. In South Africa, such people are known as Whites. They have a long history of misunderstanding Africans, with little credit to their claims that they have the best interests of Africans at heart. What options remain, then, for those who would act in the name of the state in confronting the prickly subject of witchcraft?

Witchcraft and the state. The birth of a question?

Madumo resents the failure of healers to organize themselves and cooperate in protecting the masses. Mr Zondi bemoans the increasing professionalism of witches and calls for a conjoining of the expertise of *inyangas* with political power and community action to eradicate them. Mrs Mayathula-Khoza wonders what can be done to meet the needs of a community beset by witchcraft and worries about people taking the law into their own hands. Is there a common thread here?

In the three dialogues presented above (representing innumer-able other conversations), I want to suggest that we are witnessing something like the birth of a question. This is a question that is only beginning to become relevant in Soweto (and, I would argue by extension, South Africa), but which has profound implications for the long term future of democracy. For in the long run, the ways in which this question is answered will determine the perceived moral character of political power. That question is: What is the purpose of Government'?

Prior to the transition to democracy in South Africa, it was clear to everyone in Soweto that the purpose of government was to operate the System, and the purpose of the System was to oppress and exploit black people. The Government. at least in the dying phases of apartheid, was seen as an unmitigated source of evil. Behind thc apparent face of political power, behind the image of those men like F.W. De Klerk who presented themselves to the public as the Government, right-thinking and responsible in all respects, people perceived an originary source of evil power. The hidden, secret, nature of this power fostered fantasies about an enormous capacity for causing misfortune far in excess of anything yet uncovered by investigations into covert and illicit state actions. Counterposed to the Government was the Struggle. The purpose of the Struggle was clear: Freedom. Behind the apparent disorder of the Struggle were secret organizations of freedom fighters who achieved a mythic status far in excess of their actual military achievements.

With the first democratic elections of 1994 the express purpose of government changed. The African National Congress, led by Nelson Mandela, took office brandishing a 'Reconstruction and Development Programme' (RDP) and promising a 'Better Life For All'. A state which for generations had been experienced as an alien and oppressive force was now proclaimed as the representative (and representation) of the people – the 'Rainbow Nation'. Much has been made in South African political commentary of recent years about the crisis of 'expectations' amongst black voters. Most people have yet to see the good life, and the RDP has largely disappeared from the political horizon, living on mainly in the form of sardonic jokes in the township. Disappointment alone, however, is not necessarily calamitous for a state, especially if there remain other parties to curry favor at the next election. More problematic, I would argue, are the habits that develop around the framing and atswering of the basic question: What is government for?

This question of the real purpose of government is starting to emerge in everyday political discourse in Soweto. Although rarely framed as an abstract inquiry, it constantly bubbles to the surface in talk when people ponder the moral nature of the powers that seem to be shaping (or not shaping) their lives. When the talk is of witchcraft, a source of evil and affliction for the whole community, the way the question of the purpose of government is answered is of profound importance. In common with everyone else I have spoken to about these issues in Soweto, my interlocutors above see the problem of witches as a political matter demanding community action. Yet they do not automatically see it as the responsibility of the state. I would suggest that they do not do so for two simple reasons: First, although the apartheid state provided many services, it was never particularly responsive to the needs of indigenous people and most black people saw the state, amongst other things, as a structure of discrimination and favoritism systematically biased in favor of Whites. Consequently, habits of turning to the state for assistance are shaped in terms of improving the flow of goods which previously were restricted to Whites. Second, the predominant discourses and ideologies within the ruling African National Congress – while they may countenance debates about capitalism, socialism and democracy, even 'Africanism' – are thoroughly within

the traditional frameworks of 'western' political thought and action and thus do not readily generate questions about the role of the state regarding witchcraft. However, and this is the point that needs to be stressed, whenever I have discussions with people in Soweto about the connection between the purposes of a democratic state and the problem of witches in the community is made, it seems obvious to all concerned that witchcraft is a matter that should be addressed by government.

Two years ago, when the Government of National Unity was young and untried, my friend Madumo was not so concerned with the question of *inyangas* and their power as he was when I found him in 1997. Five years ago, the question would not have entered our heads. Of course, in earlier times he had not been so badly bewitched. Many other friends in Soweto who have escaped that fate are not as preoccupied with the occult as Madumo. Nonetheless, the issue of witchcraft is immensely more salient today than it has been previously. Madumo's faith in the possibility of amalgamating *inyangas* to work for the common good comes in the wake of a general disillusionment in the capacity of government to deliver the 'better life for all' which its election slogans promised and which was sincerely believed to be the inevitable fruit of freedom. It is also formed in the context of a widespread faith in the power of collective spiritual action and the power of prayer.[9] When Mandela speaks of the 'small miracle' that was the transition to democracy, many people take him literally and thank the other-worldly force that brought it about. For Madumo, as a child of the era of 'mass action' in the struggle against apartheid, it is obvious that *inyangas* should combine in a form of collective action to remedy the ills besetting the nation as a whole. Thus Madumo's call for *inyangas* to work together to assist the government in pursuit of the common good is not totally implausible.

Madumo's call is not implausible. It is, however, mistaken. As the discussion with Mr Zondi, the healer, makes clear, the authority to heal and the capacity to cure are not bestowed by ancestors in such a manner as to make mass action by *inyangas*, or even small scale co-operation, any more effective than individual action. Mr Zondi's concern is to connect the business of healing to the power of the community – either through the state or by means of collective action – and to have healers and diviners serve as expert advisors in the identification of witches. Secular powers would take over in the apprehension and punishment of offenders once divination produces the damning evidence of their crimes. Diviners then, would serve as expert witnesses in the trials of witches and policy advisors in elaborating procedures for the effective control of witchcraft.[10] Mr Zondi, has no doubt that his profession could co-operate with state authorities to remedy the problem of witchcraft by eradicating witches. This is an updated version of the 'traditional', version of the proper relation between diviner and Chief in witchcraft matters. Mr Zondi might find this vision of a policy-role for *inyangas* appealing. The world's press, however, would descend upon Soweto and hold them up to ridicule.

For Mrs Mayathula-Khoza, despite the fact that she had never thought about the problem of witchcraft as a matter of government, the connection, when pointed out, was instantly apparent. Her worries about people 'taking the law into their own hands' gave the issue some urgency. For, as this discussion suggests, the issue of witchcraft in the community is a question of law and justice; state incapacity is readily matched by a public appetite for vigilantism, such as when the schoolboys killed Chafunya's mother. In my discussion with the Mayor, as soon as witchcraft was placed in the category of social problems besetting the community, it became obvious to her that the same methods used by government to address other issues – committee meetings, discussion, and debate – should be applied to the problem of witchcraft. Yet it is by no means obvious what these discussions could achieve.

People living outside the worlds of witches (which includes myself and virtually everyone else who has written on the subject along with the representatives of the white suburban areas in the Southern Metropolitan Areas of which Soweto forms a part) are united in conceiving of witchcraft as a matter of belief serving to motivate social action – albeit with a wide variety of associated idioms and discourses. Those who live with witches as a reality engage with witchcraft as a form of action in itself; a form of action which involves causing harm and which is something like a crime. This is where the 'ontological fault-line' of which I spoke at the opening of this essay opens up. Of course, within liberal democracies, a great deal of ontological pluralism can be permitted. You can believe in the virgin birth and the power of prayer and I can believe in the spaceship behind Hale-Bop and, so long as we respect each other's rights, we can all get along. Surely witchcraft can be accommodated within such pluralism as well? This would indeed be the case were witchcraft, in practice, simply a matter of 'belief'. However, as stressed above, witchcraft is generally understood in Soweto as a form of action, a mode of perpetrating harm from which the community must be protected. Protecting communities is very close to the central notions about the purposes of states in liberal political theory.

If witchcraft was a marginal matter in people's lives none of this would matter very much. But, as I hope the conversations reported above make clear, witchcraft does matter. And the consensus is that it is getting worse as a direct result of changes brought about by democracy. The new regime is approaching the point of reckoning where they are either seen to be doing something about the witches, or they are seen to be in league with the witches. And, as is demonstrated in the case of Chafunya's mother, along with many hundreds of similar killings in recent years throughout the country, people are accustomed to taking the law into their own hands in these matters. If those who act in the name of the state – whether as judges, police, or the Mayor of Soweto – are to avoid the charge of aiding and abetting witches by preventing people from taking the law into their own hands, they must be seen to be doing something about witchcraft. Yet treating witchcraft seriously, as any African politician must, poses a fundamental challenge for the criminal justice system within a 'modern' democratic state. For it is impossible for state authorities to recognize witchcraft as a form of action in the manner it is seen in Soweto without fundamentally compromising the basic principles of evidence and the notions of rationality, agency, and intention that constitute legal doctrines of responsibility. The nearest they could come would be some variant of the current position of accepting a sincere belief in witchcraft as a 'mitigating factor' in relation to other crimes – such as assaulting and killing people accused of being witches.

Not being a witch, I cannot rightly say in what the essence of the action that is witchcraft consists. No-one else I have ever encountered can do so either. It is perhaps a question that cannot be answered, and this is not the place to try. However, from the ways in which I have heard people in Soweto talk about witchcraft, including the three reported above, the closest I can come to saying what sort of action witchcraft is as it is spoken of in Soweto is to say that it must be some kind of work, indeed, a craft: a matter of

combining knowledge, skill, technique (and technology), and effort to produce results in the world. Is witchcraft a form of work that can be regulated by the state? I doubt it. My friends in Soweto, however, do not. And if it turns out, as I suspect it will, that the government can neither do anything about witches nor about the circumstances that are making witchcraft more prevalent, the question will be asked even more insistently: what is government for?

Furthermore, if the government fails to mitigate the misfortunes of poverty, unemployment and disease, the question will arise: To what extent are the witches responsible? In that case, too, when government seems to be about something else than securing a 'better life for all', the question must surely be asked: What role do the witches play in securing, through the state, the good life for some?

Notes

1. For a more detailed account of witchcraft in Soweto and a discussion of relevant literature, see Ashforth (1996). For a general study of witchcraft and politics in Africa, see Geschiere (1997).
2. The most accurate recent estimates of Soweto's population are the 1991 census figure of 888,212 and the Soweto in Transition Project's 1,326,035. See University of the Witwatersrand, Department of Sociology, Soweto in Transition Project, *Preliminary Report*, para. 3.1. Sowetans typically put the population figure much higher, perhaps to correspond with their sense of the significance of the place.
3. Vukile Pokwana, 'Prancing and Shrieking Fail to Yield Missing Girl', *City Press*, July 13th, 1997, p. 5.
4. In a much-publicized 'discovery' in March 1996 a *sangoma* from the Eastern Cape, Chief Nicholas Gcaleka, claimed to have recovered in Scotland the head of Hintsa, a Xhosa king who was killed by the British in 1835. The skull was found not to be Hintsa's and Gcaleka was denounced as a 'charlatan out only to make money and boost his image as a sangoma healer'. Eddie Koch, 'King's Skull Seized', *Weekly Mail and Guardian*, March 15th, 1996.
5. See MEC for Safety and Security, Northern Province, *Report of the Commission of Inquiry into Witchcraft Violence and Ritual Murders in the Northern Province of the Republic of South Africa* (1996), p. 64 ff.
6. The Cosmic Gypsy signed up for twelve years after MT told her he needed three hundred Rands for a 'legal' problem.
7. The historical record shows that ancestors of the leaders of clans, tribes, and nations had significantly greater powers than ordinary commoners and could be drawn upon to secure the common good of their descendants as a whole (see Willoughby 1928). Such notions took a beating under apartheid, although they remain current to some extent in rural ethnic enclaves. In polyglot urban communities such as are found in Soweto, however, the notion of superior collective ancestors has no purchase outside of Zionist churches. In the largest of these, the Zion Christian Church which is founded explicitly upon the model of the Pedi polity, for example, the founder Bishop Barnabas Lekganyane serves as a chief ancestor for all the members preserving the unity and fortunes of the church as a whole.
8. Chafunya was a notorious criminal who terrorized the Senaoane and Phiri neighborhoods of Soweto in the mid-1990s until he was killed in a gunfight by a young man, a high school student from Phiri, in a quarrel over a girl. When the police arrested the killer of Chafunya, the schoolboy's friends mobilized at the school grounds and marched to the police station where they caused a riot demanding his release. They then marched to Chafunya's mother's house, stoned her to death as a witch, burnt her house and began a military campaign against the other members of Chafunya's gang.
9. On March 23rd, 1994, for example, Lieutenant-Colonel Johan Botha of the South African Police was praying at his home in Nelspruit when an angel appeared and, according to *The Citizen* (a right-wing newspaper

with an impeccable record in supporting the actions of the SAP), 'told him that the peace initiative in South Africa would not succeed unless all its people joined in prayer' (Thursday, 7 April, 1994. p. 5). Botha began a campaign for a National Day of Prayer which culminated in a prayer rally at the Johanneshurg Easter Show and services around the country.

10 Such a role for *inyangas* is commonplace in the so-called People's Courts which are still periodically convened in Soweto. In my experience of these proceedings, evidence uncovered through divination is routinely accorded the same status as that presented by witnesses, especially if it endorses a preponderant sentiment in favor of the guilt or innocence of the accused.

References

Ashforth, A. 1996. 'Of Secrecy and the Commonplace: Witchcraft and Power in Soweto', *Social Research* 63 (4), Winter: 1183–1234.

Geschiere, P. 1997. *The Modernity of Witchcraft: Politics and the Occult in Postcolonial Africa* (Charlottesville and London: University Press of Virginia) (1st ed., Paris, Karthala, 1996).

Willoughby, W. C. 1928. *The Soul of the Bantu: A Sympathetic Study of the Magical Religious Practices and Belief of the Bantu Tribes of Africa* (New York: Doubleday).

Acknowledgments

Financial support for various aspects of this research has been provided by the Social Science Research Council/MacArthur Foundation Program on Peace and International Security, the Professional Staff Congress of the City University of New York (Research Grant #6-68536), the Institute for Advanced Study, Princeton, and the Harry Frank Guggenheim Foundation.

Index